Crisis in American Institutions

CRISIS IN AMERICAN INSTITUTIONS

Twelfth Edition

JEROME H. SKOLNICK

New York University

ELLIOTT CURRIE

University of California, Berkeley and Florida State University

Boston   New York   San Francisco
Mexico City   Montreal   Toronto   London   Madrid   Munich   Paris
Hong Kong   Singapore   Tokyo   Cape Town   Sydney

Senior Editor: Jeff Lasser
Editorial Assistant: Andrea Christie
Marketing Manager: Krista Groshong
Production Administrator: Michael Granger
Editorial-Production Service: Omegatype Typography, Inc.
Composition and Prepress Buyer: Linda Cox
Manufacturing Buyer: JoAnne Sweeney
Cover Administrator: Linda Knowles
Electronic Composition: Omegatype Typography, Inc.

For related titles and support materials, visit our online catalog at www.ablongman.com.

Library of Congress Cataloging-in-Publication Data

CIP Data not available at time of publication.
ISBN 0-205-37148-5

Printed in the United States of America
10   9   8   7   6   5   4   3   2   08   07   06   05   04

Contents

SYSTEMIC PROBLEMS

INSTITUTIONS IN CRISIS

Preface

As always, we are extremely gratified by the positive response to the previous edition of *Crisis in American Institutions,* but once again we have made a number of changes for this new edition.

Most importantly, we have added a new section we've called "America in the World." The idea for this section isn't entirely new—some earlier editions, for example, offered articles dealing with America's global military role. But the events of September 11, 2001, drove home the reality that it is no longer possible, if indeed it ever was, to separate what goes on within our national borders from the way our policies influence the world beyond them. In many ways, America's social problems are increasingly global problems, and in this new section we present a selection of articles that may begin to help us understand those connections.

Meanwhile, we have dropped a number of good but aging articles while adding new ones to existing sections in order to keep abreast of the ever-evolving issues in American society—including the widespread financial scandals affecting major corporations like Enron and WorldCom, the growing disparities between executive pay and corporate performance, and the troubling prevalence of white-collar crime. Each edition has provided an opportunity to review the best contemporary writing on social problems, and with each we have regretted having to drop old favorites and omit promising new work. We invariably find more good writing than we can use. This isn't surprising, since we cover a range of topics—from corporate power to racism, from the family to the environment—each of which could profitably occupy a lifetime of study and writing.

Once again, many people have helped us to make this new edition a reality. We want particularly to thank Jeff Lasser and Andrea Christie of Allyn and Bacon for their skill and patience in facilitating this revision, and Mary Young, Diana Neatrour, and the team at Omegatype Typography for their extraordinary efficiency and good cheer in producing the book under a very tight schedule. We would also like to thank the reviewers for this edition: Robert S. Bausch, Cameron University; Patrick G. Donnelly, University of Dayton; Carol Goldsmith, University of Wisconsin, Parkside; and Richard Wunderlich, The College of Saint Rose. Very special thanks, also, to Ambreen Chowdhry for her enthusiastic and crucial help in preparing the manuscript. The Center for the Study of Law and Society at the University of California, Berkeley, again offered a supportive environment, and we especially thank Rod Watanabe and Rosann Greenspan for helping to create that environment. We deeply appreciate their assistance and friendship. Finally, we are most grateful to the students and teachers who have continued to educate us about each edition's strengths and weaknesses.

Crisis in American Institutions

Introduction

Approaches to Social Problems

In the early years of the twenty-first century, American society presents us with some striking paradoxes. We are now the world's only "superpower," and our economic might is admired (and sometimes feared) throughout the world. Yet we are also a nation wracked by widespread poverty on a scale that is unknown in other industrial societies. We are a country of crowded shopping malls—and crowded prisons; a country of glittering cities inhabited by stubborn legions of homeless people. We are a nation that routinely produces new technological marvels, from Internet software to breakthroughs in genetic medicine. But we are also a nation in which more than 40 million citizens have no regular source of health care and some lack the most basic sanitation.

This book explores these paradoxes and others through a collection of some of today's best writing on social problems in America. Our contributors are social scientists, specialists in public health and the environment, and journalists skilled in reporting and analyzing social issues. We don't claim that these articles, by themselves, can resolve all of the complex issues surrounding the causes and consequences of social problems in the United States. We do believe that they challenge readers to think more clearly and more critically about a range of issues that affect us all—from violence against women to racial profiling by police, from homelessness to global warming.

In that sense, these writings fit well with the best traditions in the study of social problems in the United States. Social scientists and others have been studying these problems for a long time, and the study of social problems has never taken place in the antiseptic confines of a scientific laboratory. Social theorists, like everyone else, are deeply influenced by broader trends in the society, the economy, and the cultural and technological setting of social life. As a way of introducing the articles that follow and of placing today's debates in some historical and intellectual context, we want to spend a few pages outlining the way in which the study of social problems has developed over time and how those larger social changes have shaped its basic assumptions and guiding themes.

DEFECTIVES AND DELINQUENTS

The earliest writers on social problems in this country were straightforward moralists, staunch supporters of the virtues of thrift, hard work, sexual purity, and personal discipline. Writing at the end of the nineteenth century, they sought ways of maintaining the values of an earlier, whiter, more Protestant, and more stable America in the face of the new challenges of industrialization, urbanization, and immigration.[1]

This early social science usually concentrated on the problems of what one nineteenth-century textbook described as the "defective, dependent, and delinquent classes."[2] The causes of social problems were located in the physical constitution or moral "character" of the poor, the criminal, the insane, and other "unfortunates." For these theorists, the solution to nineteenth-century social problems lay in developing means of transforming the character of these "defective" classes, in the hope of equipping them better to succeed within a competitive, hierarchical society whose basic assumptions were never questioned. Social reformers working from these theories created, in the last part of the nineteenth and the first part of the twentieth centuries, much of the modern apparatus of "social control" in the United States: reformatories, modern prisons, institutions for the mentally ill, and the beginnings of the modern welfare system.

THE RISE OF "VALUE-FREE" SOCIAL PROBLEMS

During the first decades of this century, this straightforward moralism was increasingly discarded in favor of a more subtle, ostensibly "neutral" approach to writing about social problems. By the 1930s, the idea that the social sciences were—or could be—purely "objective" or "value-free" had come to be widely accepted. From that point until the present, social problems theory has been characterized by a tortuous attempt to prove that theories and policies serving to support the status quo are actually scientific judgments arrived at objectively. In this view, social scientists do not try to impose their own values in deciding what kinds of things will be defined and dealt with as social problems. Instead, the "scientific" student of social problems simply accepts "society's" definition of what is a problem and what is not. This approach is apparent in these statements, taken from major textbooks and articles, on what constitutes a social problem:

> Any difficulty or misbehavior of a fairly large number of persons which we wish to remove or correct.[3]

> What people think they are.[4]

> Whenever people begin to say, isn't it awful! Why don't they do something about it?[5]

> Conditions which affect sizable proportions of the population, which are out of harmony with the values of a significant segment of the population, and which people feel can be improved or eliminated.[6]

> Any substantial discrepancy between socially shared standards and actual conditions of social life.[7]

These definitions share the common idea that social problems are popularly defined. No condition is a problem unless a certain number of people in a society say it is. Because we are merely taking, as our starting point, the definitions of the problem that "other people," "society," or "significant segments of the population" provide, we are no longer in the position of moralizing about objective conditions.

The basic flaw in this happy scheme is that it does not make clear *which* segments of the population to consult when defining problems or deciding between conflicting ideas about what is problematic and what is not. In the real world, societies are divided along class, racial, sexual, and other lines, and the sociologist who proposes to follow "people's" definitions of social problems in fact generally adopts one of several competing ideologies of social problems based on those divisions. In practice, the ideology adopted has usually been not too different from that of the "unscientific" social problems writers of the nineteenth century.

These points are not new; they were raised as early as 1936 in an unusually perceptive paper called "Social Problems and the Mores," by the sociologist Willard Waller. Waller noted, for example, that discussions of poverty in the social problems literature of the 1930s were shaped by the unquestioning acceptance of the ideology of competitive capitalism:

> A simpleton would suggest that the remedy for poverty in the midst of plenty is to redistribute income. We reject this solution at once because it would interfere with the institution of private property, would destroy the incentive for thrift and hard work and disjoint the entire economic system.[8]

Waller's question is fundamental: What has been left out in a writer's choice of what are to be considered problems? What features of society are going to be taken for granted as the framework *within* which problems will be defined and resolved? In this case, the taken-for-granted framework is the principle of private property and individual competition. In general, Waller argued, "social problems are not solved because people do not want to solve them";[9] they *are* problems mainly because of people's unwillingness to alter the basic conditions from which they arise. Thus:

> Venereal disease becomes a social problem in that it arises from our family institutions and also in that the medical means which could be used to prevent it, which would unquestionably be fairly effective, cannot be employed for fear of altering the mores of chastity.[10]

For Waller, the definition of social problems was, in the broadest sense, a political issue involving the opposed ideologies of conflicting groups.

Waller's points still ring true. Most social problems writers in the United States still tacitly accept the basic structure of American society and restrict their treatment of social problems to maladjustments *within* that structure.

SOCIAL PROBLEMS IN THE 1950s: GRADUALISM AND ANTICOMMUNISM

This is not to say that the literature on social problems since the 1930s has all been the same. Books on social problems, not surprisingly, tend to reflect the preoccupations of the time when they were written. Those conceived in the 1950s, for example, reflect social and political concerns that now seem bizarre. The shadow of Mc-Carthyism and the general national hysteria over the "Communist menace" pervaded this literature. Consider the discussion of "civil liberties and subversion" in Paul B. Horton and Gerald R. Leslie's textbook *The Sociology of Social Problems*.[11] Horton and Leslie saw the "American heritage of liberty" being attacked from both Left and Right, from both "monolithic communism" and overzealous attempts to defend "our" way of life from it. Their position was resolutely "moderate." They claimed a scientific objectivity; yet, they were quite capable of moral condemnation of people whose politics were "extreme," whether Right or Left:

> Most extremists are deviants. Most extremists show a fanatical preoccupation with their cause, a suspicious distrust of other people in general, a disinterest in normal pursuits, recreations, and small talk, and a strong tendency to divide other people into enemies and allies.[12]

The preference for "normal pursuits," even "small talk," over social criticism and action was common in an age noted for its "silent generation," but it was hardly "scientific." Among the other presumably objective features of the book were the authors' "rational proposals for preserving liberty and security," including these:

> *An adequate national defense* is, needless to say, necessary in a world where an international revolutionary movement is joined to an aggressive major power. This is a military problem, not a sociological problem, and is not discussed here.
>
> *Counterespionage is essential.* Highly trained professional agencies such as the FBI and the Central Intelligence Agency can do this efficiently and without endangering personal liberties of citizens. If headline-hunting congressmen, Legion officials, or other amateurs turn G-men, they merely scare off any real spies and destroy the counterespionage effort of the professionals.[13]

The military and intelligence services themselves were not considered to be problems relevant for social science. Questions about the operation of these agencies were viewed as internal and technical, military rather than sociological, issues.

In a section on "Questions and Projects," the authors asked, "How have conservatives or reactionaries sometimes given unintentional assistance to the Communists? How have liberals sometimes given unintentional assistance to the Communists?"[14]

In the introduction to their book, Horton and Leslie considered the possibilities of social change and the proper role of social scientists in promoting it. They carefully adopted a middle ground between conservatives, to whom social problems were primarily problems of individual character, and "extremists" hoping for sudden or radical changes in social structure. They argued that the resolution of social problems "nearly always involves sweeping institutional changes" but also that such changes are "costly" and "difficult," and that therefore

> it is unrealistic to expect that these problems will be solved easily or quickly. . . . Basic solutions of social problems will come slowly, if at all. Meanwhile, however, considerable amelioration or "improvement" may be possible.[15]

Social change, according to these authors, must be gradual and realistic; it must also be guided by experts. The authors insisted that their own role, and that of social experts in general, was merely to show the public how to get what they already valued. But in this role it was folly for the "layman" to question the expert. Horton and Leslie wrote that "when experts are *agreed* upon the futility of one policy or the soundness of another, it is sheer stupidity for the layman to disagree."[16]

An elitist, Cold War liberalism and gradualism, a fear of extremism and of an international Communist conspiracy—all these were presented not as moral and political positions but as fundamental social scientific truths. The sturdy entrepreneurial and Protestant values described in Waller's paper of the 1930s gave way, in Horton and Leslie's book of the 1950s, to a general preference for moderation, anticommunism, and "normal pursuits."

THE 1960s: AFFLUENCE AND OPTIMISM

A different imagery dominated the social problems literature of the next decade. Robert K. Merton and Robert A. Nisbet's *Contemporary Social Problems*[17] was a product of the beginning of the 1960s, the period of the "New Frontier," which saw a significant shift, at least on the surface, in the focus of social concern. Americans were becoming aware of an "underdeveloped" world abroad and a "disadvantaged" world at home, both unhappily excluded from the benefits of an age of general "affluence" and well-being. New agencies of social improvement were created at home and abroad. A critique of old-style welfare efforts began to develop, along with the notion of "helping people help themselves," whether in Latin America, Harlem, or Appalachia. The idea of inclusion, of participation, in the American way of life became a political metaphor for the age. From a slightly different vantage, the idea emerged as "development" or "modernization." The social problems of the 1960s would be solved by extending the technological and intellectual resources of established American institutions into excluded, deprived, or underdeveloped places and groups. An intervention-minded government combined with an energetic social science on a scale unprecedented in this country.

In this period—very brief, as it turned out—social problems were often seen as problems of being *left out* of the American mainstream: "left behind," as the people of Appalachia were described; "traditional," like the Mexican Americans; or "underdeveloped," like most Africans, Asians, and Latin Americans. In social problems theory, these ideas were manifested in a conservative ideology that celebrated American society as a whole, coupled with a liberal critique of the conditions hindering the extension of the American way to all.

One variant of this view was given in Nisbet's introduction to *Contemporary Social Problems*. For Nisbet, social facts become problematic when they "represent interruptions in the expected or desired scheme of things; violations of the right or the proper, as a society defines these qualities; dislocations in the social patterns and relationships that a society cherishes."[18]

Nisbet's assessment of the American situation was in keeping with the exaggerated optimism of the early 1960s:

> In America today we live in what is often called an affluent society. It is a society characterized by imposing command of physical resources, high standards of private consumption, effective maintenance of public order and security, freedom from most of the uncertainties of life that plagued our ancestors, and relatively high levels of humanitarianism. There are also, of course, squalid slums, both urban and rural; occasional epidemics of disease; sudden eruptions of violence or bigotry, even in the most civilized of communities; people for whom the struggle for food and shelter yet remains obsessing and precarious. Thus, we are not free of social problems, and some of them seem to grow almost in direct proportion to our affluence.[19]

Nisbet was aware that America had not yet solved all its problems; indeed, that some seem to come with the generally glittering package that is America in the twentieth century. Yet the problems were viewed as peripheral, as occasional eruptions in the backwaters of society where modern institutions had not fully penetrated.

Like earlier theorists, Nisbet sharply separated the role of the scientific student of social problems from that of other concerned people. The social scientist, as a scientist, should not engage in moral exhortation or political action but instead concentrate on understanding. At the same time, the scientist is

> as interested as the next citizen in making the protection of society his first responsibility, in seeing society reach higher levels of moral decency, and when necessary, in promoting such legal actions as are necessary in the short run for protection or decency.[20]

Here the scientific stance masked a preference for vaguely defined values—"societal protection" and "moral decency"—that, in turn, determine what will be selected as social problems. In this instance, problems were selected according to whether they offended the values of social stability, that is, values associated with the conservative tradition in social thought.

Thus, problems were repeatedly equated with "dislocations and deviations";[21] they were problems of "dissensus," as if consensus might not also be a problem. Indeed, the entire book was divided into two sections, one dealing with "deviant behavior" and the other with "social disorganization." The articles in the text were not all of a piece. A paper by Robert S. Weiss and David Riesman on the problems of work took a different view on what constitutes a problem; the authors declared that "social forms which tend toward the suppression or frustration of meaning and purpose in life are inferior forms, whether or not they tend toward disorganization."[22] But many of the articles simply accepted the purposes of existing institutions and defined problems in terms of combating disorganization *within* those institutions. Perhaps the clearest illustration of this tendency appeared in an essay by Morris Janowitz addressing problems of the military establishment:

> It is self-evident that the military establishment, the armed forces, and their administrative organizations have become and will remain important institutions of United States society. The distinctive forms of military organization must be analyzed in order

to understand the typical sources of personal and social disorganization found in military life.[23]

The existence of a large military establishment was defined as outside the critical concern of the sociologist. The focus was not on the effect of the military on national or international life but on the problems of maladjustment within the military apparatus. The increasing scope of military activities was noted, but it was simply accepted as a fact of modern life:

> The armed forces have also become involved in a wide variety of logistical, research, and training activities. In the current international scene, they must take on many politico-military duties, including military assistance of allied powers.[24]

The implication was that the militarization of American society is not itself a problem for social analysis. And the acceptance of the place of the military in American society leads to the enlistment of social science in the service of military ends. Thus, in discussing changes in the requirements of military discipline, Janowitz noted that, in the 1960s, instead of employing "shock technique" to assimilate the recruit into the military, the problem had become how to foster "positive incentives and group loyalties through a team concept."[25] Janowitz didn't ask *what* the recruit is being assimilated *into*. The effect of primary-group relations on morale under Cold War conditions was extensively discussed, but the Cold War itself was not.

Robert Merton's epilogue to *Contemporary Social Problems,* called "Social Problems and Sociological Theory," represented a major attempt to give theoretical definition to the "field" of social problems. Merton was well aware that different interests are present in society and therefore that definitions of social problems were likely to be contested—"one group's problem will be another group's asset"—and more specifically that "those occupying strategic positions of authority and power of course carry more weight than others in deciding social policy and so, among other things, in identifying for the rest what are to be taken as significant departures from social standards."[26]

According to Merton, however, this diversity of perspectives does not mean that sociologists must succumb to relativism or abandon their position as scientific students of society's problems. The way out of the dilemma is to distinguish between "manifest" and "latent" social problems—the latter are problems also "at odds with the values of the group" but not recognized as such. The task of the sociologist is to uncover the "latent" problems, or unrecognized consequences of existing institutions and policies; in this way, "sociological inquiry does make men increasingly accountable for the outcome of their collective and institutionalized actions."[27]

The demand that social science make people accountable for their actions was a healthy departure from the false relativism of some earlier theorists. But the distinction between manifest and latent problems did not do what Merton claimed for it: It did not make the choice of problems a technical or neutral one. Actually, Merton's approach is best seen as providing a rationale for evaluating and criticizing particular policies and structures within a presumably consensual society whose basic values and institutions are not seen as problematic.

We could easily agree with Merton that "to confine the study of social problems to only those circumstances that are expressly defined as problems in the society is arbitrarily to discard a complement of conditions that are also dysfunctional to values held by people in that society."[28] But what about those values themselves? Shouldn't they be examined and, if necessary, criticized? It seems obvious to us, for example, that it is part of the sociologist's task to study and criticize the values held by people in German society during the Nazi era or by slaveholders in the antebellum American South, rather than to confine ourselves to studying conditions that might be "dysfunctional" in terms of those values. To do otherwise amounts to an acceptance by default; the social scientist becomes an expert at handling problems within the confines of an assumed consensus on basic goals and values.

The division of social problems into the two categories of *deviant behavior* and *social disorganization* reflected this acceptance, for both categories were defined as "disruptions" of an existing social order and did not question the adequacy of that social order itself. Thus:

> Whereas social disorganization refers to faults in the arrangement and working of social statuses and roles, deviant behavior refers to conduct that departs significantly from the norms set for people in their social statuses.[29]

It is not, as some critics have suggested, that this kind of analysis suggests that whatever is, is right. But it does imply that whatever *disturbs* the existing social system is the primary problem.

The sociologist's "expert" judgment, of course, may conflict with what people themselves feel to be their problems, and if so, according to Merton, the expert should prevail. Merton argued:

> We cannot take for granted a reasonably correct public imagery of social problems; of their scale, distribution, causation, consequences and persistence or change. . . . Popular perceptions are no safe guide to the magnitude of a social problem.[30]

The corollary, presumably, is that the sociologist's imagery of social problems is at least "reasonably correct," even, perhaps, where segments of the public strongly object to having their problems defined, or redefined, for them. We seem to have come back to the same condescending attitude toward the public expressed by Horton and Leslie and other sociologists of the 1950s.

This kind of attitude wasn't, of course, confined to writers on social problems. It was a major theme in the social thought and government policy of the 1960s, a decade characterized by an increasing detachment of governmental action from public knowledge and accountability—as exemplified in the growth of a vast intelligence apparatus, the repeated attempts to overthrow popularly elected governments overseas, and the whole conduct of the Vietnam War. This process was often excused on the ground that political decisions involved technical judgments that were out of the reach of ordinary people.

The conception of social problems as technical, rather than moral and political, issues was explicit in Merton and Nisbet's text. Thus, Merton suggested that "the kind of problem that is dominated by social disorganization results from instrumental and technical flaws in the social system. The system comes to operate less efficiently than it realistically might."[31]

If the problems are technical ones, then it was, of course, reasonable to view social scientists as technicians and to regard their intervention into social life as free from partisan interest. It is this, apparently, that renders the social scientist a responsible citizen, rather than a "mere" social critic or ideologue:

> Under the philosophy intrinsic to the distinction between manifest and latent social problems, the social scientist neither abdicates his intellectual and professional responsibilities nor usurps the position of sitting in judgment on his fellow men.[32]

It is apparent, however, that this kind of "philosophy" lends itself all too easily to an alignment of expertise and "professionalism" with dominant values and interests masquerading as societal consensus. This is apparent in the choice of topics offered in most textbooks. Merton and Nisbet—whose widely used textbook has gone through several editions—characteristically dealt with mental disorders, crime and delinquency, drug use, alcoholism, suicide, sexual behavior, the population crisis, race relations, family disorganization, work and automation, poverty, community disorganization, violence, and youth and politics. The book did not deal with (to take some examples from our own table of contents) corporate power, sexism, health care, the criminal justice system, and so on. The pattern of these differences is obvious: Merton and Nisbet focused most heavily on those who have, for one reason or another, failed to "make it" within the American system—delinquents, criminals, the mentally ill, drug users—and on disorganization *within* established institutions. Even when individual authors in their book attempted to analyze the system itself, the effort was usually relegated to a peripheral, or merely symbolic, place.

Despite its claim to political neutrality, the social science of the 1960s typically focused on the symptoms of social ills, rather than their sources: the culture of the poor, rather than the decisions of the rich; the "pathology" of the ghetto, rather than the problems of the economy. What "socially shared standards" dictated this choice of emphasis? In the introduction to a newer edition of *Contemporary Social Problems,* Nisbet tried to answer this question. "It may well be asked," he writes, "why these problems have been chosen by the editors," rather than other problems that "for some persons at least might be regarded as even more pressing to national policy."

> The answer is that this is a textbook in sociology. Sociology is a special science characterized by concepts and conclusions, which are based on analysis and research, yielding in turn perspectives on society and its central problems. For many decades now, sociologists have worked carefully and patiently on these problems. In other words this book is concerned not only with the presentation of major social problems but with the scientific concepts and procedures by which these problems have been, and continue to be, studied.[33]

Nisbet seems to be explaining that these problems were selected by the editors because sociologists have studied them, and not other problems, in the past. Such an argument is hardly compelling.

THE 1970s TO THE PRESENT:
A HARSHER VISION

Much of the thinking about social problems in the 1960s—and the public policies that flowed from it—tended to assume, at least implicitly, that most of the ills of American society were solvable; that a rich and technologically advanced society should be able to overcome problems like poverty, unemployment, and inadequate health care, if it had the will to do so. And so an active government launched a number of social programs and experiments designed to bring the American reality in closer harmony with the American ideal. In the 1980s, it became fashionable to say that the government attempted too much in those years, throwing vast amounts of money at social problems. In fact, though we did try a multitude of programs, the amounts we spent on them were never large. Our total federal spending on job training, public job creation, and schooling programs for low-income people, for example, never rose to as much as one-half of 1 percent of our gross national product during the 1960s.[34]

But the belief that government had taken on too big a role helped to usher in a harsher, more pessimistic perspective in the 1970s—a perspective that has dominated social policy in the United States ever since. In the context of a deeply troubled economy, the stubborn persistence of poverty and joblessness, and frightening levels of social pathology in the cities, the moderate optimism of the 1960s began to give way to a new brand of scholarly pessimism arguing that many of these problems were due to "human nature" or defective "culture"—or even genetic deficiencies. The implication was that social concern of the 1960s variety couldn't have much positive impact on social problems—and, in the view of some writers, had probably made them worse.

Writers such as Arthur Jensen resurrected long-discredited hereditary theories of racial inferiority in intelligence to explain why blacks still remained at the bottom of the educational and economic ladder, despite all the equal opportunity programs of the 1960s. Others, such as Harvard's Edward Banfield, explained the persistence of poverty and urban crime as the reflection of a distinctive "lower-class culture" that prevented the poor from thinking ahead or delaying immediate gratification. By the 1980s, Charles Murray and other critics were explaining the stubbornness of poverty as the result of the demoralization of the poor by an overly generous welfare system. The growth of urban violence was similarly explained as the result of excessive leniency with criminals; in the 1980s, when years of "getting tough" with criminals left us with still-frightful levels of crime and violence, some writers began looking for the roots of crime—and of poverty and other social pathologies as well—in faulty physiology or defective genes.

By the 1980s, in other words, American thinking about social problems had just about come full circle; we had returned to something that looked very much like the focus on "defectives, dependents, and delinquents" that characterized late-nineteenth-century social science. And the harsh social policies that flowed from this attitude were also strikingly reminiscent of the Social Darwinism of the late nineteenth century. The belief that many of our social problems (from school failure to juvenile delinquency to welfare dependency) can be traced to deficiencies in the minds, cultures, or genetic makeup of a hard-core few—or to the folly of government intervention—a belief that was so comforting to the complacent thinkers of the nineteenth century, had returned with a vengeance.

As in the past, this outlook—still hugely influential today—serves to explain away some of the most troubling expressions of the crisis in American institutions, including many we address in this book: swollen prisons, the rapid descent of millions into the ranks of the poor, minority joblessness that persists at near-Depression levels through "good" economic times and bad. And it is used to justify sharp cutbacks in many of the programs created to address those problems—even successful programs in child health care, job training, and nutrition.

By now, however, this perspective has itself come under growing criticism. Its proponents, after all, have been arguing for a long time that the poor, the jobless, and the sick are largely responsible for their own problems and that they—along with the rest of us—would be better off with less help from government. We have, accordingly, been reducing government's role as well for a long time. But the problems haven't gone away; many have grown. And so the job of developing a fresh and creative approach to social problems is once again on the agenda.

That task is certainly an urgent one. As many of the articles in this book suggest, we have reached what seems to be a crucial turning point in our policies toward social problems. Technological and economic changes are reshaping the conditions of American life with sometimes dizzying speed, and how we choose to deal with those changes will profoundly affect the character of life in the United States for many years to come.

Consider just one example: the rapidly shifting character of work in America. As suggested by several of the articles in this book (notably those by Barbara Ehrenreich and William Julius Wilson), a combination of intense global economic competition and the continuing march of new workplace technology is dramatically affecting the pattern of jobs and incomes in the United States. Whether we can harness these changes to build a more sustaining and fulfilling society will depend on how our social and political institutions respond to them—whether, for example, we are willing to make a sufficient investment in worker retraining and job creation to offset the loss of many traditional jobs, and to provide adequate wages, child care, health care and other benefits to those now at work in the lower levels of the new economy. And as American lives are more and more affected by the workings of a largely unregulated global economy, we will increasingly need to confront these issues on an international scale. More generally, the increasing interconnection between the United States and the rest of the world—dramatically revealed by the attacks on the World Trade Center in September 2001, and explored in a new section at the end of this book—has given new urgency to questions of how we will manage our role as the only "superpower" in a world that is profoundly unstable and wracked by pervasive inequality and insecurity.

These are very big questions, and in this book we can only begin to explore them, not answer them once and for all. But we believe the articles that follow can provide a strong beginning. As in earlier editions, they represent a wide range of styles and perspectives. But most of them fit comfortably within a common overall vision: a critical, democratically inclined approach to social institutions that emphasizes the potential for constructive change.

Within this very broad perspective, there is plenty of room for controversy. Our authors don't necessarily share the same theoretical positions or social or political views. The editors, for that matter, don't always agree—and we think that's as it should be. We frequently argue about many of the issues covered in this book, and this debate has continued through twelve editions. But we think this tension is fruitful, and we have tried to capture it in our selection of readings.

Our purpose is to raise issues, to provide students with the beginnings of a critical approach to the society they live in and will, we hope, help to improve. This book provides few definitive answers, and it leaves unresolved many basic theoretical and practical questions about the sources and solutions of American social problems. But its purpose will be accomplished if it helps students to begin their own process of confronting those questions.

ENDNOTES

1. C. Wright Mills, "The Professional Ideology of the Social Pathologists," in Irving L. Horowitz, ed., *Power, Politics, and People: The Collected Essays of C. Wright Mills* (New York: Ballantine, 1963).

2. Charles Richmond Henderson, *An Introduction to the Study of Defective, Dependent, and Delinquent Classes* (Boston: Heath, 1906).

3. Lawrence K. Frank, "Social Problems," *American Journal of Sociology*, 30 (January 1925), p. 463.

4. Richard C. Fuller and Richard R. Myers, "The Natural History of a Social Problem," *American Sociological Review*, 6 (June 1941), p. 320.

5. Paul B. Horton and Gerald R. Leslie, *The Sociology of Social Problems* (New York: Appleton-Century-Crofts, 1955), p. 6.

6. Arnold M. Rose, "Theory for the Study of Social Problems," *Social Problems*, 4 (January 1957), p. 190.

7. Robert K. Merton and Robert A. Nisbet, *Contemporary Social Problems* (New York: Harcourt, Brace, and World, 1961), p. 702.

8. Willard Waller, "Social Problems and the Mores," *American Sociological Review*, 1 (December 1936), p. 926.

9. *Ibid.*, p. 928.

10. *Ibid.*, p. 927.

11. Horton and Leslie, *The Sociology of Social Problems*. We refer here to the original edition in order to place the book in its historical context.

12. *Ibid.*, p. 517.

13. *Ibid.*, p. 520.

14. *Ibid.*, p. 523.

15. *Ibid.*, p. 12.

16. *Ibid.*, p. 19.

17. Merton and Nisbet, *Contemporary Social Problems*. Here, too, we refer to the first edition in order to consider the book in historical perspective. The general theoretical perspective in the book has changed little, if at all, as we will note later; there have been some

substantive changes, however—for example, the chapter by Janowitz has been dropped and new chapters added.

18. Robert A. Nisbet, "The Study of Social Problems," in *ibid.*, p. 4.

19. *Ibid.*, p. 5. The reader might compare C. Wright Mills's notion, developed during the same period, that the United States should be seen as an "overdeveloped" society; see Irving L. Horowitz, "Introduction," in Horowitz, *Power, Politics, and People*, p. 8.

20. Nisbet, "The Study of Social Problems," p. 9.

21. *Ibid.*, p. 12.

22. Robert S. Weiss and David Riesman, "Social Problems and Disorganization in the World of Work," in Merton and Nisbet, *Contemporary Social Problems*, p. 464.

23. Morris Janowitz, "The Military Establishment: Organization and Disorganization," in Merton and Nisbet, *Contemporary Social Problems*, p. 515.

24. *Ibid.*, p. 516.

25. *Ibid.*, pp. 533–534.

26. Robert K. Merton, "Social Problems and Sociological Theory," in Merton and Nisbet, *Contemporary Social Problems*, p. 706.

27. *Ibid.*, p. 710.

28. *Ibid.*, p. 711.

29. *Ibid.*, p. 723.

30. *Ibid.*, pp. 712–713.

31. *Ibid.*, p. 723.

32. *Ibid.*, p. 712.

33. Robert M. Nisbet, "The Study of Social Problems," in *ibid.*, p. 2.

34. Gary L. Burtless, "Public Spending for the Poor," in Sheldon H. Danziger and Daniel H. Weinberg, *Fighting Poverty: What Works and What Doesn't* (Cambridge, MA: Harvard University Press, 1986), p. 37.

SYSTEMIC PROBLEMS

PART ONE

Corporate Power

The myth of American capitalism is individual "free enterprise"—the vision of the hardworking, thrifty entrepreneur competing with others and constrained by the forces of the market. But the reality of American capitalism is what Ralph Nader once called "corporate collectivism": the domination of our economic life by a relative handful of large corporations.

The largest corporation in America today, Wal-Mart stores, employs a number of people greater than the populations of Dallas, San Diego, or Detroit: if they were a city, indeed, they would be the seventh largest in the United States. Wal-Mart's 2002 revenue of nearly a quarter of a trillion dollars is roughly equal to the Gross National Product of Sweden. The American corporation with the most assets—the Citigroup banking empire—has more than a trillion dollars in assets, or a sum comparable to the Gross National Product of China. The great size and power of these corporations influences virtually aspect of American life today, as the articles in the part illustrate.

As corporate business has grown in size and influence, for example, it has also become more closely entwined with government, in a variety of ways. Part of our myth of free enterprise is the idea that, unlike, say, poor people on welfare or the elderly who receive Medicare, private businesses must go it alone: they must earn their own way in the economy, or go under. But as Janice Shields points out in the article we reprint here, poor people are by no means the only recipients of government largesse: Billions of dollars in "corporate welfare" also flow to businesses, including some of America's largest. These giveaways come in a variety of forms, from subsidies to help companies sell dog food in foreign countries to complex "reforms" that allow corporations to avoid the costs of environmental or health and safety regulations. Much of this "aid to dependent corporations" is distributed with little public input, or even public knowledge. In recent years, Congress has taken some steps to rein in spending on corporate welfare. But these have been far less effective than measures to cut back on public assistance for the poor or working Americans.

This is not surprising, since the poor, unlike large corporations, have little to contribute to the campaign coffers of elected officials. As Mark Green illustrates in his article on the "cost of money," the increasingly massive flow of money into the political process has drastically reshaped politics in America, in ways that have deeply undercut the principles of democracy on which the nation was founded. Most obviously, it costs ordinary Americans vast sums of money by influencing politicians to support legislation that benefits corporations to the detriment of everyone else. But there are also more subtle effects of the growing dominance of money in American politics. By forcing legislators to spend much of their time raising money in order to get elected, it reduces the amount of time and energy they can spend on actually governing. It renders many elections uncompetitive, since only those candidates with huge financial 'war chests'—often incumbents or the independently wealthy—have much of a chance in an increasingly expensive political arena. And it fuels political apathy and cynicism—helping to explain why half of American voters stay home during presidential elections—as potential voters become increasingly convinced that politicians are essentially 'bought' and that their own votes don't matter.

One of the most prominent contributors of money to political campaigns has been the tobacco industry. A *New York Times* article once described a scene in the 1990s when a Congressman from the Midwest was seen on the floor of the House of Representatives "Cheerfully tossing out checks from tobacco companies like daisies." Clearly, that kind of money has traditionally helped the industry fight off regulation despite growing awareness of the inherent dangers of its product.

By now, there is no question that cigarettes are addictive and that the tobacco industry has known, capitalized on, and denied that fact for years. What's worse, according to Philip J. Hilts in the excerpt from his book *Smoke Screen*, is that the industry has deliberately targeted its advertising and marketing at young people—because it also knows that the overwhelming majority of smokers become hooked when they are in their teens. If they can be lured into smoking in the first place, they are very likely to become addicted—thus eventually becoming the profit-making future of the tobacco industry.

These articles all describe the growing influence of private power in the United States. That growth has been fueled, in part, by the widespread belief that the private sector can do a better job than government in addressing economic needs, and that it should be left alone by government, as much as possible, in order to get the job done most efficiently. The United States has gone much farther in this direction than most countries, with a relatively smaller role for government in economic life than in many other advanced industrial societies. And the dominance of the private sector has increased considerably in recent years, as private companies have moved in to take over many functions that used to be public ones—everything from running schools to operating prisons to providing water—one of the most basic needs of human life.

As John Luoma points out in "Water for Profit," the takeover of water systems in many cities—and countries—by a handful of large corporations was supposed to make the delivery of water more efficient. But in some places, especially in some developing countries, the results have been the opposite. Water, which had been taken for granted even by the poor, suddenly became too expensive for many to afford, and often became unhealthy as well. In the United States, most people still get their water from public utilities, but not for long, if some corporations have their way. Illustrating the reach and complexity of the modern large corporation, among the companies most prominent in the drive to privatize water is the French-based Vivendi Universal, which, among other enterprises, also owns the USA television network and the Universal motion picture studios. Luoma concludes that "If success is measured in terms of delivering an essential commodity to everyone who needs it, then the industry's record is less than encouraging." As we hear calls to turn more and more of our basic needs over to private corporations, we would do well to ponder this example.

CHAPTER 1

Getting Corporations off the Public Dole

JANICE SHIELDS

From the White House to Capitol Hill, the mantra in Washington these days is, "We want to end welfare as we know it." Billions of dollars have been cut from housing, nutrition, health, and education programs. Remaining relatively unscathed are billions in aid for dependent corporations in all its omnipresent forms. Cash subsidies, free or below-cost government services and products, tax breaks, and business-protection laws fill the corporate welfare trough and multiply. Through our research, we conservatively identified more than 150 examples of corporate welfare totaling more than $167 billion in fiscal year 1995 alone.

BROTHER, CAN YOU SPARE A BILLION?

Lockheed and Martin Marietta merged this year to form Lockheed Martin, a company that will generate $11.6 billion in annual military sales. In a scenario of bizarre federal giveaways, U.S. taxpayers will spend $1 billion to cover the costs of related plant shutdowns and employee relocations, even though 30,000 workers will lose their jobs. Another $31 million in federal money will go to top officials of the two companies, one third of their $92 million bonus package. Defense Secretary William Perry and his then deputy, John Deutch, officially approved the deal; both had been employed as consultants by Martin Marietta before joining the Pentagon. Last year the duo secretly reversed the Pentagon's 40-year ban on reimbursing expenses related to defense company acquisitions and mergers so that Martin Marietta could get $330 million in federal payments in connection with its acquisition of a defense subsidiary from General Electric. Before approving that payout, Perry and Deutch obtained waivers of an ethics regulation that prohibits Pentagon officials from dealing with former employers for one year. Ironically, Daniel M. Tellep, the chairman and CEO of Lockheed Martin, received the Public Sector Council Leadership Award in April. The goal of the council is to encourage cooperation between business and government.

The Agriculture Department's Market Promotion Program (MPP) provides more than $100 million annually in taxpayer handouts to private companies and their trade associations for overseas promotional activities, such as advertising, market research, technical assistance, and trade servicing. According to a Center for Study of Responsive Law report, five businesses each received more than $1 million from the MPP in 1993. They included Sunkist Growers, Inc. ($6.6 million), E. & J. Gallo Winery ($4.3 million), Sunsweet Growers, Inc. ($2.4 million), Dole ($1.57 million), and Brown-Forman Corporation ($1.1 million). The fiscal year 1994 budget contained promotional funding for alcohol, wine and beer ($6.34 million), mink ($1.9 million), and pet food ($1.1 million). Incredibly, while the U.S. Congress cut spending for food programs for the poor in recent rescissions packages, the MPP, which funds dog food advertisements overseas, has survived intact.

CORPORATE "FREE CHEESE"

Instead of direct cash handouts, some welfare programs provide free or below-cost government goods and services to corporations. For the beneficiaries, cost savings give the same bounce to the bottom line as do revenues from subsidies.

On April 11, 1995, the Department of Health and Human Service's National Institutes of Health announced that it had relinquished the right to require "reasonable pricing" on drugs developed in cooperation between the federal government and private industry. The reasonable pricing policy had required companies to provide documentation showing a reasonable relationship between the price of a product, the public investment in that product, and the health and safety needs of the public. The policy had been adopted in 1987 because of congressional and public criticism of the pricing of the anti-AIDS drug, AZT. Although federal scientists had done much of the work to develop the drug, Burroughs Wellcome, the pharmaceutical company that marketed AZT, initially priced AZT to cost each patient $8,000 to $10,000 per year. Now, Bristol-Myers Squibb has been given the exclusive right to commercialize the cancer drug Taxol even though Taxol was discovered, manufactured, and tested by the federal government. According to the Taxpayer Assets Project, the drug costs about $52.50 per shot to produce, but the current wholesale price is $1,022.70. Bristol-Myers Squibb, whose 1994 profits were $1.8 billion, pays no royalties to the government on the company's Taxol sales, which are expected to generate $480 million in revenues in 1995.

The federal Overseas Private Investment Corporation (OPIC) provides below-market-rate loans and political risk insurance to multinational companies that are at least 50 percent beneficially owned by U.S. citizens, to encourage private U.S. investment in developing countries. OPIC made loan commitments of $1.7 billion and insurance commitments of $6 billion during fiscal year 1994, which marked the highest level of activity in the agency's 23-year history. U.S. West, a telecommunications company, received $170 million in taxpayer-subsidized OPIC loans in 1994 even though U.S. West generated profits of $1.4 billion that year. Citibank obtained subsidized OPIC insurance coverage exceeding $388 million in 1994 even though Citibank's 1994 profits exceeded $3.4 billion.

TAX BREAKS AND LOOPHOLES

Congressional leaders have proposed cuts in corporate welfare (subsidies), but plan to use the government savings to offset federal revenue losses resulting from increases in yet another form of corporate welfare—tax breaks. The Congressional Joint Committee on Taxation (JCT) estimates that fiscal year 1995 corporate tax expenditures (bureaucratese for special tax provisions or regulations that provide tax benefits to particular taxpayers) will exceed $58 billion.

Accelerated depreciation deductions allow companies to decrease their taxable income by amounts that exceed the dollar decline in the useful life of an asset in its early years. The extra deductions reduce company tax liabilities and amount to interest-free loans from taxpayers to businesses. These "loans" show up as deferred taxes in company annual reports and, according to the JCT, create aggregate federal tax expenditures of $19 billion per year. IBM's 1994 10-K reports accumulated deferred taxes of $1.653 billion related to depreciation. Hasbro's shows deferred taxes of $64 million due to depreciation. The tax bill passed by the House of Representatives in April would continue to allow accelerated depreciation and, as an added bonus, let companies take depreciation deductions in excess of the cost of the asset. According to Department of Treasury estimates, the tax subsidy would cut government revenue an additional $14 billion per year over the long term by reducing the corporate income tax take by about 8 percent.

The JCT estimates that tax credits for companies with operations in Puerto Rico and the Virgin Islands will reduce U.S. Treasury receipts by $3.7 billion in 1995. The credit allows qualified U.S. corporations to deduct from their U.S. tax bill the amount of U.S. taxes that would have been due on profits from business operations, sales of assets, and investments in Puerto Rico and the Virgin Islands. Merck & Company's 1993 10-K reports tax savings of $158.7 million because of its Puerto Rican operations. According to Pfizer's 10-K, the company was able to reduce its statutory tax rate from 35 percent to 25.1 percent due to the effect of its partially tax-exempt operations in Puerto Rico.

REGULATORY DEFORM

The final form of corporate welfare includes business-protection laws and changes in other rules. This welfare helps companies increase revenues or cut costs, but is more difficult to quantify.

Certain industries are fighting to maintain import restrictions to control domestic supplies and reduce competition. The U.S. government currently guarantees sugar producers a minimum price, in part by limiting sugar imports. According to a U.S. General Accounting Office (GAO) study, consumers pay an average $1.4 billion in higher grocery bills annually as a result. Sugar producers claim that dropping the price support program would place 420,000 sugar-producing jobs in jeopardy—in other words, U.S. consumers are paying at least $3,333 per job ($1.4 billion/420,000). Compounding the criticisms, just 1 percent of sugar farms benefit from 42 percent of the higher revenues resulting from this corporate welfare program. According to the Center for Responsive Politics, one family enterprise alone has enjoyed $64.6 million in federal sugar benefits in 1993 and 1994—not a bad return on its federal election contributions of $1.5 million from 1979 through 1994.

Many companies have lobbied vigorously on Capitol Hill for changes in tort law that would effectively limit suits by victims of defective products, medical malpractice, and securities fraud and for reductions in the so-called regulatory burden of consumer-, worker-, and environmental-protection laws. CEOs admit that federal subsidies are small change compared to potential cost savings from tort and regulatory reform.

During the first 100 days of the 104th Congress, the House of Representatives passed legislation that would place a moratorium on new regulations and include requirements that risk assessment and cost/benefit analysis be completed for new rules. According to the Union of Concerned Scientists, estimates of costs of regulations are plagued with uncertainties and generally overstate expenses.

Two studies of the costs of regulations to the banking industry yielded widely varying results. The American Bankers Association (ABA) estimated that regulations cost 45 percent of pretax bank income; the Independent Bankers Association of America (IBAA), another trade group, estimated 24 percent. However, neither the ABA nor the IBAA studies made any attempt to quantify the benefits from complying with regulations, even though bankers, such as Charles K. Gifford of the Bank of Boston, say, "We've already proved to ourselves that we can make money making Community Reinvestment Act–related loans." Despite the divergent statistics and incomplete analyses, the bankers' congressional lobbyists are now begging for corporate welfare in the form of reduced regulation of the industry, targeting the Community Reinvestment Act, among others.

BIDDING FOR BUSINESS

Complementing federal corporate welfare programs are state and local largess, which has burgeoned as competition to retain or attract companies has intensified. The costs of the resulting jobs are outrageous. According to the American Federation of State, County and Municipal Employees, in 1993 Alabama offered tax breaks to Mercedes-Benz that were valued at $150,000 per job created; jobs created from Kentucky's tax breaks for Dofasco Steel cost $350,000 each; and Minnesota paid an incredible $558,000 per job in tax breaks for Northwest Airlines.

States and cities have even used federal grants to steal businesses from each other. Poplar Bluff, Missouri, for example, used a $205,000 U.S. Housing and Urban

Development (HUD) Community Block Grant to provide infrastructure to encourage Briggs & Stratton to relocate from Milwaukee. Schutt Sports Group accepted a low-interest HUD Block Grant loan of $500,000, funneled through the Illinois Community Development Assistance Program, for machinery and equipment to relocate 60 jobs from Knoxville to Salem, Illinois. (Proposed federal legislation would ban the utilization of federal funds by one state to lure jobs and businesses from other states.)

Rio Rancho, New Mexico, has provided a smorgasbord of incentives—lower corporate income taxes, exemption from property taxes and gross receipts taxes on equipment purchases, recruitment and training of workers, rapid grants of permits, and deep discounts on everything from moving and storage fees to utility deposits—to attract employers. In 1993 Intel announced plans to build a $1 billion plant, then crassly circulated the company's "ideal incentive matrix" among officials of competing states. A bidding war raged between New Mexico, California, Arizona, and others. Rio Rancho was declared the ultimate winner when the town offered a $114 million package of incentives and tax breaks; Intel's 1994 profits were $2.3 billion. Unfortunately, after handing out big tax breaks to attract employers, Rio Rancho could not afford schools. High school students are bused to an overcrowded Albuquerque school and local middle and elementary schools are packed to twice their capacity.

Providing tax breaks and other incentives does not guarantee anticipated results. In 1978 Volkswagen played Pennsylvania and Ohio off against each other when the company decided to open a Rabbit plant. Pennsylvania "won" after the state agreed to provide a $40 million 1.75 percent loan, which VW will not begin repaying until 1998, $25 million in highway and rail construction, $3 million in training subsidies, and five years of local tax abatements. However, only half of the 5,000 jobs that VW had promised were created and the company ended up closing the plant in less than 10 years.

General Motors requested and received $1.3 billion in tax abatements from Ypsilanti, Michigan, since 1975, including a 12-year property tax abatement for investment in GM's Willow Run facility in 1988. In 1992 GM announced plans to close Willow Run and transfer production to Texas. Ypsilanti filed suit, alleging that GM had violated agreements and representations that the company had made to obtain the abatements. The town won, but GM prevailed on appeal when the court ruled that an abatement does not carry a promise of continued employment.

STRANGE BEDFELLOWS

The prospect of rich corporations on the taxpayer dole has brought together strange bedfellows, from the conservative Cato Institute and the Competitive Enterprise Institute to the Center for Budget and Policy Priorities and Ralph Nader's Essential Information to fight to end welfare for wealthy companies. In June [1995] a coalition of the Cato Institute, the Progressive Policy Institute, and Essential Information released its first "Dirty Dozen" list of federal subsidies and grants to corporations that the three organizations unanimously recommended should be cut from the fiscal year 1996 and future budgets, for savings of more than $16 billion over five years. The list included eliminating maritime operating subsidies, OPIC loans and insurance, the MPP, the Export Enhancement Program, subsidies for military exports, and more. At a Washington press conference to announce the list, Representatives Bernard Sanders (I-Vt.), Peter A. DeFazio (D-Ore.), and Major R. Owens (D-N.Y.) spoke in support of axing corporate welfare.

CUTTING WELFARE

Groups from across the political spectrum agree that cuts should be made for several compelling reasons:

- Subsidies and grants may corrupt the relationship between business and government. For example, Commerce Secretary Ron Brown has led nine international trade missions for 170 CEOs. The Commerce Department insists that seats on the trips are awarded based on genuine needs for a government boost in closing deals. Yet, according to a *New York Times* report, the CEO of Cellular Communications International was included on a trip to India after one of President Clinton's classmates wrote to Commerce aides, noting that the CEO was a "very generous donor" to the Democratic Party.
- Subsidies and grants encourage corporate executives to focus their energies on politics instead of business. In April, the Senate voted to cut nutrition and housing programs but tabled an amendment to eliminate the MPP. During the debate, Senator Cochran declared, "I am hoping that we can increase the funding [for the MPP]." He then asked permission to include in the *Congressional Record* a copy of a letter he had received from a coalition that consisted of Sunkist, the National Wine Coalition, Dole, and other recipients of the MPP.
- Subsidies and grants create corporate winners and losers based on political decisions. The Clinton Administration is lobbying Congress to save the Advanced Technologies Program (ATP), which was budgeted to receive $340 million in taxpayer funds in 1995 to support research and development projects of private U.S.- and foreign-owned companies. However, the program has targeted only certain commercial technologies for funding, such as car manufacturing and telecommunications. Big companies such as 3M and IBM have been the big winners of ATP grants.
- Subsidies and grants disburse taxpayer monies for business costs properly borne by the private sector. The Export-Import Bank provides subsidized loans, loan guarantees, and tied-aid grants. In the 60 years since its creation, the Ex-Im Bank has lost $8 billion on its operations, according to the Congressional Budget Office. Even David Stockman and other Reagan politicians tried to get rid of the Ex-Im Bank, arguing that its practice of financing export projects with below-market interest rates amounted to "corporate welfare."

PROGRESSIVE AGENDA

Here are a number of recommendations to improve the accountability of corporate welfare programs:

- The U.S. government should consolidate and regularly report information about corporate welfare programs, expenditures, and recipients so that the number of programs and dollar costs are known. In 1994 Senators Joseph I. Lieberman (D-Conn.) and Donald W. Riegle (D-Mich.) asked the U.S. General Accounting Office to prepare a list only of the federal programs that provide management and technical assistance to businesses. The GAO concluded, "We found no particular federal office that tracks or coordinates all the various management and technical assistance programs at the different government agencies."
- Recipients should be required to provide a public report each year identifying the specific types of welfare received, the purposes and uses of that welfare, and the cost and benefits to the taxpayers. Corporations are currently not required to disclose information about government grants and subsidies received.
- Means testing should be required for corporate welfare recipients and limits should be placed on the length of time that companies may remain on welfare. A "three strikes and you're out" rule should require removal of corporate welfare abusers convicted of misdeeds from the welfare rolls.
- Public hearings should be held before new corporate welfare programs are introduced. Periodic cost/benefit analyses should be conducted to determine whether existing programs should continue.

FIGHTING BACK

Activists at the local, state, and federal level are beginning to mobilize to put pressure on legislators to rein in corporate welfare. Minnesota's Corporate Welfare Reform Law, which went into effect on August 1, 1995, requires a business that receives state or local government assistance for economic development or job growth purposes to create a net increase in jobs in Minnesota within two years of receiving the assistance. A ballot initiative has been drafted in California that if passed would allow any citizen to bring court action against a corporate welfare abuser. The end result would be that a corporation could have its privilege to do business in the state revoked if it is ruled a welfare abuser three times over a 10-year period.

These efforts should continue and spread. Failure to control and shrink corporate welfare makes a tragic mockery of the current debate on welfare reform for the neediest of our society.

CHAPTER 2

The Cost of Money

MARK GREEN

> The day may come when we'll reject the money of the rich as tainted, but it hadn't come when I left Tammany Hall at 11:25 today.
> —George Washington Plunkitt, 1905

> I don't think we buy votes. What we do is we buy a candidate's stance on issues.
> —Allen Pross, executive director of the California Medical Association's PAC, 1989

> I got $3500 over 10 years (from Enron). Heck, I'm the chairman of the committee. That wasn't a contribution. That was an insult.
> —Senator Ernest F. Hollings (D–SC), 2002

In April 2002, when President George W. Bush's approval rating—bolstered by post–September 11 patriotism—stood at 74 percent, six out of ten Americans surveyed by Greenberg Quinlan Rosner Research agreed with the following statement: "When it comes to domestic policies, the Bush administration always seems to do what the big corporations want." President Bush wasn't alone. In other polls commissioned around the same time, large majorities believed that "special-interest groups own Congress" and have too much influence over elected officials. And while 29 percent of those polled by the University of Michigan's National Election Studies in 1964 felt the government was "run by a few big interests looking out for themselves," that number rose to 76 percent in 1994.

This growing belief that big interests run Washington parallels the growing donations that big interests have sent to Washington—and the perception that money gets results.

In a study conducted by Ellen Miller for the Center for Responsive Politics, 20 percent of the members of Congress *admitted* that campaign contributions affected their voting; only half claimed contributions had no effect, and 30 percent said they weren't sure. "Let's be clear," writes Fred Wertheimer, former president of Common Cause. "Though for many years it has been taboo in most Washington circles to use the word 'corruption' to portray the political money system in action, that is precisely what's going on."

Put yourself in the shoes of a candidate. If elections cost millions of dollars to win—and given the ego and the high stakes involved, you'd sure like to win—you'll need to get the money from somewhere. Support from friends and family is a good start, but if you're like most people, it wouldn't be nearly enough to make you competitive. So whom do you count on when your personal network is exhausted? (Hint: It's not working people and advocacy groups.)

There's a huge cost involved when candidates engage in the primordial task of hunting and gathering monetary gifts from the 1 percent of wealthy Americans who do the vast majority of the contributing. And a huge cost when a Congress becomes in effect a pay-per-use system utilized only by those wealthy enough to afford the membership dues.

Most *current* incumbents try to explain away the inevitable reality that when Joe Citizen calls on line 1 and Marty the Millionaire on line 2, Marty's line is going to get picked up first. But most *former* elected officials complain about the wear and tear of the money chase on their time and their integrity.

The pay-to-play mentality has so seeped into our system that there now exist two classes of citizens. There are those for whom tax breaks, bailouts, and subsidies are granted; for whom running for and winning office is plausible; and with whom elected officials take time to meet. And then there are the rest of us—the non-donors for whom taxes go up, consumer prices rise, and influence evaporates.

In *The Godfather,* Marlon Brando's Don Corleone tells a man named Bonasera in the opening scene: "Someday, and that day may never come, I'll call upon you to do a service for me. But until that day, accept this justice as a gift on my daughter's wedding day." The only difference between Bonasera and a member of Congress is that, for the latter, that day will *surely* come.

Some lobbyists, and even some elected officials, will argue that industry campaign contributions reward a member's *past* performance, and have no implication for how he or she should behave in the *future.* But the past-future analysis is a distinction without a difference. For candidates and contributors aren't just mineral matter, with no sense of the future. Bribes are unnecessary when everyone involved in the money chase knows implicitly that gifts will keep coming if a candidate keeps supporting the industry.

Lobbyists themselves can be part of the problem. Of course, lobbyists—named for those in the 1800s who huddled in the lobbies off the floor of Congress waiting to pounce—are exercising their right to "petition government" and "redress grievances" under the First Amendment. And since members of Congress and their staffs can't know everything about everything, or even something about everything, they look to interested parties (discounting for bias) to bring key information to their attention. The problem occurs when an army of lobbyists for one interest—say, a lower capital gains rate, or bigger gas-guzzling cars—combines with big contributions from that interest to overwhelm a less vocal or invisible opposition. And 17,000 lobbyists in Washington overall—or more than 30 per member of Congress—is quite an army.

"Every day there's a cadre of special-interest lobbyists lined up outside the House chamber on the sidewalk," reports Matt Keller, legislative director of Common Cause, who's spent years lobbying on Capitol Hill. "It's like a caricature. You've got Mr. Oil Man, Mr. Gas Man, Mr. Tobacco Man. It's like something out of *The Simpsons*. These guys spend their days trying to defeat something so obviously in the best interests of the country and the planet, and they can't possibly believe in what they're doing—but money talks. It's bizarre and frightening to watch up close." . . .

THE MONEY CHASE DISCOURAGES VOTING AND CIVIC PARTICIPATION

As special-interest dollars in elections go up by the millions, voter participation goes down. While Israel reliably achieves over 80 percent turnout in its elections for prime minister, and France and the United Kingdom typically turn out about three quarters of their voting-age populations, the United States has not broken *60* percent since 1968 (see table 2.1). The turnout for American elections is no higher today than it was in the 1930s—with roughly half of eligible voters staying home in presidential elections, and nearly two thirds in congressional elections.

The 1988 presidential race between George Bush and Michael Dukakis had the worst turnout (50.1 percent) in 64 years, but that dubious honor was not held long: two cycles later, 1996's Clinton-Dole contest yielded a limp 49.1 percent. And four years after that, not even the tightness of 2000's Bush-Gore fight could inspire many more than half of registered voters to turn out. On the local level, the trends are similar: In a May 2002 Nebraska primary, a microscopic 20 percent of registered voters went to the polls, shattering the previous low mark of 36 percent.

TABLE 2.1   Turnout of Eligible Voters in Presidential Elections since 1960

Year	Percent	Year	Percent
1960	63.1	1984	53.1
1964	61.9	1988	50.1
1968	60.8	1992	55.1
1972	55.2	1996	49.1
1976	53.6	2000	51.2
1980	52.6		

Source: Federal Election Commission.

When right-wing extremist Jean-Marie Le Pen took second place in France's 2002 presidential race, legions of press attributed the accused racist's surprise finish to the large number of so-called absent voters. Soberingly, the 72 percent turnout for that race—France's lowest in nearly four decades—is higher than any U.S. turnout in the twentieth century. "The nation that prides itself on being the best example of government of, for, and by the people," notes Curtis Gans, director of the nonpartisan Committee for the Study of the American Electorate, "is rapidly becoming a nation whose participation is limited to the interested or zealous few."

Consider these regressive trends, as reflected in Robert Putnam's much discussed *Bowling Alone: The Collapse and Revival of American Community:*

- Just 11 percent of eighteen- and nineteen-year-olds eligible to vote for the first time in 1998 actually did so.
- Beyond a 25 percent decline in voting, there has been a 50 percent dip in political involvement (measured by campaign activities) over the last forty years. In 1973, a majority of Americans wrote an article, signed a petition, made a speech, or sent a letter to an elected official; twenty-one years later, most Americans did none of these.
- In 1973, two-thirds of Americans attended at least one organization or club meeting a year; in 1994, the reverse was true. Over the same time span, membership in social and civic organizations fell 16 percent, while active participation in these same groups dropped by 50 percent.
- Volunteering has diminished among nearly every age group, churchgoing has gone down 10 percent, and active involvement in church activities has plummeted by 25 to 50 percent.

"There is now a lower level of trust toward our government than at any time perhaps since the 1920s, perhaps ever," explains Gans. One reason, he says, is "the media's increasingly cynical portrayal of politics, aided by thousands of deaths in Vietnam, the Iran-Contra affair, George [H. W.] Bush's 'Read My Lips, No New Taxes' vow, and impeachment."

Gans believes that citizens watching six hours a day of TV are left with little time to do much else but work, eat, and sleep; their civic information base is unvaried and limited because it's filtered nearly exclusively through the TV screen. He points also to the increasingly stressful lives people lead today: more Americans are single, divorced, commuting, generally anxious, and therefore less likely to participate in civic affairs—including voting—when faced with a crude cost-benefit decision. Also, Gans notes, although "leaders" like Newt Gingrich and Tom DeLay call government the enemy, demagoguing against the government isn't likely to encourage participation in government.

Beyond the campaign finance arena, however, in recent years a number of plausible and promising ideas have been proposed to boost voting. One idea is the nationwide adoption of election day registration (EDR). Currently practiced by six states, EDR reduces barriers to participation by enabling voters who mistakenly think they are already registered to do so on election day. This would also solve the additional problems of voters being turned away because their registration hasn't been processed in a timely manner, or because they've been wrongly purged from voter lists. According to a report by the nonpartisan research group Demos, states using EDR in the 2000 presidential election had turnout rates nearly 12 percent higher than the national average—63.2 percent versus 51.3 percent.

Another pro-turnout initiative is 1993's "Motor Voter" Act, or the National Voter Registration Act. This historic bill, aimed at increasing participation, enabled voters to register at their department of motor vehicles, public assistance offices, or other state agencies while applying for driver's licenses or government assistance. The legislation also provided for mail-in voter registration. The results have been modest but encouraging: from 1992 to 2000, registration went up 5.2 percent.

In Oregon, voting by mail has proven to boost participation. In addition to being cost-effective (between 1995 and 1997, Oregon counties saved over $1 million in three voting-by-mail special elections), the system is obviously more convenient for voters than driving to the polls. In the 1996 Republican and Democratic presidential primaries, Oregon led the nation in turnout, with over 53.7 percent of voters mailing in their ballots. New Hampshire ranked second, with a 45 percent turnout.

Despite these signs of improvement, turnout and registration remain low among many demographic groups, including persons of low income (less than half of those making under $50,000 annually are registered, compared with 77 percent of those making $75,000 or more), communities of color (Latinos, for instance, register at approximately half the rate whites do), and young people (only 44 percent of citizens eighteen to twenty-four were registered in 1998, compared with a rate of over three fourths among senior citizens).

While from 1992 to 2000 soft money contributions increased five-fold, hard money nearly doubled, and party fund-raising tripled, voting in federal elections went *down* four percentage points overall. Obviously nothing can be done to change the statistical fact that one person's vote is highly unlikely to sway an election (although the tightness of Bush-Gore should make voters think twice). But with the combination of incumbency and money apparently predetermining election results, many voters rationally assume their vote can't really matter.

This problem is of concern not just to liberals but to all small-d democrats. "We're perilously close to not having democracy," said Paul Weyrich, a prominent conservative who heads the Free Congress Foundation. "Non-voters are voting against the system, and if we get a bit more than that, the system won't work."

THE MONEY CHASE DISCOURAGES COMPETITIVE ELECTIONS

In an age when incumbency and money are mutually reinforcing and "redistricting" is little more than a synonym for "incumbent protecting," the realistic number of potentially competitive seats in this fall's general elections can be counted on one's fingers and toes. In fact, getting reelected has become so automatic that a member of Congress is almost more likely to vacate his or her seat by *dying* than by losing.

In both 1998 and 2000, more than 98 percent of House incumbents who sought reelection won their races. (Senate challengers fared slightly better, winning 10 percent and 18 percent, respectively.) In 1996, every single one of the 113 Congress members first elected in the 1980s won his or her race for reelection. All but 4 won by 10 percent or more, and 75 won by a whopping 30 percent or more. While 142 incumbents were defeated in the 1960s, that number fell to just 97 in the 1970s, to 88 in the 1980s, and to 102 in the 1990s. . . .

The incumbent's advantage is largely predicated on money. Of course, the fact that incumbents can gerrymander districts once a decade also helps their bids for reelection but is marginal when compared with the potent mixture of money and incumbency. In 1988, incumbents ended up with twice as much in *leftover* funds as their challengers *spent.* In 2000, House incumbents outspent their challengers by better than 4 to 1 ($408.5 million to $89 million), enjoyed an 8-to-1 edge in PAC money, and by the end of October had a 13-to-1 advantage in cash on hand. Senate incumbents in 2000 raised $155.9 million, compared with $63 million by their challengers, and held a 6-to-1 edge in both PAC funds and cash on hand. . . . One can't help but conclude that the two distinct political parties in Washington have given way to one monolithic alternative: the incumbent party.

Carrying over war chests is one of the great time-honored traditions of the incumbency protection program. Amass as much cash as you possibly can—even if you have no known opponent—and then use it to intimidate potential challengers, who will drop out or never even run to begin with. Once reelection is achieved, the member of Congress carries over the war chest into the next campaign and the next and the next. In a very real sense rolling over such treasuries violates the spirit of the campaign finance contribution limits, since a John Donor may give Challenger X only $2000 for a particular campaign in a particular year but may have given Congressman Z a total of $8000 for a campaign against Challenger X ($2000 in each of four election cycles).

In Public Citizen's Congress Watch study *House Insurance: How the Permanent Congress Hoards Campaign Cash,* members of the 101st Congress were found to have over $67 million stowed away in campaign war chests *the month they took office,* "virtually assur[ing] reelection [and] certainly discourag[ing] qualified candidates from challenging the financially stronger representatives." According to the same Congress Watch report, 89 percent of House incumbents faced financially noncompetitive races in 2000, meaning they faced either no opposition or challengers with less than half their campaign resources.

The only ways to crack open this continuing "unfair advantage" are serious campaign finance reform or congressional term limits. And we'll get reform only when members of Congress start fearing limits on their terms more than they fear limits on their money.

THE MONEY CHASE CREATES "PART-TIME LEGISLATORS, FULL-TIME FUND-RAISERS"

On any given workday, you can see streams of Congress members leaving their Capitol Hill offices to go to small campaign cubicles in order to dial for dollars. "The problem is much worse than portrayed," says Senator Ron Wyden (D–OR). "The money chase is so time-consuming that people should wonder how we have time to get anything done. Yes, the day after an election, people sleep in on Wednesday. But then the money chase starts in again, day after day, year in and year out.

"In an election year," he continued, "members have cards or Blackberrys that say '8–9 Grange; 9–10 Hearing on Technology; 10–4 money calls at DCCC.' For that much of the day, a significant number of public officials are sitting in a dank office away from their public office with their tin cup out instead of thinking about how to help their constituents."

Ask anyone involved in the game, and, if they're honest, the refrain will be the same. In his autobiography, Bill Bradley wrote that, despite his fame and popularity, he had to spend 40 percent of his freshman Senate term fund-raising for re-election. One New York congressman, well known for raising tons of special-interest money, confided at a fund-raiser in early 2002, "I spend almost half my time raising money." When asked if his job performance would change if he didn't have to fund-raise incessantly, the representative didn't hesitate. "Oh yes, I'd be much more independent and effective."

Even Senator Dick Durbin (D–IL), among the hardest working of the new senators, is candid enough to admit in an interview, "Of course I won't miss votes, but after that, fund-raising has to take precedence. We'll schedule fund-raisers and then build around them." Representative Sherrod Brown (D–OH) confides that he has three full-time jobs: "Congressman, campaigner, fund-raiser."

Senator Robert C. Byrd, the longest-serving member of either chamber, put it best, calling his colleagues "part-time legislators and full-time fund-raisers." Senator Byrd told Mark Shields that during his tenure as Senate majority leader he often had to delay votes because of fund-raising conflicts. He mocked the parade of requests he endured for years: "Please, no votes Monday . . . no votes after four on Thursday . . . I've got a fund-raiser scheduled in Los Angeles . . . in New York . . . in my home state." Senator John Kerry, who refuses to take PAC money and has 55,000 donors averaging $36 each, said in the early 1990s, "A few months ago, I was out in Columbus, Ohio. And the same day I was there, across the hall was Tom Harkin of Iowa, and the next morning there was a room reserved downstairs for Bill Bradley of New Jersey. Now, that is Columbus, Ohio. That is ridiculous."

Stanley Sheinbaum, a prominent Democratic donor and activist in California, grew so frustrated with members of Congress calling to ask for money that he told a high-ranking senator he would accept his request for a meeting only "on the proviso that money not be discussed." But given the rules of engagement, is it really a surprise that incumbents regard donors more as ATMs than as people, and that donors come to resent it?

THE MONEY CHASE DETERS TALENT FROM SEEKING OFFICE

Challengers know they must make it through a "money primary" first if they ever want to reach the "voters' primary"—and the polling place of donors can turn away anyone without secure financing, which of course deters potential contenders who have more talent than funds. "At some point," argues Joshua Rosenkranz of the Brennan Center for Justice, "the spending of money is less an exercise in speech, and more an exercise in raw power—the power to dominate the conversation and to scare away all potential challengers." Of course it's impossible to calculate how many good women and men decide not to seek office because of the prohibitive costs, but most astute observers assume that it's many. As Senator Paul Wellstone (D–MN) laments, "People are giving up and not running for senator or governor because the money chase is too much."

When Elizabeth Dole aborted her run for president in October 1999, money was the single reason she cited. She pointed to the 80-to-1 fund-raising edge George W. Bush held over her. "I hoped to compensate by attracting new people to the political process, by emphasizing experience and advocating substantive issues," she told a roomful of tearful supporters. "But as important as these things may be, the bottom line remains money."

Perhaps most alarming is the case of Reubin Askew. So vast and disquieting were the demands for money in Askew's 1988 Florida Senate race that the former governor abruptly dropped out—despite opinion polls showing him with a 4-to-1 lead in the primary and a 2-to-1 advantage in the general election. "Something is seriously wrong with our system," Askew explained, "when many candidates for the Senate need to spend 75 percent of their time raising money." As Askew's issues director for the campaign, Dexter Filkins, wrote, "The need to raise so much cash so fast limited Askew's contact with the average voter—that is, one who did not donate money. We simply didn't have time for them." If Askew, a popular elected official, couldn't handle the incessant demands of fund-raising, how do you suppose an unwealthy, unfamous, and unsubsidized workingman or -woman might make out?

Of course, there's no formal "money primary" in the law or Constitution. All potential candidates are allowed to raise up to $1000 a donor per election or give themselves as much of their personal wealth as they can. "The law, in its majestic equality, permits the rich as well as the poor to sleep under bridges, to beg in the streets and steal bread," wrote Anatole France, which inspired this extrapolation from the late U.S. Appellate Court Judge J. Skelly Wright: "The law, in its majestic equality, allows the poor as well as the rich to form political action committees, to purchase the most sophisticated polling, media and direct mail techniques and to drown out each other's voices by overwhelming expenditures in political campaigns. Financial inequities . . . undermine the political proposition to which this nation is dedicated— that all men are created equal."

These financial disparities account in part for why there are so few blue-collar workers in Congress. "Do you honestly think that a butcher could get elected to the Senate today?" Senator Byrd rhetorically asked. "A garbage collector? A small grocery man? A welder?"

THE MONEY CHASE FAVORS MULTIMILLIONAIRES

When soliciting funds from individuals and PACs turns out to be inadequate to cover the costs of campaigning, candidates will often supply the requisite funds by drawing from their personal finances. In 2000, twenty-seven House and Senate candidates spent at least $500,000 of their own money on their own campaigns. Self-financing is especially pronounced for challengers and for candidates in open-seat races. Challengers in the 1996 House elections spent an average of over $40,000 of their own money, one sixth of their total campaign costs; candidates in open-seat races spent over $90,000. The average Senate challenger that year spent $645,000—one quarter of his/her total campaign costs—out of his/her own pocket.

Already, more than a third of Senate members are millionaires—and the number keeps growing. At least 50 members of the two houses are multimillionaires, among them the following senators: John Kerry, with a net worth of $675 million; Jon Corzine, $400 million; Herbert Kohl (D–WI), $300 million; Jay Rockefeller IV (D–WV), $200 million; Peter Fitzgerald (R–IL), $50 million; Mark Dayton (D–MN), $20 million; and Bill Frist (R–TN), $20 million.

Asked why so many of the deep-pocketed senators are, surprisingly, Democrats, Senator Carl Levin laughs. "It's a growing solution to Republican money. Since we can't raise as much special-interest money, we look more for candidates who can spend their own." Corzine, a former Goldman Sachs CEO, agrees. "Democratic leaders more eagerly recruited [wealthy self-financers] to relieve financial pressure on the party and because more such Democrats [than Republicans] run believing that government does good things," New Jersey's junior senator explains. "There's a tradition from FDR to JFK of Democrats who do it to fix the world and level the playing field of society."

Indeed, party leaders acknowledge that they explicitly try to recruit self-financing candidates, not necessarily the best candidates, to run. But since *Buckley v. Valeo* permits the wealthy to contribute as much to their own campaigns as they like—because the Court reasoned a person can't corrupt *himself,* never considering how such spending could corrupt the *process*—the strategy is legal, and often a winning one. Think about the thousands of hours of fund-raising that can be used for other things, like wooing party officials and opinion leaders, reaching out to voters, studying up on issues, and making news. Or the bottomless budget for television advertising that enables the candidate to flood the airwaves with her message.

Those who counter that advertisements don't force voters to vote for their candidates are correct, at least in a narrow sense. There's probably no amount of money that could persuade a majority to vote for Pat Buchanan, or to buy an Edsel. But advertising is a $600-billion-a-year industry for a reason—and the reason is that, overall, the more advertising a candidate does, the more likely he is to make the sale. Or to raise doubts about an opponent who can't afford to rebut. Put it another way: Suppose the New York Yankees are the best team in baseball; who would you bet on if the Yankees could bat in only two innings while their opponent, the worst major-league team, could bat in nine?

That said, being a multimillionaire certainly doesn't guarantee victory. Sometimes a candidate does something so self-immolating, or is found so untenable, that not even money can glide him into office. Jay Rockefeller and Jon Corzine—and even publishing magnate William Randolph Hearst, whose newspaper empire helped fund winning campaigns for Congress in 1902 and 1904—may have been successful, but Michael Huffington and Al Checchi are two examples of wealthy self-financing candidates in California who lost. Huffington, in his $30 million campaign for U.S. Senate in 1994, lost the election after attacking the immigrants flooding the state while, it was revealed, he himself had hired an illegal alien in his household. Checchi, the past head of American Airlines, lost his $40 million Democratic gubernatorial primary in 1998 after he ran a barrage of ads so brutally harsh that people began to resent *him*. Both candidates also faced opponents who were well financed and able to spend at least half their amounts—incumbent Senator Dianne Feinstein against Huffington, and now-Governor Gray Davis against Checchi.

But self-financers are starting to win major races now, which encourages other very wealthy people to try to do the same. As I mentioned earlier, multimillionaires Tony Sanchez in Texas and Douglas Forrester in New Jersey won competitive primaries in 2002. Following the success of Michael Bloomberg in New York City, five multimillionaires ran in statewide races in New York in 2002: Jane S. Hoffman (who later dropped out due to health) and Dennis Mehiel for lieutenant governor, William Mulrow for comptroller, and Tom Golisano for governor. Eliot Spitzer, the incumbent Attorney General, also significantly self-financed his initial victory in 1998.

Mark Schmitt of the Open Society Institute wrote, "The self-financed Democrats of most recent vintage . . . have all shown themselves to be as capable, liberal, and brave as their older counterparts like Jay Rockefeller. But there is no getting around the fact that the advantage of self-financed candidates has created a political plutocracy that looks less like America, economically, than at any time since before the direct election of senators."

If something doesn't change soon, there will be only three types of people running for and holding office in the future: super-fund-raisers, celebrities, and multimillionaires.

THE MONEY CHASE CORRUPTS LEGISLATION—
"BUYING SHARP'S SILENCE"

Of course, much of the $3 billion contributed to candidates in 2000 came because donors knew the candidate, believed in the candidate's philosophy, liked his/her personality, looks, religion, or race. The problem, however, is that the system is also flooded with a Niagara of contributions from economic interests seeking a return. And getting one.

A dozen years ago, the Democracy Project, a policy institute I founded, published a study attempting to analyze the costs of the private financing of elections. *Public Funding vs. Private Funding: Two Case Studies of the Benefits of Campaign Finance Reform* was an early attempt to quantify a significant and largely immeasurable problem. We started by examining how special-interest-inspired legislation can increase a product's cost to consumers, how tax breaks due to PACs increase the burden to taxpayers generally, and how legislation needed but forestalled by PACs can impose additional health and other costs on taxpayers.

The results, similar to estimates conducted more recently by groups like Public Citizen, were staggering. In *taxpayer* costs alone, the bailout of failed S&Ls cost $25 billion a year, the deregulation of tobacco (plus a farm bill authorizing manufacturers to buy stored tobacco at 90 percent discounts) cost Americans $2.1 billion a year, and loopholes won by Chicago's commodities traders hit taxpayers with a $300 million tab.

Then add new *consumer* costs. Sugar price supports (delivered to repay seventeen major sugar PACs who doled out $3.3 million to Senate and House members) cost consumers $3 billion a year. Similarly, dairy and milk price supports milked consumers by tacking an additional $9 billion onto the $45 billion shoppers already were spending on dairy.* Add to that an additional $2 billion a year on utilities, $10 billion a year on beer and wine, and $4.3 billion on health costs stemming from the passage of a much weaker version of the Clean Air Act, and the impact of PACs on American families is, in effect, a political corruption tax.

In all, the rough cost to Americans of the *private* system of financing elections was $50 billion annually. By contrast, the costs of *public* financing are modest and transparent; no serious proposals for public funding of elections have exceeded $500 million to $1 billion.

"I think most people assume—I do, certainly—that someone making an extraordinarily large contribution is going to get some kind of an extraordinary return for it," said Supreme Court Justice David H. Souter. "I think that is a pervasive assumption. And . . . there is certainly an appearance of, call it an attenuated corruption, if you will, that large contributors are simply going to get better service, whatever that service may be, from a politician than the average contributor, let alone no contributor."

---

*To put this in perspective, the market wholesale price of a gallon of milk at the time was 61 cents worldwide versus 87 cents in the United States.

CHAPTER 3

Smoke Screen

PHILIP J. HILTS

> Yes, this world is flat and boring; as for the other, bullshit! I myself go
> resigned to my fate, without hope, and to kill time while awaiting death,
> I smoke slender cigarettes thumbing my nose at the gods.
> —Jules LaForgue, 1880, France, "La Cigarette"
> quoted from *Cigarettes Are Sublime*

When I first began to write about tobacco as a regular beat at the *New York Times*, I noticed something which puzzled me: the industry answers to routine questions were predictable on every subject, except children. When this topic arose I noted a slight change in tone. I had already learned that tobacco men and women these days don't mind being rather frank in private conversation about the diseases and addiction associated with smoking. After all, the companies are still profitable, have political potency equal to that of any other group in society, and have a strong record of defending themselves against claims by injured smokers. There should be a sense of confidence. But that confidence flags when the topic turns to children. The company people become uneasy; they bristle defensively, or else fall into silence. It would be a while before I discovered the reason for this little oddity.

It is commonly said that the great attraction of the cigarette for children is that it is forbidden. "Cigarette smoking begins under the sign of the illicit," as Richard Klein puts it. "Since moralists, no less than doctors, have disapproved of tobacco from its introduction, its use constitutes a form of defiance of authority, of the laws of man and God."

There is defiance, an experiment with disobedience, but in real life it is not just the adolescent and his God at odds. Lurking behind the tree, in the background of the tableau is the agent of the tobacco trade. Unlike the tempter in Eden, the tobacco agents come to their role reluctantly. If the companies could choose, they would not intentionally lure children into smoking. Matters would be simpler if they could keep the whole business between adults and not worry about the young ones.

Unfortunately, and this is still unappreciated, it is not possible to run a cigarette business without actively working the sidewalks where the children are. This is the source of the tobacco industry's discomfort.

The trouble arises from two facts peculiar to the industry. The first is obvious enough, and in private documents beginning in the early 1960s, executives have spoken plainly about their awareness of it: the reason that tobacco is ingested steadily, over many years—not just occasionally, not just tried out—is that the nicotine in tobacco is fiercely addictive. In unguarded moments, even tobacco executives, not to appear as fools who don't understand what they are doing, acknowledge this fact of business.

To bracket the period with acknowledgments:

From 1963, Sir Charles Ellis of the British American Tobacco Company spoke of smoking as "a habit of addiction," and his American colleague Addison Yeaman wrote that nicotine "is addictive. We are, then, in the business of selling nicotine, an addictive drug effective in the release of stress mechanisms."

A more recent example, from the fall of 1994, is the commentary of Ross Johnson, at one time the chief executive officer of R. J. Reynolds Tobacco. While he held that job, he did his duty and denied the hazards of smoking and the addictive nature of it. But after he left, he was interviewed for a profile in the *Wall Street Journal*. His business acumen was noted. He was asked about whether nicotine is addictive. Outside the closed circle of the tobacco industry, he could be plain: "Of course it's addictive. That's why you smoke the stuff."

The exercise of trying to corner executives into admitting what is obvious to others has limited value, of course. But here is the second peculiar fact about the tobacco trade, which, when combined with the first, makes the companies vulnerable in both politics and law:

This addiction, fundamental to the trade, does not develop among adults. Among those over the age of 21 who take up smoking for the first time, more than 90 percent soon drop it completely. It takes more than a year, and sometimes up to three years, to establish a nicotine addiction; adults simply don't stick with it. If it were true that the companies steer clear of children, as they say, the entire industry would collapse within a single generation.

Put in market terms, the most important datum of the tobacco trade is that, among those who will be their customers for life, 89 percent have already become their customers by age 19. In fact three-quarters had already joined the ranks of users by age 17.

This knowledge appears in documents from inside certain tobacco companies. The secret of how and when nicotine addiction develops, why it does not develop in adults, and even how companies might make use of these facts, has been learned only gradually over the years by the companies, but most clearly and intensively in the wave of research that came after the scares of 1954.

Thus, the reason this topic is different from all other topics is that it is both the most crucial of all issues to the continued business, and the issue of greatest exposure for the industry. What an awful conjunction of bright and dark planets!

Because of the companies' fears, over the years the tobacco folks have become less and less candid even in private about the fact that they cannot run their businesses without the children. . . .

The logic of the situation, which may have been realized only partially in earlier years, is this: Smoking appeals to the very young not because of its nicotine, but chiefly for a number of social reasons—they need this product as a badge of daring and independence, and this is at least partly *because* it is dangerous and discouraged by authorities. Adults *do not* start smoking because that social motivation is not present; adults have already formed up their image of themselves, and found the necessary badges of independence and contrariness elsewhere. Adults most especially do not take up cigarette smoking, which is the least pleasant form of tobacco use. The cigarette aroma is not as good, and the cigarette invites deep inhaling, which leads to awful trouble with breathing and coughing that does not occur as much when pipes or cigars are used.

Once this is clear, then one may ask about the details of the young starting smoker's habit. The young smoker experiments early with a few puffs or a few cigarettes very early between ages 5 and 13, then moves on to smoke a few cigarettes daily in the next stage, between 14 and 17. The habit reaches the full usual addiction by 18 to 21 years old, at a little more than a pack a day—the average lifetime level.

In dollars, this profile means that between ages 5 and 18, the children are spending far less money and buying fewer cigarettes than their older counterparts. A child starting may spend only $100 per year on cigarettes. A confirmed smoker of a major brand might typically spend more like $800 per year.

If the product were video cameras, this annual purchase would suggest marketing to the older, more regular customer and leaving the kids alone.

But with cigarettes, it turns out that because cigarette smoking begins in a psychological need, a brand can become bound up in the very self-image of the new smoker. That creates a very high likelihood that a smoker will stay with their first regular brand for years or even for life. Brand loyalty, it is called, and it is far higher among the young and among cigarette smokers than just about anyplace else in business.

In 1950, a *U.S. Tobacco Journal* article noted that even though the industry had been extraordinarily successful in making cigarettes glamorous, and had introduced them to nearly half the adult population, "A massive potential market still exists among women and young adults, cigarette industry leaders agreed, acknowledging that recruitment of these millions of prospective smokers comprises the major objective for the immediate future and on a long term basis as well." A Philip Morris executive was quoted by the journal: "Students are tremendously loyal. If you catch them, they'll stick with you like glue."

In addition, it turns out that advertising to new smokers often does not reach directly to the candidate smoker, but is filtered through the perceptions and tastes of slightly older, model smokers. So those who take up the habit are carriers: they infect their younger peers. The most needy and insecure kids, who cannot manage their independence without props, but instead find a commercial product to use, draw in others by showing that cigarettes can work. Howard Beals, a tobacco-company-supported researcher, says that "same-sex peers" are the single strongest influence: a boy is eight times as likely to smoke if his best friend does, and a girl is six times as likely if her best friend does.

Taking the long view, investing a larger percentage of your marketing dollars in children will pay off in the future as they remain loyal and their habit grows in dollar value and becomes stable. Further, buying the most loyal smokers, those who start young, helps prevent the dangerous problem of brand-switching which occurs among adult starters more often than among young starters. Though companies have often said they advertise cigarettes to get people to switch brands, this is illogical: those who switch are the least stable, and are likely to keep switching right past your brand.

In 1957, E. Gilbert, a Philip Morris executive, wrote, "hitting the youth can be more efficient even though the cost to reach them is higher, because they are willing to experiment, they have more influence over others in their age group than they will later in life, and they are far more loyal to their starting brand."

U.S. Tobacco, a company which virtually invented a market for chewing tobacco beginning in 1970, explicitly outlined their strategy based on similar principles, creating "starter" brands that don't sell all that well in the market as a whole, but get a user started with sweet tastes and relatively low nicotine.

This situation explains the odd statistical fact that U.S. Tobacco spends half its entire advertising and promotion budget on young people who are only 2 percent of the market: They come in 2 percent at a time, year by year, and both accumulate in numbers and increase their habit later. But without the entry portal which the company punched through, the habit would not exist (and did not exist before about 1970) as a feature in young American culture.

And so it is that we see in the tobacco documents that when getting ready to target a young audience, the data that marketers prepare includes not only which brands are smoked by which sex and age group, but there is more: what percent of this brand is smoked by starters? What percent by switchers? What was the chief factor in getting this smoker started? Peer influence? Package design? Brand image?

So it is that tobacco advertising to children is misunderstood. The difficulty is that anti-smoking groups seem to have blamed advertising for people's smoking habits, whereas no rational soul believes advertising is enough to get people started smoking, or to keep them smoking. It is not to be imagined that children see Joe Camel and think, that's cool, I better start smoking. Not at all.

The role is more indirect and subtle, though still powerful enough to have a major effect on behavior. That is, powerful enough that companies spend $6 billion per year advertising. They would not do it if it did not work in some way, to some degree.

The way in which it works is this: children are just beginning to shape their image of themselves, elbowing out a niche in the world, and must somehow differentiate themselves from parents and other adults, and get out from under what the authorities in life want from them. They dress differently, sometimes shockingly. They listen to different, sometimes shocking, music. In this quest, the children are worried, insecure, seeking to make choices and have them supported by their friends or others they respect. Most obviously, their choices are supported by each other. They have learned to lean on each other for aid and assent. Sometimes older siblings lend support. But because the insecurity is great, as many supports as possible are needed.

Here is the role of advertising for children. It is not that they are messages that argue with and convince children to smoke. Rather, they exploit a natural event of human development. It is natural to rebel and separate oneself from parents and family for a time. What is so troublesome about this approach is that it exploits this natural need, offering a destructive manner of rebellion as an alternative to the more constructive varieties, such as outrageous fashion, music, and politics.

The leading companies insert themselves in the family as it develops, and lend support to a choice the children have made or are about to make. They back it up with images, and sly ads; what is already attractive for one or another reason. It gives an extra push. It helps support the idea, learned elsewhere, that smoking is a pleasurable adult activity.

And we should add, it does so without regard to the consequences, and does so for profit.

Lest you doubt the reach of the tobacco company programs, more than half the teenage smokers in America own gifts, such as lighters, knives, or tee shirts, from cigarette companies.

While much of the documentary evidence on tobacco is about plans and theories, on the subject of children we also have a sheaf of papers giving concrete detail from the industry's direct work with children, and what has come of it. . . .

Among the details the companies discover in their research was that tobacco experimentation begins, fairly often, around age five, in imitation of older siblings. More often, though, it starts about age 7 or 8, while serious efforts to learn to smoke occur at 12 or 13 years old. "Part of the thrill of adolescent smoking is the thrill of hiding it from parental wrath."

"In some cases, the beginning smoker is not just emulating the peer group in general, but copying a specific member of it that is respected and admired. . . ."

"More important reasons for this attraction are the 'forbidden fruits' aspect of cigarettes. The adolescent seeks to display his new urge for independence with a symbol, and cigarettes are such a symbol since they are associated with adulthood and at the same time the adults seek to deny them to the young."

The company thus must ally itself with the children, against "adults" and aid the child in proclaiming "his break with childhood, at least to his peers."

There is nausea, sometimes even vomiting on the first try, of course, but "this perceived failure spurs them on to try again, and not fail."

The complexities of adolescent life and parental control are reflected here. When to hide it, when to announce it ("If successfully hidden, the young smoker will announce his smoking around the age of 15 or 16"). Parents nag children to stop; this nagging leads to spiteful attempts to continue secretly. Schools do not offer a significant barrier, and "reactions to formal school lectures and films about smoking are mainly anger over a perceived intrusion on the right of the smoker to do as he wishes. . . ."

Apart from the memos already cited, which show what groups the companies target, there is other, more direct evidence of their intentions.

One example is the RJR program which was established to sell Camel cigarettes, using Joe the Camel and other inducements. The Camel campaign was not a single shot, but was one example of broader strategies outlined in RJR memos. These plans were referred to in company documents as YAS, for targeting of "young adult smokers," and as FUBYAS, for programs that worked to be the "First Usual Brand of Young Adult Smokers." These titles are somewhat deceptive, as they refer to "adults," when, for example, the first usual brand is smoked as a child, historical evidence over decades demonstrates. The appearance of the word "adult" suggests that the company, when it began these programs, was aware that internal documents should be careful not to suggest the targeting of children.

One document written in preparation for changing Camel from an older person's cigarette to the cigarette of "starters" noted, "Camel's flat to declining performance is due primarily to the share losses posted by its non-filter parent . . . it has little to offer FUBYAS."

In public, the company has said Camel promotions and advertising were aimed at those 18 to 34 years old. In the crucial graphs and charts of the confidential Camel business plans, however, the target is much narrower: 18–20-year-olds. The company's charts of the share of smokers they have succeeded in attracting reports that the huge growth among 18–20-year-olds is replacing older, quitting smokers. There is also a chart which states directly that it is not the older groups that matter for Camel, but the "Young Adult Smokers growth, driven by 18–20-year-old group."

Historical data, like that from John Pierce in San Diego, shows that, whatever group they claim to approach in documents so far exposed, they have in fact had the greatest effect on those under 18 years old.

Also, in search of objective data to supply an underpinning for the outrage of health departments, the California Department of Health carried out an extensive survey, reviewing the tobacco advertising and promotions in 5,773 stores around the state. This is the ultimate court of intention—what is actually out in the stores. This is where companies put their money. If convenience stores do not show any evidence that young people are being targeted, then we would have to begin to believe the company protestations.

All things being equal, promotions should end up evenly distributed in stores. But they are not. More promotions are placed in stores within 1,000 feet of a school than are placed in other stores. Promotions are near the candy counters more often than elsewhere. Displays are set at a height of 3 feet or lower more often than higher. In stores near schools, and in neighborhoods with a large number of children under 17, there is a distinctly greater number of signs on the outside of the store and in the windows than is the case in stores not near schools.

These disproportions do not happen by accident, as these ad placements are not only intentional, but carefully governed.

The companies deny marketing to children, of course, and offer various programs of their own—chiefly advertising which says it's illegal to smoke—to prove they are against youth smoking.

But their lobbying pattern is quite different. In 1993, riding on the tide of anti-smoking laws enacted in more than 700 towns and counties around the U.S., Congress passed an amendment to the bill re-authorizing funds for the Alcohol, Drug Abuse and Mental Health Administration, requiring each of the states to pass a law that would make cigarette sales illegal to those under the age of 18, and more importantly, requiring each state to establish a program that would actually work. In the language of the bill, the states would have to establish programs "in a manner that can reasonably be expected to reduce the extent to which tobacco products are available to individuals under the age of 18." If the states fail, in the judgment of the Secretary of Health and Human Services, then federal monies for drug abuse programs to the states could be reduced. States depend on those funds, and so it is a serious threat.

The tobacco companies and their strongest supporters in Congress have worked to delay the day when the "Synar Amendment," as it is called after its chief sponsor, the late Rep. Mike Synar of Oklahoma, takes effect. Rep. Tom Bliley, of Richmond, Virginia, now the chairman of the House Commerce Committee, threatened to challenge the law on constitutional grounds if the HHS ever tried to put an effective version of it into effect.

In a draft of the rule, HHS would require that states demonstrate their programs are effective by showing that children who try to buy cigarettes fail more than half the time. Then, over the next three years, the states must show their stores sell to minors less often than 40, 30 and 20 percent of the time.

The Tobacco Institute in comments to the federal government said this kind of regulation is outrageous, and suggested that the Synar Amendment was never intended to reduce sales to minors significantly. It suggested making sales to those under age 18 illegal, but without any rules to ensure enforcement.

The companies are on record as against most methods of enforcement, including inspections, sting operations, surveys, and holding merchants responsible for illegal sales. Instead they suggest punitive measures which would be certain not only to backfire, but to cast the enforcers in the worst possible light. They suggest targeting for arrest children who buy cigarettes rather than retailers who sell them. They also suggest arresting or fining the clerks in the stores, not the managers or owners. . . .

I pursued the matter to those who were actually responsible for carrying out the targeting of children.

I began with a memorandum first mentioned in passing by the *Wall Street Journal* in 1991. As the Joe Camel and YAS campaigns got underway in 1989, RJR executives held regional meetings with salesmen to explain just who was being targeted, and how they were to be targeted. To the executives' discomfort, they had to be rather explicit with the salesmen.

Company officials realized that making RJR products the first brands of young people would require a completely different kind of marketing than that used with regular smokers. They would be heavy on gimmicks and gifts, tee shirts, cartoon figures, fancy cigarette lighters and knives. The campaigns turned out to be some of the most successful marketing campaigns in the history of the tobacco industry, taking brands from virtually nothing to a major share of the youth market in only a few years.

One key component of the program, company officials said, was the decision to pick out convenience stores near high schools and colleges to hit with a barrage of extra premiums and promotions—from discount prices to free cigarette lighters, tee shirts and caps, as well as access to more expensive items like jackets that could be discounted with coupons from cigarette packages.

(The industry has for many years maintained that it will not advertise to anyone under 21, will not provide samples to them, will not mail samples to anyone under 21, or advertise on any billboards near schools.

The industry's code of behavior, signed by RJR, also states that "There shall be no other distribution of non-tobacco premium items bearing cigarette brand names, logos, etc. without written, signed certification that the addressee is 21 years of age or older.")

One memo, written after regional sales directors arrived back in their regions, came from J. P. McMahon, division manager in Florida. It was written on January 10, 1990, and was addressed to sales representatives in his area. "<u>VERY IMPORTANT, PLEASE READ CAREFULLY!!!</u>," it read, in underline and capital letters at the top.

"I need all of you to study the attached . . . list of monthly accounts in your [area] that are presently doing more than 100 Cartons Per Week, for purposes of denoting stores that are heavily frequented by young adult shoppers. These stores can be in close proximity to colleges, high schools or areas where there are a large number of young adults frequent the store." (Weird grammar in the original.)

As high schools and junior high schools have students from ages 11 to 18, this amounts to an explicit order to target children. The company at the time denied that was the intent, and said Mr. McMahon misunderstood orders.

However, when the FDA began to check out this tale, they found that there was another regional manager who had misunderstood. R. G. Warlick, chief in Oklahoma, wrote to his sales reps, "Due to a revision in the definition of what is a Retail Young Adult Smoker Retailer Account, you will be required to resubmit again your list of YAS accounts in your territory." So, not only had they already targeted stores where young people hang out, but now, the sales reps are to be sure to add some specific stores: "The criteria for you to utilize in identifying these accounts are as follows: All package action calls [stores that sell packs rather than cartons, that is, stores frequented by the young] located across from, adjacent to are [sic] in the general vicinity of the High Schools or College Campus (Under 30 years of age)."

Terence Sullivan, a sales rep in Florida under regional manager McMahon, said that he and others objected to the explicit targeting of junior high school and high school children. He said in an interview that while children might well pick up the habit, he did not want to be party to pitching them directly. "We were targeting kids, and I said at the time it was unethical and maybe illegal, but I was told that it was just company policy," he said.

Sullivan has since been fired by the company, and has filed a suit for wrongful dismissal in reply.

To check the tale further, I tracked down two other salesmen who worked on the campaign in Florida.

Mike Shaw, a salesman with RJR for twenty years, said the program was intended to target kids, including high school students, quite plainly.

"At just about every meeting I ever attended, the question came up, how can we get our share of the convenience store business where Philip Morris was doing so well. The convenience stores are where kids buy their cigarettes, one pack or two at a time."

"We wanted to get into that market, and used the promotional items, tee shirts, baseball caps, and one hot item were lighters, knowing full well the people we were giving these away to was kids half the time."

The YAS program, which started in 1989, he said, was the same as other promotions, only more aggressive—more premiums, more discounts.

"We actually would do exactly what those letters said," referring to the McMahon and Warlick memos. "Kids is what we're talking about; most are not adults. These are kids."

He said the idea was to designate the stores where young people were, and load them up with ads and promotions. "If you got a high school on a block, and at the end of the block you got a Seven–11, that's one YAS outlet. The criteria you would use was simple. The stores were the ones where the kids hang out."

He said the concrete description of who they were targeting was not supposed to make it into print, but was intended to be verbal. "The managers weren't supposed to write it down. These two guys who wrote it in their memos were just a little more stupid than the others. They were told to do something and they did it."

After word of the McMahon memo leaked out, mention of the McMahon memo appeared in the paper, and soon many documents about the program were destroyed. Each division office was issued a shredder, he said.

Gary Velcher, Chain Store Account Manager in South Florida for RJR, said that even though the company now says the memos got the company policy wrong, and misconstrued what was laid out at sales meetings, he was at the same sales meetings, and has read the memos.

"I find nothing inconsistent in the memos with what went on in that meeting" in Ft. Lauderdale that kicked off the YAS campaign. The YAS "campaign took a more aggressive posture than any I had ever seen. It was more overt. The purpose and intent was clearer than ever," he said.

The plan, he said, was to identify stores as "young people's hangouts" and concentrate heavily your promotions in those stores—buy two get one free, a free Camel tee shirt with four packs, and so on. He said that he was told to "make sure you never run out there, make sure there's always a chance to buy a 'deal pack' of some kind there."

He also said that when news of the McMahon memo leaked out, documents were recalled and shredded, the program was renamed, but went on as before.

Terri Sullivan said that the clearest statement he heard from RJR headquarters executives came in a question and answer period at a regional sales meeting. Someone asked exactly who the young people were that were being targeted, junior high school kids, or even younger?

The reply came back, "They got lips? We want 'em."

CHAPTER 4

Water for Profit

JOHN LUOMA

Even before the water turned brown, Gordon Certain had plenty to worry about. With his north Atlanta neighborhood in the middle of a growth boom, the president of the North Buckhead Civic Association had been busy fielding complaints about traffic, a sewer tunnel being built near a nature preserve, and developers razing tidy postwar ranch homes to make room for mansions. But nothing compared to the volume of calls and emails that flooded Certain's home office in May, when Georgia's environmental protection agency issued an alert to North Buckhead residents: Their tap water, the agency warned, wasn't safe to drink unless they boiled it first. Some neighbors, Certain recalls, had just fed formula to their baby when they heard the alert. "I had parents calling me in tears," he says. "The things that have happened to the water here have sure scared the hell out of a lot of people." A month later, another "boil water" alert came; this time, when Certain turned on his own tap, the liquid that gushed out was the color of rust, with bits of debris floating in it.

Atlanta's water service had never been without its critics; there had always been complaints about slow repairs and erroneous water bills. But the problems intensified three years ago, says Certain, after one of the world's largest private water companies took over the municipal system and promised to turn it into an "international showcase" for public-private partnerships. Instead of ushering in a new era of trouble-free drinking water, Atlanta's experiment with privatization has brought a host of new problems. This year there have been five boil-water alerts, indicating unsafe contaminants might be present. Fire hydrants have been useless for months. Leaking water mains have gone unrepaired for weeks. Despite all of this, the city's contractor—United Water, a subsidiary of French-based multinational Suez—has lobbied the City Council to add millions more to its $21-million-a-year contract.

Atlanta's experience has become Exhibit A in a heated controversy over the push by a rapidly growing global water industry to take over public water systems. At the heart of the debate are two questions: Should water, a basic necessity for human survival, be controlled by for-profit interests? And can multinational companies actually deliver on what they promise—better service and safe, affordable water?

Already, the two largest players in the industry, French-based conglomerates Suez and Vivendi Universal, manage water for 230 million people, mostly in Europe and the developing world. Now they are seeking access to a vast and relatively un-tapped market: the United States, where 85 percent of people still get their water from public utilities. Private water providers have positioned themselves as the so-lution to the developing world's water problems, notes Hugh Jackson, a policy ana-lyst at the advocacy group Public Citizen. "But it's a lot harder for them to make the case when here, in the world's center of capitalism, cities are delivering tremendous amounts of high-quality, clean, inexpensive water to people."

Yet over the past decade, hundreds of U.S. cities and counties, including Indi-anapolis and Milwaukee, have hired private companies to manage their waterworks. Currently New Orleans; Stockton, California; and Laredo, Texas, are in the process of going private, although opposition has sprung up in all three cities. Water companies have been conducting annual "fly ins" to Washington, D.C., to press their legislative agenda, lobbying for laws that would protect companies from lawsuits over contam-inated water and block municipalities from taking back troubled privatized systems. Most recently, a bipartisan group in Congress has been pushing a federal waterworks funding bill, advocated by the National Association of Water Companies, which would require cities to "consider" privatization before they can tap federal funds for upgrad-ing or expanding public utilities and would also subsidize such privatization deals.

At the municipal level the lobbying pressure is equally intense, with water com-panies actively courting local officials (the U.S. Conference of Mayors' website fea-tures a large ad from Vivendi subsidiary U.S. Filter) and spending hundreds of thousands of dollars supporting privatization in local referendums. "It's hard for local guys to turn these companies away," Massachusetts' former water commissioner Douglas MacDonald has said. "They're everywhere, with arms like an octopus."

The argument behind privatization is that only corporate efficiency can rescue the nation's aging waterworks. But if success is measured in terms of delivering an essential commodity to everyone who needs it, then the industry's record is less than encouraging. Around the world, cities with private water-management companies have been plagued by lapses in service, soaring costs, and corruption. In Manila—where the water system is controlled by Suez, San Francisco-based Bechtel, and the prominent Ayala family—water is only reliably available for two hours a day and rates have increased so dramatically that the poorest families must choose each month between either paying for water or two days' worth of food. In the Bolivian city of Cochabamba, rate increases that followed privatization sparked rioting in 2000 that left six people dead. And in Atlanta, city officials are considering cancel-ing United Water's contract as early as this winter.

"Atlanta was going to be the industry's shining example of how great privati-zation is," says Public Citizen's Jackson. "And now it's turned into our shining exam-ple about how it maybe isn't so great an idea after all."

On a cloudy August day that brought a welcome bit of drizzle to drought-parched Atlanta, Mayor Shirley Franklin lugged a seven-pound bound volume off a shelf and heaved it onto a table in her office. The report, prepared by a com-mittee she appointed shortly after taking office last January, contained the city's case against United Water. It detailed violations of federal drinking water standards, including one instance in which levels of chlorine rose to six times the level the company agreed to in its contract.

The report also listed a string of maintenance problems ranging from broken security cameras and gates to open manholes and water-main leaks that went unrepaired for weeks. Some residents had to wait months for basic repairs, even though the company's contract specifies that some repairs must be made within 15 days. In fact, United failed to complete more than half of all required repairs in 2001, and it allowed rust and debris to build up, so that when the boil-water alerts forced the company to flush the system, brown water flowed from the taps. Finally, the report noted, instead of improving collections of unpaid water bills as promised, United actually allowed collection rates to drop from 98 to 94 percent, costing the city millions of dollars.

United has succeeded at one thing, according to the city: cutting its own operating costs, chiefly by reducing the waterworks staff by 25 percent even as demand for water in burgeoning Atlanta keeps rising. Staff reductions were partly responsible for the company's service troubles, the report indicated, as were higher-than-expected repair expenses: Last year United demanded that the city provide an additional $80 million for unanticipated maintenance costs. The increase was blocked when a lone City Council member refused to sign the revised contract.

In mid-August, Mayor Franklin announced that "United Water has not lived up to its responsibility" and formally notified the company that it had 90 days to fix the problems or the city would terminate its contract. "They keep telling me they are part of a world-class corporation that can bring us world-class service," she says, offering a small smile. "So I'm giving them a chance to prove it." United has offered to spend $1 million on outside inspectors to reassure city officials that it isn't, as Franklin puts it, "cutting any corners."

It wasn't supposed to turn out this way. In 1998, when Atlanta's City Council voted to contract out its water filtration and delivery system, city officials insisted that corporate management would stave off a budget crisis and drastic rate increases, and would lower costs by more than 40 percent while improving service. (Franklin herself, then a management consultant, lobbied for one of the companies bidding on the contract.) It was the largest water-privatization program ever attempted in the United States and was expected to prompt a wave of similar contracts around the country.

Water privatization has been gaining steam since the early 1990s, when market advocates began touting it as the next logical step after deregulating electricity. Many city waterworks that were built or expanded in the 1970s are now decaying, and the cost of needed repairs is staggering. The U.S. Environmental Protection Agency estimates that U.S. cities will have to spend nearly $151 billion to upgrade or replace pipes, filters, storage tanks, and other infrastructure over the next two decades. Cities will have to spend an additional $460 billion on sewage systems—another area where the corporate water giants are making inroads.

The prospect of skyrocketing infrastructure costs prompted U.S. officials to look overseas, where privatization is already a booming business. Multinational companies now run water systems for 7 percent of the world's population, and analysts say that figure could more than double, to 17 percent, by 2015. Private water management is estimated to be a $200 billion business, and the World Bank—which has encouraged governments to sell off their utilities to reduce public debt—projects it could reach $1 trillion by 2021. *Fortune* has called water "one of the world's great business opportunities," noting that it "promises to be to the 21st century what oil was to the 20th."

The biggest contenders for this emerging market are Suez, a corporate descendant of the company that built the Suez Canal, and the media conglomerate Vivendi Universal, which owns the USA network and Universal Studios. Together, the two companies now control about 70 percent of the world's private water-delivery systems and take in a combined $60 billion in revenues. Both have spent billions in recent years expanding in the United States: In 1999, Suez bought United Water for $1 billion, and Vivendi acquired the then-largest American company, U.S. Filter, for more than $6 billion. RWE/Thames Water, a German/British conglomerate, is currently completing its merger with the biggest remaining domestic company, American Water Works.

The water companies have been expanding even more dramatically in the developing world, where antiquated, often colonial-era, water systems are no match for rapidly increasing populations. More than 1 billion people lack access to clean drinking water, notes Peter Gleick, president of the Pacific Institute for Studies in Development, Environment and Security; a recent report he co-authored points out that "half the world's people fail to receive the level of water services available in many of the cities of ancient Greece and Rome."

Yet corporate water's record in fixing those problems—or even maintaining the industrialized world's systems—has been mixed at best. In 1989 Prime Minister Margaret Thatcher pushed through a program to privatize the United Kingdom's water supply; costs to consumers soared over the following decade, despite billions in government subsidies to the water companies. In some cities, water bills rose by as much as 141 percent in the '90s, while thousands of public-sector jobs were lost. Even the conservative *Daily Mail* declared that "Britain's top ten water companies have been able to use their position as monopoly suppliers to pull off the greatest act of licensed robbery in our history."

Last year the Ghanaian government agreed to privatize local water systems as a condition for an International Monetary Fund loan. To attract investors, the government doubled water rates, setting off protests in a country where the average annual income is less than $400 a year and the water bill—for those fortunate enough to have running water—can run upwards of $110.

In Bolivia's third largest city, Cochabamba, water rates shot up 35 percent after a consortium led by Bechtel took over the city's water system in 1999; some residents found themselves paying 20 percent of their income for water. Street protests led to riots in which six people were killed; eventually, the Bolivian government voided Bechtel's contract and told company officials it could not guarantee their safety if they stayed in town.

Privatization has also spawned protests and, in some cases, dominated elections in several other countries, including Paraguay—where police last summer turned water cannons on anti-privatization protesters—Panama, Brazil, Peru, Colombia, India, Pakistan, Hungary, and South Africa.

BOX **4.1**

Water's Big Three

A handful of global companies have come to dominate the water industry by buying up dozens of smaller competitors. The three top players are based in Europe, but San Francisco-based Bechtel is a close fourth, and Enron's water division, Azurix, was muscling its way into water contracts from Ghana to India before it collapsed. A quick sketch of the Big Three:

SUEZ
- **Number of customers:** 120 million
- **Does business in:** 130 countries, including France, U.K., Argentina, Indonesia, Philippines, and Cameroon; runs water systems in dozens of cities, including Buenos Aires, Casablanca, and Amman, Jordan
- **U.S. activity:** Owns United Water, which manages systems in Atlanta, Puerto Rico, Milwaukee, and Washington, D.C., and is bidding to take over New Orleans' sewer system
- **Also owns:** Waste disposal, electricity, and gas operations; built the Suez Canal in 1858
- **Trouble spots: Nkonkobe, South Africa.** The city went to court late last year to get out of its contract with a Suez subsidiary, arguing that it could save $1.8 million by returning the water system to municipal control.
- **Buenos Aires, Argentina.** In 1992, Suez won a 30-year contract to manage the city's water and sewage systems. But because it failed to install wastewater lines fast enough, sewage has been flooding streets and basements, posing a threat to public health.

VIVENDI UNIVERSAL
- **Number of customers:** 110 million
- **Does business in:** 100 countries, including Hungary, China, South Korea, Kazakhstan, Lebanon, Chad, Romania, and Colombia
- **U.S. activity:** Owns U.S. Filter, the second-largest U.S. water company, best known for its Culligan filters; runs water systems in more than 500 communities
- **Also owns:** Universal Studios, the USA television network, and Houghton Mifflin, as well as waste disposal, energy, and telecommunications operations
- **Trouble spot: Tucuman, Argentina.** Water prices more than doubled after Vivendi took over management of local water systems throughout the province in 1995. Residents protested, and in 1998 the company withdrew from its 30-year contract.

RWE/THAMES WATER
- **Number of customers:** 51 million
- **Does business in:** 44 countries, including U.K., Germany, Turkey, and Japan
- **U.S. activity:** Acquiring American Water Works, which runs water systems in 27 states; the company also owns E'town, a water and sewage company that serves more than 50 communities in New Jersey
- **Also owns:** Electric utilities in Germany, wastewater, gas, recycling, and oil operations
- **Trouble spot: Lexington, Kentucky.** When American Water Works announced its merger with RWE/Thames in September 2001, Lexington indicated that it might try to buy out the conglomerate's local subsidiary, Kentucky-American Water. In response, the company sent letters to each of its 104,000 customers, asking them to fight a "forced government takeover." At present, the utility is still under RWE/Thames' control.

Here in the United States, some municipalities that initially jumped on the privatization bandwagon are now having second thoughts. In Milwaukee, which turned its sewage system over to United Water in 1998, an audit released in July found that a sewer tunnel was dumping raw sewage into local waterways, including Lake Michigan. Vivendi managed Puerto Rico's water and wastewater treatment for seven years, but after a territorial commission cited inaccurate billing and poor maintenance this year, its contract wasn't renewed.

Companies scrambling for lucrative municipal water contracts have also been caught up in corruption scandals. In June, Katherine Maraldo, a New Orleans Sewer and Water Board member, and Michael Stump, the former president of Professional Services Group, which ran the city's wastewater system, were convicted on bribery charges. PSG is now part of Vivendi, which is bidding to take over New Orleans' drinking-water system. And in 2001, two associates of Bridgeport, Connecticut, Mayor Joseph Ganim pled guilty to racketeering, mail fraud, and falsifying tax returns in connection with a $806,000 payment from PSG, which was negotiating for the city's $183 million water contract.

Such incidents point to a fundamental problem with allowing private companies to take over public water systems, says the Pacific Institute's Gleick. In attempting to make attractive bids for long-term contracts, companies often underestimate the cost of maintaining a water system, and so are forced to either skimp on staffing or demand more money to keep turning a profit. "At least when you have public utilities, the money they take in stays in the community," Gleick says. "With the private companies, the profits are going to go out of your community, out of your state, and probably out of your country."

Nevertheless, Troy Henry, the southern regional manager of United Water, is convinced that private water providers can do a better job than public utilities. He readily admits that his company and Atlanta city managers have had problems "dealing with the complexities of the system" in Atlanta and says the company is spending "multiple millions of dollars [to] win back the citizens' and mayor's confidence." A biomedical and electrical engineer and former manager at IBM, Henry argues that private companies can do for water delivery what Big Blue did for computing—revolutionize technology and attract "the best and the brightest and most talented people."

Perhaps Henry can mend fences in Atlanta, which he insists is United Water's—and corporate parent Suez's—"No. 1 priority." But Clair Muller, chair of the City Council's utility committee, contends that even if United Water ends up saving its Atlanta contract, it will merely have proved that privatization can work only under tight city supervision. And if tight supervision is possible, why privatize? "If government is run correctly—and that's always a big *if*—there's no profit motive," she says. "So if this is about saving money, we should always be able to do it cheaper."

In the end, the debate is about more than money. Taking responsibility for a community's water, Muller argues, is simply not the same as running a sports stadium or a cable franchise. "Water is the worst thing to privatize," she says. "It's what we need to live. I think that's key to the whole debate—are we going to lose control over functions that are essential to life?"

PART TWO

Economic Crisis

The United States is the largest economic power in the world: measured in terms of sheer output, we tower over every other country. And when we look around us it is easy to see evidence of the marvels of American productivity: an ever-changing array of high-tech devices, new medical breakthroughs, an economy transformed by computers and the Internet. We are able to communicate almost instantaneously with people around the world. No one would doubt that our economy displays enormous wealth and potential.

But at the same time, we have not been able to translate that economic power and potential into security and well-being for all Americans. Our economy remains volatile and unstable, producing recurring cycles of good times and bad. A long burst of prosperity in the 1990s was followed by a hard fall as the new century began. And even in good times, great numbers of people in the United States have been unable to make a living. The articles in this part explore some of the dimensions, consequences, and causes of America's ongoing economic crisis.

One of the most troubling, and enduring, aspects of that crisis is the inability of our economy to ensure a decent standard of living to everyone who works in it. There was a time in our history when Americans assumed that they could attain the "good life" if they got a regular job and stuck with it. But despite our tremendous economic growth, that ideal has never materialized. To be sure, the American economy has produced vast numbers of jobs, and indeed it is sometimes described as a "job machine." But many of these jobs are found in the rapidly growing "service" economy of restaurants, hotels, and other low-paying employers. For people with few skills, these jobs—many paying little more than the minimum wage—may be the only ones they will ever hold. But can they provide a decent and dignified living? Journalist Barbara Ehrenreich spent several weeks working in a restaurant job in order to find out: and her answer is no. The mathematics of the new service economy are simple and harsh: it is virtually impossible to work solely at these low-wage jobs and make enough money to pay the rent and to afford life's basic necessities. As more and more of the jobs we create fit this description, and as we steadily cut back on other sources of income support for poor people—especially poor women— these stark realities should give us pause.

Ehrenreich's article focuses on people at the lower end of the spectrum of jobs and income in America. But they are not the only ones facing difficult economic conditions.

The recession of the early twenty-first century and the decline of the stock market have also struck hard at the security of once-stable middle-class people. And in recent years, the country has been wracked by a series of devastating corporate scandals that have aggravated the economy's long-term troubles, as companies like Enron, Global Crossing, and WorldCom collapsed from the effects of predatory management and dishonest accounting practices. Enron, which was the fifth largest U.S. corporation in 2001 and earned over $138 billion in revenues, had virtually disappeared by the following year. These sudden catastrophes illustrated the fragility beneath the enormous size and power of many American corporations, and showed that this volatility extended well beyond a handful of rogue companies, to engulf many other key institutions—including Wall Street, the accounting industry, and, again, the political system, to which many of these failed corporations were major contributors, and which notably failed to oversee or regulate them effectively.

These corporate disasters often seemed to come out of the blue, and were often so complicated that it was hard even for experts to understand what had happened. But there was no mystery about the impact on the lives of tens of thousands of people who worked for these companies. We have reprinted here the Congressional testimony of a long-time worker at a plant formerly owned by Enron, which we think speaks for itself.

Not everyone, however, has been affected equally by the recent volatility and crisis of the American economy. Indeed, some have done very well, and in fact have seen their wealth grow considerably even in the face of the economy's ills. As the article we've reprinted from the business magazine *Fortune* shows, the compensation for top executives at major corporations—already stratospheric—has continued to rise, often bearing no relationship to those executives' performance in running their companies. Just when many working Americans were losing jobs and pensions or taking pay cuts, many of those at the top were doing better and better, and devising ever more intricate ways to pay themselves handsomely even if they were running their companies into the ground.

These articles describe an economy in a state of permanent disorder—one that too often is both inefficient and unfair, and that routinely fails to meet the basic needs of many Americans. But if our present economic policies seem to work so poorly for so many people, why do they continue? In "The Limits of Markets," Robert Kuttner suggests one part of the answer. For many years, economic policy in the United States has been guided by the belief that economic decisions are best left to the unimpeded workings of the "market." Accordingly, we tend to reject any degree of government intervention to rectify the injustices and imbalances that the market economy creates. But the result of that one-sided reliance on the market is a society that is both unjust and, in many ways, inefficient. Some degree of balance between market and government is necessary, Kuttner argues, if we want to create an economy that maximizes both our economic well-being and our human values.

CHAPTER 5

Nickel-and-Dimed

On (Not) Getting by in America

BARBARA EHRENREICH

A t the beginning of June 1998 I leave behind everything that normally soothes the ego and sustains the body—home, career, companion, reputation, ATM card—for a plunge into the low-wage workforce. There, I become another, occupationally much diminished "Barbara Ehrenreich"—depicted on job-application forms as a divorced homemaker whose sole work experience consists of housekeeping in a few private homes. I am terrified, at the beginning, of being unmasked for what I am: a middle-class journalist setting out to explore the world that welfare mothers are entering, at the rate of approximately 50,000 a month, as welfare reform kicks in. Happily, though, my fears turn out to be entirely unwarranted: during a month of poverty and toil, my name goes unnoticed and for the most part unuttered. In this parallel universe where my father never got out of the mines and I never got through college, I am "baby," "honey," "blondie," and, most commonly, "girl."

My first task is to find a place to live. I figure that if I can earn $7 an hour—which, from the want ads, seems doable—I can afford to spend $500 on rent, or maybe, with severe economies, $600. In the Key West area, where I live, this pretty much confines me to flophouses and trailer homes—like the one, a pleasing fifteen-minute drive from town, that has no air-conditioning, no screens, no fans, no television, and, by way of diversion, only the challenge of evading the landlord's Doberman pinscher. The big problem with this place, though, is the rent, which at $675 a month is well beyond my reach. All right, Key West is expensive. But so is New York City, or the Bay Area, or Jackson Hole, or Telluride, or Boston, or any other place where tourists and the wealthy compete for living space with the people who clean their toilets and fry their hash browns.[1] Still, it is a shock to realize that "trailer trash" has become, for me, a demographic category to aspire to.

So I decide to make the common trade-off between affordability and convenience, and go for a $500-a-month efficiency thirty miles up a two-lane highway from the employment opportunities of Key West, meaning forty-five minutes if there's no road construction and I don't get caught behind some sun-dazed Canadian tourists. I hate the drive, along a roadside studded with white crosses commemorating the more effective head-on collisions, but it's a sweet little place—a cabin, more or less, set in the swampy back yard of the converted mobile home where my landlord, an affable TV repairman, lives with his bartender girlfriend. Anthropologically speaking, a bustling trailer park would be preferable, but here I have a gleaming white floor and a firm mattress, and the few resident bugs are easily vanquished.

Besides, I am not doing this for the anthropology. My aim is nothing so mistily subjective as to "experience poverty" or find out how it "really feels" to be a long-term low-wage worker. I've had enough unchosen encounters with poverty and the world of low-wage work to know it's not a place you want to visit for touristic purposes; it just smells too much like fear. And with all my real-life assets—bank account, IRA, health insurance, multiroom home—waiting indulgently in the background, I am, of course, thoroughly insulated from the terrors that afflict the genuinely poor.

No, this is a purely objective, scientific sort of mission. The humanitarian rationale for welfare reform—as opposed to the more punitive and stingy impulses that may actually have motivated it—is that work will lift poor women out of poverty while simultaneously inflating their self-esteem and hence their future value in the labor market. Thus, whatever the hassles involved in finding child care, transportation, etc., the transition from welfare to work will end happily, in greater prosperity for all. Now there are many problems with this comforting prediction, such as the fact that the economy will inevitably undergo a downturn, eliminating many jobs. Even without a downturn, the influx of a million former welfare recipients into the low-wage labor market could depress wages by as much as 11.9 percent, according to the Economic Policy Institute (EPI) in Washington, D.C.

But is it really possible to make a living on the kinds of jobs currently available to unskilled people? Mathematically, the answer is no, as can be shown by taking $6 to $7 an hour, perhaps subtracting a dollar or two an hour for child care, multiplying by 160 hours a month, and comparing the result to the prevailing rents. According to the National Coalition for the Homeless, for example, in 1998 it took, on average nationwide, an hourly wage of $8.89 to afford a one-bedroom apartment, and the Preamble Center for Public Policy estimates that the odds against a typical welfare recipient's landing a job at such a "living wage" are about 97 to 1. If these numbers are right, low-wage work is not a solution to poverty and possibly not even to homelessness.

It may seem excessive to put this proposition to an experimental test. As certain family members keep unhelpfully reminding me, the viability of low-wage work could be tested, after a fashion, without ever leaving my study. I could just pay myself $7 an hour for eight hours a day, charge myself for room and board, and total up the numbers after a month. Why leave the people and work that I love? But I am an experimental scientist by training. In that business, you don't just sit at a desk and theorize; you plunge into the everyday chaos of nature, where surprises lurk in the most mundane measurements. Maybe, when I got into it, I would discover some hidden economies in the world of the low-wage worker. After all, if 30 percent of the workforce toils for less than $8 an hour, according to the EPI, they may have found some tricks as yet unknown to me. Maybe—who knows?—I would even be able to detect in myself the bracing psychological effects of getting out of the house, as promised by the welfare wonks at places like the Heritage Foundation. Or, on the other hand, maybe there would be unexpected costs—physical, mental, or financial—to throw off all my calculations. Ideally, I should do this with two small children in tow, that being the welfare average, but mine are grown and no one is willing to lend me theirs for a month-long vacation in penury. So this is not the perfect experiment, just a test of the best possible case: an unencumbered woman, smart and even strong, attempting to live more or less off the land.

On the morning of my first full day of job searching, I take a red pen to the want ads, which are auspiciously numerous. Everyone in Key West's booming "hospitality industry" seems to be looking for someone like me—trainable, flexible, and with suitably humble expectations as to pay. I know I possess certain traits that might be advantageous—I'm white and, I like to think, well-spoken and poised—but I decide on two rules: One, I cannot use any skills derived from my education or usual work—not that there are a lot of want ads for satirical essayists anyway. Two, I have to take the best-paid job that is offered me and of course do my best to hold it; no Marxist rants or sneaking off to read novels in the ladies' room. In addition, I rule out various occupations for one reason or another: Hotel front-desk clerk, for example, which to my surprise is regarded as unskilled and pays around $7 an hour, gets eliminated because it involves standing in one spot for eight hours a day. Waitressing is similarly something I'd like to avoid, because I remember it leaving me bone tired when I was eighteen, and I'm decades of varicosities and back pain beyond that now. Telemarketing, one of the first refuges of the suddenly indigent, can be dismissed on grounds of personality. This leaves certain supermarket jobs, such as deli clerk, or housekeeping in Key West's thousands of hotel and guest rooms. Housekeeping is especially appealing, for reasons both atavistic and practical: it's what my mother did before I came along, and it can't be too different from what I've been doing part-time, in my own home, all my life.

So I put on what I take to be a respectful-looking outfit of ironed Bermuda shorts and scooped-neck T-shirt and set out for a tour of the local hotels and supermarkets. Best Western, Econo Lodge, and HoJo's all let me fill out application forms, and these are, to my relief, interested in little more than whether I am a legal resident of the United States and have committed any felonies. My next stop is Winn-Dixie, the supermarket, which turns out to have a particularly onerous application process, featuring a fifteen-minute "interview" by computer since, apparently, no human on the premises is deemed capable of representing the corporate point of view. I am conducted to a large room decorated with posters illustrating how to look "professional" (it helps to be white and, if female, permed) and warning of the slick promises that union organizers might try to tempt me with. The interview is multiple choice: Do I have anything, such as child-care problems, that might make it hard for me to get to work on time? Do I think safety on the job is the responsibility of management? Then, popping up cunningly out of the blue: How many dollars' worth of stolen goods have I purchased in the last year? Would I turn in a fellow employee if I caught him stealing? Finally, "Are you an honest person?"

Apparently, I ace the interview, because I am told that all I have to do is show up in some doctor's office tomorrow for a urine test. This seems to be a fairly general rule: if you want to stack Cheerio boxes or vacuum hotel rooms in chemically fascist America, you have to be willing to squat down and pee in front of some health worker (who has no doubt had to do the same thing herself). The wages Winn-Dixie is offering—$6 and a couple of dimes to start with—are not enough, I decide, to compensate for this indignity.[2]

I lunch at Wendy's, where $4.99 gets you unlimited refills at the Mexican part of the Superbar, a comforting surfeit of refried beans and "cheese sauce." A teenage employee, seeing me studying the want ads, kindly offers me an application form, which I fill out, though here, too, the pay is just $6 and change an hour. Then it's off for a round of the locally owned inns and guesthouses. At "The Palms," let's call it, a bouncy manager actually takes me around to see the rooms and meet the existing housekeepers, who, I note with satisfaction, look pretty much like me—faded ex-hippie types in shorts with long hair pulled back in braids. Mostly, though, no one speaks to me or even looks at me except to proffer an application form. At my last stop, a palatial B&B, I wait twenty minutes to meet "Max," only to be told that there are no jobs now but there should be one soon, since "nobody lasts more than a couple weeks." (Because none of the people I talked to knew I was a reporter, I have changed their names to protect their privacy and, in some cases perhaps, their jobs.)

Three days go by like this, and, to my chagrin, no one out of the approximately twenty places I've applied calls me for an interview. I had been vain enough to worry about coming across as too educated for the jobs I sought, but no one even seems interested in finding out how overqualified I am. Only later will I realize that the want ads are not a reliable measure of the actual jobs available at any particular time. They are, as I should have guessed from Max's comment, the employers' insurance policy against the relentless turnover of the low-wage workforce. Most of the big hotels run ads almost continually, just to build a supply of applicants to replace the current workers as they drift away or are fired, so finding a job is just a matter of being at the right place at the right time and flexible enough to take whatever is being offered that day. This finally happens to me at a one of the big discount hotel chains, where I go, as usual, for housekeeping and am sent, instead, to try out as a waitress at the attached "family restaurant," a dismal spot with a counter and about thirty tables that looks out on a parking garage and features such tempting fare as "Pollish [sic] sausage and BBQ sauce" on 95-degree days. Phillip, the dapper young West Indian who introduces himself as the manager, interviews me with about as much enthusiasm as if he were a clerk processing me for Medicare, the principal questions being what shifts can I work and when can I start. I mutter something about being woefully out of practice as a waitress, but he's already on to the uniform: I'm to show up tomorrow wearing black slacks and black shoes; he'll provide the rust-colored polo shirt with HEARTHSIDE embroidered on it, though I might want to wear my own shirt to get to work, ha ha. At the word "tomorrow," something between fear and indignation rises in my chest. I want to say, "Thank you for your time, sir, but this is just an experiment, you know, not my actual life."

So begins my career at the Hearthside, I shall call it, one small profit center within a global discount hotel chain, where for two weeks I work from 2:00 till 10:00 P.M. for $2.43 an hour plus tips.[3] In some futile bid for gentility, the management has barred employees from using the front door, so my first day I enter through the kitchen, where a red-faced man with shoulder-length blond hair is throwing frozen steaks against the wall and yelling, "Fuck this shit!" "That's just Jack," explains Gail, the wiry middle-aged waitress who is assigned to train me. "He's on the rag again"—a condition occasioned, in this instance, by the fact that the cook on the morning shift had forgotten to thaw out the steaks. For the next eight hours, I run after the agile Gail, absorbing bits of instruction along with fragments of personal tragedy. All food must be trayed, and the reason she's so tired today is that she woke up in a cold sweat thinking of her boyfriend, who killed himself recently in an upstate prison. No refills on lemonade. And the reason he was in prison is that a few DUIs caught up with him, that's all, could have happened to anyone. Carry the creamers to the table in a monkey bowl, never in your hand. And after he was gone she spent several months living in her truck, peeing in a plastic pee bottle and reading by candlelight at night, but you can't live in a truck in the summer, since you need to have the windows down, which means anything can get in, from mosquitoes on up.

At least Gail puts to rest any fears I had of appearing overqualified. From the first day on, I find that of all the things I have left behind, such as home and identity, what I miss the most is competence. Not that I have ever felt utterly competent in the writing business, in which one day's success augurs nothing at all for the next. But in my writing life, I at least have some notion of procedure: do the research, make the outline, rough out a draft, etc. As a server, though, I am beset by requests like bees: more iced tea here, ketchup over there, a to go box for table fourteen, and where are the high chairs, anyway? Of the twenty-seven tables, up to six are usually mine at any time, though on slow afternoons or if Gail is off, I sometimes have the whole place to myself. There is the touch-screen computer-ordering system to master, which is, I suppose, meant to minimize server-cook contact, but in practice requires constant verbal fine-tuning: "That's gravy on the mashed, okay? None on the meatloaf," and so forth—while the cook scowls as if I were inventing these refinements just to torment him. Plus, something I had forgotten in the years since I was eighteen: about a third of a server's job is "side work" that's invisible to customers—sweeping, scrubbing, slicing, refilling, and restocking. If it isn't all done, every little bit of it, you're going to face the 6:00 P.M. dinner rush defenseless and probably go down in flames. I screw up dozens of times at the beginning, sustained in my shame entirely by Gail's support—"It's okay, baby, everyone does that sometime"—because, to my total surprise and despite the scientific detachment I am doing my best to maintain, I care.

The whole thing would be a lot easier if I could just skate through it as Lily Tomlin in one of her waitress skits, but I was raised by the absurd Booker T. Washingtonian precept that says: If you're going to do something, do it well. In fact, "well" isn't good enough by half. Do it better than anyone has ever done it before. Or so said my father, who must have known what he was talking about because he managed to pull himself, and us with him, up from the mile-deep copper mines of Butte to the leafy suburbs of the Northeast, ascending from boilermakers to martinis before booze beat out ambition. As in most endeavors I have encountered in my life, doing it "better than anyone" is not a reasonable goal. Still, when I wake up at 4:00 A.M. in my own cold sweat, I am not thinking about the writing deadlines I'm neglecting; I'm thinking about the table whose order I screwed up so that one of the boys didn't get his kiddie meal until the rest of the family had moved on to their Key Lime pies. That's the other powerful motivation I hadn't expected—the customers, or "patients," as I can't help thinking of them on account of the mysterious vulnerability that seems to have left them temporarily unable to feed themselves. After a few days at the Hearthside, I feel the service ethic kick in like a shot of oxytocin, the nurturance hormone. The plurality of my customers are hard-working locals—truck drivers, construction workers, even housekeepers from the attached hotel—and I want them to have the closest to a "fine dining" experience that the grubby circumstances will allow. No "you guys" for me; everyone over twelve is "sir" or "ma'am." I ply them with iced tea and coffee refills; I return, mid-meal, to inquire how everything is; I doll up their salads with chopped raw mushrooms, summer squash slices, or whatever bits of produce I can find that have survived their sojourn in the cold-storage room mold-free.

There is Benny, for example, a short, tight-muscled sewer repairman, who cannot even think of eating until he has absorbed a half hour of air-conditioning and ice water. We chat about hyperthermia and electrolytes until he is ready to order some finicky combination like soup of the day, garden salad, and a side of grits. There are the German tourists who are so touched by my pidgin "Willkommen" and "Ist alles gut?" that they actually tip. (Europeans, spoiled by their trade-union-ridden, high-wage welfare states, generally do not know that they are supposed to tip. Some restaurants, the Hearthside included, allow servers to "grat" their foreign customers, or add a tip to the bill. Since this amount is added before the customers have a chance to tip or not tip, the practice amounts to an automatic penalty for imperfect English.) There are the two dirt-smudged lesbians, just off their construction shift, who are impressed enough by my suave handling of the fly in the pina colada that they take the time to praise me to Stu, the assistant manager. There's Sam, the kindly retired cop, who has to plug up his tracheotomy hole with one finger in order to force the cigarette smoke into his lungs.

Sometimes I play with the fantasy that I am a princess who, in penance for some tiny transgression, has undertaken to feed each of her subjects by hand. But the non-princesses working with me are just as indulgent, even when this means flouting management rules—concerning, for example, the number of croutons that can go on a salad (six). "Put on all you want," Gail whispers, "as long as Stu isn't looking," She dips into her own tip money to buy biscuits and gravy for an out-of-work mechanic who's used up all his money on dental surgery, inspiring me to pick up the tab for his milk and pie. Maybe the same high levels of agape can be found throughout the "hospitality industry." I remember the poster decorating one of the apartments I looked at, which said "If you seek happiness for yourself you will never find it. Only when you seek happiness for others will it come to you," or words to that effect—an odd sentiment, it seemed to me at the time, to find in the dank one-room basement apartment of a bellhop at the Best Western. At the Hearthside, we utilize whatever bits of autonomy we have to ply our customers with the illicit calories that signal our love. It is our job as servers to assemble the salads and desserts, pouring the dressings and squirting the whipped cream. We also control the number of butter patties our customers get and the amount of sour cream on their baked potatoes. So if you wonder why Americans are so obese, consider the fact that waitresses both express their humanity and earn their tips through the covert distribution of fats.

Ten days into it, this is beginning to look like a livable lifestyle. I like Gail, who is "looking at fifty" but moves so fast she can alight in one place and then another without apparently being anywhere between them. I clown around with Lionel, the teenage Haitian busboy, and catch a few fragments of conversation with Joan, the svelte fortyish hostess and militant feminist who is the only one of us who dares to tell Jack to shut the fuck up. I even warm up to Jack when, on a slow night and to make up for a particularly unwarranted attack on my abilities, or so I imagine, he tells me about his glory days as a young man at "coronary school"—or do you say "culinary"?—in Brooklyn, where he dated a knock-out Puerto Rican chick and learned everything there is to know about food. I finish up at 10:00 or 10:30, depending on how much side work I've been able to get done during the shift, and cruise home to the tapes I snatched up at random when I left my real home—Marianne Faithfull, Tracy Chapman, Enigma, King Sunny Ade, the Violent Femmes—just drained enough for the music to set my cranium resonating but hardly dead. Midnight snack is Wheat Thins and Monterey Jack, accompanied by cheap white wine on ice and whatever AMC has to offer. To bed by 1:30 or 2:00, up at 9:00 or 10:00, read for an hour while my uniform whirls around in the landlord's washing machine, and then it's another eight hours spent following Mao's central instruction, as laid out in the Little Red Book, which was: Serve the people.

I could drift along like this, in some dreamy proletarian idyll, except for two things. One is management. If I have kept this subject on the margins thus far it is because I still flinch to think that I spent all those weeks under the surveillance of men (and later women) whose job it was to monitor my behavior for signs of sloth, theft, drug abuse, or worse. Not that managers and especially "assistant managers" in low-wage settings like this are exactly the class enemy. In the restaurant business, they are mostly former cooks or servers, still capable of pinch-hitting in the kitchen or on the floor, just as in hotels they are likely to be former clerks, and paid a salary of only about $400 a week. But everyone knows they have crossed over to the other side, which is, crudely put, corporate as opposed to human. Cooks want to prepare tasty meals; servers want to serve them graciously; but managers are there for only one reason—to make sure that money is made for some theoretical entity that exists far away in Chicago or New York, if a corporation can be said to have a physical existence at all. Reflecting on her career, Gail tells me ruefully that she had sworn, years ago, never to work for a corporation again. "They don't cut you no slack. You give and you give, and they take."

Managers can sit—for hours at a time if they want—but it's their job to see that no one else ever does, even when there's nothing to do, and this is why, for servers, slow times can be as exhausting as rushes. You start dragging out each little chore, because if the manager on duty catches you in an idle moment, he will give you something far nastier to do. So I wipe, I clean, I consolidate ketchup bottles and recheck the cheesecake supply, even tour the tables to make sure the customer evaluation forms are all standing perkily in their places—wondering all the time how many calories I burn in these strictly theatrical exercises. When, on a particularly dead afternoon, Stu finds me glancing at a *USA Today* a customer has left behind, he assigns me to vacuum the entire floor with the broken vacuum cleaner that has a handle only two feet long, and the only way to do that without incurring orthopedic damage is to proceed from spot to spot on your knees.

On my first Friday at the Hearthside there is a "mandatory meeting for all restaurant employees," which I attend, eager for insight into our overall marketing strategy and the niche (your basic Ohio cuisine with a tropical twist?) we aim to inhabit. But there is no "we" at this meeting. Phillip, our top manager except for an occasional "consultant" sent out by corporate headquarters, opens it with a sneer: "The break room—it's disgusting. Butts in the ashtrays, newspapers lying around, crumbs." This windowless little room, which also houses the time clock for the entire hotel, is where we stash our bags and civilian clothes and take our half-hour meal breaks. But a break room is not a right, he tells us. It can be taken away. We should also know that the lockers in the break room and whatever is in them can be searched at any time. Then comes gossip; there has been gossip; gossip (which seems to mean employees talking among themselves) must stop. Off-duty employees are henceforth barred from eating at the restaurant, because "other servers gather around them and gossip." When Phillip has exhausted his agenda of rebukes, Joan complains about the condition of the ladies' room and I throw in my two bits about the vacuum cleaner. But I don't see any backup coming from my fellow servers, each of whom has subsided into her own personal funk; Gail, my role model, stares sorrowfully at a point six inches from her nose. The meeting ends when Andy, one of the cooks, gets up, muttering about breaking up his day off for this almighty bullshit.

Just four days later we are suddenly summoned into the kitchen at 3:30 P.M., even though there are live tables on the floor. We all—about ten of us—stand around Phillip, who announces grimly that there has been a report of some "drug activity" on the night shift and that, as a result, we are now to be a "drug-free" workplace, meaning that all new hires will be tested, as will possibly current employees on a random basis. I am glad that this part of the kitchen is so dark, because I find myself blushing as hard as if I had been caught toking up in the ladies' room myself. I haven't been treated this way—lined up in the corridor, threatened with locker searches, peppered with carelessly aimed accusations—since junior high school. Back on the floor, Joan cracks, "Next they'll be telling us we can't have sex on the job." When I ask Stu what happened to inspire the crackdown, he just mutters about "management decisions" and takes the opportunity to upbraid Gail and me for being too generous with the rolls. From now on there's to be only one per customer, and it goes out with the dinner, not with the salad. He's also been riding the cooks, prompting Andy to come out of the kitchen and observe—with the serenity of a man whose customary implement is a butcher knife—that "Stu has a death wish today."

Later in the evening, the gossip crystallizes around the theory that Stu is himself the drug culprit, that he uses the restaurant phone to order up marijuana and sends one of the late servers out to fetch it for him. The server was caught, and she may have ratted Stu out or at least said enough to cast some suspicion on him, thus accounting for his pissy behavior. Who knows? Lionel, the busboy, entertains us for the rest of the shift by standing just behind Stu's back and sucking deliriously on an imaginary joint.

The other problem, in addition to the less-than-nurturing management style, is that this job shows no sign of being financially viable. You might imagine, from a comfortable distance, that people who live, year in and year out, on $6 to $10 an hour have discovered some survival stratagems unknown to the middle class. But no. It's not hard to get my co-workers to talk about their living situations, because housing, in almost every case, is the principal source of disruption in their lives, the first thing they fill you in on when they arrive for their shifts. After a week, I have compiled the following survey:

- Gail is sharing a room in a well-known downtown flophouse for which she and a roommate pay about $250 a week. Her roommate, a male friend, has begun hitting on her, driving her nuts, but the rent would be impossible alone.
- Claude, the Haitian cook, is desperate to get out of the two-room apartment he shares with his girlfriend and two other, unrelated, people. As far as I can determine, the other Haitian men (most of whom only speak Creole) live in similarly crowded situations.
- Annette, a twenty-year-old server who is six months pregnant and has been abandoned by her boyfriend, lives with her mother, a postal clerk.
- Marianne and her boyfriend are paying $170 a week for a one-person trailer.
- Jack, who is, at $10 an hour, the wealthiest of us, lives in the trailer he owns, paying only the $400-a-month lot fee.
- The other white cook, Andy, lives on his dry-docked boat, which, as far as I can tell from his loving descriptions, can't be more than twenty feet long. He offers to take me out on it, once it's repaired, but the offer comes with inquiries as to my marital status, so I do not follow up on it.
- Tina and her husband are paying $60 a night for a double room in a Days Inn. This is because they have no car and the Days Inn is within walking distance of the Hearthside. When Marianne, one of the breakfast servers, is tossed out of her trailer for subletting (which is against the trailer-park rules), she leaves her boyfriend and moves in with Tina and her husband.

- Joan, who had fooled me with her numerous and tasteful outfits (hostesses wear their own clothes), lives in a van she parks behind a shopping center at night and showers in Tina's motel room. The clothes are from thrift shops.[4]

It strikes me, in my middle-class solipsism, that there is gross improvidence in some of these arrangements. When Gail and I are wrapping silverware in napkins—the only task for which we are permitted to sit—she tells me she is thinking of escaping from her roommate by moving into the Days Inn herself. I am astounded: How can she even think of paying between $40 and $60 a day? But if I was afraid of sounding like a social worker, I come out just sounding like a fool. She squints at me in disbelief, "And where am I supposed to get a month's rent and a month's deposit for an apartment?" I'd been feeling pretty smug about my $500 efficiency, but of course it was made possible only by the $1,300 I had allotted myself for start-up costs when I began my low-wage life: $1,000 for the first month's rent and deposit, $100 for initial groceries and cash in my pocket, $200 stuffed away for emergencies. In poverty, as in certain propositions in physics, starting conditions are everything.

There are no secret economies that nourish the poor; on the contrary, there are a host of special costs. If you can't put up the two months' rent you need to secure an apartment, you end up paying through the nose for a room by the week. If you have only a room, with a hot plate at best, you can't save by cooking up huge lentil stews that can be frozen for the week ahead. You eat fast food, or the hot dogs and styrofoam cups of soup that can be microwaved in a convenience store. If you have no money for health insurance—and the Hearthside's niggardly plan kicks in only after three months—you go without routine care or prescription drugs and end up paying the price. Gail, for example, was fine until she ran out of money for estrogen pills. She is supposed to be on the company plan by now, but they claim to have lost her application form and need to begin the paperwork all over again. So she spends $9 per migraine pill to control the headaches she wouldn't have, she insists, if her estrogen supplements were covered. Similarly, Marianne's boyfriend lost his job as a roofer because he missed so much time after getting a cut on his foot for which he couldn't afford the prescribed antibiotic.

My own situation, when I sit down to assess it after two weeks of work, would not be much better if this were my actual life. The seductive thing about waitressing is that you don't have to wait for payday to feel a few bills in your pocket, and my tips usually cover meals and gas, plus something left over to stuff into the kitchen drawer I use as a bank. But as the tourist business slows in the summer heat, I sometimes leave work with only $20 in tips (the gross is higher, but servers share about 15 percent of their tips with the busboys and bartenders). With wages included, this amounts to about the minimum wage of $5.15 an hour. Although the sum in the drawer is piling up, at the present rare of accumulation it will be more than a hundred dollars short of my rent when the end of the month comes around. Nor can I see any expenses to cut. True, I haven't gone the lentil stew route yet, but that's because I don't have a large cooking pot, pot holders, or a ladle to stir with (which cost about $30 at Kmart, less at thrift stores), not to mention onions, carrots, and the indispensable bay leaf. I do make my lunch almost every day—usually some slow-burning, high-protein combo like frozen chicken patties with melted cheese on top and canned pinto beans on the side. Dinner is at the Hearthside, which offers its employees a choice of BLT, fish sandwich, or hamburger for only $2. The burger lasts longest, especially if it's heaped with gut-puckering jalapeños, but by midnight my stomach is growling again. . . .

How former welfare recipients and single mothers will (and do) survive in the low-wage workforce, I cannot imagine. Maybe they will figure out how to condense their lives—including child-raising, laundry, romance, and meals—into the couple of hours between full-time jobs. Maybe they will take up residence in their vehicles, if they have one. All I know is that I couldn't hold two jobs and I couldn't make enough money to live on with one. And I had advantages unthinkable to many of the long-term poor—health, stamina, a working car, and no children to care for and support. Certainly nothing in my experience contradicts the conclusion of Kathryn Edin and Laura Lein, in their recent book *Making Ends Meet: How Single Mothers Survive Welfare and Low-Wage Work,* that low-wage work actually involves more hardship and deprivation than life at the mercy of the welfare state. In the coming months and years, economic conditions for the working poor are bound to worsen, even without the almost inevitable recession. As mentioned earlier, the influx of former welfare recipients into the low-skilled workforce will have a depressing effect on both wages and the number of jobs available. A general economic downturn will only enhance these effects, and the working poor will of course be facing it without the slight, but nonetheless often saving, protection of welfare as a backup.

The thinking behind welfare reform was that even the humblest jobs are morally uplifting and psychologically buoying. In reality they are likely to be fraught with insult and stress. But I did discover one redeeming feature of the most abject low-wage work—the camaraderie of people who are, in almost all cases, far too smart and funny and caring for the work they do and the wages they're paid. The hope, of course, is that someday these people will come to know what they're worth, and take appropriate action.

ENDNOTES

1. According to the Department of Housing and Urban Development, the "fair-market rent" for an efficiency is $551 here in Monroe County, Florida. A comparable rent in the five boroughs of New York City is $704; in San Francisco, $713; and in the heart of Silicon Valley, $808. The fair-market rent for an area is defined as the amount that would be needed to pay rent plus utilities for "privately owned, decent, safe, and sanitary rental housing of a modest (non-luxury) nature with suitable amenities."

2. According to the *Monthly Labor Review* (November 1996), 28 percent of work sites surveyed in the service industry conduct drug tests (corporate workplaces have much higher rates), and the incidence of testing has risen markedly since the Eighties. The rate of testing is highest in the South (56 percent of work sites polled), with the Midwest in second place (50 percent). The drug most likely to be detected—marijuana, which can be detected in urine for weeks—is also the most innocuous, while heroin and cocaine are generally undetectable

three days after use. Prospective employees sometimes try to cheat the tests by consuming excess amounts of liquids and taking diuretics and even masking substances available through the Internet.

3. According to the Fair Labor Standards Act, employers are not required to pay "tipped employees," such as restaurant servers, more than $2.13 an hour in direct wages. However, if the sum of tips plus $2.13 an hour falls below the minimum wage, or $5.15 an hour, the employer is required to make up the difference. This fact was not mentioned by managers or otherwise publicized at either of the restaurants where I worked.

4. I could find no statistics on the number of employed people living in cars or vans, but according to the National Coalition for the Homeless's 1997 report "Myths and Facts About Homelessness," nearly one in five homeless people (in twenty-nine cities across the nation) is employed in a full- or part-time job.

CHAPTER 6

Testimony of Mr. Thomas O. Padgett

THOMAS O. PADGETT

My name is Tom Padgett. I was an employee of the Enron Corporation, with 30 years of accredited service at their Morgan's Point chemical plant in La Porte, Texas, until last August, 2001, when Enron transferred our plant to EOTT Energy Corporation. My wife, Karen, is a registered nurse whose work activity is limited now due to crippling rheumatoid arthritis. We have 3 grown children and 5 grandchildren.

I turned 59 years old last December 10, and I have worked in the chemical industry for 35 years. My job title is Senior Lab Analyst in the Quality Control Lab. My specific job functions consist of running analyses on petroleum feed stock products coming into the plant, on stream analysis of products within the plant, and final product analysis to make sure our products meet customer specifications. I work 12 hour shifts at the plant.

There are—or were—a lot of people like me at Enron. Not everyone at Enron is an energy trader or an MBA. We are also chemical plant employees and managers, electrical utility workers, and pipeline employees, just to give a few examples. We live and work in places like La Porte, Texas, Port Barre, Louisiana, and Portland, Oregon.

I am a participant in the Enron Corp. 401(k) Savings Plan. Our retirement savings and our retirement plans were based solely on my 401(k) Savings Plan with Enron. The value of our savings account on December 31, 2000 was $615,456. We still have not received our year-end statement for 2001, but, using the present value of Enron stock, we estimate that our savings account is now worth less than $15,000 dollars.

We have sacrificed over the years in order to contribute as much as we could to our 401(k) Plan account. I joined Enron from my previous job with Tenneco, and rolled our savings from my Tenneco 401(k) Plan into the Enron Plan. I continued to participate in the Enron Savings Plan after our plant was transferred to EOTT Energy.

Over the last 10 years, we were able to build up a sizable sum of money in our Enron 401(k) Plan. I made contributions to the plan by deductions from my paycheck every two weeks. My contributions were matched by Enron with the Company's stock. Under the Enron 401(k) Plan, the Company's matching contribution was made exclusively with Enron stock, and participants were required to hold the matching stock until age 50. Nearly all of our savings were invested in Enron's stock.

I was a dedicated and loyal employee to Enron, and I worked with the others in my plant and in the Company to help make Enron one of the best companies in the nation. Throughout my time with Enron, the top management of the company constantly encouraged us to invest our savings in Enron stock. I took the fact that the Company matched our savings only with Enron stock as a further endorsement of the stock as a safe retirement investment. More recent statements made by Enron's top management, including e-mails from Ken Lay, about the Company's stock also caused me to keep investing my savings into the stock. I remember, in the Fall of 2000, Enron's top executives telling us at an employee meeting and by Company e-mail that Enron's stock price was going to increase to at least $120 per share. When Mr. Skilling resigned last August, Mr. Lay told us that the Company was stronger than it had ever been.

Many people now ask why we and so many other Enron Savings Plan participants did not diversify our savings accounts. My answer is that we were loyal Enron employees, proud to be owners of what we were led to believe was a great company. I would note that our decision to invest in our retirement savings in our Company appears, from what I have seen in the newspapers and on television, to be the same as other employees in many large companies in the United States, like Procter & Gamble, General Electric and Coca-Cola.

Our stock ownership was encouraged by Enron's top management, who I now believe benefited handsomely from our commitment. Based on what we were told—repeatedly by the men at the top—I never dreamed that this disaster could have happened. We are not Wall Street analysts. I am sure that most Enron employees manage their investments themselves, like Karen and I did. The fact remains, though, that good investment decisions require honest information. We all know now that the information that we were given was false.

We also have been asked about the "lockdown" of our savings account by the Company in October 2001. I received notification from the Company approximately ten days before the lockdown that I would not be able to access my savings account for a period of about four weeks. I do not know when the lockdown period actually began. But I do know that, at about the same time, Enron released some very damaging news about the condition of the Company. By the time we were able to access our account, our Enron stock was worth less than $10 a share. The reason that Enron gave for the lockdown was to change plan administrators. What I still have not heard explained is why the Company proceeded with the lockdown at a time when they had to know that this damaging information was going to come out and cause the stock price to drop even more.

Karen and I had planned on retiring this coming June, when I will be 59½ years old. Our plans were to move to the country and possibly start a small farm or a ranch for disabled, handicapped or terminally ill children. Our idea was that this would allow these children's parents to have some special time to themselves to strengthen their relationship, knowing their child would be taken care of during this time. We had planned on spending more time with our family and grandchildren and caring for our elderly parents. Karen and I had planned on spending more time together, fishing and doing some traveling. We felt like we had enough money in our retirement savings to take care of ourselves as we grew older so we would not be a burden on our children.

Now that is all gone and our children may need to take care of us. I have lost nearly all of my retirement savings because of Enron's collapse. It appears that I will need to work for another ten years or as long as my health holds out in order to support my family. I just recently had surgery on my right hand so I can continue in my present capacity running samples in the lab.

We are not alone in this, of course. The plant where I work has approximately 100 employees and most of them had most of their 401(k) savings in Enron. There are five or six other employees in my plant that also had planned on retiring this year. Now they also will have to keep working to support their families. I am sure our experience is the same as thousands of other Enron employees. However, we are still more fortunate than some at Enron. We still have our jobs, unlike many who worked for Enron. I have a strong faith in God, and I know we will make it through this.

You have been interested to hear about our experience and I appreciate your invitation to appear before you today. As our lawmakers, I will tell you that I believe the law should protect workers and their retirement savings from what happened at Enron. Companies must be responsible for giving truthful information to their employees about their retirement investments. Our loyalty and trust as Enron employees have been betrayed, and it does not look like we will be able to recoup all of our losses from the Company or others who are responsible. But we hope that our experience and your work will prevent this happening to others.

CHAPTER 7

Have They No Shame?

JERRY USEEM

> But the pigs were so clever that they could think of a way round every difficulty.
>
> —George Orwell, *Animal Farm*

Who says CEOs don't suffer along with the rest of us? As his company's stock slid 71% last year, one corporate chief saw his compensation fall 12%. Sure, he still earned $82 million, making him the second-highest-paid executive at an S&P 500 company in 2002, according to the 360 proxy statements that had rolled in as of April 9. And yeah, he's under indictment for the wholesale looting of his company, Tyco. But at least Dennis Kozlowski set a better example than the top-paid executive, who pulled in a whopping $136 million. That was Mark Swartz, his former CFO.

Unusual, you might say, for one company to produce the two top earners in a given year. But three of the top six? Now that's truly striking—especially since the other person isn't part of Kozlowski's gang at all. It's Ed Breen, the guy hired to clean up the mess.

You'd think that in the aftermath of a scandal that made Tyco a symbol of cartoonish greed, its board might want to make a point of frugality. Yet even as it was pressuring its former officers to "disgorge" their ill-gotten gains, it was letting its new man, who became CEO last July, gorge himself on $62 million worth of cash, stock, and other prizes. By all accounts Breen is doing a fine job so far, but *still*. And the gravy train didn't stop there. Tyco's board of directors dished out another $25 million for a new CFO, plus $25 million to a *division head*, putting them both on a par with the CEOs of Wal-Mart and General Electric. At least the company, now with a new board of directors, seems to recognize the need for some limits: Its bonus scheme "now caps out at 200% of base salary," notes Breen, "whereas before it was more like 600% or 700%."

That, in a nutshell, is what a year of unprecedented uproar and outrage can do. Before, CEOs had a shot at becoming very, very, very rich. Now they're likely to get only very, very rich. More likely, in fact. FORTUNE asked Equilar, an independent provider of compensation data, to analyze CEO compensation at 100 of the largest companies that had filed proxy statements for 2002. Their findings? Average CEO compensation dropped 23% in 2002, to $15.7 million, but that's mostly because the pay of a few mega-earners fell significantly. A more telling number—median compensation, or what the middle-of-the-road CEO earned—actually *rose* 14%, to $13.2 million. This in a year when the total return of the S&P 500 was down 22.1%.

"The acid test for reform," wrote Warren Buffett in his most recent letter to shareholders, "will be CEO compensation." With most of the results now in, the acid strip is bright red: Corporate reform has failed. Not only does executive pay seem more decoupled from performance than ever, but boards are conveniently changing their definition of "performance." "From a compensation point of view," says Matt Ward, an independent pay consultant, "it's a whole new bag of tricks."

What did fall last year were monster grants of stock options, like the 20 million awarded to Apple's Steve Jobs in 2000. The declining use of options (which even Kozlowski once called a "free ride—a way to earn megabucks in a bull market") would seem cause for reformers to rejoice. But delve more closely into the data for those 100 big companies and what do you find? That every other form of compensation—including some burgeoning forms of stealth wealth—has grown.

Options not paying what they once did? Have some cold, hard cash to make up the difference. Cendant's Henry Silverman got $11 million in salary and bonus, a 41% rise, while Cendant's total stock return fell 47%. Or take Disney's Michael Eisner. After he failed to clear his bonus hurdle two years running, his board lowered the performance bar, and then—hooray!—he finally cleared it. An Olympian effort worth $5 million.

The 5% rise in median salaries and 21% jump in median bonuses was chicken feed, though, compared with the boom in restricted stock. The number of people receiving such grants rose 42%. While awarding shares outright has some advantages over options—they can ease shareholder concerns about dilution and "option overhang"—it also supplants pay-for-performance with what Matt Ward calls "pay-for-attendance."

Even more troubling is stealth wealth. "Deferred compensation" plans, for instance, let executives sock away up to 100% of their salary and bonus in a tax-advantaged account until retirement, often with the addition of a company match and above-market interest. Meanwhile, many pension plans credit executives with decades of unserved "service," even shielding them from creditors in the event of bankruptcy.

Perhaps most striking are the sums to be made at the most troubled firms. After paying huge severance packages to failed chiefs, Sprint and Lucent laid out eye-popping amounts for their would-be saviors. While reflecting the difficulty of luring anyone to a disaster scene, it also shows how much can be made in the comings and goings these days. Michael Capellas, for instance, pulled off the golden parachute *and* the golden handshake in the same week, collecting $27.8 million just for jumping from Hewlett-Packard to WorldCom. "With CEOs receiving an average of $15 million to start and $16.5 million to finish," notes Paul Hodgson of the Corporate Library, a research firm that advocates boardroom reform, "they hardly need to make any money in between."

While shocking in one sense, these developments are not wholly surprising. For several decades now, CEO pay has been governed by the Law of Unintended Compensation, which holds that any attempt to reduce compensation has the perverse result of increasing it.

- In 1989, Congress tries to cap golden parachutes by imposing an excise tax on payments above 2.99 times base salary. Result: Companies make 2.99 the new minimum and cover any excise tax for execs.
- In 1992, Congress tries to shame CEOs by requiring better disclosure of their pay. Result: CEOs see how much everyone else is making, and then try to get more.
- In 1993, Congress declares salaries over $1 million to be non-tax-exempt. Result: Companies opt for huge stock option grants while upping most salaries to $1 million.

You get the idea. Regulation is a spur to innovation, and in the pay arena innovation always means "more." As executive-pay critic Graef Crystal once put it, "The more troughs a pig feeds from, the fatter it gets."

To see all those troughs in use—and the peculiar doublespeak of the compensation realm—check out the employment contract of Bob Nardelli, the ex-GE man who joined Home Depot in late 2000. (At presstime, Home Depot had not filed the proxy for its 2002 fiscal year.) First comes the "make-whole payment." In Nardelli's case, that entailed reimbursing him for all the goodies he forfeited by leaving General Electric: $50,400 in cash, a $10 million loan, and a stock option grant of 3.5 million shares, a million of which came fully vested. The whole point of forfeiture rules is to induce CEOs to stay put. The whole point of the make-whole payment is to undermine them. It's a virtuous cycle—for the CEOs. In 1999, for instance, Hewlett-Packard made Carly Fiorina "whole" for Lucent options that soon after would have slipped deeply underwater. Says Crystal: "She stepped from one ocean liner to another just as the first one took six torpedoes from the tubes of a submarine."

Another lovely term is the "guaranteed bonus" *(bo•nus [n.] Something over and above what is normally expected)*. Nardelli's contract actually calls it the "target bonus," *(tar•get [n.] A goal to be achieved)*, but it's the same thing. Even if he drives Home Depot's stock to zero, Nardelli's bonus will be no less than $3 million. His "maximum" bonus may be no less than $4 million—his minimum maximum, in other words. But there is no maximum maximum, because "nothing contained herein shall prevent the [compensation] committee from paying an annual bonus in excess of the maximum amount." Naturally.

As an incentive to work hard, he also gets annual option grants of no fewer than 450,000 shares.

Home Depot agreed to these terms because it wanted a hot-shot executive, and Nardelli—one of three finalists for Jack Welch's corner office—fit the bill. Since Nardelli took over, Home Depot's total return is down 43.4%; in 2002, the stock was the Dow's worst performer. "You can tell the world that Home Depot got more than its money's worth when it got Bob Nardelli," declares Ken Langone, the company's lead director. Still, it's worth asking: What would Nardelli get if the board wanted a regime change?

Again, Nardelli's contract comes to the rescue. Let's say he's fired for "cause." No, wait, that's almost impossible. Because these days "cause" doesn't mean what you think it might. Let's leave Nardelli for a minute and look at 3M CEO James Mc-Nerney. In his contract

> . . . cause shall not include any one or more of the following:
> (i) bad judgment,
> (ii) negligence.

Screwing up, in other words, doesn't qualify. Would a felony conviction do the trick? Maybe. But the employment contracts of three former Kmart CEOs said it must be

> . . . a felony involving moral turpitude or any other felony unless, in the case of such other felony, the Executive (A) acted in good faith and in a manner he reasonably believed to be in, or not opposed to, the best interests of the Company and (B) had no reasonable cause to believe his conduct was unlawful.

That is, as long as the CEO believed he was acting legally and in Kmart's interests, he could be convicted of drunk driving, possession of counterfeit securities, possession of a sawed-off shotgun, reckless homicide, or "lascivious carriage"—all of which have failed to meet some courts' definition of "moral turpitude." It's a loophole so gaping (and so common) that the CEO could theoretically join the army of a foreign state—Libya, say—and *still* not get fired for "cause." Which is why, in practice, nobody ever is.

It may seem like semantic hairsplitting, but that one little word makes all the difference. Because getting canned without cause can trigger an Ed McMahon-like payday. Let's go back to Nardelli. Not only would his "incentive" Home Depot stock become instantly convertible to cash, but the company would be forced to award him *all new* stock grants upon his departure—giving him an incentive to do what, exactly, isn't clear. Then comes $20 million in cash, straight up. By contract, Home Depot will also forgive the balance of and outstanding interest on his $10 million loan. Lest he have to pay income tax on this largess himself, Home Depot will cover the bill with what's called a gross-up payment. And since that payment is itself taxable, there will be a gross-up on the gross-up. Meaning shareholders will pick up the whole gross amount.

All told, Nardelli could walk away with $82 million, estimates the Corporate Library's Hodgson—a figure that doesn't even include his deferred compensation or other benefits.

Those are the provisions spelled out in the contract. But many boards aren't afraid to hand out money willy-nilly. Consider how Texas Instruments couched its comp decision for top execs in its original 2002 proxy: The compensation committee says it followed no specific formula, only "factors it deemed relevant." (By Equilar's calculations, CEO Tom Engibous got $22.7 million while the 2002 shareholder return was –46.2%.) Playing make-believe is another option. Before the 2000 retirement of Engelhard Corp.'s longtime CEO Orin Smith, the board voted that his options should be extended "as if Mr. Smith had not retired."

As nonsensical as all this seems, board members insist there's an elemental logic to it. Everybody knows that (1) a great CEO is the key ingredient to corporate success, and (2) great CEOs are in short supply. Or so the executive recruiters and compensation consultants keep saying. "It's supply and demand," super-headhunter Gerry Roche is fond of remarking. "Everyone says, 'Get me Larry Bossidy.' How many Larry Bossidys do you think there are?"

Well, just one, according to an Internet phonebook search. But that's not the point. A headhunter "gets his gigantic search fees advancing the idea that there are only five or six people in the world who can do this job—and he knows all of them," says Joseph Daniel McCool, editor of *Executive Recruiter News*. "The shortage of CEOs is a myth." Graef Crystal puts it in Econ 101 terms: "If pay is rising, it's going to be due either to a change in supply or to a change in demand. Has there been a decrease in the supply of CEOs? No. And the business schools are churning out more people every year. Is there an increase in demand? For every company like ITT that splits into three, there are 100 that merge. So if anything, CEO pay should be *sinking*."

Why, then, isn't it? Because for all CEOs' free-market rhetoric, their pay has less to do with the market's invisible hand than with the invisible handshake. Studies have shown a link between a CEO's pay and how much the people on their compensation committee make in their day jobs—often as CEOs at other companies. Verizon's Ivan Seidenberg (2002 comp: $22.4 million), for instance, sits on the comp committee for Viacom CEO Sumner Redstone (2002 comp: $39.5 million). "Everybody is stroking everybody else," says Herb Sandler, co-CEO of Golden West Financial, whose comp last year was just $1.3 million. "It's sort of like the Golden Rule gone wrong," says Harvard Business School professor Rakesh Khurana. "CEOs do unto others as they would have them do unto them."

The situation wasn't always so. Up through the 1970s, a chief executive's pay was generally linked to that of his underlings in a geometrically proportional relationship known as the "golden triangle." But soon a new breed of compensation consultant began whispering in CEOs' ears: Look what other chiefs are making. They pointed to a "peer group" and calculated the average pay. Because some of those peers were likely to have supersized salaries, just pegging the CEO's pay to the average usually guaranteed a raise. But nobody's CEO is just "average." One compensation consultant recalls a CEO asking him with a straight face if everyone in his industry was paid at the 75th percentile.

It's easy to laugh. But it is the chase for this mathematical impossibility that leads to what Charles Elson, director of the University of Delaware's Center for Corporate Governance, calls a "closed circulation market that's ever spiraling up."

So how do we break out of this spiral? We could tell boards to grow a spine. We could tell CEOs they're embarrassing themselves. We could tell people to be outraged. But we've done all that—two years ago, ten years ago, 20 years ago. "The irrationalities and excesses . . . do not seem easy to eradicate," FORTUNE wrote in a 1982 cover story, "The Madness of Executive Compensation."

We could offer up the latest Rube Goldberg solutions for aligning CEOs' interests with their shareholders'. One proposal making the rounds, indexed options, would reward CEOs only if their stock beat a larger market index. Nifty idea, but ask a CEO to try this on for size: The value of your options, already hard to calculate, will now gyrate with some index, which, by the way, only a third of companies beat. What, no takers?

We could observe that European companies generally pay their CEOs a small fraction of what their U.S. counterparts make, yet don't seem to have any trouble "recruiting and retaining talent." We could point to a number of FORTUNE 500 companies that pay their CEOs moderately and seem to be doing just fine.

We could even mention this year's record 275 shareholder proposals to rein in executive pay. Two of them—at Hewlett-Packard and Tyco—have gotten majority votes. But management is free to ignore those mostly nonbinding resolutions and routinely does.

Nope, it's going to take more than tinkering to reverse a dynamic this powerful. And there's only one way to do it: Address a basic power imbalance. Somewhere along the line, managers—who are, after all, just hired hands—started behaving as if they owned the place. And the real owners—mostly mutual funds and pensions—started behaving as if they didn't. In fact, they voted their shares just as their hired hands told them to. Taking orders from the help might seem humiliating. But then, institutional investors (including the mutual funds you own) don't have to declare the way they vote.

That's changing. A new SEC rule that takes effect in the summer of 2004 will require it. It may seem like just another procedural tinker. But there's reason to hope it could be something more. CEOs have already proved they can't be embarrassed. But maybe owners can be. If so, they might finally provide the counterweight that is so desperately needed—and keep CEOs from stuffing their bellies at the shareholder trough.

Let's hope so. Because until the owners come back, the pigs will be running the farm.

CHAPTER 8

The Limits of Markets

ROBERT KUTTNER

The claim that the freest market produces the best economic outcome is the centerpiece of the conservative political resurgence. If the state is deemed incompetent to balance the market's instability, temper its inequality, or correct its myopia, there is not much left of the mixed economy and the modern liberal project.

Yet while conservatives resolutely tout the superiority of free markets, many liberals are equivocal about defending the mixed economy. The last two Democratic presidents have mainly offered a more temperate call for the reining in of government and the liberation of the entrepreneur. The current vogue for deregulation began under Jimmy Carter. The insistence on budget balance was embraced by Bill Clinton, whose pledge to "reinvent government" was soon submerged in a shared commitment to shrink government. Much of the economics profession, after an era of embracing a managed form of capitalism, has also reverted to a new fundamentalism about the virtues of markets. So there is today a stunning imbalance of ideology, conviction, and institutional armor between right and left.

At bottom, three big things are wrong with the utopian claims about markets. First, they misdescribe the dynamics of human motivation. Second, they ignore the fact that civil society needs realms of political rights where some things are not for sale. And third, even in the economic realm, markets price many things wrong, which means that pure markets do not yield optimal economic outcomes.

There is at the core of the celebration of markets relentless tautology. If we begin by assuming that nearly everything can be understood as a market and that markets optimize outcomes, then everything leads back to the same conclusion—marketize! If, in the event, a particular market doesn't optimize, there is only one possible conclusion—it must be insufficiently market-like. This is a no-fail system for guaranteeing that theory trumps evidence. Should some human activity not, in fact, behave like an efficient market, it must logically be the result of some interference that should be removed. It does not occur that the theory mis-specifies human behavior.

The school of experimental economics, pioneered by psychologists Daniel Kahneman and Amos Tversky, has demonstrated that people do not behave the way the model specifies. People will typically charge more to give something up than to acquire the identical article; economic theory would predict a single "market-clearing" price. People help strangers, return wallets, leave generous tips in restaurants they will never visit again, give donations to public radio when theory would predict they would rationally "free-ride," and engage in other acts that suggest they value general norms of fairness. To conceive of altruism as a special form of selfishness misses the point utterly.

Although the market model imagines a rational individual, maximizing utility in an institutional vacuum, real people also have civic and social selves. The act of voting can be shown to be irrational by the lights of economic theory, because the "benefit" derived from the likelihood of one's vote affecting the outcome is not worth the "cost." But people vote as an act of faith in the civic process, as well as to influence outcomes.

In a market, everything is potentially for sale. In a political community, some things are beyond price. One's person, one's vote, one's basic democratic rights do not belong on the auction block. We no longer allow human beings to be bought and sold via slavery (though influential Chicago economists have argued that it would be efficient to treat adoptions as auction markets). While the market keeps trying to invade the polity, we do not permit the literal sale of public office. As James Tobin wrote, commenting on the myopia of his own profession, "Any good second-year graduate student in economics could write a short examination paper proving that voluntary transactions in votes would increase the welfare of the sellers as well as the buyers."

But the issue here is not just the defense of a civic realm beyond markets or of a socially bearable income distribution. History also demonstrates that in much of economic life, pure reliance on markets produces suboptimal outcomes. Market forces, left to their own devices, lead to avoidable financial panics and depressions, which in turn lead to political chaos. Historically, government has had to intervene, not only to redress the gross inequality of market-determined income and wealth, but to rescue the market from itself when it periodically goes haywire. The state also provides oases of solidarity for economic as well as social ends, in realms that markets cannot value properly, such as education, health, public infrastructure, and clean air and water. So the fact remains that the mixed economy—a strong private sector tempered and leavened by a democratic policy—is the essential instrument of both a decent society and an efficient economy.

The second coming of laissez faire has multiple causes. In part, it reflects the faltering of economic growth in the 1970s, on the Keynesian watch. It also reflects a relative weakening of the political forces that support a mixed economy—the declining influence of the labor movement, the erosion of working-class voting turnout, the suburbanization of the Democratic Party, and the restoration of the political sway of organized business—as well as the reversion of formal economics to preKeynesian verities.

Chicago-style economists have also colonized other academic disciplines. Public Choice theory, a very influential current in political science, essentially applies the market model to politics. Supposedly, self-seeking characterizes both economic man and political man. But in economics, competition converts individual selfishness into a general good, while in politics, selfishness creates little monopolies. Public Choice claims that office holders have as their paramount goal re-election, and that groups of voters are essentially "rent seekers" looking for a free ride at public expense, rather than legitimate members of a political collectivity expressing democratic voice. Ordinary citizens are drowned out by organized interest groups, so the mythic "people" never get what they want. Thus, since the democratic process is largely a sham, as well as a drag on economic efficiency, it is best to entrust as little to the public realm as possible. Lately, nearly half the articles in major political science journals have reflected a broad Public Choice sensibility.

The Law and Economics movement, likewise, has made deep inroads into the law schools and courts, subsidized by tens of millions of dollars from right-wing foundations. The basic idea of Law and Economics is that the law, as a system of rules and rights, tends to undermine the efficiency of markets. It is the duty of judges, therefore, to make the law the servant of market efficiency rather than a realm of civic rights. Borrowing from Public Choice theory, Law and Economics scholars contend that since democratic deliberation and hence legislative intent are largely illusory, it is legitimate for courts to ignore legislative mandates—not to protect rights of minorities but to protect the efficiency of markets. Regulation is generally held to be a deadweight cost, since it cannot improve upon the outcomes that free individuals would rationally negotiate.

These intellectual currents are strategically connected to the political arena. Take the journal titled *Regulation,* published for many years by the American Enterprise Institute, and currently published by the Cato Institute. Though it offers lively policy debates over particulars, virtually every article in *Regulation* is anti-regulation. Whether the subject is worker safety, telecommunications, the environment, electric power, health care—whatever—the invariable subtext is that government screws things up and markets are self-purifying. It is hardly surprising that the organized right publishes such a journal. What is more depressing, and revealing, is that there is no comparable journal with a predisposition in favor of a mixed economy. This intellectual apparatus has become the scaffolding for the proposition that governments should leave markets alone.

MARKETS, EFFICIENCY, AND JUSTICE

The moral claim of the free market is based on the interconnected premises that markets maximize liberty, justice, and efficiency. In a market economy, individuals are free to choose, as Milton Friedman famously wrote. They are free to decide what to buy, where to shop, what businesses or professions to pursue, where to live—subject "only" to the constraints of their individual income and wealth. The extremes of wealth and poverty seemingly mock the claim that markets epitomize human freedom—a poor man has only the paltry freedoms of a meager income. But the constraints of market-determined income are presumed defensible, because of the second claim—that the purchasing power awarded by markets is economically fair. If Bill Gates has several billion dollars to spend, that is only because he has added several billions of dollars of value to the economy, as validated by the free choices of millions of consumers. An unskilled high school dropout, in contrast, has little freedom to consume, because his labor offers little of value to an employer. There may be extenuating prior circumstances of birth or fortune, but each of us is ultimately responsible for our own economic destiny.

Linking these two premises is the third claim—that markets are roughly efficient. The prices set by supply and demand reflect how the economy values goods and services. So the resulting allocation of investment is efficient, in the sense that an alternative allocation mandated by extra-market forces would reduce total output. This is why professional economists who have liberal social values as citizens generally argue that if we don't like the social consequences of market income distribution, we should redistribute after the fact rather than tamper with the market's pricing mechanism.

Of course, each of these core claims is ultimately empirical. If in fact the freest market does not truly yield the optimal level of material output, then it follows that a pure market is neither just nor conducive of maximal liberty. A tour of the actual economy reveals that some sectors lend themselves to markets that look roughly like the market of the textbook model, while others do not.

Why would markets not be efficient? The most orthodox explanation is the prevalence of what economists call "externalities." These are costs or benefits not captured by the price set by the immediate transaction. The best-known negative externality is pollution. The polluter "externalizes" the true costs of his waste products onto society by dumping them, at no personal cost, into a nearby river or spewing them into the air. If the full social cost were internalized, the price would be higher.

Positive externalities include research and education. Individuals and business firms underinvest in education and research because the benefits are diffuse. The firm that trains a worker may not capture the full return on that investment, since the worker may take a job elsewhere; the fruits of technical invention, likewise, are partly appropriated by competitors. As economists put it, the private return does not equal the social return, so we cannot rely on profit-maximizing individuals for the optimal level of investment. By the same token, if we made the education of children dependent on the private resources of parents, society as a whole would underinvest in the schooling of the next generation. There is a social return on having a well-educated workforce and citizenry. As the bumper sticker sagely puts it, "If you think education is expensive, try ignorance."

Standard economics sees externalities as exceptions. But a tour of economic life suggests that in a very large fraction of the total economy, markets do not price things appropriately. When we add up health, education, research, public infrastructure, plus structurally imperfect sectors of the economy like telecommunications, they quickly add up to more than half of society's total product. The issue is not whether to temper market verdicts, but how.

SUPER MARKETS

Even realms that are close to textbook markets can actually be enhanced by extra-market interventions. Consider your local supermarket. The pricing and supply of retail food is mostly unregulated, and fiercely competitive. Somehow, the average consumer's lack of infinite time to go shopping, and less-than-perfect information about the relative prices of a thousand products in several local stores, exactly allows the supermarket to earn a normal profit.

Supermarkets connect the retail market to the agricultural one. The supermarket also provides part of the local market for labor and capital. Though cashiers and meat cutters are not the most glamorous of jobs, the supermarket manages to pay just enough to attract people who are just competent enough to perform the jobs acceptably. If supermarket profits are below par over time, the price of its shares will fall. That also operates as a powerful signal—on where investors should put their capital, and on how executives must supervise their managers and managers their employees.

Though there may be occasional missteps, and though some supermarkets go bankrupt, the interplay of supply and demand in all of these submarkets contributes to a dynamic equilibrium. It results in prices that are "right" most of the time. The supermarket stocks, displays, and prices thousands of different highly perishable products in response to shifting consumer tastes, with almost no price regulation. Supply and demand substitutes for elaborate systems of control that would be hopelessly cumbersome to administer. No wonder the champions of the market are almost religious in their enthusiasm.

But please note that supermarkets are not perfectly efficient. Retail grocers operate on thin profit margins, but the wholesale part of the food distribution chain is famous for enormous markups. A farmer is likely to get only 10 cents out of a box of corn flakes that retails for $3.99. Secondly, even supermarkets are far from perfectly free markets. Their hygiene is regulated by government inspectors, as is most of the food they sell. Government regulations mandate the format and content of nutritional labeling. They require clear, consistent unit pricing, to rule out a variety of temptations of deceptive marketing. Moreover, many occupations in the food industry, such as meat cutter and cashier, are substantially unionized; so the labor market is not a pure free market either. Much of the food produced in the United States is grown by farmers who benefit from a variety of interferences with a laissez-faire market, contrived by government to prevent ruinous fluctuations in prices. The government also subsidizes education and technical innovation in agriculture.

So even in this nearly perfect market, a modicum of regulation is entirely compatible with the basic discipline of supply and demand, and probably enhances its efficiency by making for better-informed consumers, less-opportunistic sellers, and by placing the market's most self-cannibalizing tendencies off-limits. Because of the imperfect information of consumers, it is improbable that repealing these regulations would enhance efficiency.

SICK MARKETS

Now, however, consider a very different sector—health care. Medical care is anything but a textbook free market, yet market forces and profit motives in the health industry are rife. On the supply side, the health industry violates several conditions of a free market. Unlike the supermarket business, there is not "free entry." You cannot simply open a hospital, or hang out your shingle as a doctor. This gives health providers a degree of market power that compromises the competitive model—and raises prices. On the demand side, consumers lack the special knowledge to shop for a doctor the way they buy a car and lack perfectly free choice of health insurer. And since society has decided that nobody shall perish for lack of medical care, demand is not constrained by private purchasing power, which is inflationary.

Health care also offers substantial "positive externalities." The value to society of mass vaccinations far exceeds the profits that can be captured by the doctor or drug company. If vaccinations and other public health measures were left to private supply and demand, society would seriously underinvest. Society invests in other public health measures that markets underprovide. The health care system also depends heavily on extra-market norms—the fact that physicians and nurses are guided by ethical constraints and professional values that limit the opportunism that their specialized knowledge and power might otherwise invite.

The fact that health care is a far cry from a perfect market sets up a chain of perverse incentives. A generation ago, fee-for-service medicine combined with insurance reimbursement to stimulate excessive treatment and drive up costs. Today many managed care companies reverse the process and create incentives to deny necessary care. In either case, this is no free market. Indeed, as long as society stipulates that nobody shall die for lack of private purchasing power, it will never be a free market. That is why it requires regulation as well as subsidy.

Here is the nub of the issue. Are most markets like supermarkets—or like health markets? The conundrum of the market for health care is a signal example of an oft-neglected insight known as the General Theory of the Second Best. The theory, propounded by the economists Richard Lipsey and Kelvin Lancaster in 1956, holds that when a particular market departs significantly from a pure market, attempts to marketize partially can leave us worse off.

A Second Best market (such as health care) is not fully accountable to the market discipline of supply and demand, so typically it has acquired second-best forms of accountability—professional norms, government supervision, regulation, and subsidy—to which market forces have adapted. If the health care system is already a far cry from a free market on both the demand side and the supply side, removing one regulation and thereby making the health system more superficially market-like may well simply increase opportunism and inefficiency. In many economic realms, the second-best outcome of some price distortion offset by regulation and extra-market norms may be the best outcome practically available.

Another good Second Best illustration is the banking industry. Until the early 1970s, banking in the United States was very highly regulated. Regulation limited both the price and the quantity of banking services. Bank charters were limited. So were interest rates. Banks were subject to a variety of other regulatory constraints. Of course, banks still competed fiercely for market share and profitability, based on how well they served customers and how astutely they analyzed credit risks. Partially deregulating the banking and savings and loan industries in the 1980s violated the Theory of the Second Best. It pursued greater efficiency, but led to speculative excess. Whatever gains to the efficiency of allocation were swamped by the ensuing costs of the bailout.

THE THREE EFFICIENCIES

The saga of banking regulation raises the question of contending conceptions of efficiency. The efficiency prized by market enthusiasts is "allocative." That is, the free play of supply and demand via price signals will steer resources to the uses that provide the greatest satisfaction and the highest return. Regulation interferes with this discipline, and presumably worsens outcomes. But in markets like health care and banking, the market is far from free to begin with. Moreover, "allocative" efficiency leaves out the issues that concerned John Maynard Keynes—whether the economy as a whole has lower rates of growth and higher unemployment than it might achieve. Nor does allocative efficiency deal with the question of technical advance, which is the source of improved economic performance over time. Technical progress is the issue that concerned the other great dissenting economic theorist of the early twentieth century, Joseph Schumpeter. Standard market theory lacks a common metric to assess these three contending conceptions of efficiency.

Countermanding the allocative mechanism of the price system may depress efficiency on Adam Smith's sense. But if the result is to increase Keynesian efficiency of high growth and full employment, or the Schumpeterian efficiency of technical advance, there may well be a net economic gain. Increasing allocative efficiency when unemployment is high doesn't help. It may even hurt—to the extent that intensified competition in a depressed economy may throw more people out of work, reduce overall purchasing power, and deepen the shortfall of aggregate demand.

By the same token, if private market forces underinvest in technical innovation, then public investment and regulation can improve on market outcomes. Patents, trademarks, and copyrights are among the oldest regulatory interventions acknowledging market failure, and creating artificial property rights in innovation. As technology evolves, so necessarily does the regime of intellectual property regulation.

In my recent book, *Everything For Sale,* I examined diverse sectors of the economy. Only a minority of them operated efficiently with no regulatory interference.

Some sectors, such as banking and stock markets, entail both fiduciary responsibilities and systemic risks. In the absence of financial regulation, conflicts of interest and the tendency of money markets to speculative excess could bring down the entire economy, as financial panics periodically did in the era before regulation.

Other sectors, such as telecommunications, are necessarily a blend of monopoly power and competition. New competitors now have the right to challenge large incumbents, but often necessarily piggyback on the infrastructure of established companies that they are trying to displace. Without regulation mandating fair play, they would be crushed. The breakup of the old AT&T monopoly allows greater innovation and competition, but if the new competition is to benefit consumers it requires careful ground rules. The 1996 Telecommunications Act, complex legislation specifying terms of fair engagement, is testament for the ongoing need for discerning regulation in big, oligopolistic industries.

Similarly, in the electric power industry, where new technologies allow for new forms of competition, the old forms of regulation no longer apply. Once, a public utility was granted a monopoly; a regulatory agency guaranteed it a fair rate of return. Today, the system is evolving into one in which residential consumers and business customers will be able to choose among multiple suppliers. Yet because of the need to assure that all customers will have electric power on demand, and that incumbents will not be able to drive out new competitors, the new system still depends on regulation. A regime of regulated competition is replacing the old form of regulation of entry and price—but it is regulation nonetheless.

Regulation, of course, requires regulators. But if democratic accountability is a charade, if regulators are hopeless captives of "rent-seeking" interest groups, if public-mindedness cannot be cultivated, then the regulatory impulse is doomed. Yet because capitalism requires ground rules, it is wrong to insist that the best remedy is no regulation at all. The choice is between good regulation and bad regulation.

In the 1970s, many economists, including many relative liberals such as Charles Schultze, began attacking "command-and-control" regulation for overriding the market's pricing mechanism. Instead, they commended "incentive regulation," in which public goals would take advantage of the pricing system. What Schultze proposed in the area of pollution control, Alfred Kahn commended for electric power regulation and Alain Enthoven proposed for health insurance. But what all three, and others in this vein, tended to overlook is that incentive regulation is still regulation. It still requires competent, public-minded regulators. And because technology continues to evolve, regulation is not merely transitional.

The 1990 Clean Air Act created an innovative acid rain program that supplanted "command-and-control" regulation of sulphur dioxide emissions with a new, "market-like" system of tradable emission permits. But before this system could operate, myriad regulatory determinations were necessary. Public policy had to specify the total permissible volume of pollutants, how the new market was to be structured, and how emissions were to be monitored. This was entirely a contrived market. So was the decision to auction off portions of the broadcast spectrum. Though hailed as more "market-like" than the previous system of administrative broadcast licensing, the creation of auctions required innumerable regulatory determinations.

Unlike airline deregulation, in which the supervisory agency, the Civil Aeronautics Board, was put out of business, the Federal Communications Commission and the Environmental Protection Agency remain to monitor these experiments in incentive regulation and to make necessary course corrections. Airline deregulation has been at best a mixed success, because there is no government agency to police the results and to intervene to prevent collusive or predatory practices.

Similarly, if we are to use incentives in sectors that have previously been seen as public goods, such as education, issues of distribution inevitably arise. How public policy allocates, say, vouchers, and how it structures incentives, cannot help affecting who gets the service. The ideal of a pure market solution to a public good is a mirage.

The basic competitive discipline of a capitalist economy can coexist nicely with diverse extramarket forces; the market can even be rendered more efficient by them. These include both explicit regulatory interventions and the cultivation of extramarket norms, most notably trust, civility, and long-term reciprocity. Richard Vietor of the Harvard Business School observes in his 1994 book, *Contrived Competition,* that imperfect, partly regulated markets still are highly responsive to competitive discipline. The market turns out to be rather more resilient and adaptive than its champions admit. In markets as varied as banking, public utilities, and health care, entrepreneurs do not sicken and expire when faced with regulated competition; they simply revise their competitive strategy and go right on competing. Norms that commit society to resist short-term opportunism can make both the market and the society a healthier place. Pure markets, in contrast, commend and invite opportunism, and depress trust.

THE INEVITABILITY OF POLITICS

A review of the virtues and limits of markets necessarily takes us back to politics. Even a fervently capitalist society, it turns out, requires prior rules. Rules govern everything from basic property rights to the fair terms of engagement in complex mixed markets such as health care and telecommunications. Even the proponents of market-like incentives—managed competition in health care, tradable emissions permits for clean air, supervised deregulation of telecommunications, compensation mandates to deter unsafe workplace practices—depend, paradoxically, on discerning, public-minded regulation to make their incentive schemes work. As new, unimagined dilemmas arise, there is no fixed constitution that governs all future cases. As new products and business strategies appear and markets evolve, so necessarily does the regime of rules.

The patterns of market failure are more pervasive than most market enthusiasts acknowledge. Generally, they are the result of immutable structural characteristics of certain markets and the ubiquity of both positive and negative spillovers. In markets where the consumer is not effectively sovereign (telecommunications, public utilities, banking, airlines, pure food and drugs), or where the reliance on market verdicts would lead to socially intolerable outcomes (health care, pollution, education, gross income inequality, the buying of office or purchase of professions), a recourse purely to ineffectual market discipline would leave both consumer and society worse off than the alternative of a mix of market forces and regulatory interventions. While advocates of laissez faire presume that the regulation characteristic of an earlier stage of capitalism has been mooted by technology, competition, and better-informed consumers, they forget that the more mannered capitalism of our own era is precisely the fruit of regulation, and that the predatory tendencies persist.

Contrary to the theory of perfect markets, much of economic life is not the mechanical satisfaction of preferences or the pursuit of a single best equilibrium. On the contrary, many paths are possible—many blends of different values, many mixes of market and social, many possible distributions of income and wealth—all compatible with tolerably efficient getting and spending. The grail of a perfect market, purged of illegitimate and inefficient distortions, is a fantasy.

The real world displays a very broad spectrum of actual markets with diverse structural characteristics, and different degrees of separation from the textbook ideal. Some need little regulation, some a great deal—either to make the market mechanism work efficiently or to solve problems that the market cannot fix. Someone has to make such determinations, or we end up in a world very far from even the available set of Second Bests. In short, rules require rule setters. In a democracy, that enterprise entails democratic politics.

The market solution does not moot politics. It only alters the dynamics of influence and the mix of winners and losers. The attempt to relegate economic issues to "nonpolitical" bodies, such as the Federal Reserve, does not rise above politics either. It only removes key financial decisions from popular debate to financial elites, and lets others take the political blame. A decision to allow markets, warts and all, free rein is just one political choice among many. There is no escape from politics.

QUIS CUSTODET?

The issue of how precisely to govern markets arises in libertarian, democratic nations like the United States, and deferential, authoritarian ones like Singapore. It arises whether the welfare state is large or small, and whether the polity is expansive or restrained in its aspirations. Rule setting and the correction of market excess are necessarily public issues in social-democratic Sweden, in Christian Democratic Germany, in feudal-capitalist Japan, and in Tory Britain. The highly charged question of the proper rules undergirding a capitalist society pervaded political discourse and conflict throughout nineteenth-century America, even though the public sector then consumed less than 5 percent of the gross domestic product.

The political process, of course, can produce good sets of rules for the market, or bad ones. Thus, the quality of political life is itself a public good—perhaps the most fundamental public good. A public good, please recall, is something that markets are not capable of valuing correctly. Trust, civility, long-term commitment, and the art of consensual deliberation are the antitheses of pure markets, and the essence of effective politics.

As the economic historian Douglass North, the 1993 Nobel laureate in economics, has observed, competent public administration and governance are a source of competitive advantage for nation-states. Third-world nations and postcommunist regimes are notably disadvantaged not just by the absence of functioning markets but by the weakness of legitimate states. A vacuum of legitimate state authority does not yield efficient laissez faire; it yields mafias and militias, with whose arbitrary power would-be entrepreneurs must reckon. The marketizers advising post-Soviet Russia imagined that their challenge was to dismantle a state in order to create a market. In fact, the more difficult challenge was to constitute a state to create a market.

Norms that encourage informed civic engagement increase the likelihood of competent, responsive politics and public administration, which in turn yield a more efficient mixed economy. North writes:

> The evolution of government from its medieval, Mafia-like character to that embody-ing modern legal institutions and instruments is a major part of the history of freedom. It is a part that tends to be obscured or ignored because of the myopic vision of many economists, who persist in modeling government as nothing more than a gigantic form of theft and income redistribution.

Here, North is echoing Jefferson, who pointed out that property and liberty, as we know and value them, are not intrinsic to the state of nature but are fruits of ef-fective government.

The more that complex mixed markets require a blend of evolving rules, the more competent and responsive a public administration the enterprise requires. Strong civic institutions help constitute the state, and also serve as counterweights against excesses of both state and market. Lately, the real menace to a sustainable society has been the market's invasion of the polity, not vice versa. Big money has crowded out authentic participation. Commercial values have encroached on civic values.

Unless we are to leave society to the tender mercies of laissez faire, we need a mixed economy. Even laissez faire, for that matter, requires rules to define property rights. Either way, capitalism entails public policies, which in turn are creatures of democratic politics. The grail of a market economy untainted by politics is the most dangerous illusion of our age.

PART THREE

Inequality

There is no doubt that the United States is an extremely prosperous society, but that prosperity has not been shared by everyone. One of the most striking features of American society today, indeed, is the stark coexistence of great wealth and widespread poverty. In many respects, economic inequality is more glaring today than ever before in our recent history. But a wide gap between "haves" and "have-nots" has been with us from the beginning, and has stubbornly persisted even during good economic times.

In the 1950s and 1960s, for example, many social scientists described the United States as an "affluent" society—one in which most people could expect a steady improvement in their standard of living, great disparities in income and wealth were fast disappearing, and true poverty was soon to be a thing of the past. These perceptions were based on some undeniable facts. On average, Americans' incomes did rise substantially after World War II, and during the 1960s millions of the poor were lifted above the official poverty line. It was natural to believe that these trends would continue.

But even in the expanding economy of the 1950s and 1960s, there were important limits to what some believed was a steady march toward greater equality. For one thing, the progress in raising the overall standard of living had virtually no impact on the *distribution* of income and wealth in America—the gap between rich and poor. Throughout most of the period since World War II, the upper one-fifth of income earners received roughly 40 percent of the country's total personal income; the bottom fifth, about 5 percent. And although poverty was sharply reduced in many rural areas, it proved to be much more stubborn in the inner cities.

More recently, the trends have become much more discouraging: The limited postwar progress toward economic equality has been reversed. By the early 1980s, the spread of income inequality in the United States had begun to increase as the share of the most affluent rose while the share of the poor fell. In the 1990s, income inequality reached its most extreme level since World War II. By the turn of the new century, the top fifth of income earners took home half the nation's total income.

As Edward Wolff points out in his article on the distribution of wealth in America, the growth of inequality is actually understated if we look only at the gap in *income*—that is, the flow of cash that families and individuals receive over a given period. At least equally important is the widening gap in Americans' *wealth*—stocks and bonds, businesses, homes, and other assets. Even with a high income, a family without significant assets is vulnerable to economic insecurity. Wealth, moreover, confers a degree of economic and political influence that those without it cannot share. It's especially troubling, therefore, that the wealth gap is wider now than at any time since before the Great Depression of the 1930s, with the top 1 percent of American households cornering almost two-fifths of the country's entire net wealth.

As the economic fortunes of the richest Americans have shot upward, those of low-income Americans have deteriorated. At last count, close to 33 million Americans had incomes below the "poverty line," defined as slightly over $18,000 for a family of four in 2003. Today one American child in six lives in poverty, a far higher proportion than in most other industrial nations.

Many people are aware that poverty among children is widespread in America, but fewer realize that it is *much* more prevalent here than in other developed societies. Using data from the Luxembourg Income Study, an international comparison of levels of inequality and poverty begun in the 1980s, Lee Rainwater and Timothy Smeeding illustrate just how stark those differences are. Poor children are worse off in the United States—one of the world's most affluent countries—than in all but the poorest industrial societies. And the economic gap between affluent and poor children is wider—sometimes *much* wider—in the United States than in any other Western industrial country.

Poverty is more than a matter of income alone. One of the most devastating, and most visible, consequences of rising poverty (among other causes) has been the growth of homelessness in the United States. Elliot Liebow, an anthropologist, spent several years closely observing homeless women in and around Washington, D.C., and his article paints a compelling picture of what life is really like at the bottom of the American system of inequality. Being homeless, he reveals, means having to struggle every day for the bare essentials of life most of us take for granted—from a place to sleep to somewhere to store our belongings.

The problems of poverty and homelessness are so deeply entrenched in America that they sometimes seem like a normal backdrop of social life—part of the natural order of things. But why do we tolerate such widespread deprivation on a scale unknown in most other advanced societies? Part of the reason may be that, as Herbert Gans suggests, we have developed for those at the bottom of the social ladder a variety of "labels" that help absolve the larger society of any responsibility for their condition while emphasizing the moral and psychological failings of the poor. The most recent version is the common term *underclass,* which, Gans argues, is often used to justify the social exclusion of the poor and to deflect our attention from the broader causes of poverty. Such labels, Gans reminds us, may allow "mainstream" Americans to vent their anger and frustration at the poor, but they do not help us deal realistically with the roots of poverty or with the wider economic inequity that poverty reflects.

CHAPTER 9

Recent Trends in the Size Distribution of Household Wealth

EDWARD N. WOLFF

W hy is wealth important, over and above income? Family wealth by itself is a source of well-being, independent of the direct financial income it provides. There are four reasons. First, wealth in the form of owner-occupied housing provides services directly to its owners. Second, wealth is a source of consumption, independent of the direct money income it provides, because assets can be converted directly into cash and thus provide for immediate consumption needs. Third, the availability of financial assets can provide liquidity to a family in times of economic stress, such as occasioned by unemployment, sickness, or family break-up. Fourth, in a representative democracy, the distribution of power is often related to the distribution of wealth.

It would be foolish, of course, to expect even the best-functioning market economy to produce near-equality of wealth. The population is at different points in the life cycle, and one would expect the middle-aged and elderly to have accumulated more wealth than the young. People will have different tastes for accumulating human capital, for working and earning wages, and for saving. Entrepreneurial spirits are not distributed evenly across the population, nor is entrepreneurial success. Luck will play a role in economic outcomes. Who bought stock in Intel or Microsoft 15 years ago? Who happened to own a family farm that became coveted suburban real estate?

But even if economists can readily find reasons to be comfortable with some degree of wealth inequality, it is nonetheless troubling when that level rises substantially. In the 1970s, the level of wealth inequality in the United States was comparable to that of other developed industrialized countries. By the 1980s, the United States had become the most unequal society in terms of wealth among the advanced industrial nations. In the 1990s, the run-up in stock prices has added to the disparities in wealth. By 1997, one man, Bill Gates, was worth about as much as the 40 million American households at the bottom of the wealth distribution! . . .

The sources used for this study are the 1983, 1989, 1992, and 1995 Survey of Consumer Finances (SCF) conducted by the Federal Reserve Board. The unit of observation is the "primary economic unit" of a household, which can be a family, a single individual, or two or more unrelated individuals who share expenses. . . .

I will focus in the discussion that follows on two measures of wealth, which I will refer to as "net worth" and "financial wealth." Net worth (or marketable wealth) is defined as the current value of all marketable or fungible assets less the current value of debts. Net worth is thus the difference in value between total assets and total liabilities or debt. Total assets are defined as the sum of: 1) the gross value of owner-occupied housing; 2) other real estate owned by the household; 3) cash and demand deposits; 4) time and savings deposits, certificates of deposit, and money market accounts; 5) government bonds, corporate bonds, foreign bonds, and other financial securities; 6) the cash surrender value of life insurance plans; 7) the cash surrender value of pension plans, including IRAs, Keogh, 401(k) plans, and other defined contribution plans; 8) corporate stock and mutual funds; 9) net equity in unincorporated businesses; and 10) equity in trust funds. Total liabilities are the sum of: 1) mortgage debt; 2) consumer debt, including auto loans; and 3) other debt.

This measure of wealth is used because the primary interest here is in wealth as a store of value and therefore a source of potential consumption. Thus only assets that can be readily converted to cash (that is, "fungible" ones) are included. As a result, consumer durables (such as cars) and retirement wealth (for example, the present value of expected Social Security benefits), which are sometimes included in broader concepts of wealth, are excluded here.

The second concept of wealth, which I call "financial wealth," is more restricted. It is defined as net worth minus net equity in owner-occupied housing. Financial wealth is a more "liquid" concept than marketable wealth, since it is somewhat difficult to liquidate one's housing wealth in the short term. (Remember, just taking out a home equity loan does not alter one's wealth, since in terms of personal wealth, the lower equity in the house and new cash available for spending offset each other.) Financial wealth thus reflects the resources that may be immediately available for consumption or various forms of investments.

WEALTH HAS FALLEN FOR THE MEDIAN AMERICAN HOUSEHOLD

Median wealth for a U.S. household was about 10 percent lower in 1995 than in 1983, as shown in the first row of Table 9.1. However, the decline was not continuous. After rising by 7 percent between 1983 and 1989, median wealth fell by 17 percent from 1989 to 1995. Mean wealth is much higher than the median—four to five times as great—implying that the vast bulk of household wealth is concentrated in the richest families. Mean wealth also showed a substantial increase from 1983 to 1989 fol-

TABLE 9.1   Mean and Median Household Wealth, 1983, 1989, 1992, and 1995
(1995 Dollars)

	1983	1989	1992	1995	% Change 1983–1995
Net Worth					
Median	51,051	54,643	46,616	45,630	–10.6
Mean	198,770	227,718	221,384	204,529	2.9
Percent with zero negative net worth	15.5	17.9	18.0	18.5	
Financial Worth					
Median	11,025	13,012	10,917	9,950	–9.8
Mean	144,245	169,977	168,770	156,935	8.8
Percent with zero or negative financial wealth	25.7	26.8	28.2	28.7	

lowed by a rather precipitous decline, though overall it was 3 percent higher in 1995 than in 1983. One reason for the decline in household wealth is evident from the third row of Table 9.1, which shows that the percentage of households reporting zero or negative net worth increased from 15.5 percent in 1983 to 18.5 percent in 1995.

When equity in owner-occupied housing is subtracted, median financial wealth was less than $10,000 in 1995, indicating that the average American household had very little savings available for immediate needs. As shown in Table 9.1, the time trend for financial wealth similar to that for household net worth. In particular, the fraction of households with zero or negative financial wealth rose over this period from 26 to 29 percent.

WEALTH INEQUALITY IS STILL MUCH HIGHER IN 1995 THAN IN 1983

In 1995, the top 1 percent of families as ranked by net worth owned almost 39 percent of total household wealth; the top 20 percent of households held 84 percent. The richest 1 percent as ranked by financial wealth own 47 percent of total household financial wealth; the top 20 percent, 93 percent. A more detailed breakdown by various percentiles of the wealth distribution is presented in Table 9.2.

The figures also show that the wealth inequality, after rising steeply between 1983 and 1989, leveled off from 1989 to 1995. For example, the share of wealth held by the top 1 percent rose by 3.6 percentage points from 1983 to 1989. Then, from 1989 and 1995, the share of the top percentile grew by a more modest 1.1 percentage points, while the share of the next 9 percentiles fell by 1.3 percentage points. However, the share of the bottom two quintiles also grew by 0.9 percentage points over this time.

TABLE 9.2   The Size Distribution of Wealth, 1983, 1989, 1992, and 1995

Year	Percentage Share of Net Worth or Financial Wealth Held by							
	Top 1.0%	Next 4.0%	Next 5.0%	Next 10.0%	Top 20.0%	2nd 20.0%	3rd 20.0%	Bottom 40.0%
Net Worth								
1983	33.8	22.3	12.1	13.1	81.3	12.6	5.2	0.9
1989	37.4	21.6	11.6	13.0	83.5	12.3	4.8	−0.7
1992	37.2	22.8	11.8	12.0	83.8	11.5	4.4	0.4
1995	38.5	21.8	11.5	12.1	83.9	11.4	4.5	0.2
Financial Wealth								
1983	42.9	25.1	12.3	11.0	91.3	7.9	1.7	−0.9
1989	46.9	23.9	11.6	10.9	93.4	7.4	1.7	−2.4
1992	45.6	25.0	11.5	10.2	92.3	7.3	1.5	−1.1
1995	47.2	24.6	11.2	10.1	93.0	6.9	1.4	−1.3

Note: For the computation of percentile shares of net worth, households are ranked according to their net worth; and for percentile shares of financial wealth, households are ranked according to their financial wealth.

The trend is similar for the inequality of financial wealth. The share of the top 1 percent climbed 4.0 percentage points between 1983 and 1989. In the ensuing six years, the share of the richest 1 percent grew by another 0.3 percentage points. At the same time, the share of the next 19 percentiles declined, as did the share of the second quintile, and that of the bottom two quintiles grew by 1.1 percentage points.

Table 9.3 shows the striking changes in absolute wealth between 1983 and 1995. Over this period, the largest gains in both absolute and relative terms were made by the wealthiest households. The top 1 percent in 1995 saw their average

TABLE 9.3   Mean Wealth Holdings by Quantile, 1983, 1989, 1992, and 1995
(in thousands, 1995 dollars)

Year	Top 1%	Next 4%	Next 5%	Next 10%	Top 20%	2nd 20%	3rd 20%	Bottom 40%	All
Net Worth									
1983	6,708	1,110	482.6	260.6	808.3	124.9	51.9	4.4	198.8
1995	7,875	1,115	471.7	246.8	858.1	116.8	45.9	0.9	204.5
% Change	17.4	0.5	−2.3	−5.3	6.2	−6.5	−11.5	−79.6	2.9
Financial Wealth									
1983	6,187	906	354.0	158.7	658.3	57.0	12.3	−6.3	144.2
1995	7,400	963	352.2	158.5	730.0	54.0	11.3	−10.6	156.9
% Change	19.6	6.4	−0.5	−0.1	10.9	−5.3	−7.8	−68.3	8.8

wealth (in 1995 dollars) grow by $1.2 million or by 17 percent relative to their counterparts in 1983 (who may not necessarily be the same households). The only other group whose wealth increased was the next richest 4 percent of the wealth holders (0.5 percent). Average wealth fell for every other group, and the poorest 40 percent of households experienced the steepest decline in their wealth holdings (a fall of 80 percent). The pattern is similar for financial wealth. The average financial wealth of the richest 1 percent grew by 20 percent and that of the next richest 4 percent by 6 percent. Financial wealth fell for all other groups, with the lower wealth groups suffering the greatest declines. . . .

There are marked differences in household portfolios by level of wealth. Table 9.4 provides a breakdown for the top 1 percent of households as ranked by wealth, who had a net worth exceeding $2.4 million (in 1995 dollars), the next 19 percent, with net worth between $177,000 and $2.4 million, and the bottom 80 percent, with net worth less than $177,000. The richest 1 percent of households invested about 80 percent of their savings in investment real estate, businesses, corporate stock, and financial securities in 1995. Housing accounted for only 6 percent of their wealth, liquid assets another 8 percent, and pension accounts 5 percent. Their debt-equity ratio (the ratio of debt to net worth) was 5 percent. Among the next richest 19 percent of U.S. households, 43 percent of their wealth took the form of investment assets—real estate, business equity, stocks and bonds. Housing comprised 30 percent, liquid assets 11 percent, and pension assets 13 percent. Debt amounted to 13 percent of their net worth.

TABLE 9.4   The Composition of Household Wealth by Wealth Class in 1995
(percent of gross assets)

	All Households	Top 1%	Next 19%	Bottom 80%
Principal residence	30.4	6.4	30.1	65.9
Other real estate	11.0	11.4	13.9	5.0
Liquid assets (bank deposits, money market funds, and cash surrender value of insurance)	10.0	7.7	11.3	11.1
Pension assets	9.0	4.7	12.6	8.5
Unincorporated business equity	17.9	36.8	11.0	3.1
Corporate stock (financial securities, mutual funds, and personal trusts)	18.9	30.3	18.0	4.1
Miscellaneous assets	2.8	2.7	3.1	2.2
Total assets	100.0	100.0	100.0	100.0
Memo: Debt/net worth	19.4	4.8	12.9	73.0

In contrast, almost two-thirds of the wealth of the bottom 80 percent of households was invested in their own home. Another 11 percent went into monetary savings of one form or another and 9 percent into pension accounts. The remaining 14 percent of their wealth was about evenly split among non-home real estate, business equity, and various financial securities and corporate stock. The ratio of debt to net worth was 73 percent, much higher than for the richest 20 percent.

Another way to portray differences between the middle class and the rich is to compute the share of total assets of different types held by each group, which is done in Table 9.5. In 1995, the richest 1 percent of households (again, this group has wealth exceeding $2.4 million) held half of all outstanding stock and trust equity, almost two-thirds of financial securities and over two-thirds of business equity, and 35 percent of investment real estate. The top 10 percent as a group, with household wealth of $352,000 and over, accounted for about 90 percent of stock shares, bonds, trusts, and business equity, and about three-quarters of non-home real estate. Moreover, despite the fact that 41 percent of households owned stock shares either directly or indirectly through mutual funds, trust accounts, or various pension accounts (up from 26 percent in 1983), a more detailed breakdown than is provided in the table shows that the richest 10 percent of households accounted for 82 percent of the total value of these stocks, only slightly less than their 88 percent share of directly owned stocks and mutual funds.

In contrast, owner-occupied housing, deposits, life insurance, and pension accounts were more evenly distributed among households. The bottom 90 percent of households, with wealth less than $352,000, accounted for over two-thirds of the value of owner-occupied housing, almost 40 percent of deposits, over half of life in-

TABLE 9.5   The Percent of Total Assets Held by Wealth Class, 1995

Asset Type	Top 1.0%	Next 9.0%	Bottom 90%
Assets Held Primarily by the Wealthy			
Stocks & Mutuals	51.4	37.0	11.6
Financial securities	65.9	23.9	10.2
Trusts	49.6	38.9	11.5
Business Equity	69.5	22.2	8.3
Non-Home Real Estate	35.1	43.6	21.3
Total for Group	55.5	32.1	12.5
Assets and Liabilities Held Primarily by the Non-Wealthy			
Principal Residence	7.1	24.6	68.3
Deposits	29.4	32.9	37.7
Life Insurance	16.4	28.5	55.1
Pension Accounts	17.7	44.7	37.7
Total for Group	12.8	29.7	57.5
Total Debt	9.4	18.9	71.7

surance cash value, and almost 40 percent of the value of pension accounts. Debt was the most evenly distributed component, with the bottom 90 percent of households responsible for 72 percent of total indebtedness.

There was relatively little change between 1983 and 1995 in the concentration of ownership of particular assets, with a few exceptions. The wealthiest 10 percent of households increased its share of total financial securities from 83 percent to 90 percent of the total amount of such securities over this period and its share of total deposits from 53 percent to 62 percent. The share of total pension accounts held by the top 10 percent fell from 68 percent in 1983 to 51 percent in 1989, reflecting the growing use of IRAs by middle income families, and then rebounded to 62 percent in 1992 and 1995 from the introduction of 401(k) plans and their adoption by high-income earners. The share of total debt held by the top 10 percent also fell somewhat, from 32 to 28 percent.

THE RACIAL DIVIDE WIDENS

Households in the Survey of Current Finance are divided into four racial/ethnic groups: non-Hispanic whites; non-Hispanic blacks; Hispanics; and other races, including Asians, Native Americans, and others. The discussion here will focus on the striking differences in the wealth holdings of whites and blacks. Table 9.6 gives illustrative mean and median values for the wealth of black and white households, as well as ratios between them.

In 1995, the ratio of black/white mean and median wealth holdings was 0.17 and 0.12, respectively, and that of financial wealth still lower, at 0.11 and 0.01, respectively. Underlying these trends, average real net worth rose for white households but fell for blacks from 1983 to 1995, so that the ratio fell from 0.19 to 0.17, whereas median wealth increased among black households while falling for whites, so that the ratio increased from 7 percent to 12 percent. Average financial wealth has remained relatively constant among black households while rising among whites, so that the ratio fell from 13 percent to 11 percent over this period. The median financial wealth of black households has also remained virtually constant over these years, at roughly zero.

If one searches the wealth data for positive notes, the homeownership rate of black households did grow from 44.3 percent in 1983 to 46.8 percent in 1995; while this is about two-thirds of the white level, it does represent a relative gain, since the homeownership rate among whites increased only from 68.1 percent to 69.4 percent over this time. Also, the percentage of black households reporting zero or negative net worth fell from 34.1 percent in 1983 to 31.3 percent in 1995; while this level is twice that of white households, the proportion of white households reporting zero or negative net worth rose from 11.3 percent in 1983 to 15.0 percent in 1995.

Interestingly, it appears that the black/white wealth ratios held fairly steady from 1983 to 1992, or the relative position of blacks even improved somewhat, but then losses were sustained from 1992 to 1995. The most vivid example is that the median net worth of black households relative to white, which rose from 7 percent in 1983 to 17 percent in 1992, before slipping back to 12 percent in 1995.

TABLE 9.6   Racial Wealth Differences, 1983–1995 *(in thousands of 1995 dollars, unless otherwise noted)*

Year	Mean Values			Median Values		
	Non-Hispanic Whites	Non-Hispanic Blacks	Ratio	Non-Hispanic Whites	Non-Hispanic Blacks	Ratio
Net Worth						
1983	232.3	43.7	0.19	66.9	4.4	0.07
1989	274.8	46.1	0.17	79.4	2.0	0.03
1992	265.9	49.4	0.19	66.6	11.2	0.17
1995	242.4	40.8	0.17	61.0	7.4	0.12
Financial Wealth						
1983	171.1	22.0	0.13	18.6	0.0	0.00
1989	207.7	22.5	0.11	25.1	0.0	0.00
1992	204.7	28.2	0.14	20.5	0.1	0.01
1995	188.4	21.2	0.11	18.1	0.2	0.01

One interesting issue is why the black/white wealth ratio is so much lower than the corresponding income ratio, which stood at 48 percent in 1995, particularly in light of the fact that black families appear to save more than white families at similar income levels (Blau and Graham, 1990). One important reason is differences in inheritances. According to the SCF data, 24 percent of white households had received an inheritance in 1995, compared to 11 percent of black households, and the average bequest among inheritors was $115,000 for whites and only $32,000 for blacks.

THE YOUNG ARE GETTING POORER

The life-cycle model predicts that wealth will follow a hump-shaped pattern over life, with accumulation in early and middle adulthood, followed by the decumulation in old age (Modigliani and Brumberg, 1954). In general, the data on wealth does follow this pattern, as shown in Table 9.7. The table is scaled so that mean net worth of all households in any given year is normalized to 1.00; then, the levels for each age group is given relative to that level. Mean wealth increases with age up through age 65 or so and then falls off; however, the average wealth of elderly households (age 65 and over) still averages about 80 percent higher than the non-elderly.

Despite an apparent overall similarity in the age-wealth profiles for 1983, 1989, 1992, and 1995, some shifts in the relative holdings of wealth by age group are worth noting. From 1983 to 1995, the wealth of the youngest age group, under 35 years of age, fell in relative terms from 21 percent of the overall mean to 16 percent, and that of households between 35 and 44 years of age dropped from 71 percent to 65 percent. In contrast, the wealth of the oldest age group, age 75 and over, gained sub-

TABLE 9.7 Age-Wealth Profiles, 1983–1995
(ratio of mean net worth by age class to the overall mean)

	1983	1989	1992	1995
All	1.00	1.00	1.00	1.00
Under 35	0.21	0.29	0.20	0.16
35–44	0.71	0.72	0.71	0.65
45–54	1.53	1.50	1.42	1.39
55–64	1.67	1.58	1.82	1.81
65–74	1.93	1.61	1.59	1.71
75 and over	1.05	1.26	1.20	1.32

stantially, from 105 percent of the mean to 132 percent of it. The statistics point to a clear shifting of asset ownership away from younger towards older households. . . .

U.S. WEALTH INEQUALITY IN AN INTERNATIONAL CONTEXT

In comparing wealth distributions across countries, it is important to derive such estimates from data sources collected in a relatively comparable way. Otherwise, different sampling frames and degrees of asset coverage can lead to wildly different estimates of household wealth inequality. Table 9.8 offers estimates of the distribution of household wealth for various OECD countries in the mid-1980s, based on a variety of sources.

Take the 1983 Survey of Consumer Finances as the baseline study for the United States. The first comparison is the 1984 Statistics Canada Survey of Consumer Finances. The original survey data from the two samples shows that wealth inequality is clearly greater in the United States, with a share of the top percentile almost

TABLE 9.8 The Inequality of Household Wealth in Selected Countries, Mid-1980s

	Percent of Total Wealth Held by:	
	Top 1%	Top 5%
United States, 1983	35	56
Canada, 1984	17	38
France, 1986	26	43
Japan, 1984		25
Sweden 1985/86	16	31
Statistics Sweden, 1985/86	16.5	37
United Kingdom, 1983	25	
United Kingdom, 1986	22	

Source: Wolff (1996b). See the paper for details on sources and methods.

double that of Canada's. However, the Canadian SCF does not include a high-income supplement, as does the American SCF. When Davies (1993) adjusted the Canadian data for this, he estimated a 22–27 percent share for the top 1 percent in Canada and a 41–46 percent share for the top 5 percent, figures still well below the corresponding figures for the United States.

Estimates for Japan are shown for Japan's 1984 National Survey of Family Income and Expenditures, suggesting that wealth inequality is considerably lower in Japan than in the United States. The low wealth concentration in Japan may be due to the extremely large share that owner-occupied housing has in the Japanese household portfolio; total real estate comprised 85 percent of Japan's household net worth in 1984. Two sets of estimates are shown for Sweden in 1985/1986, one from a survey of Household Market and Non-Market Activities conducted at the University of Gothenburg, the other from a household survey conducted by Statistics Sweden. The concentration of wealth also appears to be much greater in the United States than in Sweden. Estimates from the United Kingdom are based on marketable wealth for adult individuals derived from estate duty returns, taken from the Inland Revenue Statistics (the U.K. tax authority). Previous work of mine showed a remarkably close correspondence between the concentration shares of the top 1 percent of individuals computed from U.S. estate tax data and the top 1 percent of households derived from household survey data (Wolff, 1996b). If this relation also holds for the United Kingdom, then the results suggest that wealth inequality is considerably less in the United Kingdom than in the United States.

Evidence from a variety of other sources confirms that the inequality of the U.S. wealth distribution is markedly higher than in other countries. . . .

CONCLUDING COMMENTS

The distribution of wealth in the United States became much more unequal in the 1980s, and that trend seems to be continuing, albeit at a slower pace, in the 1990s. The only households that saw their mean net worth and financial wealth rise in absolute terms between 1983 and 1995 were those in the top 20 percent of their respective distributions and the gains were particularly strong for the top 1 percent. All other groups suffered real wealth or incorrect losses, and the declines were particularly precipitous at the bottom. Slicing the numbers by black and white, or by young and old, only confirms the growth in inequality of wealth.

REFERENCES

Blau, Francine D., and John W. Graham, "Black-White Differences in Wealth and Asset Composition," *Quarterly Journal of Economics,* May 1990, *105*:2, 321–39.

Davies, James B., "The Distribution of Wealth in Canada." In Edward N. Wolff, ed., *Research in Economic Inequality, 4.* Greenwich, CT: JAI Press, 1993, 159–80.

Hurst, Erik, Ming Ching Luoh, and Frank P. Stafford, "Wealth Dynamics of American Families, 1984–1994," Institute for Social Research, University of Michigan, mimeo, August 1996.

Kennickell, Arthur B., Douglas A. McManus, and R. Louise Woodburn, "Weighting Design for the 1992 Survey of Consumer Finances," mimeo, Federal Reserve Board of Washington, March 1996.

Kennickell, Arthur B., and R. Louise Woodburn, "Estimation of Household Net Worth Using Model-Based and Design-Based Weights: Evidence from the 1989 Survey of Consumer Finances," mimeo, Federal Reserve Board of Washington, April 1992.

Kennickell, Arthur B., and R. Louise Woodburn, "Consistent Weight Design for the 1989, 1992, and 1995 SCFs, and the Distribution of Wealth," mimeo, Federal Reserve Board of Washington, June, 1997.

Modigliani, Franco, and Richard Brumberg, "Utility Analysis and the Consumption Function: An Interpretation of Cross-Section Data." In K. Kurihara, ed., *Post-Keynesian Economics*. New Brunswick, N.J.: Rutgers University Press, 1954.

Wolff, Edward N., "Trends in Household Wealth in the United States, 1962–1983 and 1983–1989," *Review of Income and Wealth*, June 1994, *40*, 143-74.

Wolff, Edward N. *TOP HEAVY: A Study of Increasing Inequality of Wealth in America*, Updated and expanded edition. New York: Free Press, 1996a.

Wolff, Edward N., "International Comparisons of Wealth Inequality," *Review of Income and Wealth*, December 1996b, *42*, 433–51.

CHAPTER 10

Doing Poorly

The Real Income of American Children in a Comparative Perspective

LEE RAINWATER

TIMOTHY M. SMEEDING

INTRODUCTION

Both poverty and inequality have increased in the United States since the late 1970s, particularly among families with children. By the official standard United States child poverty has risen steadily since the 1960s and has continued to rise in the 1990s. The question is whether these most recent increases in child poverty have been endemic in the rest of the industrial economies or whether they are unique to the United States. Cross-national comparisons of economic well-being are useful for learning how one nation is alike or different from other comparable nations, because countries which face similar economic and demographic issues may use different policy instruments to address these issues and may have very different outcomes. . . .

This paper compares the economic well-being of children in the 1980s and 1990s in 18 countries: 14 in Europe (Austria, Belgium, Denmark, Finland, France, Germany, Ireland, Italy, Luxembourg, Netherlands, Norway, Sweden, Switzerland, and the United Kingdom) and four elsewhere (Australia, Canada, Israel, and the

United States). The analysis is based on the Luxembourg Income Study (LIS) database (Smeeding, Rainwater and O'Higgns, 1990; LIS Users Guide, 1995). . . .

We compare the real spendable (disposable) incomes of well-off, average, and low income children in the United States with comparably situated children in 17 other nations. The average American child in a four person family in 1991 had a family income of $34,675.

In fact, American children who are in families in the upper 20 percent of the income distribution do very well indeed. They have much higher standards of living as measured by real spendable income than do similarly situated children in all countries, with only Switzerland and Canada being within 20 percent of the United States level. Scandinavia—e.g., Denmark, Sweden—has high-income children who live in families with three-quarters the income of the average American child. The only nations whose "rich" children live in households with incomes which are less than 60 percent of that found in the United States are Israeli and Irish children. Given that Israel and Ireland have, by far, the lowest overall real standards of living of the nations observed here, this is to be expected.

Focusing on children in the middle 20 percent we find that only in Denmark and in Canada are children as well off as are American children, although Swedish and Swiss children are almost as well off. The average child in Belgium, Germany, Norway, and Finland is only 90 percent as well off, and 80 percent or less as well off in countries like Austria, Italy, France. On the other hand, in only three countries is the average child less than three-quarters as well-off as in the United States—the United Kingdom at 72 percent, Israel at 52 percent, and Ireland at 43 percent.

At the lower end of the distribution we find a very different and surprising picture. Both national (U.S. Bureau of the Census, 1995) and international evidence suggests that the poverty rate of United States children is in the neighborhood of 20 percent. We compare the real spendable incomes of the typical poor American child—the one at the median of the bottom 10 percent—with that of comparable low-income children in other countries in Figure 10.1. We immediately see that in six countries low-income children have real standards of living at least 50 percent higher than in the United States—Switzerland, Sweden, Finland, Denmark, Belgium, and Norway. And in four other countries (Germany, Luxembourg, Netherlands, and Austria) low-income children are at least 30 percent better of than in the United States. Only in Israel and Ireland—the two nations with the lowest GDP per capita of those studied—do low-income children have a lower real standard of living than do children in the United States.

In other words, while the United States has a higher real level of income than most of our comparison countries it is the high- and middle-income children who reap the benefits (and much more the former than the latter). Low-income American children suffer in both absolute and relative terms. The average low-income child in the other 17 countries is at least one-third better off than is the average low-income American child.

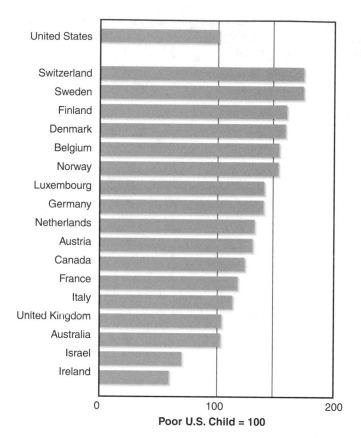

FIGURE 10.1   Comparisons of Real Income: Children in the Poorest Households

Notes: Based on Table 10.1, Column 4. See note to Table 10.1 for explanation.
Source: Luxembourg Income Study.

EVIDENCE ON CHILD POVERTY: LEVEL AND TREND

We shift now to measures of relative income within each country to examine both the level and trend in child poverty across the 18 developed nations for which we have data. . . .

Child poverty rates throughout Western Europe are below 10 percent, with the exception of 12.0 percent in Ireland, also the poorest nation in real terms of the Western European nations observed here. And in the other Western nations, most recent child poverty rates range from 11.1 percent in Israel to 14.0 percent in Australia. Clearly the United States rate of 21.5 percent stands out as the largest percentage of children in poverty among the nations observed here (Figure 10.2).

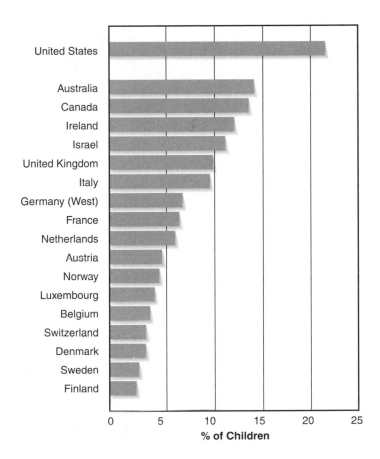

FIGURE 10.2   Child Poverty Rates in 18 Countries[a,b]

[a]Poverty is defined as percent of children living in families with adjusted disposable incomes less than 50 percent of adjusted median income for all persons. Income includes all transfers and tax benefits.

[b]Year for each estimate is most recent year in Table 10.1.

Trend

The 1980s was not a period in which the relative economic well-being of children in any of these countries was greatly improved. In two countries, there are hints of improvement from the 1970s through the 1980s to the 1990s (see Canada and Sweden in Table 10.1). But overall we have a picture of either stability or deterioration in the children's economic well-being. In the United States, Israel, and the United Kingdom there is a clear trend toward a worsening situation for children, though the most recent poverty rate for the United States suggests a leveling off of the previous increases. The 1990s results for Israel and the United Kingdom are not yet available.

TABLE 10.1 Level and Trend in Child Poverty Rates:[a] 1967–1992

Nation	Year of Survey	Period 1 <1971	Period 2 1972–1975	Period 3 1976–1981	Period 4 1982–1985	Period 5 1986–1988	Period 6 1989–
A. United States	69, 74, 79, 86, 91	13.1	17.3	18.5		22.9	21.5
B. West Europe:							
Austria	87					4.8	
Belgium	85, 88, 92				3.4	3.1	3.8
Finland	87, 91					2.9	2.5
Denmark	87, 92					5.3	3.3
France	79, 84			6.3	6.5		
Germany (West)	73, 78, 83/84, 89[b]		4.0	3.2	4.8/6.4		6.8
Ireland	87					12.0	
Italy	86, 91					10.8	9.6
Luxembourg	85				4.1		
The Netherlands	83, 87/91[c]				2.5	3.6	/6.2
Norway	79, 86, 91			3.8		3.8	4.6
Sweden	67, 75, 81, 87, 92	3.5	1.9	3.9		3.0	2.7
Switzerland	82				3.3		
United Kingdom	69, 74, 79, 86	5.3	7.0	8.5		9.9	
C. Other:							
Australia	82, 86, 90			14.0	13.1		14.0
Canada	71, 75, 81, 87, 91	15.2	14.6	13.9		13.6	13.5
Israel	79, 86			8.2		11.1	

[a]Poverty is defined as percentage of children living in households with adjusted disposable income less than 50 percent of median adjusted disposable income for all persons. Income includes all transfers and tax benefits.

[b]The slash (/) for Germany indicates that the German survey for 1973–1983 is different from that for 1984 and 1989, hence one cannot derive overall trend estimates from 1973 through 1989 from these figures.

[c]The slash (/) for The Netherlands indicates that the survey for 1983 and 1987 differs from the 1991 survey, hence one cannot derive trend estimates for 1983–1991 from these figures.

Source: Luxembourg Income Study.

Over an 18 year period, from 1969 to 1986, the child poverty rate increased from 5.3 percent to 9.9 percent in the United Kingdom and in the United States from 13.1 percent to 22.9 percent, before falling to 21.5 percent in 1991. In Israel, too, there was a deterioration during the first half of the 1980s. All of the Scandinavian countries have been able to keep child poverty below five percent, and many other European nations keep it in the 5 to 6 percent range over the 1980s and into the 1990s.

It needs to be emphasized that levels and trends in child poverty rates do not supply mirror levels and changes in overall income inequality in these nations. While the United States has the highest level of inequality among the nations observed here, Switzerland ranks third in overall inequality but very low in terms of child poverty (Gottschalk and Smeeding, 1995, Figure 3). And while patterns of increasing income inequality in the United States and in the United Kingdom are correlated with their rising child poverty rates over the longer term, the timing of increases in each nation are quite different. Inequality in the United States has continued to increase from the middle 1980s through the 1990s while child poverty has remained constant or has fallen slightly by our measure over this same period. Many nations observed here have sustained large increases in income inequality during the 1980s with no change in poverty, e.g., Sweden and Austria (Gottschalk and Smeeding, 1995, Tables 5 and 6). . . .

Differences between Two-Parent and Solo-Mother Families

A child's chance of being poor in the United States differs dramatically depending on whether he or she lives in a one- or two-parent family (Table 10.2). A child in a two-parent United States family has only about an 11 percent chance of being poor as compared to a 60 percent chance if the child lives with a lone parent who is a mother. In fact, in all countries studied, one's chance of being poor in a one-parent mother family is much higher than in two-parent families.

Because so few children in most countries live in solo-mother families the difference across countries in the percent of children living in solo-mother families has little to do with the difference in total child poverty rates. Only in the cases of Australia, Canada, and the United States would total poverty rates be noticeably lower if the proportion of solo-mother families was the average for these 17 countries. In other counties with greater than 10 percent of children in solo-mother families (Denmark, Norway, Sweden, United Kingdom), the poverty rates for single parent children are close enough to couples rates to not make a great deal of difference in the overall poverty rate. And demography is clearly not destiny; children in solo-mother families in Denmark, Finland (7 percent poverty rate), and Sweden (5 percent poverty rate) do better than children in two-parent families in many of the nations studied.

Comparing the poverty rates of children in two-parent families and in solo-mother families we note a group of countries with very low rates for both types—Sweden, Finland, Belgium, Denmark, and Luxembourg. Another group has child poverty rates in solo-mother families between roughly 20 and 40 percent but covers

TABLE 10.2   Poverty Rates for Children by Family Type[a]

Country (Year)	All Children	Children in Two-Parent Family[b]	Children in single Parent/Solo Mother Family[c]	Percent of Children in Solo Mother Families[c,d]
United States (91)	21.5	11.1	59.5	21.2
Australia (90)	14.0	7.7	56.2	12.4
Belgium (92)	3.8	3.2	10.0	8.1
Canada (91)	13.5	7.4	50.2	13.4
Denmark (91)	3.3	2.5	7.3	14.3
Finland (91)	2.5	1.9	7.5	9.5
France (84)	6.5	5.4	22.6	6.5
Germany (89)	6.8	2.9	42.7	9.9
Ireland (97)	12.0	10.5	40.5	5.3
Israel (86)	11.1	10.3	27.5	5.1
Italy (91)	9.6	9.5	13.9	4.4
Luxembourg (85)	4.1	3.6	10.0	6.8
The Netherlands (91)	6.2	3.1	39.5	8.4
Norway (91)	4.6	1.9	18.4	15.4
Sweden (92)	2.7	2.2	5.2	14.6
Switzerland (82)	3.3	1.0	25.6	6.9
United Kingdom (86)	9.9	8.4	18.7	13.0

[a]Poverty is defined as in Table 10.1.

[b]Child poverty rates in two-parent families are for those children living in situations where there are only two adults who are married, or are living together as married.

[c]Single parent/solo-mother families are children living in those situations where one female adult resides in the household. Other adults (e.g., older children) may also occupy the residence.

[d]Because some children live in other types of situations, e.g., in multiple family unit households or in lone-father units, the weighted averages of children in solo-mother and two-parent households do not add to the "all children" total.

Source: Luxembourg Income Study database.

a wide range of rates in two-parent families—Germany, Switzerland, and Norway have quite low two-parent rates. France has a middling rate and Israel, Italy, and the United Kingdom higher rates for children in two-parent households.

The combination of difference in the poverty rates of children in two-parent compared to solo-mother families and the smaller differences in the percentage of children who live in solo-mother families has an important effect on the family type composition of the poor. In five countries more than half of poor children live in solo-mother families—the United States, Australia, Germany, Switzerland, and Norway with Canada coming close at around 40 percent. At the other extreme, fewer than 15 percent of poor children are in solo-mother families in the Netherlands, Belgium, Italy, and Israel. Children in solo-mother families make up between 15 and 30 percent of the poor in Luxembourg, Ireland, France, the United Kingdom, and Sweden. Thus, the rate of feminization of poverty varies dramatically across these countries based on both the poverty rate for children in single parent units and on the percentage of children living in each type of unit.

In summary, 1 of every 8 American children is a poor child living with a solo mother. Fewer than 1 in 100 children are in the same situation in Sweden, the Netherlands, Luxembourg, Italy, Finland, and Belgium. In the United States 1 of every 10 children is a poor child living in a two-parent family and this ratio is not too different in three other countries—Ireland, Israel, and Italy. In contrast the ratio is about 1 in 50 in Finland, Germany, Norway, Sweden, and Switzerland.

The results of this paper are striking. United States low-income children have a lower real standard of living than do their counterparts in almost every other nation studied. . . .

In contrast to our low-income children, our high-income children are better off than their counterparts in every nation studied. The wide variance in child well-being found in the United States mirrors the high level of overall income inequality in our nation. This pattern is not found in other nations. While their inequality is less than in the United States, children living in families at the bottom of the distribution enjoy living standards which are significantly above those found for similar children in the United States, even in nations where overall income inequality has increased during the 1980s. . . .

CONCLUSION

All nations begin with the issue of preventing severe poverty and disadvantage for at-risk children. The major difference we note is that other nations are able to produce lower levels of child poverty than in the United States. It follows that child poverty is neither intractable nor intransigent. The United States had an elder poverty problem in 1970 which it markedly reduced through increased social security spending and greater efforts on the part of the aged to save and invest. It now has a child poverty problem which produces an intolerably low real standard of living for a large number of American children. Our high-income children do very well in real terms compared to similar children in other nations. No one wants to take away these advantages for which the parents of these children work long and hard. What is needed is a reasonable response to the real needs of low-income American children. And as other nations have shown, there is an answer that we can find if we have the national will to face up to the sobering facts presented in this paper.

CHAPTER 11

Day by Day

The Lives of Homeless Women

ELLIOT LIEBOW

On the street or in a shelter, homelessness is hard living. At first sight, one wonders why more homeless people do not kill themselves. How do they manage to slog through day after day, with no end in sight? How, in a world of unremitting grimness, do they manage to laugh, love, enjoy friends, even dance and play the fool? How, in short, do they stay fully human while body and soul are under continuous and grievous assault?

Simple physical survival is within the grasp of almost everyone willing and able to reach out for it.[1] As the women thrash about, awash in a sea of need, emergency shelters, along with public assistance in the form of cash, food stamps, and medical assistance, make it just possible for many of the women to keep their heads above water. Through the use of shelters, soup kitchens, and hospital emergency rooms, it is even possible for most homeless people who do not get public assistance to survive at some minimal level without benefit of a structured assistance program.

At their very best, however, these bare-boned elements of a life-support system merely make life possible, not necessarily tolerable or livable. Serious problems remain. Homelessness can transform what for others are little things into insurmountable hurdles. Indeed, homelessness in general puts a premium on "little things." Just as some homeless women seem to have learned (more than most of us, perhaps) to value a small gesture of friendship, a nice day, a bus token, or a little courtesy that others might take for granted or not notice at all, so too can events or circumstances that would be trivial irritants to others approach catastrophic proportions for the homeless person.[2]

For homeless women on the street, the struggle for subsistence begins at the animal level—for food, water, shelter, security, and safe sleep.[3] In contrast, homeless women in shelters usually have these things; their struggle begins at the level of human rather than animal needs—protection of one's property, health care, and avoidance of boredom. The struggle then moves rapidly to the search for companionship, modest measures of independence, dignity, and self-respect, and some hope and faith in the future. These needs are not particularly sequential or hierarchical. One can just as easily be immobilized by hopelessness and despair as by hunger and cold. Body and soul are equally in need of nurture and the women must grab whatever they can get when they can get it.[4]

* * *

For some of the women, day-by-day hardships began with the problem of getting enough sleep. A few women complained they could never get any sleep in a shelter. Grace was one of them. "There's no getting sleep in a shelter," she said. "Only rest."

There was indeed much night noise and movement. There was snoring, coughing, sneezing, wheezing, retching, farting, cries from bad dreams, occasional weeping or seizures, talking aloud to oneself or to someone else who may or may not have been present, and always movement to and from the bathroom. Grace was complaining about noise, and she found a partial remedy in ear plugs. But ear plugs could not help those women like Kathleen who were kept awake not by noise but by questions: Is this it for me? How did I end up here? How will I get out? But eventually, as the night wore on, there was a lot of snoring, and that meant that, Grace and Kathleen notwithstanding, there was a lot of sleeping, too.

Having to get up at 5:30 A.M. and be out of the shelter by 7:00 was a major hardship of shelter life. It was not simply the fact of having to get up and out, but rather that the women had to do this every day of the week, every day of the year (Thanksgiving and Christmas Day excepted), no matter what the weather or how they felt. On any given morning, as the women drifted onto the street, one might see two or three ailing women—this one with a fever or cough or headache, that one with a limp or stomach ache or other ailment—pick up their bags and walk silently into the weather.

The women especially missed Saturday and Sunday mornings, which looked just like Tuesday and Wednesday mornings. The occasional opportunity to stay in bed an extra hour or two was desperately missed. Not being able to sleep in, ever, especially on a weekend, was seen by many as a major deprivation that unfairly set them apart from the rest of the world. At 7:15, on a Sunday morning in the park, several women were looking for benches that offered some protection from the wind. The streets were empty of cars and people and the rest of the world seemed to be asleep. The women talked about how nice it would be to sleep in just one morning, just for the hell of it, or because you don't feel well, and how nice it would be to have *a* place—not even your own place, just a place—where you could go and lie down for a while without having anyone else around telling you to do this or do that.

One bitterly cold Sunday morning Betty announced she was going to the mayor's office the next day to tell him what it was like to live in a shelter and to ask him to order the county-funded shelters to allow people to remain there on Sundays, sleeping, resting, doing their nails or hair, watching TV, or whatever. "Everyone is entitled to a day of rest," she said. "Even homeless women." The women within ear-shot nodded agreement.

Some of the working women took motel rooms on weekends once or twice a month. Jane regularly disappeared on weekends. "She went to a motel for the week-end so she could sleep in," Judy explained to one of the women who asked about her. Samantha, who was working regularly, used the shelter for eating, washing, and so-cializing, but when the lights went out on Friday and Saturday nights, she left the shelter to sleep in a car so she could sleep late Saturday and Sunday mornings.

When Vicki learned she would be able to move into her own place in 10 days or so, she talked about her shelter experience as if it were already in the past. The hardest part of living in a shelter, she said, was having to get up every morning, no matter how you felt. The next worse thing was having to go out on the street and kill time—really kill time—until the shelter reopened in the evening.

* * *

Along with perennial fatigue, boredom was one of the great trials of home-lessness. Killing time was not a major problem for everyone but it was high on most women's lists of hardships.* Betty could have been speaking for most of them when she talked about the problem. On a social visit to the state psychiatric hospital where, four years earlier, she had been an inpatient in an alcoholic program, Betty sought out a nurse named Lou. They embraced and Lou asked Betty what she was doing these days. Betty said she was living in a shelter. Lou said that was a shame, and asked Betty how she spent her time.

"I walk the streets," said Betty. "Twelve hours and 15 minutes a day, every day, I walk the streets. Is that what I got sober for? To walk the streets?" Betty went on to say that she sits on a lot of park benches looking for someone to talk to. Many times there is no one, so she talks to the birds. She and the birds have done a lot of talking in her day, she said.

Months later, Betty repeated much of this at her SSI (Supplemental Security Income) hearing. She told the hearing officer about being homeless and sleeping in the night shelter. He asked what her biggest problem was, and Betty said it was stay-ing on the street for 12 hours and 15 minutes every day. She told him about the pub-lic library and park benches and the birds. Staying awake with nothing to do was a special problem, she added. You are not permitted to sleep in the library, she said, and she didn't dare fall asleep on a park bench for fear that someone would steal her bags or that a policeman would arrest her for vagrancy.

Some of the women with jobs also had trouble killing time. Like the others, Grace had to leave the shelter by 7:00 A.M. but she couldn't report to work much be-

---

*DIRECTOR: This world is a place for productive people. The idea of killing time, day after day, was an alien concept to the vigorous, enthusiastic staff. The Refuge volunteers would regu-larly suggest a plan of action which in a rational world would begin to solve a woman's prob-lems. These solutions were offered with little understanding of the complexity of these women's lives.

fore 9:00, and her job was less than a 10-minute drive away. "Have you ever tried to kill two hours in the morning, every morning, with nowhere to go and nothing to do?" she asked. "I have some tapes I can listen to in the car—some Christmas carols and some Bible readings. But two hours? Every day?"

For Sara, leaving the shelter in the morning was by far the worst time of day. That was when being homeless hit her the hardest. You can't decide what to do because it doesn't matter what you do. You're not needed anywhere, not wanted anywhere, and not expected anywhere. Nobody cares what you do.

"I can't go on, walking the streets all day and coming here at night," announced Elsie one evening. "It's not my style. It's just not my style." Some women were better than others at finding relief in a book or TV program or jigsaw puzzle at the day shelter, or in conversation with others, but relief was typically short-lived. Sleeping may also have been tried as a remedy. In the parks, the lobbies of public buildings, and the day shelters, the women did a lot of sleeping. Some of this may have been because they did not sleep well at night, or because of medication, or depression perhaps, but some of it was also a way of killing time, a way of getting through the nothing-to-do present until it was time to do something—go to the soup kitchen, show up for a clinic appointment, or return to the night shelter.

Other kinds of behavior were also aimed at killing time or making it more bearable. Many of the women, for example, regularly appeared at the night shelter or the day shelter or the soup kitchen long before they opened, even when there were no lines to give advantage to early arrivals. It was as if the rush to get to the next "event" was a way of moving from a do-nothing to a do-something state.

For much the same reasons, the women might talk about and plan for an appointment with a doctor or a caseworker that was still several days away. In part, this may have been simply a matter of paying attention to what was most important to them at the moment, but this early anticipation may have also served to bring the event prematurely into present time, thereby giving the otherwise boring and undifferentiated present some sort of focus and direction.

Sometimes the women also made what looked like a deliberate effort to take apart a group of tasks and stretch them out over several days. At any given time, for example, a woman might need to make an appointment with a caseworker, visit a clinic, see a housing office representative, go to the unemployment office, or attend to some personal business. Any two of these tasks could normally be done in a day, one in the morning and one in the afternoon, and three in one day was not always out of the question.

Having a task to do, however, was a precious resource that gave point and structure to the day when it had to be done. To do two or three tasks on the same day would be a waste of resources, so the women often seemed to go out of their way to stretch their tasks over several days.* Thus, what often seemed to be procrastination or laziness or exasperating inefficiency to those looking in from the outside

---

*KIM: I think this is overstated. Service providers are spread out all over the county. It can take several bus transfers to reach Point B. Bus stop waits and waits in line add up to many hours. Filling out applications everywhere adds up to more. Particularly when dealing with Social Services, a great deal of time is wasted on the way to brick walls and dead ends.

may well have been, from the women's point of view, an attempt to distribute structure and meaning over as many days as possible.[5]

* * *

It is all too easy to think of homeless people as having few or no possessions ("How could a homeless person have anything of value?" sneered Kim), but one of the major and most talked-about problems was storage—how to keep one's clothing, essential documents, and other belongings secure and accessible. The preservation and protection of belongings could be a major consumer of one's time, energy, and resources. A principal difficulty was the fact that most emergency shelters had only limited space for individual storage—often space for only two bags or two small cardboard boxes.* And it was not uncommon to find shelters where one could not store anything at all.[6] Even where limited storage space was available, many women were reluctant to use it because there was no guarantee that their belongings would be intact when they returned. Stealing was believed to be common: "You've got to expect these things in shelters" was heard from staff and women alike. The end result was that many homeless women who would have left their belongings behind had they had a safe place to store them were forced to take most of their belongings with them. Some wore them in layers. Others carried them. They had become, in short, bag ladies.[7]

During a discussion of Luther Place, one of the best-run shelters in downtown Washington, one of the women said Luther Place was OK but she didn't like the women there—they were all bag ladies. One of the other women objected that the women at Luther Place were no different from women in other shelters. They were bag ladies, she said, because Luther Place had no storage space.

With some important exceptions, how much "stuff" one had was inversely proportional to the length of time one had been homeless. The longer a woman had been homeless, the more likely it was that she had had to jettison belongings, often stripping down to just what she could carry. For most women, this stripping-down process was a painful exercise in triage. Much of what they carried around in bags, boxes, or suitcases was clothing. Sometimes there was an emergency food ration. Along with toilet articles, some cosmetics, maybe a can opener, a bottle of aspirin or Tylenol or a prescription drug, almost everyone carried a birth certificate, pocket-size ID, varieties of legal documents or official papers, and perhaps some rent receipts or W-2's.

More important, however, were the other, more personal things. Often there were snapshots or framed photographs of children or other family members, personal letters, a color picture of Jesus, a Bible, and other religious and inspirational reading material. There may also have been a teddy bear or a bronzed baby shoe, a

---

*DIRECTOR: Without question, dealing with the "stuff" of these women was a great source of consternation. There was absolutely no room for the women's personal belongings. There was also an underlying concern that the belongings were a health hazard: some bags were filled with old food and insects.

swizzle stick perhaps, or a matchbook cover, and some objects that looked like nothing more than a rag, a bone, a hank of hair, but which were, in fact, tokens of some treasured secret.

Given the contents of their bags, boxes, and suitcases, it is not surprising that the women were fiercely protective and possessive of them, sometimes to the patronizing amusement of outsiders. The importance of clothing and toiletries is self-evident. Moreover, the women had to carry proof of their social existence with them. Without a home address, telephone number, or job as testimony to their existence, they needed their birth certificates and other documents to prove that they existed as legal persons with rights to assert and claims to make on society.

Many of the personal things—the letters, the religious materials, the photographs, and the mementos of people, relationships, and experiences—looked back to earlier, presumably happier times. In effect, the women carried their life histories with them. To lose one's stuff, or to have to jettison some of it, was to lose connections to one's past if not the past itself. Thus, for women who had only the one or two slender boxes they may have been allowed to store in the shelter, along with what they may have carried with them, their more personal belongings tended to be strongly oriented toward the past.[8]

Many other women, however, mainly recent arrivals to homelessness or those with a car or other resources, often had far more belongings than they could carry or store in the shelters. These belongings were typically stored in their cars, public storage warehouses, a church basement, a fellow Alcoholics Anonymous member's garage, or even a garage or attic in the house of a friend or relative.

Most of the time, these nonportable possessions looked forward, not backward. They were things that were being saved for the future rather than remembrances of things past. Here, in the automobiles and the public and private storage spaces, the women kept not only clothing but pots and pans and linens and silverware, lamps and chairs, hat boxes and electric typewriters, and sometimes rugs and other heavy, major household furnishings as well. Sara regularly visited her storage unit to fondle her carefully wrapped crystal and linens. "That sustains her," said Samantha.

Clearly, the main value of these furnishings lay not in sentiment but in the hope, if not the prospect, that they would all be needed tomorrow or next week or next month when the woman would once again set up housekeeping in her own place. So long as she continued to own pots and pans and linens and things, she could remain, in her own mind at least, a temporarily dispossessed homemaker whose return to homemaking was imminent. For the woman who had to give up these furnishings, however, the prospect of returning to homemaking receded into uncertainty and she was plunged deeper into the reality of homelessness.

Past and future, then, and even one's self, were embedded in one's belongings. When Louise could no longer pay for storage and lost her belongings to auction, she was surprised at her own reaction to the loss. Her belongings had been so much a part of her, she said, that now that she's lost them, she's not sure who she is.[9]

Great sacrifices were made to store belongings, and the ever-present threat of losing them was a major source of anxiety and stress. The smallest and cheapest spaces in public storage warehouses were 5′ × 5′ and rented for $37.50 to $42.50 a month, which meant that some of the women on public assistance spent about 25 percent of their income for storage alone. Others spent much more. During her first couple of years of homelessness, while she still had money from her divorce settlement (her share of the proceeds from sale of the house), Louise paid $156 a month to store her household goods. Kim maintained a storage space in her hometown as well as one in the shelter area. Together, these cost her about $90 a month.

For many women, it was much too easy to fall behind in storage payments, and the penalties built up quickly. The "late charge," invoked one day after the monthly due date, was $10. After 10 days, management put their own lock on the storage bin, denying access to the renter until all due monies had been paid. After 30 days, the stored contents were subject to public auction.

Fierce attachment to belongings meant that many women, storing their things on a month-to-month basis and not knowing how long they would have to continue, ended up making monthly storage payments that totaled many times the original or replacement cost of what was stored. Shirley's experience was a case in point. Shirley had been behind in her storage payments for several months but had managed to stave off the loss of her things to public auction each month by last-minute fund-raising heroics. Eventually, however, she missed another deadline. Suspecting that the auction hammer had come down on the contents of her locker, Shirley and I drove to the storage facility. Yes, the auction had been held, the manager told her, but her stuff was still recoverable because no one had seen fit to bid even $5 for the contents of her $42.50-per-month locker. Shirley was dismayed. This news was probably worse than learning that someone had bought them. "The footlocker alone is worth $50," she protested. "And the chair. Isn't that a nice chair?"

To lighten the financial burden, two or even three women sometimes shared a space, but in a 5' × 5' area, the only way to accommodate additional items was to pile them ever higher. This made for a variety of storage and retrieval problems requiring a strenuous and time-consuming reorganization for each use, especially if—as when June and Peggy doubled up—big or fragile items were involved (a sofa up on end, an old, heavy IBM Selectric typewriter, several lamps, a rug, books, dishes, and more).

So important was secure and adequate storage that women sometimes allowed it to be a determining factor in important life choices. Kim turned down a new job at a much higher salary because her current job allowed her to store her belongings in a locked attic at her place of employment. The higher salary would have more than covered the cost of public storage, but Kim decided the extra money was not worth the loss of convenience and easy access to belongings stored on the job. Elsie planned to prepay six months storage costs when she thought (incorrectly) that she was getting an $800 income tax refund.

Jeanette stored her household furnishings in her 1974 Datsun B-210 station wagon. The car broke down and was towed away by police before Jeanette could assemble the money to repair it. Distraught, Jeanette traced the car to the county's Abandoned Auto Lot. We drove there to salvage some of her smaller, more valued possessions. The lot attendant told Jeanette that the next auction would be the following Friday and that she could probably buy back her car (and everything in it) for $25 or so, the going rate for junk autos. Successful bidders, he told her, would have three days in which to remove their purchases from the lot.

But Jeanette's station wagon had three flat tires, a dead battery, dead license plates, and surely a string of invisible problems as well. The cost of repurchasing the car, having it towed off the lot, and making even minimal repairs would be many times the value of the car, but Jeanette was determined to buy it back. Not for transportation, she explained, but as the only way she could retrieve and afford to keep her belongings. For her, the car had become, purely and simply, a storeroom.[10]

ENDNOTES

1. "Almost" is crucial because the issue is life and death. Some homeless people are killed by hopelessness. Some die quietly and others die violent deaths. Some die from untreated disease or injury, some freeze to death, and still others lose digits or limbs. Here is the sworn testimony of a doctor who treated homeless patients in several Washington, D.C., shelters: "During the winter of 1987/1988, I have personal knowledge that approximately 30 homeless persons . . . had one or more fingers, toes, feet, or legs amputated as a result of gangrene following frostbite. . . . I have been informed that during the winter of 1987/1988, at least 10 homeless persons froze to death." Janelle Goetcheus, MD, *Affidavit (W) in Support of Plaintiff's Memorandum*. . . .

In mild-wintered San Francisco in 1988, the death rate for homeless persons was 58% higher than that for the general population. National Coalition for the Homeless, *Safety Network* 8, no. 2 (February 1989), p. 1.

2. It was from the women that I learned to juxtapose good little things and bad little things in this way. It puts "little things" in a fresh perspective and supports Otto Jesperson's observation that the world is made up of little things; what is important is to see them largely. Cited by Geoffrey K. Pullum, *The Great Eskimo Vocabulary Hoax and Other Irreverent Essays on the Study of Language*, p. 68.

3. Contrary to popular belief, homeless persons do not have secret, ingenious, and sometimes easy ways of getting along. In fact, homeless people on the street have precisely those terrible problems that one would guess them to have. Kathleen Dockett, in her interview study of street homeless persons in Washington, D.C., reports that "a lack of access to bathing (68%) and laundry facilities were the most difficult needs to satisfy. The . . . need for sufficient sleep (63%) and safety in terms of finding a safe place to sleep (58%) were the second most difficult needs to satisfy. . . . There was a strong consensus . . . that shelters were unhealthy, dangerous, stressful." Dockett, *Street Homeless People in the District of Columbia: Characteristics and Service Needs,* pp. viii, ix. When one realizes that many homeless persons—mostly men—often choose street life over shelter life, one begins to get a sense of just how "unhealthy, dangerous, stressful" some shelters can be.

4. The chapter-by-chapter discussion of these needs is not meant to imply a hierarchy.

5. Elderly persons who live alone sometimes resort to much the same strategy of makework, a sort of remembering to forget. In the morning, a woman goes to the supermarket and buys, say, a carton of milk and a loaf of bread. Later the same morning, she says, "Oh, I forgot to get eggs," and returns to the store. Still later, "I forgot to get potatoes," or "I forgot to go to the post office," and so on through the day, thereby filling it up with things to do.

6. I helped June to move to Mount Carmel, a women's shelter in downtown D.C., and one of the most preferred shelters in the city. She moved in with seven bags, boxes, and suitcases. The sister in charge explained, almost apologetically, that June would be allowed to store only

two such items in the shelter. June went through her things. She threw some of them out and stored the remainder at the Catholic church she used to attend.

7. Of course not all bag ladies were forced into that status. Some women were or had become bag ladies for less obviously rational reasons, but they were a minority. If affordable, accessible, and secure storage space were available, surely many bag ladies would disappear.

8. In this discussion of storage, I have attempted to exclude hoarders—those women who hold on to things because they cannot let go of them. It is useful to keep in mind, however, that the storage problems of the occasional hoarder, even if self-inflicted, are as great or greater than everyone else's.

9. "To lose a home or the sum of one's belongings is to lose evidence as to who one is and where one belongs in this world." Kai T. Erikson, *Everything in Its Path: Destruction of Community in the Buffalo Creek Flood,* p. 177. See the section "The Furniture of Self" in this beautiful book for additional insights into the meanings embedded in one's house and personal possessions.

10. Jeanette did, in fact, buy back her car for $25, and she found "a Christian gas station owner" who agreed to tow it to his lot and wait for the money. The car never again moved under its own power, but Jeanette was able to keep her things there until, six weeks later, the minister of the church she attended found a church member who allowed her to store her things in his garage.

CHAPTER 12

The Underclass Label

HERBERT J. GANS

One of America's popular pejorative labels is "slum," which characterizes low-income dwellings and neighborhoods as harmful to their poor occupants and the rest of the community. In the nineteenth century, slums were often faulted for turning the deserving poor into the undeserving poor, but in the twentieth century the causality was sometimes reversed, so that poor people with "slum-dweller hearts" were accused of destroying viable buildings and neighborhoods.

After World War II, "slum" and "slum dweller" as well as "blight" all became more or less official labels when the federal government, egged on by a variety of builder and realty pressure groups, started handing out sizeable sums for the "clearance" of low-income neighborhoods unfortunate enough to fit these terms as they were defined in the 1949 U.S. Housing Act. Although by and large only slums located in areas where private enterprise could build luxury and other profitable housing were torn down, more than a million poor households lost their homes in the next twenty years, with almost nothing done for the people displaced from them.

This chapter is written with that much-told history in mind, in order to suggest that the underclass label—as well as all but the most neutrally formulated behavioral term—can have dangerous effects for the poor and for antipoverty policy. While the emphasis will be on "underclass," the dangers of related labels will be discussed as well.

Labels may be only words, but they are judgmental or normative words, which can stir institutions and individuals to punitive actions. The dangers from such labels are many, but the danger common to all behavioral labels and terms is that they focus on behavior that hides the poverty causing it, and substitutes as its cause moral or cultural or genetic failures.

"THE UNDERCLASS" AS CODE WORD

The term "underclass" has developed an attention-getting power that constitutes its first danger. The word has a technical aura that enables it to serve as a euphemism or code word to be used for labeling. Users of the label can thus hide their disapproval of the poor behind an impressively academic term. "Underclass" has also become morally ambiguous, and as it is often left undefined, people can understand it in any way they choose, including as a label.

Because "underclass" is a code word that places some of the poor *under* society and implies that they are not or should not be *in* society, users of the term can therefore favor excluding them from the rest of society without saying so. Once whites thought of slaves, "primitives," and wartime enemies as the inhuman "other," but placing some people under society may not be altogether different.

A subtler yet in some ways more insidious version of the exclusionary mechanism is the use of "underclass" as a synonym for the poor, deserving and undeserving. While not excluding anyone from society, it increases the social distance of the poor from everyone else. This distance is increased further by the contemporary tendency of elected officials and journalists to rename and upgrade the working class as the lower middle class—or even the middle class.

Because "underclass" is also used as a racial and even ethnic code word, it is a convenient device for hiding antiblack or anti-Latino feelings. As such a code word, "underclass" accommodates contemporary taboos against overt prejudice, not to mention hate speech. Such taboos sometimes paper over—and even repress—racial antagonisms that people do not want to express openly.

Ironically, the racial code word also hides the existence of very poor whites who suffer from many of the same problems as poor blacks. When used as a racial term, "underclass" blurs the extent to which the troubles of whites and blacks alike are generated by the economy and by classism or class discrimination and require class-based as well as race-based solutions.

Like other code words, "underclass" may interfere with public discussion. Disapproval of the actions of others is part of democracy, but code words make covert what needs to be overt in order for the disapproval to be questioned and debated. If openly critical terms such as "bums" and "pauper" were still in use, and if umbrella terms such as "underclass" were replaced with specific ones such as "beggars" or "welfare dependents," upset citizens could indicate clearly the faults of which they want to accuse poor people. In that case, public discussion might be able to deal more openly with the feelings the more fortunate classes hold about the poor, the actual facts about the poor, and the policy issues having to do with poverty and poverty-related behavior.

THE FLEXIBILITY OF THE LABEL

Terms and labels undergo broadening in order to adapt them for use in varying conditions. Broadening also makes labels flexible so that they can be used to stigmatize new populations, or accuse already targeted ones of new failures.

One source of harm to such populations is flexible *meaning*, which stems from the vagueness of a new word, the lack of an agreed-upon definition for it. Since Oscar Lewis once identified nearly sixty-five "traits" for his culture of poverty, there is apt precedent for the flexibility of the underclass label that replaced Lewis's term.

Flexibility becomes more harmful when pejorative prefixes can be added to otherwise descriptively used terms; for example, a female welfare recipient can also be described as a member of a permanent underclass, which suggests that she is incapable of ever escaping welfare. An underclass of young people becomes considerably more threatening when it is called "feral," and even worse is the idea of a biological underclass, which implies a genetic and thus permanent inferiority of a group of people whom public policy can render harmless only by sterilizing, imprisoning, or killing them.

Another serious danger follows from the flexibility of *subjects:* the freedom of anyone with labeling power to add further populations to the underclass, and to do so without being accountable to anyone. The poor cannot, after all, afford to bring libel and slander suits. If tenants of public housing are also assigned to the underclass, they are even more stigmatized than when they are coming from "the projects." Illegal immigrants who are refugees from a country not favored by the State Department or the Immigration and Naturalization Service are more likely candidates for public harassment or deportation if their native-born neighbors decide that their behavior marks them as members of the underclass. That they may be doing work that no one else will do or collecting entitlements for which they have paid their share of taxes becomes irrelevant once they have been assigned the label.

THE REIFICATION OF THE LABEL

A further source of danger is the reification of the label, which takes place when a definition is awarded the gift of life and label users believe there to be an actually existing and homogeneous underclass that is composed of whatever poor people are currently defined as underclass. Reification, which turns a definition into an actual set of people, hides the reality that the underclass is an imagined group that has been constructed in the minds of its definers. Once a stigmatized label is reified, however, visible signs to identify it are sure to be demanded sooner or later, and then invented, so that people bearing the signs can be harassed more easily.

Furthermore, once the signs are in place so that imagined groups can be made actual, the labels run the danger of being treated as causal mechanisms. As a result, the better-off classes may decide that being in the underclass is a cause of becoming homeless or turning to street crime. Homelessness then becomes a symptom of underclass membership, with the additional danger of the hidden policy implication: that the elimination of the underclass would end homelessness, thereby avoiding the need for affordable housing or for jobs and income grants for the homeless.

Even purely descriptive terms referring to actual people, such as "welfare recipients," can be reified and turned into causal labels. People may thus persuade themselves to believe that being on welfare is a cause of poverty, or of single-parent families. Once so persuaded, they can propose to eliminate both effects by ending welfare, and without appearing to be inhumane—which is what conservative politicians running for office, and the intellectuals supporting them, have been doing since the early 1990s. They ignore the fact that in the real world the causal arrow goes in the other direction, but they achieve their political aim, even if they also harm poor mothers and their children.

Since popular causal thinking is almost always moral as well as empirical, the reification of a label like "the underclass" usually leads to the assignment of *moral* causality. If the underclass is the cause of behavior that deviates from mainstream norms, the solution is moral condemnation, behavioral modification, or punishment by the elimination of financial aid. Thus people are blamed who are more often than not victims instead of perpetrators, which ignores the empirical causes, say, of street crime, and interferes with the development of effective anticrime policy. Blaming people may allow blamers to feel better by blowing off the steam of righteous (and in the case of crime, perfectly justified) indignation, but even justified blaming does not constitute or lead to policy for ending street crime.

A scholarly form of reification can be carried out with labels that are also scientific terms, so that the former are confused with the latter and thus obtain the legitimacy that accompanies scientific concepts. Conversely, the moral opprobrium placed on the labeled allows social scientists either to incorporate overt biases in their concepts or to relax their detachment and in the process turn scientific concepts into little more than operationalized labels.

A case in point is the operational definition of "the underclass" by Erol Ricketts and Isabel Sawhill, which has been widely used by government, scholars, and in simplified form even by popular writers. The two social scientists argue that the underclass consists of four populations: "high school dropouts," "prime-age males not regularly attached to the labor force," welfare recipients, and "female heads." Ricketts and Sawhill identify these populations as manifesting "underclass behaviors," or "dysfunctional behaviors," which they believe to be "at variance with those of mainstream populations."

The two authors indicate that they can "remain agnostic about the fundamental causes of these behaviors." Nonetheless, they actually adopt an implicit moral causality, because in defining the underclass as "people whose behavior departs from (mainstream) norms" and remaining silent about causality, they imply that the behaviors result from the violations of these values.

Ricketts and Sawhill provide no evidence, however, that the four behaviors in question are actually the result of norm violation. More important, their operational definition does not consider other causal explanations of the same behavior. No doubt some poor young people drop out of school because they reject mainstream norms for education, but Ricketts and Sawhill omit those who drop out because they have to go to work to support their families, or because they feel that their future in the job market is nil, as well as the youngsters who are forced out by school administrators and who should be called "pushouts."

Likewise, in addition to the "prime-age males" Ricketts and Sawhill believe to be jobless because they do not want to work, some of these men reject being targeted for a career of dead-end jobs, and others, most in fact, are jobless because there are no jobs for them. Indeed, the irony of the Ricketts-Sawhill definition is that when an employer goes out of business, workers who may previously have been praised as working poor but now cannot find other jobs are then banished to the underclass.

Poor mothers go on welfare for a variety of reasons. Some are working mothers who need Medicaid for their children and cannot get health benefits from their employers. Female family heads are often single because jobless men make poor breadwinners, not because they question the desirability of mainstream marriage norms.

If I read the two authors correctly, they are conducting essentially normative analyses of the four types of underclass people they have defined, even if they may not have intended to be normative. Thus, the measures they have chosen to operationalize their definitions bear some resemblance to popular pejorative labels that condemn rather than understand behavior. Conversely, Ricketts and Sawhill do not appear to consider the possibility that the failure of the mainstream economy is what prevents people from achieving the norms they are setting for the poor.

As a result, the two authors make no provision for data that measure the failures of the mainstream economy, and they do not include—or operationalize—a good deal of other information. For example, they could count home, school, and neighborhood conditions that interfere with or discourage learning, and the economic conditions that cause the disappearance of jobs and frustrate the desire for work. In addition, they might obtain information on job availability for jobless prime-age males, as well as for women on welfare—just to mention some of the relevant data that are publicly available. Until they include such data, their definition and operationalization of "underclass" are scientific only because and to the extent that their counting procedures observe the rules of science.

A different approach to the indiscriminate mixing of science and labeling, and to the reification of stereotypes, emerged in some proposals in the late 1980s to measure underclass status by poor people's answers to attitude questions: on their willingness to plan ahead, for example. Such attitude data could be found in the widely used Panel Survey of Income Dynamics. This type of question assumes not only that people should plan ahead, but that their failure to do so reflects their unwillingness, rather than their inability, to plan ahead, which has been documented in many empirical studies. Nonetheless, people whose poverty prevented them from planning ahead and who answered honestly that they did not so plan, would have been assigned a stigmatizing label—merely on the basis of their response to superficial and general questions. Fortunately this approach to "measuring" the underclass appears not to have been used so far by anyone in an influential position.

A final reification is spatial, an approach in which behavioral labels are applied to census tracts to produce "underclass areas." Such areas derive from statistical artifacts invented by the U.S. Bureau of the Census. The bureau developed the concept of "extreme poverty areas" for those places in which at least 40 percent of the people were poor. While this is inaccurate enough—especially for the 60 percent not poor—Ricketts and Sawhill subsequently identified "underclass areas," in which the proportion of people exhibiting all four of their behavioral indicators for being in the underclass was "one standard deviation above the mean *for the country as a whole.*" The two authors did not explain why they chose this measure, even though poverty is not dispersed through the country as a whole but is concentrated in the cities of the northeast, midwest, and south, the latter being also the location of the most severe rural poverty.

Most people lack the methodological skills of social scientists, and do not see the assumptions that underlie the approaches to underclass counting. Once word gets out that social scientists have identified some areas as underclass areas, however, these neighborhoods can easily be stigmatized, the population labeled accordingly and accused of whatever local meanings the term "underclass" may have acquired.

When areas become known as underclass areas, local governments and commercial enterprises obtain legitimation to withdraw or not provide facilities and services that could ameliorate the poverty of the area's inhabitants. Labeling areas as underclass can also encourage governments to choose them as locations for excess numbers of homeless shelters, drug treatment centers, and other facilities that serve the very poor and that are therefore rejected by other neighborhoods.

In fact, "underclass areas" is basically a current version of the old label "slum," which also treated indicators of poverty as behavioral failures. In the affluent economy of the post–World War II era, similar defining and subsequent counting activities were used to justify "slum clearance," and the displacement of poor people for subsidized housing for the affluent. And as in all labeling, the poor people who are labeled are left to fend for themselves.

THE DANGERS OF THE UMBRELLA EFFECT

Since "underclass" is an umbrella label that can include in its definition all the various behavioral and moral faults that label-makers and users choose to associate with it, two further dangers accrue to those it labels.

The sheer breadth of the umbrella label seems to attract alarmist writers who magnify the many kinds of moral and behavioral harmfulness attributed to people it names. A correlate of the umbrella effect is amnesia on the part of writers about the extreme and usually persistent poverty of the labeled. Thus, the more widely people believe in the validity of the underclass label, and the broader its umbrella becomes, the more likely it is that political conditions will not allow for reinstituting effective antipoverty policy. If the underclass is dangerous, and dangerous in so many different ways, it follows that the government's responsibility is to beef up the police, increase the punishments courts can demand, and create other punitive agencies that try to protect the rest of society from this dangerous class.

Umbrella labels also do harm when they lump into a single term a variety of diverse people with different problems. This ignores the reality that the people who are assigned the underclass label have in common only that their actual or imagined behaviors upset the mainstream population, or the politicians who claim to speak in its name. Using this single characteristic to classify people under one label can be disastrous, especially if politicians and voters should ever start talking about comprehensive "underclass policies," or what Christopher Jencks has called "meta solutions." For one thing, many of the people who are tagged with the label have not even deviated from mainstream norms, and yet others have done nothing illegal. An underclass policy would thus be a drastic violation of civil rights and civil liberties.

At this writing, electioneering politicians as well as angry voters still remain content with policies that harm the people who bear specific labels, such as welfare recipients, illegal immigrants, and the homeless. In the past, however, the makers of earlier umbrella labels have proposed extremely drastic policies. In 1912, Henry Goddard suggested dealing with the feebleminded by "unsexing . . . removing, from the male and female, the necessary organs for procreation." Realizing that there would be strong popular opposition both to castration and ovariectomies, he proposed instead that the next best solution was "segregation and colonization" of the feebleminded. A few decades earlier, Charles Booth had offered the same solution for an equivalent category of poor people, and not long before he was forced to resign as vice president of the United States in 1974, Spiro Agnew suggested that poor people accused of behavioral shortcomings should be rehoused in rural new towns built far away from existing cities and suburbs.

Even a thoughtful underclass policy would be dangerous, because the people forced under the underclass umbrella suffer from different kinds of poverty and, in some cases, poverty related problems, which may require different solutions. Reducing poverty for able-bodied workers requires labor market policy change; reducing it for people who cannot work calls for a humane income grant program. Enabling and encouraging young people to stay in school requires different policies than the elimination of homelessness, and ending substance abuse or street crime demands yet others. Labelers or experts who claim one policy can do it all are simply wrong.

THE HUMAN DANGERS OF LABELING

Most immediately, the underclass label poses a danger for poor people in that the agencies with which they must deal can hurt clients who are so labeled. For one thing, agencies for the poor sometimes build labels into their operating procedures and apply them to all of their clients. As a result, either evidence about actual clients is not collected, or the label is assumed to fit regardless of evidence to the contrary. Agencies responsible for public safety typically resort to this procedure as a crime prevention or deterrence measure, especially when those labeled have little legal or political power. For example, in 1993, the Denver police department compiled a roster of suspected gang members based on "clothing choices," "flashing of gang signals," or associating with known gang members. The list included two-thirds of the city's young black men, of whom only a small percentage were actual gang members.

Labeling also creates direct punitive effects of several kinds. Bruce Link's studies of people labeled as mentally ill have found that the labeling act itself can lead to depression and demoralization, which prevent those labeled from being at their best in job interviews and other competitive situations. Likewise, when poor youngsters who hang out on street corners are treated as "loiterers," they may end up with an arrest record that hurts them in later life—which is probably why middle-class teenagers who also hang out are rarely accused of loitering.

Some effects of labels are felt even earlier in children's lives. Teachers treat students differently if they think they come from broken homes. A long-term study of working-class London has found that labeling effects may even be intergenerational. Labeling of parents as delinquent makes it more likely that their children will also be labeled, adding to the numbers in both generations who are accused of delinquent or criminal behavior.

Sometimes the effect of labeling is more indirect: agencies cut off opportunities and the label turns into a self-fulfilling prophecy. When teachers label low-income or very dark-skinned students as unable to learn, they may reduce their efforts to teach them—often unintentionally, but even so students then become less able to learn. If poor youngsters accused of loitering are assumed to have grown up without the self-control thought to be supplied by male supervision, they may be harassed—sometimes to tease and entrap them into an angry response. The arrests and arrest records that inevitably follow may deprive youngsters from fatherless families of legal job opportunities, and help force them into delinquent ones. In all these cases, the self-fulfilling prophecy is used to declare the labeled guilty without evidence of misconduct.

Another variation of the entrapment process takes place in jails. John Irwin's study of San Francisco courts and jails reports that these sometimes punished defendants whether they were guilty or not, and adds that "the experience of harsh and unfairly delivered punishment frequently enrages or embitters defendants and makes it easier for them to reject the values of those who have dealt with them in this way." In this instance, as in many of the other instances when the labels are applied by penal institutions, the labeled are not necessarily "passive innocents," as Hagan and Palloni put it. Instead, labeling sometimes generates reactions, both on the part of the police and of those they arrest, that push both sides over the edge.

The direct and indirect effects of labeling even hurt the poor in seeking help, because when they evoke labels in the minds of service suppliers they may be given inferior service, the wrong service, or none at all. Services for the labeled are normally underfunded to begin with and service suppliers are frequently overworked, so that the agencies from which the poor seek help must operate under more or less permanent triage conditions. One way of deciding who will be sacrificed in triage decisions is to assume that most clients cheat, use every contact with them to determine whether they are cheating, and exclude those who can be suspected of cheating. Since clients are of lower status than service suppliers and lack any power or influence over them, the suppliers can also vent their own status frustrations on clients. An arbitrary denial of services to clients not only relieves such frustrations but also enables suppliers to make the needed triage choices. For that reason alone, poor clients who object to being mistreated are usually the first to be declared ineligible for help.

Labeling clients as cheaters encourages service suppliers to distrust them, and that distrust is increased if the suppliers fear revenge, particularly violent revenge, from these clients. Consequently, suppliers hug the rules more tightly, making no leeway in individual cases, and even punishing colleagues who bend the rules in trying to help clients. When clients, who presumably come with prejudices of their own about agency staffs, develop distrust of the staff, a spiraling effect of mutual distrust and fear is set up. This creates data to justify labeling on both sides. The mutual distrust also encourages the exchange of violence, or the preemptive strikes of staff members who fear violence from angry clients.

Admittedly, labeling of clients is only a small part of staff-client misunderstandings and client mistreatment. The previously noted lack of funds and staff, the stresses of operating in stigmatized agencies and with stigmatized clients, normal bureaucratic rules that always put the demands of the agency and its staff ahead of the needs of clients, as well as differences of class and race between staff and clients, wreak their own cumulative havoc.

The added role of labeling in reducing services is particularly serious for poor people who live at the edge of homelessness or starvation or ill health. Yet another cause for the reduction or ending of already minimal services may push them over the edge, into the streets or an emergency clinic, into chronic illness or permanent disability, or into street crime.

Nevertheless, agencies sometimes actively discourage labeled people from escaping their stigmatized status. Liebow reports a dramatic but typical incident from a women's shelter: two women were trying to escape homelessness by taking second jobs, which they were forced to give up in order to attend obligatory but aimless night meetings so as to retain their beds in the shelter. In unlabeled populations, taking second jobs would have been rewarded as upward mobility; among labeled ones it is identified as evasion of agency rules or flouting of service supplier authority, as well as evidence of the client troublemaking that is often associated with the label.

Consequently, one major ingredient in successful efforts to help the labeled poor is to remove the label. For example, scattered site housing studies suggest that such housing is successful in changing the lives of the rehoused when their origins and backgrounds are kept from their new neighbors, so that these cannot react to pejorative labels about slum dwellers.

The labels that have produced these effects are not created solely from overheated mainstream fears or imaginations. Like all stereotypes, such labels are built around a small core of truth, or apply "to a few bad apples," as lay psychology puts it. Labeling, however, punishes not only the bad apples but everybody in the population to whom the label is applied. By labeling poor young black males as potential street criminals, for example, the white and black populations fearful of being attacked may feel that they protect themselves, but at the cost of hurting and antagonizing the large majority of poor young black males who are innocent. Inevitably, however, a proportion of the innocent will react angrily to the label, and find ways of getting even with those who have labeled them. In the end, then, everyone loses, the label users as well as the labeled.

Nonetheless, labeling is only a by-product of a larger structural process that cannot be ignored. In any population that lacks enough legitimate opportunities, illegitimate ones will be created and someone will take them. When the jobs for which the poor are eligible pay such a low wage that even some of the employed will turn to drug selling or other crime to increase their incomes, the labeling process is set in motion that finally hurts many more people, poor and nonpoor, whether or not they are guilty or innocent. Still, the real guilt has to be laid at the door of the employers that pay insufficient wages and the market conditions that may give some of them little other choice.

THE INACCURACIES OF LABELS

Last but not least, labels are dangerous simply because they are inaccurate. "Underclass" is inaccurate if interpreted literally, because there can be no class that exists *under* society, as the class hierarchy extends from the top of society to its very bottom. Indeed, "underclass" is like "underworld," which is also part of society, and in fact could not long exist if it were not supplying demanded goods or services to an "overworld."

"Underclass" is also an inaccurate label because it so vague that there is no agreement on a single or simple definition. Several other labels, however, which have evolved from descriptive terms about which there is widespread consensus, offer good illustrations of how much the portraits of the labeled vary from data on actual people.

"Welfare dependent," "single-parent family," "teenage mother," and "the homeless" are relevant examples. "Welfare dependent" is a corruption of "welfare recipient," which assumes that recipients become dependent on the government by virtue of obtaining welfare. In fact, however, only 30 percent of all recipients who begin a period on welfare will stay on for more than two years, and only 7 percent will be on more than eight years, although some of those who leave it also return to it later. Further, about 20 percent of all welfare recipients report non-AFDC income, although if off-the-books employment is counted, nearly half of all recipients are working.

Some recipients would leave welfare and take their chances in the labor market if they could obtain medical insurance for their children. Still, many poor women clearly rely on AFDC and are thus dependent on the government program; what is noted less often is that often they are even more dependent on staying in the good graces of their welfare agency, which can decide to cut them off arbitrarily without a great deal of accountability.

Ironically enough, only welfare recipients are accused of being dependents; others who are subsidized by government without adding something to the economy in exchange for their subsidy are not so labeled. Students with government fellowships, home owners who receive federal tax and mortgage interest deductions, corporations that receive subsidies to stay in existence, as well as unproductive civil servants and the workers on superfluous military bases kept open to prevent the elimination of jobs, are not thought of as being dependent. Thus the economic dependency of welfare recipients is not the real issue, and the label is misnamed as well as partly inaccurate.

"Single-parent family," or at least the label, is also partly or wholly incorrect. For one thing, some families have a man in or near the household de facto if not de jure; more are embedded in an extended family in which mothers, grandmothers, and others share the parenting.

The notion that the children of such families are subject to undue school leaving, joblessness, and poverty, as well as crime and various pathologies, because they did not grow up in two-parent households is similarly incorrect. Since the modern family is not an economically productive institution, single-parenthood per se cannot logically cause poverty in the next generation, any more than growing up in a two-parent family can cause affluence. This helps to explain why well-off single parents are rarely accused of raising children who will grow up with economic or other problems. And since single-parent households are almost always poorer than other poor households, at least when their economic condition is measured properly, whatever economic effects children from such households suffer can be traced to their more extreme poverty or greater economic insecurity.

In addition, while the children of happy two-parent families are best off, all other things being equal, the children of single parents are sometimes emotionally and otherwise better off than the children of two parents who are in constant conflict. If parental conflict is more detrimental to children's well-being and performance than is single parenthood, it would explain the results of studies concluding that children of divorced parents are not uniformly worse off than those from in tact families. Since the scarcity of money is a major cause of conflict—and spouse battering—among poor parents, this also helps to explain further the unwillingness of pregnant young women to marry their partners if they are jobless. None of this argues that poor single-parent families are desirable and should be encouraged, because if there is only one parent, the economic and other burdens on her and the children are often too great, and all may suffer. But the single-parent family structure and the burdens that come with it are usually the result of poverty.

The same conclusions apply to teenage pregnancy. Unmarried adolescents who bear children constitute about half of all adolescent mothers and 8 percent of all welfare recipients, although some adult welfare recipients also became mothers in adolescence. The younger among them may be reacting to school failures as well as family conflict, which can increase the urgency of the normal desire to feel useful to and loved by someone. More to the economic point, many scholars, beginning with Frank Furstenberg, Jr., have pointed out that the babies of such mothers will be in school when their occupational chances are better.

These observations are no argument for adolescent motherhood, especially since many of the babies are actually unwanted at time of conception, and may even be the product of a young woman's defeat by her sexual partner in a power struggle over wearing a condom, or over having sex at all. Unwanted fetuses, however, seem to turn into wanted babies, partly because of lack of access to abortion facilities but perhaps also because low-income families have traditionally welcomed new arrivals. Given the limited chances for upward mobility among the poor, additional babies do not represent the same obstacle to higher status that they sometimes do among the more affluent classes.

There is not even reliable evidence that poor women in their twenties are automatically better mothers than poor girls in their teens, especially if the teenagers have already been responsible for taking care of their younger siblings. Older mothers are probably more mature, but if adolescent mothers receive more help from their mothers and grandmothers than they would if they were older, then adolescence may sometimes be an advantage. It could also be an advantage on health grounds, if the hypothesis that poor mothers are healthier as teenagers than as adults turns out to be supported by sufficient evidence. Conversely, today's poor teenagers are in the unfortunate position of becoming mothers when America's culturally dominant female role models—upper-middle-class professional women—postpone motherhood as long as possible in order to put their careers on a secure footing. Thus what may be rational behavior for poor young women is decidedly irrational according to cultural norms these days. Teenage motherhood does not thereby become desirable, but once more, the fundamental problem is the poverty that helps to make it happen.

Finally, even the homeless label can be incorrect. For one thing, label users tend to combine panhandlers with the homeless, even though the former are frequently housed. Furthermore, homeless populations differ from community to community depending on the nature of the low-income labor and housing markets, and particularly of housing vacancy rates for poor nonwhites in these communities. Even the rates of mental illness and substance abuse vary.

More important, since the mentally ill and addicted homeless were poor to begin with, curing them would not by itself significantly increase their ability to find affordable housing, or jobs that would enable them to afford such housing. Most lack occupational skills and skin colors that are needed on the job market these days, the obvious virtues of mental health and freedom from addiction notwithstanding. Jencks argues that money spent on substance abuse could be used instead for shelter, but in most communities, it is both easier and cheaper to get hard drugs and alcohol than low-income housing. It is not yet even known how many homeless people turned to alcohol or drugs because of economic problems or familial ones—or just lack of family—and then became homeless, and how many became homeless first and addicts subsequently.

While dealing with mental illness and addiction are vital, homelessness is a disease of the housing market, just as being on welfare is a disease of the job market. The mentally ill and the addicted are the most vulnerable to both of these economic diseases, but as long as there are not enough dwelling units and jobs for the poor, someone will have to be homeless and on welfare. Whether intentionally or not, the most vulnerable are almost always "selected" for most deprivations, among other reasons because they are the least able to protest or to defend themselves.

Labels, whether applied to welfare recipients, the homeless, and other poor people, cannot ever describe the labeled, because labels mainly describe their imagined behavioral and moral deviations from an assumed mainstream. Justified or not, labels express the discontents of the mainstream and those speaking for it, not the characteristics and conditions of the labeled themselves. When label users are discontented and seek people on whom they can project their frustrations, the accuracy of the resultant labels is not a major consideration. In fact, accuracy may get in the way if frustrated people want to be enraged by poor people and thus able to blame them.

Ultimately, however, even accurate labels for the poor are dangerous because the labels cannot end poverty or the criminal and offending poverty-related behavior of some of the poor, or the fear, anger, and unhappiness of the labelers. In the long run, these latter may be the most dangerous effects of labels.

PART FOUR

Racism

D uring the 1960s, the successful struggle for legislation to enforce equal op- portunity for minorities—in jobs, housing, and education—created the hope that government action would effectively remove the most important barri- ers to racial equality in American society. This sense of optimism was enhanced by the expectation of an ever-expanding economy that seemed to promise there would be room for everyone to have a chance at the good life in America.

To some extent, these expectations were borne out—for a while. Blacks and other minorities made significant social and economic progress, particularly in the 1960s, as a result of civil rights protest, government action, and an expanding econ- omy. But the urban riots of the 1960s also showed a more ominous side of the racial picture and revealed that some aspects of racial disadvantage in the United States were relatively impervious to both economic growth and the expansion of civil rights. And during the 1970s and early 1980s, some of the gains made by minorities in ear- lier years began to be reversed. Minority income fell behind as a proportion of white income, and minority poverty—especially in the inner cities—increased sharply. A combination of unfavorable economic trends, a less generous public policy, and a waning commitment to the vigorous enforcement of civil rights laws has taken its toll on minority progress in recent years. The depth of the disaster for many inner-city minorities was brutally revealed in the explosion of rioting in Los Angeles in 1992— the worst single urban civil disorder in America in this century.

Yet despite these troubling developments, some commentators have begun to argue that race is no longer very important in America. No one denies that minori- ties still suffer a variety of economic and social disadvantages. But it is now some- times argued that these disadvantages no longer have much to do with outright racial discrimination—which, in this view, has greatly diminished over time. In this argument, the high rates of unemployment and poverty among black Americans, for example, are now mainly due to problems of culture or attitudes, rather than sys- tematic barriers to economic opportunity.

The articles in this section, however, make it clear that this celebration of the end of racial discrimination is decidedly premature. Race still matters in the United States, and it matters very much.

As Douglas Massey and Nancy Denton point out in the selection from their book *American Apartheid,* there was for many years a great deal of denial about the continuing significance of racial segregation in American life. They point out that no other group has faced such systematic residential segregation as blacks have—and that there has been very little change in that pattern in recent years. Most blacks still live in neighborhoods populated mainly by other blacks; and one result is that poverty among the black population has become harshly concentrated, as have the social problems that accompany it. Moreover, blacks remain segregated in housing at every level of income, meaning that no matter how well black families succeed in the world of work, they are still likely to be trapped in isolated and segregated communities, with all that it implies for the quality of life.

Compounding the stubborn persistence of housing segregation is the unequal treatment of minorities in the criminal justice system. And no form of discrimination has led to more division between the races in contemporary America. Here too, as Jeffrey Goldberg makes clear in "The Color of Suspicion," the idea that the United States has left discrimination behind and become a "color-blind" society turns out to be a myth. Many police officers, it seems, routinely use "racial profiling" in deciding whose car will be pulled over on the freeway, or which young men will be detained and questioned on the street. Police often justify their disproportionate focus on black or Hispanic citizens on the grounds that they are, in the real world, more likely to be involved in crime or drug dealing. But the result is a much greater chance that blacks or Hispanics will wind up in the jails and prisons—and a growing anger and alienation in the face of predictably unequal treatment.

The persistence of racial segregation and stereotyping in housing and policing is matched, as many studies show, in other institutions, including education and the job market. Especially since the civil rights movement of the 1950s and 1960s, there have been many attempts to combat these problems and to promote racial equality and diversity.

One of the most important strategies to combat discrimination has been what is loosely called "affirmative action"—the requirement that institutions make special efforts to ensure a fair chance for historically underrepresented minorities. Many people wrongly believe that this means that colleges, businesses, and other institutions maintain "quotas" mandating that a certain percentage of their employees or students must be from minority groups. In fact, such quotas have been illegal since the 1970s. But universities and other institutions *have* been allowed to devise a variety of ways to increase racial and ethnic diversity.

Affirmative action has become one of most controversial social policies in the United States: many feel that it gives unfair preferences to minorities which have nothing to do with their merit or performance, while others believe that it is an essential tool to maintain a diverse community and to help redress the discriminatory policies of the past. However one feels about that issue in the abstract, it is important to put it in context. What is usually left out in the public debate over affirmative action is that many *other* groups besides minorities receive a variety of preferences in such things as admission to college, and have for a long time. Athletes, for example, have long been able to gain admission to exclusive colleges with lower grades and test scores than other applicants. And, as Daniel Golden shows, many universities now make special efforts to bend the standards in order to admit the children of wealthy parents. This is sometimes euphemistically called "development" admissions, but by whatever name, it is a kind of preference. The fact that, as one student puts it, "Everybody at Duke has something that got them in," helps to put the issue of affirmative action for minority students in better perspective.

Americans of Asian descent face complex forms of discrimination as well, as Ronald Takaki shows in "Asian Americans: The Myth of the Model Minority." According to the census, the "Asian or Pacific Islander" population is among the most rapidly increasing in the United States, and it is an extraordinarily diverse population—encompassing a wide range of groups from many different countries and very different traditions. The growth of the Asian-American population has been accompanied by many stereotypes, which, as Takaki shows, obscure the complexity of the Asian-American experience and hide continuing problems of discrimination and uneven opportunities. Part of the problem is that the very real educational and economic successes of some Asian American groups mask the difficulties faced by others—especially the growing Southeast Asian population—who face high rates of poverty, unemployment, school problems, and preventable diseases. Nor does the success of some Asian Americans mean that discrimination against them has disappeared. Despite considerable upward mobility, Asians often run into a "glass ceiling" in the job hierarchy—and sometimes face brutal, overt racism in the streets as well.

CHAPTER 13

American Apartheid

DOUGLAS S. MASSEY

NANCY A. DENTON

During the 1970s and 1980s a word disappeared from the American vocabulary. It was not in the speeches of politicians decrying the multiple ills besetting American cities. It was not spoken by government officials responsible for administering the nation's social programs. It was not mentioned by journalists reporting on the rising tide of homelessness, drugs and violence in urban America. It was not discussed by foundation executives and think-tank experts proposing new programs for unemployed parents and unwed mothers. It was not articulated by civil rights leaders speaking out against the persistence of racial inequality, and it was nowhere to be found in the thousands of pages written by social scientists on the urban underclass. The word was segregation.

Most Americans vaguely realize that urban America is still a residentially segregated society, but few appreciate the depth of black segregation or the degree to which it is maintained by ongoing institutional arrangements and contemporary individual actions. They view segregation as an unfortunate holdover from a racist past, one that is fading progressively over time. If racial residential segregation persists, they reason, it is only because civil rights laws passed during the 1960s have not had enough time to work or because many blacks still prefer to live in black neighborhoods. The residential segregation of blacks is viewed charitably as a "natural" outcome of impersonal social and economic forces, the same forces that produced Italian and Polish neighborhoods in the past and that yield Mexican and Korean areas today.

But black segregation is not comparable to the limited and transient segregation experienced by other racial and ethnic groups, now or in the past. No group in the history of the United States has ever experienced the sustained high level of residential segregation that has been imposed on blacks in large American cities for the past fifty years. This extreme racial isolation did not just happen; it was manufactured by whites through a series of self-conscious actions and purposeful institutional arrangements that continue today. Not only is the depth of black segregation unprecedented and utterly unique compared with that of other groups, but it shows little sign of change with the passage of time or improvements in socioeconomic status.

If policymakers, scholars, and the public have been reluctant to acknowledge segregation's persistence, they have likewise been blind to its consequences for American blacks. Residential segregation is not a neutral fact; it systematically undermines the social and economic well-being of blacks in the United States. Because of racial segregation, a significant share of black America is condemned to experience a social environment where poverty and joblessness are the norm, where a majority of children are born out of wedlock, where most families are on welfare, where educational failure prevails, and where social and physical deterioration abound. Through prolonged exposure to such an environment, black chances for social and economic success are drastically reduced.

Deleterious neighborhood conditions are built into the structure of the black community. They occur because segregation concentrates poverty to build a set of mutually reinforcing and self-feeding spirals of decline into black neighborhoods. When economic dislocations deprive a segregated group of employment and increase its rate of poverty, socioeconomic deprivation inevitably becomes more concentrated in neighborhoods where that group lives. The damaging social consequences that follow from increased poverty are spatially concentrated as well, creating uniquely disadvantaged environments that become progressively isolated—geographically, socially, and economically—from the rest of society.

The effect of segregation on black well-being is structural, not individual. Residential segregation lies beyond the ability of any individual to change; it constrains black life chances irrespective of personal traits, individual motivations, or private achievements. For the past twenty years this fundamental fact has been swept under the rug by policymakers, scholars, and theorists of the urban underclass. Segregation is the missing link in prior attempts to understand the plight of the urban poor. As long as blacks continue to be segregated in American cities, the United States cannot be called a race-blind society.

THE FORGOTTEN FACTOR

The present myopia regarding segregation is all the more startling because it once figured prominently in theories of racial inequality. Indeed, the ghetto was once seen as central to black subjugation in the United States. In 1944 Gunnar Myrdal wrote in *An American Dilemma* that residential segregation "is basic in a mechanical sense. It exerts its influence in an indirect and impersonal way: because Negro people do not live near white people, they cannot . . . associate with each other in the many activities founded on common neighborhood. Residential segregation . . . becomes reflected in uni-racial schools, hospitals, and other institutions" and creates "an artificial city . . . that permits any prejudice on the part of public officials to be freely vented on Negroes without hurting whites."

Kenneth B. Clark, who worked with Gunnar Myrdal as a student and later applied his research skills in the landmark *Brown v. Topeka* school integration case, placed residential segregation at the heart of the U.S. system of racial oppression. In *Dark Ghetto*, written in 1965, he argued that "the dark ghetto's invisible walls have been erected by the white society, by those who have power, both to confine those who have *no* power and to perpetuate their powerlessness. The dark ghettos are social, political, educational, and—above all—economic colonies. Their inhabitants are subject peoples, victims of the greed, cruelty, insensitivity, guilt, and fear of their masters."

Public recognition of segregation's role in perpetuating racial inequality was galvanized in the late 1960s by the riots that erupted in the nation's ghettos. In their aftermath, President Lyndon B. Johnson appointed a commission chaired by Governor Otto Kerner of Illinois to identify the causes of the violence and to propose policies to prevent its recurrence. The Kerner Commission released its report in March 1968 with the shocking admonition that the United States was "moving toward two societies, one black, one white—separate and unequal." Prominent among the causes that the commission identified for this growing racial inequality was residential segregation.

In stark, blunt language, the Kerner Commission informed white Americans that "discrimination and segregation have long permeated much of American life; they now threaten the future of every American." "Segregation and poverty have created in the racial ghetto a destructive environment totally unknown to most white Americans. What white Americans have never fully understood—but what the Negro can never forget—is that white society is deeply implicated in the ghetto. White institutions created it, white institutions maintain it, and white society condones it."

The report argued that to continue present policies was "to make permanent the division of our country into two societies; one, largely Negro and poor, located in the central cities; the other, predominantly white and affluent, located in the suburbs." Commission members rejected a strategy of ghetto enrichment coupled with abandonment of efforts to integrate, an approach they saw "as another way of choosing a permanently divided country." Rather, they insisted that the only reasonable choice for America was "a policy which combines ghetto enrichment with programs designed to encourage integration of substantial numbers of Negroes into the society outside the ghetto."

America chose differently. Following the passage of the Fair Housing Act in 1968, the problem of housing discrimination was declared solved, and residential segregation dropped off the national agenda. Civil rights leaders stopped pressing for the enforcement of open housing, political leaders increasingly debated employment and educational policies rather than housing integration, and academicians focused their theoretical scrutiny on everything from culture to family structure, to institutional racism, to federal welfare systems. Few people spoke of racial segregation as a problem or acknowledged its persisting consequences. By the end of the 1970s residential segregation became the forgotten factor in American race relations.

RACE VERSUS CLASS: AN UNEQUAL CONTEST

Before exploring the continuing causes of segregation, we assess the extent to which the geographic separation of blacks and whites may be attributed to economic differences between the two groups. In the market-driven, status-conscious society of the United States, affluent families live in different neighborhoods than poor families, and to the extent that blacks are poor and whites are affluent, the two groups will tend to be physically separated from one another. Is what appears to be racial segregation actually segregation on the basis of social class?

Economic arguments can be invoked to explain why levels of black–white segregation changed so little during the 1970s. After decades of steady improvement, black economic progress stalled in 1973, bringing about a rise in black poverty and an increase in income inequality. As the black income distribution bifurcated, middle-class families experienced downward mobility and fewer households possessed the socioeconomic resources necessary to sustain residential mobility and, hence, integration. If the economic progress of the 1950s and 1960s had been sustained into the 1970s, segregation levels might have fallen more significantly. William Clark estimates that 30%–70% of racial segregation is attributable to economic factors, which, together with urban structure and neighborhood preferences, "bear much of the explanatory weight for present residential patterns."

Arguments about whether racial segregation stems from white racism or from economic disadvantages are part of a larger debate on the relative importance of race and class in American society. Some observers hold that black social and economic problems now stem from the unusually disadvantaged class position of African Americans; they argue that black poverty has become divorced from race per se and is now perpetuated by a complex set of factors, such as joblessness, poor schooling, and family instability, that follow from the transformation of cities from manufacturing to service centers. Other investigators place greater emphasis on racism; they argue that because white prejudice and discrimination have persisted in a variety of forms, both overt and subtle, skin color remains a powerful basis of stratification in the United States.

Since the mid-1970s, the race-class debate has gone on without definitive resolution with respect to a variety of socioeconomic outcomes: employment, wealth, family stability, education, crime. But when one considers residential segregation, the argument is easily and forcefully settled: race clearly predominates. Indeed, race predominates to such an extent that speculations about what would have happened if black economic progress had continued become moot. Even if black incomes had continued to rise through the 1970s, segregation would not have declined: no matter how much blacks earned they remained spatially separated from whites. In 1980, as in the past, money did not buy entry into white neighborhoods of American cities.

The dominance of race over class is illustrated by Table 13.1, which presents black–white dissimilarity indices for three income groups within the thirty largest black communities of the United States. These data show the degree of residential segregation that blacks experience as their family income rises from under $2,500 per year to more than $50,000 per year. Although we computed segregation indices for all income categories between these two extremes, in the interest of brevity we

TABLE 13.1   Segregation by Income in Thirty Metropolitan Areas with the Largest Black Populations, 1980

Metropolitan Area	Income Category		
	Under $2,500	$25,000–$27,500	$50,000+
Northern areas			
Boston	85.1	83.9	89.1
Buffalo	85.2	80.0	90.0
Chicago	91.1	85.8	86.3
Cincinnati	81.7	70.9	74.2
Cleveland	91.6	87.1	86.4
Columbus	80.3	74.6	83.4
Detroit	88.6	85.0	86.4
Gary–Hammond–E. Chicago	90.6	89.5	90.9
Indianapolis	80.8	76.6	80.0
Kansas City	86.1	79.3	84.2
Los Angeles–Long Beach	85.4	79.8	78.9
Milwaukee	91.3	87.9	86.3
New York	86.2	81.2	78.6
Newark	85.8	79.0	77.5
Philadelphia	84.9	78.6	81.9
Pittsburgh	82.1	80.6	87.9
St. Louis	87.3	78.4	83.2
San Francisco–Oakland	79.9	73.7	72.1
Average	85.8	80.7	83.2
Southern areas			
Atlanta	82.2	77.3	78.2
Baltimore	82.4	72.3	76.8
Birmingham	46.1	40.8	45.2
Dallas–Ft. Worth	83.1	74.7	82.4
Greensboro–Winston Salem	63.2	55.1	70.8
Houston	73.8	65.5	72.7
Memphis	73.8	66.8	69.8
Miami	81.6	78.4	76.5
New Orleans	75.8	63.1	77.8
Norfolk–Virginia Beach	70.1	63.3	72.4
Tampa–St. Petersburg	81.8	76.0	85.7
Washington, D.C.	79.2	67.0	65.4
Average	74.4	66.7	72.8

Source: Nancy A. Denton and Douglas S. Massey, "Residential Segregation of Blacks, Hispanics, and Asians by Socioeconomic Status and Generation," *Social Science Quarterly* 69:4, pp. 797–817. Copyright © 1988 by the University of Texas Press. All rights reserved.

only show one middle category ($25,000–$27,500). Little is added by including other income groups, because black segregation does not vary by affluence.

Among northern metropolitan areas, for example, blacks, no matter what their income, remain very highly segregated from whites. As of 1980, black families earning under $2,500 per year experienced an average segregation index of 86, whereas those earning more than $50,000 had an average score of 83; blacks in the middle category displayed a score of 81. This pattern of constant, high segregation was replicated in virtually all northern urban areas. In Chicago, for example, the poorest blacks displayed an index of 91; the most affluent blacks had an index of 86. In New York, the respective figures were 86 and 79; and in Los Angeles they were 85 and 79. In no northern metropolitan area did blacks earning more than $50,000 per year display a segregation index lower than 72.

Although southern areas generally evinced lower levels of racial segregation, the basic pattern by income was the same: rising economic status had little or no effect on the level of segregation that blacks experienced. On average, segregation moved from 74 in the lowest income category to 73 in the highest, with a value of 67 in between. Segregation was particularly high and resistant to change in Atlanta, Baltimore, Dallas, Miami, and Tampa; but even in southern cities with relatively low levels of segregation, there was little evidence of a meaningful differential by income: the poorest blacks in Birmingham, Alabama, displayed a segregation index of 46, whereas the most affluent black families had a segregation index of 45.

One possible explanation for this pattern of constant segregation irrespective of income is that affluent blacks are not well informed about the cost and availability of housing opportunities in white neighborhoods. Reynolds Farley examined this possibility using special data collected in the University of Michigan's Detroit Area Survey. He found that blacks were quite knowledgeable about housing costs throughout the metropolitan area, even in distant white suburbs, and were well aware that they could afford to live outside the ghetto. Whatever was keeping affluent blacks out of white areas, it was not ignorance.

The uniqueness of this pattern of invariant high segregation is starkly revealed when blacks are compared with Hispanics or Asians. In the Los Angeles metropolitan area, for example, the segregation index for Hispanics earning under $2,500 in 1979 was 64, and it declined to a moderate value of 50 among those earning $50,000 or more. In the largest Latino barrio in the United States, therefore, the *poorest* Hispanics were less segregated than the *most affluent* blacks (whose score was 79). Similarly, in the San Francisco–Oakland metropolitan area, which contains the largest concentration of Asians in the United States, the Asian–white segregation index fell from 64 in the lowest income category to 52 in the highest (compared with respective black–white indices of 86 and 79). These contrasts were repeated in cities throughout the United States; Hispanic and Asian segregation generally begins at a relatively modest level among the poor and falls steadily as income rises.

Similar patterns are observed when segregation is examined by education and occupation. No matter how socioeconomic status is measured, therefore, black segregation remains universally high while that of Hispanics and Asians falls progressively as status rises. Only blacks experience a pattern of constant, high segregation that is impervious to socioeconomic influences. The persistence of racial segregation in American cities, therefore, is a matter of race and not class. The residential segregation of African Americans cannot be attributed in any meaningful way to the socioeconomic disadvantages they experience, however serious these may be.

CHAPTER 14

The Color of Suspicion

JEFFREY GOLDBERG

Sgt. Mike Lewis of the Maryland State Police is a bullnecked, megaphone-voiced, highly caffeinated drug warrior who, on this shiny May morning outside of Annapolis, is conceding defeat. The drug war is over, the good guys have lost and he has been cast as a racist. "This is the end, buddy," he says. "I can read the writing on the wall." Lewis is driving his unmarked Crown Victoria down the fast lane of Route 50, looking for bad guys. The back of his neck is burnt by the sun, and he wears his hair flat and short under his regulation Stetson.

"They're going to let the N.A.A.C.P tell us how to do traffic stops," he says. "That's what's happening. There may be a few troopers who make stops solely based on race, but this—they're going to let these people tell us how to run our department. I say, to hell with it all. I don't care if the drugs go through. I don't."

He does, of course. Mike Lewis was born to seize crack. He grew up in Salisbury, on the Eastern Shore—Jimmy Buffett country—and he watched his friends become stoners and acid freaks. Not his scene. He buzz-cut his hair away and joined the state troopers when he was 19. He's a star, the hard-charger who made one of the nation's largest seizures of crack cocaine out on Route 13. He's a national expert on hidden compartments. He can tell if a man's lying, he says, by watching the pulsing of the carotid artery in his neck. He can smell crack cocaine inside a closed automobile. He's a human drug dog, a walking polygraph machine. "I have the unique ability to distinguish between a law-abiding citizen and an up-to-no-good person," he says. "Black or white." All these skills, though, he's ready to chuck. The lawsuits accusing the Maryland State Police of harassing black drivers, the public excoriation—and most of all, the Governor of New Jersey saying that her state police profiled drivers based on race, and were wrong to do so—have twisted him up inside. "Three of my men have put in for transfers," he says. "My wife wants me to get out. I'm depressed."

What depresses Mike Lewis is that he believes he is in possession of a truth polite society is too cowardly to accept. He says that when someone tells this particular truth, his head is handed to him. "The superintendent of the New Jersey State Police told the truth and he got fired for it," Lewis says.

This is what Carl Williams said, fueling a national debate about racial profiling in law enforcement: "Today, with this drug problem, the drug problem is cocaine or marijuana. It is most likely a minority group that's involved with that." Gov. Christine Todd Whitman fired Williams, and the news ricocheted through police departments everywhere, especially those, like the Maryland State Police, already accused of racial profiling—the stopping and searching of blacks because they are black.

The way cops perceive blacks—and how those perceptions shape and mis-shape crime fighting—is now the most charged racial issue in America. The systematic harassment of black drivers in New Jersey, the shooting of Amadou Diallo, an unarmed African immigrant, by New York City police officers earlier this year, and other incidents in other states have brought the relationship between blacks and cops to a level of seemingly irreversible toxicity.

Neither side understands the other. The innocent black man, jacked-up and humiliated during a stop-and-frisk or a pretext car stop, asks: Whatever happened to the Fourth Amendment? It is no wonder, blacks say, that the police are so wildly mistrusted.

And then there's the cop, who says: Why shouldn't I look at race when I'm looking for crime? It is no state secret that blacks commit a disproportionate amount of crime, so "racial profiling" is simply good police work.

Mike Lewis wishes that all this talk of racial profiling would simply stop.

As we drive, Lewis watches a van come up on his right and pass him. A young black man is at the wheel, his left leg hanging out the window. The blood races up Lewis's face: "Look at that! That's a violation! You can't drive like that! But I'm not going to stop him. No, sir. If I do, he's just going to call me a racist."

Then Lewis notices that the van is a state government vehicle. "This is ridiculous," he says. Lewis hits his lights. The driver stops. Lewis issues him a warning and sends him on his way. The driver says nothing.

"He didn't call me a racist," Lewis says, pulling into traffic, "but I know what he was thinking." Lewis does not think of himself as a racist. "I know how to treat people," he says. "I've never had a complaint based on a race-based stop. I've got that supercharged knowledge of the Constitution that allows me to do this right."

In the old days, when he was patrolling the Eastern Shore, it was white people he arrested. "Ninety-five percent of my drug arrests were dirt-ball-type whites—marijuana, heroin, possession-weight. Then I moved to the highway, I start taking off two, three kilograms of coke, instead of two or three grams. Black guys. Suddenly I'm not the greatest trooper in the world. I'm a racist. I'm locking up blacks, but I can't help it."

His eyes gleam: "Ask me how many white people I've ever arrested for cocaine smuggling—ask me!"

I ask.

"None! Zero! I debrief hundreds of black smugglers, and I ask them, 'Why don't you hire white guys to deliver your drugs?' They just laugh at me. 'We ain't gonna trust our drugs with white boys.' That's what they say."

Mike Lewis's dream: "I dream at night about arresting white people for cocaine. I do. I try to think of innovative ways to arrest white males. But the reality is different."

A big part of Lewis's reality is a black man named Keith Hill. Lewis killed Keith Hill three years ago. Hill was speeding down Route 13 when Lewis pulled him over. He approached the car, Hill rolled down the window and Lewis smelled burning marijuana. He ordered Hill out of the car, began to search him and came up with thousands of dollars of cash and packets of marijuana. Hill suddenly resisted. What flashed through Lewis's mind was his friend Edward Plank, a trooper killed by a coke runner on this same highway a few months before.

They fought, Hill knocking Lewis into a ravine. They wrestled, and Hill went for Lewis's gun. "We were in a clinch, just breathing heavy," Lewis recalls, "and I said, 'Man, it's just pot, it's not worth it.'" But Hill kept going for the gun, Lewis tells me. He couldn't get it, and ran. He looped through a housing development and back to his car. Hill gunned the engine just as Lewis got himself in front of the car. Lewis drew his weapon and fired, striking Hill twice in the chest.

Lewis speaks often of the shooting, and of Eddie Plank's death. One day, he collects for me old newspaper stories of trooper shootouts. I'm reading them when we pass two members of his interdiction squad parked on the median of Route 13. They've stopped two cars with New York license plates filled with young black men. "What's up?" Lewis asks Gary Bromwell, a bulky, sullen trooper.

The two cars were pulled over for speeding and weaving, but that was a pretext. The goal of Lewis's unit, the criminal-interdiction unit, is to find drugs, guns and untaxed cigarettes in the cars of smugglers. However, in order to stop a suspected gunrunner or drug mule, troopers first have to find a reason in the state's traffic laws.

Bromwell issues written warnings and sends them on their way. I ask Bromwell, who is white, why he didn't ask the young men their consent to search the cars. Reasonable suspicion—anything the trooper can articulate before a judge—is enough to justify a consent search. "They're decent people," Bromwell says.

How can you tell?

"They looked me in the eye, and the driver's hand didn't shake when he handed me his license—."

Lewis interrupts: "No visible sign of contraband, no overwhelming odor of air fresheners emanating from the vehicle, no signs of hard driving"—that is, driving long hours without making stops. He is listing Drug Enforcement Administration-endorsed indicators of drug smuggling. Smugglers use air fresheners to fool drug-sniffing dogs. Signs of hard driving—"these guys drive straight through because they don't want to leave their drugs alone," Lewis says—include loose-fitting clothing, day-old beards and food wrappers on the floor. These signs, though, can also indicate the presence of college students—which is, in fact, the case here.

Did you stop them because they were black men from New York? I ask.

"Tell you the truth," Bromwell says, "we couldn't see who was driving these cars. They were speeding."

After the New York cars pull into traffic, Lewis shows Bromwell and his partner, Rob Penny, the newspaper clippings, hoping they will back him up. "Eddie Plank," he says. "Killed by a black male. My shooting—a black. Robbie Bishop, down in Georgia, killed by a black. North Carolina trooper, killed by a black."

Bromwell looks uneasy. I ask him if he believes in a connection between the race of the shooters and the crimes they commit.

"People might think it," Bromwell says, walking away, "but they don't say it." He flashes Lewis a look that says, Shut up, and quick.

WHY A COP PROFILES

This is what a cop might tell you in a moment of reckless candor: in crime fighting, race matters. When asked, most cops will declare themselves color blind. But watch them on the job for several months, and get them talking about the way policing is really done, and the truth will emerge, the truth being that cops, white and black, profile. Here's why, they say. African-Americans commit a disproportionate percentage of the types of crimes that draw the attention of the police. Blacks make up 12 percent of the population, but accounted for 58 percent of all carjackers between 1992 and 1996. (Whites accounted for 19 percent.) Victim surveys—and most victims of black criminals are black—indicate that blacks commit almost 50 percent of all robberies. Blacks and Hispanics are widely believed to be the blue-collar backbone of the country's heroin- and cocaine-distribution networks. Black males between the ages of 14 and 24 make up 1.1 percent of the country's population, yet commit more than 28 percent of its homicides. Reason, not racism, cops say, directs their attention.

Cops, white and black, know one other thing: they're not the only ones who profile. Civilians profile all the time—when they buy a house, or pick a school district, or walk down the street. Even civil rights leaders profile. "There is nothing more painful for me at this stage in my life," Jesse Jackson said several years ago, "than to walk down the street and hear footsteps and start thinking about robbery—and then look around and see somebody white and feel relieved." Jackson now says his quotation was "taken out of context." The context, he said, is that violence is the inevitable by-product of poor education and health care. But no amount of "context" matters when you fear that you are about to be mugged.

At a closed-door summit in Washington between police chiefs and black community leaders recently, the black chief of police of Charleston, S.C., Reuben Greenberg, argued that the problem facing black America is not racial profiling, but precisely the sort of black-on-black crime Jackson was talking about. "I told them that the greatest problem in the black community is the tolerance for high levels of criminality," he recalled. "Fifty percent of homicide victims are African-Americans. I asked what this meant about the value of life in this community."

The police chief in Los Angeles, Bernard Parks, who is black, argues that racial profiling is rooted in statistical reality, not racism. "It's not the fault of the police when they stop minority males or put them in jail," Parks told me. "It's the fault of the minority males for committing the crime. In my mind it is not a great revelation that if officers are looking for criminal activity, they're going to look at the kind of people who are listed on crime reports."

Chief Parks defends vigorously the idea that police can legitimately factor in race when building a profile of a criminal suspect.

"We have an issue of violent crime against jewelry salespeople," Parks says. "The predominant suspects are Colombians. We don't find Mexican-Americans, or blacks or other immigrants. It's a collection of several hundred Colombians who commit this crime. If you see six in a car in front of the Jewelry Mart, and they're waiting and watching people with briefcases, should we play the percentages and follow them? It's common sense."

What if you follow the wrong Colombian, or track an Ecuadorean by mistake? "We're not using just race," he says. "It's got to be race, plus other indicators, so that won't happen."

I asked Parks to comment on the 3-out-of-10 hypothetical. In Maryland, the state police, as part of a settlement of an American Civil Liberties Union lawsuit, reported that on a particular stretch of highway, the police came up with drugs in 3 out of every 10 consent searches. This was deemed unacceptable by the A.C.L.U. "Three out of 10?" Parks said. "That would get you into the Hall of Fame. That's a success story." He continued: "At some point, someone figured out that the drugs are being delivered by males of this color driving these kinds of vehicles at this time of night. This isn't brain surgery. The profile didn't get invented for nothing."

PROFILING IN BLACK AND WHITE

"Some blacks, I just get the sense off them that they're wild," Mark Robinson says. "I mean, you can tell. I have what you might call a profile. I pull up alongside a car with black males in it. Something doesn't match—maybe the style of the car with the guys in it. I start talking to them, you know, 'nice car,' that kind of thing, and if it doesn't seem right, I say, 'All right, let's pull it over to the side,' and we go from there."

He is quiet and self-critical, and the words sat in his mouth a while before he let them out.

"I'm guilty of it, I guess."

Guilty of what?

"Racial profiling."

His partner, Gene Jones, says: "Mark is good at finding stolen cars on the street. Real good."

We are driving late one sticky Saturday night through the beat-down neighborhood of Logan, in the northern reaches of Philadelphia. The nighttime commerce is lively, lookouts holding down their corners, sellers ready to serve the addict traffic. It's a smorgasbord for the two plainclothes officers, but their attention is soon focused on a single cluster of people, four presumptive buyers who are hurrying inside a spot the officers know is hot with drugs.

The officers pull to the curb, slide out and duck behind a corner, watching the scene unfold. The suspects are wearing backward baseball caps and low-slung pants; the woman with them is dressed like a stripper.

"Is this racial profiling?" Jones asks. A cynical half-smile shows on his face.

The four buyers are white. Jones and Robinson are black, veterans of the street who know that white people in a black neighborhood will be stopped. Automatically. Faster than a Rastafarian in Scarsdale.

"No reason for them to be around here at this time of night, nope," Jones says.

Is it possible that they're visiting college friends? I ask.

Jones and Robinson, whose intuition is informed by experience, don't know quite what to make of my suggestion.

"It could be," Jones says, indulgently. "But, uhhhh, no way."

Are you going to stop them?

"I don't know what for yet, but I'm going to stop them."

The whites step out of the building, separate and dissolve into the night before Jones gets to make his stop. Jones is unhappy; he's proud of his tracking skills. "They're hard to see in the dark, I guess," he says, smiling.

So, race is a legitimate proxy for criminality?

"No," Jones says. Few cops ever answer yes at the outset. "But it depends. I mean, you're a cop. You know who's committing the crimes. It's your neighborhood. That's how it works."

Jones and Robinson are assigned to Philadelphia's 35th Police District, one of the more drug-ridden districts in a drug-ridden city. Certain sections of Philadelphia are still very much lawless. Last year, the city hired John Timoney, who served as first deputy commissioner under William Bratton in New York City, to revive a police department that had become tragically inept. Timoney, by all accounts, has done a remarkable job reforming the department, and letting the criminal underclass know that their actions will bring consequences.

But Philadelphia is not quite Rudolph Giuliani's New York. Jones and Robinson are surprised to hear, for instance, that the smoking of marijuana in public places is actively discouraged by New York police. They express this surprise after they try to clear a drug corner of young men who continue smoking fat blunts even after Robinson and Jones alert them to the fact that they are in the presence of law-enforcement officers.

"You know, the city is cracking down on marijuana smoking," Jones tells the men. They stub out their joints—but not before one man takes one last, deep drag—and move across the street.

Jones shakes his head and says, "It's like there aren't any laws out here."

Like many black cops, Jones and Robinson have more in common with their white colleagues than they do with, say, the Rev. Al Sharpton. "The problem with black politicians is that they think the cop is automatically guilty," Jones says.

One day, while driving through a particularly rank stretch of their police district, Jones decides that I should interview drug dealers on the subject of police harassment and racial profiling. The point he hopes to make is that the complaints of racial harassment are illegitimate. Jones approaches one group of dealers, heavy-lidded young men drinking 40-ounce bottles of malt liquor. One dealer, who gives his name as Si-Bee, is asked by Jones whether the police are harassing young blacks or simply enforcing the law.

"Why can't I just sit on my corner?" Si-Bee says in response. "Unless you've got probable cause, you can't come and harass me." To which Jones replied: "Whoa. Probable cause. Big word."

"Cops come busting on us for no reason," a young man named Mustafa says. "It's just plain and simple harassment. Just messing with us."

"Which are worse?" Jones asks. "White cops or black cops?"

"Black," comes the reply, virtually in unison.

We return to the car, and Jones laughs: "That one," he says, pointing out the window, "I arrested for dealing. That one we got in a stolen car. That one, the one who wouldn't talk to me, I arrested two months ago. I'm going to court soon to testify against him."

We stop at another corner, another group of feckless youth. Same questions, same responses. I decide to switch subjects. Instead of talking about Philadelphia, I want to know what happens when they drive the New Jersey Turnpike.

"That's the worst," one young man says. "I never ride the turnpike."

I turn to Jones, waiting for a smirk.

It never comes.

"I'm going to have to agree with the brother on that one," he says.

What?

Jones, it turns out, is a staff sergeant in the New Jersey National Guard. "Yeah, when I go to Jersey for Guard weekends, I take the back roads," he says. "I won't get on the turnpike. I won't mess with those troopers."

"DRIVING WHILE BLACK," AND OTHER EXAGGERATIONS

Here's the heart of the matter, as Chief Greenberg of Charleston sees it: "You got white cops who are so dumb that they can't make a distinction between a middle-class black and an underclass black, between someone breaking the law and someone just walking down the street. Black cops too. The middle class says: 'Wait a minute. I've done everything right, I pushed all the right buttons, went to all the right schools, and they're jacking me up anyway.' That's how this starts."

So is racism or stupidity the root cause of racial profiling?

Governor Whitman, it seems, would rather vote for stupidity.

"You don't have to be racist to engage in racial profiling," she says. We are sitting in her office in the State House in Trenton. She still seems a bit astonished that her state has become the Mississippi of racial profiling.

Whitman, though burned by the behavior of her state troopers, is offering them a generous dispensation, given her definition of racial profiling. "Profiling means a police officer using cumulative knowledge and training to identify certain indicators of possible criminal activity," she told me. "Race may be one of those factors, but it cannot stand alone."

"Racial profiling," she continues, "is when race is the only factor. There's no other probable cause."

Her narrow, even myopic, definition suggests that only stone racists practice racial profiling. But the mere sight of black skin alone is not enough to spin most cops into a frenzy. "Police chiefs use that word 'solely' all the time, and it's such a red herring," says Randall Kennedy, Harvard Law professor and author of the book "Race, Crime and the Law." "Even Mark Fuhrman doesn't act solely on the basis of race."

The real question about racial profiling is this: Is it ever permissible for a law-enforcement officer to use race as one of even 5, or 10, or 20, indicators of possible criminality?

In other words, can the color of a man's skin help make him a criminal suspect?

Yes, Whitman says. She suggests she doesn't have a problem with the use of race as one of several proxies for potential criminality. "I look at Barry McCaffrey's Web site," she says, referring to the Clinton Administration's drug czar, "and it says certain ethnic groups are more likely to engage in drug smuggling."

It is true. Despite President Clinton's recent declaration that racial profiling is "morally indefensible," the Office of National Drug Control Policy's Web site helpfully lists which racial groups sell which drugs in different cities. In Denver, McCaffrey's Web site says, it is "minorities, Mexican nationals" who sell heroin. In Trenton, "crack dealers are predominantly African-American males, powdered cocaine dealers are predominantly Latino."

The link between racial minorities and drug selling is exactly what Whitman's former police superintendent, Carl Williams, was talking about. So was Williams wrong?

"His comments indicated a lack of sensitivity to the seriousness of the problem."

But was he wrong on the merits?

"If he said, 'You should never use this solely; race could be a partial indicator, taken in concert with other factors'"—she pauses, sees the road down which she's heading, and puts it in reverse—"but you can't be that broad-brushed."

"Racial profiling," is a street term, not a textbook concept. No one teaches racial profiling. "Profiling," of course, is taught. It first came to the public's notice by way of the Federal Bureau of Investigation's behavioral-science unit, which developed the most famous criminal profile of all, one that did, in fact, have a racial component—the profile of serial killers as predominantly white, male loners.

It is the Drug Enforcement Administration, however, that is at the center of the racial-profiling controversy, accused of encouraging state law-enforcement officials to build profiles of drug couriers. The D.E.A., through its 15-year-old "Operation Pipeline," finances state training programs to interdict drugs on the highway. Civil rights leaders blame the department for the burst of race-based stops, but the D.E.A. says it discourages use of race as an indicator. "It's a fear of ours, that people will use race," says Greg Williams, the D.E.A.'s operations chief.

Cops use race because it's easy, says John Crew, the A.C.L.U.'s point man on racial profiling. "The D.E.A. says the best profile for drug interdiction is no profile," he says. "They say it's a mistake to look for a certain race of drivers. That's their public line. But privately, they say, 'God knows what these people from these state and local agencies do in the field.'"

The A.C.L.U. sees an epidemic of race-based profiling. Anecdotes are plentiful, but hard numbers are scarce. Many police officials see the "racial profiling" crisis as hype. "Not to say that it doesn't happen, but it's clearly not as serious or widespread as the publicity suggests," says Chief Charles Ramsey of Washington. "I get so tired of hearing that 'Driving While Black' stuff. It's just used to the point where it has no meaning. I drive while black—I'm black. I sleep while black too. It's victimology. Black people commit traffic violations. What are we supposed to say? People get a free pass because they're black?"

HOW TO JACK UP A BLACK MAN: A PRIMER

"You know, the black people out here are different," Girolamo Renzulli says. He is formerly of New York, now serving as a Los Angeles County deputy sheriff. We are standing in the parking lot of the Lennox sheriff's station on the edge of South Central Los Angeles. Renzulli speaks in low tones.

"How so?"

"They're just, I don't know, different."

Like how?

"Wild," he says. "You'll see."

The Los Angeles Sheriff's Department does not look at black men differently than it looks at white men: it is heinous to even suggest it, the Sheriff himself, Leroy Baca, says. He has 8,000 sworn officers under his command; the Sheriff's Department polices unincorporated areas of Los Angeles County and 40 different towns.

"It's happened before," Baca will acknowledge. "When I was a lieutenant, I knew a deputy who stopped interracial couples. We removed him from the field, disciplined him and transferred him out."

Today, though, it just doesn't happen. Baca reads to me from his "Core Values" statement, which, among other items, promises that sheriff's deputies will have the "courage" to stand up to "racism, sexism, anti-Semitism and homophobia."

"Even criminals have dignity as human beings that must be honored," Baca says.

This is not necessarily an opinion shared by his men. Bobby Harris is a senior deputy at the Lennox station, who, with four other deputies, shot and killed one man this year, and, Harris says, "the year ain't over yet." Deputy Harris is not shy about sharing his position on profiling, which does not dovetail with Sheriff Baca's—at least as Baca described his position to me.

"Racial profiling is a tool we use, and don't let anyone say otherwise," Harris says. "Like up in the valley," he continues, referring to the San Fernando Valley, "I knew who all the crack sellers were—they look like Hispanics who should be cutting your lawn. They were driving cars like this one"—he points to an aging Chevy parked in the station's lot—"and all the cars had DARE stickers on them. That's just the way it is."

If it is unclear whether Sheriff Baca is sincerely oblivious to the goings-on at the Lennox station, many chiefs, I've found, are not terribly interested in knowing too much about the tactics their subordinates use to bring down the crime numbers—

crime reductions that, in this performance-driven era of policing, are key to job preservation. In Baltimore, for instance, rank-and-file officers know full well who a multi-agency drug interdiction team that operates at the city's train station is looking for.

"Everyone knows they're looking for 'Yo girls,' " says Craig Singleterry, a black Baltimore police officer. "Yo girls," Singleterry explains, are young black women with long nails and hair weaves who carry such accouterments as Fendi bags and who deliver drugs and money for dealers in New York.

"Of course we do racial profiling at the train station," says Gary McLhinney, the president of the Baltimore Fraternal Order of Police. "If 20 people get off the train and 19 are white guys in suits and one is a black female, guess who gets followed? If racial profiling is intuition and experience, I guess we all racial-profile."

Here is Baltimore's Police Commissioner, Thomas Frazier, on racial profiling: "To say that being of any particular race makes you a suspect in a particular type of crime is just wrong, and it's not done in Baltimore."

Roll call in Los Angeles, and the subject is an upcoming demonstration protesting the police killing last December of a 19-year-old woman in neighboring Riverside County. Tyisha Miller is the West Coast's Amadou Diallo. She was shot to death while slumped in her car with a gun on her lap. The police officers say they opened fire when she reached for the gun.

"I hear Al Sharpton is coming out for this," one deputy says.

"Can you believe it? They're going to turn this thing into another goddamn O.J.," another responds.

"And Jesse Jackson is coming."

"Oh, for Chrissakes."

All but two of the deputies are white. One is Hispanic, and he hangs with the whites. The other deputy is black, and he does not participate in the conversation. He instead stares at a fixed point on the wall in front of him. All of the white men in the room wear their hair in crew cuts. Many of them are ex-marines. Many also wear a tattoo of the Grim Reaper on their ankles. Deputies assigned to hard-core gang areas often tattoo themselves identically, very much like the gangs they fight. It is the white deputies who do this, in the main, and civil rights activists have loudly accused the Sheriff's Department of harboring racist gangs, identifiable by the tattoos they wear. Because of the criticism, deputies keep their tattoos a secret, even though they see nothing wrong with them. "If it was a picture of a black man hanging from a tree, I could see people getting upset," one deputy, Jeffrey Coates, told me.

Coates is perhaps the hardest-charging deputy at Lennox. He is a heavily muscled white man, a power lifter who usually wears a mustache but shaved it off for SWAT tryouts. SWAT culture frowns on facial hair.

The first time I met Coates, he was training a new deputy, a black woman named Angela Walton. Walton and Coates seemed to work well together. It can be unpleasant to be a black female deputy in Los Angeles, and Coates would rise to her defense. Once, he recalled, a suspect taunted Walton, saying, " 'I bet yo' training officer treats you real good.' "

"I wanted to beat his [expletive] face in," Coates remembered. "I told him to shut up, just shut up. Then he called me a nigger. I mean, what's that about? How am I a nigger?"

Coates was reared in Iowa, but he has an expert feel for the streets of South Central. He also seems to attract gunfire. Not long after I rode with him, he and his partner were shot at by a man with a revolver, who missed. Last year, Coates and a partner killed a man who opened fire on them from seven feet away. After the shooting, Coates paid a mandatory visit to the department psychiatrist. "He asked me how I felt. I said, 'I feel, [expletive] him.'"

"Afterward, the black newspaper wrote, 'Deputies kill another black man,'" Coates said. "But if this guy dumped me, they wouldn't have said anything." Coates doesn't have much patience for those who protest the killing of Tyisha Miller, or those who complain about racial profiling: "I say, get your own house in order. Stop the black-on-black homicide."

On one of the days we rode together, Coates and his partner for the day, Andy Ruiz, responded to a domestic call that involved an angry young black man with a tire iron. They pulled up just as the young man walked into the street. Coates grabbed the tire iron. Ruiz pulled out his 9-millimeter pistol. He later said, "I was ready to shoot him, really."

Inside the apartment the young man with the tire iron was trying to destroy, there were empty bottles of malt liquor on the television console. Coates: "You ever hear Chris Rock? He does this thing: 'Guy says, I got a job, man! Like he's proud. Well, [expletive], you supposed to have a job.'" This is an inexact recollection of a Chris Rock routine in which he delineates the differences between "blacks" and "niggers." Rock is very popular with white cops.

Coates spent one day giving me what might be called a master class in the art of the pretext stop—pulling over blacks and Hispanics, hoping to come up with dope, or guns, or information. "There's a law against almost everything as it relates to a vehicle," Coates said. Coates knows the law, and uses it.

For example, Coates spotted a type of car, a Monte Carlo, which is known to be favored by gangsters, moving along in traffic. He pulled in behind the car and studied it for a moment.

"No mud flaps," Coates said, turning on his lights.

They pulled the car over, and asked the three teenagers, shaven-headed Hispanics, to step outside. They patted them down and looked through the vehicle. The teen-agers freely admitted to being members of the South Los gang.

"Now the reason we stopped you was that you have no mud flaps on your rear tires," Coates said. "But the real reason we stopped you is because we saw that you're rolling out of your area. Why don't you turn it around and go home."

The men argued: "We're just going to Costco."

For what?

"Pet food."

"Pitbull?" Coates asked.

"Two," one of the men answered.

Coates, same day, different vehicle, a purple Buick Regal with a bumper sticker that reads, "Don't you wish you were a pimp." Coates knows the owner of the car— he put him in jail. Behind the wheel is his wife. "There's got to be some violations on that car," Coates said.

There were two women in the car, smoking, and three very small children. Not one was in a car seat. "There's something hanging from your mirror, ma'am," Coates said, covering his bases. "Now, you've got to have the baby in a car seat, O.K.?"

The Regal pulled off, and Coates shook his head. "I should take her to jail just for the secondhand smoke," he said. "Smoking inside a car with little babies? Can you believe that? This place is crazy."

Coates doesn't believe that everyone in his patrol sector is guilty of something. He told me he believes that slightly less than half are guilty of something. He has a good hit rate—most of the drivers he stops are driving without licenses or registration.

But sometimes, in his sweep of the neighborhood, he makes a wrong call. One day, while patrolling with Walton on a bleak street of boarded-up bungalows and dead-eyed black men, he stopped a car without license plates. An obvious stop, but it's what happened after the car was stopped that warrants notice. Every male Coates stops he asks to step to the police cruiser and place his hands on the hood. Coates will then pat him down for a weapon.

The man driving this particular car acceded readily to this, but he was agitated. "This is my neighborhood," he said. He was a black man in his 30's. He seemed terribly embarrassed.

Coates knew something was off when the man produced his license, registration and insurance card, the trifecta of responsibility.

"I'm sorry. I was just taking the car from the garage back home," the man said. "I should have plates, you're right."

He explained why he was nervous: "I work at Northrop. I don't want anybody to see me like this." He had his palms flat on the hood of Coates's cruiser as he was talking. Walton was standing nearby, her hand near her weapon.

Coates dismissed him without writing a citation. The man thanked the deputy profusely, and took off.

It was a troubling moment, and I asked Coates if it's his policy to remove every male from any car he stops, no matter what the cause for the stop.

"Yes. Officer safety."

"Would you do that in a different part of the county?"

"I wouldn't do it in Santa Clarita," he said, pausing—realizing, perhaps, what that sounded like. "I mean, it all depends."

Do you recognize that you might have just created an enemy on this traffic stop?

"I was polite," he responded, "I always treat people with respect." This is true— he is generally respectful, even affable. But good manners do not necessarily neutralize humiliation.

As I was leaving, I asked Coates if he wore the Grim Reaper tattoo on his ankle.

"I haven't lied to you yet," he said. "So I'm going to have to take the Fifth on that one."

PLAYING THE PERCENTAGES

The sheriff's station in Santa Clarita is located on a street named after a nearby amusement park, Magic Mountain. Santa Clarita is part of Los Angeles County, but it is geographically and culturally close to Simi Valley—and a world away from the ghettoes of South Central. Not a lot happens out in Santa Clarita, which is why sheriff's deputies patrol in single-officer cars. Deputy Sam Soehnel is assigned to patrol the middle-class and white Valencia area, as well as the small, rundown Mexican section known as Old Newhall. Most of his problems are in Old Newhall.

"A lot of Hispanics are heavy drinkers," he says. "It's cultural." If pretext stops happen at all, they happen in Old Newhall.

A typical Saturday, a typical call. Someone has found a bank door ajar. Soehnel comes to talk to the semihysterical woman who discovered the open door. "Do you think someone is locked in the vault?" she asks. The manager comes, and closes up.

"People have very active imaginations here," Deputy Soehnel says.

Imaginations run wild, for instance, when residents see a black man or a Hispanic man someplace he "shouldn't be."

"If you're in a nice area," Soehnel explains, "and you see a Hispanic guy, he just sticks out, if he's just walking around, hanging out. People will call 911. If it's off a citizen's call, I can make contact with the individual. Ascertain what they're doing in the area."

I ask if it's his policy to pull people out of their cars during traffic stops.

"It depends. A nice area, a guy in Valencia, no. But if it's somebody you're not used to seeing, unfamiliar, yes. On this job, you learn that it's the nice guys that get killed."

Recently, there was a home-invasion robbery on his beat. A black suspect. "We get a lot of 911 calls," Soehnel says. "I got a call, 'There's a black guy walking around on people's lawns.' I get there, he's wearing an electric-company uniform. This woman sees a black guy walking on her lawn and goes ballistic."

Soehnel is sympathetic. To the woman.

"You play the percentages," he says. "That's the way it works. People see a black guy, they think: 'carjacker.'"

Or rapist.

GETTING PROFILED TO DEATH

"Amadou Diallo was profiled to death," says Ben Ward, New York City's first black police commissioner. The night Diallo was killed—the night Rudolph Giuliani's experiment in "zero tolerance" came to an end—the Street Crime Unit that fired the famous 41 shots was on the hunt for a black rapist.

Ward is no Sharptonite; he was one of the first black police officials to talk openly about what he called the "the dirty little secret" of black-on-black crime. Yet he believes, he says, that most police officers are spectacularly unqualified to discern the difference between lawbreakers and honest citizens.

"The demonstrable evidence shows that they stink at identifying criminals," he says, noting that the Street Crime Unit of the N.Y.P.D. reported that its officers stopped 45,000 people in 1997 and 1998, and arrested only 9,500.

The sociologist Jerome Skolnick once wrote that police officers keep in their minds a picture of the "symbolic assailant." In his work, Skolnick identified that "symbolic assailant" as a young black man.

It's not only white cops who keep that symbolic assailant in mind when they're out on patrol.

"Sometimes, I hate the young black males because of what they do to their community," Mark Buchanan, a black antigang officer in Boston, told me. "But then I think to myself, 'If this is the way I feel, and I'm black, what must white officers think about blacks?'"

I took this question to Mike Lewis, the Maryland state trooper who thinks often—very often—about race. We were driving through a black ghetto on the back-side of Salisbury. It is, he says, a pit stop on the crack highway.

Has this job made you prejudiced? I ask.

He turned his head in surprise. It looked as is he wanted to say something, but nothing came out.

Finally, he says: "Let me tell you something. We respond to calls here, and let's say it's a domestic. We get there, 3, 4 in the morning, and the parents are cracked out, and the kids are up watching TV and eating popcorn, and the place is crawling with roaches. When I go home, the first thing I do is take a shower."

So are you prejudiced?

This is how he answers: "We arrested a Salisbury police sergeant a few months ago, for drugs. We knew he was involved with drugs. For years. He was black."

Black, black, black, black. It is what Mike Lewis sees. It is what Jeffrey Coates sees. It is tunnel vision. They understand half the equation—blacks commit more of certain types of crimes than whites. But what they don't understand is, just because blacks commit more crimes than whites doesn't mean that most blacks commit crimes.

"I see a 16-year-old white boy in a Benz, I think, 'Damn, that boy's daddy is rich.' I see a 16-year-old black, I think, 'That boy's slinging drugs,'" says Robert Richards, a black police sergeant in Baltimore who admits that tunnel vision is a hazard of the job. But like many black cops, he sees nuance where white cops see, well, black and white. "When I start thinking that way, I try to catch myself. If I'm walking down the street and I pass a black male, I realize that, chances are, he's not a criminal."

It is, in some respects, nearly impossible to sit in judgment of a Mike Lewis or a Jeffrey Coates. If Coates says he must pull black men out of their cars and search them on traffic stops, well, Coates has been shot at before, and most critics of the Sheriff's Department have not. But if Coates—and his department, by extension—believe that it is permissible to conduct pretext stops in South Central but impermissible to do so in Santa Clarita, then there's a problem.

The numbers cops cite to justify aggressive policing in black neighborhoods and on the highways tell only part of the story—an important part, but only part.

For one thing, blacks make up only 13 percent of the country's illicit drug users, but 74 percent of people who are sentenced to prison for drug possession, according to David Cole, a law professor at Georgetown University and the author of "No Equal Justice."

Common sense, then, dictates that if the police conducted pretext stops on the campus of U.C.L.A. with the same frequency as they do in South Central, a lot of whites would be arrested for drug possession, too.

Of course, this doesn't happen, because no white community is going to let the police throw a net over its children.

WHAT GETS TALKED ABOUT, AND WHAT DOESN'T

Bob Mulholland is the sort of white cop who scares even white people. He is tall and thick and his eyes are hard. He works Philadelphia's 35th Police District with Gene Jones and Mark Robinson.

The three men meet up one afternoon on a drug corner.

Jones had been talking about the unequal application of the law. He is a mash of contradictions. One moment, he will speak of the need to "fry" black drug dealers. The next, he will talk about the absurd double standard in law enforcement—the way in which white drug users know with near 100-percent certainty that they will never go to jail for marijuana possession. How they know that they will never be jacked up during a pretext stop. How white cops cut white kids a break.

"We were doing a drunk-driving checkpoint one night," he said. "And I began to notice that when the cops caught a white kid drunk, they would say things like: 'I'm going to call your father. You're in big trouble.' With black guys, they'd just arrest them. Well, I mean, black kids got fathers, too."

Jones and Robinson like Mulholland. They told me he was fair. So I asked him if he ever sees a double standard in law enforcement, if the ghetto is policed one way and a white neighborhood another.

"My job is to clear this corner of [expletives]," he says. "That's what I do."

Do you ever cut anyone slack? Maybe a student who's waiting for a bus?

"My job is to clear this corner of [expletives]," he says, again.

But would you do that equally? If this wasn't the ghetto, but a university campus, would you clear the corner of white kids drinking beer?

"I don't give a [expletive] who's on the corner. My job is to clear the corner of [expletives]."

Jones and Robinson return to their car and sit in silence.

"Well," Jones says.

"That's what you call a back-in-the-day kind of attitude," Robinson says. The "day" being the time when white cops didn't have to worry about repercussions. I ask them if they believe Mulholland would in fact apply his corner-clearing skills with equal vigor in a white neighborhood.

"No," Jones says.

"No," Robinson says.

"Sometimes, white guys come from white neighborhoods to this job," Jones says. "They don't know a lot of black people, except what they see on TV. So they think they've got to act all hard. They get scared easy.

"Bob's a good guy, though," he continues. "He's a good cop. He's not a racist." Jones and Robinson are truly perplexed. White cops are impossible to understand sometimes. Sometimes they're your friends. And sometimes. . . .

"You won't believe this," Robinson tells me one day. "I got stopped."

Really?

"Yeah, in Abington." Abington is a white suburb over the Philadelphia city line. "It was weird. I was stopped at a light, and this police officer behind me puts his lights on, so I pull it to the side, thinking he's going to pass me. I was thinking like a cop. And then another car comes. The first cop comes over to my window and says he stopped me because my inspection sticker was placed abnormally high on the windshield."

Gene Jones begins to laugh.

"I thought they were going to pull out rulers," Robinson continues. "I mean, inspection sticker too high on the windshield?"

I ask Robinson what he was wearing. "What I've got on now," a denim shirt and a baseball cap.

"Then he sees the police emblem on my car, and he says, 'Oh, you're a cop?' I said, Yeah."

Why do you think he pulled you over in Abington? I ask.

"I don't know. Maybe because my car is kind of old."

He doesn't believe this even as he says it.

"Maybe it was that other thing," he continues. "The thing we were talking about."

Mark Robinson, the cop who profiles, was just profiled, and he can't even call it by name.

CHAPTER 15

At Many Colleges, the Rich Kids Get Affirmative Action

DANIEL GOLDEN

Despite her boarding-school education and a personal tutor, Maude Bunn's SAT scores weren't high enough for a typical student to earn admission to Duke University.

But Ms. Bunn had something else going for her—coffeemakers. Her Bunn fore-bears built a fortune on them and, with Duke hoping to woo her wealthy parents as donors, she was admitted.

Afterward, her parents promptly became co-chairmen of a Duke fund-raising effort aimed at other Duke parents. "My child was given a gift, she got in, and now I'm giving back," says Maude's mother, Cissy Bunn, who declines to say how much the family has contributed to the university.

Most universities acknowledge favoring children of alumni who support their alma mater. But to attract prospective donors, colleges are also bending admissions standards to make space for children from rich or influential families that lack long-standing ties to the institutions. Through referrals and word-of-mouth, schools identify applicants from well-to-do families. Then, as soon as these students enroll, universities start soliciting gifts from their parents.

Duke says it has never traded an admission for a donation. "There's no quid pro quo, no bargains have been struck," says Peter Vaughn, director of development communications. While it won't comment on individual cases, the university notes that financial gifts from parents are used to update facilities and provide financial aid, among other things.

The formal practice of giving preference to students whose parents are wealthy—sometimes called "development admits"—has implications for the legal challenge to affirmative action, which the U.S. Supreme Court will hear April 1 [2003]. Special admissions treatment for the affluent has racial overtones, at least indirectly. Reflecting the distribution of wealth in America, the vast majority of major donors to higher education are white. Defenders of minority preference say such advantages for white applicants are precisely why affirmative action is still needed.

Top schools ranging from Stanford University to Emory University say they occasionally consider parental wealth in admission decisions. Other elite schools, such as Massachusetts Institute of Technology, say parental means don't influence them. "I understand why universities leverage parent contacts to enrich themselves," says Marilee Jones, dean of admissions at MIT. "If somebody's offering them a check, why not take it? But I honestly think it's out of control."

While children of the wealthy have long had advantages getting into colleges, a look at how "development" admissions works at Duke shows how institutionalized the process has become at some major universities.

Under-endowed compared with rivals such as Harvard, Princeton and Stanford, Duke has been particularly aggressive in snaring donors through admissions breaks. Widely considered one of the nation's top ten universities, Duke accepts 23% of its applicants and turns down more than 600 high-school valedictorians a year. Three-fourths of its students score above 1320 out of a perfect 1600 on the SATs.

Yet in recent years, Duke says it has relaxed these standards to admit 100 to 125 students annually as a result of family wealth or connections, up from about 20 a decade ago. These students aren't alumni children and were tentatively rejected, or wait-listed, in the regular admissions review. More than half of them enroll, constituting an estimated 3% to 5% of Duke's student body of 6,200.

The strategy appears to be paying off. For the last six years, Duke says it has led all universities nationwide in unrestricted gifts to its annual fund from non-alumni parents: about $3.1 million in 2001–2002. A university fund-raising campaign recently met its $2 billion goal. While 35% of alumni donate to Duke, 52% of parents of last year's freshman class contributed to the university—besides paying $35,000 in tuition and room and board.

Students admitted for development reasons graduate at a higher rate than the overall student body, Duke says, although their grades are slightly lower. These applicants are held to the same lesser standard as some top athletes; not whether they can excel, but whether they can graduate. "There's never been a case where I think the student can't be successful at Duke, and the student is admitted," says admissions director Christoph Guttentag.

Caroline Diemar, a Duke senior, says she favors maintaining minority preference for college admissions because she knows from experience that well-connected white students get a boost too. The daughter of an investment banker, she applied early to Duke despite an 1190 SAT score. Her candidacy was deferred to the spring.

She then buttressed her application with recommendations from two family friends who were Duke donors, and she was accepted. "I needed something to make me stand out," says Ms. Diemar, a sociology major with a 3.2 grade point average, below the 3.4 average of the senior class. "Everybody at Duke has something that got them in." The lesson she learned: "Networking is how you go about everything."

After she enrolled, Duke recruited Ms. Diemar's parents to serve as co-chairmen of a fund-raising effort. Her father, Robert Diemar, declined to say how much he has given to Duke. "We support all of our five children's schools," said Mr. Diemar, a Princeton alumnus. He said Duke accepted his daughter on merit.

The practice of giving preference to the children of potential donors has caused fissures on Duke's campus, with some worrying that it dilutes the student body's intellectual vitality and undermines racial and economic diversity. In November 2000, a report to the trustees by a university committee on admissions called for a one-third cut in applicants accepted for development reasons. Mr. Guttentag says he plans to reduce such admissions to about 65 this year to achieve "greater flexibility" in shaping next fall's freshman class.

Duke President Nannerl O. Keohane thinks the Supreme Court should uphold affirmative action because preferences for children of potential donors is "disproportionately favorable to white students. . . . The two are definitely linked, and it seems odd to me to allow one sort of preference, but not the other."

The University of Michigan, defendant in the affirmative action case before the Supreme Court, wants to continue to allow preferential treatment for minorities. It also gives preferential admissions treatment to children of potential donors—but only if they're white or Asian.

DISCRETIONARY POINTS

Under the 150-point "Selection Index" Michigan uses for undergraduate admissions, a review committee may award 20 "discretionary" points to children of donors, legislators, faculty members and other key supporters. Minorities underrepresented in higher education—Hispanics, African-Americans and Native Americans—qualify for an automatic 20 points, but they are ineligible for the discretionary points. The university says less than 1% of admitted students receive this edge.

The late Terry Sanford, Duke president from 1969 to 1985, practiced donor preference on a large scale. Mr. Sanford, a gregarious former North Carolina governor, used his wide circle of contacts in business, politics and the media to elevate Duke from a regional to a national university. According to Keith Brodie, Duke's president emeritus, Mr. Sanford would personally meet each year with the admissions and development directors to ensure special attention for 200 of these friends' children applying to Duke. More than 100 would ultimately enroll.

As president from 1985 to 1993, Dr. Brodie says, he removed himself from the admissions process, resisted lobbying by some trustees, and trimmed the number of underqualified students admitted due to donor preference to 20 a year. "A Duke education is too valuable an asset to squander," says Dr. Brodie, a professor of psychiatry, who was criticized as president for a lack of fund-raising zeal. "University presidents are under greater pressure than ever to raise money," he adds. "I suspect many of them have turned to admissions to help that process."

Harold Wingood, who was senior associate director of admissions under Dr. Brodie, recalls that 30 to 40 students per year were upgraded from "rejected" to "wait-list," or from "wait-list" to "admit" due to their family ties. "We'd take students in some cases with SAT scores 100 points below the mean, or just outside the top 15% of their class," says Mr. Wingood, now dean of admissions at Clark University in Worcester, Mass. "They weren't slugs, but they weren't strong enough to get in on their own."

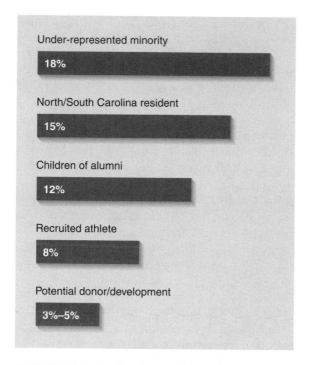

FIGURE 15.1   Study Break: Proportion of the 1,654 Current Duke University Freshmen Who Qualified for Various Admission Preferences

Note: Some students may have qualified for more than one preference, or would have qualified for admission on their academic records regardless of preference.

Source: Duke admissions office.

The numbers have increased under Ms. Keohane, Duke's current president. Duke says it admitted about 125 non-alumni children in 1998, and again in 1999, who had been tentatively rejected or wait-listed prior to considering family connections. It accepted 99 such students in 2000. Similar data aren't available for 2001 or 2002, the school says.

Ms. Keohane says she didn't intentionally increase the number of wealthy applicants given a leg up. She says "it is possible that the numbers drifted upward" during the recent $2 billion-fund-raising campaign because "more people in development expressed interest in candidates. But this was certainly not a policy directive, or even a conscious choice."

The system at Duke works this way: Through its own network and names supplied by trustees, alumni, donors and others, the development office identifies about 500 likely applicants with rich or powerful parents who are not alumni. (Children of major alumni donors are given similar preference in a separate process.) It cultivates them with campus tours and basic admissions advice; for instance, applying early increases their chances. It also relays the names to the admissions office, which returns word if any of the students forget to apply—so development can remind them.

The development office then winnows the initial 500 into at least 160 high-priority applicants. Although these names are flagged in the admissions-office computer, admissions readers evaluate them on merit, without regard to family means. About 30 to 40 are accepted, the others tentatively rejected or wait-listed. During an all-day meeting in March, Mr. Guttentag and John Piva Jr., senior vice president for development, debate these 120 cases, weighing their family's likely contribution against their academic shortcomings.

In her 2001 book, "Admissions Confidential," former Duke admissions officer Rachel Toor recalled that most admissions officers "hated to see these kids get in" because they were "the weakest part of our applicant pool." Nevertheless, most of the 120 students are admitted.

Once these children of privilege enroll, the development office enlists their parents as donors and fund raisers. According to Dr. Brodie, Duke's parent program originated as a forum for parent concerns about safety issues, but it has evolved into a fund-raising vehicle.

A committee of more than 200 non-alumni parents provides its volunteer army for the four classes currently at Duke. Committee members usually give at least $1,000 to Duke, and the eight co-chairmen and the national chairman much more—including at least two seven-figure gifts endowing faculty chairs.

Membership in the parents' committee is by invitation only and is overwhelmingly white. Lately, one affluent Chicago suburb—Lake Forest—has dominated its higher echelons. Lake Forest luminaries on the committee have included department-store heir Marshall Field V, who has given at least $100,000 to Duke; Paul Clark, chief executive of Icos Corp., a biotech firm; Robert DePree, chairman of cornmeal maker House-Autry Mills Inc.; and investment banker Willard Bunn III, Maude's father.

The Lake Forest couples are social friends, serve on many of the same Chicago-area boards and several sent their children to the same private elementary school, Lake Forest Country Day. They write recommendations to Duke for each other's children.

'PRETTY INTIMATE GROUP'

Susan DePree, Robert's wife, describes the Duke parents committee as a "pretty intimate group" but not "clubby." She declined to say how much she and her husband have contributed to Duke, but says they solicited at least one six-figure gift from a parent-committee member.

Maude Bunn, whose family lives in Lake Forest, attended an elite boarding school in Lawrenceville, N.J., where the Bunn Library opened in 1996. She says other Lake Forest parents recommended her to Duke.

Cissy Bunn acknowledges her daughter didn't fit the academic profile of a Duke student. "She's bright, she had good grades, but she doesn't meet the superstar status," Mrs. Bunn says. "Did my normal child take the place of somebody who could really make a difference in the world? Sure, yes, to an extent. But there are so many things you can lose sleep over. I'm happy for me and my child."

Maude Bunn says she initially felt very awkward at Duke because her admission "wasn't necessarily on my own merits." But these days, the sophomore says she is thriving. "The more time I've spent here, I feel more and more confident—they didn't have to take me if they didn't think I was equal to all the other students they are admitting," she says. "I'm doing just as well as everybody I know if not better." She is studying art history and wants a career in fashion.

Now her younger sister Meg, a high-school senior, is applying to Duke. Maude says the family likes Meg's chances. "The people my mother works with for fund raising told her, 'It's really hard to get the first child in,'" she says. "After that, sisters and brothers are easier." Duke says it, like many universities, gives some preference to siblings.

Mrs. Bunn says she's not twisting anyone's arm. "I told them, 'If she's qualified at all, that would be lovely,'" she says. "If she gets in, I'd be happy to stay on the parents' committee."

As college admission becomes increasingly competitive, parents try to help their children's chances in any way they can. Duke accepted Jane Hetherington in 2000, despite SAT scores in the mid-1200s and what she calls "average" grades in high school. She attributes her acceptance to a "wonderful recommendation" by Norman Christensen Jr., then dean of Duke's Nicholas School of the Environment and Earth Sciences, a graduate program. She got the recommendation after one meeting with him.

At the time, her father, John Hetherington, was vice president of Westvaco Corp., a paper-products firm that had donated to the school, sponsored research there and hired some of its graduates. Mr. Hetherington asked a family friend on the school's advisory board to have the dean interview Ms. Hetherington.

Mr. Christensen, a Duke professor, says he was impressed by Ms. Hetherington's devotion to environmental studies. The student's father later reciprocated by arranging a meeting between the school's new dean and Westvaco's chief executive officer, hoping the company would increase support for the school. Nothing came of it, says Mr. Hetherington. (Westvaco merged with Mead Corp. last year.)

"I don't feel we benefited from anything you would describe as the traditional white power structure network," says Mr. Hetherington, who is now a Republican state representative in Connecticut and favors a "sunset law" for affirmative action. He doesn't think his position affected his daughter's acceptance into college. "It worked out for some reason," he says. "In all candor, we got lucky."

CHAPTER 16

Asian Americans

The Myth of the Model Minority

RONALD TAKAKI

Today Asian Americans are celebrated as America's "model minority." In 1986, *NBC Nightly News* and the *McNeil/Lehrer Report* aired special news segments on Asian Americans and their success, and a year later, CBS's *60 Minutes* presented a glowing report on their stunning achievements in the academy. "Why are Asian Americans doing so exceptionally well in school?" Mike Wallace asked, and quickly added, "They must be doing something right. Let's bottle it." Meanwhile, *U.S. News & World Report* featured Asian-American advances in a cover story, and *Time* devoted an entire section on this meteoric minority in its special immigrants issue, "The Changing Face of America." Not to be outdone by its competitors, *Newsweek* titled the cover story of its college-campus magazine "Asian-Americans: The Drive to Excel" and a lead article of its weekly edition "Asian Americans: A 'Model Minority.'" *Fortune* went even further, applauding them as "America's Super Minority," and the *New Republic* extolled "The Triumph of Asian-Americans" as "America's greatest success story."

The celebration of Asian-American achievements in the press has been echoed in the political realm. Congratulations have come even from the White House. In a speech presented to Asian and Pacific Americans in the chief executive's mansion in 1984, President Ronald Reagan explained the significance of their success. America has a rich and diverse heritage, Reagan declared, and Americans are all descendants of immigrants in search of the "American dream." He praised Asian and Pacific Americans for helping to "preserve that dream by living up to the bedrock values" of America—the principles of "the sacred worth of human life, religious faith, community spirit, and the responsibility of parents and schools to be teachers of tolerance, hard work, fiscal responsibility, cooperation, and love." "It's no wonder," Reagan emphatically noted, "that the median incomes of Asian and Pacific-American families are much higher than the total American average." Hailing Asian and Pacific

Americans as an example for all Americans, Reagan conveyed his gratitude to them: we need "your values, your hard work" expressed within "our political system."

But in their celebration of this "model minority," the pundits and the politicians have exaggerated Asian-American "success" and have created a new myth. Their comparisons of incomes between Asians and whites fail to recognize the regional location of the Asian-American population. Concentrated in California, Hawaii, and New York, Asian Americans reside largely in states with higher incomes but also higher costs of living than the national average: 59 percent of all Asian Americans lived in these three states in 1980, compared to only 19 percent of the general population. The use of "family incomes" by Reagan and others has been very misleading, for Asian-American families have more persons working per family than white families. In 1980, white nuclear families in California had only 1.6 workers per family, compared to 2.1 for Japanese, 2.0 for immigrant Chinese, 2.2 for immigrant Filipino, and 1.8 for immigrant Korean (this last figure is actually higher, for many Korean women are unpaid family workers). Thus the family incomes of Asian Americans indicate the presence of more workers in each family, rather than higher incomes.

Actually, in terms of personal incomes, Asian Americans have not reached equality. In 1980 the mean personal income for white men in California was $23,400. While Japanese men earned a comparable income, they did so only by acquiring more education (17.7 years compared to 16.8 years for white men twenty-five to forty-four years old) and by working more hours (2,160 hours compared to 2,120 hours for white men in the same age category). In reality, then, Japanese men were still behind Caucasian men. Income inequalities for other men were more evident: Korean men earned only $19,200, or 82 percent of the income of white men, Chinese men only $15,900 or 68 percent, and Filipino men only $14,500 or 62 percent. In New York the mean personal income for white men was $21,600, compared to only $18,900 or 88 percent for Korean men, $16,500 or 76 percent for Filipino men, and only $11,200 or 52 percent for Chinese men. In the San Francisco Bay Area, Chinese-immigrant men earned only 72 percent of what their white counterparts earned, Filipino-immigrant men 68 percent, Korean-immigrant men 69 percent, and Vietnamese-immigrant men 52 percent. The incomes of Asian-American men were close to and sometimes even below those of black men (68 percent) and Mexican-American men (71 percent).

The patterns of income inequality for Asian men reflect a structural problem: Asians tend to be located in the labor market's secondary sector, where wages are low and promotional prospects minimal. Asian men are clustered as janitors, machinists, postal clerks, technicians, waiters, cooks, gardeners, and computer programmers; they can also be found in the primary sector, but here they are found mostly in the lower-tier levels as architects, engineers, computer-systems analysts, pharmacists, and schoolteachers, rather than in the upper-tier levels of management and decision making. "Labor market segmentation and restricted mobility between sectors," observed social scientists Amado Cabezas and Gary Kawaguchi, "help promote the economic interest and privilege of those with capital or those in the primary sector, who mostly are white men."

This pattern of Asian absence from the higher levels of administration is characterized as "a glass ceiling"—a barrier through which top management positions can only be seen, but not reached, by Asian Americans. While they are increasing in numbers on university campuses as students, they are virtually nonexistent as administrators: at Berkeley's University of California campus where 25 percent of the students were Asian in 1987, only one out of 102 top-level administrators was an Asian. In the United States as a whole, only 8 percent of Asian Americans in 1988 were "officials" and "managers," as compared to 12 percent for all groups. Asian Americans are even more scarce in the upper strata of the corporate hierarchy: they constituted less than half of one percent of the 29,000 officers and directors of the nation's thousand largest companies. Though they are highly educated, Asian Americans are generally not present in positions of executive leadership and decision making. "Many Asian Americans hoping to climb the corporate ladder face an arduous ascent," the *Wall Street Journal* observed. "Ironically, the same companies that pursue them for technical jobs often shun them when filling managerial and executive positions."

Asian Americans complain that they are often stereotyped as passive and told they lack the aggressiveness required in administration. The problem is not whether their culture encourages a reserved manner, they argue, but whether they have opportunities for social activities that have traditionally been the exclusive preserve of elite white men. "How do you get invited to the cocktail party and talk to the chairman?" asked Landy Eng, a former assistant vice president of Citibank. "It's a lot easier if your father or your uncle or his friend puts his arm around you at the party and says, 'Landy, let me introduce you to Walt.'" Excluded from the "old boy" network, Asian Americans are also told they are inarticulate and have an accent. Edwin Wong, a junior manager at Acurex, said: "I was given the equivalent of an ultimatum: 'Either you improve your accent or your future in getting promoted to senior management is in jeopardy.'" The accent was a perceived problem at work. "I felt that just because I had an accent a lot of Caucasians thought I was stupid." But whites with German, French, or English accents do not seem to be similarly handicapped. Asian Americans are frequently viewed as technicians rather than administrators. Thomas Campbell, a general manager at Westinghouse Electric Corp., said that Asian Americans would be happier staying in technical fields and that few of them are adept at sorting through the complexities of large-scale business. This very image can produce a reinforcing pattern: Asian-American professionals often find they "top out," reaching a promotional ceiling early in their careers. "The only jobs we could get were based on merit," explained Kumar Patel, head of the material science division at AT&T. "That is why you find most [Asian-Indian] professionals in technical rather than administrative or managerial positions." Similarly an Asian-Indian engineer who had worked for Kaiser for some twenty years told a friend: "They [management] never ever give you [Asian Indians] an executive position in the company. You can only go up so high and no more."

Asian-American "success" has emerged as the new stereotype for this ethnic minority. While this image has led many teachers and employers to view Asians as intelligent and hardworking and has opened some opportunities, it has also been harmful. Asian Americans find their diversity as individuals denied: many feel forced to conform to the "model minority" mold and want more freedom to be their individual selves, to be "extravagant." Asian university students are concentrated in the sciences and technical fields, but many of them wish they had greater opportunities to major in the social sciences and humanities. "We are educating a generation of Asian technicians," observed an Asian-American professor at Berkeley, "but the communities also need their historians and poets." Asian Americans find themselves all lumped together and their diversity as groups overlooked. Groups that are not doing well, such as the unemployed Hmong, the Downtown Chinese, the elderly Japanese, the old Filipino farm laborers, and others, have been rendered invisible. To be out of sight is also to be without social services. Thinking Asian Americans have succeeded, government officials have sometimes denied funding for social service programs designed to help Asian Americans learn English and find employment. Failing to realize that there are poor Asian families, college administrators have sometimes excluded Asian-American students from Educational Opportunity Programs (EOP), which are intended for *all* students from low-income families. Asian Americans also find themselves pitted against and resented by other racial minorities and even whites. If Asian Americans can make it on their own, pundits are asking, why can't poor blacks and whites on welfare? Even middle-class whites, who are experiencing economic difficulties because of plant closures in a deindustrializing America and the expansion of low-wage service employment, have been urged to emulate the Asian-American "model minority" and to work harder.

Indeed, the story of the Asian-American triumph offers ideological affirmation of the American Dream in an era anxiously witnessing the decline of the United States in the international economy (due to its trade imbalance and its transformation from a creditor to a debtor nation), the emergence of a new black underclass (the percentage of black female-headed families having almost doubled from 22 percent in 1960 to 40 percent in 1980), and a collapsing white middle class (the percentage of households earning a "middle-class" income falling from 28.7 percent in 1967 to 23.2 percent in 1983). Intellectually, it has been used to explain "losing ground"—why the situation of the poor has deteriorated during the last two decades of expanded government social services. According to this view, advanced by pundits like Charles Murray, the interventionist federal state, operating on the "misguided wisdom" of the 1960s, made matters worse: it created a web of welfare dependency. But this analysis has overlooked the structural problems in society and our economy, and it has led to easy cultural explanations and quick-fix prescriptions. Our difficulties, we are sternly told, stem from our waywardness: Americans have strayed from the Puritan "errand into the wilderness." They have abandoned the old American "habits of the heart." Praise for Asian-American success is America's most recent jeremiad—a renewed commitment to make America number one again and a call for a rededication to the bedrock values of hard work, thrift, and industry. Like many congratulations, this one may veil a spirit of competition, even jealousy.

Significantly, Asian-American "success" has been accompanied by the rise of a new wave of anti-Asian sentiment. On college campuses, racial slurs have surfaced in conversations on the quad: "Look out for the Asian Invasion." "M.I.T. means Made in Taiwan." "U.C.L.A. stands for University of Caucasians Living among Asians." Nasty anti-Asian graffiti have suddenly appeared on the walls of college dormitories and in the elevators of classroom buildings: "Chink, chink, cheating chink!" "Stop the Yellow Hordes." "Stop the Chinese before they flunk you out." Ugly racial incidents have broken out on college campuses. At the University of Connecticut, for example, eight Asian-American students experienced a nightmare of abuse in 1987. Four couples had boarded a college bus to attend a dance. "The dance was a formal and so we were wearing gowns," said Marta Ho, recalling the horrible evening with tears. "The bus was packed, and there was a rowdy bunch of white guys in the back of the bus. Suddenly I felt this warm sticky stuff on my hair. They were spitting on us! My friend was sitting sidewise and got hit on her face and she started screaming. Our boy friends turned around, and one of the white guys, a football player, shouted: 'You want to make something out of this, you Oriental faggots!'"

Asian-American students at the University of Connecticut and other colleges are angry, arguing that there should be no place for racism on campus and that they have as much right as anyone else to be in the university. Many of them are children of recent immigrants who had been college-educated professionals in Asia. They see how their parents had to become greengrocers, restaurant operators, and storekeepers in America, and they want to have greater career choices for themselves. Hopeful a college education can help them overcome racial obstacles, they realize the need to be serious about their studies. But white college students complain: "Asian students are nerds." This very stereotype betrays nervousness—fears that Asian-American students are raising class grade curves. White parents, especially alumni, express concern about how Asian-American students are taking away "their" slots—admission places that should have gone to their children. "Legacy" admission slots reserved for children of alumni have come to function as a kind of invisible affirmative-action program for whites. A college education has always represented a valuable economic resource, credentialing individuals for high income and status employment, and the university has recently become a contested terrain of competition between whites and Asians. In paneled offices, university administrators meet to discuss the "problem" of Asian-American "overrepresentation" in enrollments.

Paralleling the complaint about the rising numbers of Asian-American students in the university is a growing worry that there are also "too many" immigrants coming from Asia. Recent efforts to "reform" the 1965 Immigration Act seem reminiscent of the nativism prevalent in the 1880s and the 1920s. Senator Alan K. Simpson of Wyoming, for example, noted how the great majority of the new immigrants were from Latin America and Asia, and how "a substantial portion" of them did not "integrate fully" into American society. "If language and cultural separatism rise above a certain level," he warned, "the unity and political stability of the Nation will—in time—be seriously eroded. Pluralism within a united American nation has been our greatest strength. The unity comes from a common language and a core public culture of certain shared values, beliefs, and customs, which make us distinctly 'Americans.'" In the view of many supporters of immigration reform, the post-1965 immigration from Asia and Latin America threatens the traditional unity and identity of the American people. "The immigration from the turn of the century was largely a continuation of immigration from previous years in that the European stock of Americans was being maintained," explained Steve Rosen, a member of an organization lobbying for changes in the current law. "Now, we are having a large influx of third-world people, which could be potentially disruptive of our whole Judeo-Christian heritage." Significantly, in March 1988, the Senate passed a bill that would limit the entry of family members and that would provide 55,000 new visas to be awarded to "independent immigrants" on the basis of education, work experience, occupations, and "English language skills."

Political concerns usually have cultural representations. The entertainment media have begun marketing Asian stereotypes again: where Hollywood had earlier portrayed Asians as Charlie Chan displaying his wit and wisdom in his fortune cookie Confucian quotes and as the evil Fu Manchu threatening white women, the film industry has recently been presenting images of comic Asians (in *Sixteen Candles*) and criminal Asian aliens (in *Year of the Dragon*). Hollywood has entered the realm of foreign affairs. *The Deer Hunter* explained why the United States lost the war in Vietnam. In this story, young American men are sent to fight in Vietnam, but they are not psychologically prepared for the utter cruelty of physically disfigured Viet Cong clad in black pajamas. Shocked and disoriented, they collapse morally into a world of corruption, drugs, gambling, and Russian roulette. There seems to be something sinister in Asia and the people there that is beyond the capability of civilized Americans to comprehend. Upset after seeing this movie, refugee Thu-Thuy Truong exclaimed: "We didn't play Russian roulette games in Saigon! The whole thing was made up." Similarly *Apocalypse Now* portrayed lost innocence: Americans enter the heart of darkness in Vietnam and become possessed by madness (in the persona played by Marlon Brando) but are saved in the end by their own technology and violence (represented by Martin Sheen). Finally, in movies celebrating the exploits of Rambo, Hollywood has allowed Americans to win in fantasy the Vietnam War they had lost in reality. "Do we get to win this time?" snarls Rambo, our modern Natty Bumppo, a hero of limited conversation and immense patriotic rage.

Meanwhile, anti-Asian feelings and misunderstandings have been exploding violently in communities across the country, from Philadelphia, Boston, and New York to Denver and Galveston, Seattle, Portland, Monterey, and San Francisco. In Jersey City, the home of 15,000 Asian Indians, a hate letter published in a local newspaper warned: "We will go to any extreme to get Indians to move out of Jersey City. If I'm walking down the street and I see a Hindu and the setting is right, I will just hit him or her. We plan some of our more extreme attacks such as breaking windows, breaking car windows and crashing family parties. We use the phone book and look up the name Patel. Have you seen how many there are?" The letter was reportedly written by the "Dotbusters," a cruel reference to the *bindi* some Indian women wear as a sign of sanctity. Actual attacks have taken place, ranging from verbal harassments and egg throwing to serious beatings. Outside a Hoboken restaurant on September 27, 1987, a gang of youths chanting "Hindu, Hindu" beat Navroz Mody to death. A grand jury has indicted four teenagers for the murder.

Five years earlier a similarly brutal incident occurred in Detroit. There, in July, Vincent Chin, a young Chinese American, and two friends went to a bar in the late afternoon to celebrate his upcoming wedding. Two white autoworkers, Ronald Ebens and Michael Nitz, called Chin a "Jap" and cursed: "It's because of you mother-fuckers that we're out of work." A fistfight broke out, and Chin then quickly left the bar. But Ebens and Nitz took out a baseball bat from the trunk of their car and chased Chin through the streets. They finally cornered him in front of a McDonald's restaurant. Nitz held Chin while Ebens swung the bat across the victim's shins and then bludgeoned Chin to death by shattering his skull. Allowed to plead guilty to manslaughter, Ebens and Nitz were sentenced to three years' probation and fined $3,780 each. But they have not spent a single night in jail for their bloody deed. "Three thousand dollars can't even buy a good used car these days," snapped a Chinese American, "and this was the price of a life." "What kind of law is this? What kind of justice?" cried Mrs. Lily Chin, the slain man's mother. "This happened because my son is Chinese. If two Chinese killed a white person, they must go to jail, maybe for their whole lives. . . . Something is wrong with this country."

PART FIVE

Sexism

The 1960s were known as a decade of civil rights struggles, black militancy, antiwar protests, and campus disturbances. It seemed unlikely that yet another social movement could take hold and grow, but the consciousness of women's oppression could and did grow, with enormous impact over remarkably few years.

Black militancy, the student movement, the antiwar movement, youth militancy, and radicalism all affirmed freedom, equality, and liberation, but none of these was thought to be particularly necessary or applicable to women, especially by radical men. Ironically, it was political experience with radical men that led radical women to the consciousness of women as a distinctly oppressed group and, therefore, a group with distinctive interests.

The feminism that emerged in the 1970s was in fact both novel and part of a long and often painful series of movements for the liberation of women. Women's rights proposals were first heard more than a century ago. But the movement for the equality of women ground to a halt when the emergencies of the Depression and World War II pushed aside feminist concerns. With victory, both sexes gratefully resumed the middle-class dream of family, security, and upward mobility. These years of the late 1940s and early 1950s were the years of "The Feminine Mystique,"[1] when the *domestic* role of women dominated American culture.

When women began, in the 1970s, once again to reassert themselves and claimed to be able to be doctors and lawyers and bankers and pilots, they were met with derision. The "Long Amnesia" had taken hold and stereotyped women's roles into those of the 1940s and 1950s. People, especially men, had come to regard female domesticity almost as a natural phenomenon. Nevertheless, women persevered, and, in what was historically a brief period, it became inconceivable to see no female faces broadcasting the news, granting loans, and training to be jet pilots at the U.S. Air Force Academy.

By the twenty-first century most young women in American were growing up in a world so greatly changed from the 1950s that for many these battles seemed like pieces of a long-ago past. But the struggle for real equality between the sexes is hardly over, for reasons suggested by the readings in this part. Although the idea of male supremacy may be on the way out in most industrialized nations, there is still, in many respects, a long way to go. Part of the problem is the stubborn persistence of sexist norms and attitudes, which, though often subtle, still shape the life chances of men and women in very different ways. And another part of the problem is that the changes in gender roles and expectations that *have* taken place have not affected all women equally.

Among the most dangerous of lingering sexist attitudes and practices are those that still promote the idea that men have the right to dominate women in intimate relationships. Despite several decades of activism and advances in the laws against domestic violence, violence against women remains a problem of massive and tragic dimensions in the United States. The "privilege" of men to abuse their spouses no longer exists in the law, but as James Ptacek argues in the article we reprint here, such abuse is still routinely justified, in a variety of ways, by the men who engage in it.

The ways in which society undermines women's chances can also be quite subtle, as Peggy Orenstein shows in "Learning Silence." Orenstein observed a California school that enjoys an exemplary curriculum. But she also found operating in the school a "hidden curriculum" that delivers unstated lessons—a "running subtext"—undermining girls' confidence in their ability to learn, especially in crucial subjects like science and math. Girls and boys are also given subtle but effective cues on how to behave in the classroom and where to locate themselves in the school's culture and social organization. Orenstein concludes that these faint but compelling lessons have the effect of teaching students their proper place in the status hierarchy of the larger society.

One of the most profound shifts in women's status in recent years has been the movement of many women into professional and high-level managerial jobs which had been largely closed to them in the past. The extent of this occupational revolution is sometimes exaggerated: among the officers of the largest 500 American corporations, for example, fewer than 16 percent were female in 2002, and only seven of those 500 companies had a female chief executive officer.[2] But the changes have been much slower when it comes to conditions in the lower-level jobs that are still disproportionately held by women—often women of color. As Pierrette Hondagneu-Sotelo shows in her description of domestic household workers in California, the women who do these jobs are typically immigrants as well. The conditions they frequently face on the job—low pay, long hours, isolation, and sometimes harsh treatment by employers—illustrate how traditional gender expectations linger even in the most 'modern' of settings.

ENDNOTES

1. Betty Friedan, *The Feminine Mystique,* New York: Norton, 1963.
2. Editorial, "Working women go it alone," *USA Today,* May 9, 2003.

CHAPTER 17

The Tactics and Strategies of Men Who Batter

JAMES PTACEK

[T]he privilege, ancient though it be, to beat her with a stick, to pull her hair, choke her, spit in her face or kick her about the floor, or to inflict upon her like indignities, is not now acknowledged by our law.
—Judge Charles Pelham, *Fulgham v. The State, 46 ALA. 146–147 (1871)*

AFFIDAVIT: Describe in detail the most recent incidents of abuse. State what happened, the dates, who did what to whom, and describe any injuries. Also describe any history of abuse.
—Instructions for obtaining a restraining order in Massachusetts Courts (MGLC209A)

One of the first laws against wife battering was passed in the Massachusetts Bay Colony in 1641 (Pleck, 1987). More a symbolic act than the beginning of criminal prosecution of batterers, the law was rarely enforced and does not seem to have survived the Revolutionary War (Pleck, 1987, 1983). In the late 1800s, a period of active political campaigns by women to increase the penalties for wife battering and rape, a series of state supreme court decisions, such as the one cited previously, established that the "privilege" of battering women no longer found legitimation in law (Pleck, 1983). In spite of these changes, another century would pass before laws against the battering of women began to be enforced with any regularity (Pleck, 1987; Lerman, 1981).

In the 1990s, after two decades of renewed feminist activism, violence by men against their intimate partners is more visible than ever before. Indeed, intimate violence has become bureaucratized; the complaint forms for restraining orders now contain the language shown in the epigraph, which indicates that while the "privilege" of men to abuse women is no longer acknowledged in the written law, the fact of its widespread occurrence is now openly conceded. In the glare of recent media attention to crimes against women, courts are now hearing the testimony of abused women in an unprecedented manner. Yet, there is already evidence of a backlash against the modest gains made by women in terms of recent legislation and much needed remedies within the criminal justice system for abused women. Ancient characterizations of women as liars and manipulators who exaggerate their suffering have assumed new forms in public discourse; some lawyers and judges claim that women are dishonestly seeking restraining orders to gain advantage in divorce cases, win child support settlements, or unfairly displace men from the marital home. Such misogynist allegations deny both the commonness and severity of violence against women in modern society (Mahoney, 1991; Ritmeester and Pence, 1992). At a 1993 forum on restraining orders sponsored by the Dorchester [Massachusetts] Bar Association, one defense attorney summed up this misogynist perspective bluntly: "Of the fifty to sixty thousand restraining orders issued, how many women get charged with perjury?"

Given the high levels of conflict inherent in the opposing views about why women seek restraining orders, it is increasingly important for researchers to understand the nature of the events that women are reporting to the courts. More specifically, both the means and the ends of intimate violence must be detailed. This chapter presents an analysis of the tactics and strategies employed by men, as reported by women in restraining order complaint forms. The term *tactics* refers to the types of violence and abuse men use against women. The term *strategies* refers to the goals of this violence and abusiveness—that is, what these men were trying to accomplish with their assaults. Essentially, this is an analysis of the motives of men who batter from the perspectives of battered women. . . .

This section examines the testimony by women on the motivation of violent intimate partners, as contained in requests for restraining orders in two Massachusetts criminal courts: the Dorchester and Quincy district courts. The Dorchester District Court serves a working-class and poor population, predominantly Black and Latino; the Quincy District Court serves a middle- and working-class population, largely White. In 1992, these were two of the busiest lower criminal courts in Massachusetts; 2,251 restraining orders were filed in the Dorchester court; 1,695 restraining orders were filed in the Quincy court (Massachusetts Trial Court, 1993). In 1992, the Dorchester court was the second highest court statewide in restraining order filings; Quincy the sixth highest court. A record high of over 53,000 requests for restraining orders were filed in Massachusetts in 1992 (Massachusetts Office for Victim Assistance, 1993).

A random sample of 100 cases filed in 1992 were selected for study; 50 cases drawn from the Dorchester District Court and 50 cases from the Quincy District Court. Every fifth case selected involved a woman seeking an order against a husband, ex-husband, boyfriend, or ex-boyfriend, beginning on the same date in each court. In Massachusetts, court records on restraining orders are officially open to the public, in recognition of "the public's general right to examine and evaluate the quality of justice done in its courts" (Massachusetts Trial Court, 1990). Qualitative and quantitative data from the original complaint forms and the court orders issued by the judges were gathered in order to construct a profile of the relationships of the women to the defendants. The women's affidavits are also part of the court files. These affidavits are written statements, signed under penalty of perjury, which women file as part of the restraining order request. In their own words, written out in longhand, women detail the range of violence and abuse that prompted them to seek court protection. . . .

THE STRATEGIES OF MEN WHO BATTER

One of the major objectives of the present research was to determine how women who seek restraining orders describe the logic of the violence and abuse used by their intimate partners. By interpreting violence in terms of strategies, this study draws from the sociology of emotions, as developed by Arlie Hochschild (1975, 1979, 1983, 1989, 1991). Two of her concepts are useful here: gender ideology and gender strategy. *Gender ideology* is a set of beliefs about men, women, and relationships—beliefs that have deep emotional anchors. As they emerge from adolescence, Hochschild claims, individuals come to embrace or identify with a set of cultural ideals about manhood and womanhood. A *gender strategy* is the attempt to implement this ideology in daily life, including the emotional preparations necessary to follow this plan of action (Hochschild, 1989). In their affidavits, women are often eloquent in their descriptions of the strategic goals of the batterers' abusiveness. While it would be necessary to talk with the men named as defendants to fully explore their gender ideologies, nevertheless these affidavits suggest outlines of the deeply held beliefs by men regarding what they are entitled to as husbands, fathers, boyfriends, and as ex-partners.

Out of the randomly selected sample of 100 cases, exactly one half of the women gave some indication of the objectives behind their partner's violence and abuse. The types of strategies described in these affidavits can be characterized as: (1) attacks on the women's attempt to leave the relationship; (2) punishment, coercion, and retaliation against the women's actions concerning children; (3) coercion or retaliation against the women's pursuit of court or police remedies; and (4) assaults upon the women's challenges to drinking behavior, to sexual entitlement, and to other dimensions of male authority. Each of these strategies is described here.

Attempts to Deny a Woman's Efforts to Separate

In a feminist critique of legal discourse on battered women, Martha R. Mahoney (1991) prescribes a new concept to describe the kinds of assaults men use to curb the autonomy of women, specifically those assaults designed to prevent women from leaving, force women to return, or retaliate against women after they have left.

Discussions of "why does she stay?" focus less on the coercive actions of the batterer than on the failures of the battered woman, Mahoney states. What is needed is a way to alter our perceptions of battering to refocus public attention on the struggle for power and control that is implicated in battering, a struggle that is only intensified when women attempt to separate themselves from violent intimate partners. Drawing from her own experience and the stories of other women who have suffered violence in relationships, Mahoney coins the new term *separation assault.*

There is a significant difference, Mahoney insists, between stating that a woman's attempt to separate "triggered" a man's violence, and saying that his violence represents an assault "on separation itself" (Mahoney, 1991: 66). The latter view highlights the strategy behind the assault: to deny women their autonomy. *Separation assault* names the violence and abuse that keep women in destructive relationships and terrorize them after they leave. Mahoney's analysis parallels that of other researchers who have examined the subjectivity of women in violent relationships (Dobash and Dobash, 1984; Gordon, 1988; Kelly, 1988). Liz Kelly (1988: 23), for instance, states that "male violence arises out of men's power and women's resistance to it." In particular, a number of researchers have found that men are often violent when women attempt to leave the relationship (Dobash and Dobash, 1984; Gordon, 1988; Wilson and Daly, 1992). Desmond Ellis (1993) and Ellis and Walter S. DeKeseredy (1989) have, for example, given particular attention to violence against separated and divorced women. Using the term *post-separation woman abuse*, Ellis associates an increased risk of violence with a woman's assertion of independence. Mahoney is concerned, however, that this term neglects attacks on the very decision to leave; she argues that these attacks on autonomy occur while women are still in relationships with their batterers. In the previous description of the relationship status of the women seeking restraining orders at Dorchester and Quincy courts, it was noted that most of the relationships have either ended or, at the very least have changed status dramatically. Mahoney's concept of "separation assault" finds substantial support in the present data. Fully 48 percent of the affidavits ($n = 24$) describe motivations that fit the kinds of attacks on the subjectivity of women that she identifies in her work. Violence and abuse aimed at *preventing women from separating* was reported by 18 percent of the women who identified the motives of their intimate partners. Women described being assaulted for attempts to get a divorce; being physically prevented from leaving abusive situations; and suffering violence and abuse for their efforts to get the batterers to leave. The following statements from court documents illustrate the kinds of testimony given by women who seek restraining orders.

> [He] has repeatedly threatened to kill me threatened to burn down my home threatened to wreck my car pushed shoved me thrown things at me, broken furniture and household items every time I have tried to discuss divorce/separation. He said he would not leave voluntarily. I would have to get a restraining order and if I did I wouldn't live to get to probate court.

> I have asked him many times to leave but every time I do he will punch me and physically abuse me.

We are like a prisoner in the home. . . . My husband told the kids that I can't get him out of there. . . . By breaking the door he is proving to me that I can't do anything.

Violence and abuse are clearly part of the plan of action for these men; in each case, the men are repeatedly attacking any movement by the women toward independence. This stifling of subjectivity is also reported by women who have left; 8 percent of the women indicated that their former partners made threats or attempts at physically *forcing them to return to the relationship.*

When we got to his car he choked me when I asked him to please leave. He also said, "If you don't stay with me I will kill you."

The defendant has said in a telephone conversation, and in person, that he would be coming to my wedding. . . . He said he would like to kidnap me and take me away.

[My estranged husband] offered me a ride home in his car. After I got into the car he tried [to force] me to have sex with him.

In another 22 percent of the cases, women reported violence and abuse in *retaliation for leaving.*

[I] have tried to end the relationship, but fearful, intimidated . . . [once he] came to my office, cried and threatened suicide if I left him. Finally, I ended it . . . and since [then] . . . threats to use any means. . . . He has a gun permit.

[He] called me at my place of employment and threatened me. He told me that if he couldn't have me, no one will and also that he wanted to "cut my heart out."

[My ex-partner] found some jewelry from my male friend. He began questioning me then started calling me dirty names. Then I asked him to leave my home—he didn't. He argued with me and threatened me, then he started choking me pushing me on the bed.

These attempts to maintain a coercive connection with women reportedly occurred even years after the relationship had ended. The following examples describe incidents between intimate partners that occurred a year or more after the couples had been separated.

[He] called my house three times saying things like he was going to beat me up and also my boyfriend.

[He] came to the window and started to threaten [my male] companion. I went out of the building to try to intervene. . . . [He] threatened bodily harm with a [piece of lumber] . . . police . . . arrived and arrested the defendant. I am now in fear of my life.

The sense that not only marriage, but even a past dating relationship entitles these men to possess or control the women is apparent throughout these accounts. Adrienne Rich describes this kind of gender ideology as follows:

> It would seem that a man experiences the violation of some profound "right" when a woman leaves him: the "right" to her services, however lacking in mutuality the relationship. Through patriarchal socialization, men learn to think in terms of their "rights" where rights are not actually the issue: in areas like sexual behavior, maternal behavior, which are seen, not as springing from a woman's choice and affections but as behavior to which a man is entitled *as a male* (Rich, 1979: 220).

Rich identifies "father-right" and "husband-right" as forms of this entitlement. In the violent relationships encountered throughout the restraining order documents, this entitlement appears to have been extended to include both cohabiting and dating relationships. There now seems to be a belief in "boyfriend-right" even "ex-boyfriend-right" and "ex-husband-right."

Women who demonstrate independence or who are no longer willing to remain with these men are, according to the affidavits, verbally degraded: They are called "whores," "bitches," and other misogynist names. These sexually demeaning terms serve to transform and dehumanize women in the minds of these men. Such "transformations" are a common practice among men to avoid dealing with women as peers (Astrachan, 1986). Such verbal assaults also serve as emotional preparation for further attacks on women, just as the use of the term *gook* by U.S. troops in Vietnam facilitated violence against Vietnamese soldiers and civilians (Lifton, 1992).

Mahoney (1991: 68) argues that separation violence represents "the main reason women seek protective orders." Taken together, attacks and abuse aimed at preventing any separation by these women, forcing the women to return, or retaliating after they leave are described in nearly half (48 percent) of the affidavits that recount strategies on the part of the intimate partner. The evidence from this investigation supports Mahoney's assessment. While previous research on restraining orders has not identified the motives of violent men, the findings from the present study are consistent with research showing that many women face increased danger following separation (Browne, 1987; Ellis, 1992; Sonkin, Martin, and Walker, 1985).

Punishment, Coercion, and Retaliation Concerning Children

Motherhood profoundly affects the experiences of violence and abuse, Mahoney argues. Yet both the law and much feminist legal theory, she claims, assume "that women with children are individual actors" (Mahoney, 1991: 19). A mother's connections with her children are "existential, social and extremely practical," Mahoney states; "in many significant ways—our 'selves' simply are not single" (Mahoney, 1991: 20). Of the 100 randomly selected cases in the present study, over three-quarters ($n = 76$) of the women were mothers. Underscoring the relevance of motherhood to violence and abuse, 7 percent of the women describe violence and abuse suffered while they were pregnant. One woman reported being assaulted while holding her baby in her arms. Eleven percent of the women detailed physical abuse, sexual abuse, or threats directed against children, while 5 percent were threatened with the potential kidnapping of their children. The situational circumstances of the abuse are also relevant to children, especially when women are not living with the fathers of their children. In 9 percent of the cases, women reported violence or abuse taking place during those times when they were either dropping the children off with their fathers or picking the children up from their fathers.

In the 22 percent (n = 11) of the affidavits in which goals were indicated, the women described the violence and abuse as centering on the parental authority or responsibilities of the abusive partner. Eight percent of the women described their abuse as *punishment for questioning men's authority over the children,* as shown in these accounts:

> He then became extremely abusive after I told him that I didn't like his language and how he was treating my daughter—with his language. . . . He then kicked her. . . . I was also physically abused.

> [He] called our [daughter] names. . . . I asked him to stop because she started to cry and got scared. . . . He then went into our bedroom and started to smash things. All our pictures of the children, lights. . . . When he was doing this all he was screaming. Terrible dirty dirty words to me.

From these descriptions, there seems to be an expectation on the part of the men that their authority as fathers should not have been questioned, regardless of how abusive they had become. These men seemed to be saying that women, whether as wives or unmarried partners, ought to defer to the rights of men as fathers.

Threats and violence aimed at *coercing custody and child care decisions* were reported in another 8 percent of the women's affidavits.

> He said he would get someone to kill me and make it look like an accident so he could get custody of our son.

> Threatened to kill me if I was going to try to take his daughter away from him. He also stated that if he was to go and take her from where ever she is, no one will be able to stop him even if he has to hurt them.

> He got furious and threatened to kill me if I send her to a day care [instead of having him baby sit the child]. . . . He said if I got a restraining order, the police won't be here all the time, and he can kill me then.

These threats against women and their children represent another kind of assault on the autonomy of women. From the perspectives of these three men, father-right is not incompatible with criminal threats and cruelty toward mothers and their own children.

Another dimension of father-right is expressed in the violence and threats by the men in *retaliation for women seeking child support.* This strategy was detailed in 6 percent of the women's statements.

> The defendant . . . and myself engaged in a very heated argument about financial support for our child. . . . As a result he became very violent striking me in the head with his closed fist, also attempting to strangle me.

> [He] called to tell me he was sending court papers to _____ court regarding child support. [He] does not want to pay child support because he doesn't see my [child]. Then . . . he called back and told me I would be hurt very soon. . . . He then called [a third time] and told me he would be at my house [within minutes]. I called the police.

If unquestioned authority over children is one dimension of father-right, another expression of it is a refusal to accept material obligations toward one's children. This is a common means of expressing hostility toward women for separation. The severity of the threats and violence in these cases indicates the level of bitterness and desperation among some men at losing their relationships. Here again, separation is not really a solution for these women, but rather shifts the ground in a continuing power struggle to matters involving their children. Batterers' counseling programs have long understood that estranged fathers will often use children as weapons against their former wives or partners. This is a central theme of the Duluth Domestic Abuse Intervention Project's work with batterers (Pence and Paymar, 1986; Paymar, 1993). Emerge, the Boston area batterers' counseling and education program, has developed a checklist for their work with men that identifies thirty-four violent and controlling behaviors towards children (Emerge, n.d.).

Retaliation and Coercion Concerning Court and Police Actions

In 12 percent ($n = 6$) of the accounts of motives, women testified that the violence or abuse was related to legal actions that they had taken besides those involving custody and child support. These actions against which men retaliated included calling the police; being somehow responsible, in men's eyes, for convictions and sentences for rape; and taking out restraining orders that lead to convictions and sentences for violating the orders. Here are several examples of the women's testimony.

> Kicked me in my back. Hit me in the back of my head. Threatening to get a gun and shoot because I called the police.

> He thought I called the police (I have called them in the past) and he grabbed me, dragged me by my hair into the kitchen and threatened to kill me. He has repeatedly threatened to kill me and threatened me with kitchen knives.

> He was released [from prison four days ago] since then I have been receiving crank calls all times of the night . . . stating that I will not get away with this he will pay me back.

[He] came into my home and physically abused me. . . . [He] just got out of jail [three days before] for violating a restraining order. . . . [He] told me several times [that night] that he's going to kill me.

This testimony frames the dilemma of legal intervention in the starkest terms: These are nightmare stories. They represent the terror that the legal system will only make matters worse. Among other goals of their violence, these men are seeking *vengeance against women for being held accountable to the law.* The men act as if the privacy of the home ought to protect their privileges, including the right to abuse women, and that any breach of this protective cloak represents a betrayal that merits retaliation.

Two other affidavits identified *retaliation and coercion regarding divorce* as strategies.

[He] has put me in fear and is behaving aggressively with abusive language over the phone [and] when he returns children to me. He is especially angry over the recent court orders for me to have exclusive use and occupancy of our marital home. . . .

[He] told me he wants a divorce but he wasn't going to move out and if I don't get it . . . he'll make me wish I had. . . . My husband has threatened me and threatened to destroy my property and my job. . . . My husband believes in payback. Please help me.

This kind of disregard for the law and the courts produces extraordinary fear and despair in women. When Judge Albert Kramer, former presiding justice at Quincy District Court testified at a public hearing about batterers' defiance of the law, he made the following observations about batterers who came before the bench:

[W]hen we are dealing with batterers and perpetrators of domestic violence, more than any other violent offender, they are the most dangerous and with them you have the most potential for harm. . . . There is no other group of perpetrators of violence that is more tenaciously resistant to court orders and court efforts to curb their violence and prevent their almost relentless pursuit of their victims (Kramer, 1992b).

The "ancient privileges" of husband-right and father-right—along with their modern equivalents as boyfriend-right and ex-partner-right—represent for many men a more compelling moral order than that symbolized by the courts. How well the courts are negating these patriarchal privileges is the focus of much recent research (Buzawa and Buzawa, 1992, 1993; Gondolf, 1992; Harrell et al., 1993; Hilton, 1993; Klein, 1994; Knudsen and Miller, 1991; Steinman, 1991; Viano, 1992).

Retaliation for Other Perceived Challenges to Male Authority

In 12 percent ($n = 6$) of the affidavits, women recount how the violence and abuse converged on two matters deemed essential by some men to the fulfillment of masculinity in the United States: drinking and sexuality. In one-quarter ($n = 25$) of the 100 restraining order complaint forms, women described their abusers as drinking, drunk, or involved with drugs and alcohol. But alcohol or drugs do not supply strategies in themselves, in the sense of the goals of violence and abuse by men. Rather, alcohol figures into these goals when the drinking behavior meets intolerance. In 6 percent of the complaint forms, women noted that they were abused after raising the issue of drinking behavior with their partners. The goal of this violence and abuse appears to be, at least in part, the men's *defense of their prerogative to get drunk at will,* regardless of the consequences.

> When I was five months pregnant we had an argument over how he's an alcoholic and how he's treated me. I was trying to tell him that he needs help. He got real angry and started pushing me. . . . He grabbed me and pushed me down hard into the [furniture]. . . . I spent the night in the hospital . . . he knows he hurts me, he knows I suffer. He does it deliberately.

> [I] questioned the defendant about his drinking because he's not supposed to be drinking, he's on probation. The defendant got angry and gestured with a beer bottle. . . . The police came because someone had called—he had been yelling and punching.

The guiding premises of this kind of violence would seem to be that men have the inviolable right to drink, along with the license to act irresponsibly, which drinking provides. Notions that battering is mostly drunken, "impulsive" violence, however, do not account for the routinized, repetitious nature of a man's drinking behavior, nor for the defense of this behavior when the perpetrator knows the consequences of his behavior for others.

The sexual entitlement and possessiveness of men has already been addressed with respect to separation assault. Beyond these assaults on women who attempt to separate from violent partners, there are additional strategies related to the men's belief in nonreciprocal sexual "rights." Two affidavits recount *assaults on a woman's questioning of a man's affairs.*

> [My husband] was drunk and I caught him talking on the phone with his girlfriend that he has. And I started yelling at him so he hit me and I left. . . . I'm afraid he'll kill me.

> [My husband] is and has been having extra marital affairs with another woman. This morning he threatened to hit me when I notified him that I knew about his affair.

The familiar double standard appears to be operating in these cases: Not only are men entitled to nonreciprocated sexual latitude, but women are not even allowed to bring it up.

Another woman reported her husband's *jealous verbal attacks and extreme possessiveness.*

> [H]e accused me of sleeping with my daughter's boyfriend. . . . I was called a whore and a bitch and the angry hurtful words just kept on [for the past five months]. . . . I am a grown woman and I am not allowed to speak to a male or even say hello unless it's someone he associates with.

Accusations that a woman is secretly sleeping around represent more than a feeling of jealousy; such accusations represent the abusive man's strategy, based on deeply felt entitlements, to circumscribe a woman's social life and make her negotiate the world outside the family household only through him.

Lastly, there is a residual group of affidavits in which women named revenge as a goal without further specification.

> [He called and said] he is sick of the way things are going and that he was going to meet me on my job and take care of me. . . . [Later] He grabbed me and, putting his hand on his gun, told me that he would "blow my goddamn brains out." . . . [I] phoned the police.

> [He] began calling my home making threats against my life "I will kill you." . . . [The next day] he came to my door. I did not open it, he started screaming that he would get me one way or the other. He also screamed many vulgar statements and then drove away.

Neither of these were isolated incidents, according to the accounts; they were part of a pattern of similarly threatening acts by these men.

Threats to kill a woman, made repeatedly over a period of weeks or months, are a form of psychological torture (Herman, 1992; Romero, 1985; Russell, 1990; Tifft, 1993). Again, threats to kill were reported in 24 percent of the sample of 100 cases. The parallels between the tactics used against battered women and the means of torture used against political prisoners have prompted some feminist researchers and activists to call woman battering a violation of international human rights (Schuler, 1992; Bunch and Carrillo, 1991; Carrillo, 1992; Chapman, 1990).

Table 17.1 summarizes the types of strategies described in the sworn statements by women. The gender ideologies of many of the men depicted in these accounts appear to be held with extraordinary tenacity, self-righteousness, and depth of feeling. There is additional evidence that as a group, the men appearing in these restraining order files have histories of being violent and of being charged with both violent and nonviolent crimes. While criminal records of the men named as defendants in these orders were not obtained, a recent study of 644 restraining orders at

TABLE 17.1 Men's Strategies Reported in Affidavits of 50 Women

	n	%
Separation assault	24	48%
Punishment, coercion, and retaliation concerning children	11	22
Retaliation or coercion regarding women's legal action	6	12
Retaliation against other perceived challenges to men's authority		
In response to challenges to his drinking behavior	3	6
In response to questions regarding his relationship with other women	2	4
In response to actions arousing his jealousy	1	2
Unspecified vengeance	3	6
	50	100%

Quincy District Court (Klein, 1994) found that 78 percent of the men named as defendants had a previous record of criminal complaints; 43 percent had records of violent crimes against persons. The average number of prior criminal complaints was 13. On a statewide basis, a study found that nearly 80 percent of the first 8,500 men identified in restraining orders had prior criminal records (Cochran, 1992).

There are two important implications of these findings. First, a large number of these men have what Cardarelli (personal communication, 1994) calls a "proficiency" at being violent. In comparison to the women who are or were their wives or partners, violence is a well-rehearsed tactic of control, rehearsed both physically and also in terms of the emotional preparation for acting violently. If a man has been arrested for assault and battery on another man, his partner likely knows this. This colors the negotiations between them, whether or not they live together. A threat by this man that he will kill her has credibility. Even when a man's criminal record is for nonviolent offenses, such as drunk driving or drug possession, threats to physically harm a woman may draw power from this other evidence of lawlessness. While the incompleteness of these court documents must be kept in mind, both the testimony of the women and the research associated with restraining orders in Massachusetts provide ample reason for high levels of fear on the part of women who seek restraining orders.

SUMMARY

Violence against women by intimate partners persists as a widespread social phenomenon, despite the development of new resources, the creation of laws prohibiting it, and the remedies available to women from the courts. Sylvia Walby (1989, 1990) states that the patterning of violence against women represents a distinct social structure. She makes her argument based on the ritualized forms that this violence assumes; the common availability of violence as a resource for men; the routine consequences violence has on women's lives; and the traditional reluctance of the state to intervene.

The personal accounts of women seeking restraining orders in two of the busiest courts in Massachusetts provide a unique sketch of the kinds of violence and abuse to which these women are subjected by their intimate partners. Contradicting the popular image of battered women who seek restraining orders, the present research found the number of women living apart from their abusive partners to far outnumber those living with such partners. An examination of the affidavits of these women reveals a variety of physical, sexual, psychological, and economic tactics used by abusive men, most of which are criminal in nature. The women's testimony in these affidavits gives rise to four main themes derived from the kinds of strategies that motivated their partner's violence and abuse. First, nearly half of the incidents correspond to the definition of separation assault previously discussed where violence is used either to prevent separation, to coerce a return, or to retaliate for departure (Mahoney, 1991). The remaining themes revolve around strategies aimed at asserting their rights as fathers; reacting to legal actions pursued by the women; and finally, violence directed to any perceived challenge to male authority.

The consequences of battering identified in these documents include not only physical injuries to both women and their children, but also the terror of being threatened with murder, destruction of property, economic losses, and the disruption of being forced to leave home. Violence also colors what Dobash and Dobash (1978, 1979: 127–133) call the "negotiation of daily life," the discussion and allocation of money, time, and other resources in family households. These are resources over which men generally have greater control. Given the inferior position of women in the paid labor force and their greater responsibility for their children, women must negotiate for these resources from a subordinate position. What the affidavits used in the present research show is that after separation or even divorce, women are often still forced to negotiate child support, child custody decisions, and visitation under threats of violence. The term *domestic violence*, therefore, loses meaning when the web of fear and terror is spread this widely.

The evidence from these 100 restraining order case files challenges claims that the increase in restraining orders is the result of attempts by women to gain leverage in divorce settlements, win battles over child support, or claim the marital home. Half of the women seeking restraining orders in the present study were not married to their defendants; thus, they were unable to seek any advantages associated with divorce. In addition, the majority of women with children did not request child support as part of the restraining order, and most who did request such support did not receive it. Advocates for battered women volunteering at these courts report that women with children are often too afraid to ask for child support. Furthermore, since most women seeking orders are not living with the defendants, most are not even seeking to have a man removed from their home.

What women are asking for is an end to violence, terror, and harassment aimed at limiting their autonomy. More than 120 years after Judge Pelham condemned the practice of men beating women with objects, pulling women by the hair, choking them, spitting in their faces, and kicking them, these identical practices were found in a random sample of 100 restraining order files. The testimony of the women in these affidavits frames the question "What are the best ways to support the moves by women toward independence and break the ancient, yet modern, control that batterers exercise over their lives?"

REFERENCES

Browne, A. (1987). *When battered women kill.* New York: Macmillan/Free Press.

Bunch, C., & Carillo, R. (1991). *Gender violence: A development and human rights issue.* New Brunswick, NJ: Center for Women's Global Leadership, Douglass College, Rutgers University.

Buzawa, E. S., & Buzawa, C. G. (1990). *Domestic violence: The criminal justice response.* Newbury Park, CA: Sage.

——— (1992). *Domestic violence: The changing criminal justice response.* Westport, CT: Auburn House.

——— (1993). The impact of arrest on domestic assault. Special issue of the *American Behavioral Scientist, 36*(5).

Carillo, R. (1992). *Battered dreams: Violence against women as an obstacle to development.* New York: UNIFEM/United Nations Development Fund for Women.

Chapman, J. R. (1990). Violence against women as a violation of human rights. *Social Justice, 17*(2): 54–70.

Cochran, D. (1992). *Over 8500 domestic restraining orders filed since September in Massachusetts.* Boston: Office of the Commissioner of Probation.

Dobash, R. E., & Dobash, R. P. (1978). *The negotiation of daily life and the "provocation" of violence: A patriarchal concept in support of the wife beater.* Paper presented at the 9th World Congress of Sociology, Uppsala, Sweden.

——— (1979). *Violence against wives: A case against the patriarchy.* New York: Free Press.

——— (1984). The nature and antecedents of violent events. *British Journal of Criminology, 24*(3): 269–288.

Ellis, D. (1992). Woman abuse among separated and divorced women: The relevance of social support. In E. C. Viano (Ed.), *Intimate violence: Interdisciplinary perspectives* (pp. 177–189). Washington, DC: Hemisphere.

Ellis, D., & DeKeseredy, W. S. (1989). Marital status and woman abuse: The DAD model. *International Journal of Sociology of the Family, 19:* 67–87.

Emerge. (n.d.). *Violent and controlling behavior toward children.* Checklist available from Emerge: A counseling and educational program for abusive men, 18 Hurley Street, Cambridge, MA 02141.

Gondolf, E. W. (1992). *Court response to "protection from abuse" petitions.* Unpublished paper available from the author at the Mid-Atlantic Addiction Training Institute, Indiana University of Pennsylvania, Indiana, PA 15705.

Gordon, L. (1988). *Heroes of their own lives: The politics and history of family violence, Boston 1880–1960.* New York: Viking.

Harrell, A., Smith, B., & Newmark, L. (1993, May). *Court processing and the effects of restraining orders for domestic violence victims.* Washington, DC: The Urban Institute.

Hilton, N. Z. (Ed.). (1993). *Legal responses to wife assault.* Newbury Park, CA: Sage.

Hochschild, A. R. (1975). The sociology of feeling and emotion: Selected possibilities. In M. Millman & R. M. Kanter (Eds.), *Another voice: Feminist perspectives on social life and social science* (pp. 280–307). Garden City, NY: Anchor Books.

——— (1979). Emotion work, feeling rules, and social structure. *American Journal of Sociology, 85*(3): 551–575.

——— (1983). *The managed heart: Commercialization of human feeling.* Berkeley: University of California Press.

——— (1991). The economy of gratitude. In M. Hutter (Ed.), *The family experience: A reader in cultural diversity* (pp. 499–515). New York: Macmillan.

Hochschild, A. R., & Machung, A. (1989). *The second shift: Working parents and the revolution at home.* New York: Viking.

Kelly, L. (1988a). How women define their experiences of violence. In K. Yllŏ & M. Bograd (Eds.), *Feminist perspectives on wife abuse* (pp. 114–132). Newbury Park, CA: Sage.

——— (1988b). *Surviving sexual violence.* Minneapolis: University of Minnesota Press.

Klein, A. (1994). *Recidivism in a population of court-restrained batterers after two years.* Unpublished dissertation, Northeastern University.

Knudsen, D. D., & Miller, J. (Eds.). (1991). *Abused and battered: Social and legal responses to family violence.* New York: Aldine de Gruyter.

Kramer, A. L. (1992a). Statement to the Massachusetts joint committee on the judiciary: Written testimony. Quincy, MA: Quincy District Court.

——— (1992b). Statement to the women's legislative caucus hearing on domestic violence, March 2: Oral testimony. Quincy, MA: Quincy Districy Court.

Lerman, L. (1981). Criminal prosecution of wife beaters. *Response to Violence in the Family, 4*(3): 1–19.

Lifton, R. J. (1992). *Home from the war: Learning from Vietnam veterans.* Boston: Beacon Press.

Mahoney, M. R. (1991). Legal images of battered women: Redefining the issue of separation. *Michigan Law Review, 1:* 43–49.

Massachusetts Office for Victim Assistance. (1993, May). *A guide to domestic violence court advocacy in Massachusetts.* Massachusetts Office for Victim Assistance, Boston.

Massachusetts Trial Court. (1993). *Interim annual report, 1992.* Office of the Chief Administrative Justice, Massachusetts Trial Court.

Paymar, M. (1993). *Violent no more: Helping men end domestic abuse.* Alameda, CA: Hunter House.

Pence, E., & Paymar, M. (1986). *Power and control: Tactics of men who batter.* Minnesota Program Development, Inc., Duluth, MN.

Pleck, E. (1983). Feminist responses to "crimes against women," 1868–1896. *Signs, 8*(3): 451–470.

——— (1987). *Domestic tyranny: The making of American social policy against family violence from colonial times to the present.* New York: Oxford University Press.

Romero, M. (1985). A comparison between strategies used on prisoners of war and battered wives. *Sex Roles, 13:* 537–547.

Russell, D. E. H. (1982). *Rape in marriage.* New York: Macmillan.

——— (1990). *Rape in marriage* (rev. ed.). Bloomington: Indiana University Press.

Schuler, M. (Ed.). (1992). *Freedom from violence: Women's strategies from around the world.* New York: OEF International/UNIFEM.

Sonkin, D. J., Martin, D., & Walker, L. E. A. (Eds.). (1985). *The male batterer: A treatment approach.* New York: Springer.

Steinman, M. (1991). Coordinated criminal justice interventions and recidivism among batterers. In M. Steinman (Ed.), *Women battering: Policy responses* (pp. 221–236). Cincinnati: Anderson.

Tifft, L. L. (1993). *Battering of women: The failure of intervention and the case for prevention.* Boulder, CO: Westview Press.

Viano, E. C. (Ed.). (1992). *Intimate violence: Interdisciplinary perspectives.* Washington, DC: Hemisphere.

Walby, S. (1989). Theorizing patriarchy. *Sociology, 23*(2): 213–234.

——— (1990). *Theorizing patriarchy.* Oxford: Basil Blackwell.

Wilson, M. I., & Daly, M. (1992). Who kills whom in spouse killings? On the exceptional sex ratio of spousal homicides in the United States. *Criminology, 30*(2): 189–215.

CHAPTER 18

Learning Silence

PEGGY ORENSTEIN

Weston, California, sits at the far reaches of the San Francisco Bay Area. The drive from the city takes one through a series of bedroom communities, carefully planned idylls in which, as the miles roll by, the tax brackets leap upward, the politics swing right, and the people fade to white. But Weston is different: once an oddly matched blend of country folk and chemical plant workers, this is an old town, the kind of place where people still gather curbside under the bunting-swathed lampposts of Maple Street to watch the Fourth of July parade. Many of the businesses in Weston's center—doughnut shops, ladies' clothing stores, a few hard drinkers' bars, and picked-over antiquaries—haven't changed hands in over thirty years. There are a few fern bars and one café serving espresso here, but if people want high tone, they go to the city.

Not that Weston has remained suspended in time. The ramshackle houses downtown may still be populated by the families of mechanics, plant workers, and, in shoddy apartment complexes, a small community of working poor, but the hills that ring the town's edge have been gobbled up by tract homes where young professionals have hunkered down—a safe distance from urban ills—to raise their children. There's even a clean, modern supermarket by the freeway, built expressly for the new suburbanites, with a multiplex cinema across the street for their occasional evenings out.

The only place where Weston's two populations converge regularly is at Weston Middle School, a crumbling Spanish-style edifice just up the street from the post office, city hall, and, more important to the student body, a McDonald's. This is the town's sole middle school, and as such, it serves nearly nine hundred students a year from this disparate population. The bumper stickers on the cars dropping off the children reflect the mix: Toyota vans advertising the local NPR affiliate pull up behind rusty pickups that proclaim: "My wife said if I buy another gun she'll divorce me; God, I'll miss her!" There is also a staunch Christian population here—Mormons, Seventh-Day Adventists, and other, less austere sects whose cars remind other residents that "Jesus Loves You!"

In recent years, Weston Middle School has fulfilled its mandate well: the school entrance is draped with a "California Distinguished School" banner, earned last year by the students' estimable standardized test scores as well as the staff's exemplary performance. The teachers are an impressive, enthusiastic group who routinely seek methods of instruction that will inspire a little more engagement, a little more effort on the part of their pupils: an eighth-grade history teacher uses a karaoke microphone to juice up his lessons; an English teacher videotapes students performing original poems to bring literature to life; a science teacher offers extra credit to students who join him in cleaning up the banks of a local river. There is also some concern about gender issues in education: Weston's history teachers have embraced the new, more inclusive textbooks adopted by the state of California; in English, students write essays on their views about abortion and read, among other books, *Streams to the River, River to the Sea,* a historical novel which recasts Sacagawea as an intrepid female hero.

Yet the overt curriculum, as fine as it may be, is never the only force operating in a classroom. There is something else as well. The "hidden curriculum" comprises the unstated lessons that students learn in school: it is the running subtext through which teachers communicate behavioral norms and individual status in the school culture, the process of socialization that cues children into their place in the hierarchy of larger society. Once used to describe the ways in which the education system works to reproduce class systems in our culture, the "hidden curriculum" has recently been applied to the ways in which schools help reinforce gender roles, whether they intend to or not.

THE DAILY GRIND: LESSONS IN THE HIDDEN CURRICULUM

Amy Wilkinson has looked forward to being an eighth grader forever—at least for the last two years, which, when you're thirteen, seems like the same thing. By the second week of September she's settled comfortably into her role as one of the school's reigning elite. Each morning before class, she lounges with a group of about twenty other eighth-grade girls and boys in the most visible spot on campus: at the base of the schoolyard, between one of the portable classrooms that was constructed in the late 1970s and the old oak tree in the overflow parking lot. The group trades gossip, flirts, or simply stands around, basking in its own importance and killing time before the morning bell.

At 8:15 on Tuesday the crowd has already convened, and Amy is standing among a knot of girls, laughing. She is fuller-figured than she'd like to be, wide-hipped and heavy-limbed with curly, blond hair, cornflower-blue eyes, and a sharply up-turned nose. With the help of her mother, who is a drama coach, she has become the school's star actress: last year she played Eliza in Weston's production of *My Fair Lady.* Although she earns solid grades in all of her subjects—she'll make the honor roll this fall—drama is her passion, she says, because "I love entertaining people, and I love putting on characters."

Also, no doubt, because she loves the spotlight: this morning, when she mentions a boy I haven't met, Amy turns, puts her hands on her hips, anchors her feet shoulder width apart, and bellows across the schoolyard, "Greg! Get over here! You have to meet Peggy."

She smiles wryly as Greg, looking startled, begins to make his way across the schoolyard for an introduction. "I'm not exactly shy," she says, her hands still on her hips. "I'm *bold.*"

Amy is bold. And brassy, and strong-willed. Like any teenager, she tries on and discards different selves as if they were so many pairs of Girbaud jeans, searching ruthlessly for a perfect fit. During a morning chat just before the school year began, she told me that her parents tried to coach her on how to respond to my questions. "They told me to tell you that they want me to be my own person," she complained. "My mother *told* me to tell you that. I do want to be my own person, but it's like, you're interviewing me about who I am and she's telling me what to say—that's not my own person, is it?"

When the morning bell rings, Amy and her friends cut off their conversations, scoop up their books, and jostle toward the school's entrance. Inside, Weston's hallways smell chalky, papery, and a little sweaty from gym class. The wood-railed staircases at either end of the two-story main building are worn thin in the middle from the scuffle of hundreds of pairs of sneakers pounding them at forty-eight-minute intervals for nearly seventy-five years. Amy's mother, Sharon, and her grandmother both attended this school. So will her two younger sisters. Her father, a mechanic who works on big rigs, is a more recent Weston recruit: he grew up in Georgia and came here after he and Sharon were married.

Amy grabs my hand, pulling me along like a small child or a slightly addled new student: within three minutes we have threaded our way through the dull-yellow hallways to her locker and then upstairs to room 238, Mrs. Richter's math class.

The twenty-two students that stream through the door with us run the gamut of physical maturity. Some of the boys are as small and compact as fourth graders, their legs sticking out of their shorts like pipe cleaners. A few are trapped in the agony of a growth spurt, and still others cultivate downy beards. The girls' physiques are less extreme: most are nearly their full height, and all but a few have already weathered the brunt of puberty. They wear topknots or ponytails, and their shirts are tucked neatly into their jeans.

Mrs. Richter, a ruddy, athletic woman with a powerful voice, has arranged the chairs in a three-sided square, two rows deep. Amy walks to the far side of the room and, as she takes her seat, falls into a typically feminine pose: she crosses her legs, folds her arms across her chest, and hunches forward toward her desk, seeming to shrink into herself. The sauciness of the playground disappears, and, in fact, she says hardly a word during class. Meanwhile, the boys, especially those who are more physically mature, sprawl in their chairs, stretching their legs long, expanding into the available space.

Nate, a gawky, sanguine boy who has shaved his head except for a small thatch that's hidden under an Oakland A's cap, leans his chair back on two legs and, although the bell has already rung, begins a noisy conversation with his friend Kyle.

Mrs. Richter turns to him, "What's all the discussion about, Nate?" she asks.

"*He's* talking to *me*," Nate answers, pointing to Kyle. Mrs. Richter writes Nate's name on the chalkboard as a warning toward detention and he yells out in protest. They begin to quibble over the justice of her decision, their first—but certainly not their last—power struggle of the day. As they argue, Allison, a tall, angular girl who once told me, "My goal is to be the best wife and mother I can be," raises her hand to ask a question. Mrs. Richter, finishing up with Nate, doesn't notice.

"Get your homework out, everyone!" the teacher booms, and walks among the students, checking to make sure no one has shirked on her or his assignment. Allison, who sits in the front row nearest both the blackboard and the teacher, waits patiently for another moment, then, realizing she's not getting results, puts her hand down. When Mrs. Richter walks toward her, Allison tries another tack, calling out her question. Still, she gets no response, so she gives up.

As a homework assignment, the students have divided their papers into one hundred squares, color-coding each square prime or composite—prime being those numbers which are divisible only by one and themselves, and composite being everything else. Mrs. Richter asks them to call out the prime numbers they've found, starting with the tens.

Nate is the first to shout, "Eleven!" The rest of the class chimes in a second later. As they move through the twenties and thirties, Nate, Kyle, and Kevin, who sit near one another at the back of the class, call out louder and louder, casually competing for both quickest response and the highest decibel level. Mrs. Richter lets the boys' behavior slide, although they are intimidating other students.

"Okay," Mrs. Richter says when they've reached one hundred. "Now, what do you think of one hundred and three? Prime or composite?"

Kyle, who is skinny and a little pop-eyed, yells out, "Prime!" but Mrs. Richter turns away from him to give someone else a turn. Unlike Allison, who gave up when she was ignored, Kyle isn't willing to cede his teacher's attention. He begins to bounce in his chair and chant, "*Prime! Prime! Prime!*" Then, when he turns out to be right, he rebukes the teacher, saying, "*See,* I told you."

When the girls in Mrs. Richter's class do speak, they follow the rules. When Allison has another question, she raises her hand again and waits her turn; this time, the teacher responds. When Amy volunteers her sole answer of the period, she raises her hand, too. She gives the wrong answer to an easy multiplication problem, turns crimson, and flips her head forward so her hair falls over her face.

Occasionally, the girls shout out answers, but generally they are to the easiest, lowest-risk questions, such as the factors of four or six. And their stabs at public recognition depend on the boys' largesse: when the girls venture responses to more complex questions the boys quickly become territorial, shouting them down with their own answers. Nate and Kyle are particularly adept at overpowering Renee, who, I've been told by the teacher, is the brightest girl in the class. (On a subsequent visit, I will see her lay her head on her desk when Nate overwhelms her and mutter, "I hate this class.")

Mrs. Richter doesn't say anything to condone the boys' aggressiveness, but she doesn't have to: they insist on—and receive—her attention even when she consciously tries to shift it elsewhere in order to make the class more equitable.

After the previous day's homework is corrected, Mrs. Richter begins a new lesson, on the use of exponents.

"What does three to the third power mean?" she asks the class.

"*I know!*" shouts Kyle.

Instead of calling on Kyle, who has already answered more than his share of questions, the teacher turns to Dawn, a somewhat more voluble girl who has plucked her eyebrows down to a few hairs.

"Do you know, Dawn?"

Dawn hesitates, and begins "Well, you count the number of threes and . . . "

"*But I know!*" interrupts Kyle. "*I know!*"

Mrs. Richter deliberately ignores him, but Dawn is rattled: she never finishes her sentence, she just stops.

"*I know! ME!*" Kyle shouts again, and then before Dawn recovers herself he blurts, "*It's three times three times three!*"

At this point, Mrs. Richter gives in. She turns away from Dawn, who is staring blankly, and nods at Kyle. "Yes," she says. "Three times three times three. Does everyone get it?"

"*YES!*" shouts Kyle; Dawn says nothing.

Mrs. Richter picks up the chalk. "Let's do some others," she says.

"Let me!" says Kyle.

"I'll pick on whoever raises their hand," she tells him.

Nate, Kyle, and two other boys immediately shoot up their hands, fingers squeezed tight and straight in what looks like a salute.

"Don't you want to wait and hear the problem first?" she asks, laughing.

They drop their hands briefly. She writes 8^4 on the board. "Okay, what would that look like written out?"

Although a third of the class raises their hands to answer—including a number of students who haven't yet said a word—she calls on Kyle anyway.

"Eight times eight times eight times eight," he says triumphantly, as the other students drop their hands.

When the bell rings, I ask Amy about the mistake she made in class and the embarrassment it caused her. She blushes again.

"Oh yeah," she says. "That's about the only time I ever talked in there. I'll never do that again."

BAD CHEMISTRY: "GUYS LIKE IT WHEN YOU ACT ALL HELPLESS"

It is another late-fall morning under the oak tree at Weston. Amy, Becca, and Evie huddle together slightly apart from the other students, the intimate turn to their shoulders making it clear that they're exchanging the juiciest gossip. A squadron of seventh-grade boys on bicycles zips by and the girls look up, annoyed, sidling to the left to avoid being hit.

A few seconds later, Becca, usually the most reserved of her friends, shrieks.

"*Get that away from me!*"

The bikers are forgotten as the girls scatter, screaming, their faces flushed, revealing Carl Ross, a boy from Evie's math class, whose feet are firmly planted where the girls once stood. An uncapped jar labeled "Felicia" dangles from his left hand. Until a minute ago, it held a large spider he'd captured for extra credit in science class. Felicia is currently hanging from a dead pine needle in his other hand, her legs tucked in and body contracted in fear.

Becca runs about ten feet and turns around. When she smiles, she reveals a mouth full of braces. "I'm *deathly* afraid of spiders," she says, her eyes shining as she looks back at her tormentor.

The other two girls run up to her. "God, me too!" Amy says breathlessly, clutching her friend's arms. "When I saw *Arachnophobia* my dad had to go check my room for me. He had to look under the bed!"

Evie's cheeks are pink and her dark hair is falling from its bun. She tucks the wayward wisps back in place as a second boy lets the bug drop from his finger by a lengthening strand of web. "Yuck, how disgusting," she says, widening her eyes. "I hope he doesn't come near me with that."

As a woman standing among these girls, I wasn't sure how to react. I desperately wanted them to stand up to the boys who increasingly joined in the game. I wanted them to be brave, to marvel at the spider's jewel-green body, to ask for a turn at holding it and watching it try to spin its escape. But I felt the pressure too: a real girl, a girl who wants a boy to like her, runs screaming from spiders. The more she likes a boy, the more she allows him to terrorize her, and the more helpless she pretends to be. Showing any real interest in spiders would've been imprudent for the girls, a denial of their newly important femininity. During my year at Weston, I saw girls run from spiders innumerable times; with each flight toward traditional femininity, I thought about who has permission, who has the right in our culture, to explore the natural world, to get dirty and muddy, to think spiders and worms and frogs are neat, to bring them in for extra credit in science. In fact, to be engaged in science at all.

"I'm not *really* afraid of that stuff, except snakes and blood," Amy admits later, after the hoopla. "But guys like it if you act all helpless and girly, so you do."

As with math, there is a circular relationship among girls' affection for science, their self-esteem, and their career plans. But unlike in math, the achievement gap between girls and boys in science is actually widening: the National Assessment of Educational Progress found that, for thirteen-year-olds, gender differences in all areas of science performance except biology actually increased during the 1980s, with boys' skills improving and girls' slipping during that time. This is particularly disturbing when one considers that today's young people are growing up in an era of rapid technological change; without a solid grounding in science, girls will not only be unable to participate in shaping that change, they will be helpless in the face of it.

Certainly, the culture outside the classroom discourages scientific competence in girls. Boys still have more casual exposure to science—whether it's light meters, chemistry sets, or, like Carl and his friends, spiders—and they're more likely to have computers at home. Science toys are still marketed almost exclusively toward boys, with boys featured on packages (or, worse still, girls *watching* boys) and the world of video games seems constructed with an entirely male audience in mind.

In school, girls opt out—or are pushed out—of science at every stage of advancement. In high school, boys and girls take introductory biology and chemistry in similar numbers, but far more boys go on to physics or advanced chemistry, while girls, if they take science at all, continue with biology. And although the numbers of women who pursue the sciences has skyrocketed, there were formerly so few that even huge jumps yield small results: for instance, the number of female engineers grew 131 percent during the 1980s, but women still make up only 8 percent of that field. In fact, a scant 16 percent of currently employed scientists are female, and that figure may well have peaked: by the late 1980s, the numbers of women pursuing degrees in science and engineering (excluding the social sciences) had leveled off and was dropping, especially in advanced physics and computer science.

Nonetheless, in spite of the achievement gap, today's girls believe that they can excel in science; the trouble is, boys (perhaps prejudiced by the overreaction to spiders and snakes) do not share that belief about their female classmates. Because of that disparity, science laboratory groups—in which boys grab equipment from girls, perform experiments for them, and ridicule girls' contributions—can become less an opportunity for partnership than a microcosm of unintended lessons about gender.

Amy's science class is taught by Mr. Sinclair, a mustachioed fellow with a receding hairline, who chose teaching as a profession during what he describes as his idealistic youth in the late 1960s. He periodically considers changing careers, mostly for financial reasons, but he enjoys his work too much to quit. Instead, he stays sharp by attending conferences on science instruction, subscribing to newsletters, seeking out new ways to teach. He tries hard to be creative because, he says, the kids tend not to like physical science very much. But judging from what happens in his classroom, it's really the girls who don't like it.

Like Mrs. Richter, Mr. Sinclair never intentionally discriminates against the girls in his class; both he and the other eighth-grade science teacher at Weston—who is also male—are quick to point out the few girls who do participate (although in further conversation I found that many of those girls felt neither affection nor affinity for the subject). What I saw instead, even more than in the math classes I observed, was a kind of passive resistance to participation by the girls that went unquestioned by the teacher. Call it gender bias by omission. When, week after week, boys raised their hands to ask or answer questions in far greater numbers than girls, when only boys shouted out responses, when boys enthusiastically offered up extra-credit demonstrations, the teacher simply didn't notice.

The very morning that Amy flees shrieking from Felicia the spider, Mr. Sinclair invites me to observe as her section of his physical science class performs an easy, fun experiment called "The Cartesian Diver." Each group of three students is given an empty dishwashing liquid bottle, an eyedropper, and a beaker of water. The idea is to fill the bottle with water, drop in the dropper, and, through some magical process that the students must determine (which turns out to be placing a little water in the dropper in advance, then squeezing the bottle to cause mass displacement), make the dropper sink and float at will.

In Amy's lab group there is another girl, Donna, and a boy, Liam, who sits between them. Liam performs the experiment as the two girls watch, occasionally offering encouragement, but no criticism. When he is successful, Amy squeals and pats him on the arm. Eventually Liam lets Donna and Amy each try the diver exactly once; then he recovers it and continues to play.

In another group of two girls and one boy directly behind Amy, Roger stands behind the girls, supervising . . . sort of.

"You're doing it wrong, ha-ha," he taunts in a singsong voice. Roger has a long rattail and a pierced ear; he wears an oversized tie-dyed T-shirt. The girls, who have styled their long blond hair identically, huddle together, trying to ignore him, and continue to attempt the experiment. Roger watches them a moment longer, then grabs the bottle from them, pours the water into the beaker and walks away with the dropper. The girls do not protest. When he comes back a few minutes later, the girls have refilled the bottle, but, still uncertain about how to proceed, have decided to empty it again and start over.

"Oh, smart," Roger says sarcastically. "*Real* smart." He grabs the bottle again. "*I'll* do it." He refills the bottle, puts the dropper in, and completes the experiment while the girls watch in silence.

I wander to the far corner of the room, where Allison, from Amy's math class, and Karla, a round-faced Latina girl with deep dimples and black hair pulled into a topknot, are having trouble with their diver. There are several girls sitting around them, yet they have asked a boy for help.

"I told him he could do it for us because he has man's hands," Karla, who once told me she wants to be an astronaut, tells me, smiling.

A second boy is watching the scene. When his friend completes the experiment, he pumps his fist in the air. "Yes!" he says. "A *man* had to do it!"

"But *how* did you do it?" Allison asks.

"I have magic hands," the first boy answers. "*Man* hands," and he laughs.

The girls laugh too—acting appropriately "helpless and girly"—but they never learn how to do the experiment. Instead, like the girls in the other groups, they have become outsiders in the learning process, passive observers rather than competent participants. In truth, "man hands" do complete most of the experiments in the room.

CHAPTER 19

Doméstica

PIERRETTE HONDAGNEU-SOTELO

I magine that you are a young woman, newly arrived in the United States. You are penniless—no, hugely in debt from making the trip—you do not speak English, and you are without a passport or any other legitimizing documents. Vilified in political campaigns as an "illegal," or simply scorned as a "Mexican," you live as a fugitive. You know only a distant cousin, a childhood friend, or perhaps an older brother whose wife is determined to cut your stay in their already-crowded apartment to a minimum. What do you do? You take a live-in job; or as the women say, *te encierras*. You lock yourself up. . . .

Who are these women who come to the United States in search of jobs, and what are those jobs like? Domestic work is organized in different ways, and in this chapter I describe live-in, live-out, and housecleaning jobs and profile some of the Latina immigrants who do them and how they feel about their work. . . .

LIVE-IN NANNY/HOUSEKEEPER JOBS

For Maribel Centeno, newly arrived from Guatemala City in 1989 at age twenty-two and without supportive family and friends with whom to stay, taking a live-in job made a lot of sense. She knew that she wouldn't have to spend money on room and board, and that she could soon begin saving to pay off her debts. Getting a live-in job through an agency was easy. The *señora*, in her rudimentary Spanish, only asked where she was from, and if she had a husband and children. Chuckling, Maribel recalled her initial misunderstanding when the *señora*, using her index forger, had drawn an imaginary "2" and "3" in the palm of her hand. "I thought to myself, well, she must have two or three bedrooms, so I said, fine. 'No,' she said. 'Really, really big.' She started counting, 'One, two, three, four . . . two-three rooms.' It was twenty-three rooms! I thought, *huy!* On a piece of paper, she wrote '$80 a week,' and she said, 'You, child, and entire house.' So I thought, well, I have to do what I have to do, and I happily said, 'Yes.' "

"I arrived on Monday at dawn," she recalled, "and I went to the job on Wednesday evening." When the *señora* and the child spoke to her, Maribel remembered "just laughing and feeling useless. I couldn't understand anything." On that first evening, the *señora* put on classical music, which Maribel quickly identified. "I said, 'Beethoven.' She said, 'Yeah,' and began asking me in English, 'You like it?' I said 'Yes,' or perhaps I said, '*Sí*,' and she began playing other cassettes, CDs. They had Richard Clayderman and I recognized it, and when I said that, she stopped in her tracks, her jaw fell open, and she just stared at me. She must have been thinking, 'No schooling, no preparation, no English, how does she know this music?' " But the *señora*, perhaps because of the language difficulty, or perhaps because she felt upstaged by her live-in's knowledge of classical music, never did ask. Maribel desperately wanted the *señora* to respect her, to recognize that she was smart, educated, and cultivated in the arts. In spite of her best status-signaling efforts, "They treated me," she said, "the same as any other girl from the countryside." She never got the verbal recognition that she desired from the *señora*.

Maribel summed up her experiences with her first live-in job this way: "The pay was bad. The treatment was, how shall I say? It was cordial, a little, uh, not racist, but with very little consideration, very little respect." She liked caring for the little seven year-old boy, but keeping after the cleaning of the twenty-three-room house, filled with marble floors and glass tables, proved physically impossible. She eventually quit not because of the polishing and scrubbing, but because being ignored devastated her socially.

Compared to many other Latina immigrants' first live-in jobs, Maribel Centeno's was relatively good. She was not on call during all her waking hours and throughout the night, the parents were engaged with the child, and she was not required to sleep in a child's bedroom or on a cot tucked away in the laundry room. But having a private room filled with amenities did not mean she had privacy or the ability to do simple things one might take for granted. "I had my own room, with my own television, VCR, my private bath, and closet, and a kind of sitting room—but everything in miniature, Thumbelina style," she said. "I had privacy in that respect. But I couldn't do many things. If I wanted to walk around in a T-shirt, or just feel like I was home, I couldn't do that. If I was hungry in the evening, I wouldn't come out to grab a banana because I'd have to walk through the family room, and then everybody's watching and having to smell the banana. I could never feel at home, never. Never, never, never! There's always something invisible that tells you this is not your house, you just work here."

It is the rare California home that offers separate maid's quarters, but that doesn't stop families from hiring live-ins; nor does it stop newly arrived Latina migrant workers from taking jobs they urgently need. When live-ins cannot even retreat to their own rooms, work seeps into their sleep and their dreams. There is no time off from the job, and they say they feel confined, trapped, imprisoned.

"I lose a lot of sleep," said Margarita Gutiérrez, a twenty-four-year-old Mexicana who worked as a live-in nanny/housekeeper. At her job in a modest-sized condominium in Pasadena, she slept in a corner of a three-year-old child's bedroom. Consequently, she found herself on call day and night with the child, who sometimes went several days without seeing her mother because of the latter's schedule at an insurance company. Margarita was obliged to be on her job twenty-four hours a day; and like other live-in nanny/housekeepers I interviewed, she claimed that she could scarcely find time to shower or brush her teeth. "I go to bed fine," she reported, "and then I wake up at two or three in the morning with the girl asking for water, or food." After the child went back to sleep, Margarita would lie awake, thinking about how to leave her job but finding it hard to even walk out into the kitchen. Live-in employees like Margarita literally have no space and no time they can claim as their own.

Working in a larger home or staying in plush, private quarters is no guarantee of privacy or refuge from the job. Forty-four-year-old Elvia Lucero worked as a live-in at a sprawling, canyon-side residence, where she was in charge of looking after twins, two five-year-old girls. On numerous occasions when I visited her there, I saw that she occupied her own bedroom, a beautifully decorated one outfitted with delicate antiques, plush white carpet, and a stenciled border of pink roses painstakingly painted on the wall by the employer. It looked serene and inviting, but it was only three steps away from the twins' room. Every night one of the twins crawled into bed with Elvia. Elvia disliked this, but said she couldn't break the girl of the habit. And the parents' room lay tucked away at the opposite end of the large (more than 3,000 square feet), L-shaped house.

Regardless of the size of the home and the splendor of the accommodations, the boundaries that we might normally take for granted disappear in live-in jobs. They have, as Evelyn Nakano Glenn has noted, "no clear line between work and non-work time," and the line between job space and private space is similarly blurred.[1] Live-in nanny/housekeepers are at once socially isolated and surrounded by other people's territory; during the hours they remain on the employers' premises, their space, like their time, belongs to another. The sensation of being among others while remaining invisible, unknown and apart, of never being able to leave the margins, makes many live-in employees sad, lonely, and depressed. Melancholy sets in and doesn't necessarily lift on the weekends.

Rules and regulations may extend around the clock. Some employers restrict the ability of their live-in employees to receive telephone calls, entertain friends, attend evening ESL classes, or see boyfriends during the workweek. Other employers do not impose these sorts of restrictions, but because their homes are located on remote hillsides, in suburban enclaves, or in gated communities, their live-in nanny/housekeepers are effectively kept away from anything resembling social life or public culture. A Spanish-language radio station, or maybe a *telenovela*, may serve as their only link to the outside world.

Food—the way some employers hoard it, waste it, deny it, or just simply do not even have any of it in their kitchens—is a frequent topic of discussion among Latina live-in nanny/housekeepers. These women are talking not about counting calories but about the social meaning of food on the job. Almost no one works with a written contract, but anyone taking a live-in job that includes "room and board" would assume that adequate meals will be included. But what constitutes an adequate meal? Everyone has a different idea, and using the subject like a secret handshake,

Latina domestic workers often greet one another by talking about the problems of managing food and meals on the job. Inevitably, food enters their conversations.

No one feels the indignities of food more deeply than do live-in employees, who may not leave the job for up to six days at a time. For them, the workplace necessarily becomes the place of daily sustenance. In some of the homes where they work, the employers are out all day. When these adults return home, they may only snack, keeping on hand little besides hot dogs, packets of macaroni and cheese, cereal, and peanut butter for the children. Such foods are considered neither nutritious nor appetizing by Latina immigrants, many of whom are accustomed to sitting down to meals prepared with fresh vegetables, rice, beans, and meat. In some employers' homes, the cupboards are literally bare. Gladys Villedas recalled that at one of her live-in jobs, the *señora* had graciously said, " 'Go ahead, help yourself to anything in the kitchen.' But at times," she recalled, "there was nothing, nothing in the refrigerator! There was nothing to eat!" Even in lavish kitchens outfitted with Subzero refrigerators and imported cabinetry, food may be scarce. A celebrity photograper of luxury homes that appear in posh magazines described to a reporter what he sees when he opens the doors of some of Beverly Hills' refrigerators: "Rows of cans of Diet Coke, and maybe a few remains of pizza."[2]

Further down the class ladder, some employers go to great lengths to economize on food bills. Margarita Gutiérrez claimed that at her live-in job, the husband did the weekly grocery shopping, but he bought things in small quantities—say, two potatoes that would be served in half portions, or a quarter of a watermelon to last a household of five all week. He rationed out the bottled water and warned her that milk would make her fat. Lately, she said, he was taking both her and the children to an upscale grocery market where they gave free samples of gourmet cheeses, breads, and dips, urging them all to fill up on the freebies. "I never thought," exclaimed Margarita, formerly a secretary in Mexico City, "that I would come to this country to experience hunger!"

Many women who work as live-ins are keenly aware of how food and meals underline the boundaries between them and the families for whom they work. "I never ate with them," recalled Maribel Centeno of her first live-in job. "First of all, she never said, 'Come and join us,' and secondly, I just avoided being around when they were about to eat." Why did she avoid mealtime? "I didn't feel I was part of that family. I knew they liked me, but only because of the good work I did, and because of the affection I showered on the boy; but apart from that, I was just like the gardener, like the pool man, just one more of their staff." Sitting down to share a meal symbolizes membership in a family, and Latina employees, for the most part, know they are not just like one of the family.

Food scarcity is not endemic to all of the households where these women work. In some homes, ample quantities of fresh fruits, cheeses, and chicken stock the kitchens. Some employer families readily share all of their food, but in other households, certain higher-quality, expensive food items may remain off-limits to the live-in employees, who are instructed to eat hot dogs with the children. One Latina live-in nanny/housekeeper told me that in her employers' substantial pantry, little "DO NOT TOUCH" signs signaled which food items were not available to her; and another said that her employer was always defrosting freezer-burned leftovers for her to eat, some of it dating back nearly a decade.

Other women felt subtle pressure to remain unobtrusive, humble, and self-effacing, so they held back from eating even when they were hungry. They talked a lot about how these unspoken rules apply to fruit. "Look, if they [the employers] buy fruit, they buy three bananas, two apples, two pears. So if I eat one, who took it? It's me," one woman said, "they'll know it's me." Another nanny/housekeeper recalled: "They would bring home fruit, but without them having to say it, you just knew these were not intended for you. You understand this right away, you get it." Or as another put it, "*Las Americanas* have their apples counted out, one for each day of the week." Even fruits growing in the garden are sometimes contested. In Southern California's agriculture-friendly climate, many a residential home boasts fruit trees that hang heavy with oranges, plums, and peaches, and when the Latina women who work in these homes pick the fruit, they sometimes get in trouble.[3] Eventually, many of the women solve the food problem by buying and bringing in their own food; early on Monday mornings, you see them walking with their plastic grocery bags, carting, say, a sack of apples, some chicken, and maybe some prepared food in plastic containers.

The issue of food captures the essence of how Latina live-in domestic workers feel about their jobs. It symbolizes the extent to which the families they work for draw the boundaries of exclusion or inclusion, and it marks the degree to which those families recognize the live-in nanny/housekeepers as human beings who have basic human needs. When they first take their jobs, most live-in nanny/housekeepers do not anticipate spending any of their meager wages on food to eat while on the job, but in the end, most do—and sometimes the food they buy is eaten by members of the family for whom they work.

Although there is a wide range of pay, many Latina domestic workers in live-in jobs earn less than minimum wage for marathon hours: 93 percent of the live-in workers I surveyed in the mid-1990s were earning less than $5 an hour (79 percent of them below minimum wage, which was then $4.25), and they reported working an average of sixty-four hours a week.[4] Some of the most astoundingly low rates were paid for live-in jobs in the households of other working-class Latino immigrants, which provide some women their first job when they arrive in Los Angeles. Carmen Vasquez, for example, had spent several years working as a live-in for two Mexican families, earning only $50 a week. By comparison, her current salary of $170 a week, which she was earning as a live-in nanny/housekeeper in the hillside home of an attorney and a teacher, seemed a princely sum.

Many people assume that the rich pay more than do families of modest means, but working as a live-in in an exclusive, wealthy neighborhood, or in a twenty-three-room house, provides no guarantee of a high salary. Early one Monday morning in the fall of 1995, I was standing with a group of live-in nanny/housekeepers on a corner across the street from the Beverly Hills Hotel. As they were waiting to be picked up by their employers, a large Mercedes sedan with two women (a daughter and mother or mother-in-law?) approached, rolled down the windows, and asked if anyone was interested in a $150-a-week live-in job. A few women jotted down the phone number, and no one was shocked by the offer. Gore Vidal once commented that no one is allowed to fail within a two-mile radius of the Beverly Hills Hotel, but it turns out that plenty of women in that vicinity are failing in the salary department. In some of the most affluent Westside areas of Los Angeles—in Malibu, Pacific Palisades, and Bel Air—there are live-in nanny/housekeepers earning $150 a week. And in 1999, the *Los Angeles Times* Sunday classified ads still listed live-in nanny/housekeeper jobs with pay as low as $100 and $125.[5] Salaries for live-in jobs, however, do go considerably higher. The best-paid live-in employee whom I interviewed was Patricia Paredes, a Mexicana who spoke impeccable English and who had legal status, substantial experience, and references. She told me that she currently earned $450 a week at her live-in job. She had been promised a raise to $550, after a room remodel was finished, when she would assume weekend housecleaning in that same home. With such a relatively high weekly salary she felt compelled to stay in a live-in job during the week, away from her husband and three young daughters who remained on the east side of Los Angeles. The salary level required that sacrifice.

But once they experience it, most women are repelled by live-in jobs. The lack of privacy, the mandated separation from family and friends, the round-the-clock hours, the food issues, the low pay, and especially the constant loneliness prompt most Latina immigrants to seek other job arrangements. Some young, single women who learn to speak English fluently try to move up the ranks into higher-paying live-in jobs. As soon as they can, however, the majority attempt to leave live-in work altogether. Most live-in nanny/housekeepers have been in the United States for five years or less; among the live-in nanny/housekeepers I interviewed, only two (Carmen Vasquez and the relatively high-earning Patricia Paredes) had been in the United States for longer than that. Like African American women earlier in the century, who tired of what the historian Elizabeth Clark-Lewis has called "the soul-destroying hollowness of live-in domestic work,"[6] most Latina immigrants try to find other options.

Until the early 1900s, live-in jobs were the most common form of paid domestic work in the United States, but through the first half of the twentieth century they were gradually supplanted by domestic "day work."[7] Live-in work never completely disappeared, however, and in the last decades of the twentieth century, it revived with vigor, given new life by the needs of American families with working parents and young children—and, as we have seen, by the needs of newly arrived Latina immigrants, many of them unmarried and unattached to families. When these women try to move up from live-in domestic work, they see few job alternatives. Often, the best they can do is switch to another form of paid domestic work, either as a live-out nanny/housekeeper or as a weekly housecleaner. When they do such day work, they are better able to circumscribe their work hours, and they earn more money in less time.[8] . . .

JOB STRUCTURES

Live-in and live-out nanny/housekeepers find that the spatial and social isolation of the job intensifies their craving for personal contact. Typically they work for only one employer, and spend each day at the home of the same family. With the exception of those hired by very high income families who simultaneously employ several domestic workers, they generally have no co-workers with whom to speak. The job is, as one employer conceded, "a lonesome one." Nanny/housekeepers may be alone for most of the day, or they may spend the entire day with infants. If they are lucky, they may meet up for an hour or two with a group of nannies at a public park, or on arranged play dates.

Nanny/housekeepers with live-in jobs are the most isolated. They work long hours—on average, more than sixty hours a week—leaving the employer's home only on Saturday afternoons, when they retreat to a shared apartment or a rented room until Monday morning. During the rest of the week, they remain confined to their work site. Without anyone to speak with day after day, many of them become emotionally distraught and depressed. It is little wonder that they often seek more personalistic relations with the only adults they see, their employers.

Erlinda Castro, a middle-aged Guatemalan woman and mother of five, had spent three years working as a live-in housekeeper in three different households before finally establishing her route of weekly housecleaning jobs. In the first of her live-in jobs, she worked for a family whom she described as good employers, because they paid her what she had expected to earn and because they did not pile on an unreasonable number of duties. The school-age children were gone for most of the day, and her job tasks seemed fair and physically manageable. The employers did not criticize her work, and they never insulted or yelled at her. Unlike many other live-ins, she had her own room and there was food for her to eat. Yet Erlinda found her employers cold and impersonal, unresponsive to her attempts to engage them in conversation; and she told me that their aloofness drove her out of the job.

"I would greet the *señora*, 'Good morning, *señora* Judy,' " she recalled. "They spoke a little Spanish, but the *señor* never spoke. If I greeted him, maybe in between his teeth he would mutter, 'Heh,' just like that. That's how one is often treated, and it feels cruel. You leave your own home, leaving everything behind only to find hostility. You're useful to them only because you clean, wash, iron, cook—that's the only reason. There is no affection. There is nothing." She expected some warmth and affection, but instead she found a void. Erlinda Castro entered the home of these employers directly after leaving her home and five children in Guatemala. On weekends she visited with her husband, whom she had joined in Los Angeles. It was her first experience with paid domestic work, and although she was not put off by the pay, the job tasks, or the low status of the job, the impersonal treatment became intolerable. "I felt bad, really bad. I couldn't go on with that, with nothing more than, 'Good morning, *señora*' and, 'Good night, *señora*.' Nothing else. They would say nothing, nothing, absolutely nothing to me! They would only speak to me to give me orders." Erlinda stayed on that job for approximately one year, leaving it for another live-in job that a friend had told her about.

Being treated as though one is invisible is a complaint commonly voiced by domestic workers of color working for white employers. As the historian David Katzman has noted in his study of the occupation in the South, "One peculiar and most degrading aspect of domestic service was the requisite of invisibility. The ideal servant . . . would be invisible and silent[,] . . . sensitive to the moods and whims of those around them, but undemanding of family warmth, love or security."[9] In her early 1980s ethnographic research, for which she posed as a housecleaner, Judith Rollins revealed a telling moment: an employer and her teenage son conducted an entire conversation about personal issues in her presence. "This situation was," Rollins wrote in her field notes, "the most peculiar feeling of the day: being there and not being there."[10] At different times, African American, Japanese American, and Chicana domestic workers in the United States have had the same disturbing experience.[11]

Some domestic workers see personalism as the antidote to these indignities and humiliations. Verbal interaction affords them respect and recognition on the job. Elvira Areola, a Mexicana, had worked for eleven years for one family. I interviewed her several days after an acrimonious fight with her employer—a disagreement that became physical—had left her jobless and without an income. As a single mother, she found herself in a frightening position. Still, she expressed no regrets, partly because the almost completely nonverbal relationship that she had maintained for several years with the *patrona* had been so strained. Her female employer had not worked and was physically present in the home, yet they hardly interacted. "I would arrive [in the morning] and sometimes she wouldn't greet me until two in the afternoon. . . . I'd be in the kitchen, and she'd walk in but wouldn't say anything. She would ignore me, as if to say, 'I'm alone in my house and there's no one else here.' Sometimes she wouldn't speak to me the whole day . . . she'd act as if I was a chair, a table, as if her house was supposedly all clean without me being there." Her dissatisfaction with the lack of appreciation and verbal recognition was echoed in the accounts of many other women.

ENDNOTES

1. Glenn 1986:141.
2. Lacher 1997:E1.
3. One nanny/housekeeper told me that a *señora* had admonished her for picking a bag of fruit, and wanted to charge her for it; another claimed that her employer had said she would rather watch the fruit fall off the branches and rot than see her eat it.
4. Many Latina domestic workers do not know the amount of their hourly wages; and because the lines between their work and nonwork tend to blur, live-in nanny/housekeepers have particular difficulty calculating them. In the survey questionnaire I asked live-in nanny/housekeepers how many days a week they worked, what time they began their job, and what time they ended, and I asked them to estimate how many hours off they had during an average workday (39 percent said they had no time off, but 32 percent said they had a break of between one and three hours). Forty-seven percent of the women said they began their workday at 7 A.M. or earlier, with 62 percent ending their workday at 7 P.M. or later. With the majority of them (71 percent) working five days a week, their average workweek was sixty-four hours. This estimate may at first glance appear inflated; but consider a prototypical live-in nanny/housekeeper who works, say, five days a week, from 7 A.M. until 9 P.M., with one and a half hours off during the children's nap time (when she might take a break to lie down or watch

television). Her on-duty work hours would total sixty-four and a half hours per week. The weekly pay of live-in nanny/housekeepers surveyed ranged from $130 to $400, averaging $242. Dividing this figure by sixty-four yields an hourly wage of $3.80. None of the live-in nanny/housekeepers were charged for room and board—this practice is regulated by law—but 86 percent said they brought food with them to their jobs. The majority reported being paid in cash.

5. See, e.g., Employment Classified Section 2, *Los Angeles Times,* June 6, 1999, G9.

6. Clark-Lewis 1994:123. "After an average of seven years," she notes in her analysis of African American women who had migrated from the South to Washington, D.C., in the early twentieth century, "all of the migrant women grew to dread their live-in situation. They saw their occupation as harming all aspects of their life" (124). Nearly all of these women transitioned into day work in private homes. This pattern is being repeated by Latina immigrants in Los Angeles today, and it reflects local labor market opportunities and constraints. In Houston, Texas, where many Mayan Guatemalan immigrant women today work as live-ins, research by Jacqueline Maria Hagan (1998) points to the tremendous obstacles they face in leaving live-in work. In Houston, housecleaning is dominated by better-established immigrant women, by Chicanas and, more recently, by the commercial cleaning companies—so it is hard for the Maya to secure those jobs. Moreover, Hagan finds that over time, the Mayan women who take live-in jobs see their own social networks contract, further reducing their internal job mobility.

7. Several factors explain the shift to day work, including urbanization, interurban transportation systems, and smaller private residences. Historians have also credited the job preferences of African American domestic workers, who rejected the constraints of live-in work and chose to live with their own families and communities, with helping to promote this shift in the urban North after 1900 (Katzman 1981; Clark-Lewis 1994:129–35). In many urban regions of the United States, the shift to day work accelerated during World War I, so that live-out arrangements eventually became more prevalent (Katzman 1981; Palmer 1989). Elsewhere, and for different groups of domestic workers, these transitions happened later in the twentieth century. Evelyn Nakano Glenn (1986:143) notes that Japanese immigrant and Japanese American women employed in domestic work in the San Francisco Bay Area moved out of live-in jobs and into modernized day work in the years after World War II.

8. Katzman 1981; Glenn 1986.

9. Katzman 1981:188.

10. Rollins 1985:208.

11. Rollins 1985; Glenn 1986; Romero 1992; Dill 1994.

INSTITUTIONS IN CRISIS

PART SIX

The Family

Is there a crisis in the American family? Certainly it is a time of change for the family, and for many families it is also a time of trouble. The "traditional" family, with the husband as the sole source of financial support and the wife as a full-time homebody, still exists, of course, but it is now a statistical minority. Increasingly large numbers of women, married or not, have entered the labor force. Others live in unconventional intimate arrangements and contribute to the increasing diversity of American family lifestyles. All of this diversity, this permissiveness, if you will, seems to many to be menacing the integrity and stability of the American family.

Still, the American family will doubtless remain with us for a long time. It may look less and less like the conventional family of suburbia in the 1950s—with its traditional male and female roles—but the family will nevertheless continue, with accompanying transformations, readjustments, and problems.

These changes do not, however, necessarily signal decline or decay. To conclude that the family is declining, one must point to a historical era when things were rosier. Certainly, the ideal of home, motherhood, and apple pie is part of our romantic mythology, but the myth did not always match the experience.

Nevertheless, many Americans—men and women, husbands and wives, parents and children—are experiencing marked uncertainties and anxieties. We have known deep changes in family life and in society. But our understanding of how to interpret these changes—and to deal with them—has been impaired by lack of knowledge about the relationship between family life and society, particularly about the impact of social forces upon the everyday workings of family life.

America has become a high-risk, high-stress society, and family life has been feeling the strain. Economic booms and recessions, the trade-offs between time spent at work and family time generate pressures for families and those living within them. This is especially true as economic inequality and homelessness have hardened into stubbornly persistent features of American life. But the middle-class family has also been hit uncommonly hard by economic decline. Layoffs among blue- and white-collar workers have resulted in downward social mobility for suburban as well as inner-city families, while others have prospered.

Sixteen years after the publication of her classic *Worlds of Pain,* Lillian B. Rubin undertook a new study of working-class families, which shows how the lack of a social safety net and the economic upheavals of the last two decades have undermined family life among "ordinary" Americans and, not so incidentally, have contributed to racial and ethnic antagonisms. In the selection we reprint here, Rubin describes how the pressures of time and the absence of child care and other supports have brought enormous stresses to working families—stresses that affect virtually every realm of family life, from sexuality to child rearing. "Time and money," Rubin concludes, are the "precious commodities in short supply."

As Rubin's research suggests, part of the problem for all too many American families is that we lack anything approaching a comprehensive national policy that could ease the strain between parenting and work. In the 1990s, some steps have been taken to develop new national policies regarding family leaves and child care. But are these efforts adequate? Not if we compare the American approach with that of European countries.

In her article "More than Welcome," Brittany Shahmehri, an American journalist living in Sweden, gives us an in-depth description of that country's extensive supports for families, which are among the most generous in the world. The centerpiece of the Swedish approach is a guaranteed leave of absence from work for new parents when their children are born, which is not only far longer than our own brief parental leave, but is also paid. The generous parental leave, moreover, is only one of many "family-friendly" policies in Sweden, which provides an approach to nurturing families and children that contrasts conspicuously with the distinctly minimal efforts in the United States. The heart of the difference is that in Sweden, as in some other European countries, it is assumed that society as a whole has an interest in—and a responsibility for—the well-being of *all* children.

Families in poor inner-city neighborhoods face all the problems generally facing working-class families, and more. Elijah Anderson's continuing ethnographic study of an inner-city neighborhood in Philadelphia distinguishes between two family types, the "decent" and the "street" or "ghetto"—terms which residents themselves use in making judgments ascribing status to resident families. Anderson shows the difficulties and dilemmas faced by parents, and especially by single mothers, in maintaining "decent" values for their children in the face of an alienated and embittered "street" culture.

CHAPTER 20

Families on the Fault Line

LILLIAN B. RUBIN

It's hardly news that child care is an enormous headache and expense for all two-job families. In many professional middle-class families, where the child-care bill can be $1,500–2,000 a month, it competes with the mortgage payment as the biggest single monthly expenditure. Problematic as this may be, however, these families are the lucky ones when compared to working-class families, many of whom don't earn much more than the cost of child care in these upper middle-class families. Even the families in this study at the highest end of the earnings scale, those who earn $42,000 a year, can't dream of such costly arrangements.

For most working-class families, therefore, child care often is patched together in ways that leave parents anxious and children in jeopardy. "Care for the little ones, that's a real big problem," says Beverly Waldov, a thirty-year-old white mother of three children, the youngest two, products of a second marriage, under three years old. "My oldest girl is nine, so she's not such a problem. I hate the idea of her being a latchkey kid, but what can I do? We don't even have the money to put the little ones in one of those good day-care places, so I don't have any choice with her. She's just got to be able to take care of herself after school," she says, her words a contest between anxiety and hope.

"We have a kind of complicated arrangement for the little kids. Two days a week, my mom takes care of them. We pay her, but at least I don't have to worry when they're with her; I know it's fine. But she works the rest of the time, so the other days we take them to this woman's house. It's the best we can afford, but it's not great because she keeps too many kids, and I know they don't get good attention. Especially the little one; she's just a baby, you know." She pauses and looks away, anguished. "She's so clingy when I bring her home; she can't let go of me, like nobody's paid her any mind all day. But it's not like I have a choice. We barely make it now; if I stop working, we'd be in real trouble."

Even such makeshift solutions don't work for many families. Some speak of being unable to afford day care at all. "We couldn't pay our bills if we had to pay for somebody to take care of the kids."

Some say they're unwilling to leave the children in the care of strangers. "I just don't believe someone else should be raising our kids, that's all."

Some have tried a variety of child-care arrangements, only to have them fail in a moment of need. "We tried a whole bunch of things, and maybe they work for a little while," says Faye Ensey, a black twenty-eight-year-old office worker. "But what happens when your kid gets sick? Or when the baby sitter's kids get sick? I lost two jobs in a row because my kids kept getting sick and I couldn't go to work. Or else I couldn't take my little one to the baby sitter because her kids were sick. They finally fired me for absenteeism. I didn't really blame them, but it felt terrible anyway. It's such a hassle, I sometimes think I'd be glad to just stay home. But we can't afford for me not to work, so we had to figure out something else."

For such families, that "something else" is the decision to take jobs on different shifts—a decision made by one-fifth of the families in this study. With one working days and the other on swing or graveyard, one parent is home with the children at all times. "We were getting along okay before Daryl junior was born, because Shona, my daughter, was getting on. You know, she didn't need somebody with her all the time, so we could both work days," explains Daryl Adams, a black thirty-year-old postal clerk with a ten-year-old daughter and a nine-month-old son. "I used to work the early shift—seven to three—so I'd get home a little bit after she got here. It worked out okay. But then this here big surprise came along." He stops, smiles down fondly at his young son and runs his hand over his nearly bald head.

"Now between the two of us working, we don't make enough money to pay for child care and have anything left over, so this is the only way we can manage. Besides, both of us, Alesha and me, we think it's better for one of us to be here, not just for the baby, for my daughter, too. She's growing up and, you know, I think maybe they need even more watching than when they were younger. She's coming to the time when she could get into all kinds of trouble if we're not here to put the brakes on."

But the cost such arrangements exact on a marriage can be very high. When I asked these husbands and wives when they have time to talk, more often than not I got a look of annoyance at a question that, on its face, seemed stupid to them. "Talk? How can we talk when we hardly see each other?" "Talk? What's that?" "Talk? Ha, that's a joke."

Mostly, conversation is limited to the logistics that take place at shift-changing time when children and chores are handed off from one to the other. With children dancing around underfoot, the incoming parent gets a quick summary of the day's or night's events, a list of reminders about things to be done, perhaps about what's cooking in the pot on the stove. "Sometimes when I'm coming home and it's been a hard day, I think: Wouldn't it be wonderful if I could just sit down with Leon for half an hour and we could have a quiet beer together?" thirty-one-year-old Emma Guerrero, a Latina baker, says wistfully.

But it's not to be. If the arriving spouse gets home early enough, there may be an hour when both are there together. But with the pressures of the workday fresh for one and awaiting the other, and with children clamoring for parental attention, this isn't a promising moment for any serious conversation. "I usually get home about forty-five minutes or so before my wife has to leave for work," says Ralph Jo, a thirty-six-year-old Asian repairman whose children, ages three and five, are the product of a second marriage. "So we try to take a few minutes just to make contact. But it's hard with the kids and all. Most days the whole time gets spent with taking care of business—you know, who did what, what the kids need, what's for supper, what bill collector was hassling her while I was gone—all the damn garbage of living. It makes me nuts."

Most of the time even this brief hour isn't available. Then the ritual changing of the guard takes only a few minutes—a quick peck on the cheek in greeting, a few words, and it's over. "It's like we pass each other. He comes in; I go out; that's it."

Some of the luckier couples work different shifts on the same days, so they're home together on weekends. But even in these families there's so little time for normal family life that there's hardly any room for anyone or anything outside. There's so much to do when I get home that there's no time for anything but the chores and the kids," says Daryl's wife, Alesha Adams. "I never get to see anybody or do anything else anymore and, even so, I'm always feeling upset and guilty because there's not enough time for them. Daryl leaves a few minutes after I get home, and the rest of the night is like a blur—Shona's homework, getting the kids fed and down for the night, cleaning up, getting everything ready for tomorrow. I don't know; there's always something I'm running around doing. I sometimes feel like—What do you call them?—one of those whirling dervishes, rushing around all the time and never getting everything done.

"Then on the weekends, you sort of want to make things nice for the kids—and for us, too. It's the only time we're here together, like a real family, so we always eat with the kids. And we try to take them someplace nice one of the days, like to the park or something. But sometimes we're too tired, or there's too many other catch-up things you have to do. I don't even get to see my sister anymore. She's been working weekends for the last year or so, and I'm too busy week nights, so there's no time.

"I don't mean to complain; we're lucky in a lot of ways. We've got two great kids, and we're a pretty good team, Daryl and me. But I worry sometimes. When you live on this kind of schedule, communication's not so good."

For those whose days off don't match, the problems of sustaining both the couple relationship and family life are magnified enormously. "The last two years have been hell for us," says thirty-five-year-old Tina Mulvaney, a white mother of two teenagers. "My son got into bad company and had some trouble, so Mike and I decided one of us had to be home. But we can't make it without my check, so I can't quit.

"Mike drives a cab and I work in a hospital, so we figured one of us could transfer to nights. We talked it over and decided it would be best if I was here during the day and he was here at night. He controls the kids, especially my son, better than I do. When he lays down the law, they listen." She interrupts her narrative to reflect on the difficulty of raising children. "You know, when they were little, I used to think about how much easier it would be when they got older. But now I see it's not true; that's when you really have to begin to worry about them. This is when they need someone to be here all the time to make sure they stay out of trouble."

She stops again, this time fighting tears, then takes up where she led off. "So now Mike works days and I work graveyard. I hate it, but it's the only answer; at least this way somebody's here all the time. I get home about 8:30 in the morning.

The kids and Mike are gone. It's the best time of the day because it's the only time I have a little quiet here. I clean up the house a little, do the shopping and the laundry and whatever, then I go to sleep for a couple of hours until the kids come home from school.

"Mike gets home at five; we eat; then he takes over for the night, and I go back to sleep for another couple of hours. I try to get up by 9 so we can all have a little time together, but I'm so tired that I don't make it a lot of times. And by 10, he's sleeping because he has to be up by 6 in the morning. So if I don't get up, we hardly see each other at all. Mike's here on weekends, but I'm not. Right now I have Tuesday and Wednesday off. I keep hoping for a Monday–Friday shift but it's what everybody wants, and I don't have the seniority yet. It's hard, very hard; there's no time to live or anything," she concludes with a listless sigh.

Even in families where wife and husband work the same shift, there's less time for leisure pursuits and social activities than ever before, not just because both parents work full-time but also because people work longer hours now than they did twenty years ago. Two decades ago, weekends saw occasional family outings, Friday-evening bowling, a Saturday trip to the shopping mall, a Sunday with extended family, once in a while an evening out without the children. In summer, when the children weren't in school, a week night might find the family paying a short visit to a friend, a relative, or a neighbor. Now almost everyone I speak with complains that it's hard to find time for even these occasional outings. Instead, most off-work hours are spent trying to catch up with the dozens of family and household tasks that were left undone during the regular work week. When they aren't doing chores, parents guiltily try to do in two days a week what usually takes seven—that is, to establish a sense of family life for themselves and their children.

"Leisure," snorts Peter Pittman, a twenty-eight-year-old African-American father of two, married six years. "With both of us working like we do, there's no time for anything. We got two little kids; I commute better than an hour each way to my job. Then we live here for half rent because I take care of the place for the landlord. So if somebody's got a complaint, I've got to take care of it, you know, fix it myself or get the landlord to get somebody out to do it if I can't. Most things I can do myself, but it takes time. I sometimes wonder what this life's all about, because this sure ain't what I call living. We don't go anyplace; we don't do anything; Christ, we hardly have time to go to the toilet. There's always some damn thing that's waiting that you've got to do."

Clearly, such complaints aren't unique to the working class. The pressures of time, the impoverishment of social life, the anxieties about child care, the fear that children will live in a world of increasing scarcity, the threat of divorce—all these are part of family life today, regardless of class. Nevertheless, there are important differences between those in the higher reaches of the class structure and the families of the working class. The simple fact that middle-class families have more discretionary income is enough to make a big difference in the quality of their social life. For they generally have enough money to pay for a baby-sitter once in a while so that parents can have some time to themselves; enough, too, for a family vacation, for tickets to a concert, a play, or a movie. At $7.50 a ticket in a New York or San Francisco movie house, a working-class couple will settle for a $3.00 rental that the whole family can watch together.

Finding time and energy for sex is also a problem, one that's obviously an issue for two-job families of any class. But it's harder to resolve in working-class families because they have so few resources with which to buy some time and privacy for themselves. Ask about their sex lives and you'll be met with an angry, "What's that?" or a wistful, "I wish." When it happens, it is, as one woman put it, "on the run"—a situation that's particularly unsatisfactory for most women. For them, the pleasure of sex is related to the whole of the interaction—to a sense of intimacy and connection, to at least a few relaxed, loving moments. When they can't have these, they're likely to avoid sex altogether—a situation the men find equally unsatisfactory.

"Sex?" asks Lisa Scranton, a white twenty-nine-year-old mother of three who feigns a puzzled frown, as if she doesn't quite know the meaning of the word. "Oh yeah, that; I remember now," she says, her lips smiling, her eyes sad. "At the beginning, when we first got together, it was WOW, real hot, great. But after a while it cools down, doesn't it? Right now, it's down the toilet. I wonder, does it happen to everybody like that?" she asks dejectedly.

"I guess the worst is when you work different shifts like we do and you get to see each other maybe six minutes a day. There's no time for sex. Sometimes we try to steal a few minutes for ourselves but, I don't know, I can't get into it that way. He can. You know how men are; they can do it any time. Give them two minutes, and they can get off. But it takes me time; I mean, I like to feel close, and you can't do that in three minutes. And there's the kids; they're right here all the time. I don't want to do it if it means being interrupted. Then he gets mad, so sometimes I do. But it's a problem, a real problem."

The men aren't content with these quick sexual exchanges either. But for them it's generally better than no sex at all, while for the women it's often the other way around. "You want to talk about sex, huh?" asks Lisa's husband, Chuck, his voice crackling with anger. "Yeah, I don't mind; it's fine, only I got nothing to talk about. Far as I'm concerned, that's one of the things I found out about marriage. You get married, you give up sex. We hardly ever do it anymore, and when we do, it's like she's doing me a favor.

"Christ, I know the way we've got to do things now isn't great," he protests, running a hand through his hair agitatedly. "We don't see each other but a few minutes a day, but I don't see why we can't take five and have a little fun in the sack. Sure, I like it better when we've got more time, too. But for her, if it can't be perfect, she gets all wound and uptight and it's like . . . " He stops, groping for words, then explodes, "It's like screwing a cold fish."

She isn't just a "cold fish," however. The problems they face are deeper than that. For once such conflicts arise, spontaneity takes flight and sex becomes a problem that needs attention rather than a time out for pleasure and renewal. Between times, therefore, he's busy calculating how much time has passed: "It's been over two weeks"; nursing his wounds: "I don't want to have to beg her"; feeling deprived and angry: "I don't know why I got married." When they finally do come together, he's disappointed. How could it be otherwise, given the mix of feelings he brings to the bed with him—the frustration and anger, the humiliation of feeling he has to beg her, the wounded sense of manhood.

Meanwhile, she, too, is preoccupied with sex, not with thoughts of pleasure but with figuring out how much time she has before, as she puts it, "he walks around with his mouth stuck out. I know I'm in real big trouble if we don't do it once a week. So I make sure we do, even if I don't want to." She doesn't say those words to him, of course. But he knows. And it's precisely this, the knowledge that she's servicing him rather than desiring him that's so hard for him to take.

The sexual arena is one of the most common places to find a "his and her" marriage—one marriage, two different sex lives. Each partner has a different story to tell; each is convinced that his or her version is the real one. A husband says mournfully, "I'm lucky if we get to make love once a week." His wife reports with irritation, "It's two, sometimes three times a week." It's impossible to know whose account is closest to the reality. And it's irrelevant. If that's what they were after, they could keep tabs and get it straight. But facts and feelings are often at war in family life. And nowhere does right or wrong, true or false count for less than in their sexual interactions. It isn't that people arbitrarily distort the truth. They simply report their experience, and it's feeling, not fact, that dominates that experience; feeling, not fact, that is their truth.

But it's also true that, especially for women, the difference in frequency of sexual desire can be a response—sometimes conscious, sometimes not—to other conflicts in the marriage. It isn't that men never withhold sex as a weapon in the family wars, only that they're much more likely than women to be able to split sex from emotion, to feel their anger and still experience sexual desire. For a man, too, a sexual connection with his wife can relieve the pressures and tensions of the day, can make him feel whole again, even if they've barely spoken a word to each other.

For a woman it's different. What happens—or, more likely, what doesn't happen—in the kitchen, the living room, and the laundry room profoundly affects what's possible in the bedroom. When she feels distant, unconnected, angry; when her pressured life leaves her feeling fragmented; when she hasn't had a real conversation with her husband for a couple of days, sex is very far from either her mind or her loins. "I run around busy all the time, and he just sits there, so by the time we go to bed, I'm too tired," explains Linda Bloodworth, a white thirty-one-year-old telephone operator.

"Do you think your lack of sexual response has something to do with your anger at your husband's refusal to participate more fully in the household?" I ask.

Her eyes smoldering, her voice tight, she snaps, "No, I'm just tired, that's all." Then noticing something in my response, she adds, "I know what you're thinking, I saw that look. But really, I don't think it's *because* I'm angry; I really am tired. I have to admit, though, that I tell him if he helped more, maybe I wouldn't be so tired all the time. And," she adds defiantly, "maybe I wouldn't be."

Some couples, of course, manage their sexual relationship with greater ease. Often that's because they have less conflict in other areas of living. But whether they accommodate well or poorly, for all two-job families, sex requires a level of attention and concern that leaves most people wanting much of the time. "It's a problem, and I tell you, it has to be well planned," explains thirty-four-year-old Dan Stolman, a black construction worker. "But we manage okay, we make dates or try to slip it in when the baby's asleep and my daughter's out with a friend or something. I don't mean things are great in that department. I'm not always satisfied and neither is Lorraine. But what can you do? We try to do the best we can. Sex isn't all there is to a marriage, you know. We get along really well, so that makes up for a lot.

"What I really miss is that we don't ever make love anymore. I mean, we have sex like I said, but we don't have the kind of time you need to make love. We talk about getting away for an overnight by ourselves once in a while. Lorraine's mother would come watch the kids if we asked her; the problem is we don't have any extra cash to spare right now."

Time and money—precious commodities in short supply. These are the twin plagues of family life, the missing ingredients that combine to create families that are both frantic and fragile. Yet there's no mystery about what would alleviate the crisis that now threatens to engulf them: A job that pays a living wage, quality child-care facilities at rates people can pay, health care for all, parental leave, flexible work schedules, decent and affordable housing, a shorter work week so that parents and children have time to spend together, tax breaks for those in need rather than for those in greed, to mention just a few. These are the policies we need to put in place if we're to have any hope of making our families stable and healthy.

CHAPTER 21

More Than Welcome

Families Come First in Sweden

BRITTANY SHAHMEHRI

Recently, my husband's laptop needed repair, and he called technical support to arrange for service. When he explained the problem, the phone representative at the multinational computer company said, "I'm going to recommend level-two support, but the technician will have to call you tomorrow to schedule an appointment. Today he's home with his sick kid."

When we still lived in the US, my husband might have wondered what a sick child had to do with his laptop. But last year we moved to Sweden, where parents not only are legally entitled to stay home with their sick children, but also get paid for doing so. Most amazing is that there's no shame in it. For fathers as well as mothers, it is assumed that when your child is sick, you are going to take care of him or her. That's more important than fixing someone's laptop on the spot. The computer company knows it and my husband's employer knows it. In almost every circumstance, the laptop can wait a day.

Even visiting tourists can see that Sweden has a child-friendly culture. A stroller logo is as common as the wheelchair logo in public restrooms and elevators. Buses accommodate strollers, and trains have places for children to play. (By the way, the children ride free.) Gas stations often have tiny working toilets as well as the standard toilets, as do zoos and other places that cater to children. "Amazing," I thought, the first time I visited.

But on closer examination, all of this is just window dressing. Sweden has one of the most generous parental leave policies in the world. Parents of each newborn or newly adopted child share 450 paid days to care for that child. The childcare system is of extremely high quality, offers a wide range of options, and is subsidized for all families. Parents are legally entitled to work reduced hours at their current jobs until their children reach the age of eight (when they formally enter school), and can take up to 60 paid days to take care of sick children. Toss in protected time to nurse a baby on the job and tuition-free universities, and to an American working parent, it sounds like utopia!

WHY SUCH WIDESPREAD SUPPORT?

According to Dr. Irene Wennemo, a Swedish family policy expert, the question of supporting families in Sweden is generally framed in terms of how the state should implement policies and what level of resources should be invested. "It's very accepted here that the state should be responsible for the living standard of children," Wennemo told me. "Children aren't a private thing; society has a responsibility for part of the cost."

Most of the reasons for this are self-evident. Children are members of society. It's not good for people, especially children, to live in poverty. Children should have equal opportunities. It's necessary for society that people have children, so it should be easy to combine working and having children. It's good for men and women to have equal access to both work and family.

"If you want a society in which it is accepted that both partners go out and work, then you have to take people's needs seriously," states Gunnar Andersson, a sociologist at Lund University. "Both school and child care must be really good, and there must be much more flexibility for all."[1]

"This is what our parents worked for," explains Anneli Elfwén, a Swedish midwife with two young sons. In the 1950s most Swedish women stayed home with the children. When women began to enter the workforce in the late 1960s, the need for stronger family policy became clear. The modern versions of parental leave policy and subsidized child care were implemented in the early 1970s and met with wide popular support. When I asked Elfwén why support for family policy was so widespread, she laughed, "Maybe we get it in the breastmilk. It's very natural for us."

HOW IT WORKS

When Elfwén's first son, Simon, was born in 1995, Elfwén was entitled to the same parental leave benefits that are offered to all Swedish families. She and her husband could share the 450 days of leave as they pleased, though one month was reserved for her, and one for her husband; and if either of them chose not to take their individual time, they would forfeit it.

One of the most unique aspects of Swedish parental leave is that it can be taken part time. Elfwén and her husband used the flexibility in their schedules to extend the time Simon spent at home with one of his parents. Between paid leave, flexible jobs, and the help of grandparents, the Elfwéns juggled a two-career, two-parent family. When their second son, Olle, was born in 1998, he, too, was entitled to 450 days of his parents' time. This made it possible for Elfwén to maintain the career that she loves, while keeping her children home until they were about three. The parental leave made all the difference.

Parents can continue to work reduced hours until their children reach the age of eight. This option was chosen by a couple I know, both schoolteachers. The mother took one day a week off, the father one day, and they staggered their hours on remaining days, so that their children spent less time in child care. Both parents were able to maintain professional lives while sharing the responsibility for raising their children.

CHOICES IN CHILD CARE

When it was time for the Elfwéns to decide on a preschool for Simon, they selected a Waldorf school with low student-teacher ratios and organic vegetarian meals. There are also traditional preschools, Christian schools, Montessori schools, cooperative schools, and even daycare centers that focus on gender equality. Families pay the county rather than the childcare center, and the amount depends on each family's household income. This means that, with few exceptions, parents can send their child to any childcare center without consideration to finances. So a single mother studying at university might pay $30.00 a month for her child to attend a school, while a family with three children and a household income of $40,000 would pay around $240 a month to have their three children in the same school. As of 2002, there will be a cap of $115 a month for the first child, ramping down according to income.

Of course, things are not perfect. It can be difficult to find a spot in the middle of the year, so it's necessary to plan ahead. The school we chose for my four year old did not suit him, so we kept him home while waiting for a place in a new school. In looking at the options, however, we were impressed with the low student-teacher ratios at all the preschools we visited, and the consistently high quality of care.

SEPARATE TAXATION AND CHILD ALLOWANCES

A few other odds and ends round out the package. People are taxed individually in Sweden, so a woman's income won't fall into a high tax bracket just because the household income is high. In addition, cash payments take the place of tax deductions for children. Each month, about $95.00 per child is deposited into the account of every family with a child, from the unemployed to the royal family. Families with more than two children receive a small bonus, so for my three children, we get a cash payment of $300 a month. Many families turn the money over to their children when they reach the age of 15 so they can learn to handle a checking account and manage their clothing and leisure purchases.

THE EMPLOYER'S ROLE

In Sweden, creating balance between work and family life is not left solely to the government and individual families. Section five of the Swedish Equal Opportunity Act reads, "An employer shall facilitate the combination of gainful employment and parenthood with respect to both female and male employees." Employers, in other words, are legally obligated to help employees combine parenthood and work. Employees who believe that an employer has directly violated this principle can take their case to the office of the Equal Opportunity Ombudsman (JämO).

Claes Lundkvist filed one of the eight cases registered with JämO last year regarding parenthood and employment. Lundkvist, a broadcast journalist for Swedish Radio, generally took his children to daycare each morning, and his wife, a physiotherapist with her own business, picked them up at the end of the day. But a new contract required Lundkvist to transfer to a branch more than an hour away. His working hours were inflexible as well. "My wife was very stressed taking all the responsibility," Lundkvist says. "It didn't work." After looking at JämO's Web page, he decided to pursue the issue.

The involvement of fathers as parents should be encouraged, according to JämO: "Employers may have an old-fashioned view of parenthood, or think that 'your wife can take care of that,' when the husband wants to be free to care for sick children or asks for more flexible working hours in order to combine work and family."[2] Changing the attitude of such employers is one of JämO's goals. JämO accepted Lundkvist's case, recognizing that without some adjustment in his new situation, his ability to combine work and family would be seriously impaired. The case initially met with resistance from Lundkvist's employers, and as he was a contract worker, JämO's power was limited. Lundkvist has since, however, negotiated a solution that does offer some flexibility.

With each case filed, the resulting publicity strengthens the public debate about men's rights and responsibilities as fathers. "It's hard to change gender roles," says Tommy Ferrarini, a PhD student at the Institute of Social Research in Stockholm who is currently doing research on family policy. But Ferrarini believes measures such as parental leave time allotted for the father shift social expectations: "It puts pressure on the employers when something becomes a right. It's all very individualized. . . . [This means] increased individual autonomy for the mother, the father, and the children. You give both parents the possibility of self-fulfillment."

WHAT FAMILY POLICY MEANS FOR WOMEN

Swedish mothers don't think they are doing it all, and they don't think the system is perfect. Some women have jobs that are more flexible than others; some are happier with their child care than others. While men are doing a larger share of the housework than in the past, couples still fight about who does the laundry. You'd be hard-pressed to find a Swedish mom who would call herself a superwoman.

Observing the situation, however, I see women who come pretty close to fulfilling the American "superwoman" myth. The vast majority of women have careers. With the help of their partners, they juggle children and work and birthday parties and still manage to make it to aerobics every week.

In the US, in contrast, the superwoman myth operates in a male-dominated corporate culture, and society views accepting help as a weakness. If you are granted a day off, you should be grateful. If your husband takes two unpaid weeks at the birth of a child, he should be grateful. If his company calls after a week and asks him to come back early (as my husband's company did), he should apologize when he says no, and then thank them for understanding.

In Sweden, you can certainly say "thank you" if you like, but no one has done you any favors. Among CEOs and entrepreneurs, you may see a more male-dominated culture, but even there, people are still likely to take a good portion of the five to eight weeks vacation they receive annually.

Swedish women face many of the same problems as their American counterparts. Their career advancement slows while children are young, and juggling everything can be very challenging. But women in Sweden do not have to do it alone. Families are supported by society, both financially and culturally. This means that women also give back to society, and not just in tax dollars—though even there, their contribution is substantial. Having women in the workplace changes the culture. Today, 43 percent of representatives in the Swedish Parliament and half of all State Ministers are women. In the long run, that will have an effect on the tone of the government as well as the laws that are passed.

CHILDREN ARE PEOPLE, TOO

Children in Sweden are not considered merely a lifestyle choice. They're members of society in their own right. Flexibility and support for families means that parents are better able to meet the needs of their children, something the children deserve. This approach offers myriad benefits to children, both emotionally and physically. Recent studies have suggested that "parental leave has favorable and possibly cost-effective impacts on pediatric health."[3] The same studies also indicate that with longer parental leaves, child and infant mortality rates go down.[4]

Respect for children is an important aspect of Swedish culture. Sweden has a Children's Ombudsman who represents children and young people in public debates, the ultimate goal being that young people can make their voices heard and gain respect for their views. In line with this, corporal punishment of any kind is illegal. Though controversial when it was first proposed, a Parliamentary Minister put the issue into context: "In a free democracy like our own, we use words as arguments, not blows. . . . If we can't convince our children with words, we will never convince them with violence."[5]

Children in Sweden are people, not property. Family policy is very much about creating a better situation for men and women who choose to have families, but at its core, family policy is all about children. A society that cherishes and respects children must make it possible for every child to be raised with certain minimal standards. Ensuring healthcare coverage, making sure children have enough to eat, and keeping children free of the risks that inevitably accompany poverty are a few modest goals. In Sweden, every child is entitled to be home with his or her parents for the first year of life. That is the minimum standard the society has chosen.

What that means is that any child you see on the street had access to her parents for the most important time in her development, and has access to free, high-quality medical and dental care. You know that she has enough food to eat, and that she likely attends a well-run preschool. That child has advocates in government and the support of society. Who will that child become? Right now it doesn't matter. The bottom line is that she lives in a society that values her just the way she is.

NOTES

1. Kristina Hultman, "A Step Away from a Childless Society?" *New Life: A Gender Equality Magazine for New Parents* (Stockholm: Swedish Government Division for Gender Equality, 2001): 10.

2. "What Is JämO?," a brochure published by the Equal Opportunity Ombudsman's office; see *www.jamombud.se.*

3. C. J. Ruhm, "Parental Leave and Child Health," *NBER Working Paper* no. W6554 (Cambridge, MA: National Bureau of Economic Research, 1998): 27.

4. Sheila Kamerman, "Parental Leave Policies: An Essential Ingredient in Early Childhood Education and Care Policies," *Social Policy Report 14,* no. 2 (2000): 10.

5. Louise Sylwander, "The Swedish Corporal Punishment Ban—More Than Twenty Years of Experience," Barnombudsmannen website, *www.bo.se* (choose the British flag for English).

For additional information about Sweden, see the following article in a past issue of *Mothering:* "Swedish Parents Don't Spank," no. 63.

CHAPTER 22

Decent and Street Families

ELIJAH ANDERSON

Almost everyone residing in poor inner-city neighborhoods is struggling financially and therefore feels a certain distance from the rest of America, but there are degrees of alienation, captured by the terms "decent" and "street" or "ghetto," suggesting social types. The decent family and the street family in a real sense represent two poles of value orientation, two contrasting conceptual categories. The labels "decent" and "street," which the residents themselves use, amount to evaluative judgments that confer status on local residents. The labeling is often the result of a social contest among individuals and families of the neighborhood. Individuals of either orientation may coexist in the same extended family. Moreover, decent residents may judge themselves to be so while judging others to be of the street, and street individuals often present themselves as decent, while drawing distinctions between themselves and still other people. There is also quite a bit of circumstantial behavior—that is, one person may at different times exhibit both decent and street orientations, depending on the circumstances. Although these designations result from much social jockeying, there do exist concrete features that define each conceptual category, forming a social typology.

The resulting labels are used by residents of inner-city communities to characterize themselves and one another, and understanding them is part of understanding life in the inner-city neighborhood. Most residents are decent or are trying to be. The same family is likely to have members who are strongly oriented toward decency and civility, whereas other members are oriented toward the street—and to all that it implies. There is also a great deal of "code-switching": a person may behave according to either set of rules, depending on the situation. Decent people, especially young people, often put a premium on the ability to code-switch. They share many of the middle-class values of the wider white society but know that the open display of such values carries little weight on the street: it doesn't provide the emblems that say, "I can take care of myself." Hence such people develop a repertoire of behaviors that do provide that security. Those strongly associated with the street, who have less exposure to the wider society, may have difficulty code-switching; imbued with the code of the street, they either don't know the rules for decent behavior or may see little value in displaying such knowledge.

At the extreme of the street-oriented group are those who make up the criminal element. People in this class are profound casualties of the social and economic system, and they tend to embrace the street code wholeheartedly. They tend to lack not only a decent education—though some are highly intelligent—but also an outlook that would allow them to see far beyond their immediate circumstances. Rather, many pride themselves on living the "thug life," actively defying not simply the wider social conventions but the law itself. They sometimes model themselves after successful local drug dealers and rap artists like Tupac Shakur and Snoop Doggy Dogg, and they take heart from professional athletes who confront the system and stand up for themselves. In their view, policemen, public officials, and corporate heads are unworthy of respect and hold little moral authority. Highly alienated and embittered, they exude generalized contempt for the wider scheme of things and for a system they are sure has nothing but contempt for them.

Members of this group are among the most desperate and most alienated people of the inner city. For them, people and situations are best approached both as objects of exploitation and as challenges possibly "having a trick to them," and in most situations their goal is to avoid being "caught up in the trick bag." Theirs is a cynical outlook, and trust of others is severely lacking, even trust of those they are close to. Consistently, they tend to approach all persons and situations as part of life's obstacles, as things to subdue or to "get over." To get over, individuals develop an effective "hustle" or "game plan," setting themselves up in a position to prevail by being "slick" and outsmarting others. In line with this, one must always be wary of one's counterparts, to assume that they are involved with you only for what they can get out of the situation.

Correspondingly, life in public often features an intense competition for scarce social goods in which "winners" totally dominate "losers" and in which losing can be a fate worse than death. So one must be on one's guard constantly. One is not always able to trust others fully, in part because so much is at stake socially, but also because everyone else is understood to be so deprived. In these circumstances, violence is quite prevalent—in families, in schools, and in the streets—becoming a way of public life that is effectively governed by the code of the street.

Decent and street families deal with the code of the street in various ways. An understanding of the dynamics of these families is thus critical to an understanding of the dynamics of the code. It is important to understand here that the family one emerges from is distinct from the "family" one finds in the streets. For street-oriented people especially, the family outside competes with blood relatives for an individual's loyalties and commitments. Nevertheless, blood relatives always come first. The folklore of the street says, in effect, that if I will fight and "take up for" my friend, then you know what I will do for my own brother, cousin, nephew, aunt, sister, or mother—and vice versa. Blood is thicker than mud.

DECENT FAMILIES

In decent families there is almost always a real concern with and a certain amount of hope for the future. Such attitudes are often expressed in a drive to work "to have something" or "to build a good life," while at the same time trying to "make do with what you have." This means working hard, saving money for material things, and raising children—any "child you touch"—to try to make something out of themselves. Decent families tend to accept mainstream values more fully than street families, and they attempt to instill them in their children. Probably the most meaningful description of the mission of the decent family, as seen by members and outsiders alike, is to instill "backbone" and a sense of responsibility in its younger members. In their efforts toward this goal, decent parents are much more able and willing than street-oriented ones to ally themselves with outside institutions such as schools and churches. They value hard work and self-reliance and are willing to sacrifice for their children: they harbor hopes for a better future for their children, if not for themselves. Rather than dwelling on the hardships and inequities facing them, many such decent people, particularly the increasing number of grandmothers raising grandchildren, often see their difficult situation as a test from God and derive great support from their faith and church community.

The role of the "man of the house" is significant. Working-class black families have traditionally placed a high value on male authority. Generally, the man is seen as the "head of household," with the woman as his partner and the children as their subjects. His role includes protecting the family from threats, at times literally putting his body in the line of fire on the street. In return he expects to rule his household and to get respect from the other members, and he encourages his sons to grow up with the same expectations. Being a breadwinner or good provider is often a moral issue, and a man unable to provide for a family invites disrespect from his partner. Many young men who lack the resources to do so often say, "I can't play house," and opt out of forming a family, perhaps leaving the woman and any children to fend for themselves.

Intact nuclear families, although in the minority in the impoverished inner city, provide powerful role models. Typically, husband and wife work at low-paying jobs, sometimes juggling more than one such job each. They may be aided financially by the contributions of a teenage child who works part-time. Such families, along with other such local families, are often vigilant in their desire to keep the children away from the streets.

In public such an intact family makes a striking picture as the man may take pains to show he is in complete control—with the woman and the children following his lead. On the inner-city streets this appearance helps him play his role as protector, and he may exhibit exaggerated concern for his family, particularly when other males are near. His actions and words, including loud and deep-voiced assertions to get his small children in line, let strangers know: "This is my family, and I am in charge." He signals that he is capable of protecting them and that his family is not to be messed with.

I witnessed such a display one Saturday afternoon at the Gallery, an indoor shopping mall with a primarily black, Hispanic, and working- to middle-class white clientele. Rasheed Taylor, his wife, Iisha, and their children, Rhonda, Jimmy, and Malika, wandered about the crowded food court looking for a place to sit down to eat. They finally found a table next to mine. Before sitting down, Mr. Taylor asked me if the seats were available, to which I replied they were. He then summoned his family, and they walked forward promptly and in an orderly way to take the seats. The three children sat on one side and the parents on the other. Mr. Taylor took food requests and with a stern look in his eye told the children to stay seated until he and his wife returned with the food. The children nodded attentively. After the adults left, the children seemed to relax, talking more freely and playing with one another. When the parents returned, the kids straightened up again, received their food, and began to eat, displaying quiet and gracious manners all the while. It was very clear to everybody looking on that Mr. Taylor was in charge of this family, with everyone showing him utter deference and respect.

Extremely aware of the problematic and often dangerous environment in which they reside, decent parents tend to be strict in their child-rearing practices, encouraging children to respect authority and walk a straight moral line. They sometimes display an almost obsessive concern about trouble of any kind and encourage their children to avoid people and situations that might lead to it. But this is very difficult, since the decent and the street families live in such close proximity. Marge, a slight, forty-three-year-old, married, decent parent of five who resides in such a neighborhood, relates her experience:

But you know what happens now? I have five children. Or I had five children—my oldest son got killed in a car accident. My children have always been different [decent]. And sometimes we have to act that way [street] that other people act to show them that you're not gonna be intimidated, that my child is gonna go to the store, they're gonna come out here and play, they're gonna go to school. You don't wanta do that, but you can't go to them and talk. 'Cause I've tried that. I've tried to go to people and say, "Listen. These are children. Let's try to make them get along." I remember years ago my sons had some expensive baseball mitts and bats that was given to them. I didn't buy them. They got them from Mr. Lee because he had the baseball team. And so he gave my sons some baseball bats and gloves. At that time the park at Twenty-seventh and Girard was Fred Jackson Stadium; they call it Ruth Bloom now. My sons played baseball there. So one little boy wanted to borrow some of the gloves and the bat. I told my children, "Don't let him hold [use] the gloves and the bat." But they let him hold them anyway. So he told them that when he finished with them he would put them on the porch. I told them they were never going to see them again, and they were never put on the porch. So I went to his mother, that was my neighbor, and I approached her very nicely and I said, "Johnny didn't bring Terry and Curtis's gloves and bat back." You know, she cursed me out! I was shocked. [She said,] "He doesn't have to take a so-and-so bat and a ball." And that woman really shocked me and hurt my feelings. I said, "Forget it. Just forget it." She was really ignorant. But I had to—even though I didn't get ignorant [get on her level] 'cause my son was there—but I had to say *some* negative things to her to let her know that I was just shocked. But I've been here [residing in this neighborhood] twenty-two years, and in twenty-two years I've had at least ten different, separate incidents that I had to go out and talk to somebody, to the point that I told my children, "No more." Somebody's gonna get hurt 'cause they don't know when to stop.

OK, my daughter, Annette, she went to Germantown High. So she was in about the ninth grade, had never had a fight in her life. She came from the store one day, and she told me about this girl that kept pickin' on her. She came up on the porch, and she said, "Mommy, come to the door. I want to show you this girl that keeps picking on me." Of course. Anybody that bothered them, I always wanted to see who it was in case I had to go see their parents or whatever. So I came and looked over the railing on the porch, and me and my daughter were lookin' down the street in that direction, not really at her [which could have been taken as offensive]. The girl came up and said, "Who the fuck are you lookin' at?" I said to my daughter, "Don't say anything." So I said to the girl, "You better go home. You better take your little butt home." OK. So she did go home. That afternoon, my daughter was sitting on the steps of the porch and reading a book— now this is a child who never had a fight, gets good grades. I think I raised her extremely well. She's a biochemist now. She's sitting on the step, reading her little book, and the girl came up to her, said something to her. I wasn't even out there, and so by the time my sons came to get me, my daughter and her were fighting. That was the first fight that she ever had in her life, and she was in the ninth grade. So I went out there and separated them. The girl went around the corner. When she came back, she had twenty different people with her. But I knew what was gonna happen. So—those same baseball bats I told you about—I told my son to get the baseball bats from the hallway. I said, "We're not gonna get off the porch, but if we have to, if they come up here, we're gonna have to do something." So they came back, and I had to actually coax them off like I was a little tough, like I'm not gonna take it. And I said to my sons, "If they come up here, we're gonna pay they ass back," and all that kind of stuff. And that's how I got them off us. I mean, it was about twenty of them, friends, family, neighbors.

As I indicated above, people who define themselves as decent tend themselves to be polite and considerate of others and teach their children to be the same way. But this is sometimes difficult, mainly because of the social environment in which they reside, and they often perceive a need to "get ignorant"—to act aggressively, even to threaten violence. For whether a certain child gets picked on may well depend not just on the reputation of the child but, equally important, on how "bad" the child's family is known to be. How many people the child can gather together for the purposes of defense or revenge often emerges as a critical issue. Thus social relations can become practical matters of personal defense. Violence can come at any time, and many persons feel a great need to be ready to defend themselves.

At home, at work, and in church, decent parents strive to maintain a positive mental attitude and a spirit of cooperation. When disciplining their children, they tend to use corporal punishment, but unlike street parents, who can often be observed lashing out at their children, they may explain the reason for the spanking.

These parents express their care and love for teenage children by guarding against the appearance of any kind of "loose" behavior (violence, drug use, staying out very late) that might be associated with the streets. In this regard, they are vigilant, observing children's peers as well and sometimes embarrassing their own children by voicing value judgments in front of friends.

These same parents are aware, however, that the right material things as well as a certain amount of cash are essential to young people's survival on the street. So they may purchase expensive things for their children, even when money is tight, in order that the children will be less tempted to turn to the drug trade or other aspects of the underground economy for money.

THE DECENT SINGLE MOTHER

A single mother with children—the majority of decent families in the impoverished sections of the inner city are of this type— must work even harder to neutralize the draw of the street, and she does so mainly by being strict and by instilling decent values in her children. She may live with her mother or other relatives and friends, or she may simply receive help with child care from her extended family. In raising her children, she often must press others to defer to her authority; but without a strong man of the house, a figure boys in particular are prepared to respect, she is at some disadvantage with regard not only to her own sons and daughters but also to the young men of the streets. These men may test her ability to control her household by attempting to date her daughters or to draw her sons into the streets. A mother on her own often feels she must be constantly on guard and exhibit a great deal of determination.

Diane, a single mother of four sons, three of whom are grown, offers a case in point. Diane is forty-six years old, of average height, heavyset, and light-complexioned. One of her sons is a night watchman at the utility company, and another is a security guard at a downtown store. Diane herself works as an aide in a day care center. In describing her situation, she has this to say:

> It really is pretty bad around here. There's quite a few grandmothers taking care of kids. They mothers out here on crack. There's quite a few of 'em. The drugs are terrible. Now, I got a fifteen-year-old boy, and I do everything I can to keep him straight. 'Cause they [drug dealers and users] all on the corner. You can't say you not in it, 'cause we in a bad area. They be all on the corner. They be sittin' in front of apartments takin' the crack. And constantly, every day, I have to stay on 'em and make sure everything's OK. Which is real bad, I never seen it this bad. And I been around here since '81, and I never seen it this bad. At nights they be roamin' up and down the streets, and they be droppin' the caps [used crack vials] all in front of your door. And when the kids out there playin', you gotta like sweep 'em up. It's harder for me now to try to keep my fifteen-year-old under control. Right now, he likes to do auto mechanics, hook up radios in people's cars, and long as I keep 'im interested in that, I'm OK. But it's not a day that goes by that I'm not

in fear. 'Cause right now he got friends that's sellin' it. They, you know, got a whole lot of money and stuff. And I get him to come and mop floors [she works part-time as a janitor], and I give him a few dollars. I say, "As long as you got a roof over yo' head, son, don't worry about nothin' else."

It's just a constant struggle tryin' to raise yo' kids in this time. It's very hard. They [boys on the street] say to him, "Man, why you got to go in the house?" And they keep sittin' right on my stoop. If he go somewhere, I got to know where he's at and who he's with. And they be tellin' him [come with us]. He say, "No, man, I got to stay on these steps. I don't want no problem with my mama!" Now, I been a single parent for fifteen years. So far, I don't have any problems. I have four sons. I got just the one that's not grown, the fifteen-year-old. Everyone else is grown. My oldest is thirty-five. I'm tryin'. Not that easy. I got just one more, now. Then I'll be all right. If I need help, the older ones'll help me. Most of the time, I keep track myself. I told him I'll kill him if I catch him out here sellin'. And I know most of the drug dealers. He better not. I'm gon' hurt him. They better not give him nothin'. He better not do nothin' for them. I tell him, "I know some of your friends are dealers. [You can] speak to 'em, but don't let me catch you hangin' on the corner. I done struggled too hard to try to take care of you. I'm not gon' let you throw your life away."

When me and my husband separated in '79, I figured I had to do it. He was out there drivin' trucks and never home. I had to teach my kids how to play ball and this and that. I said, "If I have to be a single parent, I'll do it." It used to be the gangs, and you fought 'em, and it was over. But now if you fight somebody, they may come back and kill you. It's a whole lot different now. You got to be street-smart to get along. My boy doesn't like to fight. I took him out of school, put him in a home course. The staff does what it wants to. [They] just work for a paycheck.

You tell the kid, now you can't pick their friends, so you do what you can. I try to tell mine, "You gon' be out there with the bad [street kids], you can't do what they do. You got to use your own mind." Every day, if I don't get up and say a prayer, I can't make it. I can't make it. I watch him closely. If he go somewhere, I have to know where he at. And when I leave him, or if he go to them girlfriends' houses, I tell the parents, "If you not responsible, he can't stay." I'm not gon' have no teenager making no baby.

These comments show how one decent inner-city parent makes sense of the breakdown in civility, order, and morality she sees occurring in her community and how she copes. When Diane was a child, and even when her older sons were growing up, gang fights were common, but they generally took the form of an air-clearing brawl. Today many community residents feel that if you run afoul of a gang or an individual, somebody may simply kill you. Note that the schools are included among the institutions seen to have abdicated their responsibilities, a widespread belief among many inner-city parents. . . .

The inner-city community is actually quite diverse economically; various people are doing fairly well, whereas others are very poor but decent and still others are utterly and profoundly suffering, alienated, and angry. Such is the social terrain the decent family must navigate and negotiate in order to remain whole as well as secure. This situation creates a major dilemma for decent families who are trying to raise their children to remain decent even though they must negotiate the streets. These parents want their children to value educations, jobs, and a future, but they also want them to get their fair share of respect and the props that go with it—and not to be dissed or attacked or shot.

PART SEVEN

The Environment

I t's sometimes said that in America today, everyone has become an environmentalist. If so, this represents a large change in a relatively short time. The environmental movement in the United States only took off in the 1960s and 1970s. Yet today many practices that seemed revolutionary in those days are now routine. School children learn about the virtues of recycling in the classroom; corporations run magazine advertisements urging the public to recognize their commitment to clean air and water. The vast majority of Americans, according to opinion polls, believe that maintaining a clean environment is worth whatever it costs.

These changes have been so pervasive and so rapid that some now insist that the battle against environmental destruction has been largely won and we can now relax our concern. Others think that we've already gone too far in the pursuit of environmental quality, to the point where cumbersome regulations are hobbling the economy and lowering our standard of living.

But as the articles in this part make clear, any complacency about the state of the environment is unwarranted. It's true that important gains have been made against some environmental problems. But for others, progress is slow at best, and at the same time, new and gravely threatening problems have emerged that were largely unforeseen only a few decades ago. One recent report, for example, estimates that nearly half the American population continues to breathe unhealthy levels of ozone, a toxic air pollutant that has been implicated in many kinds of respiratory disease.[1] Another tells us that there may no longer be *any* streams or rivers left in the United States that are free from chemical contamination.[2]

Indeed, Barry Commoner argues that we have "failed" to live up to the promise of the environmental movement. While some victories—such as the sharp reduction of lead in the air we breathe—have been won, the overall picture is one of stagnation. With some exceptions, levels of pollutants in the air have declined only moderately, and the rate of decline has slowed considerably since the 1970s. We are "stuck," Commoner believes, for a very basic reason: We have mainly tried to deal with pollution *after* it is produced, rather than preventing it in the first place—in effect, attacking only the symptoms, not the disease. Taking pollution prevention more seriously, he believes, would require dramatic changes in our systems of production and therefore challenge the dominance of private interests over the public good.

And so we are moving instead toward an easier but ultimately ineffective approach: searching for "acceptable" levels of pollution that will not interfere with industry's ability to set the terms of environmental discussion.

One result of this choice is that environmental problems have become increasingly concentrated among America's most disadvantaged people—one more aspect of the growing inequality we've charted in previous sections of this book. As Robert Bullard shows, blacks, Hispanics, and Native Americans now carry much more than their share of the burden of environmental pollution. They are more likely to live near toxic waste dumps and other hazardous facilities, they breathe the most polluted air, and they suffer more often from lead poisoning and contaminated water supplies. Moreover, violations of pollution regulations are likely to be prosecuted much more zealously in white than in minority communities. In other words, the benefits of economic growth—jobs and income—go disproportionately to the affluent, while the toxic *costs* of growth are allotted to the poor, turning some poor communities into "sacrifice zones."

Another troubling indication of the limits of our success with the environment is that, although some traditional environmental threats have eased, new and even more disturbing ones have appeared. Among them are long-term changes in the earth's atmosphere, including global warming and the depletion of the ozone layer that helps, among other things, to protect humans from the sun's radiation. In "The Heat is on," Ross Gelbspan contends that, despite a concerted campaign to deny the seriousness of the threat of global warming, it is very real indeed. The extremes of weather experienced in the United States in recent years, he argues, are a forewarning of worse environmental disruptions in the future that could, in turn, bring unprecedented economic and social dislocations for generations to come.

Attacking global warming at the source—by, for example, reducing the burning of fossil fuels—may be the best way to avoid that scenario. But there has been considerable resistance to such steps by some corporations and governments, including our own, mainly on the ground that they would hurt the economy. As Gelbspan points out, however, the health of the economy ultimately depends on the state of the environment, not the other way around; and if we are not careful, the ongoing insult to the earth's atmosphere could bring economic as well as ecological havoc.

ENDNOTES

1. American Lung Association, *State of the Air: 2003*, New York, NY, May 2003.
2. John Heilprin, "Report Paints Gloomy U.S. Ecological Picture," Associated Press, September 25, 2002.

CHAPTER 23

Why We Have Failed

BARRY COMMONER

In 1970, in response to growing concern, the U.S. Congress began a massive effort to undo the pollution damage of the preceding decades. In short order, legislators in Washington passed the National Environmental Protection Act (NEPA) and created the Environmental Protection Agency (EPA) to administer it. These two events are the cornerstone of what is indisputably the world's most vigorous pollution control effort, a model for other nations and a template for dozens of laws and amendments passed since. Now, nearly 20 years later, it is time to ask an important and perhaps embarrassing question: how far have we progressed toward the goal of restoring the quality of the environment?

The answer is indeed humbling. Apart from a few notable exceptions, environmental quality has improved only slightly, and in some cases worsened. Since 1975, emissions of sulfur dioxide and carbon monoxide are down by about 19 percent, but nitrogen oxides are up about 4 percent. Overall improvement in major pollutants amounts to only about 15 to 20 percent, and the rate of improvement has actually slowed considerably.

There are several notable and heartening exceptions. Pollution levels of a few chemicals—DDT and PCBs in wildlife and people, mercury in the fish of the Great Lakes, strontium 90 in the food chain and phosphate pollution in some local rivers—have been reduced by 70 percent or more. Levels of airborne lead have declined more than 90 percent since 1975.

The successes explain what works and what does not. Every success on the very short list of significant environmental quality improvements reflects the same remedial action: production of the pollutant has been stopped. DDT and PCB levels have dropped because their production and use have been banned. Mercury is much less prevalent because it is no longer used to manufacture chlorine. Lead has been taken out of gasoline. And strontium has decayed to low levels because the United States and the Soviet Union had the good sense to stop the atmospheric nuclear bomb tests that produced it.

The lesson is plain: pollution prevention works; pollution control does not. Only where production technology has been changed to eliminate the pollutant has the environment been substantially improved. Where it remains unchanged, where an attempt is made to trap the pollutant in an appended control device—the automobile's catalytic converter or the power plant's scrubber—environmental improvement is modest or nil. When a pollutant is attacked at the point of origin, it can be eliminated. But once it is produced, it is too late.

PROGRESS AND POLLUTION

Most of our environmental problems are the inevitable result of the sweeping technological changes that transformed the U.S. economic system after World War II: the large, high-powered cars; the shift from fuel-efficient railroads to gas-guzzling trucks and cars, the substitution of fertilizers for manure and crop rotation and of toxic synthetic pesticides for ladybugs and birds.

By 1970, it was clear that these technological changes were the root cause of environmental pollution. But the environmental laws now in place do not address the technological origin of pollutants. I remember the incredulity in Senator Edmund Muskie's voice during NEPA hearings when he asked me whether I was really testifying that the technology that generated postwar economic progress was also the cause of pollution. I was.

Because environmental legislation ignored the origin of the assault on environmental quality, it has dealt only with its subsequent problems—in effect defining the disease as a collection of symptoms. As a result, all environmental legislation mandates only palliative measures. The notion of preventing pollution—the only measure that really works—has yet to be given any administrative force.

The goal established by the Clean Air Act in 1970 could have been met if the EPA had confronted the auto industry with a demand for fundamental changes in engine design, changes that were practical and possible. And had American farmers been required to reduce the high rate of nitrogen fertilization nitrate water pollution would now be falling instead of increasing.

If the railroads and mass transit were expanded, if the electric power system were decentralized and increasingly based on cogenerators and solar sources, if American homes were weatherized, fuel consumption and air pollution would be sharply reduced. If brewers were forbidden to put plastic nooses on six-packs of beer, if supermarkets were not allowed to wrap polyvinyl chloride film around everything in sight, if McDonald's restaurants could rediscover the paper plate, if the use of plastics was cut back to those things considered worth the social costs (say, artificial hearts or video tape), then we could push back the petrochemical industry's toxic invasion of the biosphere.

Of course, all this is easier said than done. I am fully aware that what I am proposing is no small thing. It means that sweeping changes in the major systems of production—agriculture, industry, power production and transportation—would be undertaken for a social purpose: environmental improvement. This represents social (as contrasted with private) governance of the means of production—an idea that is so foreign to what passes for our national ideology that even to mention it violates a deep-seated taboo.

The major consequence of this powerful taboo is the failure to reach the goals in environmental quality that motivated the legislation of the 1970s.

RISK AND PUBLIC MORALITY

In the absence of a prevention policy, the EPA adopted a convoluted pollution control process. First, the EPA must estimate the degree of harm represented by different levels of the numerous environmental pollutants. Next, some "acceptable" level of harm is chosen (for example, a cancer risk of one in a million) and emission and/or ambient concentration standards that can presumably achieve that risk level are established.

Polluters are then expected to respond by introducing control measures (such as automobile exhaust catalysts or power plant stack scrubbers) that will bring emissions to the required levels. If the regulation survives the inevitable challenges from industry (and in recent years from the administration itself), the polluters will invest in the appropriate control systems. Catalysts are attached to cars, and scrubbers to the power plants and trash-burning incinerators. If all goes well—and it frequently does not—at least some areas of the country and some production facilities are then in compliance with the regulation.

The net result is that an "acceptable" pollution level is frozen in place. Industry, having invested heavily in equipment designed to reach just the required level, is unlikely to invest in further improvements.

Clearly, this process is the opposite of the preventive approach to public health. It strives not for the continuous improvement of environmental health, but for the social acceptance of some, hopefully low, risk to health. By contrast, the preventive approach aims at progressively reducing the risk to health. It does not mandate some socially convenient stopping point. The medical professions, after all, did not decide that the smallpox prevention program could stop when the risk reached one in a million. They kept on, and the disease has now been wiped out worldwide.

How do you decide when to stop, where to set the standard for acceptable pollution? The current fashion is to submit the question to a risk/benefit analysis. Since the pollutants' ultimate effect can often be assessed by the number of lives lost, the risk/benefit analysis requires that a value be placed on human life. Such reckoning often bases that value on lifelong earning power, so that a poor person's life is worth less than a rich person's. So, on the risk/benefit scale, the poor can be exposed to more pollution than the rich. In fact, this is what is happening in the United States: the burden of an environmental risk—say the siting of a municipal incinerator or a hazardous waste landfill—falls disproportionally on poor people, who lack the political and financial clout to deter the risk.

In this way, risk/benefit analysis—a seemingly straightforward numerical computation—conceals a profound, unresolved moral question: should poor people be subjected to a more severe environmental burden than rich people, simply because they lack the resources to evade it? Since in practice the risk/benefit equation masquerades as science, it relieves society of the duty to confront this question. One result of failing to adopt the preventive approach is that the regulatory agencies have been driven into positions that seriously diminish the force of social morality.

THE REAL SOLUTION

The fate of Alar, the pesticide used to enhance the marketability of apples, provides a recent instructive example of what prevention means. Like many other petrochemical products, Alar poses a health risk. It has been proven to induce cancer in test animals. As in many other such cases, a debate has flourished over the extent of the hazard to people, especially children, and over what standards should be applied to limit exposure to "acceptable" levels.

In June, Alar broke out of the pattern when the manufacturer, Uniroyal, decided that regardless of the toxicological uncertainties, Alar would be taken off the market. They acted simply because parents were unhappy about raising their children on apple juice that represented *any* threat to their health. Food after all, is supposed to be good for you.

This is a clear-cut example of the benefits of prevention, as opposed to control. Pollution prevention means identifying the source of the pollutant in the production process, eliminating it from that process and substituting a more environmentally benign method of production. This differentiates it from source reduction (reducing the amount of the pollutant produced, ether through altering processes or simple housekeeping) and pollution control. Once a pollutant is eliminated, the elaborate system of risk assessment, standard stating and the inevitable debates and litigation become irrelevant.

Instituting the practice of prevention rather than control will require the courage to challenge the taboo against questioning the dominance of private interests over the public interest. But I suggest that we begin with an open public discussion of what has gone wrong, and why. That is the necessary first step on the road toward realizing the nation's unswerving goal—restoring the quality of the environment.

CHAPTER 24

Environmental Racism

ROBERT D. BULLARD

Despite the recent attempts by federal agencies to reduce environmental and health threats in the United States, inequities persist.[1] If a community is poor or inhabited largely by people of color, there is a good chance that it receives less protection than a community that is affluent or white.[2] This situation is a result of the country's environmental policies, most of which "distribute the costs in a regressive pattern while providing disproportionate benefits for the educated and wealthy."[3] Even the Environmental Protection Agency (EPA) was not designed to address environmental policies and practices that result in unfair outcomes. The agency has yet to conduct a single piece of disparate impact research using primary data. In fact, the current environmental protection paradigm has institutionalized unequal enforcement; traded human health for profit; placed the burden of proof on the "victims" rather than on the polluting industry; legitimated human exposure to harmful substances; promoted "risky" technologies such as incinerators; exploited the vulnerability of economically and politically disenfranchised communities; subsidized ecological destruction; created an industry around risk assessment; delayed cleanup actions; and failed to develop pollution prevention as the overarching and dominant strategy. As a result, low-income and minority communities continue to bear greater health and environmental burdens, while the more affluent and whites receive the bulk of the benefits.[4]

The geographic distribution of both minorities and the poor has been found to be highly correlated to the distribution of air pollution; abandoned toxic waste dumps; lead poisoning in children; and contaminated fish consumption.[5] Virtually all studies of exposure to outdoor air pollution have found significant differences in exposure by income and race. Moreover, the race correlation is even stronger than the class correlation.[6] The National Wildlife Federation recently reviewed some 64 studies of environmental disparities; in all but one, disparities were found by either race or income, and disparities by race were more numerous than those by income. When race and income were compared for significance, race proved to be the more important factor in 22 out of 30 tests.[7] And researchers at Argonne National Laboratory recently found that:

> In 1990, 437 of the 3,109 counties and independent cities failed to meet at least one of the EPA ambient air quality standards. . . . 57 percent of whites, 65 percent of African-Americans, and 80 percent of Hispanics live in 437 counties with substandard air quality. Out of the whole population, a total of 33 percent of whites, 50 percent of African-Americans, and 60 percent of Hispanics live in the 136 counties in which two or more air pollutants exceed standards. The percentage living in the 29 counties designated as nonattainment areas for three or more pollutants are 12 percent of whites, 20 percent of African-Americans, and 31 percent of Hispanics.[8]

The public health community has very little information on the magnitude of many air pollution–related health problems. For example, scientists are at a loss to explain the rising number of deaths from asthma in recent years. However, it is known that persons suffering from asthma are particularly sensitive to the effects of carbon monoxide, sulfur dioxide, particulate matter, ozone, and oxides of nitrogen.[9]

Current environmental decisionmaking operates at the juncture of science, technology, economics, politics, special interests, and ethics and mirrors the larger social milieu where discrimination is institutionalized. Unequal environmental protection undermines three basic types of equity: procedural, geographic, and social.

PROCEDURAL EQUITY

Procedural equity refers to fairness—that is, to the extent that governing rules, regulations, evaluation criteria, and enforcement are applied in a nondiscriminatory way. Unequal protection results from nonscientific and undemocratic decisions, such as exclusionary practices, conflicts of interest, public hearings held in remote locations and at inconvenient times, and use of only English to communicate with and conduct hearings for non-English-speaking communities.

A 1992 study by staff writers from the *National Law Journal* uncovered glaring inequities in the way EPA enforces its Superfund laws:

> There is a racial divide in the way the U.S. government cleans up toxic waste sites and punishes polluters. White communities see faster action, better results and stiffer penalties than communities where blacks, Hispanics and other minorities live. This unequal protection often occurs whether the community is wealthy or poor.[10]

After examining census data, civil court dockets, and EPA's own record of performance at 1,177 Superfund toxic waste sites, the authors of the *National Law Journal* report revealed the following:

- Penalties applied under hazardous waste population were 500 percent higher than penalties at sites with the greatest minority population. Penalties averaged out at $335,566 at sites in white areas but just $55,318 at sites in minority areas.

- The disparity in penalties applied under the toxic waste law correlates with race alone, not income. The average penalty in areas with the lowest median income is $113,491—3 percent more than the average penalty in areas with the highest median income.
- For all the federal environmental laws aimed at protecting citizens from air, water, and waste pollution, penalties for noncompliance were 46 percent higher in white communities than in minority communities.
- Under the Superfund cleanup program, abandoned hazardous waste sites in minority areas take 20 percent longer to be placed on the National Priority List than do those in white areas.
- In more than half of the 10 autonomous regions that administer EPA programs around the country, action on cleanup at Superfund sites begins from 12 to 42 percent later at minority sites than at white sites.
- For minority sites, EPA chooses "containment," the capping or walling off of a hazardous waste dump site, 7 percent more frequently than the cleanup method preferred under the law: permanent "treatment" to eliminate the waste or rid it of its toxins. For white sites, EPA orders permanent treatment 22 percent more often than containment.[11]

These findings suggest that unequal environmental protection is placing communities of color at risk. The *National Law Journal* study supplements the findings of several earlier studies and reinforces what grassroots activists have been saying all along: Not only are people of color differentially affected by industrial pollution but they can expect different treatment from the government.[12]

GEOGRAPHIC EQUITY

Geographic equity refers to the location and spatial configuration of communities and their proximity to environmental hazards and locally unwanted land uses (LULUs), such as landfills, incinerators, sewage treatment plants, lead smelters, refineries, and other noxious facilities. Hazardous waste incinerators are not randomly scattered across the landscape. Communities with hazardous waste incinerators generally have large minority populations, low incomes, and low property values.[13]

A 1990 Greenpeace report, *Playing with Fire,* found that communities with existing incinerators have 89 percent more people of color than the national average; communities where incinerators are proposed for construction have minority populations that are 60 percent higher than the national average; the average income in communities with existing incinerators is 15 percent lower than the national average; property values in communities that host incinerators are 38 percent lower than the national average; and average property values are 35 percent lower in communities where incinerators have been proposed.[14]

The industrial encroachment into Chicago's Southside neighborhoods is a classic example of geographic inequity. Chicago is the nation's third largest city and one of the most racially segregated cities in the country. More than 92 percent of the city's 1.1 million African American residents live in racially segregated areas. The Altgeld

Gardens housing project, located on the city's southeast side, is one of these segregated enclaves. The neighborhood is home to 150,000 residents, of whom 70 percent are African American and 11 percent are Latino.

Altgeld Gardens is encircled by municipal and hazardous waste landfills, toxic waste incinerators, grain elevators, sewage treatment facilities, smelters, steel mills, and a host of other polluting industries.[15] Because of its location, Hazel Johnson, a community organizer in the neighborhood, has dubbed the area a "toxic doughnut." There are 50 active or closed commercial hazardous waste landfills; 100 factories, including 7 chemical plants and 5 steel mills; and 103 abandoned toxic waste dumps. . . .[16]

In the Los Angeles air basin, 71 percent of African Americans and 50 percent of Latinos live in areas with the most polluted air whereas only 34 percent of whites live in highly polluted areas.[17] The "dirtiest" zip code in California (90058) is sandwiched between South-Central Los Angeles and East Los Angeles. The one-square-mile area is saturated with abandoned toxic waste sites, freeways, smokestacks, and wastewater pipes from polluting industries. Some 18 industrial firms in 1989 discharged more than 33 million pounds of waste chemicals into the environment.

Unequal protection may result from land-use decisions that determine the location of residential amenities and disamenities. Unincorporated communities of poor African Americans suffer a "triple" vulnerability to noxious facility siting.[18] For example, Wallace, Louisiana, a small unincorporated African American community located on the Mississippi River, was rezoned from residential to industrial use by the mostly white officials of St. John the Baptist Parish to allow construction of a Formosa Plastics Corporation plant. The company's plants have been major sources of pollution in Baton Rouge, Louisiana; Point Comfort, Texas; Delaware City, Delaware; and its home country of Taiwan.[19] Wallace residents have filed a lawsuit challenging the rezoning action as racially motivated.

Environmental justice advocates have sought to persuade federal, state, and local governments to adopt policies that address distributive impacts, concentration, enforcement, and compliance concerns. Some states have tried to use a "fair share" approach to come closer to geographic equity. In 1990, New York City adopted a fair share legislative model designed to ensure that every borough and every community within each borough bears its fair share of noxious facilities. Public hearings have begun to address risk burdens in New York City's boroughs.

Testimony at a hearing on environmental disparities in the Bronx points to concerns raised by African Americans and Puerto Ricans who see their neighborhoods threatened by garbage transfer stations, salvage yards, and recycling centers:

> On the Hunts Point peninsula alone there are at least thirty private transfer stations, a large-scale Department of Environmental Protection (DEP) sewage treatment plant and a sludge dewatering facility, two Department of Sanitation (DOS) marine transfer stations, a citywide private regulated medical waste incinerator, a proposed DOS resource recovery facility and three proposed DEP sludge processing facilities. That all of the facilities listed above are located immediately adjacent to the Hunts Point Food Center, the biggest wholesale food and meat distribution facility of its kind in the United States, and

the largest source of employment in the South Bronx, is disconcerting. A policy whereby low-income and minority communities have become the "dumping grounds" for unwanted land uses, works to create an environment of disincentives to community-based development initiatives. It also undermines existing businesses.[20]

Some communities form a special case for environmental justice. For example, Native American reservations are geographic entities but are also quasi-sovereign nations. Because of less stringent environmental regulations than those at the state and federal levels, Native American reservations from New York to California have become prime targets for risky technologies.[21] Indian nations do not fall under state jurisdiction. Similarly, reservations have been described as the "lands the feds forgot."[22] More than 100 industries, ranging from solid waste landfills to hazardous waste incinerators and nuclear waste storage facilities, have targeted reservations.[23]

SOCIAL EQUITY

Social equity refers to the role of sociological factors, such as race, ethnicity, class, culture, lifestyles, and political power, in environmental decisionmaking. Poor people and people of color often work in the most dangerous jobs and live in the most polluted neighborhoods, and their children are exposed to all kinds of environmental toxins on the playground and in their homes and schools.

Some government actions have created and exacerbated environmental inequity. More stringent environmental regulations have driven noxious facilities to follow the path of least resistance toward poor, overburdened communities. Governments have even funded studies that justify targeting economically disenfranchised communities for noxious facilities. Cerrell Associates, Inc., a Los Angeles–based consulting firm, advised the state of California on facility siting and concluded that "ideally . . . officials and companies should look for lower socioeconomic neighborhoods that are also in a heavy industrial area with little, if any commercial activity."[24]

The first state-of-the-art solid waste incinerator slated to be built in Los Angeles was proposed for the South-Central Los Angeles neighborhood. The city-sponsored project was defeated by local residents.[25] The two permits granted by the California Department of Health Services for state-of-the-art toxic waste incinerators were proposed for mostly Latino communities: Vernon, near East Los Angeles, and Kettleman City, a farm worker community in the agriculturally rich Central Valley. Kettleman City has 1,200 residents, of which 95 percent are Latino. It is home to the largest hazardous waste incinerator west of the Mississippi River. The Vernon proposal was defeated but the Kettleman City proposal is still pending. . . .

The solution to unequal protection lies in the realm of environmental justice for all people. No community—rich or poor, black or white—should be allowed to become a "sacrifice zone." The lessons from the civil rights struggles around housing, employment, education, and public accommodations over the past four decades suggest that environmental justice requires a legislative foundation. It is not enough to demonstrate the existence of unjust and unfair conditions; the practices that cause the conditions must be made illegal.

ENDNOTES

1. U.S. Environmental Protection Agency, *Environmental Equity: Reducing Risk for All Communities* (Washington, D.C., 1992); and K. Sexton and Y. Banks Anderson, eds., "Equity in Environmental Health: Research Issues and Needs," *Toxicology and Industrial Health* 9 (September/October 1993).

2. R. D. Bullard, "Solid Waste Sites and the Black Houston Community," *Sociological Inquiry* 53, nos. 2 and 3 (1983): 273–88; idem, *Invisible Houston: The Black Experience in Boom and Bust* (College Station, Tex.: Texas A&M University Press, 1987); idem, *Dumping in Dixie: Race, Class, and Environmental Quality* (Boulder, Colo.: Westview Press, 1990); idem, *Confronting Environmental Racism: Voices from the Grassroots* (Boston, Mass.: South End Press, forthcoming); D. Russell, "Environmental Racism," *American Journal* 11 no. 2 (1989): 22–32; M. Lavelle and M. Coyle, "Unequal Protection," *National Law Journal*, 21 September 1992, 1–2; R. Austin and M. Schill, "Black, Brown, Poor, and Poisoned: Minority Grassroots Environmentalism and the Quest for Eco-Justice," *Kansas Journal of Law and Public Policy* 1 (1991): 69–82; R. Godsil, "Remedying Environmental Racism," *Michigan Law Review* 90 (1991): 394–427; and B. Bryant and P. Mohae, eds., *Race and the Incidence of Environmental Hazards: A Time for Discourse* (Boulder, Colo.: Westview Press, 1992).

3. R. B. Stewart, "Paradoxes of Liberty, Integrity, and Fraternity: The Collective Nature of Environmental Quality and Judicial Review of Administration Action," *Environmental Law* 7, no. 3 (1977): 474–76; M. A. Freeman, "The Distribution of Environmental Quality," in A. V. Kneese and B. T. Bower, eds., *Environmental Quality Analysis* (Baltimore, Md.: Johns Hopkins University Press for Resources for the Future, 1972); W. J. Kruvant, "People, Energy, and Pollution," in D. K. Newman and D. Day, eds., *American Energy Consumer* (Cambridge, Mass.: Ballinger, 1972), 125–67; and L. Gianessi, H. M. Peskin, and E. Wolff, "The Distributional Effects of Uniform Air Pollution Policy in the U.S.," *Quarterly Journal of Economics* 56, no. 1 (1979): 281–301.

4. Freeman, note 3 above; Kruvant, note 3 above; Bullard, 1983 and 1990, note 2 above; P. Asch and J. J. Seneca, "Some Evidence on the Distribution of Air Quality," *Land Economics* 54, no. 3 (1978): 278–97; United Church of Christ Commission for Racial Justice, *Toxic Wastes and Race in the United States: A National Study of the Racial and Socioeconomic Characteristics of Communities with Hazardous Waste Sites* (New York: United Church of Christ, 1987); Russell, note 2 above: R. D. Bullard and B. H. Wright, "Environmentalism and the Policies of Equity: Emergent Trends in the Black Community," *Mid-American Review of Sociology* 12, no. 2 (1987): 21–37; idem, "The Quest for Environmental Equity: Mobilizing the African American Community for Social Change," Society and Natural Resources 3, no. 4 (1990): 301–11; M. Gelobter. "The Distribution of Air Pollution by Income and Race" (paper presented at the Second Symposium on Social Science in Resource Management, Urbana, Ill., June 1988); R. D. Bullard and J. R. Feagin, "Racism and the City," in M. Gottdiener and C. V. Pickvance, eds., *Urban Life in Transition* (Newbury Park, Calif.: Sage, 1991), 55–76; R. D. Bullard, "Urban Infrastructure: Social, Environmental, and Health Risks to African Americans," in B. J. Tidwell,

ed., *The State of Black America 1992* (New York: National Urban League, 1992), 183–96; P. Ong and E. Blumenberg, "Race and Environmentalism" (paper prepared for the Graduate School of Architecture and Urban Planning, University of California at Los Angeles, 14 March 1990); and B. H. Wright and R. D. Bullard, "Hazards in the Workplace and Black Health," *National Journal of Sociology* 4, no. 1 (1990): 45–62.

5. Freeman, note 3 above; Gianessi, Peskin, and Wolff, note 3 above; Gelobter, note 4 above; D. R. Wernette and L. A. Nieves, "Breathing Polluted Air," *EPA Journal* 18, no. 1 (1992): 16–17; Bullard, 1983, 1987, and 1990, note 2 above; R. D. Bullard, "Environmental Racism," *Environmental Protection* 2 (June 1991): 25–26; L. A. Nieves, "Not in Whose Backyard? Minority Population Concentrations and Noxious Facility Sites" (paper presented at the Annual Meeting of the American Association for the Advancement of Science, Chicago, 9 February 1992); United Church of Christ, note 4 above; Agency for Toxic Substances and Disease Registry, *The Nature and Extent of Lead Poisoning in Children in the United States: A Report to Congress* (Atlanta, Ga.: U.S. Department of Health and Human Services, 1988); K. Florini et al., *Legacy of Lead: America's Continuing Epidemic of Childhood Lead Poisoning* (Washington, D.C.: Environmental Defense Fund, 1990); and P. West, J. M. Fly, F. Larkin, and P. Marans, "Minority Anglers and Toxic Fish Consumption: Evidence of the State-Wide Survey of Michigan," in B. Bryant and P. Mohai, eds., *The Proceedings of the Michigan Conference on Race and the Incidence of Environmental Hazards* (Ann Arbor, Mich.: University of Michigan School of Natural Resources, 1990), 108–22.

6. Gelobter, note 4 above; and M. Gelobter, "Toward a Model of Environmental Discrimination," in Bryant and Mohai, eds., note 5 above, pages 87–107.

7. B. Goldman, *Not Just Prosperity: Achieving Sustainability with Environmental Justice* (Washington, D.C.: National Wildlife Federation Corporate Conservation Council, 1994), 8.

8. Wernette and Nieves, note 5 above, pages 16–17.

9. H. P. Mak, P. Johnson, H. Abbey, and R. C. Talamo, "Prevalence of Asthma and Health Service Utilization of Asthmatic Children in an Inner City," *Journal of Allergy and Clinical Immunology* 70 (1982): 367–72; I. F. Goldstein and A. L. Weinstein, "Air Pollution and Asthma: Effects of Exposure to Short-Term Sulfur Dioxide Peaks," *Environmental Research* 40 (1986): 332–45; J. Schwartz et al., "Predictors of Asthma and Persistent Wheeze in a National Sample of Children in the United States," *American Review of Respiratory Disease* 142 (1990): 555–62; U.S. Environmental Protection Agency, note 1 above; and E. Mann, *L.A.'s Lethal Air: New Strategies for Policy, Organizing and Action* (Los Angeles: Labor/Community Strategy Center, 1991).

10. Lavelle and Coyle, note 2 above, pages 1–2.

11. Ibid., 2.

12. Bullard, 1983 and 1990, note 2 above; Gelobter, note 4 above; and United Church of Christ, note 4 above.

13. Bullard, 1983 and 1990, note 2 above; P. Costner and J. Thornton, *Playing with Fire* (Washington, D.C.: Greenpeace, 1990); and United Church of Christ, note 4 above.

14. Costner and Thornton, note 13 above.

15. M. H. Brown, *The Toxic Cloud: The Poisoning of America's Air* (New York: Harper and Row, 1987); and J. Summerhays, *Estimation and Evaluation of Cancer Risks Attributable to Air Pollution in Southeast Chicago* (Washington, D.C.: U.S. Environmental Protection Agency, 1989).

16. *Greenpeace Magazine*, "Home Street, USA: Living with Pollution," October/November/December 1991, 8–13.

17. Mann, note 9 above; and J. Kay, "Fighting Toxic Racism: L.A.'s Minority Neighborhood Is the 'Dirtiest' in the State," *San Francisco Examiner*, 7 April 1991, A1.

18. Bullard, 1990, note 2 above.

19. K. C. Colquette and E. A. Henry Robertson, "Environmental Racism: The Causes, Consequences, and Commendations," *Tulane Environmental Law Journal* 5, no. 1 (1991): 153–207.

20. F. Ferrer, "Testimony by the Office of Bronx Borough President," in *Proceedings from the Public Hearing on Minorities and the Environment: An Exploration into the Effects of Environmental Policies, Practices, and Conditions on Minority and Low-Income Communities* (Bronx, N.Y.: Bronx Planning Office, 20 September 1991).

21. B. Angel, *The Toxic Threat to Indian Lands: A Greenpeace Report* (San Francisco, Calif.: Greenpeace, 1992); and J. Kay, "Indian Lands Targeted for Waste Disposal Sites," *San Francisco Examiner,* 10 April 1991, A1.

22. M. Ambler, "The Lands the Feds Forgot," *Sierra,* May/June 1989, 44.

23. Angel, note 22 above; C. Beasley, "Of Poverty and Pollution: Deadly Threat on Native Lands," *Buzzworm* 2, no. 5 (1990): 39–45; and R. Tomsho, "Dumping Grounds: Indian Tribes Contend with Some of the Worst of America's Pollution," *Wall Street Journal,* 29 November 1990, A1.

24. Cerrell Associates, Inc., *Political Difficulties Facing Waste-to-Energy Conversion Plant Siting* (Los Angeles: California Waste Management Board, 1984).

25. L. Blumberg and R. Gottlieb, *War on Waste: Can America Win Its Battle with Garbage?* (Washington, D.C.: Island Press, 1989).

CHAPTER 25

The Heat Is On

ROSS GELBSPAN

After my lawn had burned away to straw last summer, and the local papers announced that the season had been one of the driest in the recorded history of New England, I found myself wondering how long we can go on pretending that nothing is amiss with the world's weather. It wasn't just the fifty ducks near my house that had died when falling water levels in a creek exposed them to botulism-infested mud, or the five hundred people dead in the Midwest from an unexpected heat wave that followed the season's second "one-hundred-year flood" in three years. It was also the news from New Orleans (overrun by an extraordinary number of cockroaches and termites after a fifth consecutive winter without a killing frost), from Spain (suffering a fourth year of drought in a region that ordinarily enjoys a rainfall of 84 inches a year), and from London (Britain's meteorological office reporting the driest summer since 1727 and the hottest since 1659).

The reports of changes in the world's climate have been with us for fifteen or twenty years, most urgently since 1988, when Dr. James Hansen, director of NASA's Goddard Institute for Space Studies, declared that the era of global warming was at hand. As a newspaper correspondent who had reported on the United Nations Conferences on the environment in Stockholm in 1972 and Rio in 1992, I understood something of the ill effects apt to result from the extravagant burning of oil and coal. New record-setting weather extremes seem to have become as commonplace as traffic accidents, and three simple facts have long been known: the distance from the surface of the earth to the far edge of the inner atmosphere is only twelve miles; the annual amount of carbon dioxide forced into that limited space is six billion tons; and the ten hottest years in recorded human history have all occurred since 1980. The facts beg a question that is as simple to ask as it is hard to answer. What do we do with what we know?

The question became more pointed in September, when the 2,500 climate scientists serving on the Intergovernmental Panel on Climate Change issued a new statement on the prospect of forthcoming catastrophe. Never before had the IPCC (called into existence in 1988) come to so unambiguous a conclusion. Always in years past there had been people saying that we didn't yet know enough, or that the evidence was problematical, or our system of computer simulation was subject to too many uncertainties. Not this year. The panel flatly announced that the earth had entered a period of climatic instability likely to cause "widespread economic, social and environmental dislocation over the next century." The continuing emission of greenhouse gases would create protracted, crop-destroying droughts in continental interiors, a host of new and recurring diseases, hurricanes of extraordinary malevolence, and rising sea levels that could inundate island nations and low-lying coastal rims on the continents.

I came across the report in the *New York Times* during the same week that the island of St. Thomas was blasted to shambles by one of thirteen hurricanes that roiled the Caribbean this fall. Scientists speak the language of probability. They prefer to avoid making statements that cannot be further corrected, reinterpreted, modified, or proven wrong. If its September announcement was uncharacteristically bold, possibly it was because the IPCC scientists understood that they were addressing their remarks to people profoundly unwilling to hear what they had to say.

That resistance is understandable, given the immensity of the stakes. The energy industries now constitute the largest single enterprise known to mankind. Moreover, they are indivisible from automobile, farming, shipping, air freight, and banking interests, as well as from the governments dependent on oil revenues for their very existence. With annual sales in excess of one trillion dollars and daily sales of more than two billion dollars, the oil industry alone supports the economies of the Middle East and large segments of the economies of Russia, Mexico, Venezuela, Nigeria, Indonesia, Norway, and Great Britain. Begin to enforce restriction on the consumption of oil and coal, and the effects on the global economy—unemployment, depression, social breakdown, and war—might lay waste to what we have come to call civilization. It is no wonder that for the last five or six years many of the world's politicians and most of the world's news media have been promoting the perception that the worries about the weather are overwrought. Ever since the IPCC first set out to devise strategies whereby the nations of the world might reduce their carbon dioxide emissions and thus ward off a rise in the average global temperature on the order of 4 or 5 degrees Celsius (roughly equal in magnitude to the difference between the last ice age and the current climate period), the energy industry has been conducting, not unreasonably, a ferocious public relations campaign meant to sell the notion that science, any science, is always a matter of uncertainty. Yet on reading the news from the IPCC, I wondered how the oil company publicists would confront the most recent series of geophysical events and scientific findings. To wit:

- A 48-by-22-mile chunk of the Larsen Ice Shelf in the Antarctic broke off last March, exposing rocks that had been buried for 200,000 years and prompting Rodolfo del Valle of the Argentine Antarctic Institute to tell the Associated Press, "Last November we predicted the [ice shelf] would crack in ten years, but it has happened in barely two months."
- In April, researchers discovered a 70 percent decline in the population of zooplankton off the coast of southern California, raising questions about the

survival of several species of that feed on it. Scientists have linked the change to 1 to 2 degree C increase in the surface water temperature over the last four decades.

- A recent series of articles in *The Lancet,* a British medical journal, linked changes in climate patterns to the spread of infectious diseases around the world. The *Aedes aegypti* mosquito, which spreads dengue fever and yellow fever, has traditionally been unable to survive at altitudes higher than 1,000 meters above sea level. But these mosquitoes are now being reported at 1,500 meters in Costa Rica and at 2,200 meters in Colombia. Ocean warming has triggered algae blooms linked to outbreaks of cholera in India, Bangladesh, and the Pacific coast of South America, where, in 1991, the disease infected more than 400,000 people.

- In a paper published in *Science* in April, David J. Thomson, of the AT&T Bell Laboratories, concluded that the .6 degree C warming of the average global temperature over the past century correlates directly with the buildup of atmospheric carbon dioxide. Separate findings by a team of scientists at the National Oceanic and Atmospheric Administration's National Climatic Data Center indicate that growing weather extremes in the United States are due, by a probability of 90 percent, to rising levels of greenhouse gases.

- Scientists previously believed that the transitions between ice ages and more moderate climatic periods occur gradually, over centuries. But researchers from the Woods Hole Oceanographic Institution, examining deep ocean sediment and ice core samples, found that these shifts, with their temperature changes of up to 7 degrees C, have occurred within three to four decades—a virtual nanosecond in geological time. Over the last 70,000 years, the earth's climate has snapped into radically different temperature regimes. "Our results suggest that the present climate system is very delicately poised," said researcher Scott Lehman. "Shifts could happen very rapidly if conditions are right, and we cannot predict when that will occur." His cautionary tone is underscored by findings that the end of the last ice age, some 8,000 years ago, was preceded by a series of extreme oscillations in which severe regional deep freezes alternated with warming spikes. As the North Atlantic warmed, Arctic snowmelts and increased rainfall diluted the salt content of the ocean, which, in turn, redirected the ocean's warming current from a northeasterly direction to one that ran nearly due east. Should such an episode occur today, say researchers, "the present climate of Britain and Norway would change suddenly to that of Greenland."

These items (and many like them) would seem to be alarming news—far more important than the candidacy of Colin Powell, or even whether Newt Gingrich believes the government should feed poor children—worthy of a national debate or the sustained attention of Congress. But the signs and portents have been largely ignored, relegated to the environmental press and the oddball margins of the mass media. More often than not, the news about the accelerating retreat of the world's glaciers or the heat- and insect-stressed Canadian forests comes qualified with the observation that the question of global warming never can be conclusively resolved. The confusion is intentional, expensively gift wrapped by the energy industries.

Capital keeps its nose to the wind. The people who run the world's oil and coal companies know that the march of science, and of political action, may be slowed by disinformation. In the last year and a half, one of the leading oil industry public relations outlets, the Global Climate Coalition, has spent more than a million dollars to downplay the threat of climate change. It expects to spend another $850,000 on the issue next year. Similarly, the National Coal Association spent more than $700,000 on the global climate issue in 1992 and 1993. In 1993 alone, the American Petroleum Institute, just one of fifty-four industry members of the GCC, paid $1.8 million to the public relations firm of Burson-Marsteller partly in an effort to defeat a proposed tax on fossil fuels. For perspective, this is only slightly less than the combined yearly expenditures on global warming of the five major environmental groups that focus on climate issues—about $2.1 million, according to officials of the Environmental Defence Fund, the Natural Resources Defense Council, the Sierra Club, the Union of Concerned Scientists, and the World Wildlife Fund.

For the most part the industry has relied on a small band of skeptics—Dr. Richard S. Lindzen, Dr. Pat Michaels, Dr. Robert Balling, Dr. Sherwood Idso, and Dr. S. Fred Singer, among others—who have proven extraordinarily adept at draining the issue of all sense of crisis. Through their frequent pronouncements in the press and on radio and television, they have helped to create the illusion that the question is hopelessly mired in unknowns. Most damaging has been their influence on decision makers; their contrarian views have allowed conservative Republicans such as Representative Dana Rohrabacher (R., Calif.) to dismiss legitimate research concerns as "liberal claptrap" and have provided the basis for the recent round of budget cuts to those government science programs designed to monitor the health of the planet.

Last May, Minnesota held hearings in St. Paul to determine the environmental cost of coal burning by state power plants. Three of the skeptics—Lindzen, Michaels, and Balling—were hired as expert witnesses to testify on behalf of Western Fuels Association, a $400 million consortium of coal suppliers and coal-fired utilities.[1]

An especially aggressive industry player, Western Fuels was quite candid about its strategy in two annual reports: "[T]here has been a close to universal impulse in the trade association community here in Washington to concede the scientific premise of global warming . . . while arguing over policy prescriptions that would be the least disruptive to our economy. . . . We have disagreed, and do disagree, with this strategy." "When [the climate change] controversy first erupted . . . scientists were found who are skeptical about much of what seemed generally accepted about the potential for climate change." Among them were Michaels, Balling, and S. Fred Singer.

Lindzen, a distinguished professor of meteorology at MIT, testified in St. Paul that the maximum probable warming of the atmosphere in the face of a doubling of carbon dioxide emissions over the next century would amount to no more than a negligible .3 degrees C. Michaels, who teaches climatology at the University of Virginia, stated that he foresaw no increase in the rate of sea level rise—another feared precursor of global warming. Balling, who works on climate issues at Arizona State University, declared that the increase in emissions would boost the average global temperature by no more than one degree.

At first glance, these attacks appear defensible, given their focus on the black holes of uncertainty that mark our current knowledge of the planet's exquisitely interrelated climate system. The skeptics emphasize the inadequacy of a major climate research tool known as a General Circulation Model, and our ignorance of carbon dioxide exchange between the oceans and the atmosphere and of the various roles of clouds. They have repeatedly pointed out that although the world's output of carbon dioxide has exploded since 1940, there has been no corresponding increase in the global temperature. The larger scientific community, by contrast, holds that this is due to the masking effect of low-level sulfur particulates, which exert a temporary cooling effect on the earth, and to a time lag in the oceans' absorption and release of carbon dioxide.

But while the skeptics portray themselves as besieged truth-seekers fending off irresponsible environmental doomsayers, their testimony in St. Paul and elsewhere revealed the source and scope of their funding for the first time. Michaels has received more than $115,000 over the last four years from coal and energy interests. *World Climate Review,* a quarterly he founded that routinely debunks climate concerns, was funded by Western Fuels. Over the last six years, either alone or with colleagues, Balling has received more than $200,000 from coal and oil interests in Great Britain, Germany, and elsewhere. Balling (along with Sherwood Idso) has also taken money from Cyprus Minerals, a mining company that has been a major funder of People for the West—a militantly anti-environmental "Wise Use" group. Lindzen, for his part, charges oil and coal interests $2,500 a day for his consulting services; his 1991 trip to testify before a Senate committee was paid for by Western Fuels, and a speech he wrote, entitled "Global Warming: the Origin and Nature of Alleged Scientific Consensus," was underwritten by OPEC. Singer, who last winter proposed a $95,000 publicity project to "stem the tide towards ever more onerous controls on energy use," has received consulting fees from Exxon, Shell, Unocal, Arco, and Sun Oil, and has warned them that they face the same threat as the chemical firms that produced chlorofluorocarbons (CFCs), a class of chemicals found to be depleting atmospheric ozone. "It took only five years to go from . . . a simple freeze of production [of CFCs]," Singer has written, ". . . to the 1992 decision of a complete production phase-out—all on the basis of quite insubstantial science."[2]

The skeptics assert flatly that their science is untainted by funding. Nevertheless, in this persistent and well-funded campaign of denial they have become interchangeable ornaments on the hood of a high-powered engine of disinformation. Their dissenting opinions are amplified beyond all proportion through the media while the concerns of the dominant majority of the world's scientific establishment are marginalized.[3] By keeping the discussion focused on whether there is a problem in the first place, they have effectively silenced the debate over what to do about it.

Last spring's IPCC conference in Berlin is a good example. Delegations from 170 nations met to negotiate targets and timetables for reducing the world's carbon dioxide emissions. The efforts of the conference ultimately foundered on foot-dragging by the United States and Japan and active resistance from the OPEC nations. Leading the fight for the most dramatic reductions—to 60 percent of 1990 levels—was a coalition of small island nations from the Caribbean and the Pacific that fear being flooded out of existence. They were supported by most western European governments, but China and India, with their vast coal resources, argued that until the United States significantly cuts its own emissions, their obligation to develop their own economies outranked their obligation to the global environment. In the end, OPEC, supported by the United States, Japan, Australia, Canada, and New Zealand, rejected calls to limit emissions, declaring emission limits premature.

As the natural crisis escalates, so will the forces of institutional and societal denial. If, at the cost of corporate pocket change, industrial giants can control the publicly perceived reality of the condition of the planet and the state of our scientific knowledge, what would they do if their survival were truly put at risk? Billions would be spent on the creation of information and the control of politicians. Glad-handing oil company ads on the op-ed page of the *New York Times* (from a quarter-page pronouncement by Mobil last September 28: "There's a lot of good news out there") would give way to a new stream of selective findings by privatized scientists. Long before the planet itself collapsed, democracy would break apart under the stress of "natural" disasters. It is not difficult to foresee that in an ecological state of emergency our political liberties would be the first casualties.

Thus, the question must be asked: can civilization change the way it operates? For 5,000 years, we have thought of ourselves as dependent children of the earth, flourishing or perishing according to the whims of nature. But with the explosion of the power of our technology and the size of our population, our activities have grown to the proportion of geological forces, affecting the major systems of the planet. Short of the Atlantic washing away half of Florida, the abstract notion that the old anomalies have become the new norm is difficult to grasp. Dr. James McCarthy of Harvard, who has supervised the work of climate scientists from sixty nations, puts it this way: "If the last 150 years had been marked by the kind of climate instability we are now seeing, the world would never have been able to support its present population of 5 billion people." We live in a world of man-size urgencies, measured in hours or days. What unfolds slowly is not, by our lights, urgent, and it will therefore take a collective act of imagination to understand the extremity of the situation we now confront. The lag time in our planet's ecological systems will undoubtedly delay these decisions, and even if the nations of the world were to agree tomorrow on a plan to phase out oil and coal and convert to renewable energies, an equivalent lag time in human affairs would delay its implementation for years. What too many people refuse to understand is that the global economy's existence depends upon the global environment, not the other way around. One cannot negotiate jobs, development, or rates of economic growth with nature.

What of the standard list of palliatives—carbon taxes, more energy-efficient buildings, a revival of public transportation? The ideas are attractive, but the thinking is too small. Even were the United States to halve its own carbon dioxide contribution, this cutback would soon be overwhelmed by the coming development of industry and housing and schools in China and India and Mexico for all their billions of citizens. No solution can work that does not provide ample energy resources for the development of all the world's nations.

So here is an informal proposal—at best a starting point for a conversation—from one man who is not an expert. What if we turned the deserts of the world into electricity farms? Let the Middle East countries keep their oil royalties as solar royalties. What if the world mobilized around a ten-year project to phase out all fossil fuels, to develop renewable energy technologies, to extend those technologies to every corner of the world? What if, to minimize the conflict of so massive a dislocation, the world's energy companies were put in charge of the transition—answering only to an international regulatory body and an enforceable timetable? Grant them the same profit margins for solar electricity and hydrogen fuel they now receive for petroleum and coal. Give them the licenses for all renewable energy technologies. Assure them the same relative position in the world's economy they now enjoy at the end of the project.

Are these ideas mere dreams? Perhaps, but there are historical reasons to have hope. Four years ago a significant fraction of humanity overturned its Communist system in a historical blink of an eye. Eight years ago the world's governments joined together in Montreal to regulate CFCs. Technology is not the issue. The atomic bomb was developed in two and a half years. Putting a man on the moon took eleven. Surely, given the same sense of urgency, we can develop new energy systems in ten years. Most of the technology is already available to us or soon will be. We have the knowledge, the energy, and the hunger for jobs to get it done. And we are different in one unmeasurable way from previous generations: ours is the first to be educated about the larger world by the global reach of electronic information.

The leaders of the oil and coal industry, along with their skeptical scientists, relentlessly accuse environmentalists of overstating the climatic threat to destroy capitalism. Must a transformation that is merely technological dislodge the keystone of the economic order? I don't know. But I do know that technology changes the way we conceive of the world. To transform our economy would oblige us to understand the limits of the planet. That understanding alone might seed the culture with a more organic concept of ourselves and our connectedness to the earth. And corporations, it is useful to remember, are not only obstacles on the road to the future. They are also crucibles of technology and organizing engines of production, the modern expression of mankind's drive for creativity. The industrialist is no less human than the poet, and both the climate scientist and the oil company operator inhabit the same planet, suffer the same short life span, harbor the same hopes for their children.

Each summer, our family walks the deep north Maine woods in search of adventure and a sense of renewal. The trip this year was different for me; I was visited by premonitions of the coming sickness of the forest, haunted by unwelcome and indescribably sad imaginings. They intruded at unexpected moments. One night while listening to a dialogue of loons on a black lake I suddenly experienced a momentary feeling of bottomless grief. Struck by the recognition of how fragile was the frame of the world, and how easily it could be shattered by our mutual distrust and

confusion, I feared that the cause of survival would be lost to the greed and alienation and shortsightedness that dog our few last steps to the threshold of the millennium. My dream of reconfiguring the global economy was probably nothing
more than the hopeless longing of a reporter, not a social thinker or macroeconomic
engineer.

But I am also a husband and a father, a son, and a grandson. And someday
perhaps a grandfather. Our history is rich with visionaries urging us to change our
ways of thinking, asking questions about the meaning of the past and the shape of
the future. Now the questions are being posed, in a language we don't yet fully understand, by the oceans. I have promised myself that next summer I will keep my
lawn watered, at least as long as the water holds out.

ENDNOTES

1. In 1991, Western Fuels spent an estimated $250,000 to produce and distribute a video
entitled "The Greening of Planet Earth," which was shown frequently inside the Bush White
House as well as within the governments of OPEC. In near-evangelical tones, the video
promises that a new age of agricultural abundance will result from increasing concentrations
of carbon dioxide. It portrays a world where vast areas of desert are reclaimed by the carbon
dioxide–forced growth of new grasslands, where the earth's diminishing forests are replen-
ished by a nurturing atmosphere. Unfortunately, it overlooks the bugs. Experts note that even
a minor elevation in temperature would trigger an explosion in the planet's insect population,
leading to potentially significant disruptions in food supplies from crop damage as well as to
a surge in insect-borne diseases. It appears that Western Fuels' video fails to tell people what
the termites in New Orleans may be trying to tell them now.

2. Contrary to his assertion, however, virtually all relevant researchers say the link between
CFCs and ozone depletion is based on unassailably solid scientific evidence. As if to under-
score the point, in May the research director of the European Union Commission estimated
that last winter's ozone loss will result in about 80,000 additional cases of skin cancer in Europe. This fall, the three scientists who discovered the CFC-ozone link won the Nobel Prize for
Chemistry.

3. The industry's public relations arsenal, however, is made up of much more than a few
sympathetic scientists. Last March, the Global Climate Coalition distributed a report by Accu-
Weather Inc. that denied any significant increase in extreme weather events. The report flies
in the face of contradictory evidence cited by officials of the insurance industry, which, during the 1980s, paid an average of $3 billion a year to victims of natural disasters—a figure that
has jumped to $10 billion a year in this decade. A top official of a Swiss reinsurance firm told
the World Watch Institute: "There is a significant body of scientific evidence indicating that
[the recent] record insured loss from natural catastrophes was not a random occurrence."
More succinctly, the president of the Reinsurance Association of America said climate change
"could bankrupt the industry."

PART EIGHT

Work and Welfare

Americans pride themselves on their commitment to the "work ethic." And despite predictions in the 1950s and 1960s that we were on the verge of becoming a "leisure" society, work remains central to the lives of most of us. It is how, as adults, we make a living, define our identities, and find our place in the scheme of things. Ideally, work is one of the most important ways in which we are enabled to participate in a larger human community.

But the reality of work, for all too many people, has always fallen short of the ideal. In the nineteenth century, many social theorists and social critics argued that for the great bulk of people in the emerging industrial societies, work had become a source of torment and exploitation rather than fulfillment. Karl Marx, one of the most influential of those critics, put it this way:

> What constitutes the alienation of labour? First, that the work is *external* to the worker, that it is not part of his nature; and that, consequently, he does not fulfill himself in his work but denies himself, has a feeling of misery rather than well-being, does not develop freely his mental and physical energies but is physically exhausted and mentally debased. The worker, therefore, feels himself at home only during his leisure time, whereas at work he feels homeless. His work is not voluntary but imposed, *forced labour.* It is not satisfaction of a need, but only a *means* for satisfying other needs. Its alien character is clearly shown by the fact that as soon as there is no physical or other compulsion it is avoided like the plague.[1]

Today, as we move into the twenty-first century, the concerns of the nineteenth-century critics have become, if anything, more urgent. An array of rapid economic and technological changes has made the link between work and well-being more and more problematic. The increasingly competitive global economy has put new strains on the institution of work—radically reshaping the workplace, eliminating jobs, and lowering incomes and benefits for many of those who do work steadily. The three articles in this part explore these themes in detail.

In the first, the economist Richard B. Freeman shows that while these changes have affected workers around the world, they have had an unusually destructive impact on *American* workers, who were once widely considered to be better off than their counterparts in Europe. Today the opposite is true. European workers are typically paid more, have longer vacations and shorter workweeks, and enjoy a much more generous set of social benefits.

That helps explain why, as we've seen earlier, poverty is both broader and deeper in America than in most European countries. We are often told that the United States has become a high-tech economy in which most jobs require considerable education and skill and are rewarded accordingly. But the reality is less bright. Our economy has indeed produced many high-skill, high-wage jobs in recent years, but it has also produced a far greater number of low-level ones, paying only the minimum wage or a little above it. This means increased stress and hardship for growing numbers of American workers and their families; beyond that, it has undercut one of the basic tenets of the American ethos: the conviction that hard work will lead to economic security and personal fulfillment. For more and more Americans, that is only a dream.

If succeeding through work is becoming increasingly problematic for many "mainstream" Americans, it is even more so for the inner-city poor, who have been the worst victims of the changing nature of work in America. As far back as the 1950s, many observers warned that the looming decline in manufacturing employment would have devastating consequences for the inner cities—already wracked by crime, drugs, and family disruption—if we failed to develop alternative ways to put people to work. For the most part, however, we didn't heed those warnings. The results, as William Julius Wilson's article shows, are exactly what was predicted. Deindustrialization has laid waste to job prospects in the inner cities, bringing a corresponding—but hardly surprising—deepening of social problems in its wake.

It might seem logical that we would have responded to this massive loss of jobs by creating new ones to take their place. For the most part, however, that is not what we did. One reason for our reluctance to invest directly in new jobs was the widespread belief that the lack of jobs wasn't the real problem: that, as it was often said, anybody could get a job if they really wanted one. Instead, many people blamed the stubborn poverty and other problems of the urban "underclass" on the system we had established to help the casualties of economic insecurity—the welfare system. In fact, the provision of welfare in America had always been minimal, compared with other advanced industrial countries.

But the growing belief that an overly generous welfare system caused joblessness and poverty by undermining the work ethic and encouraging dependency has nevertheless prevailed in American social policy. In the 1990s, the nation embarked on a controversial welfare "reform" designed to get people off the welfare rolls and into jobs—without much concern about whether there were enough jobs available to accommodate them, at wages that could realistically support a family. But was the welfare system itself really the problem? Recent evidence on the effects of welfare reform suggests that though this policy did manage to move many people off of the welfare rolls, it was far less successful in moving them out of poverty. And despite the radical shrinking of the welfare system, the inner city problems described by Wilson remain very much with us.

That a great deal was, and is, wrong with our welfare system cannot be denied. But as Rosemary L. Bray shows in her autobiographical account of growing up on welfare, much of the newly fashionable view of welfare families held by more fortunate Americans is misleading and self-serving. Bray's mother, who scrambled to raise four children, send them to private schools, and ultimately turn them into "working, taxpaying adults," bears little resemblance to the stereotype of welfare women as lazy consumers of government handouts. Bray acknowledges that not all women on welfare are equally motivated. But her story of one family's successful use of the welfare system to help them move up from poverty should make us think twice about the idea that welfare's impact is uniformly negative.

ENDNOTE

1. Quoted in Shlomo Avineri, *The Social and Political Thought of Karl Marx* (Cambridge, Eng.: Cambridge University Press, 1971), p. 106.

CHAPTER 26

How Labor Fares in Advanced Economies

RICHARD B. FREEMAN

In 1909 Samuel Gompers, a founder of the American labor movement and president of the American Federation of Labor, visited Europe to examine "from an American viewpoint . . . life and conditions of working men in Great Britain, France, Holland, Germany, Italy, etc." Gompers was struck by the poor living standard of Europeans compared with Americans: "Poverty such as exists in Belgium and Holland can hardly be conceived by the average dweller in an American city." Gompers noted many ways in which Europe could learn from the United States, ranging from provision of running water to efficient operation of railroads, areas in which Europe was "half a century behind time." But nowhere did he find lessons for the United States from Europe. On the union front, which concerned him most, "the national [labor] movement in no foreign country can compare with the American Federation of Labor."

Throughout the twentieth century, economic and social developments broadly validated Gompers' "America first" view of the labor scene. Through two world wars and the recoveries that followed them, the United States led the world in productivity, real wages, and conditions at the workplace. During the cold war, American unions were preeminent defenders of free enterprise and supporters of independent unions overseas. American business dominated world markets and pioneered the consumer society.

The evidence in this book shows that at the approach of the twenty-first century the situation for American labor is quite different. Labor productivity and living standards are high in the United States, but this country no longer dominates other advanced economies in providing good jobs at good wages. American work arrangements, modes of pay, training, and labor representation are not clearly superior to those in other countries. Low-paid workers in the United States earn so much less than the average that they have worse standards of living than comparable workers in Europe or Japan. Japanese firms that offer lifetime employment, job rotation, enterprise unions, and bonus payments outcompete American firms in many markets. German firms with apprenticeship programs, works councils, and workers on boards of directors, train workers better and empower them at the workplace in ways that American firms do not. Countries whose conditions horrified Gompers are among the most prosperous in the world, as any tourist to Belgium or Holland will attest. Productivity and real wages are increasing less rapidly in the United States than in Europe and Japan.

PAY AND POVERTY

The well-being of wage and salary workers depends on their rate of pay, which is related to, but not identical with, labor productivity. In his 1909 survey, Gompers reported low rates of pay for workers in Europe, which he transformed into dollars using the exchange rates of that era. Column 1 of Table 26.1 records hourly compensation of production workers in manufacturing in 1992 across countries, also transformed into dollars by exchange rates. The position of American workers is different than it was in earlier decades. At 1992 exchange rates Americans received low pay compared with workers in other advanced countries. Hourly compensation was 60 percent higher in Germany than in the United States, 50 percent higher in Sweden, 44 percent higher in Switzerland, 36 percent higher in Belgium (which Gompers saw as a disaster case), and so on. Given comparable levels of productivity, American workers are a low-wage bargain in the developed world.

However, pay comparisons based on exchange rates, while an appropriate guide to some business investment decisions, are misleading as an indicator of standards of living. Hourly compensation in PPP, given in column 2 of Table 26.1, tells a very different story. Measured in purchasing power, the United States is not *the* leader in pay it once was, but it trails only Germany, the Netherlands, and (Gompers would be stunned) Belgium. The difference in the U.S. position between columns 1 and 2 is that at 1992 exchange rates, consumer prices were much higher in Europe and Japan than in the United States. Adjusting for price differences via PPP rates greatly improves the relative American position.

But as with productivity, the growth rate of real wages (wages adjusted for inflation) in the United States portends a worsened relative position for American workers by the year 2000. The real earnings of manufacturing workers in the United States fell in the 1980s, whereas the real earnings of manufacturing workers in Europe rose by 1.2 percent per year and the real earnings of those in Japan rose by 1.6 percent per year. If 1980s rates of growth of real earnings are maintained in other countries, and the United States manages to keep real earnings from falling (which would be an improvement over the 1980s), American workers will drop from near the top of the earnings table to the lower middle ranks (see column 3 of Table 26.1). If real earnings of American manufacturing workers fall in the 1990s at the same rate as in the 1980s, the United States will drop to the fourth lowest position. Some countries will undoubtedly do better in the 1990s than they did in the 1980s while others

TABLE 26.1 Hourly Compensation of Production Workers in Manufacturing in Advanced Countries, Relative to the United States

Country	Hourly Compensation in Exchange Rates 1992[a]	Hourly Compensation in Purchasing Power 1992[b]	Hourly Compensation Projected to the Year 2000[c]
United States	100	100	100
Major Countries			
Japan	100	66	75
Germany	160	119	135
France	104	85	91
United Kingdom	91	82	98
Italy	120	100	105
Canada	105	97	96
Smaller Countries			
Australia	80	81	76
Austria	122	95	107
Belgium	136	113	114
Denmark	124	82	85
Netherlands	128	103	104
Norway	143	93	100
Spain	83	74	87
Sweden	150	80	92
Switzerland	144	89	95

[a]Column 1 data from U.S. Bureau of Labor Statistics, *International Comparisons of Hourly Compensation Costs for Production Workers in Manufacturing,* 1992 Report 844 (Washington D.C.: U.S. GPO, 1993), Table 1.

[b]Column 2 data adjusted by taking hourly compensation from Table 2 of the report and purchasing power parity figures for 1990 from OECD, 1992d (Table 1.3).

[c]Column 3 data based on projecting 1979–1990 growth of real hourly earnings in manufacturing from OECD, 1992b (Table 9.2) for each country except the United States, where I have made the more optimistic assumption of constant real earnings as opposed to the annual drop of 1 percent in the 1979–1990 period in the OECD figures.

will undoubtedly do worse, but the general pattern is clear: a falling position for the United States.

Since most workers are not production workers in manufacturing, you may wonder whether the earnings of these workers provide a valid comparison of well-being across countries. As an indicator of the position of *average* workers, the pay figures in Table 26.1 are broadly representative. Estimates of annual compensation for employees in the business sector, which covers the vast bulk of employees, confirm the story about the fall of the United States from its position as the high-wage country.

Average earnings are, however, misleading in one important sense. The *distribution* of wages (and incomes) is more unequal in the United States than in other advanced countries. Lower paid workers do much worse compared with the average in the United States than in other advanced countries, while well-paid workers do much better. Figure 26.1 documents this with two statistics: the ratio of the hourly (weekly) earnings at the lowest decile of the earnings distribution (earnings that exceed those of just 10 percent of the male work force) to the median; and the ratio of the earnings of men in the top decile (those whose earnings exceed 90 percent of workers) also relative to the median. American men in the bottom decile earn just 38 percent of median earnings—barely half as much as Europeans in the bottom decile receive relative to the European median, and just 62 percent as much as Japanese in the bottom decile relative to the Japanese median. In contrast, men in the top decile do relatively better compared with the median in the United States than in other countries. The stories about U.S. executives being well paid as compared with those in other countries are true, but it isn't only executives who do well: so do other American workers near the top of the earnings distribution.

Since average earnings in the United States are comparable in purchasing power to average earnings in countries like Germany or Norway or Belgium, the evidence that low-paid American workers are further below the average than low-paid workers in other countries implies that low-paid Americans have lower earnings and living standards than low-paid workers in those countries. Indeed I estimate that among men in the bottom decile, Americans earn roughly 45 percent of what Germans earn, 54 percent as much as Norwegians, half as much as Italians, and so on. Among bottom decile workers, if the United States is scaled at 100 as in the table, European earnings are 144 and Japanese earnings are 106. Even worse, low-paid Americans have lower real earnings than workers in all advanced countries for which

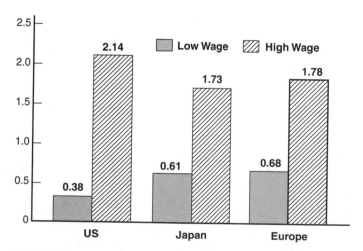

FIGURE 26.1   Pay of Low-Wage and High-Wage Workers Relative to Median: United States, Japan, and Europe

Source: Calculated from OECD, 1993b (Table 5.2) with European estimated as a weighted average using 1988 employment for weights, from OECD, 1990b.

there are comparable data—which is due largely to the fall in their real earnings. The low and falling real pay of less skilled Americans contributes to the high and rising rates of child poverty, and to the extensive homelessness and large "underclass" that differentiate American society from that of other advanced countries. . . .

Mandated Rights and Benefits

There are large country differences in the legal rights of workers at the workplace and in the nonwage benefits—pensions, unemployment benefits, health insurance, occupational disability insurance, and the like—that governments require employers to provide or fund. In Europe the Common Market's Social Charter commits EEC countries (except for the United Kingdom, which opted out of the charter) to provide "social rights of workers" in employment, remuneration, social protection, safety at the workplace, retirement benefits, and so on. As a general rule, European countries mandate greater rights and benefits for workers than does the United States. By legal statute European workers have, in addition to the works councils described earlier, the following workplace-related rights or benefits:

- Extensive vacation and holiday time
- Sickness leave, including pay during the leave
- Maternity leave, including pay during the leave
- Advance notice of dismissals
- Severance pay on dismissal
- Unemployment benefits that last longer than U.S. benefits
- Social security pension benefits comparable to U.S. benefits

The United States does not regulate vacations, sickness leave, or severance pay, and it did not legislate maternity leave until the late 1980s and early 1990s (Table 26.2). In addition, the United States did not require firms to give workers early warning of mass dismissals until 1988. Provision of most benefits is the province of collective bargaining or the individual firms seeking to attract or retain employees, and the benefits and rights that American workers gain through collective bargaining or competitive market forces fall short of those that Europeans gain through legal mandates.

In some situations mandating may be the only way for the labor market to provide benefits or to attain the desired level of benefits. A single firm can face problems in providing benefits when workers differ in their potential use of the benefit. For instance, if firm A offers good sickness benefits, it risks attracting sickly workers, whose use of the benefit may make it too costly to maintain. If every firm offered the benefit, the sickly would be employed more or less randomly among firms, and no single firm would face excessive costs. Similarly, if an insurance company sold unemployment insurance on the open market it would face grave problems, as workers in cyclically sensitive industries or in firms in trouble would seek insurance in large numbers, while those whose jobs were secure would not buy any. Mandating provides a way around these difficulties, though at the cost of forcing uniform

TABLE 26.2   Statutory Regulations Governing Benefits and Rights to Workers in European Countries and United States, 1991

Benefits and Rights	Europe	United States
Public Holidays	12	8–10
Annual Vacation	4 weeks	no statute
Sickness Leave		
Maximum weeks of leave	54	no statute
Percentage of earnings paid during sickness	62 percent	
Maternity Leave		
Maximum weeks of leave	18	13
Percentage of earnings paid during leave	89 percent	0
Severance Pay		
Percentage of workers with severance pay	72 percent	no statute
Unemployment Insurance		
Months covered	16	6
Percentage of earnings paid during unemployment	47 percent	50 percent

Notes: Tabulated from Ehrenberg, 1993 (Tables 2.3, 2.4, 2.5, and 5.1); and from OECD, 1991 (Table 7.2), where I used the replacement rate for persons without a spouse working, and gave Portugal thirteen months of unemployment coverage. I have formed EEC figures by weighting country figures by 1988 employment, as given in OECD, 1990b. Public holidays figures exclude Denmark and the U.K.; vacation data exclude Italy and the U.K. Belgium has an indefinite duration of unemployment insurance and is excluded. Most of the data are for Common Market countries; included are Belgium, Denmark, France, Germany, Greece, Ireland, Italy, Netherlands, Portugal, Spain, and the United Kingdom. The severance pay figures include Austria and the Scandinavian countries.

conditions onto workers who might do better with other arrangements. The woman who would trade the maternity leave benefit for a few extra cents in her paycheck cannot do so when the state mandates maternity leave.

The greater benefits and job security that European workers have compared with Americans are costly. The compensation that employers pay a worker consists not only of wages paid for time worked but also payroll taxes for socially mandated benefits and wages paid for vacations and other time not worked. The nonwage components of compensation are markedly higher in some European countries, such as Italy, Belgium, and France, than in the United States. Employers often complain that employer-paid payroll taxes and mandated benefits add to their labor bill, but most economists believe that in the long run workers pay for these benefits in the form of lower wages. A European who costs her employer the same amount of money *per hour worked* as an American will receive a 20 to 25 percent lower hourly wage as a trade-off for a longer paid vacation and greater mandated social insurance benefits. In addition, many European workers pay a greater share of their wages in the form of payroll taxes and income tax. There is, in short, a price for the vacation and other benefits that Europeans obtain.

Welfare State

Finally, advanced countries differ in the state welfare support they provide persons outside the work force and the working poor. Some welfare benefits require that individuals have a history of work (social security pensions) or that the person be currently employed (the American Earned Income Tax Credit, which pays money to low-income workers as a form of negative income tax, or Swedish daycare subsidies, which require that the child's mother work at least part-time). When the state mandates benefits solely to workers or to those who have worked, the programs have a "workfare" flavor: they give people an extra incentive to find a job and to work for the amount of time that qualifies them for the benefits.

Other state welfare benefits are paid to people regardless of work status, such as family income allowances that provide money for every child in a family or national health insurance, which covers all citizens. Universal benefits also change the incentive to work. If the government provides health care for all citizens, regardless of work status, a worker may be more willing to change jobs, to go on strike, or otherwise to risk losing a job than if his health benefits were tied to his job. In general, the greater the *social wage*—defined as the resources provided people as citizens regardless of their work status—the smaller will be the need to work and the higher the wage that people will demand to work.

Other benefits are limited to people who may be incapable of working, such as the disabled; to the elderly who have retired; to able-bodied persons who cannot find work—the unemployed; or to children in single-parent families, when the single parent lacks work. By providing money for not working, these programs reduce the incentive to work and risk creating a "welfare trap," wherein the recipient's income would drop if he or she obtained a job. For example, the American Aid to Families with Dependent Children program provides health benefits that many small, low-wage employers cannot afford to provide, so that its potential disincentive effect is substantial, and goes beyond the loss of the income benefits. Single mothers in countries that have subsidized daycare for young children and national health insurance, such as France, face a very different set of incentives than those in the United States.

The welfare state affects the labor market in other ways as well. In a society in which many families are headed by a single parent, welfare benefits will affect the resources invested in children and presumably the qualifications of future generations of workers. In European countries with large state welfare programs, welfare is itself a major employer in the job market: a large share of women workers in Sweden, for example, are government employees. Last but not least, since welfare benefits are paid from taxes, the size of the welfare budget affects tax rates and take-home pay.

European countries generally have more extensive state welfare programs than the United States, for which citizens pay a larger percent of GDP per person in taxes. Some countries, notably Sweden, link most benefits to work, so that welfare becomes workfare. Almost all of the countries have generous unemployment benefit systems (Table 26.2) and provide housing and other subsidies that enable many persons to live for extended periods without a job. Lacking such an extensive state welfare system, the United States relies to a greater degree on the private sector to provide welfare-type benefits. Most retired Americans receive, in addition to their Social Security check, a pension from their employer. Americans donate time and money to charitable organizations that care for the needy to a far greater extent than citizens do in other countries. But even so the United States has a low ranking in the provision of welfare and the extent of the social wage or safety net that is guaranteed to citizens. This means that more than in other developed countries, the critical dimension in determining the economic well-being of Americans is how they fare in the labor market.

CHAPTER 27

The Political Economy and Urban Racial Tensions

WILLIAM JULIUS WILSON

Recent books such as Andrew Hacker's *Two Nations* (1992) and Derrick Bell's *Faces at the Bottom of the Well* (1992) promote the view that racial antagonisms are so deep seated, so primordial that feelings of pessimism about whether America can overcome racist sentiments and actions are justified. The events surrounding the recent rebellion in Los Angeles, the worst race riot in the nation's history, aggravated these feelings. However, in this atmosphere of heightened racial awareness we forget or overlook the fact that racial antagonisms are products of situations—economic situations, political situations, and social situations.

To understand the manifestation of racial antagonisms during certain periods, is to comprehend, from both analytic and policy perspectives, the situations that increase and reduce them. As revealed in the title I have chosen for this paper ("The Political Economy and Urban Racial Tensions"), I shall try to demonstrate this important point by showing how the interrelations of political policies and economic and social processes directly and indirectly affect racial tensions in urban America. . . .

POLITICAL POLICIES, ECONOMIC PROCESSES, AND THE CITY–SUBURBAN RACIAL DIVIDE

Since 1960, the proportion of whites inside central cities has decreased steadily, while the proportion of minorities has increased. In 1960 the nation's population was evenly divided between cities, suburbs, and rural areas (Weir 1993). By 1990, both urban and rural populations had declined, leaving suburbs with nearly half of the nation's population. The urban population dipped to 31 percent by 1990. As cities lost population they became poorer and more minority in their racial and ethnic composition. Thus in the eyes of many in the dominant white population, the minorities symbolize the ugly urban scene left behind. Today, the divide between the suburbs and the city is, in many respects, a racial divide. For example, whereas 68 percent of all the residents in the city of Chicago were minority in 1990— blacks (1,074,471), Hispanics (545,852), and Asian & others (152,487), and whites (1,056,048)—83 percent of all suburban residents in the Chicago metropolitan area were white. Across the nation, in 1990, whereas 74 percent of the dominant white population lived in suburban and rural areas, a majority of blacks and Latinos resided in urban areas.

These demographic changes relate to the declining influence of American cities and provided the foundation for the New Federalism, an important political development that has increased the significance of race in metropolitan areas. Beginning in 1980, the federal government drastically reduced its support for basic urban programs. The Reagan and Bush administrations sharply cut spending on direct aid to cities, including general revenue sharing, urban mass transit, public service jobs and job training, compensatory education, social service block grants, local public works, economic development assistance, and urban development action grants. In 1980 the Federal contribution to city budgets was 18 percent; by 1990 it had dropped to 6.4 percent. In addition, the most recent economic recession sharply reduced urban revenues that the cities themselves generated, thereby creating budget deficits that resulted in further cutbacks in basic services and programs, and increases in local taxes (Caraley 1992).

The combination of the New Federalism, which resulted in the sharp cuts in federal aid to local and state governments, and the recession created for many cities, especially the older cities of the East and Midwest, the worst fiscal and service crisis since the Depression. Cities have become increasingly under-serviced and many have been on the brink of bankruptcy. They have therefore not been in a position to combat effectively three unhealthy social conditions that have emerged or become prominent since 1980: (1) the outbreaks of crack-cocaine addiction and the murders and other violent crimes that have accompanied them; (2) the AIDS epidemic and its escalating public health costs; and (3) the sharp rise in the homeless population not only for individuals, but for whole families as well (Caraley 1990).

Fiscally strapped cities have had to watch in helpless frustration as these problems escalated during the 1980s and made the larger city itself seem like a less attractive place in which to live. Accordingly, many urban residents with the economic means have followed the worn-out path from the central city to the suburbs and other areas, thereby shrinking the tax base and further reducing city revenue.

The growing suburbanization of the population influences the extent to which national politicians will support increased federal aid to large cities and to the poor. Indeed, we can associate the sharp drop in federal support for basic urban programs since 1980 with the declining political influence of cities and the rising influence of electoral coalitions in the suburbs (Weir 1993). Suburbs cast 36 percent of the vote for President in 1968, 48 percent in 1988, and a majority of the vote in the 1992 election.

In each of the three presidential elections prior to the 1992 election, the Democratic presidential candidate scored huge majorities in the large cities only to lose an overwhelming majority of the states where these cities are located. This naked reality is one of the reasons why the successful Clinton Presidential campaign designed a careful strategy to capture more support from voters who do not reside in central cities.

However, although there is a clear racial divide between the central city and the suburbs, racial tensions in the metropolitan areas continue to be concentrated in the central city. They affect the relations and patterns of interaction between blacks, other minorities, and the whites who remain, especially lower income whites.

RACIAL TENSIONS IN THE CENTRAL CITY

Like inner-city minorities, lower-income whites have felt the full impact of the urban fiscal crisis in the United States. Moreover, lower-income whites are more constrained by financial exigencies to remain in the central city than their middle-class counterparts and thereby suffer the strains of crime, higher taxes, poorer services, and inferior public schools. Furthermore, unlike the more affluent whites who choose to remain in the wealthier sections of the central city, they cannot easily escape the problems of deteriorating public schools by sending their children to private schools, and this problem has grown with the sharp decline in urban parochial schools in the United States.

Many of these people originally bought relatively inexpensive homes near their industrial jobs. Because of the deconcentration of industry, the racially changing neighborhood bordering their communities, the problems of neighborhood crime, and the surplus of central-city housing created by the population shift to the suburbs, housing values in their neighborhoods have failed to keep pace with those in the suburbs. As the industries that employ them become suburbanized, a growing number of lower-income whites in our central cities find that not only are they trapped in their neighborhoods because of the high costs of suburban housing, but they are physically removed from job opportunities as well. This situation increases the potential for racial tension as they compete with blacks and the rapidly growing Latino population for access to and control of the remaining decent schools, housing, and neighborhoods in the fiscally strained central city.

Thus the racial struggle for power and privilege in the central city is essentially a struggle between the have-nots; it is a struggle over access to and control of decent housing and decent neighborhoods, as exposed by the black–white friction over attempts to integrate the working-class ethnic neighborhoods of Marquette Park on Chicago's South Side; it is a struggle over access to and control of local public schools, as most dramatically demonstrated in the racial violence that followed attempts to bus black children from the Boston ghettos of Roxbury and Dorchester to the working-class neighborhoods of South Boston and Charlestown in the 1970s; finally, it is a struggle over political control of the central city, as exhibited in cities like Chicago, Newark, Cleveland, and New York in recent years when the race of the mayoralty candidate was the basis for racial antagonism and fear that engulfed the election campaign.

In some cases the conflicts between working-class whites and blacks are expressed in ethnic terms. Thus in a city such as Chicago, white working-class ethnics are stressing that their ethnic institutions and unique ways of life are being threatened by black encroachment on their neighborhoods, the increase of black crime, and the growth of black militancy. The emphasis is not simply that blacks pose a threat to whites but that they also pose a threat to, say, the Polish in Gage Park, the Irish in Brighton Park, the Italians in Cicero, or the Serbians, Rumanians, and Croatians in Hegewich. These communities are a few of the many ethic enclaves in the Chicago area threatened by the possibilities of a black invasion, and their response has been to stress not only the interests of whites but the interests of their specific ethnic group as well. The primary issue is whether neighborhood ethnic churches and private ethnic schools can survive if whites leave their communities in great numbers and move either to other parts of the cities or to the suburbs. The threatened survival of ethnic social clubs and the possible loss of ethnic friends are also crucial issues that contribute to the anxiety in these communities.

Although the focus of much of the racial tension has been on black and white encounters, in many urban neighborhoods incidents of ethnic antagonisms involve Latinos. According to several demographic projections, the Latino population, which in 1990 had exceeded 22 million in the United States, will replace African-Americans as the nation's largest minority group between 1997 and 2005. They already outnumber African-Americans in Houston and Los Angeles and are rapidly approaching the number of blacks in Dallas and New York. In cities as different as Houston, Los Angeles, and Philadelphia, "competition between blacks and Hispanic citizens over the drawing of legislative districts and the allotment of seats is intensifying" (Rohter 1993, p. 11). In areas of changing populations, Latino residents increasingly complain that black officials currently in office cannot represent their concerns and interests (Rohter 1993).

The tensions between blacks and Latinos in Miami, as one example, have emerged over competition for jobs and government contracts, the distribution of political power, and claims on public services. It would be a mistake to view the encounters between the two groups solely in racial terms, however. In Dade County there is a tendency for the black Cubans, Dominicans, Puerto Ricans, and Panamanians to define themselves by their language and culture and not by the color of their skin. Indeed, largely because of the willingness of Hispanic whites and Hispanic blacks to live together and mix with Haitians and other Caribbean blacks in neighborhoods relatively free of racial tension, Dade County is experiencing the most rapid desegregation of housing in the nation (Rohter 1993).

On the other hand, native-born, English speaking African-Americans continue to be the most segregated group in Miami. They are concentrated in neighborhoods that represent high levels of joblessness and clearly identifiable pockets of poverty in the northeast section of Dade County (Rohter 1993). Although there has been some movement of higher income groups from these neighborhoods in recent years, the poorer blacks are more likely to be trapped because of the combination of extreme economic marginality and residential segregation.

RACE AND THE NEW URBAN POVERTY

The problems faced by blacks in poor segregated communities are even more severe in the older cities of the East and Midwest. Indeed, there is a new poverty in our nation's metropolises that has far ranging consequences for the quality of life in urban areas, including race relations. By the "new urban poverty," I mean poor segregated neighborhoods in which a substantial majority of individual adults are either unemployed or have dropped out of the labor force. For example, in 1990 only one in three adults (35%) ages 16 and over in the twelve Chicago community areas with poverty rates that exceeded 40 percent held a job.[1] Each of these community areas, located on the South and West sides of the city, is overwhelmingly black. We can add to these twelve high jobless areas three additional predominantly black community areas, with rates of poverty of 29, 30, and 36 percent respectively, where only four in ten (42%) adults worked in 1990. Thus, in these fifteen black community areas, representing a total population of 425,125, only 37 percent of all the adults were gainfully employed in 1990. By contrast, 54 percent of the adults in the seventeen other predominantly black community areas in Chicago, with a total population of 545,408, worked in 1990. This was close to the city-wide figure of 57 percent. Finally, except for one largely Asian community area with an employment rate of 46 percent, and one largely Latino community area with an employment rate of 49 percent, a majority of the adults held a job in each of the forty-five other community areas of Chicago.[2]

To repeat, the new urban poverty represents poor segregated neighborhoods in which a substantial majority of the adults are not working. To illustrate the magnitude of the changes that have occurred in inner-city ghetto neighborhoods in recent years, let me take the three Chicago community areas (Douglas, Grand Boulevard, and Washington Park) featured in St. Clair Drake and Horace Cayton's classic book entitled *Black Metropolis*, published in 1945. These three community areas, located on the South Side of the city of Chicago, represent the historic core of Chicago's black belt.

A majority of adults were gainfully employed in these three areas in 1950, five years after the publication of *Black Metropolis*, but by 1990 only four in ten in Douglas worked, one in three in Washington Park, and one in four in Grand Boulevard. In 1950, 69 percent of all males 14 and over worked in the Bronzeville neighborhoods of Douglas, Grand Boulevard, and Washington Park; by 1990 only 37 percent of all males 16 and over held jobs in these three neighborhoods.[3]

Upon the publication of the first edition of *Black Metropolis* in 1945, there was much greater class integration in the black community. As Drake and Cayton pointed out, Bronzeville residents had limited success in "sorting themselves out into broad community areas designated as 'lower class' and 'middle class.' . . . Instead of middle class areas, Bronzeville tends to have middle-class buildings in all areas, or a few middle-class blocks here and there" (pp. 658–660). Though they may have lived on different streets, blacks of all classes in inner-city areas such as Bronzeville lived in the same community and shopped at the same stores. Their children went to the same schools and played in the same parks. Although there was some class antagonism, their neighborhoods were more stable than the inner-city neighborhoods of today; in short, they featured higher levels of social organization.

By "social organization" I mean the extent to which the residents of a neighborhood are able to maintain effective social control and realize their common values. There are two major dimensions of neighborhood social organization: (1) the prevalence, strength, and interdependence of social networks; and (2) the extent of collective supervision that the residents direct and the personal responsibility they assume in addressing neighborhood problems (Sampson 1992).

Both formal institutions and informal networks reflect social organization. In other words, neighborhood social organization depends on the extent of local friendship ties, the degree of social cohesion, the level of resident participation in formal and informal voluntary associations, the density and stability of formal organizations, and the nature of informal social controls. Neighborhoods that integrate the adults by an extensive set of obligations, expectations, and social networks are in a better position to control and supervise the activities and behavior of children, and monitor developments—e.g., the breaking up of congregations of youth on street corners and the supervision of youth leisure time activities (Sampson 1992).

Neighborhoods plagued with high levels of joblessness are more likely to experience problems of social organization. The two go hand-in-hand. High rates of joblessness trigger other problems in the neighborhood that adversely affect social organization, ranging from crime, gang violence, and drug trafficking to family break-ups and problems in the organization of family life. Consider, for example, the problems of drug trafficking and violent crime. As many studies have revealed, the decline of legitimate employment opportunities among inner-city residents builds up incentives to sell drugs (Fagan 1993). The distribution of crack in a neighborhood attracts individuals involved in violence and other crimes. Violent persons in the crack marketplace help shape its social organization and its impact on the neighborhood. Neighborhoods plagued by high levels of joblessness, insufficient economic opportunities, and high residential mobility are unable to control the volatile drug market and the violent crimes related to it (Fagan 1993, Sampson 1986). As informal controls weaken in such areas, the social processes that regulate behavior change (Sampson 1988).

A more direct relationship between joblessness and violent crime is revealed in recent longitudinal research by Delbert Elliott (1992) of the University of Colorado, a study based on National Youth Survey data from 1976 to 1989, covering ages 11 to 30. As Elliott (1992) points out, the transition from adolescence to adulthood usually results in a sharp drop in most crimes, including serious violent behavior, as individuals take on new adult roles and responsibilities. "Participation in serious violent offending (aggravated assault, forcible rape, and robbery) increases from ages 11 to 12 to ages 15 and 16 then declines dramatically with advancing age" (Elliott 1992, p. 14). Although black and white males reveal similar age curves, "the negative slope of the age curve for blacks after age 20 is substantially less than that of whites" (p. 15).

The black–white differential in the percentage of males involved in serious violent crime, although almost even at age 11, increases to 3:2 over the remaining years of adolescence, and teaches a differential of nearly 4:1 during the late twenties. However, when Elliott (1992) only compared employed black and white males, he found no significant differences between the two groups in rates of suspension or termination of violent behavior by age 21. Employed black males experienced a precipitous decline in serious violent behavior following their adolescent period. Accordingly, a major reason for the substantial overall racial gap in the termination of violent behavior following the adolescent period is the large proportion of jobless black males, whose serious violent behavior was more likely to extend into adulthood.[4] The new poverty neighborhoods feature a high concentration of jobless males and, as a result, experience rates of violent criminal behavior that exceed those of other urban neighborhoods.

Also, consider the important relationship between joblessness and the organization of family life. Work is not simply a way to make a living and support one's family. It also constitutes the framework for daily behavior and patterns of interaction because of the disciplines and regularities it imposes. Thus in the absence of regular employment, what is lacking is not only a place in which to work and the receipt of regular income, but also a coherent organization of the present, that is, a system of concrete expectations and goals. Regular employment provides the anchor for the temporal and spatial aspects of daily life. In the absence of regular employment, life, including family life, becomes more incoherent. Persistent unemployment and irregular employment hinder rational planning in daily life, the necessary condition of adaptation to an industrial economy (Bourdieu 1965). This problem is most severe for a jobless family in a low employment neighborhood. The family's lack of rational planning is more likely to be shared and therefore reinforced by other families in the neighborhood. The problems of family organization and neighborhood social organization are mutually reinforcing.

FACTORS ASSOCIATED WITH THE INCREASE IN NEIGHBORHOOD JOBLESSNESS AND DECLINE OF SOCIAL ORGANIZATION

Although high jobless neighborhoods also feature concentrated poverty, high rates of neighborhood poverty are less likely to trigger problems of social organization if the residents are working. To repeat, in previous years the working poor stood out in neighborhoods like Bronzeville. Today the non-working poor predominate in such neighborhoods. What accounts for the rise in the proportion of jobless adults in inner-city communities such as Bronzeville?

An easy explanation is racial segregation. However, as we shall soon see, a race-specific argument is not sufficient to explain recent changes in neighborhoods like Bronzeville. After all, Bronzeville was just as segregated in 1950 as it is today, yet the level of employment was much higher back then.

Nonetheless, racial segregation does matter. If large segments of the African-American population had not been historically segregated in inner-city ghettos we would not be talking about the new urban poverty. The segregated ghetto is not the result of voluntary or positive decisions of the residents to live there. As Douglas Massey and Nancy Denton (1993) have carefully documented, the segregated ghetto is the product of systematic racial practices such as restrictive convenants, redlining by banks and insurance companies, zoning, panic peddling by real estate agents, and the creation of massive public housing projects in low-income areas. Moreover, urban renewal and forced migration uprooted many urban black communities. Freeway networks built through the hearts of many cities in the 1950s produced the most dramatic changes. Many viable low-income communities were destroyed. Furthermore, discrimination in employment and inferior educational opportunities further restricted black residential mobility.

Segregated ghettos are less conducive to employment and employment preparation than other areas of the city. Segregation in ghettos exacerbates employment problems because it embraces weak informal employment networks, contributes to the social isolation of individuals and families, and therefore reduces their chances of acquiring the human capital skills that facilitate mobility in a society. Since no other group in society experiences the degree of segregation, isolation, and poverty concentration as African-Americans, they are far more likely to be at a disadvantage when they have to compete with other groups in society, including other "discriminated against" groups, for resources and privileges.

But, to repeat, neighborhoods like Bronzeville were highly segregated decades ago when employment rates were much higher. Given the existence of segregation, one then has to account for the ways in which other changes in society interact with segregation to produce the recent escalating rates of joblessness and problems of social organization. Several factors stand out.

Prominent among these is the impact of changes in the economy, changes that have had an adverse effect on poor urban blacks, especially black males. In 1950, 69 percent of all males 14 and over worked in the Bronzeville neighborhoods of Douglas, Grand Boulevard, and Washington Park, and in 1960, 64 percent of this group were employed. However, by 1990 only 37 percent of all males 16 and over held jobs in these three neighborhoods.[5]

Thirty and forty years ago, the overwhelming majority of black males were working. Many of them were poor, but they held regular jobs around which their daily family life was organized. When black males looked for work, employers considered whether they had strong backs because they would be working in a factory or in the back room of a shop doing heavy lifting and labor. They faced discrimination and a job ceiling, but they were working. The work was hard and they were hired. Now, economic restructuring has broken the figurative back of the black working population.

Data from our Urban Poverty and Family Life Study show that 57 percent of Chicago's employed inner-city black fathers (aged 15 and over and without bachelor degrees) who were born between 1950 and 1955 worked in manufacturing industries in 1974. By 1987 that figure fell to 27 percent. Of those born between 1956 and 1960, 52 percent worked in manufacturing industries as late as 1978. By 1987 that figure had declined to 28 percent.[6]

The loss of traditional manufacturing and other blue-collar jobs in Chicago has resulted in increased joblessness among inner-city black males and a concentration in low-wage, high-turnover laborer and service-sector jobs. Embedded in segregated ghetto neighborhoods that are not conducive to employment, inner-city black males fall further behind their white and their Hispanic male counterparts, especially when the labor market is slack. Hispanics "continue to funnel into manufacturing because employers prefer" them "over blacks, and they like to hire by referrals from current employees, which Hispanics can readily furnish, being already embedded in migration networks" (Krogh, p. 12). Inner-city black men grow bitter about and resent their employment prospects and often manifest or express these feelings in their harsh, often dehumanizing, low-wage work settings.

Their attitudes and actions create the widely shared perception that they are undesirable workers. The perception then becomes the basis for employer decisions to deny them employment, especially when the economy is weak and many workers are seeking jobs. The employment woes of inner-city black males gradually grows over the long term not only because employers are turning more to the expanding immigrant and female labor force, but also because the number of jobs that require contact with the public continues to climb. Because of the increasing shift to service industries, employers have a greater need for workers who can effectively serve and relate to the consumer. Our research reveals that they believe that such qualities are lacking among black males from segregated inner-city neighborhoods.

The position of inner-city black women in the labor market is also problematic. Their high degree of social isolation in poor segregated neighborhoods, as reflected in social networks, reduces their employment prospects. Although our research indicates that employers consider them more desirable as workers than the inner-city black men, their social isolation decreases their ability to develop language and other job-related skills necessary in an economy that rewards employees who can work and communicate effectively with the public.

The increase in the proportion of jobless adults in the inner city is also related to the outmigration of large numbers of employed adults from working and middle-class families. The declining proportion of non-poor families and increasing and prolonged joblessness in the new poverty neighborhoods make it considerably more difficult to sustain basic neighborhood institutions. In the face of increasing joblessness, stores, banks, credit institutions, restaurants, and professional services lose regular and potential patrons. Churches experience dwindling numbers of parishioners and shrinking resources; recreational facilities, block clubs, community groups, and other informal organizations also suffer. As these organizations decline, the means of formal and informal social control in the neighborhood become weaker. Levels of crime and street violence increase as a result, leading to further deterioration of the neighborhood.

As the neighborhood disintegrates, those who are able to leave do so, including many working and middle-class families. The lower population density created by the outmigration exacerbates the problem. Abandoned buildings increase and provide a haven for crack dens and criminal enterprises that establish footholds in the community. Precipitous declines in density also make it more difficult to sustain or develop a sense of community or for people to experience a feeling of safety in numbers. (Jargowsky 1994, p. 18)

The neighborhoods with many black working families stand in sharp contrast to the new poverty areas. Research that we have conducted on the social organization of Chicago neighborhoods reveals that in addition to much lower levels of perceived unemployment than in the poor neighborhoods, black working and middle-class neighborhoods also have much higher levels of perceived social control and cohesion, organizational services, and social support.

The rise of new poverty neighborhoods represents a movement from what the historian Allan Spear (1967) has called an institutional ghetto—which duplicates the structure and activities of the larger society, as portrayed in Drake and Cayton's description of Bronzeville—to an unstable ghetto, which lacks the capability to provide basic opportunities, resources, and adequate social controls.

NEW POVERTY NEIGHBORHOODS AND URBAN RACIAL TENSIONS

The problems associated with the high joblessness and declining social organization (e.g., individual crime, hustling activities, gang violence) in inner-city ghetto neighborhoods often spill over into other parts of the city, including the ethnic enclaves. The result is not only hostile class antagonisms in the higher income black neighborhoods near these communities, but heightened levels of racial animosity, especially among lower income white ethnic and Latino groups whose communities border or are in proximity to the high jobless neighborhoods.

The problems in the new poverty neighborhoods have also created racial antagonisms among some of the higher income groups in the city. The new poverty in ghetto neighborhoods has sapped the vitality of local business and other institutions, and it has led to fewer and shabbier movie theaters, bowling alleys, restaurants, public parks and playgrounds, and other recreational facilities. Therefore residents of inner-city neighborhoods more often seek leisure activity in other areas of the city, where they come into brief contact with citizens of different racial, ethnic, or class backgrounds. Sharp differences in cultural style and patterns of interaction that reflect the social isolation of neighborhood networks often lead to clashes.

Some behavior of residents in socially isolated inner-city ghetto neighborhoods—e.g., the tendency to enjoy a movie in a communal spirit by carrying on a running conversation with friends and relatives during the movie or reacting in an unrestrained manner to what they see on the screen—offends the sensibilities of or is considered inappropriate by other groups, particularly the black and white middle classes. Their expression of disapproval, either overtly or with subtle hostile glances, tends to trigger belligerent responses from the inner-city ghetto residents who then purposefully intensify the behavior that is the source of middle-class concerns. The white, and even the black middle class, then exercise their option and exit, to use Albert Hirschman's (1970) term, by taking their patronage elsewhere, expressing resentment and experiencing intensified feelings of racial or class antagonisms as they depart.

The areas left behind then become the domain of the inner-city ghetto residents. The more expensive restaurants and other establishments that serve the higher income groups in these areas, having lost their regular patrons, soon close down and are replaced by fast-food chains and other local businesses that cater to the needs or reflect the economic and cultural resources of the new clientele. White and black middle-class citizens, in particular, complain bitterly about how certain conveniently located areas of the central city have changed following the influx of ghetto residents.

DEMAGOGIC MESSAGES

I want to make a final point about economic, political, and social situations that have contributed to the rise of racial antagonisms in urban areas. During periods of hard economic times, it is important that political leaders channel the frustrations of citizens in positive or constructive directions. However, for the last few years just the opposite frequently occurred. In a time of heightened economic insecurities, the negative racial rhetoric of some highly visible white and black spokespersons increased racial tensions and channeled frustrations in ways that severely divide the racial groups. During hard economic times people become more receptive to demagogic messages that deflect attention from the real source of their problems. Instead of associating their declining real incomes, increasing job insecurity, growing pessimism about the future with failed economic and political policies, these messages force them to turn on each other—race against race.

As the new urban poverty has sapped the vitality of many inner-city communities, many of these messages associate inner-city crime, family breakdown, and welfare receipt with individual shortcomings. Blame the victim arguments resonate with many urban Americans because of their very simplicity. They not only reinforce the salient belief that joblessness and poverty reflect individual inadequacies, but discourage support for new and stronger programs to combat inner-city social dislocations as well.

WHAT MUST BE DONE?

I have outlined some of the situations that inflate racial antagonisms in cities like Chicago—namely those that involve the interrelation of recent political policies and economic and social processes (including the emergence of the new urban poverty). Let me conclude this paper with some thoughts on social policy that build on this situational perspective.

I believe that it will be difficult to address racial tensions in our cities unless we tackle the problems of shrinking revenue and inadequate social services, and the gradual disappearance of work in certain neighborhoods. The city has become a less desirable place in which to live, and the economic and social gap between the cities and suburbs is growing. The groups left behind compete, often along racial lines, for the declining resources, including the remaining decent schools, housing, and neighborhoods. The rise of the new urban poverty neighborhoods exacerbates the problems. Their high rates of joblessness and social disorganization create problems that not only affect the residents in these neighborhoods but that spill over into other parts of the larger city as well. All of these factors aggravate race relations and elevate racial tensions.

Ideally it would be great if we could restore the federal contribution to the city budget that existed in 1980, and sharply increase the employment base. However, regardless of changes in federal urban policy, the fiscal crisis in the cities would be significantly eased if the employment base could be substantially increased. Indeed, the social dislocations caused by the steady disappearance of work have led to a wide range of urban social problems, including racial tensions. Increased employment would help stabilize the new poverty neighborhood, halt the precipitous decline in density, and ultimately enhance the quality of race relations in urban areas. The employment situation in inner-city ghetto neighborhoods would improve if the United States' economy, which is now experiencing an upturn, could produce low levels of unemployment over a long period of time.

I say this because in slack labor markets employers are—and indeed, can afford to be—more selective in recruiting and in granting promotions. They overemphasize job prerequisites and exaggerate experience. In such an economic climax, disadvantaged minorities suffer disproportionately and the level of employer discrimination rises. In contrast, in a tight labor market, job vacancies are numerous, unemployment is of short duration, and wages are higher. Moreover, in a tight labor market the labor force expands because increased job opportunities not only reduce unemployment but also draw into the labor force those workers who, in periods when the labor market is slack, respond to fading job prospects by dropping out of the labor force altogether. Accordingly, in a tight labor market the status of disadvantaged minorities improves because of lower unemployment, higher wages, and better jobs (Tobin 1965).

Moreover, affirmative action and other anti-bias programs are more successful in tight labor markets than in slack ones. Not only are sufficient positions available for many qualified workers, but also employers, facing a labor shortage, are not as resistant to affirmative action. Furthermore, a favorable economic climate encourages supporters of affirmative action to push such programs because they perceive greater chances for success. Finally, non-minority workers are less resistant to affirmative action when there are sufficient jobs available because they are less likely to see minorities as a threat to their own employment.

However, a rising tide does not necessarily lift all boats. Special additional steps to rescue many inner-city residents from the throes of joblessness should be considered, even if the economy remains healthy. Such steps might include the creation of job information data banks in the new poverty neighborhoods and subsidized car pools to increase access to suburban jobs. Training or apprenticeship programs that lead to stable employment should also be considered.

Nonetheless, because of their level of training and education, many of the jobs to which the inner-city poor have access are at or below the minimum wage and are not covered by health insurance. However, recent policies created and proposed by the Clinton Administration could make such jobs more attractive. By 1996, the expanded Earned Income Tax Credit will increase the earnings from a minimum-wage job to $7 an hour. If this benefit is paid on a monthly basis and is combined with health care, the condition of workers in the low-wage sector would improve significantly, and the rate of employment would rise.

Finally, given the situational basis of much of today's racial tensions, I think that there are some immediate and practical steps that the President of the United States can take to help create the atmosphere for serious efforts and programs to improve racial relations. I am referring to the need for strong political and moral leadership to help combat racial antagonisms. In particular, the need to create and strongly emphasize a message that unites, not divides, racial groups.

It is important to appreciate that the poor and the working classes of all racial groups struggle to make ends meet, and even the middle class has experienced a decline in its living standard. Indeed, Americans across racial and class boundaries worry about unemployment and job security, declining real wages, escalating medical and housing costs, child care programs, the sharp decline in the quality of public education, and crime and drug trafficking in their neighborhoods. Given these concerns, perhaps the President ought to advance a new public rhetoric that does two things: focuses on problems that afflict not only the poor, but the working and middle classes as well; and emphasizes integrative programs that contribute to the social and economic improvement of all groups in society, not just the truly disadvantaged segments of the population. In short a public rhetoric that reflects a vision of racial unity.

The President of the United States has the unique capacity to command nationwide attention from the media and the general public, the capacity to get them to consider seriously a vision of racial unity and of where we are and where we should go.

I am talking about a vision that promotes values of racial and inter-group harmony and unity; rejects the commonly held view that race is so divisive in this country that whites, blacks, Latinos, and other ethnic groups cannot work together in a common cause; recognizes that if a message from a political leader is tailored to a white audience, racial minorities draw back, just as whites draw back when a message is tailored to racial minority audiences; realizes that if the message emphasizes issues and programs that concern the families of all racial and ethnic groups, individuals of these various groups will see their mutual interests and join in a multi-racial coalition to move America forward; promotes the idea that Americans across racial and class boundaries have common interests and concerns including concerns about unemployment and job security, declining real wages, escalating medical and housing costs, child care programs, the sharp decline in the quality of public education, and crime and drug trafficking in neighborhoods; sees the application of programs to combat these problems as beneficial to all Americans, not just the truly disadvantaged among us; recognizes that since demographic shifts have decreased the urban white population and sharply increased the proportion of minorities in the cities, the divide between the suburbs and the central city is, in many respects, a racial divide and that it is vitally important, therefore, to emphasize city–suburban cooperation, not separation; and, finally, pushes the idea that all groups, including those in the throes of the new urban poverty, should be able to achieve full membership in society because the problems of economic and social marginality are associated with inequities in the larger society, not with group deficiencies.

If the President were to promote vigorously this vision, efforts designed to address both the causes and symptoms of racial tensions in cities like New York, Chicago, Philadelphia, Miami, and Los Angeles would have a greater chance for success.

ENDNOTES

1. The figures on adult employment presented in this paragraph are based on calculations from data provided by the 1990 U.S. Bureau of the Census and the *Local Community Fact Book for Chicago*, 1950. The adult employment rates represent the number of employed individuals (14 and over in 1950 and 16 over in 1990) among the total number of adults in a given area. Those who are not employed include both the individuals who are members of the labor force but are not working and those who have dropped out or are not part of the labor force. Those who are not in the labor force "consists mainly of students, housewives, retired workers, seasonal workers enumerated in an 'off' season who were not looking for work, inmates of institutions, disabled persons, and persons doing only incidental unpaid family work" (*The Chicago Fact Book Consortium*, 1984, p. xxv).

2. A community area is a statistical unit derived by urban sociologists at the University of Chicago for the 1930 census in order to analyze varying conditions within the city of Chicago. These delineations were originally drawn up on the basis of settlement and history of the area, local identification and trade patterns, local institutions, and natural and artificial barriers. Needless to say, there have been major shifts in population and land use since then. But these units remain useful to trace changes over time, and they continue to capture much of the contemporary reality of Chicago neighborhoods.

3. The figures on male employment are based on calculations from data provided by the 1990 U.S. Bureau of the Census and the *Local Community Fact Book for Chicago*, 1950.

4. In Elliott's study 75 percent of the black males who were employed between the ages of 18–20 had terminated their involvement in violent behavior by age 21, compared to only 52 percent of those who were unemployed between the ages of 18–20. Racial differences remained for persons who were not in a marriage/partner relationship or who were unemployed.

5. The figures on male employment are based on calculations from data provided by the 1990 U.S Bureau of the Census and the *Local Community Fact Book for Chicago*, 1950.

6. For a discussion of these findings, see Marilyn Krogh, "A Description of the Work Histories of Fathers Living in the Inner-City of Chicago." Working paper, Center for the Study of Urban Inequality, University of Chicago, 1993. *The Urban Poverty and Family Life Study*

(UPFLS) includes a survey of 2,495 households in Chicago's inner-city neighborhoods conducted in 1987 and 1988; a second survey of a subsample of 175 respondents from the larger survey who were reinterviewed solely with open-ended questions on their perceptions of the opportunity structure and life chances; a survey of a stratified random sample of 185 employers, designed to reflect the distribution of employment across industry and firm size in the Chicago metropolitan area, conducted in 1988; and comprehensive ethnographic research, including participant observation research and life-history interviews conducted in 1987 and 1988 by ten research assistants in a representative sample of black, Hispanic, and white inner-city neighborhoods.

The UPFLS was supported by grants from the Ford Foundation, the Rockefeller Foundation, the Joyce Foundation, the Carnegie Corporation, the Lloyd A. Fry Foundation, the William T. Grant Foundation, the Spencer Foundation, the Woods Charitable Fund, the Chicago Community Trust, the Institute for Research on Poverty, and the U.S Department of Health and Human Services.

REFERENCES

Bell, Derrick. 1992. *Faces at the Bottom of the Well: The Permanence of Racism.* New York: Basic Books.

Caraley, Demetrios. 1992. "Washington Abandons the Cities," *Political Science Quarterly,* 107, Spring.

Drake, St. Clair and Horace Cayton. 1945. *Black Metropolis: A Study of Negro Life in a Northern City.* New York: Harcourt, Brace, Jovanovich, Inc.

Elliott, Delbert S. 1992. "Longitudinal Research in Criminology: Premise and Practice." Paper presented at the NATO Conference on Cross-National Longitudinal Research on Criminal Behavior, Frankfurt, Germany, July 19–25.

Fagan, Jeffrey. 1993. "Drug Selling and Licit Income in Distressed Neighborhoods: The Economic Lives of Street-Level Drug Users and Dealers," in *Drugs, Crime and Social Isolation* (edited by G. Peterson and A. Harold Washington). Urban Institute Press.

Hacker, Andrew. 1992. *Two Nations: Black and White, Separate, Hostile and Unequal.* New York: Charles Scribner's Sons.

Hirschman, Albert O. 1970. *Exit, Voice, and Loyalty: Responses to Decline in Firms, Organizations, and States.* Cambridge, Mass.: Harvard University Press.

Jargowsky, Paul A. 1994. "Ghetto Poverty Among Blacks in the 1980's," *Journal of Policy Analysis and Management,* Vol. 13, pp. 288–310.

Krogh, Marilyn. 1993. "A Description of the Work Histories of Fathers Living in the Inner-City of Chicago." *Working paper,* Center for the Study of Urban Inequality, University of Chicago.

Massey, Douglas S. and Nancy A. Denton. 1993. *American Apartheid: Segregation and the Making of the Underclass.* Cambridge, Mass.: Harvard University Press.

Rohter, Larry. 1993. "As Hispanic Presence Grows, So Does Black Anger." *New York Times,* June 20, p. 11.

Sampson, Robert J. 1986. "Crime in Cities: The Effects of Formal and Informal Social Control" in *Communities and Crime* (edited by Albert J. Reiss, Jr., and Michael Tonry) 271–310. Chicago: University of Chicago Press.

Sampson, Robert J. 1992. "Integrating Family and Community-Level Dimensions of Social Organization: Delinquency and Crime in the Inner-City of Chicago." Paper presented at

the International Workshop: "Integrating Individual and Ecological Aspects on Crime."
Stockholm, Sweden, August 31–September 5, 1992.

Sampson, Robert J. and William Julius Wilson. 1993. "Toward a Theory of Race, Crime, and
Urban Inequality," in *Crime and Inequality* (edited by John Hagan and Ruth Peterson).
Stanford University Press, in press.

Spear, Allan. 1967. *Black Chicago: The Making of a Negro Ghetto.* Chicago: University of Chicago
Press.

Tobin, James. 1965. "On Improving the Economic Status of the Negro." *Daedalus,* 94,
pp. 878–898.

Wacquant, Loic J. D. and William Julius Wilson. 1989. "Poverty, Joblessness, and the Social
Transformation of the Inner City" in *Welfare Policy for the 1990s* (edited by Phoebe Cot-
tingham and David Ellwood), 70–102. Cambridge: Harvard University Press.

Weir, Margaret. 1993. "Race and Urban Poverty: Comparing Europe and America." Center for
American Political Studies, Harvard University, Occasional Paper 93–9, March.

Wilson, William Julius. 1987. *The Truly Disadvantaged: The Inner City, the Underclass, and
Public Policy.* Chicago: University of Chicago Press.

CHAPTER **28**

So How Did I Get Here?

Growing Up on Welfare

ROSEMARY L. BRAY

G rowing up on welfare was a story I had planned to tell a long time from now, when I had children of my own. My childhood on Aid to Families with Dependent Children (A.F.D.C.) was going to be one of those stories I would tell my kids about the bad old days, an urban legend equivalent to Abe Lincoln studying by firelight. But I know now I cannot wait, because in spite of a wealth of evidence about the true nature of welfare and poverty in America, the debate has turned ugly, vicious and racist. The "welfare question" has become the race question and the woman question in disguise, and so far the answers bode well for no one.

In both blunt and coded terms, comfortable Americans more and more often bemoan the waste of their tax money on lazy black women with a love of copulation, a horror of birth control and a lack of interest in marriage. Were it not for the experiences of half my life, were I not black and female and of a certain age, perhaps I would be like so many people who blindly accept the lies and distortions, half-truths and wrongheaded notions about welfare. But for better or worse, I do know better. I know more than I want to know about being poor. I know that the welfare system is designed to be inadequate, to leave its constituents on the edge of survival. I know because I've been there.

And finally, I know that perhaps even more dependent on welfare than its recipients are the large number of Americans who would rather accept this patchwork of economic horrors than fully address the real needs of real people.

My mother came to Chicago in 1947 with a fourth-grade education, cut short by working in the Mississippi fields. She pressed shirts in a laundry for a while and later waited tables in a restaurant, where she met my father. Mercurial and independent, with a sixth-grade education, my Arkansas-born father worked at whatever came to hand. He owned a lunch wagon for a time and prepared food for hours in our kitchen on the nights before he took the wagon out. Sometimes he hauled junk and sold it in the open-air markets of Maxwell Street on Sunday mornings. Eight years after they met—seven years after they married—I was born. My father made her quit her job; her work, he told her, was taking care of me. By the time I was 4, I had a sister, a brother and another brother on the way. My parents, like most other American couples of the 1950's, had their own American dream—a husband who worked, a wife who stayed home, a family of smiling children. But as was true for so many African-American couples, their American dream was an illusion.

The house on the corner of Berkeley Avenue and 45th Street is long gone. The other houses still stand, but today the neighborhood is an emptier, bleaker place. When we moved there, it was a street of old limestones with beveled glass windows, all falling into vague disrepair. Home was a four-room apartment on the first floor, in what must have been the public rooms of a formerly grand house. The rent was $110 a month. All of us kids slept in the big front room. Because I was the oldest, I had a bed of my own, near a big plate-glass window.

My mother and father had been married for several years before she realized he was a gambler who would never stay away from the track. By the time we moved to Berkeley Avenue, Daddy was spending more time gambling, and bringing home less and less money and more and more anger. Mama's simplest requests were met with rage. They fought once for hours when she asked for money to buy a tube of lipstick. It didn't help that I always seemed to need a doctor. I had allergies and bronchitis so severe that I nearly died one Sunday after church when I was about 3.

It was around this time that my mother decided to sign up for A.F.D.C. She explained to the caseworker that Daddy wasn't home much, and when he was he didn't have any money. Daddy was furious; Mama was adamant. "There were times when we hardly had a loaf of bread in here," she told me years later. "It was close. I wasn't going to let you all go hungry."

Going on welfare closed a door between my parents that never reopened. She joined the ranks of unskilled women who were forced to turn to the state for the security their men could not provide. In the sterile relationship between herself and the State of Illinois, Mama found an autonomy denied her by my father. It was she who could decide, at last, some part of her own fate and ours. A.F.D.C. relegated marginally productive men like my father to the ranks of failed patriarchs who no longer controlled the destiny of their families. Like so many of his peers, he could no longer afford the luxury of a woman who did as she was told because her economic life depended on it. Daddy became one of the shadow men who walked out back doors as caseworkers came in through the front. Why did he acquiesce? For all his anger, for all his frightening brutality, he loved us, so much that he swallowed his pride and periodically ceased to exist so that we might survive.

In 1960, the year my mother went on public aid, the poverty threshold for a family of five in the United States was $3,560 and the monthly payment to a family of five from the State of Illinois was $182.56, a total of $2,190.72 a year. Once the $110 rent was paid, Mama was left with $72.56 a month to take care of all the other expenses. By any standard, we were poor. All our lives were proscribed by the narrow line between not quite and just enough.

What did it take to live?

It took the kindness of friends as well as strangers, the charity of churches, low expectations, deprivation and patience. I can't begin to count the hours spent in long lines, long waits, long walks in pursuit of basic things. A visit to a local clinic (one housing doctors, a dentist and pharmacy in an incredibly crowded series of rooms) invariably took the better part of a day; I never saw the same doctor twice.

It took, as well, a turning of our collective backs on the letter of a law that required reporting even a small and important miracle like a present of $5. All families have their secrets, but I remember the weight of an extra burden. In a world where caseworkers were empowered to probe into every nook and cranny of our lives, silence became defense. Even now, there are things I will not publicly discuss because I cannot shake the fear that we might be hounded by the state, eager to prosecute us for the crime of survival.

All my memories of our years on A.F.D.C. are seasoned with unease. It's painful to remember how much every penny counted, how even a gap of 25 cents could make a difference in any given week. Few people understand how precarious life is from welfare check to welfare check, how the word "extra" has no meaning. Late mail, a bureaucratic mix-up . . . and a carefully planned method of survival lies in tatters.

What made our lives work as well as they did was my mother's genius at making do—worn into her by a childhood of rural poverty—along with her vivid imagination. She worked at home endlessly, shopped ruthlessly, bargained, cajoled, charmed. Her food store of choice was the one that stocked pork and beans, creamed corn, sardines, Vienna sausages and potted meat all at 10 cents a can. Clothing was the stuff of rummage sales, trips to Goodwill and bargain basements, where thin cotton and polyester reigned supreme. Our shoes came from a discount store that sold two pairs for $5.

It was an uphill climb, but there was no time for reflection; we were too busy with our everyday lives. Yet I remember how much it pained me to know that Mama, who recruited a neighbor to help her teach me how to read when I was 3, found herself left behind by her eldest daughter, then by each of us in turn. Her biggest worry was that we would grow up uneducated, so Mama enrolled us in parochial school.

When one caseworker angrily questioned how she could afford to send four children to St. Ambrose School, my mother, who emphatically declared "My kids need an education," told her it was none of her business. (In fact, the school had a volume discount of sorts; the price of tuition dropped with each child you sent. I still don't know quite how she managed it.) She organized our lives around church and school, including Mass every morning at 7:45. My brother was an altar boy; I laid out the vestments each afternoon for the next day's Mass. She volunteered as a chaperone for every class trip, sat with us as we did homework she did not understand herself. She and my father reminded us again and again and again that every book, every test, every page of homework was in fact a ticket out and away from the life we lived.

My life on welfare ended on June 4, 1976—a month after my 21st birthday, two weeks after I graduated from Yale. My father, eaten up with cancer and rage, lived just long enough to know the oldest two of us had graduated from college and were on our own. Before the decade ended, all of us had left the welfare rolls. The eldest of my brothers worked at the post office, assumed support of my mother (who also went to work, as a companion to an elderly woman) and earned his master's degree at night. My sister married and got a job at a bank. My baby brother parked cars and found a wife. Mama's biggest job was done at last; the investment made in our lives by the State of Illinois had come to fruition. Five people on welfare for 18 years had become five working, taxpaying adults. Three of us went to college, two of us finished; one of us has an advanced degree; all of us can take care of ourselves.

Ours was a best-case phenomenon, based on the synergy of church and state, the government and the private sector and the thousand points of light that we called friends and neighbors. But there was something more: What fueled our dreams and fired our belief that our lives could change for the better was the promise of the civil rights movement and the war on poverty—for millions of African-Americans the defining events of the 1960's. Caught up in the heady atmosphere of imminent change, our world was filled not only with issues and ideas but with amazing images of black people engaged in the struggle for long-denied rights and freedoms. We knew other people lived differently than we did, we knew we didn't have much, but we didn't mind, because we knew it wouldn't be long. My mother borrowed a phrase I had read to her once from Dick Gregory's autobiography: Not poor, just broke. She would repeat it often, as often as she sang hymns in the kitchen. She loved to sing a spiritual Mahalia Jackson had made famous: "Move On Up a Little Higher." Like so many others, Mama was singing about earth as well as heaven.

These are the things I remember every time I read another article outlining America's welfare crisis. The rage I feel about the welfare debate comes from listening to a host of lies, distortions and exaggerations—and taking them personally.

I am no fool. I know of few women—on welfare or off—with my mother's grace and courage and stamina. I know not all women on welfare are cut from the same cloth. Some are lazy; some are ground down. Some are too young; many are without husbands. A few have made welfare fraud a lucrative career; a great many more have pushed the rules on outside income to their very limits.

I also know that none of these things justify our making welfare a test of character and worthiness, rather than an acknowledgment of need. Near-sainthood should not be a requirement for financial and medical assistance.

But all manner of sociologists and policy gurus continue to equate issues that simply aren't equivalent—welfare, race, rates of poverty, crime, marriage and childbirth—and to reach conclusions that serve to demonize the poor. More than one social arbiter would have us believe that we have all been mistaken for the last 30 years—that the efforts to relieve the most severe effects of poverty have not only failed but have served instead to increase and expand the ranks of the poor. In keeping women, children and men from starvation, we are told, we have also kept them from self-sufficiency. In our zeal to do good, we have undermined the work ethic, the family and thus, by association, the country itself.

So how did I get here?

Despite attempts to misconstrue and discredit the social programs and policies that changed—even saved—my life, certain facts remain. Poverty was reduced by 39 percent between 1960 and 1990, according to the Census Bureau, from 22.2 percent to 13.5 percent of the nation's population. That is far too many poor people, but the rate is considerably lower than it might have been if we had thrown up our hands and reminded ourselves that the poor will always be with us. Of black women considered "highly dependent," that is, on welfare for more than seven years, 81 percent of their daughters grow up to live productive lives off the welfare rolls, a 1992 Congressional report stated; the 19 percent who become second-generation welfare recipients can hardly be said to constitute an epidemic of welfare dependency. The vast majority of African-Americans are now working or middle class, an achievement that occurred in the past 30 years, most specifically between 1960 and 1973, the years of expansion in the very same social programs that it is so popular now to savage. Those were the same years in which I changed from girl to woman, learned to read and think, graduated from high school and college, came to be a working woman, a taxpayer, a citizen.

In spite of all the successes we know of, in spite of the reality that the typical welfare recipient is a white woman with young children, ideologues have continued to fashion from whole cloth the specter of the mythical black welfare mother, complete with a prodigious reproductive capacity and a galling laziness, accompanied by the uncaring and equally lazy black man in her life who will not work, will not marry her and will not support his family.

Why has this myth been promoted by some of the best (and the worst) people in government, academia, journalism and industry? One explanation may be that the constant presence of poverty frustrates even the best-intentioned among us. It may also be because the myth allows for denial about who the poor in America really are and for denial about the depth and intransigence of racism regardless of economic status. And because getting tough on welfare is for some a first-class career move; what better way to win a position in the next administration than to trash those people least able to respond? And, finally, because it serves to assure white Americans that lazy black people aren't getting away with anything.

Many of these prescriptions for saving America from the welfare plague not only reflect an insistent, if sometimes unconscious, racism but rest on the bedrock of patriarchy. They are rooted in the fantasy of a male presence as a path to social and economic salvation and in its corollary—the image of woman as passive chattel, constitutionally so afflicted by her condition that the only recourse is to transfer her care from the hands of the state to the hands of a man with a job. The largely ineffectual plans to create jobs for men in communities ravaged by disinvestment, the state-sponsored dragnets for men who cannot or will not support their children, the exhortations for women on welfare to find themselves a man and get married, all are the institutional expressions of the same worn cultural illusion—that women and children without a man are fundamentally damaged goods. Men are such a boon, the reasoning goes, because they make more money than women do.

Were we truly serious about an end to poverty among women and children, we would take the logical next step. We would figure out how to make sure women who did a dollar's worth of work got a dollar's worth of pay. We would make sure that women could go to work with their minds at ease, knowing their children were well cared for. What women on welfare need, in large measure, are the things key to the life of every adult woman: economic security and autonomy. Women need the skills and the legitimate opportunity to earn a living for ourselves as well as for people who may rely on us; we need the freedom to make choices to improve our own lives and the lives of those dear to us.

"The real problem is not welfare," says Kathryn Edin, a professor of sociology at Rutgers University and a scholar in residence at the Russell Sage Foundation. "The real problem is the nature of low-wage work and lack of support for these workers— most of whom happen to be women raising their children alone."

Completing a five-year study of single mothers—some low-wage workers, some welfare recipients—Edin is quantifying what common sense and bitter experience have told millions of women who rotate off and on the welfare rolls: Women, particularly unskilled women with children, get the worst jobs available, with the least amount of health care, and are the most frequently laid off. "The workplace is not oriented toward people who have family responsibilities," she says. "Most jobs are set up assuming that someone else is minding the kids and doesn't need assistance."

But the writers and scholars and politicians who wax most rhapsodic about the need to replace welfare with work make their harsh judgments from the comfortable and supportive environs of offices and libraries and think tanks. If they need to go to the bathroom midsentence, there is no one timing their absence. If they take longer than a half-hour for lunch, there is no one waiting to dock their pay. If their baby sitter gets sick, there is no risk of someone having taken their place at work by the next morning. Yet these are conditions that low-wage women routinely face, which inevitably lead to the cyclical nature of their welfare histories. These are the realities that many of the most vocal and widely quoted critics of welfare routinely ignore. In his book "The End of Equality," for example, Mickey Kaus discusses social and economic inequity, referring to David Ellwood's study on long-term welfare dependency without ever mentioning that it counts anyone who uses the services for at least one month as having been on welfare for the entire year.

In the heated atmosphere of the welfare debate, the larger society is encouraged to believe that women on welfare have so violated the social contract that they have forfeited all rights common to those of us lucky enough not to be poor. In no area is this attitude more clearly demonstrated than in issues of sexuality and childbearing. Consider the following: A Philadelphia Inquirer editorial of Dec. 12, 1990, urges the use of Norplant contraceptive inserts for welfare recipients—in spite of repeated warnings from women's health groups of its dangerous side effects—in the belief that the drug "could be invaluable in breaking the cycle of inner-city poverty." (The newspaper apologized for the editorial after it met widespread criticism, both within and outside the paper.) A California judge orders a woman on welfare, convicted of abusing two of her four children, to use Norplant; the judge's decision was appealed. The Washington state legislature considers approving cash payments of up to $10,000 for women on welfare who agree to be sterilized. These and other proposals, all centering on women's reproductive capacities, were advanced in spite of evidence that welfare recipients have fewer children than those not on welfare.

The punitive energy behind these and so many other Draconian actions and proposals goes beyond the desire to decrease welfare costs; it cuts to the heart of the nation's racial and sexual hysteria. Generated neither by law nor by fully informed public debate, these actions amount to social control over "those people on welfare"—a control many Americans feel they have bought and paid for every April 15. The question is obvious: If citizens were really aware of who receives welfare in America, however inadequate it is, if they acknowledged that white women and children were welfare's primary beneficiaries, would most of these things be happening?

Welfare has become a code word now. One that enables white Americans to mask their sometimes malignant, sometimes benign racism behind false concerns about the suffering ghetto poor and their negative impact on the rest of us. It has become the vehicle many so-called tough thinkers use to undermine compassionate policy and engineer the reduction of social programs.

So how *did* I get here?

I kept my drawers up and my dress down, to quote my mother. I didn't end up pregnant because I had better things to do. I knew I did because my uneducated, Southern-born parents told me so. Their faith, their focus on our futures are a far cry from the thesis of Nicholas Lemann, whose widely acclaimed book *The Promised Land* perpetuates the myth of black Southern sharecropping society as a primary source of black urban malaise. Most important, my family and I had every reason to believe that I had better things to do and that when I got older I would be able to do them. I had a mission, a calling, work to do that only I could do. And that is knowledge transmitted not just by parents, or school, or churches. It is a palpable thing, available by osmosis from the culture of the neighborhood and the world at large.

Add to this formula a whopping dose of dumb luck. It was my sixth-grade teacher, Sister Maria Sarto, who identified in me the first signs of a stifling boredom and told my mother that I needed a tougher, more challenging curriculum than her school could provide. It was she who then tracked down the private Francis W. Parker School, which agreed to give me a scholarship if I passed the admissions test.

Had I been born a few years earlier, or a decade later, I might now be living on welfare in the Robert Taylor Homes or working as a hospital nurse's aide for $6.67 an hour. People who think such things could never have happened to me haven't met enough poor people to know better. The avenue of escape can be very narrow indeed. The hope and energy of the 1960's—fueled not only by a growing economy but by all the passions of a great national quest—is long gone. The sense of possibility I knew has been replaced with the popular cultural currency that money and those who have it are everything and those without are nothing.

Much has been made of the culture of the underclass, the culture of poverty, as though they were the free-floating illnesses of the African-American poor, rendering them immune to other influences: the widespread American culture of greed, for example, or of cynicism. It is a thinly veiled continuation of the endless projection of "dis-ease" onto black life, a convenient way to sidestep a more painful debate about the loss of meaning in American life that has made our entire nation depressed and dispirited. The malaise that has overtaken our country is hardly confined to African-Americans or the poor, and if both groups should disappear tomorrow, our nation would still find itself in crisis. To talk of the black "underclass threat" to the public sphere, as Mickey Kaus does, to demonize the poor among us and thus by association all of us—ultimately this does more damage to the body politic than a dozen welfare queens.

When I walk down the streets of my Harlem neighborhood, I see women like my mother, hustling, struggling, walking their children to school and walking them back home. And I also see women who have lost both energy and faith, talking loud, hanging out. I see the shadow men of a new generation, floating by with a few dollars and a toy, then drifting away to the shelters they call home. And I see, a dozen times a day, the little girls my sister and I used to be, the little boys my brothers once were.

Even the grudging, inadequate public help I once had is fading fast for them. The time and patience they will need to re-create themselves is vanishing under pressure for the big, quick fix and the crushing load of blame being heaped upon them. In the big cities and the small towns of America, we have let theory, ideology and mythology about welfare and poverty overtake these children and their parents.

PART NINE

Health and Medical Care

The social stratification of health and illness is one of the most devastating inequalities in American society. Despite our enormous wealth and technological potential, the United States still lags behind most other advanced industrial societies on many measures of health and access to health care. Americans have lower life expectancies and higher rates of infant death than citizens of many other developed countries; and some groups—including the urban and rural poor—still suffer shockingly high levels of preventable diseases and inadequate health care services. These problems are hardly new ones. In 1967, a National Advisory Commission on Health Manpower noted that the health statistics of the American poor "occasionally resemble the health statistics of a developing country."[1] Unfortunately, despite several decades of economic growth and stunning advances in medical technology, the same statement could still be made.

To be sure, for those who can afford it, the United States offers some of the best medical care in the world. Yet most Americans are less fortunate. One of the most striking differences between the United States and almost every other advanced society is our lack of any comprehensive system of national health insurance that makes adequate health care available to all citizens as a matter of right. More than 40 million Americans—almost 15 percent of the population—had no health insurance coverage at all during 2001. A recent study estimates that a much larger number—almost one out of three non-elderly Americans—go without health insurance at some point over the course of two years.[2] The proportions are even higher among some groups—notably the young, minorities, and the working poor. Many studies have shown that providing health insurance for everyone would not be hugely expensive, measured against the more than $1 trillion the United States now spends on health care. But we have not moved to make health care for all a reality, and in some respects have gone backwards in recent years, as health care "reforms" have led to ever more intensive efforts to cut costs and as pinched budgets have decimated the ability of states and counties to supply adequate care.

Why don't we have a system that provides health care to everyone? One reason is the American mistrust of government we've encountered already. We have, accordingly, left it up to the "market" to provide even the most basic care, except for the elderly and for those poor enough to be on welfare, whose medical care is partly subsidized by government. But our extreme reliance on the private market to deliver medical care sets us apart from virtually every other advanced society—including our northern neighbor, Canada. Many people have argued that Canada's much-praised universal health care system should be a model for the United States; others criticize it as a cumbersome example of heavy-handed government control. As the selection here by Pat Armstrong and Hugh Armstrong makes clear, Canada's system, while by no means perfect, isn't what some of its American opponents claim. It is not "socialized medicine": Most doctors work for themselves, not for the government, and Canadians can pick any doctor they choose. And it is *less* bureaucratic than the U.S. system, not more. Meanwhile, it has managed to keep Canadians' health costs relatively low compared with ours, while ensuring access to care for everyone. As a result, vast majorities of Canadians are deeply committed to their system, and wouldn't dream of replacing it with the one that prevails south of their border.

Our tendency to leave things to the mercies of the private "market" also extends to our treatment of the elderly. In "The Shame of Our Nursing Homes," Eric Bates describes in disturbing detail some of the realities of care for the nation's nursing home residents, who are subjects of what he calls "the nation's longest running experiment in privatization." Driven by the aim of maximizing their profits, many nursing home companies—part of a business worth over $87 billion a year in the late 1990s—have routinely skimped on patient care, with results that are often degrading and sometimes deadly. Why hasn't government moved more effectively to deal with these abuses—especially since the money that subsidizes the profits of these corporations comes from tax-supported programs like Medicaid and Medicare? In part, Bates suggests, because of the troubling political issue we examined in Part One: the nursing home companies have been big financial contributors to elected officials.

These articles point to the larger reality that America's public commitment to health care is minimal, especially when we compare ourselves to many other nations. As Laurie Garrett shows in her article on "The Return of Infectious Disease," that weak commitment to investing in our public system of health care and disease control may have ominous implications for the future. One of the most troubling medical developments in recent years has been the reemergence of diseases we thought had been conquered once and for all, and the emergence of new ones with especially devastating consequences—from AIDS to the Ebola virus and, more recently, SARS. There are many reasons for this, including the increasingly rapid movement of populations across the world, which allows diseases to spread far more quickly and efficiently than in the past. But another reason for the growth of the threat of infectious disease is that we have persistently cut back funding for the public agencies that might help to control it. From basic research to mosquito control, support for prevention work is fading just as the danger from both old and new diseases is rising. The results, Garrett concludes, could be catastrophic.

The final article, "Cater to the Children," charting the troubling history of the lead industry's effort to mislead the public about the dangers of lead paint, illustrates another way in which the pursuit of private gain can have devastating and enduring consequences for the health of Americans. As the authors point out, it is well known that lead is extremely dangerous, especially to children, and that exposure to lead paint has resulted in a public health disaster of tragic proportions. What is less well known is that the lead industry knew about the dangers of lead paint for decades, but promoted it anyway—using the image of fresh-faced children to sell its product and even going so far as to try to convince parents and others that lead paint was good for you. This history shows, in especially stark terms, how what may appear at first to be simply a medical problem turns out, on closer inspection, to be another example of the deleterious consequences of ignoring the public welfare in the interest of private profit.

ENDNOTES

1. Report of the National Advisory Commission on Health Manpower, quoted in R. M. Titmuss, "Ethics and Economics of Medical Care," in *Commitment to Welfare* (New York: Pantheon, 1968), p. 268.

2. Vicki Kemper, "Study finds more lack health insurance," *Los Angeles Times*, March 5, 2003.

CHAPTER 29

Universal Health Care

What the United States Can Learn from the Canadian Experience

PAT ARMSTRONG

HUGH ARMSTRONG

with CLAUDIA FEGAN, M.D.

A sk any Canadian, "What is the difference between Canada and the United States?" Virtually every one of them will say "health care."

A remarkable 96 percent of Canadians prefer their health care system to the U.S. model.[1] And this support is not simply a reflection of Canadian nationalism in the face of a very large neighbor, although medicare certainly plays a central role as a "defining national characteristic."[2] Over the years, poll after poll has repeatedly demonstrated that health care is Canada's best-loved social program. An overwhelming majority of Canadians persistently say they want to keep their health care system.

In 1994, the Canadian government appointed a National Forum on Health to examine the current state and future possibilities of the health system. The focus groups and surveys conducted by the forum found that "the provision of health care services continues to receive strong and passionate support" among Canadians.[3] Similarly, the president of a major polling firm reported recently that among government programs "only the health care system received approval from a majority of Canadians." He went on to point out that the support even crosses social class lines. Otherwise strong differences in class values "don't occur to the same extent in the area of health care, perhaps because everyone can see themselves as becoming sick at some point."[4]

The current system is so popular that all Canadian politicians represent themselves as defenders of this sacred trust. Perhaps more surprisingly, so do many corporations in the private sector. Indeed, a major health insurance company has declared in a recent advertisement that it "believes strongly in the sanctity of Canadian medicare."[5]

The most important explanation for this support can be found in what are known as the five principles of the Canada Health Act. These are criteria for funding set out by the federal government, criteria the provinces* must follow in order to receive financial support for their health care services. Simply put, these principles require that core medical services be universal, portable, accessible, comprehensive, and publicly administered. In other words, all Canadians must have access to the medical services they require. These services must include all that is medically necessary, and must be provided regardless of age, prior condition, location, or employment. And they must be provided without regard to ability to pay. Canadian medicare was designed to allocate care on the basis of need, not individual finances.

And it worked. The system has delivered on the promised access to care. While "the number of uninsured Americans had risen to more than 40 million"[6] in 1995, virtually every Canadian is covered for essential care. This contrast in access to care can be traced to the basic philosophical approach used to fund services in Canada. As one 1981 task force put it, "Canadians are endeavouring to develop a health care system directed at health needs—not a competitive system to serve an illness market."[7]

This is made possible by the single-payer system. For the most part, health care in Canada is not *provided* by the government. It is *paid for* by governments. It is a public insurance system, a system in which governments at various levels pay for health services. Most of these services themselves are provided by nonprofit organizations or by doctors working on a fee-for-service basis. It is public payment for private practice and private provision.[8] This single-payer system has made care in Canada cheaper than in the United States, both because it significantly reduces administrative costs and because it allows for more coherent management of services.

Until medicare was introduced, Canadian health care costs were growing as fast as those in the United States. But "the period of the most rapid escalation *ended* with the establishment of universal coverage"[9] paid for from public funds. Even more startling is the fact that *public* spending on health care accounts for virtually the same proportion of each country's total economy. Yet, Canada covers the whole population and the United States covers only the elderly, the very poor, the military, and some of the disabled.

With the government as the main purchaser of services, health care is not only cheaper for individual taxpayers. It is also cheaper for employers, especially for those employers facing unions strong enough to successfully demand full health care coverage. In the United States, Chrysler pays more for health care than it pays for steel.[10] In Canada, Chrysler does not have to pay for basic hospital or medical costs and therefore its employee costs are lower. Workers' compensation in Canada does not have to cover these basic costs either, and thus this protection too is cheaper for the Canadian employer.

---

*Canada has a federal system with ten provinces and two (soon to be three) territories, each with its own health department. Although huge in size, the territories are tiny in population terms. Throughout this book "provinces" will be used to refer to both provinces and territories.

With the single-payer scheme for many essential services, Canadians have a one-tier system. The rich and the poor go to the same hospitals and doctors. Neither receives a bill and the rich cannot buy quicker access, preferred status, or better facilities. What is covered by the public insurance system cannot be covered by a private insurer and doctors are not allowed to bill above the prescribed rate for services covered by the public insurance. Sharing facilities and services means that the entire population has a vested interest in maintaining the quality of care.

For more than a quarter century, Canada has been providing this comprehensive, accessible and high-quality care, without billing individuals for services or relating care to financial status. Equally important, it has done so more efficiently and at least as effectively as the competitive system serving an illness market in the United States. It is not surprising, then, that 96 percent of Canadians prefer their system to the American way. It is somewhat more surprising that a majority of Americans also prefer the Canadian system to that in the United States.[11] After all, health care services are very similar on both sides of the border.

In both countries, hospitals form the core of the system. And an operating room in one country looks much like one in the other. Hospitals in both countries offer high-tech services. On both sides of the border, most hospitals are owned by non-government organizations and function largely as independent entities. Hospitals in both countries vary in size and degree of specialization, although teaching hospitals across the continent tend to be large and diverse. Once in the door, it would be difficult to tell Toronto Hospital from the hospital in *Chicago Hope*.

Similarly, it would be difficult to identify which doctors are Canadian and which are American. Not only do both kinds wear white coats and stethoscopes, but the majority of doctors are paid on a fee-for-service basis. They are formally governed by agencies primarily made up of peers, intended to protect both patients and providers. Across North America, specialties are very similar and so are medical techniques. Indeed, research is freely shared and even jointly conducted across the border. Like hospitals, doctors' offices look virtually the same in Canada and the United States. Marcus Welby could be a Canadian.

Although doctors in both countries have fought hard to gain a monopoly over diagnosis and other medical practices, most of the actual patient care is provided by nurses of various kinds. Even the categories of nurses are basically the same on both sides of the border, as is their range of skills. Nurses are the main care providers both in and out of the hospital setting.

The settings where nurses and others provide care include long-term care facilities of various sorts. Homes for the elderly, nursing homes, and group homes are common everywhere in North America. And in both countries a great deal of care is provided in the home, often with assistance from home care nurses or other aides.

If health care is so similar in both countries, why is there such a strong preference for the Canadian system evident across the border as well as at home? Again, the explanation can be found mainly in the five principles on which Canadian health care delivery is based. And these in turn are related to the single-payer system and the insistence on one-tier delivery. They offer the most likely reasons for both Canadians and Americans preferring the Canadian approach. . . .

Is Canada's single-payer health care system perfect? Of course not. But it has been improved in a variety of ways since its inception, and the fact that it is paid for by public insurance makes it more sensitive to public opinion than are systems based on the profit motive. Problems remain, but they are not those commonly cited by media and other critics of public health insurance. It is to the problems, imagined and real, of Canadian medicare that we now turn.

WHAT THE PROBLEMS ARE NOT

I. Finances

Comparisons of public spending in Canada and other industrialized countries show two things. The Canadian level of public expenditure is in line with levels elsewhere, and it is very much under control. These conclusions hold, however public spending is measured.

Critics have argued that the Canadian public system spends both too much and too little on health care. At the height of the debt and deficit hysteria that swept through Canada, all social programs came under attack. These programs, including health care, were blamed for causing the debt through profligate overspending.

The charge did not stand up to careful scrutiny, however. In an analysis published by Statistics Canada's leading economic journal, two highly respected economists demonstrated that the growth in spending on all social programs, indeed on all programs, accounted for virtually none of the federal debt accumulated by the late 1980s. Rather, the debt was primarily attributable to a combination of reductions in corporate taxes and increases in real interest rates, or to the cost to the government (and others) of borrowing money.[12] Spending on social programs in general, and on health care in particular, is not the problem.

Some U.S. critics of the Canadian health care system have claimed that it is too expensive in light of the heavy tax burden it creates. Like health care spending, however, the level of taxes in Canada is about average in comparison with the levels in other industrialized countries. Both Canadian payroll taxes and fringe benefit costs are among the lowest, in large measure because of Canada's public, universal, and quite comprehensive health care system. Moreover, as the *World Competitiveness Report 1991* pointed out, publicly funded health care was a major factor placing Canada as high as fifth in its world competitiveness rankings.[13]

At the same time, some critics on both sides of the border have argued that on certain items Canada spends too little to provide adequate care. There is, however, little evidence that spending more would result in better or more accessible care. When public and private spending are combined, Canada spends much less on health care than the United States. Yet for less money, Canada provides more hospital beds relative to population and the average lengths of stay in its hospitals are longer. The United States does have slightly more doctors, and many more of its doctors are specialists, but there is research to indicate that this represents excess capacity more than it represents what is needed for quality care.[14] In the midst of American plenty, moreover, there remain considerable shortages because the pri-

TABLE 29.1   Public Spending on Health Care
Selected Industrialized Countries

Country	Percentage of GDP 1995	Percentage of all public spending, 1994*
Germany	8.2	18.4
France	7.7	13.6
Switzerland	7.1	18.6
Belgium	7.0	12.6
Canada	6.9	14.5
Iceland	6.9	17.7
Netherlands	6.8	12.2
United States	6.6	16.4

*The figure for Iceland's percentage of all public spending refers to 1995; for the United States it refers to 1993.

Source: Organisation for Economic Co-operation and Development, "OECD Health Data 97." http://www.oecd.org/statlist.htm (updated July 8, 1997), Health I Table.

vate system in the United States has greater difficulty distributing care equitably and efficiently. A 1996 study found that "problems in getting needed medical care affect about 17 million uninsured adults and 17 million insured adults in America."[15] This happens to very few Canadians.

There is no way to determine scientifically the appropriate amount to spend on health care. The allocation of society's resources is as much a matter of values as it is of evidence. For their part, Canadians have made it abundantly clear that they want to continue to devote a significant proportion of their tax dollars to health care. Canadians do not feel that they spend too much on their medicare system. Nor do they feel that they receive inadequate returns on their investment.

II. *Waiting Lists*

The rich cannot buy their way to the front of the line in the Canadian health care system. A few of them, and some U.S. critics, have as a result taken to complaining about the delays experienced before certain procedures are carried out. There are several aspects of the waiting list issue that merit consideration.

First, every society is almost certain to impose at least some waiting time for some health care procedures on at least some of its members. Every country in the world, including both Canada and the United States, does so now and always has. To do otherwise would be possible, after enough providers were trained and facilities built, but it would be done at the cost of other priorities, including those that affect the social determinants of health. Just as one would not build the capacity of a mass transit system so that everyone has a comfortable seat during rush hour, so too with health care. The issue is not whether there should be rationing and waiting, but the principles that should govern the rationing and waiting.

Second, it should be made crystal clear that Canadians rarely wait for care that is required immediately. And, given that there are no financial costs to the individual at the point of receiving care, there is little incentive for patients to wait until their problems are severe. Most of the reports on waiting times that circulate widely refer to elective surgery, not to care that is required immediately.

Third, it should be remembered that Canadians have become so accustomed to readily accessible care that is portable throughout the country and that comes without cost to the individual that any waiting is considered intolerable. Surveys suggesting that waiting times have increased may thus leave a misleading impression. They may refer to increases in waiting times from a very low base, rather than the actual time people have to wait.

Fourth, we have scant comparative data in Canada, or in other countries, that would provide a solid basis for assessing the actual amounts of time people wait for care, or the consequences of their waits. How long, for example, do the "working poor" in the United States wait for diabetes diagnosis or for cataract surgery? In Canada, does waiting for elective surgery have long-term negative consequences? What are the consequences of waiting for different kinds of elective surgery? No discussion of waiting times can be adequate without such information.

Finally, and perhaps most importantly, the example of cardiac surgery in Ontario demonstrates that public systems are in a position to address waiting list problems when they are revealed. As the National Forum on Health explains,

> Experience . . . suggests that public health care can reduce waiting lists without increasing spending. The key is to ensure that waiting lists are structured and prioritized, and that incentives are in place to ensure that patients are served before their risk, or their degree of suffering, becomes unacceptably high. The solution is management, monitoring, and evaluation—not a bewildering array of public and private alternatives.[16]

III. Bureaucracy and Privacy

The beauty of the Canadian system lies in its simplicity. First, there were two short pieces of legislation, one on hospital insurance and then another on physician insurance. In 1984, these were consolidated and expanded into the Canada Health Act, another short and simple piece of legislation. Basically, the Canada Health Act lays down the five principles for the federal contribution to the funding of provincial health care programs. It therefore allows for diversity among and within provinces without creating enormous amounts of surveillance work. Health services have remained largely the way they were before medicare, except that now the bills are sent to a single payer in each province.

The consequence is less bureaucracy for both providers and patients. Because everyone belongs to the system, there is no need for fat files on each individual. Because the bills are paid from one source with little hassle, there is no need for detailed accounts of the supplies and services used by individuals, no need to hire collection agencies, and few resources spent on court battles over liability.

When Tommy Douglas first proposed to introduce public insurance coverage for doctors' services, one of the specters raised by his political opponents was that the confidentiality of individual health records would be lost. Public insurance was equated with government snooping into everyone's health file.

Ironically, however, personal health records and other personal records are much more likely to be invaded by private insurance companies competing to avoid high risks than by the public insurance agency. With everyone enrolled in a universal public scheme, there is no need to check individual medical histories or any other personal information to decide on program eligibility. And with everyone enrolled, there is also no reason to check on credit ratings, or on employment histories and status. Neither patients nor providers need to gain prior approval before undergoing tests or treatments, thus further reducing the situations in which outsiders demand personal health information. With hospitals operating under global budgets within a universal scheme, there is no need for financial administrators inside or outside the hospital to examine individual patient files.

All this contrasts sharply with private health insurance schemes. Private insurers have a financial incentive not only to enroll the best risks but also to specify as precisely as possible the services to be covered. A family history of cancer, a gay lifestyle, a clearly dangerous job or high job turnover could all mean a person is a risk. To make their enrollment and coverage decisions, private insurers need access to detailed personal medical, financial, and employment histories; to test results; and to physician and hospital practice patterns. Not incidently, they also need detailed reports on what individual physicians do, so their risk of incurring costs can be assessed. These requirements mean more bureaucracy and less privacy.

Drug prescription records may appear to provide an exception to the general rule that a public system protects privacy better. In Ontario, for example, the government has funded the establishment of a computer network that allows pharmacists to coordinate personal records on the filling of drug prescriptions. This integrated computer system enables pharmacists to watch out for drugs that may interact in harmful ways and for drugs that may be over-prescribed. The system could also enable the public insurance agency to monitor the prescribing patterns of individual doctors and the prescription drugs purchased by individual patients. It has been set up, however, on a voluntary basis, and the government and its public health insurance agency have no privileged access to individual prescription drug records.

What a public system does allow for is more information on, and more choice about, who has access to information on individual health files and on provider patterns. Again to use the example of Ontario, patient rights advocates have successfully pressed for legislation that severely restricts access to personal information on the diagnosis and treatment of mental illness. Not even parents and other relatives responsible for providing care, let alone insurance companies and governments, have access to the files without the permission of the adult patient.

IV. Choices and Abuses

Unlike the United States, which funds individuals who meet predetermined criteria, Canada has decided to fund services for everyone through a public system. As a result, Canadians have many more health care choices than do Americans. They are not prevented by predetermined criteria from qualifying for care. Individual Canadian patients and family physicians choose without outside interference who will be seen how often and by whom. On referral from a family physician, Canadian patients can go to any specialist or hospital, as frequently as medically appropriate and for as long as medically necessary.

Doctors too enjoy a wide range of choices, and freedom from supervision. There is little restriction on where they locate. In fact, a recent court decision in British Columbia struck down a provision in the fee schedule that penalized new entrants to medicine if they chose to set up their practices in heavily served urban areas. In this instance, the problem appears to be too much individual choice in the public system, not too little.[17] Physicians are guaranteed that their fees will be paid at the negotiated rate, and only very seldom are their activities scrutinized. Usually the monitoring of physicians' fees simply takes the form of letters sent to a random sample of patients inquiring whether they visited a specific physician on a specific date. The fee-for-service system under which nine out of ten Canadian doctors are paid allows them considerable choice about their hours of work and, ultimately, about how much income they will receive.

Like doctors, nurses and most other care providers in the public system must meet the health profession's standards of their province in order to practice in it. Most of the many female care providers are unionized, improving their choices in terms of pay, benefits, and working conditions.[18] The stability of a publicly financed system has been an important factor in this high rate of unionization.

The other side of choice is abuse. Within Canada, the claim is at times made that patients overuse their system, abusing their right to free choice and "free" care. This complaint is frequently combined with a call for user fees. The argument is advanced that such fees would simultaneously make people appreciate the benefits of the system more and make them be more careful about using it, thus ensuring more appropriate utilization.

There is very little evidence, however, of widespread abuse of access to care by Canadians. Nor is there evidence that user fees would prevent any of the abuse that does exist. One difficulty with attempting to collect such evidence concerns the definition of abuse. Those who use the system are unlikely to think that they are abusing it. Ask any patient waiting in a hospital emergency room, painfully or anxiously, whether *others* are there for frivolous reasons. Many will say that others do not look like they need immediate care. But they will be firmly convinced that their own visit is urgent and justified.

Furthermore, much of what might be defined as inappropriate use of the system would be so defined *after* diagnosis. Hindsight has 20/20 vision, as the saying goes. A mother may rush her screaming child to emergency only to discover that the problem is an earache that could have been dealt with by the family physician during regular office hours. But the earache could also have been an indication of a much more serious condition, and urgent care was sought precisely to find this out. When abuse is defined as use that is not medically necessary, the research that does exist has found very little abuse by patients.[19]

As a team of Canadian researchers has concluded from a thorough analysis of the uses of user fees,

> it is difficult to see how *patient*-initiated abuse *could* make up a large share of overall health care use and costs, because patients have little control over most of the decisions about the use of care. Call-back visits, referrals, hospital admissions and prescriptions, for example, all depend on the judgment and approval of a physician. No doubt there are some patients who "demand" a hospital procedure or a prescription, but the picture of patients eagerly requesting surgery or wanting to take medication just because the services are "free" makes even advocates of user charges laugh.[20]

At the same time, there is some evidence that the public insurance system encourages appropriate use in Canada. A study by Kevin Gorey published in a 1997 issue of the *American Journal of Public Health* found that "compared to their Detroit counterparts, poor women in Toronto have a survival rate for breast cancer that is 30 percent higher, for ovarian cancer that is 38 percent higher and for cervical cancer that is 48 percent higher." Moreover, "Toronto women have survival rates more than 50 percent above that of women in Detroit's poorest districts for lung, stomach and pancreatic cancer." Even after accounting for race and for the standards for measuring poverty, the differences remain.[21] The research suggests that Canadian medicare, with no user charges at the point of service, encourages appropriate and timely use, while user charges and other provisions that limit choice make the U.S. health care system less effective.

V. *Quality, Technology, Research, and Innovation*

Although it must be conceded that the Canadian system is more equitable than the U.S. alternative, it is on occasion argued that the quality of care is inferior in Canada, especially when it comes to advances related to research and technology. As we have seen, measuring quality is no simple task, and neither country is very good at it. Too much of the research on both sides of the border focuses on costs, measuring quality in terms of dollars spent and efficiency in terms of dollars saved. On both sides of the border, we know much more about expenditures per person than we do about whether these expenditures are worthwhile in terms of health outcomes.

As a result, researchers in both Canada and the United States have turned increasingly to the development of new and better ways to assess the quality of the care that is delivered. Especially for a country with a small population, Canada has a significant number of research organizations devoted to the assessment of quality in the delivery of health services. There are, for example, major centers at several universities in the provinces of British Columbia, Ontario, and Quebec that bring together multidisciplinary teams to examine health policy issues. The province of Manitoba has a Centre for Health Policy and Evaluation that maintains a database for hospital discharge information, enabling it to assess both the accessibility and the quality of care. Ontario's Institute for Clinical Evaluative Sciences

(ICES) regularly produces a practice atlas that documents variations in practice patterns across the province, in an effort to prompt medical and other practitioners to evaluate whether they are following the most appropriate procedures. The Saskatchewan Health Services Utilization Review Commission (HSURC) has conducted and publicized a wide range of studies to help providers decide on the best approaches to care.

These and similar research organizations receive the bulk of their funding from the public purse. There are also national and provincial granting councils that provide financial support to individual researchers and teams of researchers based in hospitals and universities in every part of the country.[22] Lesser amounts come from a variety of charitable foundations. Partly as a result of this tax-supported investment in research, Canadians proportionately publish virtually as many articles in medical journals as do their U.S. counterparts.[23]

All this research activity leads to a number of conclusions. First, Canada devotes considerable time and resources to health-related research, and this research is frequently the basis for innovations in practice. Second, none of the research on quality reveals the existence of significant differences in the quality of health care in Canada and the United States. Although there is relatively more technology in the U.S., there is little evidence to show that all this technology is necessary or related to better quality care. There is, however, evidence that Canada distributes its technology more appropriately and equitably. Third, although neither country has developed very rigorous ways of measuring quality, the establishment of well-funded research centers in Canada with mandates to focus on evaluation and utilization concerns may bode well for the future.[24] The existence of a publicly administered health care system in Canada enhances the likelihood that research conducted there and abroad will be translated into improved care.

ENDNOTES

1. These results come from a 1993 Gallup poll cited in Nicole Nolan, "Bitter Medicine," *In These Times* (Jan. 20, 1997), p. 16.

2. National Forum on Health, "Values Working Group Synthesis Report," *Canada Health Action: Building on the Legacy,* Vol. II, *Synthesis Reports and Issues Papers* (Ottawa: Minister of Public Works and Government Services, 1997), p. 5.

3. National Forum on Health, "Values Working Group," p. 11.

4. Frank Graves, "Canadian Health Care—What Are the Facts? An Overview of Public Opinion in Canada," in *Access to Quality Health Care for All Canadians* (Ottawa: Canadian Medical Association, 1996), pp. 18–19.

5. In *Maclean's* (Dec. 2, 1996), pp. 50–51.

6. *UC Berkeley Wellness Newsletter* (May 1997).

7. Quoted in Malcolm G. Taylor, *Health Insurance and Canadian Public Policy: The Seven Decisions That Created the Canadian Health Insurance System and Their Consequences,* 2nd ed. (Kingston and Montreal: McGill–Queen's University Press, 1989), p. 433.

8. To borrow the titles from two books on Canadian approaches to the organization of social services: C. David Naylor, *Private Practices, Public Payment: Canadian Medicine and the Politics of Health Insurance 1911–1966* (Kingston: McGill–Queen's University Press, 1986);

Josephine Rekart, *Public Funds, Private Provision* (Vancouver: University of British Columbia Press, 1994).

9. Robert Evans, "Health Care Reform: 'The Issue From Hell'," *Policy Options* (July–Aug. 1993), p. 37 (emphasis in original).

10. David U. Himmelstein and Steffie Woolhandler, *The National Health Program Book* (Monroe, ME: Common Courage Press, 1994), p. 40.

11. Robert J. Blendon and Humphrey Taylor, "Views on Health Care: Public Opinion in Three Nations," *Health Affairs* 8:1 (spring 1989), p. 152, where it is reported that 61 percent of Americans "would prefer the Canadian system of national health insurance" to the system they have now.

12. H. Mimoto and P. Cross, "The Growth of the Federal Debt," *Canadian Economic Observer* (June 1991), pp. 1–17.

13. World Economic Forum, *World Competitiveness Report 1991* (Lausanne, Switzerland: Institut pour l'étude des méthodes de direction de l'entreprise, 1992).

14. Tom Closson and Margaret Catt, "Funding System Incentives and the Restructuring of Health Care," *Canadian Journal of Public Health* 87:2 (March–April 1996), Table IV.

15. Reported in Robert Pear, "Health Costs Pose Problem for Millions, A Study Finds," *New York Times* (October 23, 1996), p. A4.

16. National Forum on Health, "Striking a Balance Working Group Synthesis Report," *Canada Health Action: Building on the Legacy,* Vol. II, *Synthesis Reports and Issues Papers* (Ottawa: Minister of Public Works and Government Services, 1997), p. 39.

17. Miro Cernetig and Robert Matas, "B.C. Can't Limit Where MDs Set Up Practices, Court Rules," Toronto *Globe and Mail* (Aug. 2, 1997), pp. A1, A7. Contrast this situation to that in the United States where, according to a recent report, at least 5 percent of new graduates in eleven of twenty-four specialties cannot find full-time positions anywhere, and "most job offers come from far-flung places, not urban areas." Leah Beth Ward, "Heartening Signs for Specialty M.D.'s," *New York Times* (Aug. 4, 1996), p. F8, reporting on a study in a March 1996 issue of the *Journal of the American Medical Association.*

18. Between 75 and 80 percent of registered nurses employed in the Canadian health care system are unionized, as against between 10 and 15 percent in the United States. Kit Costello, "Canadian Nurses—Our Northern Neighbors Fight Similar Battles," *California Nurse* 93:6 (June–July 1997), p. 12. Salaries for Canadian nurses averaged $US 39,161 for 37.5 hours work a week in 1992, as against $34,192 for 39.5 hours in the United States. Judith Shindul-Rothschild and Suzanne Gordon, "Single-Payer Versus Managed Competition: Implications for Nurses," *Journal of Nursing Education* 33:5 (May 1994), p. 204.

19. Greg L. Stoddart et al., "Why Not User Charges? The Real Issues," a discussion paper prepared for the [Ontario] Premier's Council on Health, Well-being and Social Justice (Sept. 1993), pp. 5–6.

20. Stoddart et al., "Why Not User Charges?," p. 5 (emphasis in original).

21. Jane Coutts, "Medicare Gives Poor a Better Chance," Toronto *Globe and Mail* (Aug. 1, 1997), p. A1.

22. See National Forum on Health, "Creating a Culture of Evidence-Based Decision-Making," *Canada Health Action: Building on the Legacy,* Vol. II, *Synthesis Reports and Issues Papers* (Ottawa: Minister of Public Works and Government Services, 1997), esp. pp. 21–23.

23. David U. Himmelstein and Steffie Woolhandler, *The National Health Program Book* (Monroe, ME: Common Courage Press, 1994), p. 109. In 1990, the U.S. figure was 526 articles per million population, while the Canadian figure was 520. Both were well behind Israel, Sweden, and the United Kingdom, but well ahead of Germany and Japan.

24. Noralou P. Roos et al., "Population Health and Health Care Use: An Information System for Policy Makers," *Milbank Quarterly* 74:1 (spring 1996), pp. 3–31.

CHAPTER **30**

The Shame of Our Nursing Homes

ERIC BATES

The day before Kimberly Holdford left on a camping trip with her husband and twin girls in June of 1997, she stopped by a nursing home to visit her grandmother. It had been a month since Jewel Elizabeth Forester entered the Beverly Health and Rehabilitation Center in Jacksonville, Arkansas, to recover from a bout with the flu that had left her severely dehydrated. She hated the facility. Beverly aides seldom bathed her and often neglected to take her to the bathroom, leaving her caked in dried feces and sobbing in shame. Holdford didn't know what to do; Beverly was the only nearby nursing home with an available bed. "We're understaffed," she recalls an aide telling her. "We don't have enough people to do the job."

At 80, Forester remained feisty and sharp-witted, tackling crossword puzzles and reveling in the afternoon soaps. But on the day before the camping trip, Holdford found her groggy and disoriented. "What's wrong with my grandmother?" she asked the nursing staff. "She won't wake up." Assured that a doctor would be called, Holdford reluctantly left for the weekend.

But no one at Beverly called the doctor. The next day Forester was screaming in pain and moaning in her sleep. Aides tried to calm her down because she was disturbing other patients. On Monday a respiratory therapist found Forester nearly comatose. She was rushed to the hospital, where doctors found three times the maximum therapeutic level of a drug called digoxin in her system. The nursing home had administered an overdose of the drug, even though it had been warned that Forester had trouble tolerating the medication.

"What followed was nine days of the worst deathwatch you ever saw in your life," recalls Robert Holdford, Kimberly's husband. "She was screaming and moaning as her organs shut down from the overdose. She suffered an agonizing death because of Beverly."

Nor was Forester the only patient at the home to suffer from substandard care. With too small a staff to turn and feed them, some residents developed bone-deep wounds; one was hospitalized weighing only eighty-one pounds. Last September a 58-year-old man died after an untrained and unlicensed nurse punctured his stomach lining when she tried to reinsert a feeding tube.

Dan Springer, a vice president at Beverly, calls the facility "an aberration," but the company has acknowledged that things were seriously amiss. "We knew that we had some problems," a top executive told reporters after the home was finally shut down by the state. "It was horrible."

Such horror stories involving nursing homes have become almost commonplace. For three decades, federal and state investigations have repeatedly documented widespread understaffing, misuse of medication and restraints, even physical attacks on patients. Yet thousands of vulnerable citizens remain confined in depressing, debilitating—and often deadly—institutions like the one in Jacksonville. Last summer, a federal study found that nearly one-third of all nursing homes in California had been cited for violations that caused death or life-threatening harm to patients. Federal officials charged with policing dangerous homes "generally took a lenient stance," William Scanlon, director of health financing and systems issues for the US General Accounting Office (GAO), testified before a Senate panel in July. "Homes can repeatedly harm residents without facing sanctions."

Federal officials are promising to subject nursing homes to closer scrutiny in the coming months. President Clinton has ordered a crack-down on repeat offenders, the Justice Department is investigating charges of fraud and abuse, and Congress is poised to reshape Medicare and other programs that pay for long-term care. Yet such efforts focus more on cutting costs than improving care; they fail to recognize that standards remain lax and reforms fall short because of the very nature of nursing homes. Facilities that care for nearly 2 million elderly and disabled residents form a lucrative private industry that profits directly from pain—while taxpayers foot the bill. Nursing homes ring up $87 billion of business each year, and more than 75 cents of every dollar comes from public funds through Medicaid and Medicare. The less of that money homes spend on care, the more they pocket for themselves and their shareholders. To insure those profits, nursing homes are careful not to skimp when it comes to investing in politics: The industry gives millions in contributions to state and federal officials, insuring weak public oversight.

At a time when Republicans and Democrats alike are clamoring to let big business run everything from prisons to schools, nursing homes represent the nation's longest-running experiment in privatization—one that, after half a century, offers a graphic portrayal of what happens when private interests are permitted to monopolize public services. While the industry is currently struggling to adjust to new limits on Medicare spending, nursing homes still rely on a generous flow of public subsidies. Leading the for-profit field is Beverly Enterprises, which controls more nursing-home beds than any other firm in the nation. Founded in 1963 as privatization accelerated, the company now owns 561 homes like the one in Jacksonville, which is located just a few hours down the road from its corporate headquarters in Ft. Smith, Arkansas. Although Beverly posted a loss last year, it remains an industry giant. In 1997 the company enjoyed after-tax profits of $58.5 million on revenues of $3.2 billion.

The money did little to help elderly residents like Jewel Forester. "I trusted them not to let her come to harm," says Kimberly Holdford, looking at a photo of her grandmother. "Instead, this sweet little old woman who loved me all my life suffered a brutal death. Somebody has got to stop these big corporations from hurting our old people. They're supposed to be in the healthcare business, not the money-making business. All they care about is keeping profits up."

From colonial times, caring for the elderly poor has been a responsibility of government. At first, officials tried not only to pass the buck but to make a few as well. Until the 1820s villages and cities confronted with growing numbers of impoverished citizens routinely auctioned them off to families who provided squalid accommodations in return for grueling work. An observer at one Saturday-night auction at a village tavern noted that citizens "could speculate upon the bodily vigor and the probable capacity for hard labor of a half-witted boy, a forlorn-looking widow, or a halt and tottering old man." But as abuses—and profits—mounted, cities and counties began to operate their own poorhouses for the sick and aged. The expression "over the hill" comes from an 1871 ballad that depicts the plight of an old woman cast out by her children to live in a government-run workhouse.

As industrial mechanization eliminated jobs after World War I, the public began to protest overcrowding and illness in county poorhouses. Reformers often seemed less concerned about aiding the poor, however, than about keeping them away from the well-to-do. "Worthy people are thrown together with moral derelicts, with dope addicts, with prostitutes, bums, drunks—with whatever dregs of society happen to need the institution's shelter at the moment," the New York Commission on Old Age Security complained in a 1930 report. "People of culture and refinement," the commission noted, were forced to share services "with the crude and ignorant and feebleminded."

Spurred by scandals over conditions in public poorhouses, federal lawmakers decided to hand the elderly over to private industry. In 1935 Congress specifically framed the Social Security Act to prohibit cash payments to any "inmate of a public institution." Those over 65 received small monthly pensions, but none of the money could go to government-run homes for the aged. The massive transfer of tax dollars to private business fueled the creation of for-profit homes. Almost overnight, operators set up facilities to exploit pensioners. Sometimes little changed but the name. In Minnesota, private owners removed a large sign identifying "Dodge County Poor Farm," replacing it with one reading "Fairview Rest Home." The federal government soon began making direct payments to private nursing homes and providing low-interest loans for construction, insuring the fledgling industry a handsome profit. "So rapidly has the nursing home developed during the past 20 years," two observers noted in 1955, "that its history seems more like an eruption than an evolutionary development."

The eruption became volcanic in 1965, when Congress created Medicaid to assist the elderly poor and Medicare to provide health insurance for the aged. The two programs provided a huge profusion of public money into the nursing homes, with few strings attached. Most states limited the number of homes, thus insuring a supply of patients to fill the beds. They also reimbursed homes for all expenses, from mortgage and depreciation on the building to the staff and supplies inside—in essence, giving owners a blank check that virtually guaranteed them a healthy profit on their investment. Before long, global corporations like ITT rushed to cash in on the industry. With backing from Wall Street, the number of homes soared from 13,000 in 1967 to more than 23,000 in 1969.

"That was when nursing homes moved away from mom-and-pop operations to large, for-profit enterprises," says Charles Phillips, director of the Myers Research Institute in Beachwood, Ohio. "They were more interested in real estate transactions than healthcare. They shuffled properties back and forth between subsidiaries, jacking up property costs to increase reimbursement. Our current long-term-care system is fundamentally a creature of government policy. Those real estate ventures became the source of corporate empires."

Today those empires represent a booming business. With the number of elderly citizens needing long-term care expected to double over the next two decades, Wall Street sees a steady stream of customers for nursing homes—with a guaranteed flow of cash consisting almost entirely of public funds. "We believe nursing homes are well positioned to capitalize on this growing opportunity," the investment bank Hambrecht & Quist recently advised investors, predicting that corporate chains would boost profits by laying off staff members, cutting wages and doubling patient loads. With the help of large institutional investors like Goldman Sachs and Lazard Frères, nursing-home chains are also making shareholders happy by swallowing competitors at a record pace. Last year two of the largest chains in the country merged with two fellow giants, creating parent companies with annual revenues of about $3 billion each. Thanks to their big financial backers, seven chains now collect 20 cents of every dollar spent on nursing homes nationwide (see Box 30.1).

The oldest and largest chain is Beverly Enterprises. Founded by a California accountant at the outset of the federal bonanza, the company quickly earned him $10 million on his initial investment of $5,700. In the seventies, backed by the influential Arkansas brokerage house of Stephens, Inc., Beverly led the industry in a frenzied buying spree, adding nearly 1,000 nursing homes in less than a decade. "No other chain has been able to put together as successful an acquisition formula," reported a study by the Food and Allied Service Trades of the AFL-CIO.

For a time, Beverly found, bigger was better. For five years in the eighties the chain maintained an annual return on equity of 23 percent—the fifth-highest rate of any healthcare company nationwide. But unable to manage its far-flung network of nursing homes, Beverly lost $60 million in 1987 and began selling off facilities to avoid a hostile takeover. "We probably grew too fast," acknowledged David Banks, a former typewriter salesman and Stephens executive who now heads Beverly.

Led by Banks, the company also moved to Arkansas, where it enjoyed legal advice from a young attorney at the Rose Law Firm named Hillary Clinton and political support from her husband, Bill, in the governor's mansion. In one deal that demonstrated the kind of favoritism Beverly enjoyed, a state board approved $81 million in tax-free revenue bonds that would have given the company badly needed cash to pay its debts—without creating a single new job. Clinton, who appears to

BOX **30.1**

More Beds, More Money

Beverly Enterprises controls more than 60,000 nursing-home beds, more than any other company worldwide. But six other chains also enjoy significant shares of the industry, rapidly placing more patients in the hands of big conglomerates.

- Integrated Health Services (Owings Mills, Maryland). The chain moved into the front ranks of the industry when it acquired rival Horizon/CMS Healthcare for $1.2 billion. It now boasts 42,600 beds and revenues of $3 billion.
- Vencor (Louisville, Kentucky). The chain drew fire last year when it evicted low-income residents to make way for wealthier clientele. With 38,300 beds, it enjoys revenues of $3 billion.
- Sun Healthcare Group (Albuquerque, New Mexico). After a buying spree that brought it two smaller chains, Sun has vaulted into the big leagues with 44,000 beds and $3.2 billion in revenues.

- HCR Manor Care (Toledo, Ohio). A merger between two industry giants formed a new chain with 47,000 beds and revenues of $2.2 billion. Chairman Stewart Bainum Jr. immediately promised "future acquisitions, at the lowest cost of capital in the industry."
- Mariner Post-Acute Network (Atlanta, Georgia). Another member of the billion-dollar club, formed by the merger of Mariner Health Group and Paragon Health Network. Dogged by allegations of racketeering at a former nursing home in Tampa, the chain controls 48,100 beds and $2.7 billion in revenues.
- Genesis Health Ventures (Kennett Square, Pennsylvania). The company bought a pharmaceutical chain and sponsored a real estate investment trust for some of its 37,700 beds, boosting revenues to $1.4 billion.   E.B.

Source: All figures are from company officials; revenues are for the latest available twelve-month period.

have originally seen the deal as a way to help woo the company to Arkansas, backed away from it only after Steve Clark, his attorney general, revealed that a lobbyist had offered him $100,000 in campaign gifts if he supported the bond handout. "The only way this proposal can be described," Clark told a meeting of startled officials unused to hearing criticism of Beverly, "is one which is the product of the arrogance of wealth and the arrogance of power." Even Clinton was forced to concede that the deal went too far. "They were trying to milk this bond system," he said.

While Beverly executives and shareholders profited from the company's rapid growth during the eighties, many patients suffered. Across the nation, health officials filed reports on Beverly nursing homes documenting filthy living conditions, infected bedsores and painful deaths. The State of Washington banned the company from opening any new homes because of its poor track record. The chain bowed out of Maine after inspectors there cited it for substandard conditions. A Missouri grand jury investigated reports of Beverly patients with gaping wounds. Texas suspended Medicaid payments to twenty-four of the company's homes because of health hazards. California fined the firm $724,000 and put it on probation after accusing Beverly of contributing to the deaths of nine patients. At one home, inspectors found that ants had swarmed over the body of a woman, entering her respiratory system through a wound in her throat. "Something is very wrong at Beverly Enterprises," a deputy attorney general in California concluded. Beverly considered it business as usual. "We pretty much mirror the industry," said CEO Banks at the time of the California investigation.

Beverly certainly mirrors the industry in the way it cashes in on Medicaid and Medicare. To improve the bottom line, homes have funneled as much money as possible into property, administrative salaries and ancillary services like drugs and physical therapy, while cutting corners on patient care and staff wages. Many facilities have only one registered nurse on duty, relying on skeleton staffs of nurse's aides to provide almost all the hands-on care for dozens of patients. Most earn little more than the minimum wage and received only seventy-five hours of training for difficult jobs that require them to monitor and feed patients and move frail and disabled residents with little assistance. Annual turnover industrywide is nearly 100 percent.

"They're short-staffing," says an aide at a Beverly home in Center Point, Alabama. "If you have twenty residents, it means you can't spend as much time with them as you should. You don't give residents the kind of care they deserve."

In nursing homes, skimping on labor costs can be lethal. In Minnesota, investigators found that at least eight residents at Beverly homes died after receiving inadequate care and supervision between 1986 and 1988. Myrtle Schneuer, 83, choked to death after a nurse's aide gave her bacon and toast, despite a doctor's order to feed her only soft food because she had difficulty swallowing. Lucy Gralish, 79, suffered for three hours after a heart attack before the home called a doctor. Joy Scales, 65, died of a skull fracture after an aide left her unattended on the toilet, contrary to her doctor's orders. "So much of this goes right back to the question of staffing and corner-cutting," James Varpness, the Minnesota ombudsman for older residents at the time, told reporters. "Why are people being left unattended on toilets so that they fall off and fracture their skull? It's because the nursing staff has too much to do and something else that needs to get done."

In many homes there are still too few aides to do the job. In 1993 two dozen employees at a Beverly home in Yreka, California, signed a letter to David Banks, warning him that staffing was dangerously low. "We are jeopardizing the safety of our residents as well as our own," the employees wrote. "It is a matter of time before a tragedy occurs that may have been preventable." They were right. In 1995 a suit was filed alleging that Reba Gregory, a 69-year-old resident, had been dropped by a nursing aide who was trying to move her from her bed without assistance, fracturing her right hip and shoulder. Last March a jury awarded Gregory a record $95.1 million—later reduced by a judge to $3 million—after evidence showed that time sheets the company originally claimed were destroyed had in fact been doctored to reflect nonexistent staffing.

Beverly has also repeatedly broken the law to prevent its 65,000 employees from joining a union to improve staffing and conditions. Last August the National Labor Relations Board issued an unusual corporationwide "cease and desist" order against the company for 240 violations of labor laws in eighteen states including threats, coercion and surveillance of employees. A study of federal contractors by the GAO ranked Beverly among the fifteen worst violators of federal labor laws.

Beverly and others in the industry complain that Medicaid rates are simply too low to pay for decent staffing and adequate care. In Arkansas, where Beverly owns one of every six nursing-home beds, Medicaid reimburses the industry an average of $63.99 a day for each resident—only two-thirds the national average. But the low rates don't stop companies like Beverly from enjoying big profits. According to the latest available figures, Arkansas nursing homes rank second to last in the nation in median spending on direct care for patients and dead last in staffing levels. Such miserliness enables them to post the eighth-highest profit margin nationwide—nearly double the US average. Seven of the twenty most profitable homes in the state belong to Beverly.

Even when the company claims a loss, it still finds ways to make money. The home in Jacksonville, where Jewel Forester died of an overdose, reported a loss of $859,000 for fiscal 1998, which ended last June. But cost reports filed with the state show that the "loss" included nearly $309,000 in "management fees and home office costs" that the home passed along to corporate headquarters. According to proxy statements, David Banks and two other Beverly executives topped $1 million in compensation for 1997.

When it comes to compensating nurse's aides, however, Beverly and other chains plead poverty. In Arkansas, where nursing homes pay half of their 25,000 employees only $5.15 an hour, the industry didn't want to use any of its profits to raise the minimum wage as mandated by Congress. So during the closing days of the 1997 state legislative session, lobbyists snuck an amendment into the budget requiring taxpayers to reimburse nursing homes for any increase in the minimum wage. Republican Governor Mike Huckabee vetoed the bill, but lawmakers easily overrode him. The measure could end up costing taxpayers more than $17 million.

Privatized nursing homes have other, less direct ways of raiding the public treasury. Until recently, the big money for conglomerates like Beverly has been in what are considered ancillary services—drugs, diapers, ventilators, speech therapy and other supplies and care that nursing-home patients often need. Medicare billings for physical and occupational therapy, for example, rose to $7 billion in 1996—double the 1993 rate and six times the 1990 rate. Such hefty reimbursements gave Beverly and other companies an incentive to create subsidiary firms to supply ancillary services to their own nursing homes. That way, they could bill taxpayers for the retail prices they pay their subsidiaries, rather than the lower costs the companies actually incur.

"These services typically are provided by outside contractors or through wholly-owned subsidiaries of nursing home companies that focused on maximizing revenues, not pursuing cost-effective care," Beverly notes in its latest annual report. Although the company says a new Medicare plan that caps some payments has prompted it to hire its own staff therapists, it acknowledges in the report that "there has been little incentive to reduce costs or pursue operating efficiencies, even though the result is higher costs for the government and other payors."

"Higher costs" for taxpayers means "higher profits" for Beverly. An internal company report on rehabilitative therapy shows the company has made much larger returns on ancillary services than cost reports for individual nursing homes indicate. In the first eleven months of 1994, according to the report, Beverly made revenues of $671 million on rehabilitative therapy—yet the services cost the company only $360 million. That's an annual return of 46 percent on revenues. In 1994 Beverly cleared more than $1 million on therapy every day—and almost all of it came from taxpayers.

"It's big money, and it's hidden money," says Elma Holder, founder of the National Citizens Coalition for Nursing Home Reform. "They have a set of books that show they're losing money on one side, and yet they're making money hand over fist on the other side."

Other internal documents show similar profit rates, even in homes where Beverly claims it has been unable to make money. In Texas, for example, the chain paid $100,000 to settle claims at a home where a resident's sore foot had been ignored for forty-three days until it rotted off her leg. In another case a judge awarded $55 million to the estate of a woman who died in 1994 from an infection caused by bedsores, including a bone-deep wound the size of a grapefruit at her tailbone. In 1997, calling the regulatory environment in Texas "punitive," Beverly sold its forty-nine nursing homes in that state to a company called Complete Care Services for $143 million in cash. But what Beverly claimed was a dry well looked more like a gusher to the new owners. According to internal documents, one investor who contributed $6 million expected to make $3.5 million in cash, management fees and interest in the first year—an immediate return of nearly 58 percent.

Nursing homes can enjoy even higher returns, of course, if they simply provide no services at all in return for government subsidies. A 1996 report by the GAO on Medicare payments to nursing homes found that "fraud and abusive billing practices are frequent and widespread." The federal government, the report added, allows homes to bill Medicare without confirming that "the care or items were necessary or were delivered as claimed." As a result, the program is highly vulnerable to exploitation.

A recent government audit showed that nursing homes billed Medicare for more than $3 billion in improper claims in 1996 and 1997. Another report estimated that taxpayers may be losing 15 cents of every Medicare dollar to fraud. In one case a Georgia company was certified to bill the insurance program for therapy services even though it had no salaried therapists. A clerical employee in a storefront office simply served as a shell company that subcontracted with two uncertified providers, adding a markup of 80 percent on every bill. Another company was a "paper organization" with no staff at all, enabling its "owner" to add $170,000 in administrative costs to Medicare bills over a six-month period.

Last July Beverly announced that the Justice Department had launched an investigation into whether the company improperly billed Medicare for labor costs between 1990 and 1997. Two former Beverly employees have been called before a California grand jury, and Blue Cross of California is also reviewing its dealings with the company. Investors reacted angrily to the news. In October Beverly shareholders filed a class-action suit alleging that the company "engaged in a scheme to inflate billings to Medicare" by shifting labor costs at homes that weren't Medicare-certified to those that were.

Beverly says it is cooperating with investigators, but the company is quick to knock the government for its approach to inspections. "We believe the system that regulates nursing homes is punitive, subjective and inequitable," says vice-president Dan Springer. "Rather than the government finding problems, finding facilities and upsetting the lives of good people, why not flip the tables and work in partnership?" He adds that Beverly has devised a "report card" to evaluate its own operations. "There is no arguing that there are places where care needs to be improved. But there are instances where the process as it's implemented today doesn't recognize the positive things that go on in nursing homes."

It's no secret why companies like Beverly see "positive things" in nursing homes: With the number of elderly Americans requiring long-term care projected to reach 14 million by the year 2020, the industry is virtually guaranteed a profitable future. As with other public services that have been privatized, however, the question is: What is a reasonable profit, and how can taxpayers insure they're getting their money's worth? Congress has responded to the soaring costs of nursing homes by moving Medicare and other federal programs into managed care, which caps costs at set levels. But lowering costs doesn't automatically improve the quality of care. A new reimbursement plan that took effect on January 1 gives nursing homes a fixed amount for services, then allows them to spend the money however they see fit. "The less you spend, the more you make," says Elma Holder of the Citizens Coalition.

For its part, the industry knows how to use its political and financial clout to block any meaningful reform. In 1978, on a trip to Arkansas to testify about nursing-home abuses, Holder found herself being driven to the airport by an ambitious attorney general named Bill Clinton. "I remember him saying he would never take any money from corporations that ran nursing homes," she recalls. "I was quite impressed with this man, of course, that he would say that." In 1996 Clinton raised $1.1 million from nursing-home owners, including several who attended breakfasts at the White House. The following year, at the President's recommendation, Democrats named Alan Solomont, a Massachusetts nursing-home magnate who lobbied for weaker federal enforcement, the party's new finance chairman.

Beverly has contributed more than $100,000 to federal candidates and their parties since 1995, and its board of directors enjoys high-powered contacts on both sides of the aisle. Republicans on the board include Edith Holiday, the White House Cabinet liaison during the Bush Administration, and Carolyne Davis, who served under President Reagan as administrator of the Health Care Financing Administration, the federal agency responsible for overseeing nursing homes. Democrats include Beryl Anthony, a former US representative and chair of the Democratic Congressional Campaign Committee. The industry also uses its influence to block reforms at the state level. In Beverly's home state of Arkansas, an analysis of campaign contributions shows that nursing homes were the second-largest donor to state legislative candidates in 1994.

Given the political clout of companies like Beverly, it's hard to imagine lawmakers getting behind the reform proposals advocated for years by patients and their families. But with the cost of long-term care skyrocketing, some officials are starting to listen. Advocates say more money should be directed at keeping people out of nursing homes—by providing adult daycare, home health aides and other community-based programs that keep people healthy and independent. They also point to model facilities, like the nonprofit Hampton Woods in rural North Carolina or the state-run Benton Services Center in Arkansas, that invest in providing top-flight nursing care rather than maximizing profits.

The most promising reform efforts focus on the most direct and effective way to improve care: Require homes that rely on public funds to hire more nurses and aides. Advocates in sixteen states have convinced lawmakers to introduce measures that would raise minimum staffing levels, forcing homes to provide at least four hours of direct care each day. It's a seemingly simple idea, but it strikes at the heart of industry profits. Nursing homes would have to spend tax dollars directly on care rather than funneling money into lucrative sidelines. "It's the most serious issue we face," says Holder of the Citizens Coalition. "Common sense would tell you that you can't achieve good care if you don't have enough staffing, but no one wants to talk about it because of the cost involved."

Despite the cost—and opposition from nursing homes—staffing standards are gaining support from those traditionally supportive of the industry. In Arkansas, lawmakers are expected to vote in the next few weeks on a bill mandating that nursing homes hire more aides—and pay stiff penalties for understaffing. The measure's sponsor is State Senator John Brown, a conservative Republican who generally knocks government regulation in favor of "free enterprise." On a recent sunny afternoon Brown stands in a hallway of the state capitol in Little Rock, at the bottom of a marble staircase leading to the governor's office, and caucuses with patient advocates about how to pay for the increased staffing.

"We have to talk about where the money's going to come from," Brown says.

"How about profits?" suggests Virginia Vollmer, a member of Arkansas Advocates for Nursing Home Residents.

Brown surprises her by nodding in agreement. "But we've got to look behind their published numbers," he says. "Whether it's the way they report expenses or amortize interest, there are different accounting ploys that homes can use to make money. By and large they have a pretty good return. We're paying them hundreds of millions of dollars, but in too many cases they're endangering people rather than caring for them."

The advocates are encouraged, but they remain skeptical. "I don't know that any of the increased staffing will come out of the industry's pockets," says Jim Porter, whose mother died in a Beverly home in Little Rock last November. "It will probably all come out of the taxpayer's pocket. That's the shame of it." Like Senator Brown, Porter is hardly an antibusiness activist. The chairman of the Arkansas Entertainer's Hall of Fame and a Beverly investor, Porter called CEO David Banks personally after witnessing the inadequate care at his mother's nursing home. "I told him they weren't paying the salary they need to get and keep the help they need," Porter recalls. "He said he knew they were having problems and he'd get things in order. But he didn't."

Porter has a simple explanation for why care at Beverly and other nursing homes remains substandard. "Greed," he says. "They don't want to pay these nurse's aides more because it would be money out of their profits. It's as simple as that." He also has a simple idea of how to improve care: Return nursing homes to public control. Given the history of abuses at county homes and the current political climate, it's not a proposal that's likely to gain much ground. But it does suggest the depth of frustration with a privatized system that profits from pain—and the importance of remembering who ultimately pays the price.

"Perhaps nursing homes should be taken over by the state, county or city," Porter says. "Each one of them could be run for less by the government, because there wouldn't be an owner sitting there siphoning off hundreds of thousands of dollars. Imagine what kind of care we could provide with all those profits."

CHAPTER 31

The Return of Infectious Disease

LAURIE GARRETT

THE POST-ANTIBIOTIC ERA

Since World War II, public health strategy has focused on the eradication of microbes. Using powerful medical weaponry developed during the postwar period—antibiotics, antimalarials, and vaccines—political and scientific leaders in the United States and around the world pursued a military-style campaign to obliterate viral, bacterial, and parasitic enemies. The goal was nothing less than pushing humanity through what was termed the "health transition," leaving the age of infectious disease permanently behind. By the turn of the century, it was thought, most of the world's population would live long lives ended only by the "chronics"—cancer, heart disease, and Alzheimer's.

The optimism culminated in 1978 when the member states of the United Nations signed the "Health for All, 2000" accord. The agreement set ambitious goals for the eradication of disease, predicting that even the poorest nations would undergo a health transition before the millennium, with life expectancies rising markedly. It was certainly reasonable in 1978 to take a rosy view of Homo sapiens' ancient struggle with the microbes; antibiotics, pesticides, chloroquine and other powerful antimicrobials, vaccines, and striking improvements in water treatment and food preparation technologies had provided what seemed an imposing armamentarium. The year before, the World Health Organization(WHO) had announced that the last known case of smallpox had been tracked down in Ethiopia and cured.

The grandiose optimism rested on two false assumptions: that microbes were biologically stationary targets and that diseases could be geographically sequestered. Each contributed to the smug sense of immunity from infectious diseases that characterized health professionals in North America and Europe.

Anything but stationary, microbes and the insects, rodents, and other animals that transmit them are in a constant state of biological flux and evolution. Darwin noted that certain genetic mutations allow plants and animals to better adapt to environmental conditions and so produce more offspring; this process of natural selection, he argued, was the mechanism of evolution. Less than a decade after the U.S. military first supplied penicillin to its field physicians in the Pacific theater, geneticist Joshua Lederberg demonstrated that natural selection was operating in the bacterial world. Strains of staphylococcus and streptococcus that happened to carry genes for resistance to the drugs arose and flourished where drug-susceptible strains had been driven out. Use of antibiotics was selecting for ever-more-resistant bugs.

More recently scientists have witnessed an alarming mechanism of microbial adaptation and change—one less dependent on random inherited genetic advantage. The genetic blueprints of some microbes contain DNA and RNA codes that command mutation under stress, offer escapes from antibiotics and other drugs, marshal collective behaviors conducive to group survival, and allow the microbes and their progeny to scour their environments for potentially useful genetic material. Such material is present in stable rings or pieces of DNA and RNA, known as plasmids and transposons, that move freely among microorganisms, even jumping between species of bacteria, fungi, and parasites. Some plasmids carry the genes for resistance to five or more different families of antibiotics, or dozens of individual drugs. Others confer greater powers of infectivity, virulence, resistance to disinfectants or chlorine, even such subtly important characteristics as the ability to tolerate higher temperatures or more acidic conditions. Microbes have appeared that can grow on a bar of soap, swim unabashed in bleach, and ignore doses of penicillin logarithmically larger than those effective in 1950.

In the microbial soup, then, is a vast, constantly changing lending library of genetic material that offers humanity's minute predators myriad ways to outmaneuver the drug arsenal. And the arsenal, large as it might seem, is limited. In 1994 the Food and Drug Administration licensed only three new antimicrobial drugs, two of them for the treatment of AIDS and none an antibacterial. Research and development has ground to a near halt now that the easy approaches to killing viruses, bacteria, fungi, and parasites—those that mimic the ways competing microbes kill one another in their endless tiny battles throughout the human gastrointestinal tract—have been exploited. Researchers have run out of ideas for countering many microbial scourges, and the lack of profitability has stifled the development of drugs to combat organisms that are currently found predominantly in poor countries. "The pipeline is dry. We really have a global crisis," James Hughes, director of the National Center for Infectious Diseases at the Centers for Disease Control and Prevention (CDC) in Atlanta, said recently.

DISEASES WITHOUT BORDERS

During the 1960s, 1970s, and 1980s, the World Bank and the International Monetary Fund devised investment policies based on the assumption that economic modernization should come first and improved health would naturally follow. Today the World Bank recognizes that a nation in which more than ten percent of the working-age population is chronically ill cannot be expected to reach higher levels of development without investment in health infrastructure. Furthermore, the bank acknowledges that few societies spend health care dollars effectively for the poor, among whom the potential for the outbreak of infectious disease is greatest. Most of the achievements in infectious disease control have resulted from grand international efforts such as the expanded program for childhood immunization mounted by the U.N. Children's Emergency Fund and WHO's smallpox eradication drive. At the local level, particularly in politically unstable poor countries, few genuine successes can be cited.

Geographic sequestration was crucial in all postwar health planning, but diseases can no longer be expected to remain in their country or region of origin. Even before commercial air travel, swine flu in 1918–19 managed to circumnavigate the planet five times in 18 months, killing 22 million people, 500,000 in the United States. How many more victims could a similarly lethal strain of influenza claim in 1996, when some half a billion passengers will board airline flights?

Every day one million people cross an international border. One million a week travel between the industrial and developing worlds. And as people move, unwanted microbial hitchhikers tag along. In the nineteenth century most diseases and infections that travelers carried manifested themselves during the long sea voyages that were the primary means of covering great distances. Recognizing the symptoms, the authorities at ports of entry could quarantine contagious individuals or take other action. In the age of jet travel, however, a person incubating a disease such as Ebola can board a plane, travel 12,000 miles, pass unnoticed through customs and immigration, take a domestic carrier to a remote destination, and still not develop symptoms for several days, infecting many other people before his condition is noticeable.

Surveillance at airports has proved grossly inadequate and is often biologically irrational, given that incubation periods for many incurable contagious diseases may exceed 21 days. And when a recent traveler's symptoms become apparent, days or weeks after his journey, the task of identifying fellow passengers, locating them, and bringing them to the authorities for medical examination is costly and sometimes impossible. The British and U.S. governments both spent millions of dollars in 1976 trying to track down 522 people exposed during a flight from Sierra Leone to Washington, D.C., to a Peace Corps volunteer infected with the Lassa virus, an organism that produces gruesome hemorrhagic disease in its victims. The U.S. government eventually tracked down 505 passengers, scattered over 21 states; British Airways and the British government located 95, some of whom were also on the U.S. list. None tested positive for the virus.

In the fall of 1994 the New York City Department of Health and the U.S. Immigration and Naturalization Service took steps to prevent plague-infected passengers from India from disembarking at New York's John F. Kennedy International Airport. All airport and federal personnel who had direct contact with passengers were trained to recognize symptoms of *Yersinia pestis* infection. Potential plague carriers were, if possible, to be identified while still on the tarmac, so fellow passengers could be examined. Of ten putative carriers identified in New York, only two were discovered at the airport; the majority had long since entered the community. Fortunately, none of the ten proved to have plague. Health authorities came away with the lesson that airport-based screening is expensive and does not work.

Humanity is on the move worldwide, fleeing impoverishment, religious and ethnic intolerance, and high-intensity localized warfare that targets civilians. People are abandoning their homes for new destinations on an unprecedented scale, both in terms of absolute numbers and as a percentage of population. In 1994 at least 110 million people immigrated, another 30 million moved from rural to urban areas within their own country, and 23 million more were displaced by war or social unrest, according to the U.N. High Commissioner for Refugees and the Worldwatch Institute. This human mobility affords microbes greatly increased opportunities for movement.

THE CITY AS VECTOR

Population expansion raises the statistical probability that pathogens will be transmitted, whether from person to person or vector—insect, rodent, or other—to person. Human density is rising rapidly worldwide. Seven countries now have overall population densities exceeding 2,000 people per square mile, and 43 have densities greater than 500 people per square mile. (The U.S. average, by contrast, is 74.)

High density need not doom a nation to epidemics and unusual outbreaks of disease if sewage and water systems, housing, and public health provisions are adequate. The Netherlands, for example, with 1,180 people per square mile, ranks among the top 20 countries for good health and life expectancy. But the areas in which density is increasing most are not those capable of providing such infrastructural support. They are, rather, the poorest on earth. Even countries with low overall density may have cities that have become focuses for extraordinary overpopulation, from the point of view of public health. Some of these urban agglomerations have only one toilet for every 750 or more people.

Most people on the move around the world come to burgeoning metropolises like India's Surat (where pneumonic plague struck in 1994) and Zaire's Kikwit (site of the 1995 Ebola epidemic) that offer few fundamental amenities. These new centers of urbanization typically lack sewage systems, paved roads, housing, safe drinking water, medical facilities, and schools adequate to serve even the most affluent residents. They are squalid sites of destitution where hundreds of thousands live much as they would in poor villages, yet so jammed together as to ensure astronomical transmission rates for airborne, waterborne, sexually transmitted, and contact-transmission microbes.

But such centers are often only staging areas for the waves of impoverished people that are drawn there. The next stop is a megacity with a population of ten million or more. In the nineteenth century only two cities on earth—London and New York—even approached that size. Five years from now there will be 24 megacities, most in poor developing countries: São Paulo, Calcutta, Bombay, Istanbul, Bangkok, Tehran, Jakarta, Cairo, Mexico City, Karachi, and the like. There the woes of cities like Surat are magnified many times over. Yet even the developing world's megacities are way stations for those who most aggressively seek a better life. All paths ultimately lead these people—and the microbes they may carry—to the United States, Canada, and Western Europe.

Urbanization and global migration propel radical changes in human behavior as well as in the ecological relationship between microbes and humans. Almost invariably in large cities, sex industries arise and multiple-partner sex becomes more common, prompting rapid increases in sexually transmitted diseases. Black market access to antimicrobials is greater in urban centers, leading to overuse or outright misuse of the precious drugs and the emergence of resistant bacteria and parasites. Intravenous drug abusers' practice of sharing syringes is a ready vehicle for the transmission of microbes. Underfunded urban health facilities often become unhygienic centers for the dissemination of disease rather than its control.

THE EMBLEMATIC NEW DISEASE

All these factors played out dramatically during the 1980s, allowing an obscure organism to amplify and spread to the point that WHO estimates it has infected a cumulative total of 30 million people and become endemic to every country in the world. Genetic studies of the human immunodeficiency virus that causes AIDS indicate that it is probably more than a century old, yet HIV infected perhaps less than .001 percent of the world population until the mid-1970s. Then the virus surged because of sweeping social changes: African urbanization; American and European intravenous drug use and homosexual bathhouse activity; the Uganda-Tanzania war of 1977–79, in which rape was used as a tool of ethnic cleansing; and the growth of the American blood products industry and the international marketing of its contaminated goods. Government denial and societal prejudice everywhere in the world led to inappropriate public health interventions or plain inaction, further abetting HIV transmission and slowing research for treatment or a cure.

The estimated direct (medical) and indirect (loss of productive labor force and family-impact) costs of the disease are expected to top $500 billion by the year 2000, according to the Global AIDS Policy Coalition at Harvard University. The U.S. Agency for International Development predicts that by then some 11 percent of children under 15 in sub-Saharan Africa will be AIDS orphans, and that infant mortality will soar fivefold in some African and Asian nations, due to the loss of parental care among children orphaned by AIDS and its most common opportunistic infection, tuberculosis. Life expectancy in the African and Asian nations hit hardest by AIDS will plummet to an astonishing low of 25 years by 2010, the agency forecasts.

Medical experts now recognize that any microbe, including ones previously unknown to science, can take similar advantage of conditions in human society, going from isolated cases camouflaged by generally high levels of disease to become a global threat. Furthermore, old organisms, aided by mankind's misuse of disinfectants and drugs, can take on new, more lethal forms.

A White House–appointed interagency working group on emerging and reemerging infectious diseases estimates that at least 29 previously unknown diseases have appeared since 1973 and 20 well-known ones have reemerged, often in new drug-resistant or deadlier forms. According to the group, total direct and indirect costs of infectious disease in the United States in 1993 were more than $120 billion; combined federal, state, and municipal government expenditures that year for infectious disease control were only $74.2 million (neither figure includes AIDS, other sexually transmitted diseases, or tuberculosis). . . .

A WORLD AT RISK

A 1995 WHO survey of global capacity to identify and respond to threats from emerging diseases reached troubling conclusions. Only six laboratories in the world, the study found, met security and safety standards that would make them suitable sites for research on the world's deadliest microbes, including those that cause Ebola, Marburg, and Lassa fever. Local political instability threatens to compromise the security of the two labs in Russia, and budget cuts threaten to do the same to the two in the United States (the army's facility at Fort Detrick and the CDC in Atlanta) and the one in Britain. In another survey, WHO sent samples of hantaviruses (such as Sin Nombre, which caused the 1993 outbreak in New Mexico) and organisms that cause dengue, yellow fever, malaria, and other diseases to the world's 35 leading disease-monitoring facilities. Only one—the CDC—correctly identified all the organisms; most got fewer than half right.

Convinced that newly emerging diseases, whether natural or engineered, could endanger national security, the CDC requested $125 million from Congress in 1994 to bolster what it termed a grossly inadequate system of surveillance and response; it received $7.3 million. After two years of inquiry by a panel of experts, the Institute of Medicine, a division of the National Academy of Sciences, declared the situation a crisis.

Today's reality is best reflected in New York City's battle with tuberculosis. Control of the W-strain of the disease—which first appeared in the city in 1991–92, is resistant to every available drug, and kills half its victims—has already cost more than $1 billion. Despite such spending, there were 3,000 TB cases in the city in 1994, some of which were the W-strain. According to the surgeon general's annual reports from the 1970s and 1980s, tuberculosis was supposed to be eradicated from the United States by 2000. During the Bush administration the CDC told state authorities they could safely lower their fiscal commitments to TB control because victory was imminent. Now public health officials are fighting to get levels down to where they were in 1985—a far cry from elimination. New York's crisis is a result of both immigration pressure (some cases originated overseas) and the collapse of the local public health infrastructure.

National preparedness has further eroded over the past five years in the face of budgetary constraints. Just as WHO cannot intercede in an epidemic unless it receives an invitation from the afflicted country, the CDC may not enter a U.S. state without a request from the state government. The U.S. system rests on an increasingly shaky network of disease surveillance and response by states and territories. A 1992 survey for the CDC showed that 12 states had no one on staff to monitor microbial contamination of local food and water; 67 percent of the states and territories had less than one employee monitoring the food and water of every one million residents. And only a handful of states were monitoring hospitals for the appearance of unusual or drug-resistant microbes.

State capacity rests on county and municipal public health, and there too weaknesses are acute. In October, dengue hemorrhagic fever, which had been creeping steadily northward from Brazil over the past eight years, with devastating results, struck in Texas. Most Texas counties had slashed their mosquito control budgets and were ill prepared to combat the aggressive Tiger mosquitoes from Southeast Asia that carry the virus. In Los Angeles County that month, a $2 billion budget shortfall drove officials to close all but 10 of the 45 public health clinics and to attempt to sell four of the county's six public hospitals. Congress is contemplating enormous cuts in Medicare and Medicaid spending, which the American Public Health Association predicts would result in a widespread increase in infectious disease.

PRESCRIPTIONS FOR NATIONAL HEALTH

Bolstering research capacity, enhancing disease surveillance capabilities, revitalizing sagging basic public health systems, rationing powerful drugs to avoid the emergence of drug-resistant organisms, and improving infection control practices at hospitals are only stopgap measures. National security warrants bolder steps.

One priority is finding scientifically valid ways to use polymerase chain reaction (popularly known as DNA fingerprinting), field investigations, chemical and biological export records, and local legal instruments to track the development of new or reemergent lethal organisms, whether natural or bioweapons. The effort should focus not only on microbes directly dangerous to humans but on those that could pose major threats to crops or livestock.

Most emerging diseases are first detected by health providers working at the primary-care level. Currently there is no system, even in the United States, whereby the providers can notify relevant authorities and be assured that their alarm will be investigated promptly. In much of the world, the notifiers' reward is penalties levied against them, primarily because states want to hush up the problem. But Internet access is improving worldwide, and a small investment would give physicians an electronic highway to international health authorities that bypassed government roadblocks and obfuscation.

Only three diseases—cholera, plague, and yellow fever—are subject to international regulation, permitting U.N. and national authorities to interfere as necessary in the global traffic of goods and persons to stave off cross-border epidemics. The World Health Assembly, the legislative arm of WHO, recommended at its 1995 annual meeting in Geneva that the United Nations consider both expanding the list of regulated diseases and finding new ways to monitor the broad movement of disease. The Ebola outbreak in Kikwit demonstrated that a team of international scientists can be mobilized to swiftly contain a remote, localized epidemic caused by known nonairborne agents.

Were a major epidemic to imperil the United States, the Office of Emergency Preparedness and the National Disaster Medical System (part of the Department of Health and Human Services) would be at the helm. The office has 4,200 private-sector doctors and nurses throughout the 50 states who are at its disposal and committed to rapid mobilization in case of emergency. The system is sound but should be bolstered. Participants should be supplied with protective suits, respirators, mobile containment laboratories, and adequate local isolation facilities.

As for potential threats from biological weapons, the U.S. Department of Energy has identified serious lapses in Russian and Ukrainian compliance with the Biological Weapons Convention. Large stockpiles of bioweapons are believed to remain, and employees of the Soviet program for biological warfare are still on the state payroll. Arsenals are also thought to exist in other nations, although intelligence on this is weak. The location and destruction of such weapons is a critical priority. Meanwhile, scientists in the United States and Europe are identifying the genes in bacteria and viruses that code for virulence and modes of transmission. Better understanding of the genetic mechanisms will allow scientists to manipulate existing organisms, endowing them with dangerous capabilities. It would seem prudent for the United States and the international community to examine that potential now and consider options for the control of such research or its fruits.

To guard against the proliferation of blood-associated diseases, the blood and animal exports industries must be closely regulated, plasma donors must be screened for infections, and an internationally acceptable watchdog agency must be designated to monitor reports of the appearance of new forms of such diseases. The export of research animals played a role in a serious incident in Germany in which vaccine workers were infected with the Marburg virus and in an Ebola scare in Virginia in which imported monkeys died from the disease.

Nobel laureate Joshua Lederberg of Rockefeller University has characterized the solutions to the threat of disease emergence as multitudinous, largely straightforward and commonsensical, and international in scope; "the bad news," he says, "is they will cost money."

Budgets, particularly for health care, are being cut at all levels of government. Dustin Hoffman made more money last year playing a disease control scientist in the movie *Outbreak* than the combined annual budgets for the U.S. National Center for Infectious Diseases and the U.N. Programme on AIDS/HIV.

CHAPTER 32

Cater to the Children

GERALD MARKOWITZ

DAVID ROSNER

According to the Centers for Disease Control and Prevention, it is estimated that 1 of every 20 children in the United States suffers from subclinical lead poisoning,[1] and a recent article in *Science* argues that "paint appears to be the major source of childhood lead poisoning in the United States."[2] Yet it is only during the past 15 years that the history of this tragic situation has been addressed in any detail,[3–7] primarily through the documentation of childhood lead poisoning in the public health and medical literature of the first half of the 20th century. Here we analyze the role and influence of the lead industry in shaping popular and professional opinion about lead and lead paint products. Specifically, we discuss how the Lead Industries Association (LIA, the trade group representing lead pigment manufacturers) and its member companies sought to assuage growing public and professional concerns about the dangers to children of lead-based paint. Often employing the image of children themselves, the LIA and its members engaged in aggressive marketing and advertising campaigns to persuade the public of their product's appropriateness for indoor use. . . .

The continuing use of lead paint into and after the 1950s cannot be understood without an appreciation of the enormous resources the lead industry devoted to allaying public health concerns from the 1920s through the early 1950s. Whatever responsibility the public health community had for this tragedy pales in comparison with the power and determination of the industry in perpetuating the use of lead-based paint. The lead industry, as a sponsor of research and as a clearinghouse of information about lead, was positioned to be in the forefront of efforts to prevent lead exposure in children. Instead, the industry placed its own economic interests ahead of the welfare of the nation's children.

MEDICAL KNOWLEDGE OF THE DANGERS OF LEAD-BASED PAINT

Historians have shown that knowledge of the dangers of lead poisoning to workers and children can be traced back into the 19th century[8,9] and that in the first third of the 20th century a broad scientific literature on the subject accumulated in Australia, England, and the United States. Alice Hamilton and others documented lead hazards among American workers in the pigment manufacturing, battery, painting, plumbing, ceramics, pottery, and other industries.[10,11] In 1921 the president of the National Lead Company, Edward J. Cornish, wrote to David Edsall, the dean of Harvard Medical School, saying that lead manufacturers, as a result of "fifty to sixty years" experience, agreed that "lead is a poison when it enters the stomach of man—whether it comes directly from the ores and mines and smelting works" or from the ordinary forms of carbonate of lead, lead oxides, and sulfate and sulfide of lead.[12]

At the same time, others began to systematically document the dangers of lead to children. In 1904, J. Lockhart Gibson, an Australian, was among the first English-language authors to directly link lead-based paint to childhood lead poisoning, specifically noting the dangers to children from painted walls and verandas of houses.[13] A year later, he urged, "[T]he use of lead paint within the reach of children should be prohibited by law."[14(p753)] In 1908 another Australian, Jefferis Turner, delivered a presidential address to the Section of Diseases of Children of the Australasian Medical Congress in which he noted that lead poisoning was due to paint powder that stuck to children's fingers, which they then bit or sucked.[15] In 1914, Americans Henry Thomas and Kenneth Blackfan, the latter a physician at Johns Hopkins Department of Pediatrics in Baltimore, detailed the case of a boy from Baltimore who died of lead poisoning after ingesting white lead paint from the railing of his crib.[16] In 1917, Blackfan reviewed the English-language literature on lead poisoning in children, noting specifically cases of children who chewed the white paint from their cribs.[17] By the mid-1920s, there was strong and ample evidence of the toxicity of lead paint to children, to painters, and to others who worked with lead as studies detailed the harm caused by lead dust, the dangers of cumulative doses of lead, the special vulnerability of children, and the harm lead caused to the nervous system in particular.[18]

Outside the United States, the dangers represented by lead paint manufacturing and application led to many countries' enacting bans or restrictions on the use of white lead for interior paint: France, Belgium, and Austria in 1909; Tunisia and Greece in 1922; Czechoslovakia in 1924; Great Britain, Sweden, and Belgium in 1926; Poland in 1927; Spain and Yugoslavia in 1931; and Cuba in 1934.[19] In 1922, the Third International Labor Conference of the League of Nations recommended the banning of white lead for interior use.[20] In the United States and Canada, there were calls for the use of non–lead-based paints in interiors. As early as 1913, Alice Hamilton wrote that "the total prohibition for lead paint for use in interior work would do more than anything else to improve conditions in the painting trade."[21] By the early 1930s, a consensus developed among specialists that lead paint posed a hazard to children.[22-27] Robert Kehoe, medical director for the Ethyl Gasoline Corporation and director of the Kettering Laboratories of the University of Cincinnati, perhaps the nation's leading expert on lead poisoning, concluded that "strenuous efforts must be devoted to eliminating lead from [children's] environment,"[28] especially since safer alternatives to lead, specifically titanium- and zinc-based paints, existed throughout the late 19th and early 20th centuries. In 1914, the director of the scientific section of the Paint Manufacturers' Association noted with approval the development of "sanitary leadless" paints and predicted that "lead poisoning will be done away with almost entirely."[29]

Despite the accumulating evidence of lead paint's dangers to young children, the industry did nothing to discourage the use of lead paint on walls and woodwork or to warn the general public or public health authorities of the dangers inherent in the product. In fact, it did the opposite: it engaged in an energetic promotion of lead paint for both exterior and interior uses from the 1920s through the Second World War. For a portion of that period, white lead in paint was "the most important outlet for pig lead metal,"[30] according to the LIA, which was organized in 1928 to promote the use of lead.[31] A can of pure white lead paint was composed of huge amounts of lead, creating a large market for mining companies and pigment manufacturers.[32]

Within 6 months of the LIA's founding, its secretary, Felix Wormser, noted, "Of late the lead industries have been receiving much undesirable publicity regarding lead poisoning."[33] A year later, the *United States Daily*, a newspaper "Presenting the Official News of the Legislative, Executive and Judicial Branches of the Federal Government," ran a front-page story on lead poisoning and children: "Lead poisoning as a result of chewing paint from toys, cradles and woodwork is now regarded as a more frequent occurrence among children than formerly."[34]

The reaction of the lead industry to growing negative publicity was to assure the public as well as the public health community that such fears were unfounded and that there was no reason to suspect that toys were being painted with lead pigments. In 1933, Charles F. McKahinn and Edward C. Vogt, pediatricians at Harvard Medical School and Boston's Infants' and Children's Hospitals, published an article in the *Journal of the American Medical Association* in which they mentioned a personal communication from Felix Wormser that led them to believe that "the lead industry and the manufacturers of cribs and toys . . . have cooperated by substituting other types of pigments for the lead pigments formerly used."[35(p1131)] Two years later, a major toy company acknowledged that it had been assured that its toys were safe but had found that the toys had been painted with lead. On investigation, the company found that the paint manufacturers were "willing to sign an agreement that the paint furnished would be non-poisonous, but only a few agreed that they would furnish materials that were entirely free of lead."[36] Another company responded to an inquiry from the Children's Bureau by informing the bureau that "we found that lead in the form of Lead Chromate was being used extensively in colored finishes [of toys]."[37]

Throughout the 1930s and 1940s, continuing reports of poisoned children and workers caused heightened concern among the lead pigment manufacturers, despite the LIA's assurances to the public health community. At the annual meeting of LIA members in June 1935, Wormser noted, "Hardly a day goes by but what this subject receives some attention at the headquarters of the Association." The threat of negative publicity about the health problems associated with lead was so serious that Wormser told the members, "[I]f all other reasons for the establishment of a cooperative organization in the lead industries were to disappear, the health problem alone would be sufficient warrant for its establishment."[38,39] The LIA responded to the undesirable publicity by seeking to rebut research findings and other news of lead's toxicity, whether to children or adults.

Sometimes even major corporations were intimidated. In the early 1930s, the Metropolitan Life Insurance Company had reported on the potential hazards to children from lead, and shortly thereafter Louis Dublin, the respected statistician at the Metropolitan, wrote to the US Children's Bureau requesting that because of the "strong remonstrance by the Lead Industries Association" about the publicity resulting from the earlier article, the Bureau refrain from mentioning "[t]he Metropolitan, either directly or by inference, in connection with whatever releases you may make." The Metropolitan official explained that "you will readily understand that we wish to avoid any controversy with the lead people."[40]

In 1939, the National Paint, Varnish and Lacquer Association (NPVLA), a trade group representing pigment and paint manufacturers, among others, privately acknowledged its "responsibility to the public and the protection of the industry itself with respect to the use of toxic materials in the industry's products."[41] In a letter marked "CONFIDENTIAL Not for Publication," the association informed its members that "the vital factor concerning toxic materials is to intelligently safeguard the public." The letter said that manufacturers should apply "every precautionary measure in manufacturing, in selling and in use where toxic materials are likely to or do enter a product" and noted that "children's toys, equipment, furniture, etc. are not the only consideration." It warned NPVLA members that toxic materials "may enter the body through the lungs . . . through the skin, or through the mouth or stomach." The letter specifically pointed out that lead compounds such as white lead, red lead, litharge, and lead chromate "may be considered as toxic if they find their way into the stomach."

The NPVLA reproduced for its members a set of legal principles established by the Manufacturing Chemists' Association regarding the labeling of dangerous products. The first principle was "A manufacturer who puts out a dangerous article or substance without accompanying it with a warning as to its dangerous properties is ordinarily liable for any damage which results from such failure to warn." Even when a product was widely understood to be dangerous, the Manufacturing Chemists' Association suggested that warnings be included. Further, the legal principles stated, "The manufacturer must know the qualities of his product and cannot escape liability on the ground that he did not know it to be dangerous." The NPVLA letter concluded by calling on NPVLA members to make a "sincere effort in taking advantage of every possible precaution in the use of toxic materials in manufacturing, selling and in use."[42]

DO NOT FORGET THE CHILDREN

The lead pigment manufacturers did not act on the NPVLA's advice. Rather, they actively sought to promote the use of lead in general and the safety of lead for interior uses in particular. Sherwin-Williams' logo was a can of paint poured over the entire globe, with the slogan "Covers the Earth." The Dutch Boy logo of National Lead Company paints was a familiar symbol in the fast half of the 20th century and was an essential part of the company's marketing strategy for white lead. In addition to appealing to master painters, homeowners, wives, and mothers, National Lead sought to influence generations of owners by marketing directly to children. In fact, children were a prime target of the company's advertising campaign from early on, even before the LIA was founded. In a promotion to paint distributors, the company advised store owners, "Do Not Forget the Children."[43] In the 1920s, National Lead produced "A Paint Book for Girls and Boys" titled *The Dutch Boy's Lead Party.* Its cover showed the Dutch Boy, bucket and brush in hand, looking at lead soldiers, light bulbs, shoe soles, and other members of the "lead family."[44] The Dutch Boy also promoted the use of lead paint in schoolrooms, suggesting that summer was the best time to "get after the school trustees to have each room repainted" with "flat paint made of Dutch Boy white-lead and flatting oil."[45]

By the late 1920s and into the Depression, as information about lead paint's danger to children continued to accumulate—and after the LIA had acknowledged the inappropriateness of using lead paint on children's toys and furniture—the National Lead Company used the Dutch Boy to promote the use of lead in children's rooms. In one of its several paint books for children, National Lead suggested that its paint "conquers Old Man Gloom":

> The girl and boy felt very blue
> Their toys were old and shabby too,
> They couldn't play in such a place,
> The room was really a disgrace.
>
> This famous Dutch Boy Lead of mine
> Can make this playroom fairly shine
> Let's start our painting right away
> You'll find the work is only play.

The booklet shows the Dutch Boy mixing white lead with colors and painting walls and furniture.[46]

To emphasize the benign qualities of lead paint, a National Lead Company's advertisement depicted a child in a bathtub scrubbing himself with a brush. His Dutch Boy cap, clothes, and shoes were slung on a chair, and a can of Dutch Boy All-Purpose Soft Paste and paintbrush sat on the floor next to him. The caption read, "Takes a Scrubbing with a Smile."[47] Another promotion showed a crawling infant touching a painted wall. The caption proclaimed, "There is no cause for worry when fingerprint smudges or dirt spots appear on a wall painted with Dutch Boy white-lead."[48] The explicit message was that it was easy to clean the wall; the implicit message was that it was safe for toddlers to touch woodwork and walls covered with lead paint. The theme of children painting appeared in numerous advertisements and articles.[49,50(p77)]

Even in 1949, National Lead remained particularly proud of its marketing campaign directed at children.

> souvenir figures [of the Dutch Boy Painter] in the form of paper weights, statuettes, etc. The appeal was particularly strong to children and the company has never overlooked the opportunity to plant the trademark image in young and receptive minds. One of the most successful promotions for many years was a child's paint book containing paper chips of paint from which the pictures (including, of course, several Dutch Boys) could be colored. . . . The company still will loan a Dutch Boy costume—cap, wig, shirt, overalls and wooden shoes—to any person who writes in and asks for it for any reasonable purpose, and the little painter has graced thousands of parades and masquerades.[51]

This marketing of the Dutch Boy image was seen as an essential element of National Lead Company's increasing profitability; the company's sales rose from $80 million in 1939 to more than $320 million in 1948. The continuing use of the Dutch Boy image was understood by the broader marketing industry as a clever method of improving the image of National Lead. In 1949, one marketing journal noted that "putting the boy, with his wooden keg and brush, in the attitude of a house painter, gave animation to the subject, tied him up with the product and suggested that the quality of the paint was so good that even a child could use it."[52]

In addition to portraying children in its advertisements, the pigment industry emphasized lead paint's "healthful" qualities. As early as 1923, National Lead advertisements in *National Geographic Magazine* promoted the idea that "lead helps to guard your health."[53] Throughout the 1920s, National Lead advertisements in *The Modern Hospital* called the company's tinted paint "the doctor's assistant" because of its cheerful color and the fact that it could be washed with soap and water. The ads assured readers that walls covered with National Lead paint "do not chip, peel or scale."[54] In 1930 the ads suggested, "Every room in a modern hospital deserves a Dutch Boy quality painting job."[55]

In the early 1930s the LIA produced a book, *Useful Information About Lead*, that suggested that the "prospective paint user" would be well advised to use paints containing a high percentage of lead, "the higher the better." A section called "White Lead in Paint" stated that "well painted buildings, both inside and out, go hand in hand with improved sanitation." The book included no warnings about the dangers of lead, despite the fact that the book was produced "to disseminate accurate information regarding lead products and how they best may be used." It included pictures of home and hotel interiors with captions such as "White lead paint is widely used for home interiors."[56] The theme of safety continued to be used to promote lead paint through the early war years. In 1943 Eagle Picher advertisements in *National Painters Magazine* urged professional painters to use "four arguments with prospects—you'll find they really sell paint jobs." The fourth argument was that "Eagle White Lead is just about the purest, safest, most fool-proof paint you or anybody else can use."[57]

THE WHITE LEAD PROMOTION CAMPAIGN

In addition to specific companies' ads, in 1938 the lead industry as a whole, through the LIA, began its White Lead Promotion Campaign, the single largest activity undertaken by the LIA up until that date. The purpose of the campaign was to increase interest in white lead in paint because the LIA recognized that "white lead is also constantly subject to attack from the health standpoint."[58] The LIA thought that there was a "morale problem" and that advertising would help "to offset the stigma attached to lead because of attacks made upon it by consumer organizations." The association believed the campaign would "help to dispel fear or apprehension about its use."[59]

Early in the promotion campaign, LIA secretary Felix Wormser made it clear that white lead was being promoted for use in interiors.[60] In a 1938 article, the LIA's *Lead* magazine produced an elaborate economic rationale for using lead paint in residential housing, specifically in low-cost construction.[61] The magazine continued to promote white lead for interiors of low-cost homes in its July 1939 issue. In an article on decorating plywood structures, the magazine showed pictures of a recreation room and a kitchen painted with white lead.[62]

Two representatives of the LIA, Seldon Brown and W. L. Frazee, traveled throughout the country visiting officials of public and private institutions in efforts to convince them to use white lead. The LIA specifically targeted markets in urban areas. In mid-October 1940 the LIA reported, "In the course of his work with government officials in the neighborhoods of New York City, our representative also conducted a survey of painting practices of 36 real estate developments. A separate report of this survey has been sent to interested members."[63] Brown reported his success with the Brooklyn Brewcourt Management Company: "Through a demonstration of the true costs of white lead as compared with mixed paint for interiors, Mr. Kilman plans to use white lead on several jobs and probably all future works."[64]

In 1940 the campaign was expanded to include municipal, state, and county institutions. Brown specifically marketed white lead paint for public schools, noting in reports to the association whether institutions he visited used mixed paint or white lead on both exterior and interior walls. The LIA claimed that Brown made a total of 427 calls in his first 2 years on the job, of which 380 were to state, county, and miscellaneous institutions. Brown was particularly insistent on pushing white lead for interior use. When he visited one superintendent of maintenance for Seattle's public school system, Brown initially met with resistance. The superintendent, he reported was "completely sold on white lead for exteriors, but can't see the value of white lead for interiors and [I] was not able to convince him. It was suggested that a demonstration of white lead and flat wall paint be [run] for this department by a lead salesman."[65] Brown also reported on his ability to sell the virtues of white lead to those who knew little about it.[66-69] In Flint, Mich, the superintendent of maintenance for the Board of Education was "very interested in our description of the qualities of interior white lead. [He] said that he thought that white lead was going out because he has heard so little about it. [He knew] nothing about white lead for interiors. [But he] plans to run comparative tests between white lead and present mixed paint used on interiors."[70,71]

In addition to selling to schools, the LIA marketed lead paint to cities, hotels, and even health departments. Frazee reported that he had visited Little Rock, Ark, where he convinced a local hotel manager to have "his entire hotel, inside and out, done with lead and lead reducing oil."[72,73] In Pierce County, Washington, the LIA representative visited the county health department, where he "explained properties of interior white lead paint, stressing sanitary aspects of a highly desirable and washable surface."[74]

In addition, the White Lead Promotion Campaign comprised an advertising campaign, the placement of articles promoting the use of white lead in trade and popular journals, and mailings. In 1939, *Dutch Boy Painter* magazine announced a "big, new, cooperative advertising effort in behalf of white-lead. . . . A series of large-size advertisements in such widely read magazines as the *Saturday Evening Post, Colliers, American Home, Country Gentleman,* and *Better Homes and Gardens* will bring the white-lead story to the public in general and to home-owners in particular." The magazine campaign would produce "67,570,526 separate messages that will be carried in the publications named."[75,76]

In 1940, the secretary of the LIA praised the campaign's success in countering concerns about lead's effect on human health:

> One beneficial result of our campaign is the good will it is building up for lead in general. I have always felt that the cultivation of good will for our metal and publicity about the indispensable work it does for mankind is something that lead needs more than other common metals because lead in many forms is constantly under attack on account of its toxic qualities. Our campaign helps to meet this issue.[77]

The LIA saw its promotional campaign as an important antidote to the negative publicity that lead was receiving in the national press: "[I]n the long run [the campaign] will share in dispelling anxiety about [lead's] use. In any event the problem remains serious for our industry. Hardly a day passes but what this office has to devote some attention to lead poisoning," said Wormser in 1941.[78]

THE DANGERS OF LEAD PAINT BECOME NATIONAL NEWS

In December 1943 the issue of lead poisoning from paint among children, already familiar to those in the industry and to some pediatricians and public health professionals, became national news. *Time* magazine reported on an article by pediatricians Randolph Byers and Elizabeth Lord in the *American Journal of Diseases of*

Children. The *Time* article noted that parents' lack of understanding of the dangers of lead-based paint led many to use this toxic material on toys, cribs, and window-sills. When children chewed the painted surfaces, a variety of physical and nervous disorders resulted. "All but one child, Dr. Lord discovered, were school failures. Only five had normal I.Q.s, and four of the five were so erratic that they could not learn easily."[79] The reaction of the LIA secretary was to deny the reliability of Byers and Lord's data; he went so far as to pay a personal visit to Byers in Boston. In a preliminary report on the *Time* piece, the LIA maintained that the assumption regarding the relationship between lead poisoning in early infancy and later mental retardation had not been proven and that many of the cases of lead poisoning had "never been conclusively proven."[80]

The LIA's denials of the dangers posed by lead paint came despite detailed warnings from Robert Kehoe that the association's position was indefensible. Shortly after publication of the Byers and Lord article and the *Time* article, Robert Kehoe wrote to Wormser, "I am disposed to agree with the conclusions arrived at by the authors, and to believe that their evidence, if not entirely adequate, is worthy of very serious consideration." He informed the head of the LIA that in his own work he had seen "serious mental retardation in children that have recovered from lead poisoning."[81] Kehoe left no doubt that he would be willing to assist the board of LIA, but he objected to Wormser's denial of the importance of paint in causing lead poisoning in children. Kehoe argued that the position of the LIA was insupportable. "Unfortunately for Wormser's thesis, comparable results have been obtained in almost every other area of the United States where there have been facilities that enable accurate investigation of this type to be made."[82] "Small children crawl about on the floor and contaminate themselves pretty generally with every kind of dust or dirt that is within their environment. Eventually everything they get on their hands goes into their mouths, and therefore considerably greater opportunities exist for the dangerous exposure of small children of a variety of materials."[83,84]

But the LIA refused to accept the mounting research and evidence of lead poisoning. In December 1945, the association proposed a campaign to counteract the "medical and public misinformation usually amounting to actual prejudice against lead, because of its toxic qualities, [and which] is a subject of vital importance to all the lead industries in the United States." The LIA complained, "If anything, the problem has become even more serious in the last five years than ever before, owing primarily to the spread of considerable anti-lead propaganda and also to occasional faulty medical research which has penetrated deep into medical annals and caused many physicians and hospitals to assume erroneous positions on the question of lead poisoning." The LIA believed that the issue was "so fundamental" to the future welfare of the lead industries and the continued manufacture and use of many important lead products, such as white lead, red lead, litharge, sheet lead, and pipe lead, that unless immediate attention were paid to the problem "the opposing forces may grow strong enough to do us injury which it would take years of work to correct." As a result, the LIA outlined a safety and hygiene program, one purpose of which was to address the existing literature saying that lead represented a health hazard to the worker and the consumer.[85]

In 1946 the problem intensified: Wormser reported to the LIA that

> attention to the serious problem faced by all the lead industries because of the toxic nature of our metal is occupying a growing rather than a diminishing amount of the Association's time. This is largely owing to attacks upon lead that cannot be ignored for, if unchallenged, they may very easily lead to the sponsoring of totally unwarranted State and Federal legislation of a regulatory or prohibitive character. . . . Suffice it to say here that this is an unending battle from which we can only withdraw at our peril.[86]

In general, Wormser continued to argue that the danger to the public was minimal.[87]

As late as 1952, the LIA continued to promote the usefulness of white lead in both interior and exterior coverings. In its book *Lead in Modern Industry*, the LIA noted that "white lead adds more desirable qualities to paint than any other white pigment and has practically no undesirable qualities to nullify its advantages." The book continued, "the profitable application of white lead is not confined to exterior use. Pure white lead paints can be utilized to advantage for interior decoration, particularly in public and traditional buildings where elaborate decoration is used and it is very expensive and inconvenient to repaint often."[88]

In summaries of his activities in 1952, the director of health and safety of the LIA, Manfred Bowditch, called childhood lead poisoning "a major 'headache' and a source of much adverse publicity." He counted 197 reports of lead poisoning in 9 cities, of which 40 cases were fatal, although he noted that this was an "incomplete" estimate, especially for New York City.[89] In New York, 44 cases were reported, of which 14 were fatal. Between 1951 and 1953, according to George M. Wheatly of the American Pediatrics Association, "there were 94 deaths and 165 cases of childhood lead poisoning . . . in New York, Chicago, Cincinnati, St. Louis, and Baltimore."[90]

Reports from health departments, publicized in the popular press, were demonstrating the widespread nature of the lead paint hazard. In 1952 the LIA collected "nearly 500 newspaper clippings featuring lead poisoning, often in sizable headlines."[91] In 1956 the LIA noted that a headline in the New York *Daily News,* "Lead Poisoning Killed 10 Kids in Brooklyn in '55, Highest Toll in the City," was "based largely on data from the Health Department."[92] In addition to "the common run of newspaper studies on childhood and other types of plumbism," the LIA noted 2 "items of adverse publicity transcending [them] in importance." In July 1956 *Parade* magazine, which reached more than 7 million readers of 50 newspapers across the country, ran an article titled "Don't Let YOUR Child Get Lead Poisoning," and the CBS television network carried a broadcast on childhood lead poisoning.[93]

BLAMING THE VICTIMS

The LIA recognized as early as 1952 that to continue fighting a rearguard action attacking the extent of the lead poisoning problem would be "prohibitively expensive and time-consuming."[94] But the association continued to deflect responsibility for this tragedy away from the industry itself, placing the blame on poverty, not on the lead industry: "The major source of trouble is the flaking of lead paint in the ancient slum dwellings of our older cities, [and] the problem of lead poisoning in children will be with us for as long as there are slums."[95] Bowditch acknowledged "that the overwhelmingly major source of lead poisoning in children is from structural lead paints chewed from painted surfaces, picked up or off in the form of flakes, or adhering to bits of plaster and subsequently ingested." But who was responsible for this condition? According to Bowditch and the LIA, "Childhood lead poisoning is essentially a problem of slum dwellings and relatively ignorant parents." He maintained that lead poisoning was "almost wholly confined to the older cities of the eastern third of the country" and that "until we can find means to (a) get rid of our slums and (b) educate the relatively ineducable parent, the problem will continue to plague us."[96]

The president of the NPVLA, Joseph F. Battley, elaborated on this theme but used contemporary psychological explanations to rationalize away corporate responsibility for the pollution of children's environments. There might be dietary deficiencies, he said, but even "a well-fed child may still be emotionally hungry because he does not receive as much loving attention as he needs. Another may suffer from a sense of insecurity. To gain the comfort and reassurance they crave, they often place inedible objects [i.e., flaking paint] in their mouths."[97] As late as 1959, lead poisoning was still "a headache" for the industry.[98]

In the 1940s and early 1950s, state and local health departments sought to warn consumers about the dangers lead paint presented to children and others. The industry organized to oppose these efforts. Early labeling regulations in California in 1945 and Maryland in 1949 were opposed by the LIA and NPVLA, and the LIA took credit for the repeal of Maryland's statute.[99] Confronted with pressure in a number of localities and states for increased regulation, the NPVLA's counsel suggested that "the best course to pursue from the standpoint of the industries interested in the use of lead as a pigment and otherwise is to launch a campaign of education directed at the legislatures to forestall any further unnecessary legislation."[100]

In May 1954, the New York City Health Department proposed a sanitary code provision that would have banned the sale in the city of paints containing more than 1% lead and would have required lead paint to be labeled as poisonous and not for interior use.[101] This was consistent with the recommendations of the American Medical Association, which suggested labels saying "WARNING: This paint contains an amount of lead which may be POISONOUS and should not be used to paint children's toys or furniture or interior surfaces in dwelling units which might be chewed by children."[102] Both the NPVLA and the LIA opposed such wording. They supported and helped to develop the standard adopted in 1955 by the voluntary American Standards Association, which did not require the use of the word "poison."[103] New York City's regulation limited the amount of lead in interior paints to 1% but did not include the more explicit warning, and the industry adopted the same voluntary standard. Even in 1958, the LIA continued to oppose "any legislation of a prohibitory nature."[104]

Although the industry claimed that it had stopped using lead in interior paints in the 1940s, and it is clear that other pigments increasingly replaced lead during that time, lead continued to be present in paints sold for interior use well into the 1950s. In one survey commissioned by the US Department of Housing and Urban Development, "about one third of [Pittsburgh's] dwelling units built in [1940–1959] had surfaces with high (2 mg/cm^2 or more) concentrations of lead and nearly 10 per cent of the rooms tested had such lead levels."[105] In 1970, federal legislation prohibited the use of lead paint in federally financed and subsidized housing, and the Consumer Products Safety Commission prohibited the use of all lead paint after February 27, 1978. Yet in 1971, the New York City Health Department tested 76 paints and "found eight of them with amounts of lead ranging from 2.6 to 10.8 percent."[106]

A TERRIBLE LEGACY

Despite the medical evidence concerning the dangers to children of lead-based paint, the reports from Baltimore and other cities of lead poisoning of children, occasional articles in the popular press concerning the dangers of lead-based paint, and internal correspondence from leading lead authorities around the country acknowledging that lead paint was a serious hazard, the industry neither removed lead from paint nor warned consumers of its danger until very late in the game. In fact, at critical moments during this long history, the lead industry actually misled the public health community, assuring it that lead paint was not being used on toys, interior surfaces, or cribs. The industry also consciously used children in its advertising and promotion campaigns in ways that aggravated the public health crisis. By employing children in its marketing strategies, the industry reinforced the public's perception that lead paint was safe, thereby countering the increasing medical, public health, and popular literature documenting lead paint's dangers. This terrible legacy still haunts us today, as more and more cities become aware of the enormous intellectual, physical, emotional, and economic costs of the decades during which an entire industry ignored the growing evidence of lead's impact on children's health and shaped Americans' understanding of the dangers posed by lead.

ENDNOTES

1. Centers for Disease Control and Prevention, *Morbidity and Mortality Weekly Report* 46 (1997): 141, cited in B. P. Lanphear, "The Paradox of Lead Poisoning Prevention," *Science* 281 (1998): 1617–1618.

2. B. P. Lanphear, "The Paradox of Lead Poisoning Prevention." See also D. Ryan, B. Levy, S. Pollack, and B. Walker, Jr, "Protecting Children From Lead Poisoning and Building Healthy Communities," *American Journal of Public Health* 89 (1999): 822–824.

3. D. Rosner and G. Markowitz, "A 'Gift of God'? The Public Health Controversy Over Leaded Gasoline During the 1920s," *American Journal of Public Health* 75 (1985): 344–352; W. Graebner, "Hegemony Through Science: Information Engineering and Lead Toxicology,

1925–1965," in *Dying for Work: Workers' Safety and Health in Twentieth Century America,* ed. D. Rosner and G. Markowitz (Bloomington: Indiana University Press, 1987), 140–159.

4. R. Rabin, "Warnings Unheeded: A History of Child Lead Poisoning," *American Journal of Public Health* 79 (1989): 1668–1674; E. Silbergeld, "Preventing Lead Poisoning in Children," *Annual Review of Public Health* 18 (1997): 187–210; P. Reich, *The Hour of Lead: A Brief History of Lead Poisoning in the United States Over the Past Century, and of Efforts by the Lead Industry to Delay Regulation* (Washington, DC: Environmental Defense Fund, 1992); R. Wedeen, "Shaping Environmental Research: The Lead Industries Association 1928–1946," *Mount Sinai Journal of Medicine* 62 (1995): 386–389.

5. Elizabeth Fee's article on lead poisoning among children in Baltimore (E. Fee, "Public Health in Practice: An Early Confrontation With the 'Silent Epidemic' of Childhood Lead Paint Poisoning," *Journal of the History of Medicine and Allied Sciences* 45 [1990]: 588) was perhaps the most detailed community study.

6. C. C. Sellers, *Hazards of the Job: From Industrial Disease to Environmental Health Science* (Chapel Hill: University of North Carolina Press, 1997).

7. C. Warren, *Brush with Death: A Social History of Lead Poisoning* (Baltimore, Md: Johns Hopkins University Press, forthcoming). To date, this is perhaps the most detailed and sophisticated analysis of the ways that lead has been introduced into the broader environment.

8. See *Lead Diseases: A Treatise from the French of L. Tanqueral des Planches,* trans. S. L. Dana (Lowell, 1848). Boston, Mass: Tappan, Whittmore & Mason.

9. M. D. Stewart, "Notes on Some Obscure Cases of Poisoning by Lead Chromate Manifested Chiefly by Encephalopathy," *Medical News* 1 (1887): 676–681.

10. A. Hamilton, "Industrial Diseases, With Special Reference to the Trades in Which Women are Employed," *Charities and the Commons* 20 (1908): 655, 658. See also T. Legge and K. Goadby, *Lead Poisoning and Lead Absorption* (New York, NY: Longmont, Green & Co, 1912), 35; T. Oliver, *Lead Poisoning: From the Industrial, Medical, and Social Points of View* (New York, NY: Paul B. Hombre, 1914), vii, 55–65.

11. US Department of Commerce and Labor, Bureau of Labor, "List of Industrial Poisons," *Bulletin* 86 (1910): 163.

12. Edward J. Cornish to David Edsall, 12 May 1921, courtesy of Christopher Sellers.

13. J. L. Gibson, "A Plea for Painted Railings and Painted Walls of Rooms as the Source of Lead Poisoning Amongst Queensland Children," *Australasian Medical Gazette* (1904): 149–153. See also J. C. Burnham, "Biomedical Communication and the Reaction to the Queensland Childhood Lead Poisoning Cases Elsewhere in the World," *Medical History* 43 (1999): 155–172.

14. J. L. Gibson, "The Importance of Lumbar Puncture in the Plumbic Ocular Neuritis of Children," *Australian Medical Congress Transactions* 11 (1905): 750–754.

15. A. J. Turner, "Lead Poisoning in Childhood," *Australasian Medical Congress* (1908): 2–9; J. L. Gibson, "Plumbic Ocular Neuritis in Queensland Children," *British Medical Journal* 2 (1908): 1488–1490; T. Oliver, "A Lecture on Lead Poisoning and the Race," *British Medical Journal* 1911 (May 13): 1096–1098.

16. H. M. Thomas and K. D. Blackfan, "Recurrent Meningitis, Due to Lead in a Child of Five Years," *American Journal of Diseases of Children* 8 (1914): 377–380; A. Breinl and W. J. Young, "The Occurrence of Lead Poisoning Amongst North Queensland Children," *Annals of Tropical Medicine and Parasitology* 8 (1914): 575–590; J. L. Gibson, "The Diagnosis, Prophylaxis and Treatment of Plumbic Ocular Neuritis Amongst Queensland Children," *Medical Journal of Australia* 2 (1917): 201–204.

17. K. D. Blackfan, "Lead Poisoning in Children with Especial Reference to Lead as a Cause of Convulsions," *American Journal of the Medical Sciences* 153 (1917): 877–887.

18. See, for example, R. Strong, "Meningitis, Caused by Lead Poisoning, in a Child of Nineteen Months," *Archives of Pediatrics* 37 (1920): 532–537; L. E. Holt, "General and Functional Nervous Diseases," chap 2 in *The Diseases of Infancy and Childhood for the Use of Students and Practitioners of Medicine,* 8th ed (New York, NY: Appleton & Co, 1923); L. E. Holt, "Lead Poisoning in Infancy," *American Journal of Diseases of Children* 25 (1923): 229–233; Council of the Queensland Branch BMA, "An Historical Account of the Occurrence and Causation of Lead Poisoning Among Queensland Children," *Medical Journal of Australia* 1 (1922): 148–152; J. Ruddock, "Lead Poisoning in Children With Special Reference to Pica," *Journal of the American Medical Association* 82 (1924): 1682–1684; C. V. Weller, "Some Clinical Aspects of Lead Meningo-Encephalopathy," *Annals of Clinical Medicine* 3 (1925): 604–613; C. F. McKhann, "Lead Poisoning in Children," *American Journal of Diseases of Children* 32 (1926): 386–392; L. W. Holloway, "Lead Poisoning in Children," *Journal of the Florida Medical Association* 13 (1926): 94–100; F. L. Hoffman, "Deaths from Lead Poisoning," *U.S. Bureau of Labor Statistics Bulletin* 426 (1927): 33–34 (Hoffman lists 11 boys and 8 girls under the age of 18 years who died from lead poisoning; a number of these children were poisoned by paint from windows, walls, toys, or cribs).

19. E. E. Pratt, *Occupational Diseases, A Preliminary Report on Lead Poisoning in the City of New York* (Albany, NY: J. B. Lyon & Co, 1912), 373–377; T. Oliver, *Lead Poisoning: From the Industrial, Medical, and Social Points of View* (New York, NY: Paul B. Hoeber, 1914), 56–57; F. L. Hoffman, *Lead-Poisoning Legislation and Statistics* (Newark, NJ: Prudential Press, 1933); International Labour Office, *White-Lead: Data Collected by the International Labour Office in Regard to the Use of White Lead in the Painting Industry,* Studies and Reports, Series F, Industrial Hygiene, No. 11 (Geneva, Switzerland: International Labour Office, 1927).

20. "Prohibition of White Lead in Belgium," *American Journal of Public Health* 13 (1923): 337.

21. A. Hamilton, "Hygiene of the Painters' Trade," *Bureau of Labor Statistics Bulletin* 120 (1913): 66.

22. N. Porritt, "Cumulative Effects of Infinitesimal Doses of Lead," *British Medical Journal* (1931): 92–94.

23. Hoffman, *Lead-Poisoning Legislation and Statistics.*

24. C. F. McKhann, "Lead Poisoning in Children," *Archives of Neurology and Psychiatry* 27 (1932): 294–304.

25. E. Vogt, "Roentgenologic Diagnosis of Lead Poisoning in Infants and Children," *Journal of the American Medical Association* 98 (1932): 125–129.

26. "If Your Children Chew Paint," *Scientific American* 149 (1933): 291.

27. C. F. McKhann and E. C. Vogt, "Lead Poisoning in Children," *Journal of the American Medical Association* 149 (1933): 1131–1135.

28. R. Kehoe, abstract of discussion in C. F. McKhann and E. C. Vogt, "Lead Poisoning in Children," *Journal of the American Medical Association* 101 (1933): 1131–1135.

29. H. A. Gardner, *The Toxic and Antiseptic Properties of Paints,* Bulletin 41 of the Educational Bureau of the Paint Manufacturers' Association (Philadelphia, Penn: Paint Manufacturers' Association, 1914), 12.

30. Report of the Secretary, Annual Meeting of the Lead Industries Association, 5 June 1934, New York City Law Department Lead Industries Association Documents (hereafter cited as LIA Papers). See Christian Warren, "Toxic Purity: How America Became a Nation of White-Leaders," *Business History Review* (forthcoming).

31. [Wormser?] to William J. Donovan, 21 September 1928, National Archives, Federal Trade Commission Documents.

32. Wormser to Members Supporting the White Lead Promotion Program, 20 February 1939, Bulletin No. 1, LIA Papers.

33. LIA Directors Meeting, 29 May 1929, LIA Papers.

34. "Lead-Free Paint on Furniture and Toys to Protect Children," *United States Daily,* 20 November 1930, p. 1.

35. McKahnn and Vogt, "Lead Poisoning in Children."

36. The A. Shoenhut Company to Ella Oppenheimer, Children's Bureau, 17 April 1935, National Archives, Record Group 102 (Children's Bureau), Central File, 1933–1936, File: Diseases Due to Metallic, 4-5-17.

37. Newark Varnish Works to Ella Oppenheimer, 25 April 1935, National Archives, Record Group 102 (Children's Bureau), Central File, 1933–1936, File: Diseases Due to Metallic, 4-5-17.

38. LIA Annual Meeting, 13 June 1935, LIA Papers.

39. LIA Board of Directors Meeting, 17 January 1940, Exhibit A, "Report of the Secretary," LIA Papers.

40. Louis Dublin to Ella Oppenheimer, 14 September 1993, courtesy of Christian Warren.

41. NPVLA Executive Committee Minutes, 11 July 1939, LIA Papers.

42. NPVLA letter "To Class 'A' Members," 18 July 1939, LIA Papers.

43. "Do Not Forget The Children—Some Day They May Be Customers," *The Dutch Boy Painter* (August 1920): 126.

44. "The Dutch Boy's Lead Party," *The Dutch Boy Painter* (July 1924): 139.

45. "When the School Room is Empty," *The Dutch Boy Painter* (July 1924): back page.

46. *The Dutch Boy Conquers Old Man Gloom—A Paint Book for Boys and Girls* (New York, NY: National Lead Company, 1930).

47. "Takes a Scrubbing with a Smile" (advertisement), *The Modern Hospital* 48 (1937): 35.

48. "Fingerprints," *The Dutch Boy Painter* (August 1927): 117.

49. *Dutch Boy Painter–Carter Times* (January–February 1931 and September–October 1931).

50. "Types of Stencils . . . How to Use Them," *Dutch Boy Painter–Carter Times* (1933): 75–80.

51. National Lead Company Sales Manual, "Important" [ca 1949], LIA Papers.

52. National Lead Company, *Modern Packaging,* April 1949.

53. "Lead Helps to Guard Your Health" (advertisement), *National Geographic Magazine* (November 1923): 44.

54. "Clean and Bright Hospital Walls" (advertisement), *The Modern Hospital* (July 1921): 171; "Color—the Doctor's Assistant," *The Modern Hospital* (July 1922): 169.

55. "Every Room in a Modern Hospital Deserves a Dutch Boy Quality Painting Job" (advertisement), *The Modern Hospital* (July 1930).

56. Lead Industries Association, *Useful Information About Lead,* 1st ed (New York, NY: Lead Industries Association, 1931), 49–53, 104.

57. "These 4 Points Will Help You Sell Paint Jobs TODAY!" *National Painters Magazine* (1943).

58. Wormser to Members Supporting the White Lead Promotion Program, LIA Papers, Letter, February 20, 1939.

59. LIA Advisory Committee, White Lead Promotion, Minutes of 10th Meeting, 20 October 1941, LIA Papers.

60. LIA Advisory Committee, White Lead Promotion, Minutes of 2nd Meeting, 12 April 1939, LIA Papers.

61. "White Lead Paint Economical for Interiors," *Lead* 8 (1938): 7, LIA Papers.

62. "Modern Exteriors, Interiors Combine Plywood and White Lead," *Lead* 9 (1939): 5, LIA Papers; the same issue of *Lead* contained other articles about interior decoration of low-cost housing: "Successful Low Cost Homes Benefit with White Lead," p. 11; "A New Simplified

White Lead Painting Guide," p. 5; "Lead Products Aid in Pierce Foundation Experimental Home: Low Cost House Styled with White Lead and Flashed with Sheet Lead," p. 10.

63. LIA Advisory Committee, White Lead Promotion, Minutes of 8th Meeting, 18 October 1940, Exhibit A, Progress Report, LIA Papers.

64. White Lead Promotion Campaign, Bulletin 37, 23 May 1941, LIA Papers.

65. White Lead Promotion Campaign, Annual Summary, 11 October 1940, LIA Papers.

66. White Lead Promotion Campaign, Bulletin 42, 23 January 1942, LIA Papers.

67. White Lead Promotion Campaign, Bulletin 47, 20 May 1942, LIA Papers.

68. White Lead Promotion Campaign, Bulletin 40, 2 October 1941, LIA Papers.

69. White Lead Promotion Campaign, Bulletin 43, 23 February 1942, LIA Papers.

70. White Lead Promotion Campaign, Bulletin 40.

71. White Lead Promotion Campaign, Bulletin 32, 15 January 1941, LIA Papers.

72. White Lead Promotion Campaign, Bulletin 25, 11 October 1940, LIA Papers.

73. White Lead Promotion Campaign, Bulletin 32.

74. White Lead Promotion Campaign, Annual Summary, October 11, 1940.

75. "Lead Industry Begins Campaign to Advertise White-Lead," *The Dutch Boy Painter* 32 (1939): 27, LIA Papers.

76. Board of Directors Meeting, 16 May 1939, Secretary's Report, "Summarizing the Activities of the Lead Industries Association for 1938," LIA Papers.

77. Report of the Secretary, Annual Meeting, 6 June 1940, LIA Papers.

78. Annual Report, 22 September 1941, LIA Papers.

79. "Paint Eaters," *Time*, 20 December 1943, 49.

80. Lead Industries Association, "Preliminary Report of Investigation of 'Time' Article 'Paint Eaters,' " *Lead Hygiene and Safety Bulletin* (1944): 40.

81. Kehoe to Wormser, 7 February 1944, LIA Papers.

82. Kehoe to J. H. Schaefer (Vice President, Ethyl Corp), 29 January 1945, Box 90, LIA Papers.

83. Kehoe to Dr. R. L. Gorrell, City-County Health Unit, Las Animas County, Trinidad Colo, 5 September 1945, LIA Papers.

84. Kehoe to R. H. Kotte, 14 February 1951, LIA Papers.

85. Executive Committee Meeting, Exhibit D, 28 December 1945, LIA Papers.

86. LIA Annual Meeting, Minutes, Report of the Secretary, 26 April 1946.

87. F. Wormser, "Facts and Fallacies of Lead Exposure" (1946), 10 [courtesy of Christian Warren].

88. Lead Industries Association, *Lead in Modern Industry* (New York, NY: Lead Industries Association, 1952), 153–54; this book continued to be promoted by the LIA until at least 1962. See "Lead Library of Technical Information," *Lead* (1962), 26.

89. Manfred Bowditch to Ziegfield, "1952 Activities," 16 December 1952; "Lead Hygiene" (minutes of the Annual Meeting, 9–10 April 1953), LIA Papers.

90. *New York Times*, 9 November 1954, p. 26.

91. "Lead Hygiene," LIA Papers.

92. Quarterly Report of the Secretary, 2 April 1956, LIA Papers.

93. Quarterly Report of the Secretary, 1 October 1956, LIA Papers.

94. Bowditch to Ziegfield, 16 December 1952, courtesy of Christian Warren.

95. Report of Health and Safety Division, Manfred Bowditch, Director, Annual Meeting, 24–25 April 1957, LIA Papers.

96. Bowditch to Kehoe, 26 December 1957, courtesy of Christian Warren.

97. National Paint, Varnish and Lacquer Association, "Watch Your Child's 'Eating Habits'!"

98. Annual Report for 1959, LIA Papers.

99. Annual Meeting, Report of the Secretary, 13–14 April 1950, LIA Papers.

100. T. J. McDowell, "Suggested Cause of Action for NPVL Association Re: Labeling Laws," [ca July 1954] in NPVLA, Minutes, Subcommittee on Model Labeling, 15 July 1954, LIA Papers.

101. J. Trichter (Assistant Commissioner of Environmental Sanitation, New York City Department of Health) to C. W. Slocum (Devoe & Reynolds [paint] Company), 24 August 1954, LIA Papers.

102. B. E. Conley (Secretary, American Medical Association) to J. Trichter, 9 September 1954, LIA Papers.

103. American Standards Association, "American Standards Specifications to Minimize Hazards to Children from Residual Surface Coating Materials" (Z66.1-1955), approved 16 February 1955.

104. Quarterly Report of the Secretary, 10 January 1958, LIA Papers.

105. Rabin, "Warnings Unheeded," 1672.

106. Ibid.

PART TEN

The Schools

Hardly a year goes by without another dire report on the sad state of America's public schools. Although they are often reasonably satisfied with the schools their own children attend, many Americans believe that the schools in *general* are falling apart. Bad schools are routinely blamed for a host of our national problems, from uneven economic growth to youth violence.

As many commentators have pointed out, the popular image of the schools is more than a little misleading. *Overall,* the public schools are not as bad as they are often said to be. They are educating more children, from a wider range of backgrounds—and often with more difficult problems—than ever before. Scores on achievement tests, which fell disturbingly in the 1970s, aren't falling any more. More American students go on to college than those of most other industrial countries—and our system of higher education remains one of the best in the world, drawing students from every part of the globe.

Nevertheless, there are a number of serious problems with American schools, and the articles in this part help us to separate the real ones from those that are mostly mythical.

Perhaps the most fundamental of those problems is the persistence of deep inequalities in schooling that continue to divide America's schoolchildren into educational haves and have-nots. At their best, schools—both private and public—offer students high-quality teaching, substantial resources, and excellent facilities. But at their worst, American schools can be astonishingly bad—offering dilapidated and aging classrooms, few resources, and an educational experience that cannot possibly prepare the young for a productive role in society. Unsurprisingly, these "savage inequalities," in the words of the writer Jonathan Kozol, fall along lines of income and race.

Michael Johnston, a young teacher fresh out of Yale, went to teach in a troubled, largely black high school in Greenville, Mississippi, which embodied all of these problems. In the selection from his book about that experience that we reprint here, Johnston describes one of the ways in which such schools shortchange their students, with results that are not only wasteful but, as in this case, can be tragic. Unwilling or unable to deal seriously with one student's academic deficiencies, the school system keeps promoting him anyway—which only increases his inability to do the work the schools require, and deepens his frustration and anger. When this neglect ultimately leads to violence, it surprises no one.

The problems that Johnston describes in one Mississippi high school are part of a broader pattern in which educational resources, like others, are increasingly distributed in markedly unequal ways. Earlier sections have charted a shift upward in wealth and income, as well as political influence, in the United States. But these aren't the only realms in which that upward tilt has taken place. Education is another. We have always prided ourselves on the inclusiveness of our system of public education, as a symbol and embodiment of fundamental American values. What has traditionally made college, for example, a way of moving upward for generations of lower-income Americans was that a college education could be had for free, or nearly so—meaning that the opportunity to gain a higher education was separated from one's ability to pay. But as Ellen Mutari and Melaku Lakew show, going to college today, even at many public universities, increasingly means long hours of outside work, the burden of taking on heavy student loans, or "maxing out" credit cards—a reality that may not be news to many readers of this book. As college becomes less and less affordable, it becomes that much harder for working people to achieve the American Dream through their own efforts.

In "Reading, Writing, and . . . Buying?," the editors of *Consumer Reports* magazine point to another growing problem in the schools—the increasing penetration of commercial advertising into the classroom. Schoolchildren represent a vast potential market for a wide variety of consumer goods; a market that, until recently, has been largely untapped. But many corporations have been moving aggressively to find ways of selling their products to the captive school audience, including everything from commercial-laden "news" channels on TV to cafeteria menus advertising brand-name foods. As the authors point out, all of this represents a troubling breakdown of the distinction between education and sales, between the quest for learning and the quest for profit: and it could profoundly alter the purpose of education in the United States.

CHAPTER 33

In the Deep Heart's Core

MICHAEL JOHNSTON

Two months after school began a new student entered my second-block class. When he first appeared at my door in the middle of my second block, I suspected that he was a troublemaker looking for a good prank. As he continued knocking on the door I could no longer ignore him. Months of being fooled by tricksters had taught me to demand a copy of his schedule before I let him cross my room's threshold. Much to my surprise, he pulled a crumpled schedule from his pocket. I scanned the page for my name: "English II: Johnston, 227. Jevon Jenkins." He stood barely six feet tall, but was the heaviest student I had seen on campus. Jevon was dark-skinned but his face was splotched with patches of brighter skin, as if he'd been severely burned. His arms were covered from wrist to biceps with tattoos; two I recognized as familiar gang emblems, the Deuces and CCP—the Carver Circle Posse. His vacant stare implied that he was incapable of humor or affection, cold enough that a visible show of disinterest might take some serious conjuring.

He did not seem to know anyone in the classroom, and after I approved his schedule he walked to the opposite corner of the room without instruction. He sat in one of the three wide rectangular desks I had placed along the back wall. He was too large to fit in one of the regular desks. Emmanuel, one of the student band directors, had already taken the large desk on the other side of the room, so I couldn't contest Jevon's seat choice. My biggest trouble with Emmanuel was that I would often find him at his desk composing classical music rather than working on the current assignment.

Jevon carried no accessories whatsoever—no backpack, jacket, pen, notebook; nothing. Sadly, this was rather common at Greenville High School; it was in part a protest because locker privileges had been revoked two years earlier due to security concerns. Students had to transport all their belongings and all their books, and setting them down even for a minute meant exposure to theft or vandalism. For some students, their refusal to acquire school supplies articulated their attitudes toward school in general: They would agree to show up each day as the law and their parents mandated, and they would sometimes agree not to keep others from learning, but this did not mean they had to expend their own time and energy to help the process run more smoothly. I guessed that even Jevon's pockets were empty, except for perhaps a lighter and a crumpled up cigarette.

Jevon acted much like the rest of the students on their first day: passive, restrained, calculating. After his comfort level grew, he made casual acquaintance with a few of the marginal characters who occupied the back of the room. One of them, Bryant, who generally was in school only two days a week, had taken a liking to Jevon, mostly due to a common interest in obtaining cigarettes and drug paraphernalia during the day. Toward the end of his second week, Jevon asked to go to the bathroom, saying his stomach hurt horribly and he had been sick all morning. Since this was his first request, I granted it. Naturally I continued the class, but some thirty minutes later I noticed that Jevon's desk was still empty. As the rest of the class was making sporadic efforts at some independent work, I ventured out into the hallway to search for Jevon. Much to my surprise, when I stepped into the hallway he was but a few feet away.

"Where have you been for the last thirty minutes?"

"I've been in the bathroom. Sick. I don't feel so good." He looked at the floor, deferential but not penitent. He was lying and he didn't care that I knew.

Perhaps he was curious to see how I'd handle an obvious lie that I could not prove. He still looked at the ground and shifted his feet like a boy. I looked at his tattoos; there was one on each forearm that I could not decipher, each set off by long scars that ran down his arms. In this moment when he was caught, his idiosyncrasies were still boyish, but I could feel them evolving into more worrisome habits. I chose to handle the situation by straddling a line of discipline, assuring him he couldn't expect bathroom privileges in the future. He nodded indifferently and passed back into the room. In the back of the room his surly partner, Bryant, looked up, and as he did I saw a wide smile spread across Jevon's face—the first I had ever seen. I realized then that I had erred on the side of leniency, and the effect would become obvious.

Jevon soon missed three days while the class was at work on group projects, and he returned on the day before the project's culmination. I had almost forgotten about him when the tardy bell rang for second block. As the crowd cleared, dispersing with haste into their various rooms, a solitary figure was revealed lumbering down the hall. Jevon was late, had missed a number of days, and was about to miss the test grade that the next day's projects represented.

When he reached the doorway, I told him that he had fallen behind on an assignment that was due the following day, and that he needed to work hard that day in order to receive a passing grade. He looked straight through me. Whatever he had seen in the three days of his absence, its intensity had made human figures inconsequential. I handed him a copy of the presentation topics and told him to get started right away. Without looking at it, he collected it the way a truck collects an insect on its windshield. He did not greet the small cadre of boys with whom he had grown familiar, nor did he acknowledge the rest of his classmates. Slightly disturbed by his manner, I watched him all the way to his seat. Noticing my attention, the students grew anxious themselves. I chose to disregard Jevon, and to do my best to proceed with the business of class.

Once I had gotten the students started on their work, I returned my attention to Jevon. Though I hadn't studied him closely during my instructions, I did notice that he was working on something, and I was moderately pleased. Perhaps his new disposition was in fact a wake-up call to the urgency of his own situation.

But as I started back toward Jevon's desk, I soon saw the fruits of his labor: On his desk he had spread out hundreds of shreds from the paper I had handed him. I told him that he must clean up the shredded paper and obtain a copy of the assignment from someone else before the class was over. He looked up and, with his eyes trained on me, swept the shreds off his desk and watched them sprinkle to the ground. Then he propped his big elbow on the desk and extended his pudgy middle finger directly at me.

I sent him to the principal's office.

The next occurrence was less than two weeks later. I was down in the annex during my conference period when I noticed Mr. Taylor, the history teacher, marching his class out into the open field behind the annex. I saw Jevon in the back of the group. Somehow Jevon noticed me up in the second-floor window, and when Mr. Taylor looked the other way, Jevon held his giant arm aloft and once again shot me the middle finger. Not wanting to engage in a disciplinary struggle with a student in someone else's class, I walked away from the window and thought for a minute. While running errands, I found myself in the downstairs annex ten minutes later when Mr. Taylor's class came filing in from the field. Jevon was again at the end of the line. Knowing he was coming I waited outside the door to see if he would acknowledge his earlier gesture. He swaggered toward me, smiling. He stared at me with a wry grin and then suddenly threw both of his hands toward me in a defiant gesture that mimicked rap stars.

"What you gonna do, huh?" he sneered. "What you gonna do?"

He continued staring at me as he passed close enough to threaten a punch, and certainly close enough to deliver one. Then he curled his hand into a gun, pointed it at the lockers and fired, releasing a guttural boom as his arm kicked back from the explosion. He turned toward me as he continued walking, holding his phony smoking gun aloft as he watched imaginary gunpowder swirl off the barrel.

As he reached the end of the hallway, he pointed his makeshift gun directly at me and said, "See that! That's what happens if I fail!"

He turned away and with a wide enticing smile he let his pudgy brown hand relax. I looked at my watch; in twenty-two minutes Jevon would be arriving in my room for second block.

I decided to turn to Mr. Hudson, the assistant principal, for advice. Mr. Hudson and Mr. Amos together made up the entire administration of Greenville High School. Mr. Hudson spent the entire day dealing with discipline. Every time a teacher "wrote up" a student—filled out a disciplinary referral form—the student was sent to Mr. Hudson's office. Mr. Hudson hollered at kids when they needed to be hollered at, and told them to shut their traps when they needed to shut them. The only complaint I ever heard about Mr. Hudson was that he too readily believed in the inherent goodness of the students he disciplined. He was blessed with the patience of a father and the devotion of a preacher.

There was a similarity between the entrance to Mr. Hudson's office and the local street corner on a Friday night: Both were bustling with riffraff waiting for something to happen. For repeat offenders this area became a reliable and often enjoyable hangout spot, a perch from which they could heckle any passersby, knowing they were already in trouble. For predominantly good kids who took pride in their reputation as decent students, being spotted on the wall outside Mr. Hudson's office was Greenville High's version of the Puritan stocks, an obvious social stigma. On this particular morning, business was a bit quieter than usual, since the penitent outnumbered the proud.

Like a seasoned FBI agent, Mr. Hudson responded to my mention of Jevon Jenkins with the wistful frustration over the one that kept getting away.

"Yeah, we've been tracking him now for some time. What we got to do is get enough of a paper trail on him that we can take him to a hearing."

The hearing was the school district's highest court. It was a small and sundry court, presided over by the school board, where the defendant was present and the plaintiff—the school's representative (usually Mr. Hudson) or a slighted teacher—brought forth testimony and witnesses to bear upon the defendant's guilt. This elaborate legal process was necessary because the school board could hand out the severest form of disciplinary punishment—it could either dismiss students or refer them to alternative settings, in our case Garrett Hall, the alternative school.

Mr. Hudson raised his head from his papers to give me my assignment: "Document everything you got. Each event on a separate referral form, and bring them all to me, and we'll get this started. For now we'll see if we can get you a parent conference. Ms. Coris has been having some trouble with him too."

I returned to my room and began to write up the events, waiting for the toll of the bell. I had just begun the second referral when the bell rang and the first of my second-block students filtered through the door. Mr. Taylor's class was only two doors down from mine, so Jevon was always one of the first to arrive. I did not go to the doorway to look for him. Instead, I stayed in the room and conversed with the two students who had already arrived. A moment later Jevon arrived without salutation and proceeded disinterestedly to his place in the corner. We were a good deal of the way through class before I heard from Jevon again. As before, he had been occupied with some labor at his desk. I didn't suspect that it was the assignment the rest of the class was working on, but he seemed to be doing some writing of his own kind: harmless enough. He raised his hand to call me back to his desk.

He had a blank notebook sitting squarely on his desk and I wondered what had happened to the fruits of his labor. He asked plainly if he could go to the bathroom. Without pleading he told me that he would not take long and I could watch him from the doorway if I liked. The boys' bathroom was in direct sight of my doorway. With my monitoring, his trip could not last long enough to commit either of the most common bathroom offenses: gambling and smoking. I conceded, more out of curiosity than courtesy, anxious to see if he was trying to get himself into trouble or steer clear of it. I granted his request and returned to the front of the room. As I did so, out of the corner of my eye I caught Jevon flashing a toothy smile at his partner, Bryant. I watched Jevon raise his considerable body from his desk and stand in front of Bryant, and watched Bryant reach into his backpack and pull something out, placing it furtively in Jevon's hands. Bryant smiled sheepishly at me and quickly returned his eyes to his blank paper. Jevon also put his head down and moved slowly but steadily towards the door.

I stepped in front of the door. "You need to give me whatever's in that hand."

"What? There ain't nothing."

"Give it to me, Jevon, or you go back to your seat."

By now Jevon and I had taken center stage; the entire class looked up from their papers to see how this would be resolved. Jevon no longer wished to deny that there was something in his hand; he simply refused to turn it over. I looked at the thickness of his hand and I knew that any attempt to force it from him would be futile, but I refused to let him out of my supervision with it.

"I'm just going to the bathroom. Just let me go to the bathroom, you already said I could." His eyes did not once raise to meet mine.

"It comes to me or you go to your seat, Jevon. It's that simple."

He thought for a minute, shuffling one foot and raising his head a little to look back toward the class. I moved slightly from the doorway, in part because I believed he had made his decision to return to his seat, and in part because I feared he was on the verge of snapping and barging out the door. He turned without comment or ceremony and returned to his desk. The class shifted in their seats and mumbled a few comments. Some minutes later I was leaning over a student's desk proofreading an essay when I heard a chair squeak. I raised my eyes to see Jevon, backpack in hand, rising from his desk and walking, without urgency, toward the door. He made no show of defiance or disrespect, but simply chose to leave. I knew that to call to him with any urgency would only weaken my already debilitated position.

He had made up his mind, and that decision included disregarding consequences. I knew it would be worthless to threaten him with them now.

"I'll see you in the office, Jevon," I called after him. Disconcerted, I looked back over to his desk. A muffled laughter erupted from the two boys who sat closest to Jevon. I walked over to get a better look.

In the middle of the desk, in permanent black marker, Jevon had drawn an incredibly graphic picture of a man and woman having sex. The drawing itself was about the size of a notebook pad, and it was placed so perfectly in the center of the desk that it seemed almost like a place mat awaiting future visitors. I sent all my referrals to Mr. Hudson that afternoon, including the new one, and three days later I had a parent conference scheduled with Jevon's mother.

I had forgotten about the conference, and was busy preparing for my second block, when Jevon's mother poked her head in my doorway.

"Hello, are you Mr. Johnston?"

A bit surprised, I told her I was.

"I am Jevon Jenkins's mother. I'm here for a conference." Julie Coris, Jevon's French teacher, entered the room right behind her. The three of us sat down, Jevon's mother and I obviously unfamiliar with what should happen next.

Julie started by telling Jevon's mother that the source of his problems in her class were not his fault. Jevon had been placed in her French II class, though he had never taken French I. Julie told her that she had gone to the counselor several times to request a schedule change. However, the counselors said that since Jevon had arrived a month and a half late, all other classes were full and they wanted to leave him there and "see how he does." Julie concluded with a clear prognosis: "There is no way Jevon will pass."

"Yes," Jevon's mother said, "that's what I'm wondering, is does he have any chance to pass at all? If he starts doing all his work and he gets some makeup work?"

My fantasy of Jevon completing makeup work was snuffed by Julie's abrupt response: "No, there is just no way."

His mother then turned to make me the same offer; I glanced through the grade book at the string of zeros and naked boxes where grades were meant to be, wincing like a salesman offered a low price. For a moment I thought of Corelle's heroic makeup efforts.

"He seems capable of doing the work, that doesn't seem to be the problem. But he's very far behind in many of the basic skills, and I am not sure he would be able to catch up with the rest of the kids," I told her. I watched her eyes, and I glanced back toward Jevon's cave in the back of the room. I imagined him as a student rather than a menace, and I couldn't let this offer slip away. "But as far as the numbers go, if he worked hard for the rest of the year, and made up all the assignments that he has missed . . . yes, he could still pass."

She was visually pleased and sensed that it was her turn to speak.

"Well, see, this has all gone back so far, but when we finally brought him to Greenville High they had told me that he was all on grade level, but then he got in trouble so fast that we had to send him back to that military school again, and so we've never even gotten to figure out where he's really at."

Julie and I sensed that we had happened upon a clue to the riddle we had both been studying for weeks, and we pressed her to tell us Jevon's story from the beginning. It was so unbelievable, and so obvious, that I scratched down notes as quickly as I could, hoping to find some ledge in the wall of Jevon's past, a place where he and I could perhaps find a foothold and begin to climb again. By the time the story was over, I could see all the little places along the way where she had lost the small but invaluable battles, and the moment when she finally gave up, handing her boy over to God, unaware that often it is not God who comes first to claim those who have been left to him.

She said that Jevon was born in Jackson and spent his first three years of school there. He presented such discipline problems in the second grade that she and his teachers decided to send him to an "alternative school" for a year. I had never heard of a third grader being sent to alternative school, but if it resembled the alternative schools at the high school level then it must have been an eye-opening experience for a seven-year-old. As most teachers will acknowledge, a good portion of disciplinary problems arises from the defense mechanisms of students who feel insecure about their ability to do the work. Even Jevon's mother acknowledged that the situation was no different for Jevon; part of his problem, she said, stemmed from the fact that he wasn't as "quick" as the rest of the kids. After the year at the alternative school, Jevon was returned to fourth grade at his old school. If Jevon had not left for alternative school, he would have been retained in the second grade, based on his academic ability. Instead, he was sent to the alternative school for disciplinary reasons and after one year returned as a fourth grader.

This kind of mistake is notorious in public schools. In the Delta it has grown so common that many families use it as a strategy for promotion: If a child is failing a grade, send him to stay with an aunt in a neighboring county, where he will be enrolled in a grade based on his age. After a few months, return that child to the old school system where he will again be placed in a grade level according to his age, thereby executing a promotion without any work.

Jevon continued to exhibit the same behavior when he returned to the public elementary school in Jackson, so before Christmas he was sent back to the alternative school for another year. He returned a year later and was admitted to the fifth grade. As is common, the alternative school had made some inroads at curtailing his insolence, but had not seriously addressed his academic deficiencies; as a result, Jevon failed the fifth grade two years in a row. Since Jevon was then thirteen years old and already weighed more than two hundred pounds, the principal thought it emotionally unhealthy to retain Jevon for another year in the elementary school. The principal was at a loss: He couldn't in good faith promote a student who did not have the necessary skills, but neither could he retain a student who was so socially and emotionally removed from his peers that interaction was likely to be unhealthy for both parties. The answer with Jevon always seemed to be, "Send him to someone else." With some assistance from the principal, Jevon's mother decided to send him to Boys' Town in Memphis, a much larger, better resourced, privately run school for troubled boys. He spent two years at Boys' Town. Convinced that Jevon had made some progress, his mother and he moved to Greenville. Now fifteen years old, with his last formal school experience having been in the fifth grade, Jevon enrolled as a freshman at Greenville High School.

To no one's surprise, Jevon was well behind his classmates academically, and was socially uncomfortable because he had not been in a normal school environment since the fifth grade. He was unsuccessful in two tries at that level. Also to no one's surprise, his anxiety manifested itself in a continual display of discipline problems. Before he had the chance to illustrate that he was failing due to inadequate academic preparation, Jevon was removed from Greenville High School before Thanksgiving for fighting, and placed in Garrett Hall. The alternative school obtained a record of Jevon's past, and informed him that if he could successfully complete what it outlined as the skill requirements for sixth, seventh, and eighth grades during the eight months that he was there, he could return to the ninth grade.

Apparently Jevon worked diligently over those months, and he was reinstated to the ninth grade at Greenville High School the following year. But again his disciplinary problems persisted, and his academic preparation was inadequate; again he was removed before the semester was over. This time he was sent to the Dogwood School. The Dogwood School was both more militaristic and more evangelical than any of the others, believing that enough exposure to regimentation and to the Bible could cure anyone. Unfortunately, Dogwood ran on a different schedule from Greenville High, so it was not until October that he was released from Dogwood and enrolled in Greenville High School as a tenth grader.

This is why Jevon arrived two months late to English II, French II, world history, and algebra II. He was expected to outrace his peers to compensate for the missed lessons, although the last time he had successfully passed a course in school was ten years earlier, in the second grade. Counselors placed him in French II and English II, despite the fact that he had never taken—never mind passed—English I or French I. As his mother finished her story I sat enraged, wanting to burn public education to the ground and start again just for Jevon. I glanced over her shoulder at the calendar: It was almost Thanksgiving, and Jevon was right on schedule.

To his credit, Jevon lasted until Christmas. He failed my class with a sixty, despite some marked improvements. One day the following semester, I picked up the newspaper as I waited for a faculty meeting to begin, and recognized Jevon's photograph on the front page. I wanted not to read it, already knowing what it would say. Jevon had been arrested and convicted of three different offenses. Two instances of armed robbery did not surprise me; it was the third that broke my heart. Jevon had also been convicted of sexually assaulting a seven-year-old girl. A coldness opened inside me, and I turned to the teacher next to me, who had young children.

"How old is a child when he's in second grade?"

"Seven."

"That's what I was afraid of."

CHAPTER 34

Class Conflict

The Rising Costs of College

ELLEN MUTARI

MELAKU LAKEW

Brigit M. just graduated from a public college in southern New Jersey with a 4.0 GPA. Putting herself through college with a full course load, she worked 25 to 30 hours a week off campus as a waitress, plus 8 to 12 hours a week on campus as a writing and economics tutor. She had a scholarship, but, as she says, "You think a full scholarship is great, but it doesn't cover books, transportation, and health care costs." She was lucky to have a flexible employer who was willing to accommodate her course schedule. But the time juggle was still difficult: "It was hard to come home from work at 11:00 P.M. and still have to write a paper that was due for an 8:30 A.M. class."

Brigit is one of almost six million working students in the United States. Many of these students do much more than put in a few hours in the school cafeteria or library. They cannot afford a college education without working long hours at one or more off-campus jobs, taking on heavy student loans, and using credit cards to fill in the gaps. The costs of college have skyrocketed, increasing faster than inflation, family incomes, and taxpayer funding of public institutions and financial aid programs. Full-time annual tuition now ranges from an average of $1,627 for a public community college to $15,380 on average for a private college or university. Total costs—including books and fees—are much higher. The total cost of attending a public community college on a full-time basis averages $7,265 a year, while a four-year public university averages $10,889, and a private college or university typically costs $19,443. Today's college students face tremendous monetary pressures.

Many Americans believe in education as a way of ensuring economic opportunity. Politicians and business leaders trumpet college education as means out of poverty, a by-your-own-bootstraps way of attaining the American Dream. Yet college is becoming less and less affordable, especially for students from lower-income families. Tuition at public and private institutions is rising faster than most families' incomes, according to a 2002 study by the National Center for Public Policy and Higher Education. Consequently, families paying college tuition today are shelling out much larger percentages of their incomes than families did twenty years ago. In 1980, the poorest one-fifth, or quintile, of Americans could pay tuition at a public two-year college with only 6% of their family income. By 2000, this percentage had doubled to 12% of family income. Four-year colleges and universities, including public-sector ones, take an even bigger bite out of tight family budgets. Tuition at a private college represents 25% of the annual income of the poorest quintile of families—up from 13% in 1980. It is not only the poorest families that are losing ground. Middle-class incomes have also failed to keep pace with rising tuition. Only the wealthiest families, those in the top income quintile—who since the 1980s have benefited from inflated stock prices, as well as tax cuts and other economic policies skewed toward the rich—have soaring incomes to match escalating tuition costs.

Why is tuition rising so fast? One reason is that colleges and universities are receiving less funding of other kinds; tuition is replacing other revenue sources such as donations, grants, contracts, and perhaps most significantly, state government appropriations to public-sector institutions. In fact, state appropriations to public two-year colleges, four-year undergraduate schools with some graduate programs, and research universities actually fell between the 1988–89 and 1997–98 academic years, and stayed level for four-year bachelor's institutions. The anti-tax, anti-government, anti-public services rhetoric and policies of the past few decades have undermined states' financial support for public institutions of higher learning. Yet these are the institutions with the explicit mission of making college accessible to all. The short-sighted mentality of "tax cuts today" has eroded our nation's public investment in human capital, much as it has our public infrastructure of roads, schools, and bridges.

STUDENTS WORKING OVERTIME

The gap between total costs and aid for full-time students is significant, averaging $5,631 a year at public community colleges and $6,904 at public four-year institutions. For students attending private colleges and universities, the gap is over $10,000.

More and more, students make up this shortfall with paid work. Almost three-fourths of all full-time college students work while attending school, reports the U.S. Department of Education in its 1999–2000 National Postsecondary Student Aid Survey (NPSAS). This figure is up four percentage points since the 1995–96 survey, and accounts for both on- and off-campus jobs, as well as work-study positions. While we might expect to see older, non-traditional students working, the U.S. Bureau of Labor Statistics reports high rates of employment even among traditional-age college students (those between 16 and 24 years old). These are the students we

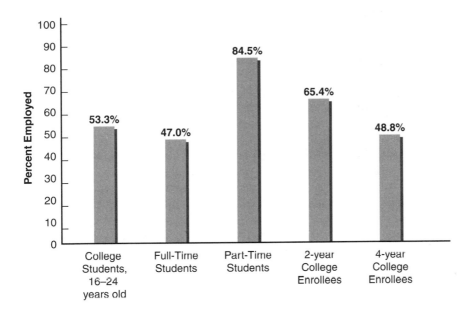

FIGURE 34.1 **Rates of Employment Among College Students 16–24 Years Old, October 2001**

Source: U.S. Bureau of Labor Statistics, "College Enrollment and Work Activity of 2001 High School Graduates," News Release USDL 02-288.

would most expect to receive parental support so that they could focus on classes and social life. But over half of these college students were holding down jobs (see Figure 34.1). Even young people who are full-time students and those enrolled in four-year colleges are employed at high rates, 47.0% and 48.8% respectively. For part-time students, employment rates are substantially higher, at 84.5%. Is this because working people choose to attend college on a part-time basis? Or because the costs of college require so many work hours that students cannot take a full-time course load?

Students' work hours indicate that they are paying for more than an occasional pizza in the dorm. Some 71% of full-time students who work are putting in more than the 15 hours per week one might expect of an on-campus work-study job, according to a summary of the NPSAS findings by the State Public Interest Research Groups' (PIRGs) Higher Education Project (see Figure 34.2). One out of five of these students working over 15 hours per week holds down the equivalent of a full-time job—balancing 35 or more weekly hours of paid work against a full-time course load.

Horace K. is a senior majoring in business, a member of the Student Senate, and a prominent student leader on campus. He works 14 hours a week between Sunday and Wednesday at his campus Student Development office. He has another 15- to 20-hour job at the local mall on Fridays, Saturdays, and Sundays. Saturday he is at the mall all day, then Sunday he follows his shift at the mall with a night shift at his on-campus job. Horace points out, "If I don't work, there's no way to buy

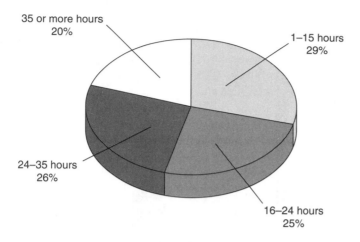

35 or more hours
20%

1–15 hours
29%

24–35 hours
26%

16–24 hours
25%

FIGURE 34.2   Distribution of Full-Time Students Who Work, by Hours Worked per Week, 1999–2000

Source: Tracey King and Ellynne Bannon, *At What Cost? The Price That Working Students Pay For A College Education,* The State PIRGs' Higher Education Project, 2002.

books, food, and things of that nature." He feels lucky to have these jobs. After his first year, he was told he no longer qualified for work-study jobs because his father earned "too much." He could not find an on-campus job, there was no bus to the mall, and he did not have a car. His summer jobs paid for a car so he could commute to the mall.

While many students report educational benefits from their experiences in the work world, they also say that working has negative impacts on their grades, library access, class choices, and ability to get help with course work. For example, Auliya A., a first-year student, was told she had to attend an all-day orientation for her new job at an Atlantic City casino, forcing her to choose between employment and a quiz in one of her classes. Persistence in college studies, especially rates of completion, tend to be lower among students working full-time. One out of five first-year students working 35 or more weekly hours did not finish the school year, compared with only one out of 17 students working fewer than 15 hours per week. According to the PIRG study, the longer a student's weekly work hours, the lower the benefits and the higher the drawbacks they report. The conclusion of the PIRG findings seems to be that a moderate amount of paid work (less than 16 hours per week) yields a positive engagement with the world, but that long work hours harm academic achievement and students' overall college experience.

Of course, students from families with annual incomes of less than $20,000 are more likely to work, and to work longer hours, than those with family incomes of $100,000 or more. These students cite necessities such as tuition, fees, or living expenses as the primary reason for working, while well-off students work for spending money and job experience. According to the PIRG report, half of low-income students who work indicate that they could not afford to continue their studies without a job. Almost one-third (32%) of students from low-income families said that their grades suffered because of their paid jobs, while 23% of students from wealthy families voiced the same concern.

INCREASING DEBT BURDEN

The same students who are working long hours to pay their rising tuition bills are likely to rely on financial aid. Indeed, seven out of ten full-time students receive financial aid. Unfortunately, financial aid does not help as much as it once did. Pell grants are the most important needs-based aid program for low-income college students. Growing out of the War on Poverty and Great Society initiatives of the 1960s, federal Pell grants were created in 1972 as the core program for low-income and working-class college students. Grant aid per student, though, has not kept pace with the rate of tuition increases. Consider how far a Pell grant stretches. The maximum Pell grant of $4,000 represents only 39% of the average cost of attending a four-year public institution. Back in 1975–76, by contrast, the maximum Pell grant was equivalent to 84% of that cost. Grant aid programs originally reflected a vision that higher education should be accessible to all students, but today Congress is undermining that vision by allowing funding to erode.

As grant programs have become stingier, student loans (including federally guaranteed loans) have come to comprise a greater portion of financial aid. Because she worked so many hours, Brigit managed to graduate with only around $5,000 of debt. But this is far less than average. Various studies estimate that average student debt upon completion of a four-year degree falls between $12,000 and $19,000, depending on research methodology. Students are graduating from college shouldering more than a gown: their monthly debt payments typically amount to $150 to $200, and last for 10 years.

At least student loans have reasonable interest rates. That makes them quite different from the high-interest credit card debts many students pile up. Credit card companies aggressively market their wares to college students they know are struggling to make ends meet. Issuers customize their standards for college students, lowering or eliminating experience ratings and income requirements. "When you're a freshman," explains Horace, "you apply and you can get any kind of credit you want." Concern about aggressive marketing to students who may not understand the implications of carrying debt has led some universities to put limits on how their students can be solicited. Nonetheless, approximately two-thirds of college students have at least one credit card; these students carry an average balance of $2,748, according to one study reported by the General Accounting Office. Approximately 15% of students with cards have balances over $1,000. The degree to which students use their cards for direct college costs is hard to pin down. The GAO found studies indicating that as many as 21% of card users paid tuition with their cards and 7% used them for room and board.

Horace's story is instructive. He is graduating with $17,000 in debt from a series of government-subsidized and unsubsidized loans. None of his financial aid was grant aid. At one time, he also had $6,000 in credit card debt. During his first year, he says, he would "walk down the hallways, sign up for a card, and get free t-shirts." Enticed by the aggressive marketing, he wound up with six cards that he used to pay for tuition and books until he found steady employment. He has gradually paid off four of the cards, but still owes $2,000 between two of them.

SOCIETY'S COSTS AND BENEFITS

There is a silver lining for students who struggle with course work and paid work, tuition bills and credit card bills. A college education brings tremendous benefits— both tangible economic gains and personal growth. College, as most students today recognize, is an "investment good," and the economic returns are substantial. The U.S. Census Bureau found that in 2000, college graduates earned 80% more than people with a high school diploma. As the U.S. economy has shifted from a manufacturing base, where jobs requiring only a high school diploma were plentiful, to a high-tech, "information-based" service economy, the demand for college graduates has escalated. Of course, the service economy also involves plenty of jobs in sectors like retail and food service. But even when a college degree is unnecessary for explicit job content, employers increasingly use it as a screening device to identify workers who they think will be hard-working and obedient.

So going to college is a little like buying a house: those who can afford the upfront costs reap great financial rewards later. This economic reality has boosted college enrollments despite the financial difficulties. The college enrollment rate of graduating high school students has risen for several decades, peaking in 1997 at 67%. There was a slight reversal as the rate fell to 63% for the high school class of 2000.

The market, however, now has the upper hand in determining who will have access to higher education. Both the federal government and the states have been shifting their responsibility for providing adequate resources for higher education to the private sector and students themselves. Markets allow the well-to-do to pay for tutors, college preparatory courses, and private college education for their children, who go on to keep the so-called "family tradition," while working-class and poorer students are more likely to be excluded from educational opportunities that can transform their lives.

Treating higher education like any other commodity to be distributed by market forces is a dangerous approach. Even the most narrow-minded economists agree that improving access to education generates benefits for society as a whole— it produces what economists call "positive externalities." Better access to education creates higher levels of skill and knowledge in the workforce, for instance. It also allows for the fuller use of one of our most valuable economic resources—our youth.

But restricting access to higher education is wrong for reasons much deeper than the fact that it "underutilizes" people. Education offers people an opportunity to expand their interests, understand human relationships, and develop a moral compass—it is not just job training, but a basis of human development. As Stanford education professor and feminist economist Myra Strober notes, economic theory is "ill suited to convey the complex and transformational goals" of education. It also fails to identify what is really wrong with leaving access to the market: education and development should be for everyone, not just those who can pay.

Viewed from this perspective, access to education should be considered a basic social right due to all people, like health care, child care, and adequate income. In most other highly-industrialized countries, people expect their government to guarantee the opportunities and material support needed to live decently: it is part of government's public purpose to provide for social rights. Access to an affordable education is one of those rights—but one that is now threatened as rising costs collide with declining aid.

CHAPTER 35

Reading, Writing, and . . . Buying?

CONSUMER REPORTS

Gavin Wahl of Palisade, Colo., arrived home from first grade last year toting free book covers with ads for Frosted Flakes, Lay's potato chips, and deodorant. Then 6-year-old Gavin proclaimed Pizza Hut as his favorite pizza. "We don't even go to Pizza Hut," says George Wahl, Gavin's father. He attributes his son's comment to the school's Pizza Hut reading program, which rewards children with pizza coupons.

Gavin also told his parents about a school movie on tooth care. "I'm supposed to brush with Sparkle Crest," he said.

That was the last straw for his father. "He told me what to buy," George Wahl says in disgust. "Now the school is going to be a conduit for this kind of thing."

Advertising to kids is nothing new. But these days, there's a disturbing difference in the quantity and quality of such ads:

- This has become the "decade of sponsored schools and commercialized classrooms," according to a new study that tracked increased media reports of commercialism in the schools by the University of Wisconsin at Milwaukee's Center for the Analysis of Commercialism in Education. The center is a nonprofit research group that receives support from Consumer's Union.
- Not only is advertising in schools pervasive, but some sponsored classroom materials give a biased view of public-policy issues. Workbooks that address global warming, for example, subtly steer class lessons in directions advantageous to the sponsor.
- Outside of school, marketers are milking the "nag factor." They're pitching to kids traditionally "adult" purchases such as cars, vacations, and telephone lines—and are even feeding kids arguments they can make—hoping parents will cave in to their kids' requests.

THE IMPACT

No matter what parents may think of these practices, one thing is clear: Advertisers are winning. Spending by youngsters ages 4 to 12 has tripled in the 1990s, rising to $24.4 billion last year, according to a leading market researchrer, James U. McNeal of Texas A&M University. Moreover, last year children influenced purchases totalling nearly eight times that amount, McNeal says.

At a minimum, ads take power away from parents, says Diane Levin, a professor of education at Boston's Wheelock College who has studied how children respond to toy advertising. "The industry says parents need to decide what's appropriate," she says, "but then they go about using every marketing ploy they can to make it harder for parents to assert their authority." One example she cites: the gift registry at Toys 'R' Us, in which a child generates a list of favored toys by pointing at them with an electronic wand. The message to kids, she says, is that "anything that's out there I can want and nag to get."

Commercial messages in schools also undermine the authority and credibility of teachers and principals. In schools that bolster their budgets by granting exclusive contracts to soft-drink companies, how seriously can students be expected to follow admonitions to limit soda in favor of healthful snacks? Who can forget the headlines from March, when a high school principal suspended an Evans, Ga., student for wearing a Pepsi shirt on the school's "Coke in Education Day"?

As for today's marketers, "These are kids who grew up with advertising. They don't see a problem," says Ellen Wartella, dean of the University of Texas College of Communication. Wartella's research dates back to the 1970s, when she demonstrated that young children have difficulty telling the difference between advertising and other programming.

"I'm not sure we can go back to an age when children weren't commercialized," Wartella adds. "But we certainly have to have standards that say not everything goes."

As of now, we don't. The Federal Trade Commission, the government agency that has done the most recently to protect children, has focused on cases of fraud and deception, not fairness. Watchdog groups such as the Center for Media Education (202 628-2620; *www.cme.org*) have taken it upon themselves to alert the public to marketplace excesses.

Parents themselves don't like advertising's effect on children, according to a 1997 survey by Roper Starch Worldwide. Nearly 80 percent of adults said that marketing and advertising exploit kids by convincing them to buy things that are bad for them or that they don't need.

George Wahl is in this majority. The idea that Gavin will be "a Pepsi drinker for life, and this is something that was planted in his head when he was a toddler, to me that's offensive," he says.

AD CAMPAIGNS

Market researchers probe virtually every aspect of kids' lives, going beyond how kids shop to sample their most intimate thoughts and feelings.

Last year, according to the child-marketing newsletter Selling to Kids, Roper Starch Worldwide and Just Kids Inc. studied kids' daydreams and fantasies, so that these could be incorporated into marketing and advertising programs. They found that 80 percent of U.S. kids daydream about helping people and 24 percent about protecting the environment. Such data, the newsletter says, can provide dividends for companies savvy enough to form the right strategic alliances with environmental groups.

Researchers even try to gauge how effectively kids nag their parents. Recently, Selling to Kids described a study by Western International Media, "The Nag Factor," which found that 3- to 8-year-olds were 14 percent more likely to get parents to buy a toy if they emphasized that the toy was important to them. "It's not just getting kids to whine, it's giving them a specific reason to ask for the product," a Western International official says in the newsletter.

Marketers also play on kids' emotional needs. Gene Del Vecchio, a senior partner at advertising agency Ogilvy & Mather Worldwide, regales attendees at child-marketing conferences with techniques featured from his recent book "Creating Ever-Cool: A Marketer's Guide to a Kid's Heart." Del Vecchio's key principle for making a product cool: "Satisfy a kid's timeless emotional need(s) but routinely dress it up in a current fad or trend." These needs include empowerment (because kids are lowest in society's power structure), peer approval, gender identification, and the desire to be a couple of years older.

How do marketers view children? Brochures from industry conferences refer to goals such as "successful ways of reaching kids and their gatekeepers in schools." Other brochures say:

- "Today's savvy kids are tomorrow's loyal customers. It's not enough to throw crayons and a placemat at a child and expect any kind of loyalty. Kids need more sophisticated and challenging ways to learn about your product or service—and to remember you fondly for years to come."
- "Kids are intensely concerned about the environment. . . . Find out how you can put these findings to work for you in giving the 'cool' factor to your marketing strategy."
- "We will explore creating an intimate relationship with teens—one based on an intimate understanding of their lives and instincts, and reflecting them back in advertising."

SCHOOLS ON THE BLOCK

It's easy to understand why marketers focus on schools. Sponsoring educational programs achieves several goals: It builds good community relations by associating a company with a good cause; it penetrates a six-hour time period—9 a.m. to 3 p.m.—that's been traditionally off-limits to advertisers; and it gains priceless credibility for a company through association with trusted teachers.

Educators themselves have not yet come to terms with the issues raised by commercialism in schools. The University of Wisconsin study found little discussion of these issues in publications by and for educators.

The University of Wisconsin media analysis followed several types of school-house commercialism: sponsorship of school events; exclusive sales of products like soft drinks; incentive programs such as collecting product labels; appropriation of space such as walls and bulletin boards; sponsored educational materials; and provision of electronic equipment or programming in return for the right to advertise. (The report is posted at *www.uwm.edu/Dept/CACE.*)

Here are some ways kids now receive commercial messages in school:

- Eight million students are required to watch Channel One, a news broadcast that includes commercials.
- More than half of American classrooms—25 million students—receive advertising-laden book covers, and 6 million schoolchildren receive advertising-filled cafeteria menus.
- Scholastic Inc., a respected educational publisher, continues to trade on its reputation by producing sponsored educational material for a variety of marketers under the Scholastic name, some of it thinly veiled promotions for Hollywood blockbusters.

Some school materials engage in subtle politicking. Teacher and student guides for Chevron's free school video on the Greenhouse effect contain valid information about global warming, but they also steer students in the industry's direction (one of the biggest man-made causes of these gases is automobile emissions). For example, most scientists now agree that global warming is occurring. But the guide repeatedly stresses disagreements among scientists over the issue. One exercise encourages students to discuss "What, if anything, can be done to safeguard the public against errors in judgment by policymakers, who may be reacting to political pressures?"

In another activity, students must decide whether certain scenarios promote or reduce atmospheric greenhouse gases. An obvious contributor to the problem—the single-driver automobile trip—isn't mentioned.

The value of influencing teachers has also not been lost on a group of oil, chemical, pharmaceutical, and other companies who fund the Keystone Science School in Keystone, Colo., a division of the nonprofit Keystone Center. In the school's annual Key Issues program, companies committed to "changing and enhancing the way science and environmental issues are taught in classrooms"—companies such as Dow Chemical, DuPont, and Union Carbide—sponsor hundreds of teachers. The stated mission is to help teachers understand various viewpoints; to be sure, the corporate viewpoint is among them. A liaison from the sponsoring company can help teachers maintain their corporate relationship through the years.

THE HOME FRONT

Even in the home, where television ads aimed at kids have been standard fare for decades, marketers are finding ways to increase their presence.

For example, parents who leave their set tuned to the Public Broadcasting System, confident that their kids are getting a break from advertising, are in for a rude surprise. "Barney & Friends," "Arthur," and other favorite shows feature ads for Chuck E. Cheese's, McDonald's, and Kellogg's Frosted Flakes. Donna Williams, a PBS spokeswoman, called them "enhanced underwriting credits," and some do offer positive educational messages. But the likes of Ronald McDonald asking, "Did somebody say McDonald's?" on PBS member station WNET in New York breaches the station's sponsorship guidelines, which prohibit the appearance of company mascots. The ad was deemed appropriate because, overall, it's noncommercial and promotes "using your imagination," says Katherine Schultheis of WNET.

Marketers are also running child-oriented ads for whole categories of products—such as cars and vacations—traditionally associated with adults. Last year, kids ages 4 to 12 influenced $188 billion in purchases—$17.7 billion in car sales alone, according to market researcher McNeal. It's no wonder, then, that Chevrolet ran a two-page spread for its Venture minivan in Sports Illustrated for Kids, with appealing scrapbook photos of Mom, Dad, the kids, and the family dog.

Now that many families have embraced the home computer, millions of children surf the World Wide Web, a trend marketers have quickly picked up on. The web has become a gold mine for companies that practice database marketing—using mailing lists of children to target them with advertising. Here's how it works: Companies use eye-catching graphics, interactive games, and chat rooms to attract children, then collect their name, address, and other information, often without a parent's knowledge. In a report to Congress this June, the FTC noted that 89 percent of the children's web sites it surveyed collect personal information from children, while less than 10 percent provide for parental control, such as the ability to review, correct, or delete information. The commission recommended that Congress pass legislation to let parents take control back from marketers.

Marketing and issue messages on the web are no less useful than sponsored school materials for shaping kids' views on public-policy issues. On Shell's G-Whiz Kids site (*www.shellus.com/whizkid*), for example, kids earn a "Certificate of Advanced Energy Studies" by teaching others about Shell's reasons why "gasoline is fueling America's future." Chevron's kids' site (*www.chevroncars.com*) teaches children that America's security and way of life depend on oil, "the fuel that makes our country go."

PART ELEVEN

Crime and Justice

In recent years, crime has often been perceived by the public as America's number one social problem. Violent crime has made many Americans afraid to walk their streets at night, and has greatly diminished the quality of life in many parts of the United States. And though levels of violent crime are not as high as they were at their peak in the early 1990s, they remain higher than those of other advanced industrial societies—despite dramatic increases in the number of people who have been put behind bars.

Many Americans believe that we have been shockingly lenient with criminals. In the excerpt we reprint here, Elliott Currie argues that this is a myth, and examines the factual underpinnings of this myth—as well as the belief that our investments in prisons are cost effective and efficacious. The reality is that we tend to be quite punitive with those "street" criminals we actually catch—considerably more so than most other countries. And, with more than two million people in our jails and prisons on any given day, we are becoming more so all the time.

Politicians, however, looking for quick fixes to the crime problem, have passed a variety of even more punitive measures in recent years—including so-called three strikes and you're out laws, mandating 25-year to life sentences for criminals convicted of three felonies. In California, the third felony may be a relatively minor offense, such as stealing a bicycle or possessing a small amount of drugs. Despite the harshness of this law, it has been recently upheld by the U.S. Supreme Court, which ruled in 2003 that a sentence of 25 years to life for stealing three golf clubs did not constitute the "cruel and unusual punishment" prohibited by our constitution.

These laws are surely "tough," but are they effective? Jerome H. Skolnick calls California's three-strikes law a "wild pitch"—arguing that the law is too rigid and will result in a vast and costly expansion of the prison system into a home for aged and low-level offenders. In response, John J. DiIulio maintains that, as a nation, we are actually soft on criminals, allowing some of the most dangerous to bargain their way into lesser charges at the front end of the system, while releasing them early to parole and community supervision at the back. In his reply, Skolnick says that DiIulio's generalizations are inaccurate, and offers data to show why.

From 1994, when the law was passed, to 1999, 47,861 felons were sentenced under its provisions. This figure includes 5,419 who have received sentences of at least 25 years to life under the law. Three strikes has also generated sharp racial disparities. African Americans were arrested for felonies at 4.7 times the rate of whites and imprisoned for a third "strike" at more than 13 times the rate of whites, suggesting that prosecutors charge such strikes differently depending on the skin color of the defendant.

California is not unique in this respect. One of the most striking, and disturbing, developments in American criminal justice has been the great increases in the number of African Americans behind bars. As of 2002, roughly 12 percent of black men aged 25–34 were currently in jail or prison, and the U.S. Department of Justice estimates that more than one in four of all black men will spend some time in a state or federal prison during their lifetime.[1]

The article by Philippe Bourgois puts a human face on such statistics. Bourgois, an anthropologist, spent several years "hanging out" with a group of young drug dealers in New York City. He concluded that drugs in the inner city are a symptom of a profound "social marginalization and alienation" and that the underground economy of drug dealing has become the fastest-growing "equal opportunity employer" for poor young men. For though selling drugs actually brings in a relatively meager "salary" for the majority of dealers, it compares favorably with the low-wage, dead-end jobs that are the only legitimate work most of them have ever experienced. It is young men like these who increasingly make up our swollen prison population.

At the other end of the scale is another kind of criminal—the affluent offenders, often corporate executives, who commit so-called "white collar" crimes. The term was coined by an American criminologist, Edwin Sutherland, in the 1930s to mean crimes committed by otherwise "respectable" people in the course of their business. It has long been understood that these "respectable" offenders are treated very differently by the criminal justice system than the ones who appear in the articles by Bourgois and Skolnick. They are far less likely to ever see the inside of a prison or jail, and unlikely, on the whole, to stay long if they do. But the article here by Ken Silverstein shows something more: that even companies that are repeat offenders, whose crimes kill and injure people and who may receive substantial fines as a result, are often rewarded by billions of dollars in government contracts. Indeed, some of the biggest government contractors in America are also among the worst and most persistent violators of federal environmental and health and safety laws. In this case, if in few others, we are indeed lenient in our treatment of criminals.

ENDNOTE

1. U.S. Bureau of Justice Statistics, *Prisons at Midyear 2002,* Washington, DC, April 2003: U.S. Bureau of Justice Statistics, *Lifetime Likelihood of Going to Prison,* Washington, DC, 1997.

CHAPTER 36

The Myth of Leniency

ELLIOTT CURRIE

Many Americans believe that the main reason we remain a frighteningly violent country is that we are shockingly lenient with criminals. That would seem, at first glance, a difficult position to maintain in the country that boasts the developed world's highest imprisonment rate. And, in fact, the idea that serious, violent criminals are treated leniently in the United States *is* a myth. But it is a myth that is deeply entrenched in the public imagination. How is it possible to maintain that America is "soft" on criminals in the face of the enormous increases in punishment in recent years?

One way to make this case is simply to downplay the magnitude of our recent increases in incarceration. Thus James Q. Wilson speaks of our "inching up" the costs of offending in recent years, a jarringly peculiar way to describe the quintupling of the prison population. Others simply sidestep the extraordinary growth of imprisonment and argue that misguided liberal policies allow most offenders to go unpunished and vast numbers of "known violent predators," in the phrase of the conservative Council on Crime in America, to run loose. William Bennett, John J. DiIulio, and James P. Walters, the authors of the leading recent conservative tract on crime, put it this way in the course of arguing for "more incarceration":

> Today and every day the "justice" system permits known, convicted, violent and repeat criminals, adult and juvenile, to get away with murder and mayhem on the streets. Criminals who have repeatedly violated the life, liberty, and property of others are routinely set free to do it all over again.

The myth of leniency is propped up by several "facts" that have been recycled repeatedly in popular and academic publications across the country in recent years. It is common to read, for example, that the overwhelming majority of violent criminals are let off without punishment, and that indeed "only 1 in 100" violent crimes results in a prison sentence; that in the rare cases when offenders are punished, the sentences they receive, even for heinous crimes, are shockingly, even ludicrously, short and that most violent criminals are not put in prison at all but are "community-based"—that is, on pretrial release, probation, or parole—an arrangement that allows them to commit further heinous crimes. All of these "facts" carry the same basic message: the heart of our crime problem lies in misguided leniency—"the failure to restrain known violent offenders," as the Council on Crime in America puts it. Contrary to what the figures on the swollen prisons would seem to tell us, the reality is that we are letting most criminals off with little or no punishment—and they are repaying us by murdering, raping, and robbing with impunity.

The prescription that follows from this diagnosis is short on specifics, but its general direction is clear. "Our view," writes the Council,

> is that America needs to put more violent and repeat criminals, adult and juvenile, behind bars longer, to see to it that truth-in-sentencing and such kindred laws as are presently on the books are fully and faithfully executed, and to begin reinventing probation and parole agencies in ways that will enable them to supervise their charges, enforce the law, and enhance public safety.

It is important to be clear: no one denies that serious offenders are sometimes let off lightly, or that we should do all we can to prevent such miscarriages of justice. But these critics are saying something more: that lenient sentencing and "revolving-door justice" are the norm in America and are responsible for America's continuing crime problem. What do we make of this argument? How do we square this picture of dramatic leniency with the reality of bursting prisons?

We can't. All of these claims are at best disingenuous, at worst painfully transparent distortions of the way criminal justice in America really works.

Consider first the statement, repeated over and over again by John DiIulio and the Council and picked up by opinion-page editors around the country, that "only 1 in 100 violent crimes results in a prison sentence." The figure itself is technically correct. In 1992, for example, there were over 10 million crimes of violence recorded in the annual survey of criminal victimization carried out by the U.S. Bureau of Justice Statistics; and, as Bennett, DiIulio, and Walters put it, "only about 100,000 persons convicted of a violent crime went to state prison." But do the numbers really tell us that "revolving-door justice" lets the wicked off with a slap on the wrist, or less?

Not at all. To begin with, it is important to understand that the majority of violent crimes are not serious ones. Thus, in 1995, 6.2 million were "simple assaults"; almost 5 million—more than half of all violent crimes—"simple assaults without injury." We are talking here about schoolyard fights or minor barroom altercations, which few would argue should result in a state prison sentence. (Most assaults, too, are "attempted" or "threatened," not "completed.") Another bit of sleight of hand is that the figure of 100,000 sent to state prison conveniently leaves out those who go to local jails, federal prisons, or juvenile institutions—implying that not going to state prison means that the offender is set free, which distorts the picture considerably.

But there is a much more fundamental problem. It is indeed true that most crimes—including many very serious ones—don't result in punishment. As every serious student of crime knows, however, that isn't primarily because the justice system is lenient with offenders; it is because the vast majority of crimes do not enter the criminal justice system at all. The Council on Crime in America provides the basic figures itself: of the more than 10 million violent crimes picked up in the national victim survey in 1992, only a little over 4 million were even *reported* to police. To be sure, more serious crimes of violence (as well as crimes like auto theft, which are reported in order to collect insurance) are more often reported. But even for robbery and assault the percentages are relatively low, and they are lower still for rape and domestic violence (more than 9 in 10 motor vehicle thefts, but only two-thirds of robberies, half of aggravated assaults, and one third of rapes are reported to the police, according to the victim surveys). And of those violent crimes that *are* reported, other than homicide, the majority do not result in an arrest (are not "cleared," in the language of criminal justice). Of those 10 million violent victimizations, just 641,000 led to an arrest at all. Hence, that "1 in 100" figure has already been transformed beyond recognition—for only 6 in 100 even enter the system. And once in the system, more offenses are dropped for lack of evidence, or otherwise dismissed, or the defendant is acquitted. The result is that the 10 million crimes are followed by only about 165,000 *convictions*—meaning that most offenses never arrive at the stage of sentencing at all.

A recent analysis, conducted by the *Los Angeles Times,* of 32 homicides that took place in the course of one week in the summer of 1994 in Los Angeles County illustrates how difficult it can be to bring a crime to the sentencing stage—even for a crime that is among those *most* likely to result in arrest and conviction. Nearly half of the 32 murder cases in that week did not result in an arrest; of those that did, a fifth were dismissed, or the suspects released or acquitted. A look at the circumstances of these cases shows some of the reasons why:

> Francisco Robert Vasquez, 20, is shot numerous times in an East Los Angeles alley. Vasquez may have been killed by fellow gang members, police say. Empty shell casings are found at the scene. But no gun is found and no suspects are arrested.

> Near MacArthur Park, at a drug sales corner controlled by 18th Street gang members, Louie Herrera, 27, is killed in a burst of gunfire. A suspect is identified, but charges are dropped after a witness becomes uncooperative, then disappears.

As these cases show, homicides that take place in the murky world of urban gangs and drugs are hard to solve. And the difficulty of achieving solid arrests and convictions is even greater for most other serious offenses. It follows that if we can improve our ability to make good arrests, and to convict those arrested, we might be able to make significant inroads against violent crime—an issue to which we'll return (indeed, the proportion of violent-crime cases that result in convictions has already increased in recent years). But it is *not* true that the gap between the large number of violent crimes committed and the much smaller number that are punished results from our leniency toward convicted offenders—from the fact that, as DiIulio puts it, "our criminal justice system is not handing down sentences to fit the crimes."

If our concern is whether we are encouraging crime by failing to punish known offenders, the real question is how many of those who are actually caught and convicted are then put behind bars. And here the evidence is unequivocal. We've already seen that the chances of incarceration for violent offenses have risen sharply in recent years in the United States; as a result, the probability that a convicted violent offender will go behind bars is very high indeed, and for repeat offenders a virtual certainty. In 1994, 77 percent of offenders convicted of felony robbery went to prison; another 11 percent went to jail, making the total incarcerated almost 9 in 10. Similarly, 88 percent of felons convicted of rape were incarcerated, four out of five of them in prison. Keep in mind that these are *averages* that lump together first-time offenders with repeaters, and less serious versions of these crimes with more serious ones. The kinds of offenders that critics like DiIulio say are now allowed to roam free—serious, violent repeaters—have been going behind bars routinely for many years, and the proportion has risen substantially since the 1970s.

But what about the *severity* of their sentences? Isn't it true that even those we do send to prison get out after a laughably short time—thus both subverting justice and encouraging predators? Here too the myth of leniency is widespread. Many Americans believe that we generally let convicted criminals off with a slap on the wrist, even those guilty of heinous offenses; John DiIulio insists that "hard time for hardened criminals is rare." Once again, that view would seem hard to reconcile with the enormous increases in imprisonment over the past twenty-five years. How is it possible to make this argument? What evidence is offered in its support?

Here is one example. In 1993 Senator Phil Gramm, later to run for president, wrote an op-ed piece in the *New York Times* entitled "Don't Let Judges Set Crooks Free." Gramm wrote that America was "deluged by a tidal wave of crime," and he identified the "main culprit" as "a criminal justice system in which the cost of committing crimes is so shamelessly cheap that it fails to deter potential criminals." Years of "soft sentencing" had brought "a dramatic decline in the cost of committing a crime and a dramatic increase in crime." As evidence, Gramm pointed to a study by an economist named Morgan Reynolds, of Texas A&M University, which has been widely cited by proponents of the myth of leniency. Reynolds's study purported to estimate the amount of time offenders committing various kinds of crimes could "expect to serve" in prison as of 1990. And the calculations are indeed starting. According to Gramm, a murderer can "expect" to spend just 1.8 years in prison. A rape earns 60 days. A robbery, according to these "findings," results in 23 days behind bars, and a car theft just a day and a half. Proof positive, according to Gramm, that a "soft" justice system is responsible for the tidal wave of crime.

The figures have been used over and over again to demonstrate the extraordinary leniency of the American justice system. And were the implications drawn from them even remotely true it would indeed be a scandal. If judges were in fact sentencing rapists to just two months behind bars and letting robbers free in less than a month, we would have a bizarre justice system indeed. But anyone who has ever followed a serious criminal trial, or known anyone who was actually sentenced to prison, knows instantly that there is something very wrong with these figures.

The standard data on the length of sentences for various crimes are published by the U.S. Bureau of Justice Statistics on the basis of periodic surveys of prison systems across the country. There are complexities involved in measuring the length of the time prisoners actually serve; it makes a considerable difference, for example, whether we try to measure it by looking at average time served by prisoners who are *released* or by estimating the time that will be served by offenders now going *into* prison. The figures on time served by released prisoners reflect the sentencing and parole policies in force some years before, when they were sentenced, while the expected time to be served for new admissions is what a convicted offender can *now* expect—which, under current conditions, will be longer. But however we measure it, the average time serious offenders spend behind bars bears no resemblance to the numbers cited by Gramm.

Among offenders sentenced in 1994—the most recent year available—the estimated time to be served in prison for murder was 127 months, or about 10 years. That figure, it should be noted, markedly understates the penalties for murder, for two reasons. First, it includes what in most states is called "nonnegligent manslaughter," a lesser offense that carries a far lower sentence than murder, and thus brings down the average. Even more importantly, the figure of 10 years does *not* include the roughly 27 percent of murderers who are sentenced to life imprisonment or death, which reduces the average far more. But even with these sentences excluded, the current penalty for murder is still many times higher than the figure Gramm provides. The same disparity holds true for the other crimes as well. The average expected time to be served for a convicted rapist in 1994 was not 60 days but 85 *months,* or just over 7 years. For robbery it was not 23 days but 51 *months,* or well over 4 years.

These figures on expected time to be served also put into perspective the frequent complaint that because of parole and "good time" provisions, most prisoners serve only a fraction of the sentence handed down in court—another sign of leniency run wild. In 1994, the Justice Department estimated that offenders sentenced for violent crimes would serve on average about 46 percent of their sentences, 54 percent for rape. But whether this is an indication of leniency obviously depends on the length of the original sentence. If all first-time robbers were sentenced to fifty-year terms, the fact that they wound up serving just half of that sentence would probably not trouble even the most punitive among us. The United States, as we've seen, generally imposes very harsh sentences by international standards; the widespread use of sentence reductions serves only to bring our average time served for serious violent crimes roughly into line with some (but not all) other advanced industrial countries. Robbers sentenced in 1994 received an average term of not quite 10 years, of which they would probably serve 4 years and 3 months. Rapists received over 13 years on average and could expect to serve over 7.

Note too that the time that offenders are likely to serve behind bars for some offenses has risen with stunning rapidity in recent years, as sentences have gotten harsher and as parole and "good time" provisions have increasingly come under siege. In just four years, from 1990 to 1994, the estimated time to be served in state prison for murder went up by two years and for rape by eleven months. Among newly committed state prison inmates generally, the estimated minimum time to be served rose from an average of thirty-one months in 1985 to forty-three months in 1995.

It is sometimes claimed that average prison sentences have *decreased* in recent years—proof, again, that we have in fact become "softer," not harder, on criminals.

The U.S. Bureau of Justice Statistics, during the Bush administration, released statistics purporting to show that "there is no evidence that the time served in prison, prior to the first release on a sentence, has been increasing"—that indeed the median time served by state prison inmates had dropped from 17 months in 1981 to 13 months in 1988. The implication was that despite the "get tough" campaigns of the 1970s and 1980s we were, oddly enough, more lenient at the end of the period than at the beginning. That was highly unlikely on the face of it, and the bureau's own chart showed that time served had risen for robbery and sexual assault and stayed level for homicide—while falling for lesser crimes, notably drug offenses and larceny. And there lies the key to the overall drop in the average time served in prison. Drug offenders were 8 percent of the inmate population in 1980 and 26 percent by 1993; violent offenders fell from 57 to 45 percent of the total. Since, with some important exceptions, drug offenders were being sentenced to shorter terms, that meant a flood of inmates with less severe sentences entering the persons, bringing down the average. Think of what happens when a river floods: say the usual depth of the river is twenty feet. The flood submerges hundreds of square miles of surrounding countryside under five feet of water. The *average* depth of the water has accordingly fallen considerably—small comfort, of course, to those whose homes and farms are now underwater.

Now, reasonable people may disagree about whether the existing sentences for violent crimes are appropriate. Some may feel that an average of seven years in prison for a rape is too little. But these actual sentence lengths are light-years away from the figures cited by Gramm (and others) to demonstrate that "soft sentencing" has flooded the nation with crime. What accounts for this wide disparity? Where did Reynolds get his numbers? The trick, again (as with the "1 in 100" figure) is that the numbers have very little to do with how "toughly" or "leniently" we are treating offenders in the courts—with "soft sentencing"—but primarily with the low rates of *arrest* for most offenses. Reynolds's figure of 23 days for robbery is derived by dividing the average time served by the robbers who are arrested and convicted *by the total number of robberies committed,* whether anyone is ever caught or not, much less convicted. It is true that, by this calculation, the "average cost" of a robbery is low—but that is because the average robbery isn't followed by an arrest, much less a conviction. Thus in 1994 about 1.3 million robberies took place, of which about 619,000 were reported to the police. But there were fewer than 46,000 adult felony convictions for robbery, of which almost all—more than 40,000—resulted in some incarceration in a jail or prison; and as we've seen, robbers who went to prison could expect to stay for well over 4 years. Again, if we could improve our ability to catch robbers in the first place, we might substantially increase the "average cost" of robberies. But it is pure sleight of hand to argue, as Gramm and others do, that weak *sentencing* practices account for the numbers, or that we treat the robbers we catch with shocking leniency.

Indeed, what the figures on the relatively low percentage of crime resulting in punishment really add up to is a profound argument for a greater emphasis on crime *prevention*—as opposed to punishment after the fact. For even if we assume that we could boost our capacity to apprehend robbers, no one seriously argues that we will ever arrive at the point where most robberies result in an arrest; and therefore no amount of increasing punishment will make as much difference as its proponents hope. That is surely not the conclusion that the purveyors of the "1 in 100" figure intended. But it is the only one that stands the test of hard scrutiny.

The fact that we already give relatively lengthy sentences to violent criminals—especially repeaters—helps explain why the rash of "three strikes and you're out" laws passed in recent years have in practice had much less impact than many people expected. Critics of these laws thought states would go broke trying to accommodate a flood of new prisoners; supporters thought large drops in violent crime were sure to come as huge numbers of violent predators roaming the streets finally got their just desserts. What has actually happened confounds both expectations, especially in those jurisdictions—which include most of the states as well as the federal government—where three-strikes laws are aimed solely at violent repeat offenders. As a study by the Campaign for an Effective Crime Policy has shown, none of those states has put many violent offenders away under their new laws. That is surely not because prosecutors are unwilling to charge offenders under the "tough" statutes. It may be in part because some judges, in some jurisdictions, are still managing to sentence offenders in ways that circumvent the harshest provisions of these laws. But it is *mainly* because most repeat violent offenders who come before the courts in these states would have been sentenced to "hard" time under the laws that already existed.

In California, where the three-strikes law was broadly drawn to target relatively low-level property and drug offenders as well as violent repeaters (any felony can trigger a third strike, leading to a mandatory sentence of twenty-five years to life), the number of people sentenced under the law has, unsurprisingly, been higher. But the proportion of *violent* offenders sentenced has still been relatively low. As of 1995, more people had been sentenced under California's three-strikes law for simple marijuana possession than for murder, rape, and kidnapping combined, and more for drug possession generally than for *all* violent offenses. Even in that state, where legislators led a stampede to pass the three-strikes law by arguing that hordes of violent repeaters were roaming the streets unpunished, the number of offenders given third *or second* "strikes" for a violent offense was fewer than 3,000 over the first two years of the law. And most of those violent offenders would have gone to prison *without* the new law. Before the passage of the three-strikes law, California already had on the books a mandatory five-year "enhancement" for the second conviction for many felonies, as well as a "habitual offender" statute providing for life imprisonment (with a minimum of twenty years before parole) for violent offenders who had caused "great bodily harm" to victims and had already served two prison sentences for similar offenses. In short, California's prisons have not been flooded with repeat violent offenders by the three-strikes law, mainly because such offenders were already being sentenced to relatively "tough" terms *before* the new law.

Again, no one denies that truly dangerous people sometimes slip out of the system. But to acknowledge that mistakes do occur is not the same as believing that the system as a whole is "soft" on serious violent criminals. And ironically, the wholesale return of genuinely "bad apples" to the streets has sometimes happened precisely because of unreflective efforts to "get tough," notably in states where dangerous criminals have been released to make room in overcrowded prisons for far less serious offenders incarcerated under mandatory sentences. The most studied case is Florida, where—despite the addition of 25,000 new prison beds—a huge influx of drug offenders during the 1980s resulted in massive prison overcrowding, forcing the state to establish an early-release program, which deposited tens of thousands of offenders who did *not* have mandatory sentences onto the streets. That number included a great many violent criminals, even robbers and rapists, most of whom received little serious supervision once in the community. (The state legislature has recently shifted its policy, to target incarceration on violent offenders and seek out alternatives for the nonviolent.)

With occasional exceptions, then, it remains true that serious, violent criminals, especially if they are repeaters, are likely to do hard time if caught and convicted. But what about the fact that so many violent criminals are out on bail, or on probation or parole? Doesn't that show that we are shockingly "soft"? Wouldn't cracking down on such people by abolishing parole altogether—and putting many of those now on probation behind bars—have a dramatic effect on the crime rate?

Probably not. Here the problems are more genuine. But they are more complicated, and more difficult to solve, than critics like the Council on Crime in America would have us believe. Their argument begins with the undisputed observation that, at any given point, more people who have committed crimes are under some form of "community" supervision than in prison and that the number of "community-based" offenders has grown along with the rise in the prison population. (Between 1980 and 1994, the number of prison inmates increased at an annual average of 8.4 percent, the parole population by 8.5 percent, and the probation population by 7.2 percent.) But it is not apparent why this should be taken as evidence of a "weak" justice system. John DiIulio, for example, argues that the fact that in 1991, 590,000 people who had been convicted of a violent crime were "residing in our communities" on parole or probation, while only 372,000 were in prison, represents "another sobering example of how the scales are tipping" toward the criminal. But that conclusion doesn't follow. Unless we believe that everyone accused of a crime ought to be detained until trial, that everyone convicted of an offense—no matter how minor—should be sent to jail or prison, and that all of those sent to prison should stay there for the rest of their lives, it is not clear why the sheer fact of growth in the number of people on pretrial release, probation, or parole is a sign of either leniency or bad policy.

The real issue is whether we are allowing the *wrong* people to remain free—whether large numbers of "known violent predators" who ought to be behind bars are being released into the community. The Council on Crime in America insists that they are, and points to statistics showing that large proportions of violent crimes (up to a third, depending on the jurisdiction and the offense) are committed by offenders who are on probation, parole, or pretrial release. Many Americans likewise believe that large numbers of predators are routinely released to community supervision, and their belief is fed by sensational media anecdotes about horrible crimes committed by parolees and offenders released on bail. Again, no one denies that such tragedies happen, or that we should do all we can to prevent them. But do these figures really tell us that we are typically lenient with "known, violent predators"?

No. To begin with, the numbers, though (usually) technically correct, are, once again, misleadingly presented. The Washington-based Sentencing Project offers this useful example: suppose in a given county there are a thousand offenders under pretrial release. There are also three murders, one of which was committed by an offender under pretrial supervision. Thus the *proportion of murders* accounted for by pretrial releasees is a substantial one-third. But the other side of the coin is that *only one in one thousand* pretrial releasees committed a murder—which suggests that trying to prevent that murder by incarcerating all the offenders we now release before trial would be extraordinarily expensive and indeed, for practical purposes, probably impossible.

There is another, even more fundamental, problem with the assertion that we are letting hordes of violent offenders go free even though we *know* they are dangerous characters. Consider this example. A young man is arrested in a big, crime-ridden city for a minor drug deal. Because he has no prior arrests and no known history of violence, he is given a year's probation. While on probation he kills an acquaintance in a fight. Is it meaningful to say the murder resulted from the "failure to restrain" a known violent offender? Not really, because it is hard to conceive of a reasonable argument that would have justified putting him in prison for a long time on the strength of what was known about him. Could we improve our capacity to *predict* which among the vast pool of minor offenders who come into the courts are truly dangerous—thus ensuring that the violent do not elude our control? Maybe. But it is important to remember that our criminal justice systems *already* try to do just that, and many have adopted elaborate risk-assessment procedures, backed by considerable research and experience, to guide those decisions. Hence, realistically, our ability to get *much* better at predicting which of those offenders poses a high enough risk to justify lengthy incarceration is limited.

What holds for probation also applies to parole. Many people believe that if we abolished parole altogether, we could sharply reduce violent crime, and that belief is based in part on the reality that heinous crimes are sometimes committed by people on parole. But unless we believe that everyone convicted of a crime of violence—of whatever seriousness—should stay in prison for the rest of their lives, most *will* at some point be released to the community—and it is not clear why it would be better for them to be in the community *without* supervision than with it. The real question, for both probation and parole, is whether we can do a better job than we now do of monitoring and supervising offenders in the community and thereby reduce the risks that they will do harm. And here the answer is certainly yes. Many probation and parole agencies in the United States, especially in the big cities, are stretched well past the point of effectiveness, their ability to provide meaningful supervision of offenders drastically eroded by years of fiscal starvation and caseloads that can run into the hundreds. The Council on Crime in America, to their credit, reject the idea that all offenders necessarily belong behind bars and suggest that improving the capacity of parole and probation agencies to supervise them outside prison walls makes eminent sense. What they do *not* say, however, is that one of the main reasons why the effectiveness of the probation and parole systems has been so badly compromised is that we have systematically disparaged what they do as "soft" on crime while diverting the money we could have used to improve them into the prisons. We desperately need better community supervision of offenders. But we are unlikely to get it unless we rein in the rush toward indiscriminate incarceration.

As importantly, if we want to prevent crimes committed by "community-based" offenders, we will need to invest more in programs to provide those we *do* incarcerate with a better chance of succeeding on the outside when they are released, as nearly all of them will be. But it should be obvious that if we make no effort to improve the capacity of ex-offenders to live and work productively outside prison walls, we shouldn't profess great surprise when many of them fail—especially if they are also returning to communities with few and perhaps diminishing opportunities for success. And we should not blame that failure on the leniency of the justice system.

CHAPTER 37

Wild Pitch

"Three Strikes, You're Out" and Other Bad Calls on Crime

JEROME H. SKOLNICK

According to the pundits, the polls, and the politicians, violent crime is now America's number one problem. If the problems were properly defined and the lessons of past efforts were fully absorbed, this could be an opportunity to set national crime policy on a positive course. Instead, it is a dangerous moment. Intuition is driving the country toward desperate and ineffectual responses that will drive up prison costs, divert tax dollars from other vital purposes, and leave the public as insecure and dissatisfied as ever.

The pressures pushing federal and state politicians to vie for the distinction of being toughest on crime do not come only from apprehensive voters and the tabloid press. Some of the leading organs of elite opinion, notably the *Wall Street Journal*, have celebrated gut-level, impulsive reactions. In one *Journal* column ("Crime Solution: Lock 'em Up"), Ben J. Wattenberg writes that criminologists don't know what works.

What works is what everyone intuitively knows: "A thug in prison cannot shoot your sister." In another *Journal* column ("The People Want Revenge"), the conservative intellectual Paul Johnson argues that government is failing ordinary people by ignoring their retributive wishes. Ordinary people, he writes, want neither to understand criminals nor to reform them. "They want them punished as severely and cheaply as possible."

Johnson is partly right and mostly wrong. Ordinary people want more than anything to walk the streets safely and to protect their families and their homes. Intuitively, like Wattenberg, many believe that more prisons and longer sentences offer safety along with punishment. But, especially in dealing with crime, intuition isn't always a sound basis for judgment.

The United States already has the highest rate of imprisonment of any major nation. The prisons have expanded enormously in recent years in part because of get-tough measures sending low-level drug offenders to jail. Intuitions were wrong: the available evidence does not suggest that imprisoning those offenders has made the public safer.

The current symbol of the intuitive lock-'em-up response is "three strikes and you're out"—life sentences for criminals convicted of three violent or serious felonies. The catchy slogan appears to have mesmerized politicians from one coast to the other and across party lines. Three-strikes fever began in the fall of 1993 in the wake of the intense media coverage of the abduction and murder of a 12-year-old California girl, Polly Klaas, who was the victim, according to police, of a criminal with a long and violent record. California's Republican Governor Pete Wilson took up the call for three strikes, and on March 7 the California legislature overwhelmingly approved the proposal. Even New York Governor Mario Cuomo endorsed a three strikes measure. The U.S. Senate has passed a crime bill that adopts three strikes as well as a major expansion of the federal role in financing state prisons and stiffening state sentencing policy. In his 1994 State of the Union address, President Clinton singled out the Senate legislation and three strikes for praise.

But will three strikes work? Teenagers and young men in their twenties commit the vast majority of violent offenses. The National Youth Survey, conducted by Colorado criminologist Delbert S. Elliott, found that serious violent offenses (aggravated-assault, rape, and robbery involving some injury or weapon) peak at age 17. The rate is half as much at age 24 and declines significantly as offenders mature into their thirties.

If we impose life sentences on serious violent offenders on their third conviction —after they have served two sentences—we will generally do so in the twilight of their criminal careers. Three strikes laws will eventually fill our prisons with geriatric offenders, whose care will be increasingly expensive when their propensities to commit crime are at the lowest.

Take the case of "Albert," described in the *New York Times* not long ago by Mimi Silbert, president of the Delancey Street Foundation in San Francisco. At age 10, Albert was the youngest member of a barrio gang. By the time he was sent to San Quentin at the age of 19, he had committed 27 armed robberies and fathered two children. Now 36, he is a plumber and substitute teacher who has for years been crime-free, drug-free, and violence-free. According to Silbert, the Delancey Street program has turned around the lives of more than 10,000 Alberts in the past 23 years.

To imprison the Alberts of the world for life makes sense if the purpose is retribution. But if life imprisonment is supposed to increase public safety, we will be disappointed with the results. To achieve that purpose, we need to focus on preventing violent crimes committed by high-risk youths. That is where the real problem lies.

The best that can be said of some three-strikes proposals is that they would be drawn so narrowly that they would have little effect. The impact depends on which felonies count as strikes. Richard H. Girgenti, director of the New York State Division of Criminal Justice Services, says that the measure supported by Governor

Cuomo would affect only 300 people a year and be coupled with the release of non-violent prisoners. President Clinton is also supporting a version of three strikes that is more narrowly drawn than California's. Proposals like California's, however, will result in incarcerating thousands of convicts into middle and old age.

REGRESSING TO THE MEAN

Before Governor Wilson signed the most draconian of the three-strikes bill introduced in the legislature, district attorneys across the state assailed the measure, arguing that it would clog courts, cost too much money, and result in disproportionate sentences for nonviolent offenders. So potent is the political crime panic in California that the pleas of the prosecutors were rebuffed.

The prospect in California is ominous. Even without three-strikes legislation, California is already the nation's biggest jailer, with one out of eight American prisoners occupying its cells. During the past 16 years, its prison population has grown 600 percent, while violent crime in the state has increased 40 percent. As Franklin E. Zimring and Gordon Hawkins demonstrate in a recent issue of the *British Journal of Criminology,* correctional growth in California was "in a class by itself" during the 1980s. The three next largest state prison systems (New York, Texas, and Florida) experienced half the growth of California, and western European systems about a quarter.

To pay for a five-fold increase in the corrections budget since 1980, Californians have had to sacrifice other services. Education especially has suffered. Ten years ago, California devoted 14 percent of its state budget to higher education and 4 percent to prisons. Today it devotes 9 percent to both.

The balance is now expected to shift sharply in favor of prisons. To pay for three strikes, California expects to spend $10.5 billion by the year 2001. The California Department of Corrections has estimated that three strikes will require the state to add 20 more prisons to the existing 28 and the 12 already on the drawing board. By 2001, there will be 109,000 more prisoners behind bars serving life sentences. A total of 275,621 more people are expected to be imprisoned over the next 30 years—the equivalent of building an electric fence around the city of Anaheim. By the year 2027 the cost of housing extra inmates is projected to hit $5.7 billion a year.

But will California be better off in 2027—indeed, will it have less crime—if it has 20 more prisons for aging offenders instead of 20 more college campuses for the young?

Of course, Wilson and other politicians are worrying about the next elections, not the next century. By the time the twice-convicted get out of prison, commit a third major offense, and are convicted and sentenced to life terms, Wilson and the others supporting three strikes will be out—that is, out of office, leaving future generations a legacy of an ineffectual and costly crime policy. To avoid that result, political leaders need to stop trying to out-tough one another and start trying to out-reason each other.

THE LIMITS OF INTUITION

H. L. A. Hart, the noted legal philosopher, once observed that the Enlightenment made the form and severity of punishment "a matter to be *thought* about, to be *reasoned* about, and *argued,* and not merely a matter to be left to feelings and sentiment." Those aspirations ought still to be our guide.

The current push to enact three strikes proposals is reminiscent of the movement in the 1970s to enact mandatory sentencing laws, another effort to get tough, reduce judicial discretion, and appease the public furies. But mandatory sentencing has not yielded any discernible reduction in crime. Indeed, the result has been mainly to shift discretionary decision-making upstream in the criminal justice system since the laws have continued to allow great latitude in bringing charges and plea bargaining.

Ironically, mandatory sentencing allowed the serial freedom of Richard Allen Davis, the accused murderer of Polly Klaas. Before 1977, California had a system of indeterminate prison sentencing for felony offenders. For such felonies as second-degree murder, robbery, rape, and kidnapping, a convict might receive a sentence of 1 to 25 years, or even one year to life. The objective was to tailor sentences to behavior, to confine the most dangerous convicts longer, and to provide incentives for self-improvement. However, in 1977, declaring that the goal of imprisonment was punishment rather than rehabilitation, the state adopted supposedly tougher mandatory sentences. Richard Allen Davis benefited from two mandated sentence reductions, despite the prescient pre-sentencing report of a county probation officer who warned of Davis's "accelerating potential for violence" after his second major conviction. Under indeterminate sentencing, someone with Davis's personality and criminal history would likely have been imprisoned far longer than the mandated six years for his first set of offenses.

Most criminologists and policy analysts do not support the reliance on expanded prisons and the rigidities of habitual offender laws. Some, like David Rothman, have apologized for their naiveté joining the movement to establish determinate sentencing in the 1970s and now recognize that it has been a failure.

Others, like John J. DiIulio, Jr., take a harder line, although the hardness of DiIulio's line seems to depend on his forum. In a January 1994 column appearing—where else?—in the *Wall Street Journal,* DiIulio supported the superficially toughest provisions of the Senate crime bill. (The *Journal*'s headline writers called the column "Let 'em Rot," a title that DiIulio later protested, though his own text was scarcely less draconian.) But writing in *The American Prospect* in the fall of 1990 ("Getting Prisons Straight") and with Anne Thomson Piehl in the fall of 1991 for the *Brookings Review,* DiIulio's message was more tempered.

The Brookings article reviews the debate over the cost-effectiveness of prisons. Imprisonment costs between $20,000 to $50,000 per prisoner per year. But is that price worth the benefit of limiting the crimes that could have been committed by prisoners if they were on the street? "Based on existing statistical evidence," write DiIulio and Piehl, "the relationship between crime rates and imprisonment is ambiguous." This is hardly a mandate for "letting 'em rot." DiIulio and Piehl recognize that the certainty of punishment is more effective than the length and that "even if we find that 'prison pays' at the margin, it would not mean that every convicted criminal deserves prison; it would not mean that it is cost effective to imprison every convicted felon." I agree and so do most criminologists. Does DiIulio read DiIulio?

THE RISE OF IMPRISONMENT

Two trends are responsible for the increase in imprisonment. First, the courts are imposing longer sentences for such nonviolent felonies as larceny, theft, and motor vehicle theft. In 1992 these accounted for 60.9 percent of crime in America, according to the Federal Bureau of Investigation's Uniform Crime Reports.

Second, drugs have become the driving force of crime. More than half of all violent offenders are under the influence of alcohol or drugs (most often alcohol) when they commit their crimes. The National Institute of Justice has shown that in 23 American cities, the percentage of arrested and booked males testing positive for any of ten illegal drugs ranged from a low of 48 percent in Omaha to 79 percent in Philadelphia. The median cities, Fort Lauderdale and Miami, checked out at 62 percent.

There has been an explosion of arrests and convictions and increasingly longer sentences for possessing and selling drugs. A Justice Department study, completed last summer but withheld from the public until February this year, found that of the 90,000 federal prison inmates, one-fifth are low-level drug offenders with no current or prior violence or previous prison time. They are jamming the prisons.

The federal prison population, through mandated and determinate sentences, has tripled in the past decade. Under current policy, it will rise by 50 percent by the century's turn, with drug offenders accounting for 60 percent of the additional prisoners. Three-strikes legislation will doubtless solidify our already singular position as the top jailer of the civilized world.

THE FEAR FACTOR

The lock-'em-up approach plays to people's fear of crime, which is rising, while actual crime rates are stabilizing or declining. This is by no means to argue that fear of crime is unjustified. Crime has risen enormously in the United States in the last quarter-century, but it is no more serious in 1994 than it was in 1991. The FBI's crime index declined 4 percent from 1991 to 1992.

In California, a legislative report released in January indicates that the overall crime rate per 100,000 people declined slightly from 1991 to 1992, dropping from 3,503.3 to 3,491.5. Violent crimes—homicide, forcible rape, robbery, and aggravated assault—rose slightly, from 1,079.8 to 1,103.9. Early figures for 1993 show a small decline.

On the other coast, New York City reported a slight decline in homicides, 1,960 in 1993, compared with 1,995 in 1992, and they are clustered in 12 of the city's 75 police districts, places like East New York and the South Bronx. "On the east side of

Manhattan," writes Matthew Purdy in the *New York Times,* "in the neighborhood of United Nations diplomats and quiet streets of exclusive apartments, the gunfire might as well be in a distant city."

So why, when crime rates are flat, has crime become America's number one problem in the polls? Part of the answer is that fear of crime rises with publicity, especially on television. Polly Klaas's murder, the killing of tourists in Florida, the roadside murder of the father of former basketball star Michael Jordan, and the killing of commuters on a Long Island Railroad train sent a scary message to the majority of Americans who do not reside in the inner cities. The message seemed to be that random violence is everywhere and you are no longer safe—not in your suburban home, commuter train, or automobile—and the police and the courts cannot or will not protect you.

A recent and as yet unpublished study by Zimring and Hawkins argues that America's problem is not crime per se but random violence. They compare Los Angeles and Sydney, Australia. Both cities have a population of 3.6 million, and both are multicultural (although Sydney is less so). Crime in Sydney is a serious annoyance but not a major threat. My wife and I, like other tourists, walked through Sydney at night last spring with no fear of being assaulted.

Sydney's crime pattern explains the difference. Its burglary rate is actually 10 percent higher than L.A.'s, and its theft rate is 73 percent of L.A.'s. But its robbery and homicide rates are strikingly lower, with only 12.5 percent of L.A.'s robbery rate and only 7.3 percent of L.A.'s homicide rate.

Americans and Australians don't like any kind of crime, but most auto thefts and many burglaries are annoying rather than terrifying. It is random violent crime, like a shooting in a fast-food restaurant, that is driving fear.

Violent crime, as I suggested earlier, is chiefly the work of young men between the ages of 15 and 24. The magnitude of teenage male involvement in violent crime is frightening. "At the peak age (17)," Delbert Elliott writes, "36 percent of African-American (black) males and 25 percent of non-Hispanic (white) males report one or more serious violent offenses." Nor are young women free of violence. One in five African-American females and one in ten white females report having committed a serious violent offense.

Blacks are more likely than whites to continue their violence into their adult years. Elliott considers this finding to be an important insight into the high arrest and incarceration rates of young adult black males. As teenagers, black and white males are roughly comparable in their disposition to violence. "Yet," Elliott writes, "once involved in a lifestyle that includes serious forms of violence, theft, and substance use, persons from disadvantaged families and neighborhoods find it very difficult to escape. They have fewer opportunities for conventional adult roles, and they are more deeply embedded in and dependent upon the gangs and the illicit economy that flourish in their neighborhoods."

The key to reformation, Elliott argues, is the capacity to make the transition into conventional adult work and family roles. His data show that those who successfully make the change give up their involvement in violence. Confinement in what will surely be overcrowded prisons can scarcely facilitate that transition, while community-based programs like Delancey Street have proven successful.

Just as violent crime is concentrated among the young, so is drug use. Drug treatment must be a key feature of crime prevention both in prisons and outside. There is some good news here. In early 1994, President Clinton and a half-dozen cabinet members visited a Maryland prison that boasts a model drug-treatment program to announce a national drug strategy that sharply increases spending for drug treatment and rehabilitation. Although the major share of the anti-drug budget, 59 percent, is still allocated to law enforcement, the change is in the right direction. A number of jurisdictions across the country have developed promising court-ordered rehabilitation programs that seem to be succeeding in reducing both drug use and the criminality of drug-using offenders.

Drugs are one area where get-tough policies to disrupt supply have been a signal failure, both internationally and domestically. Interdiction and efforts to suppress drug agriculture and manufacture within such countries as Peru and Colombia have run up against what I have called "the Darwinian Trafficker Dilemma." Such efforts undercut the marginally efficient traffickers, while the fittest—the most efficient, the best organized, the most ruthless, the most corrupting of police and judges—survive. Cocaine prices, the best measure of success or failure, dropped precipitously in the late 1980s. They have recovered somewhat, but likely more from monopolistic pricing than government interference.

Domestically, get-tough intuitions have inspired us to threaten drug kingpins with long prison terms or death. Partly, we wish to punish and incapacitate them, but mostly we wish to deter others from following in their felonious paths. Unfortunately, such policies are undermined by the "Felix Mitchell Dilemma," which I named in honor of the West Coast's once notorious kingpin, who received a life sentence in the 1980s, albeit a short one since he was murdered in federal prison. Mitchell's sentence and early demise did not deter drug sellers in the Bay Area. On the contrary, drug sales continued and, with Mitchell's monopolistic pricing eliminated, competition reduced the price of crack. The main effect of Mitchell's imprisonment was to destabilize the market, lower drug prices, and increase violence as rival gang members challenged each other for market share. Drug-related drive-by shootings, street homicides, and felonious assaults increased.

Recently, two of Mitchell's successors, Timothy Bluitt and Marvin Johnson, were arrested and sent to prison. So will peace finally come to the streets? "When a guy like Bluitt goes down, someone takes his place and gets an even bigger slice of the pie," an anonymous federal agent told the *San Francisco Chronicle* this past January. "The whole process is about consolidating turf and power."

Youngsters who sell drugs in Oakland, Denver, Detroit, South Central Los Angeles, Atlanta, and New York are part of generations who have learned to see crime as economic opportunity. This does not excuse their behavior, but it does intensify our need to break the cycle of poverty, abuse, and violence that dominates their lives. Prisons do not deter criminals partly because the Mitchells and Bluitts do not rationally calculate choices with the same points of reference that legislators employ. Drug dealers already face the death penalty on the streets.

History reminds us that gang violence is not novel, but it has not always been so lethal. The benchmark sociological study of the urban gang is Frederick Thrasher's research on 1,313 Chicago gangs published in 1927. The disorder and violence of these gangs appalled Thrasher, who observed that they were beyond the ordinary controls of police and other social agencies. He described gang youth, of which only 7.2 percent were "Negro," as "lawless, godless, wild." Why didn't more of them kill each other? They fought with fists and knives, not assault weapons.

PREVENTING VIOLENT CRIME

If violent crime prevention is our strategic aim, we need to test tactics. We need to go beyond the Brady Bill and introduce a tight regulatory system on weapons and ammunition, and we need more research and analysis to figure out what control system would be most effective. Successful gun and ammunition control would do far more to stem the tide of life-threatening violence than expensive prisons with mandated sentences.

The Senate crime bill, however, promises to increase the nation's rate of imprisonment. Besides its three strikes provisions, the legislation incorporates Senator Robert Byrd's $3 billion regional prison proposal. If enacted, states can apply to house their prisoners in 10 regional prisons, each with a capacity of 2,500 inmates.

To qualify, states must adopt "truth in sentencing" laws mandating that offenders convicted of violent crimes serve "at least 80 percent of the sentence ordered," the current average served by federal offenders. They also must approve pretrial detention laws similar to those in the federal system. And the states must ensure that four categories of crime—murder, firearms offenses resulting in death or serious bodily injury, sex offenses broadly defined, and child abuse—are punished as severely as they are under federal law. In effect, the Senate crime bill federalizes sentencing policy.

According to H. Scott Wallace of the National Legal Aid and Defender's Association, the mandate will add about 12,000 prisoners to the average state's correctional population but will offer only about 3 percent of the space needed to house them.

The most costly provision of the Senate crime bill—$9 billion worth—is its proposal for 100,000 more police, a measure endorsed by the administration. Its potential value in reducing crime is unclear. We need more research on constructive policing, including community policing, which can be either an effective approach or merely a fashionable buzzword. We need to address the deficiencies of police culture revealed in the corruption uncovered by New York City's Mollen Commission and the excessive force revealed on the Rodney King beating videotape. More police may help in some places but not much in others. And they are very expensive.

A leading police researcher, David H. Bayley, has explained the ten-for-one rule of police visibility: ten cops must be hired to put one officer on the street. Only about two-thirds of police are uniformed patrol officers. They work three shifts, take vacation and sick leave, and require periodic retraining. Consequently 100,000 new officers will mean only about 10,000 on the street for any one shift for the entire United States.

Even if we were to have more and better police, there is no guarantee they will deter crime. Criminologists have found no marginal effect on crime rates from putting more cops on the street. Indeed, Congress and the president need look no farther than down their own streets to discover that simply increasing police doesn't necessarily make the streets safe. Washington, D.C., boasts the highest police-per-resident ratio in the nation with one cop for every 150 civilians. It is also America's homicide capital.

We might get more bang for the patrolling buck by investing in para-police, or the police corps, or private police, rather than by paying for more fully sworn and expensive officers. Under the leadership of former Chief Raymond Davis, Santa Ana, California, had the most effective community-oriented policing department in the nation. Davis, who faced a weak police union, could innovate with community- and service-oriented civilians who wore blue uniforms but carried no guns—a new and cost-effective blue line.

The crime bill allocates approximately $3 billion for boot camps, another get-tough favorite. Criminologist Doris MacKenzie has found, contrary to intuition, no significant difference between camp graduates and former prison inmates in the rate at which they return to prison. Similarly, a General Accounting Office report concluded that there is no evidence that boot camps reduce recidivism.

If the public wants boot camps primarily for retribution, it doesn't matter whether they work. Under the Eighth Amendment's bar on cruel and unusual punishment, we're not permitted to impose corporal punishment with whips and clubs. In boot camps, however, we can require painful exercises and hard and demeaning labor to teach these miscreant youth a message of retribution. But if correctional boot camps are intended to resocialize youth and to prepare for them noncriminal civilian life, the camps are inadequate.

We need to experiment with boot camps plus—the "plus" including skills training, education, jobs, community reconstruction. Conservatives who stress moral revitalization and family values as an antidote to youth crime have the right idea. Yet they rarely if ever, consider how important are the structural underpinnings—education, opportunity, employment, family functioning, community support—for developing such values.

Eventually, we are going to have to choose between our retributive urges and the possibilities of crime prevention. We cannot fool ourselves into thinking they are the same. One punishment meted out by criminal law is a blunt and largely ineffectual instrument of public protection. It deters some, it incapacitates others, and it does send a limited moral message. But if we want primarily to enhance public safety by preventing crime, we need to mistrust our intuitions and adopt strategies and tactics that have been researched, tested, and critically evaluated. In short, we need to embrace the values of the enlightenment over those of the dark ages.

Instant Replay

Three Strikes Was the Right Call

John J. DiIulio Jr.

Jerome H. Skolnick's essay on crime policy ("Wild Pitch: 'Three Strikes, You're Out' and Other Bad Calls on Crime," Spring 1994), omitted some important facts and ignored several valid arguments.

Echoing the anti-incarceration consensus within criminology, Skolnick asserts that life without parole for thrice-convicted violent felons is a bad policy idea, a "wild pitch." Actually, it's more of an underhanded lob to career criminals, most of whom would hardly be affected by it. In 1991 there were about 35,000 new court commitments to federal prisons. Less than 6 percent of federal prisoners were sentenced for violent crimes. About 30 percent of the 142,000 persons committed to state prisons were sentenced for violent crimes. If 10 percent of all prisoners sentenced for violent crimes were on their "third strike," then the law would have affected some 4,500 persons in a corrections population of nearly 4.5 million. Love it or hate it, "three strikes" would have little impact on the size of prison populations, and would do nothing to plug the worm's hole of phoney "mandatory minimum" laws. These laws have put about three-quarters of all convicts—over 3 million criminals—on the streets under "supervision" that in most cases means a monthly chat with an overworked, underpaid probation or parole agent.

Millions of crimes are committed each year by convicted offenders whom the system didn't keep behind bars. Within three years of their release, persons convicted of property crimes are about as likely to commit a violent crime as persons convicted of violent crimes in the first place. And please, no more nonsense about "intermediate sanctions." Recent studies show that fully half of all probationers don't even comply with the basic terms of their sentences (pay fines, do community service, accept drug treatment) before being released from custody, and only one-fifth of the violators are ever disciplined in any way. Meanwhile, repeat criminals who beat the system inflict hundreds of billions of dollars in damages on their victims and society each year.

Skolnick may think the Polly Klaas tragedy is mere sensationalism, but all the data show that the system routinely permits known predatory criminals to plea bargain their way to lesser charges at the front end, only to give them numerous get-out-of-jail-free cards at the back end. In 1991 thirty-four states released more than 325,000 prisoners combined, 90 percent of them to community-based supervision. About half of these offenders had served *a year or less* in prison before their releases. On average, they served 35 percent of their time in confinement. This average held pretty well for all types of offenders. Thus, murderers received a maximum sentence of 20 years but served under 8 years (below 40 percent of their sentences) in prison, while drug traffickers (organized traffickers, *not* mere possessors) received an average of 4 years and served about 14 months (35 percent of their sentence) before release. The state-level data paint the same bleak picture in finer detail. In New Jersey, for example, the typical prisoner had 9 arrests, and 6 convictions, committed over a dozen serious crimes (excluding *all* drug crimes) in the year prior to his incarceration, had about a 50–50 chance of victimizing again after his release, and was most likely to victimize poor and minority citizens.

No Americans suffer more from permissive penal practices than the law-abiding minority citizens of inner city neighborhoods. Middle-class and affluent Americans are spending record amounts on private security devices, rent-a-cops, and other measures intended to make the environments in which they live relatively impervious to crime. That spending, in conjunction with now commonplace danger-avoidance behaviors (don't walk alone or ride the subway at night, don't drive through "bad neighborhoods"), help explain the recent decrease in crime rates nationally. But poor folks can't afford private security measures. Instead, they rely mainly on a "justice system" that virtually invites the criminally deviant to prey upon the truly disadvantaged.

Like most criminologists, Skolnick obscures the public protection value of imprisonment behind criminologically *de rigueur* rhetoric about the steep increase in the rate of incarceration, the U.S. having the highest incarceration rate in the world, etc. But he doesn't mention that the rate increase in community-based supervision has been even steeper. Nor does he note that only 6 percent of state prisoners are nonviolent first-time offenders. The federal system, in which prisoners must serve at least 85 percent of their time behind bars, consists largely of "non-violent" drug dealers with multiple convictions. My Princeton colleague, Ethan Nadelmann, has made a number of powerful arguments for decriminalizing drugs. He's persuaded me on some points, but not all, and not on the bottom line of legalization. But most criminologists who balk at mandatory prison terms for drug merchants lack the courage of their criminological convictions. Rather than asserting that we're locking up too many harmless people for too long, criminologists ought to get specific—identify these people, and tell us, on a jurisdiction-by-jurisdiction basis, precisely what classes of criminals they would like to let out sooner.

I agree with Skolnick that it is irrational to wait until career criminals are drifting into their less crime-prone years before slapping them with long sentences. James Q. Wilson and others made that case years ago. But there are at least four other considerations. First, the differences among the criminal classes in prison today are not that wide. We're not talking about criminals—we're talking about plea-bargain-gorged *convicted and imprisoned criminals*—the vast majority of whom carry a criminal portfolio featuring multiple property crimes, multiple violent crimes, or both.

Second, it's true that older criminals commit fewer and less serious crimes than do younger criminals. But less crime isn't no crime and we don't have any reliable way of predicting which prisoners are harmless "geriatric inmates" and which are still dangerous. (Ask the Massachusetts authorities who recently got burnt by a 61-year-old released prisoner who murdered again.)

Third, if we're really so concerned about waiting too long before hammering repeat criminals with heavy sentences, why not support "two strikes" laws that incarcerate them while they're hot—if not for life, then for 15- to 20-years with no good time and no parole? California and dozens of other states are moving in this direction. Godspeed to them. Of course, when pressed most criminologists want only "violent" crimes to count as a "strike"—major drug felonies, carjacking at knife-point, etc., aren't supposed to count. These folks have to stop decriminalizing things without admitting it, and without telling the rest of us why. This goes especially for all their hypocritical cheers for gun control. New Jersey, like many states, has dozens of tough gun laws. But the penalties for gun law violations aren't strictly enforced. Would those who want more restrictions on guns also favor making serious gun-law violations a "strike"? I would.

Fourth, society has a right not only to protect itself from convicted criminals but to express its moral outrage at their acts by, among other things, keeping them behind bars. For example, what is the right moral posture when it comes to cases like the 73-year-old man recently sentenced to life without parole for the 1963 murder of civil rights worker Medgar Evers? In my view, the public and their elected leaders have a better grasp of the moral *and* empirical issues at stake than do most of our country's criminologists.

Skolnick and most other criminologists are sure that prison is not the answer. But what, precisely, is the question? If the question's how to solve America's crime problem, plus all the rest of its urban problems, then prison is no answer. But if the question is what can protect the public from violent and repeat criminals, then prison is a very good answer indeed. Professionally, criminologists should not ignore the data on how little time most violent and repeat criminals spend behind bars. Morally they should not ignore the pleas of a majority of Americans of every demographic description. Nor should they belittle the lived experiences of the Klaas family and others that, like my own, have suffered the murder of a loved one at the hands of a released repeat criminal, or had their lives and property trifled with or ruined by thugs whom the system let loose. We can forgive the public, which has become so frustrated with America's revolving door justice that it applauds Singapore's institutionalized canings.

As Skolnick noted, the "100,000 cops" provision of the crime bill would actually mean about 10,000 around-the-clock cops distributed by Congress among hundreds of jurisdictions. The federal bucks are just seed dollars that will dry up in a half-decade, leaving the states and cities to bite the bullet. Still, with artful administration by the Office of Justice Programs (read: not the 1970s saga of the Law Enforcement Assistance Administration revisited), there is still the chance that the community policing provisions of the bill could be married to its manpower provisions. At least that's what the academics (including David Bayley, author of the 10-for-1 rule cited by Skolnick) and government officials who joined me at Brookings for a session with the Justice Department hope will happen.

In the 1980s Skolnick and other criminologists made excellent arguments for community policing. But community policing was oversold as a do-more-with-less strategy. You can't just retrain cops and put more of them on foot patrol. Many big city police forces have contracted. The thin blue line is stretched too thin, especially in the underserved inner city where crime is out of control. Community policing should be embraced for what it is—a do-better-with-more strategy. The cheap talk's over, the bill's due, and it includes more money for more cops. The public is willing to pay; criminologists should belly up to the bar, too, and endorse more police.

Skolnick has cited my January 1994 op-ed on crime for the *Wall Street Journal*, which had also recently run pieces on crime by syndicated columnist Ben Wattenberg, historian Paul Johnson, and several others. In that op-ed, I supported what President Clinton said on crime in his State of the Union address, and condemned Attorney General Reno and other liberal elites who respond with doublespeak to the public's legitimate calls for tougher anti-crime measures. Skolnick compares this op-ed to a 1990 article I published in *The American Prospect*, and a 1991 article I co-authored for the *Brookings Review*. Finding my "message" to be "more tempered" in these essays than it was in the op-ed, he writes that the "hardness of DiIulio's line seems to depend on his forum." He concludes by asking, "Does DiIulio read DiIulio?"

For the record, my *TAP* article was mainly about prison rehabilitation programs, including drug treatment. I have continued to write on that issue, done what I could to encourage Senate Republicans and others not to throw the drug treatment baby out with the crime bill bath water, and accepted a public tribute on that score from Democratic Congressman Charles Schumer of New York. I'm for more prisons, stiffer and enforced sentences, and whatever rehabilitation programs work to cut costs and reduce recidivism. But there's no need to genuflect at the prisoner rehabilitation altar in an op-ed that calls for tougher sentencing.

Whether or not imprisoning Peter keeps Paul honest, with Peter locked up, society saves itself from the crimes he might have continued to commit. And by keeping him behind bars for all or most of his term, society spares itself the crimes that might have followed his early release. For example, between 1987 and 1991 Florida parolees committed some 25,000 new crimes, including 5,000 violent crimes and 346 murders. The *Brookings Review* article referenced by Skolnick was a cost-benefit analysis of imprisonment based on official criminal records and prisoner self-report data, which revealed that in the year prior to incarceration, the typical prisoner committed about a dozen serious offenses, excluding all drug crimes. The study found that for most prisoners "prison pays" (i.e., the social benefits of incarceration are nearly 1.4 times the social costs).

Last year I completed another major prisoner self-report survey. The results, which will be published this year, indicate that the benefits of imprisonment are even greater than reported in the *Brookings* study. Still, as I wrote in the first study, "the relationship between imprisonment rates and crime rates is ambiguous." Finding that prison pays at the margin does "not mean that it is cost-effective to imprison every convicted felon."

Amazingly, however, Skolnick and other criminologists have repeatedly cited those obvious cautions and ignored the major finding of the study—namely, that contrary to all their assertions, *prison pays*. Incarcerating a greater fraction of convicted felons would yield positive social benefits, and quite dramatic ones if we factored in even a small deterrence benefit and included even a tiny fraction of all drug crimes.

Skolnick notes that the *Journal* tagged my January 1994 article "Let 'em Rot." As I made clear in my blistering top-of-the-letters-page response, the *Journal* editors' title has everything to do with the casual callousness of some conservative elites and nothing to do with either the public's concerns about crime or my views, backed by extensive research, on the practical attainability and moral necessity of humane (not luxurious) prison administration. Still, Skolnick asserted that my "message" in the piece was as "draconian" as the title.

If criminologists like Skolnick think it's "draconian" to want most violent and repeat criminals to spend most of their time behind bars, to be fed up with fake get-tough measures, to condemn liberal elites who just don't get it, and to want what majorities of every demographic group in America wants in the way of effective justice, then so be it. That says more about the perversity of the criminologists' message (prisons are teeming with petty criminals, Americans are a punitive people, voters are fools, politicians are weathervanes, drugs ought to be decriminalized, and the "experts" always know best) than it does about any venue-sensitive changes in my writing. And since Skolnick liked tarring me with a title against which I had publicly protested, let me note that last November I wrote an op-ed for, if I may imitate Skolnick—where else?—*The New York Times.* My loud, clear, and on-the-record "message" on prisons (more!) was exactly the same there as in the criminologically incorrect *Journal* piece. But the *Times* billed the article "Save the Children."

Jerome H. Skolnick Replies

John DiIulio's response is shot through with overheated generalizations. His first paragraph contains his first big—no, colossal—error, namely that three strikes "would have little impact on the size of prison populations." That's not true in California, the nation's most populous state, where three strikes is currently on the books.

DiIulio assumes that only "violent" felonies count as "strikes," but the California law itemizes "serious" felonies as well. Consequently, California is expected to imprison an additional 3,850 as a result of the Three Strikes law next year.

DiIulio estimates that three strikes will affect a total of only 4,500 felons in all state prisons in a given year based on 1991 estimates of prison population. Subtract 3,850 from 4,500 and you have only 650 additional felons incarcerated for life, in a given year, as a result of the three strikes laws impending in other states. That's not believable.

DiIulio's point would be better made as follows: the impact of three strikes laws on the size of prison populations will depend on how legislatures define third offenses that count as "strikes." DiIulio himself doesn't see much difference between property offenders and violent offenders. He mistrusts intermediate sanctions as well, although he fails to mention how starved parole and probation services are in comparison to prisons. DiIulio disavows "Let 'em rot" as his maxim, but "Lock 'em up" seems to be advised.

California's legislature has plenty of DiIulio-like thinkers. Consequently, the Department of Corrections expects significant increases in prison population as a result of three strikes, and so will other states if they follow California's lead. Moreover, since these are life sentences, their impact on prison population increases with time.

Even before three strikes legislation passed in California, the Department of Corrections predicted that its 1999 population would be more than seven times what it was in 1980. The CDC now predicts that three strikes will enlarge this number by more than half again.

The CDC estimates that three strikes will require at least 20 new prisons, in addition to the dozen already under construction. Eventually, in 2027–28, California is expected to incarcerate 272,438 criminals—the equivalent of building an electric fence around the city of Anaheim.

Interestingly, nobody, including three strikes supporters such as Governor Pete Wilson, disputes these figures. What they warrant instead is that prisons save money.

In New Jersey, where the Senate unanimously approved a three strikes law on May 12, Louis F. Kosco, the bill's sponsor, echoed this theme to a *New York Times* reporter who questioned how cash-strapped governments will cover the cost of booming prison populations. "Each time they go through the revolving door, repeat offenders cost the state a great deal in legal and parole expenses," he said. "And we must take into account the economic and social costs. . . ." George Romero, Chief Economist of the California Governor's Office of Planning and Research, issued a report in late February which estimates the amount of these savings. The average criminal, he says, hits the rest of us up for around $200,000 a year.

Consequently, although Californians will spend $383 million to imprison an estimated additional 3,580 under the three strikes law now in effect, the state will save, Romero computes, $716 million. California will really strike it rich in 2027, when the state can count on imprisoning 272,438 at a whopping savings of $54 billion compared to a measly $6.3 billion in prison costs. But three false assumptions undermine the report's conclusions:

First, the report assumes a finite group of criminals. If we keep them locked up for life or close to it, crime, the report assumes, will tumble significantly. The fallacy is this: serious violent crime is committed primarily by 15–24 year old males. The rate declines when they move into their thirties, as DiIulio acknowledges.

As Gottfredson and Hirschi assert convincingly in their recent *A General Theory of Crime,* the serious, predatory offenses said to be associated with career criminals are actually committed by young people "some of whom go on committing them for awhile, but most of whom spend their . . . late twenties running afoul of the authorities over alcohol, drugs and family squabbles." Even Sheldon and Eleanor Glueck, after a lifetime of research, report a substantial reduction in serious criminality in the 25–31 age range. If we lock them up for life as three strikes demands, they will be replaced by younger criminals. Geriatric cases will fill the prisons, while offenders will remain youthful. In the end, the public is no safer.

Second, there is no such animal as "the average criminal" or an "average murderer." The eight-year figure supplied by DiIulio includes premeditated murderers, and those who kill accidentally while driving under the influence. Both deserve punishment, but criminal law sensibly distinguishes their respective moral culpability. Sensible public policy should not penalize all felons, even violent felons, with equal, mandated, discretionless severity. Three strikes laws, and Romero's analysis, tend to treat all felons equally. This is neither morally justified nor fiscally sound.

Finally, prison costs are certain while savings are speculative. While shelling out for the five-fold increase in corrections since 1980, Californians have had to sacrifice other services in education, health, and welfare. California's public schools, which once ranked near the top, now rank near the bottom, close to Mississippi's. Its higher education system has been ravaged by the need to offer a generous retirement package to many of its most distinguished faculty because it can no longer afford to pay them without firing twice as many junior faculty.

Three strikes will shift the budget balance sharply in favor of prisons and away from educational and social services, in the absence of which teenage crime will flourish. Vast "savings" from expanded prisons are the 1994 crime control version of voodoo economics.

Even without three strikes legislation, California is already the nation's biggest jailer, with one out of eight American prisoners occupying its cells. California's prison system has grown twice as much as the systems in the next three largest states (New York, Texas, and Florida) and four times as much as Western Europe's.

If high rates of imprisonment (recall DiIulio wants "more prisons, stiffer and enforced sentences") lead to feelings of public safety, Californians should feel twice as safe as New Yorkers, Texans, and Floridians and four times as safe as citizens of France. They don't. As Joan Petersilia and Peter Reuter conclude in their RAND book *Urban America: Policy Choices for Los Angeles and the Nation,* California locks up too many people, often for the wrong offenses (drug offenders accounted for 26 percent of California prisoners in 1990, up from 11 percent in 1980) and has too little to show for it in enhanced public safety.

As reports of these facts are filtering through, the public and the press are beginning to reconsider. For example, a 70-year-old San Francisco woman refused to testify against an addict-burglar who had broken into her car. She didn't think he deserved a life sentence and called the Three Strikes law "a holocaust for the poor" in a local newspaper.

Even the Klaas family has come out against the current law, saying they were bamboozled into supporting it in a time of grief. They support a more moderate bill that eliminates household burglaries as strikes. The California three strikes law is tough and dumb, and anyone remotely familiar with the criminal justice system understands that.

According to DiIulio, I and other criminologists are out of touch with the concerns of middle class Americans. This is hyperbolic nonsense. Granted, most criminologists are skeptical that expanding imprisonment by mandating life sentences is a solution to America's crime problem. But we are skeptical for the very reason that DiIulio is: "If the question's how to solve America's crime problem . . . then prison is no answer." If we starve education and social services to pay for excessively long prison sentences, if we concentrate on building prisons at the expense of schools, crime will increase and public safety will suffer.

The criminal sanction is both an expression of moral outrage and a method of controlling crime. Unfortunately, the two goals are not always in sync. The call for long, mandated prison sentences is a response to moral outrage. Some criminals should be locked up for decades, even for life, to protect the public. For that goal we need more, rather than less, discretion from judges and parole boards.

Likewise, it makes no sense to mandate five-year sentences for an 18-year-old caught selling drugs, unless we simply want to express moral outrage. Someone else will almost certainly take his place. (See Daniel Feldman, "Imprisoner's Dilemma," *TAP* Summer 1993.)

Yes, time served for violent felonies has decreased in the last ten years. Two trends are responsible. We've been sending more nonviolent offenders to state prison because local jails are overcrowded, and we've been locking up parolees who flunk their drug tests. The latter account for about 25 percent of California's prison population.

DiIulio's rantings about criminologists as "elitists" belie a central truth. Criminologists are deeply concerned with controlling crime, especially in communities of disadvantage. I didn't write, as DiIulio claims, that the Polly Klaas tragedy is "mere sensationalism." I did say that had supposedly "soft-on-crime" indeterminate sentencing been in effect, Richard Allen Davis would not have been released.

I also tried to account for the fact that at a time when crime rates are flat or declining in California (and the nation), crime has become America's number one concern. Klaas's murder, plus a number of other highly publicized crimes, I wrote, "have sent a scary message to the majority of Americans who do not live in the inner city." Polly was an especially lovely, vivacious girl with a winning smile. And she was white and became "America's daughter." But the fact remains, a teenager's chances of being murdered in east Oakland or southeast Washington D.C. are considerably higher than in Petaluma, a bucolic northern California suburb.

What most criminologists question are policies directing funds away from crime prevention measures in disadvantaged communities and toward the expensive financing of mandated life sentences, especially for those convicted of nonviolent felonies. If crime control is the issue, criminologists have a lot to contribute. If moral outrage is what it's all about, the ranters and ravers will win the day.

Nor are criminologists opposed to appropriate, just, and effective incapacitation. When thoughtfully applied, it can protect the public against repeatedly violent criminals. True, we will make mistakes. The answer, however, is not to eliminate discretion, but to use it wisely, as is done in Minnesota's widely acclaimed sentencing guideline system.

Even DiIulio agrees imprisoning criminals for decades when they are beyond their high crime years makes no sense. He wants to hammer them while they're hot. The issue then becomes what does it mean to hammer, for which offenses, and how hot?

I agree that prosecutors will soften the impact of three strikes in California and other states. Prosecutors are the most powerful actors in the criminal justice system.

They can and will bargain, no matter what the legislation says. Even so, California and other states that follow its model will experience a vast expansion of imprisonment.

Let me conclude on a personal note. This business of argument by "elite" name calling (including Janet Reno in that category, no less) scarcely advances the debate. Besides, how can a Princeton professor and contributor to the *Brookings Review* and *The American Prospect* classify others as elites and himself as an ordinary working stiff? C'mon, let's be real. If the cultural revolution were to come to America, John DiIulio and I would be sentenced to plow the fields together side by side.

CHAPTER 38

Workaday World, Crack Economy

PHILIPPE BOURGOIS

I was forced into crack against my will. When I first moved to East Harlem—"El Barrio"—as a newlywed in the spring of 1985, I was looking for an inexpensive New York City apartment from which I could write about the experience of poverty and ethnic segregation in the heart of one of the most expensive cities in the world. I was interested in the political economy of inner-city street culture. I wanted to probe the Achilles' heel of the richest industrialized nation in the world by documenting how it imposes racial segregation and economic marginalization on so many of its Latino/a and African-American citizens.

My original subject was the entire underground (untaxed) economy, from curbside car repairing and baby-sitting to unlicensed off-track betting and drug dealing. I had never even heard of crack when I first arrived in the neighborhood—no one knew about this particular substance yet, because this brittle compound of cocaine and baking soda processed into efficiently smokable pellets was not yet available as a mass-marketed product. By the end of the year, however, most of my friends, neighbors and acquaintances had been swept into the multibillion-dollar crack cyclone: selling it, smoking it, fretting over it. I followed them, and I watched the murder rate in the projects opposite my crumbling tenement apartment spiral into one of the highest in Manhattan.

But this essay is not about crack, or drugs, per se. Substance abuse in the inner city is merely a symptom—and a vivid symbol—of deeper dynamics of social marginalization and alienation. Of course, on an immediately visible personal level, addiction and substance abuse are among the most immediate, brutal facts shaping daily life on the street. Most important, however, the two dozen street dealers and their families that I befriended were not interested in talking primarily about drugs. On the contrary, they wanted me to learn all about their daily struggles for subsistence and dignity at the poverty line.

Through the 1980s and 1990s, slightly more than one in three families in El Barrio have received public assistance. Female heads of these impoverished households have to supplement their meager checks in order to keep their children alive. Many are mothers who make extra money by baby-sitting their neighbors' children, or by housekeeping for a paying boarder. Others may bartend at one of the half-dozen social clubs and after-hours dancing spots scattered throughout the neighborhood. Some work "off the books" in their living rooms as seamstresses for garment contractors. Finally, many also find themselves obliged to establish amorous relationships with men who are willing to make cash contributions to their household expenses.

Male income-generating strategies in the underground economy are more publicly visible. Some men repair cars on the curb; others wait on stoops for unlicensed construction subcontractors to pick them up for fly-by-night demolition jobs or window renovation projects. Many sell "numbers"—the street's version of off-track betting. The most visible cohorts hawk "nickels and dimes" of one illegal drug or another. They are part of the most robust, multibillion-dollar sector of the booming underground economy. Cocaine and crack, in particular during the mid-1980s and through the early 1990s, followed by heroin in the mid-1990s, have become the fastest-growing—if not the only—equal-opportunity employers of men in Harlem. Retail drug sales easily outcompete other income-generating opportunities, whether legal or illegal.

Why should these young men and women take the subway to work minimum-wage jobs—or even double-minimum-wage jobs—in downtown offices when they can usually earn more, at least in the short run, by selling drugs on the street corner in front of their apartment or schoolyard? In fact, I am always surprised that so many inner-city men and women remain in the legal economy and work nine-to-five plus overtime, barely making ends meet. According to the 1990 Census of East Harlem, 48 percent of all males and 35 percent of females over 16 were employed in officially reported jobs, compared with a citywide average of 64 percent for men and 49 percent for women. In the census tracts surrounding my apartment, 53 percent of all men over 16 years of age (1,923 out of 3,647) and 28 percent of all women over 16 (1,307 out of 4,626) were working legally in officially censused jobs. An additional 17 percent of the civilian labor force was unemployed but actively looking for work, compared with 16 percent for El Barrio as a whole, and 9 percent for all of New York City.

"IF I WAS WORKING LEGAL . . ."

Street dealers tend to brag to outsiders and to themselves about how much money they make each night. In fact, their income is almost never as consistently high as they report it to be. Most street sellers, like my friend Primo (who, along with other friends and co-workers, allowed me to tape hundreds of hours of conversation with him over five years), are paid on a piece-rate commission basis. When converted into an hourly wage, this is often a relatively paltry sum. According to my calculations, the workers in the Game Room crackhouse, for example, averaged slightly less than double the legal minimum wage—between 7 and 8 dollars an hour. There were plenty of exceptional nights, however, when they made up to ten times minimum wage—and these are the nights they remember when they reminisce. They forget about all the other shifts when they were unable to work because of police raids, and they certainly do not count as forfeited working hours the nights they spent in jail.

This was brought home to me symbolically one night as Primo and his co-worker Caesar were shutting down the Game Room. Caesar unscrewed the fuses in the electrical box to disconnect the video games. Primo had finished stashing the leftover bundles of crack vials inside a hollowed-out live electrical socket and was counting the night's thick wad of receipts. I was struck by how thin the handful of bills was that he separated out and folded neatly into his personal billfold. Primo and Caesar then eagerly lowered the iron riot gates over the Game Room's windows and snapped shut the heavy Yale padlocks. They were moving with the smooth, hurried gestures of workers preparing to go home after an honest day's hard labor. Marveling at the universality in the body language of workers rushing at closing time, I felt an urge to compare the wages paid by this alternative economy. I grabbed Primo's wallet out of his back pocket, carefully giving a wide berth to the fatter wad in his front pocket that represented Ray's share of the night's income—and that could cost Primo his life if it were waylaid. Unexpectedly, I pulled out fifteen dollars' worth of food stamps along with two $20 bills. After an embarrassed giggle, Primo stammered that his mother had added him to her food-stamp allotment.

> *Primo:* I gave my girl, Maria, half of it. I said, "Here take it, use it if you need it for whatever." And then the other half I still got it in my wallet for emergencies.
>
> Like that, we always got a couple of dollars here and there, to survive with. Because tonight, straight cash, I only got garbage. Forty dollars! Do you believe that?

At the same time that wages can be relatively low in the crack economy, working conditions are often inferior to those in the legal economy. Aside from the obvious dangers of being shot, or of going to prison, the physical work space of most crackhouses is usually unpleasant. The infrastructure of the Game Room, for example, was much worse than that of any legal retail outfit in East Harlem: There was no bathroom, no running water, no telephone, no heat in the winter and no air conditioning in the summer. Primo occasionally complained:

> Everything that you see here [sweeping his arm at the scratched and dented video games, the walls with peeling paint, the floor slippery with litter, the filthy windows pasted over with ripped movie posters] is fucked up. It sucks, man [pointing at the red 40-watt bare bulb hanging from an exposed fixture in the middle of the room and exuding a sickly twilight].

Indeed, the only furnishings besides the video games were a few grimy milk crates and bent aluminum stools. Worse yet, a smell of urine and vomit usually permeated the locale. For a few months Primo was able to maintain a rudimentary sound system, but it was eventually beaten to a pulp during one of Caesar's drunken rages. Of course, the deficient infrastructure was only one part of the depressing working conditions.

> *Primo:* Plus I don't like to see people fucked up [handing over three vials to a nervously pacing customer]. This is fucked-up shit. I don't like this crack dealing. Word up.
> [gunshots in the distance] Hear that?

In private, especially in the last few years of my residence, Primo admitted that he wanted to go back to the legal economy.

> *Primo:* I just fuck up the money here. I rather be legal.
> *Philippe:* But you wouldn't be the head man on the block with so many girlfriends.
> *Primo:* I might have women on my dick right now but I would be much cooler if I was working legal. I wouldn't be drinking and the coke wouldn't be there every night.
> Plus if I was working legally I would have women on my dick too, because I would have money.
> *Philippe:* But you make more money here than you could ever make working legit.
> *Primo:* O.K. So you want the money but you really don't want to do the job.
> I really hate it, man. Hate it! I hate the people! I hate the environment! I hate the whole shit, man! But it's like you get caught up with it. You do it, and you say, "Ay, fuck it today!" Another day, another dollar. [pointing at an emaciated customer who was just entering] But I don't really, really think that I would have hoped that I can say I'm gonna be richer one day. I can't say that. I think about it, but I'm just living day to day.
> If I was working legal, I wouldn't be hanging out so much. I wouldn't be treating you. [pointing to the 16-ounce can of Colt 45 in my hand] In a job, you know, my environment would change . . . totally. Cause I'd have different friends. Right after work I'd go out with a co-worker, for lunch, for dinner. After work I may go home; I'm too tired for hanging out—I know I gotta work tomorrow.
> After working a legal job, I'm pretty sure I'd be good.

BURNED IN THE FIRE ECONOMY

The problem is that Primo's good intentions do not lead anywhere when the only legal jobs he can compete for fail to provide him with a livable wage. None of the crack dealers were explicitly conscious of the links between their limited options in the legal economy, their addiction to drugs and their dependence on the crack economy for economic survival and personal dignity. Nevertheless, all of Primo's colleagues and employees told stories of rejecting what they considered to be intolerable working conditions at entry-level jobs.

Most entered the legal labor market at exceptionally young ages. By the time they were 12, they were bagging and delivering groceries at the supermarket for tips, stocking beer off the books in local bodegas or running errands. Before reaching 21, however, virtually none had fulfilled their early childhood dreams of finding stable, well-paid legal work.

The problem is structural: From the 1950s through the 1980s second-generation inner-city Puerto Ricans were trapped in the most vulnerable niche of a factory-based economy that was rapidly being replaced by service industries. Between 1950 and 1990, the proportion of factory jobs in New York City decreased approximately three-fold at the same time that service-sector jobs doubled. The Department of City Planning calculates that more than 800,000 industrial jobs were lost from the 1960s through the early 1990s, while the total number of jobs of all categories remained more or less constant at 3.5 million.

Few scholars have noted the cultural dislocations of the new service economy. These cultural clashes have been most pronounced in the office-work service jobs that have multiplied because of the dramatic expansion of the finance, real estate and insurance (FIRE) sector in New York City. Service work in professional offices is the most dynamic place for ambitious inner-city youths to find entry-level jobs if they aspire to upward mobility. Employment as mailroom clerks, photocopiers and messengers in the highrise office corridors of the financial district propels many into a wrenching cultural confrontation with the upper-middle-class white world. Obedience to the norms of highrise, office-corridor culture is in direct contradiction to street culture's definitions of personal dignity especially for males who are socialized not to accept public subordination.

Most of the dealers have not completely withdrawn from the legal economy. On the contrary—they are precariously perched on its edge. Their poverty remains their only constant as they alternate between street-level crack dealing and just-above-minimum-wage legal employment. The working-class jobs they manage to find are objectively recognized to be among the least desirable in U.S. society; hence the following list of just a few of the jobs held by some of the Game Room regulars during the years I knew them: unlicensed asbestos remover, home attendant, street-corner flier distributor, deep-fat fry cook and night-shift security guard on the violent ward at the municipal hospital for the criminally insane.

The stable factory-worker incomes that might have allowed Caesar and Primo to support families have largely disappeared from the inner city. Perhaps if their social network had not been confined to the weakest sector of manufacturing in a period of rapid job loss, their teenage working-class dreams might have stabilized them for long enough to enable them to adapt to the restructuring of the local economy. Instead, they find themselves propelled headlong into an explosive confrontation between their sense of cultural dignity versus the humiliating interpersonal subordination of service work.

Workers like Caesar and Primo appear inarticulate to their professional supervisors when they try to imitate the language of power in the workplace; they stumble pathetically over the enunciation of unfamiliar words. They cannot decipher the hastily scribbled instructions—rife with mysterious abbreviations—that are left for them by harried office managers on diminutive Post-its. The "common sense" of white-collar work is foreign to them; they do not, for example, understand the logic in filing triplicate copies of memos or for postdating invoices. When they attempt to improvise or show initiative, they fail miserably and instead appear inefficient—or even hostile—for failing to follow "clearly specified" instructions.

In the highrise office buildings of midtown Manhattan or Wall Street, newly employed inner-city high school dropouts suddenly realize they look like idiotic buffoons to the men and women for whom they work. But people like Primo and Caesar have not passively accepted their structural victimization. On the contrary, by embroiling themselves in the underground economy and proudly embracing street culture, they are seeking an alternative to their social marginalization. In the process, on a daily level, they become the actual agents administering their own destruction and their community's suffering.

Both Primo and Caesar experienced deep humiliation and insecurity in their attempts to penetrate the foreign, hostile world of highrise office corridors. Primo had bitter memories of being the mailroom clerk and errand boy at a now-defunct professional trade magazine. The only time he explicitly admitted to having experienced racism was when he described how he was treated at that particular work setting.

> *Primo:* I had a prejudiced boss. . . . When she was talking to people she would say, "He's illiterate," as if I was really that stupid that I couldn't understand what she was talking about.
>
> So what I did one day—you see they had this big dictionary right there on the desk, a big heavy motherfucker—so what I just did was open up the dictionary, and I just looked up the word, "illiterate." And that's when I saw what she was calling me.
>
> So she's saying that I'm stupid or something. I'm stupid! [pointing to himself with both thumbs and making a hulking face] "He doesn't know shit."

In contrast, in the underground economy Primo never had to risk this kind of threat to his self-worth.

> *Primo:* Ray would never disrespect me that way; he wouldn't tell me that because he's illiterate too, plus I've got more education than him. I almost got a G.E.D.

The contemporary street sensitivity to being dissed immediately emerges in these memories of office humiliation. The machismo of street culture exacerbates the sense of insult experienced by men because the majority of office supervisors at the entry level are women. In the lowest recesses of New York City's FIRE sector, tens of thousands of messengers, photocopy machine operators and security guards serving the Fortune 500 companies are brusquely ordered about by young white executives—often female—who sometimes make bimonthly salaries superior to their underlings' yearly wages. The extraordinary wealth of Manhattan's financial district exacerbates the sense of sexist-racist insult associated with performing just-above-minimum-wage labor.

"I DON'T EVEN GOT A DRESS SHIRT"

Several months earlier, I had watched Primo drop out of a "motivational training" employment program in the basement of his mother's housing project, run by former heroin addicts who had just received a multimillion-dollar private sector grant for their innovative approach to training the "unemployable." Primo felt profoundly disrespected by the program, and he focused his discontent on the humiliation he faced because of his inappropriate wardrobe. The fundamental philosophy of such motivational job-training programs is that "these people have an attitude problem." They take a boot-camp approach to their unemployed clients, ripping their self-esteem apart during the first week in order to build them back up with an epiphanic realization that they want to find jobs as security guards, messengers and data-input clerks in just-above-minimum-wage service-sector positions. The program's highest success rate had been with middle-aged African-American women who wanted to terminate their relationship to welfare once their children leave home.

I originally had a "bad attitude" toward the premise of psychologically motivating and manipulating people to accept boring, poorly paid jobs. At the same time, however, the violence and self-destruction I was witnessing at the Game Room was convincing me that it is better to be exploited at work than to be outside the legal labor market. In any case, I persuaded Primo and a half-dozen of his Game Room associates to sign up for the program. Even Caesar was tempted to join.

None of the crack dealers lasted for more than three sessions. Primo was the first to drop out, after the first day. For several weeks he avoided talking about the experience. I repeatedly pressed him to explain why he "just didn't show up" at the sessions. Only after repeated badgering on my part did he finally express the deep sense of shame and vulnerability he experienced whenever he attempted to venture into the legal labor market.

> *Philippe:* Yo Primo, listen to me. I worry that there's something taking place that you're not aware of, in terms of yourself. Like the coke that you be sniffing all the time; it's like every night.
>
> *Primo:* What do you mean?
>
> *Philippe:* Like not showing up at the job training. You say it's just procrastination, but I'm scared that it's something deeper that you're not dealing with. . . .
>
> *Primo:* The truth though—listen Felipe—my biggest worry was the dress code, 'cause my gear is limited. I don't even got a dress shirt, I only got one pair of shoes, and you can't wear sneakers at that program. They wear ties too—don't they? Well, I ain't even got ties—I only got the one you lent me.
>
> I would've been there three weeks in the same gear: T-shirt and jeans. *Estoy jodido como un bón!* [I'm all fucked up like a bum!]
>
> *Philippe:* What the fuck kinda bullshit excuse are you talking about? Don't tell me you were thinking that shit. No one notices how people are dressed.
>
> *Primo:* Yo, Felipe, this is for real! Listen to me! I was thinking about that shit hard. Hell yeah!
>
> Hell, yes, they would notice if somebody's wearing a fucked-up tie and shirt.
>
> I don't want to be in a program all *abochornado* [bumlike]. I probably won't even concentrate, getting dished, like . . . and being looked at like a sucker. Dirty jeans . . . or like old jeans, because I would have to wear jeans, 'cause I only got one slack. Word though! I only got two dress shirts and one of them is missing buttons.
>
> I didn't want to tell you about that because it's like a poor excuse, but that was the only shit I was really thinking about. At the time I just said, "Well, I just don't show up."

And Felipe, I'm a stupid [very] skinny nigga'. So I have to be careful how I dress, otherwise people will think I be on the stem [a crack addict who smokes out of a glass-stem pipe].

Philippe: [nervously] Oh shit. I'm even skinnier than you. People must think I'm a total drug addict.

Primo: Don't worry. You're white.

CHAPTER 39

Unjust Rewards

KEN SILVERSTEIN

In 1989, an explosion ripped through a Phillips Petroleum chemical plant in Pasadena, Texas, killing 23 workers and injuring more than 100. Federal officials fined the company $4 million, citing "clear evidence that the explosion was avoidable had recognized safety practices been followed." In 1999 and 2000, two more explosions at the plant left another 3 workers dead and 73 injured. Phillips was hit with an additional $2.3 million in fines for ignoring safety hazards.

In 1994, a worker was killed in an explosion at an Arizona factory run by TRW, the nation's leading maker of air bags. The company, which had a record of violating workplace laws at the plant, settled criminal charges in the case for $1.7 million. Officials later discovered that TRW, in a move "clearly approved by management," was illegally dumping chemical waste from the plant at landfills in three states. Last year, the company paid a record $24 million in civil and criminal penalties.

In 1999, a jury found Koch Industries guilty of negligence in the deaths of two teenagers killed in a fire caused by a corroded pipeline. The following year, the Kansas-based energy giant paid $30 million—the largest civil penalty in the history of the Clean Water Act—for illegally discharging 3 million gallons of crude oil in six states. Last year, Koch paid $25 million to settle charges that it lied about how much oil it was pumping out of federal lands, cheating the government in nearly 25,000 separate transactions.

Phillips, TRW, and Koch have more in common than a history of repeatedly violating workplace and environmental laws. They also rank among the nation's largest government contractors. Between 1995 and 2000, the three corporations received a combined total of $10.4 billion in federal business—at the same time that regulatory agencies and federal courts were citing the companies for jeopardizing the safety of their employees, polluting the nation's air and water, and even defrauding the government.

That's not supposed to happen. Federal contracting officers are charged with reviewing the record of companies that do business with the government and barring those that fail to demonstrate "a satisfactory record of integrity and business ethics." But officials are given no guidelines to follow in making such decisions, and there's no centralized system they can consult to inform them of corporate wrong-doing. As a result, a government report concluded in 2000, those responsible for awarding federal contracts are "extremely reluctant" to take action, even when they are aware of violations. And in the rare instances when the rule is enforced, it is almost always employed against small companies with little clout in Washington.

Shortly before leaving office, President Clinton issued a new order to provide clear guidelines for deciding which firms share in the roughly $200 billion in federal contracts awarded each year. The new "contractor responsibility rule"—championed by Vice President Al Gore and developed after two years of congressional testimony and public hearings—specified that federal officials should weigh "evidence of repeated, pervasive, or significant violations of the law." Officials were told to consider whether a company has cheated on prior contracts or violated laws involving the environment, workplace safety, labor rights, consumer protection, or antitrust activities.

The measure was never implemented. In one of his first acts as president, George W. Bush put the rule on hold after only 11 days in office, saying the issue needed further study. With big business suing to block the new guidelines, Bush revoked the rule 11 months later.

Some 80,000 contractors do at least $25,000 in business with the federal government each year, and the great majority comply with the law. But a six-month investigation by *Mother Jones* of the nation's 200 largest contractors found that the government continues to award lucrative contracts to dozens of companies that it has repeatedly cited for serious violations of workplace and environmental laws. The government's own database of contractors was matched with lists of the worst violations documented by the Environmental Protection Agency (EPA) and the Occupational Safety and Health Administration (OSHA) between 1995 and 2000. Among the findings:

• Forty-six of the biggest contractors were prosecuted by the Justice Department and ordered to pay cleanup costs after they refused to take responsibility for dumping hazardous waste and other environmental violations. General Electric—which received nearly $9.8 billion from the government, making it the nation's 10th-largest contractor—topped the list with 27 cases of pollution for which it was held solely or jointly liable.

• Fifty-five of the top contractors were cited for a total of 1,375 violations of workplace safety law that posed a risk of death or serious physical harm to workers. Ford Motor, which ranks 177th among contractors with $442 million in federal business, led the OSHA list with 292 violations deemed "serious" by federal officials. In 1999, six workers were killed and dozens injured when a boiler exploded at Ford's River Rouge Complex in Dearborn, Michigan. The company was hit with a $1.5 million fine after an internal memo revealed that Ford had decided not to replace safety equipment on the aging boilers because it would then have to fully upgrade them to meet "all present safety standards."

TABLE 39.1   The Dirty Dozen: Federal Contractors with Both EPA and OSHA
Violations, Ranked by Penalties (1995–2000)

	Contracts (in millions)	Rank as Contractor	EPA Violations	OSHA Violations	Total Penalties
Ford Motor	$442	177	12	292	$6,082,271
TRW	10,267	9	3	79	5,745,234
Archer Daniels Midland	471	168	4	93	1,676,850
ExxonMobil	2,173	43	20	5	1,481,400
E.J. DuPont de Nemours	446	175	17	23	956,700
Avondale Industries	1,347	66	1	73	759,100
General Motors	4,854	18	21	14	418,393
General Electric	9,777	10	27	48	369,363
Olin Corp.	1,310	68	7	4	168,500
Atlantic Richfield	675	138	10	1	150,600
DaimlerChrysler	1,575	54	7	166	130,121
Textron	5,507	17	4	78	111,215

ABOUT THE DATA

The "contractor responsibility rule" revoked by President Bush required officials to review a company's recent history of violating federal laws. To determine which contractors have the worst records in two significant areas covered by the rule—the environment and workplace safety—*Mother Jones* compiled a list of 200 corporations that did the most business with the government between 1995 and 2000. The list was then matched to two federal databases: a list of companies prosecuted by the Justice Department and found liable for environmental violations, and a list of firms cited by the Occupational Safety and Health Administration for posing a serious risk of injury or death to workers. Database work was conducted by Ron Nixon of Investigative Reporters and Editors, a nonprofit organization based in Columbia, Missouri. Additional reporting was provided by George Sanchez, with documentation from the Project on Government Oversight, a research group based in Washington, D.C. A complete list of violations committed by the top 200 contractors is available online at *www.motherjones.com.*

- Thirty-four leading contractors were penalized for violating both environmental and workplace safety rules. The firms were hit with a total of $12.6 million in EPA penalties and $5.9 million in OSHA fines—costs more than covered by the $229 billion in federal contracts they were awarded during the same period.

"It is clear that, in many cases, the government continues to do business with contractors who violate laws, sometimes repeatedly," concludes a 2000 report by the Federal Acquisition Regulatory Council, the agency that oversees federal contractors. Others put it more bluntly. "Government should not do business with crooks," says Rep. George Miller (D-Calif.), who has demanded that the White House make public any closed-door meetings it had with corporate lobbyists to discuss killing the contractor responsibility rule. Bush's decision, Miller says, "sends a message to contractors that the government doesn't care if you underpay your workers, or expose them to toxic hazards, or destroy the public lands—the government will do business with you anyway."

During Bill Clinton's second term in office, a coalition of labor, civil rights, and consumer groups lobbied the government to crack down on contractor misconduct. Backed by Miller and other congressional allies, they pointed to numerous studies documenting the extent of the problem. A 1995 report by the Government Accounting Office revealed that 80 major federal contractors had violated the National Labor Relations Act by seeking to suppress unions. Another GAO report found that in 1994 alone, OSHA imposed fines of $15,000 or more on each of 261 companies that had received a combined $38 billion in federal contracts. Noting that some contractors place workers "at substantial risk of injury or illness," the report added that the "prospect of debarment or suspension can provide impetus for a contractor to undertake remedial measures to improve working conditions."

In July 1999, Clinton declared his support for the reform coalition and announced plans to revise the rule. What emerged over the next two years was a set of specific guidelines for federal contracting officers to follow in determining a company's eligibility. The new rule created a hierarchy of violations to be considered, topped by convictions for contract fraud. It stipulated that only repeated and serious wrongdoing, not administrative complaints, should be weighed. And it acknowledged a need for flexibility, noting that companies with serious violations might continue to receive contracts if they "correct the conditions that led to the misconduct."

"We view this fundamentally as empowering the government to do what every business in the world does, which is not to be forced to do business with people it doesn't trust," said Joshua Gotbaum, who helped draft the rule as controller of the Office of Management and Budget.

Clinton's move generated a fast and furious reaction from business and industry. The Business Roundtable, the U.S. Chamber of Commerce, and the National Association of Manufacturers launched a fierce lobbying campaign against the new rule. Despite a provision stating that only a pattern of "pervasive" and "significant" abuses would be considered, business opponents argued that the guidelines gave contracting officers excessive discretion to arbitrarily torpedo a contractor. "The proposed rules would allow contract officers to blacklist firms without regard to the number, nature, or severity of violations," said the National Center for Policy Analysis, a business-backed think tank. "Suspicions raised by rivals or disgruntled employees could cost firms millions, if not billions, of dollars."

To fight the measure, the business coalition hired Linda Fuselier of the Capitol Group, a high-powered lobbyist who had previously helped insurance firms avoid cleanup costs at Superfund waste sites. Opponents flooded officials with hundreds of comments opposing the guidelines. And when Clinton formally issued the new rule in December 2000, they went to federal court seeking to get the provision thrown out.

The court never had to decide the issue. A month later, when Bush took office, he immediately moved to postpone the rule. On January 31, 2001, federal agencies were quietly ordered to delay implementing it for six months—without issuing a public notice or soliciting comment. The Congressional Research Service issued an opinion concluding that the secret suspension of the rule was probably illegal, but the move went virtually unreported in the media. When Bush finally revoked the rule while vacationing at his Texas ranch last December, corporate executives and their allies in Congress hailed the decision. "There was never any rational basis or need for additional standards, since existing regulations already ensure the government does not do business with unethical companies," declared Rep. Thomas Davis III, a Republican from Virginia.

In reality, the government makes little effort to review contractors' records—and even the most diligent contracting officer would find it almost impossible to do so. The government does not maintain a central database to store information on contractors' records of compliance with the law. The EPA and OSHA maintain their own lists of corporate violations, but parent companies are not linked to their subsidiaries, which can number in the hundreds. OSHA makes some of its records available online, but the EPA and many other agencies do not. "There's no process built into the review system," says Gary Bass, executive director of OMB Watch, a Washington-based advocate of government accountability. "Just finding the right information is complicated and time-consuming."

As a result, even contractors that commit the most obvious violations are never suspended or debarred. One GAO study found that the government continues to award business to defense contractors that have committed fraud on prior contracts. General Dynamics, the nation's fifth-largest contractor, paid the government nearly $2 million in 1995 to resolve charges that it falsified employee time cards to bill the Pentagon for thousands of hours that were never worked on a contract for testing F-16 fighters. Northrop Grumman, the nation's fourth-largest contractor, paid nearly $6.7 million in 2000 to settle two separate cases in which it was charged with inflating the costs of parts and materials for warplanes. Yet the two defense giants continue to receive federal contracts, collecting a combined total of $38 billion between 1995 and 2000.

Opponents argue that the government already has the power to force contractors to clean up their act, without cutting them off from federal business. In addition, some contractors can be difficult to replace. The Pentagon, for example, maintains that it cannot afford to ban large defense contractors who provide specialized services and products, and the government is reluctant to take away contracts from nursing homes that commit Medicare fraud, fearing that patients will be hurt. "Debarment and suspension isn't practical," says Steven Schooner, a lawyer in the Office of Federal Procurement Policy under Clinton. "If the government needs the goods they produce, it's the only one that loses."

But while big contractors are all but immune from scrutiny, the government has no qualms about denying business to smaller operations that violate the law. Some 24,000 contractors are currently barred from government work, and almost all are small firms or individuals like Kenneth Hansen, a Kansas dentist banned from receiving federal funds to provide care for low-income patients because he defaulted on $164,800 in student loans. "We never take down the big guys," concedes Schooner, now a government-contracts law professor at George Washington University.

The review of environmental and workplace violations by *Mother Jones* reveals that many big contractors could have been forced to forfeit federal business had Bush not interceded on their behalf. Consider the record of ExxonMobil, which became the nation's 43rd-largest contractor when the two oil giants merged in 1999. Between 1995 and 2000, the firms received a total of $2.2 billion from the government for everything from renting fuel storage space to the Pentagon to selling oil to the Commerce Department. At the same time, they were openly disregarding the law. ExxonMobil has been held liable, either on its own or with other companies, in 20 cases in which it refused to clean up Superfund sites or take responsibility for air and water violations. The company is a partner in Colonial Pipeline, an Atlanta-based firm that the Justice Department sued in 2000 for multiple spills in nine states. In one incident, a pipeline rupture poured 950,000 gallons of diesel fuel into the Reedy River in South Carolina, killing 35,000 fish and other wildlife. In 1995, Mobil was hit with a $98,500 fine for its failure to inspect equipment at a refinery in Torrance, California, where 28 workers were injured in an explosion. In 1999, authorities discovered that Exxon had knowingly contaminated water supplies near a refinery in Benicia, California, with benzene and toluene, both of which cause cancer and birth defects.

One of the federal contractors with the worst record of workplace violations is Avondale Industries, which builds ships for the Navy. Between 1990 and 1996, nine workers died at Avondale's shipyard outside New Orleans, a death rate nearly three times that at other Navy shipyards. In 1999, OSHA inspectors uncovered hundreds of violations of safety and health standards, including Avondale's failure to provide safe scaffolding or training for employees who work at dangerous heights. OSHA hit the company with $717,000 in fines, among the largest ever imposed on a shipbuilder. "The stiff penalties are warranted," said then-Secretary of Labor Alexis Herman. "Workers should not have to risk their lives for their livelihood."

Yet just a month after the fines, the government awarded Avondale $22 million to work on amphibious assault ships at the New Orleans yard. The following year, three more workers were killed in accidents at the Avondale yard. One of the victims, 33-year-old Faustino Mendoza, died of head injuries when he fell 80 feet from scaffolding that lacked required safety features—the same problem that had been found during the most recent inspection. OSHA fined Avondale $49,000 for the "repeat" violation, but the penalty amounted to a tiny fraction of the $1.3 billion the firm received in federal business between 1995 and 2000. (Last year, Avondale became a subsidiary of Northrop Grumman.)

Another contractor with a pattern of workplace abuses is Tyson Foods, which received more than $163 million between 1995 and 2000, mostly for supplying poultry to government agencies. In 1999, seven workers died at plants run by Tyson or its independent operators. One of the victims was a 15-year-old boy—hired in violation of child-labor laws—who was electrocuted at a Tyson plant in Arkansas. The company has also attempted to buy influence with federal officials. In 1997, Tyson pleaded guilty to giving former Agriculture Secretary Michael Espy more than $12,000 in "gratuities" while the firm had issues before his department.

Even though the current federal rule requires contractors like Tyson, Avondale, and ExxonMobil to demonstrate "integrity and business ethics," they are in no danger of being barred from receiving federal business under the current standard. Indeed, the government continues to award major contracts to companies that have both defrauded the government *and* violated environmental and workplace laws.

TRW, the nation's ninth-largest contractor, supplies the government with everything from military satellites and spacecraft to auto parts and hand tools. Yet the company's subsidiaries have been cited for cheating the government on defense contracts, and last year it settled two cases in which it forced its employees to work off the clock and mishandled pension payments. In 1997, TRW was also listed in a "rogues' gallery" of OSHA violators in a study by *Business and Management Practices*. In just two years, the magazine found, the company racked up 67 violations and $113,202 in fines. In a single inspection in December 1999, OSHA cited TRW for 43 serious and repeat violations at an auto-parts plant in Michigan.

Some of TRW's most egregious offenses took place at two air-bag plants that lie at the foot of the Superstition Mountains near Mesa, Arizona. Within two years after they opened in 1989, the factories had experienced dozens of fires and explosions, and were the target of at least six investigations by state regulators. "There were explosions so big that they felt like earthquakes," says Bunny Bertleson, who lives less than two miles from one of the plants. "Then clouds would come blowing out of the stacks."

The cause of the blasts was sodium azide, a highly volatile chemical that triggers the explosion that inflates air bags upon impact. Sodium azide is also highly toxic. It can damage the heart, kidneys, and nervous system if it is inhaled or comes into contact with the skin or eyes. Acute exposure can cause death.

A string of injuries suffered by workers at the Mesa plants drew the attention of state regulators. Employees frequently reported feeling queasy and dizzy, a condition they dubbed the "azide buzz," but say the company failed to address the problem. "There was constant pressure to get the production numbers up," recalls Felipe Chavez, a former employee. "That was the only priority." TRW insists that such exposure is rare, and that employee safety is "our highest priority." But in 1994, a spark detonated a small quantity of sodium azide, killing one worker and injuring six. The following year, the Mesa fire chief shut down one of the plants for two days, calling it an "imminent threat to both life and property."

The Arizona attorney general's office had already taken TRW to court and won consent orders requiring it to halt the fires, which were releasing sodium azide into the air, and to properly manage hazardous waste at the plants. In 1995, after the company failed to take safety steps it had promised to make to settle prior charges, a state superior court ordered TRW to pay $1.7 million—the largest corporate criminal consent judgment in state history.

But neither court-ordered fines nor injuries to workers prompted TRW to clean up its act. In 1997, an anonymous caller informed a state environmental agency that TRW was illegally storing wastewater laced with sodium azide at one of its Mesa plants. Following up on the tip, state investigators discovered that the company had illegally disposed of hundreds of thousands of gallons of chemical wastewater at landfills in Arizona, Utah, and California. The Arizona attorney general's office determined that the dumping was not "the work of low-level employees" but involved the "approval or acquiescence" of management.

Given the scope of the illegal dumping and TRW's history of breaking its promises, the state pressed criminal charges against the company. In a statement, TRW said that "the errors that occurred did not result in harm to the environment, local residents, or our employees." But last year, the company agreed to pay $24 million to the government for the illegal dumping—the largest such consent agreement in history.

Yet the company's pattern of lawbreaking has not harmed its ability to do business with the government. Between 1995 and 2000, when most of the illegal dumping and other abuses took place, TRW received nearly $10.3 billion in federal contracts—more than 400 times the amount it agreed to pay for its environmental crimes. After the company was caught dumping sodium azide, federal officials reviewed its violations and decided that it should remain eligible to work for the government. Last year, TRW received another $2.5 billion in federal contracts.

PART TWELVE

America in the World

The events of September 11, 2001, drove home for Americans the reality that we are part of a global community that is connected, for better or worse, in multiple and intricate ways—and that what happens in our own country cannot be divorced from what happens in the rest of the world. To an important extent, of course, that has always been true. America has never existed in pristine isolation from the rest of the globe. We are, for one thing, a nation of immigrants, and we cannot understand our history without understanding the importance of the international slave trade in the eighteenth and nineteenth centuries, for example, or the impact of social changes in countries as diverse as Ireland, Poland, and Mexico on our development as a society.

But the world is even more tightly connected today than in the past, with the increasing speed of transportation and communication and the continued movement of vast numbers of people across nations and continents because of war, oppression, or economic insecurity. More than ever, it is impossible to think about many social problems in America without setting them in the context of the changes that are reshaping the wider world. In this section, we introduce some of the most important of them.

We begin with a wide-ranging discussion by Moises Naim, editor of the journal *Foreign Policy*, of five global social problems—the international trade in drugs, arms, intellectual property, people, and money. Our efforts to deal with these problems, Naim argues, have been badly flawed, in part because we have tried to deal with them as if they were merely problems of law enforcement, when in fact they have become something much larger and more complex. We are probably most familiar with the drug trade, which, after decades of efforts at control, now amounts to a business worth an estimated $400 billion a year, roughly equivalent to the entire economic output of Spain. But we have also made little headway against the trade in small arms, which accounts for 1,000 deaths a *day* around the world. These

global businesses, nimble, decentralized, and hugely profitable, have easily outma-
neuvered resource-poor governments. If we want to have a greater impact on them,
Naim argues, we will need, among other things, to invest more in international agencies to control them. Today, for example, Interpol, the main international police
agency, has an annual budget that is less than the cost of one of the more advanced
boats or airplanes now used by international drug traffickers.

Naim's analysis suggests that these problems are partly of our own making—
a reflection of our own global policies. In the excerpt from his book *Blowback,*
Chalmers Johnson extends this point, arguing that the spread of American power
around the world has bred a host of troubling, unforeseen consequences. We do not
always recognize those consequences as being the results of our own intervention,
of course—but, Johnson argues, they often are. American economic policies, for
example, imposed partly through international agencies such as the International
Monetary Fund, can undermine economies halfway around the world: when this
happens, it is often assumed to be the natural effect of an abstract process of "globalization." Johnson argues that we have created a global "empire" based on extending American military and economic power "to every corner of the world." But we
have paid far too little attention to the consequences—especially the effect on how
we are viewed by the people around the world whose lives are being shaped by these
policies. We may, as a result, be breeding a global crisis of massive proportions. The
growth of international terrorism, Johnson argues, is only the most dramatic expression of that crisis. *Blowback* was written before the events of September 11,
2001, but they only confirm the importance of his disturbing analysis.

Most Americans, as Johnson points out, are unaware of the full extent of our
involvements in various parts of the world, and may know even less about the reasons behind them. But our policies toward other countries are hardly random: from
the beginning, they have been influenced by complex and shifting economic and
political interests. As Michael Klare shows, one of the most important motives behind America's foreign policy (and that of many other countries) has been the desire to ensure a steady supply of energy—which, in our petroleum-driven economy,
prominently includes oil. Concern over securing oil supplies helped to shape the political landscape of the contemporary Middle East, with all its volatility and tragedy;
helped precipitate World War II; and, more recently, has been a backdrop for our two
wars with Iraq. And as oil reserves inevitably dwindle, Klare points out, conflict over
them is likely to increase.

One of the most troubling consequences of global instability and insecurity
today is the continuing threat from what are now often called "weapons of mass destruction." The danger of nuclear weapons, in particular, represents another example of the unanticipated consequences of policies we adopted without thinking much
about the long term. During the Cold War with the Soviet Union, both sides amassed
a huge arsenal of nuclear weapons and the materials to build them. Today, that arsenal remains to haunt us. Despite considerable efforts to reduce them, both the U.S.
and the former Soviet Union still have large stores of nuclear material; and, at least
in Russia, it is poorly guarded. It takes less than 18 pounds of plutonium to produce
a basic nuclear weapon; Russia has an estimated 140 *tons* of weapons-grade pluto-

nium. At the same time, the number of countries possessing actual nuclear weapons has grown, and now includes India and Pakistan—two poor and troubled nations that have been intermittently at war with each other for years. For more than half a century, America's nuclear scientists have produced a "Doomsday Clock" that symbolically marks the level of nuclear danger in the world. Midnight stands for nuclear catastrophe; according to the clock, we are only seven minutes away. As the scientists note, there has been progress in some areas toward reducing the threat of nuclear weapons. But in a volatile and uncertain world, there is still a long way to go.

CHAPTER 40

Five Wars We're Losing

MOISES NAIM

T he persistence of al Qaeda underscores how hard it is for governments to stamp out stateless, decentralized networks that move freely, quickly, and stealthily across national borders to engage in terror. The intense media coverage devoted to the war on terrorism, however, obscures five other similar global wars that pit governments against agile, well-financed networks of highly dedicated individuals. These are the fights against the illegal international trade in drugs, arms, intellectual property, people, and money. Religious zeal or political goals drive terrorists, but the promise of enormous financial gain motivates those who battle governments in these five wars. Tragically, profit is no less a motivator for murder, mayhem, and global insecurity than religious fanaticism.

In one form or another, governments have been fighting these five wars for centuries. And losing them. Indeed, thanks to the changes spurred by globalization over the last decade, their losing streak has become even more pronounced. To be sure, nation-states have benefited from the information revolution, stronger political and economic linkages, and the shrinking importance of geographic distance. Unfortunately, criminal networks have benefited even more. Never fettered by the niceties of sovereignty, they are now increasingly free of geographic constraints. Moreover, globalization has not only expanded illegal markets and boosted the size and the resources of criminal networks, it has also imposed more burdens on governments: Tighter public budgets, decentralization, privatization, deregulation, and a more open environment for international trade and investment all make the task of fighting global criminals more difficult. Governments are made up of cumbersome bureaucracies that generally cooperate with difficulty, but drug traffickers, arms dealers, alien smugglers, counterfeiters, and money launderers have refined networking to a high science, entering into complex and improbable strategic alliances that span cultures and continents.

Defeating these foes may prove impossible. But the first steps to reversing their recent dramatic gains must be to recognize the fundamental similarities among the five wars and to treat these conflicts not as law enforcement problems but as a new global trend that shapes the world as much as confrontations between nation-states did in the past. Customs officials, police officers, lawyers, and judges alone will never win these wars. Governments must recruit and deploy more spies, soldiers, diplomats, and economists who understand how to use incentives and regulations to steer markets away from bad social outcomes. But changing the skill set of government combatants alone will not end these wars. Their doctrines and institutions also need a major overhaul.

THE FIVE WARS

Pick up any newspaper anywhere in the world, any day, and you will find news about illegal migrants, drug busts, smuggled weapons, laundered money, or counterfeit goods. The global nature of these five wars was unimaginable just a decade ago. The resources—financial, human, institutional, technological—deployed by the combatants have reached unfathomable orders of magnitude. So have the numbers of victims. The tactics and tricks of both sides boggle the mind. Yet if you cut through the fog of daily headlines and orchestrated photo ops, one inescapable truth emerges: The world's governments are fighting a qualitatively new phenomenon with obsolete tools, inadequate laws, inefficient bureaucratic arrangements, and ineffective strategies. Not surprisingly, the evidence shows that governments are losing.

Drugs

The best known of the five wars is, of course, the war on drugs. In 1999, the United Nations' "Human Development Report" calculated the annual trade in illicit drugs at $400 billion, roughly the size of the Spanish economy and about 8 percent of world trade. Many countries are reporting an increase in drug use. Feeding this habit is a global supply chain that uses everything from passenger jets that can carry shipments of cocaine worth $500 million in a single trip to custom-built submarines that ply the waters between Colombia and Puerto Rico. To foil eavesdroppers, drug smugglers use "cloned" cell phones and broadband radio receivers while also relying on complex financial structures that blend legitimate and illegitimate enterprises with elaborate fronts and structures of cross-ownership.

The United States spends between $35 billion and $40 billion each year on the war on drugs; most of this money is spent on interdiction and intelligence. But the creativity and boldness of drug cartels has routinely outstripped steady increases in government resources. Responding to tighter security at the U.S.-Mexican border, drug smugglers built a tunnel to move tons of drugs and billions of dollars in cash until authorities discovered it in March 2002. Over the last decade, the success of the Bolivian and Peruvian governments in eradicating coca plantations has shifted production to Colombia. Now, the U.S.-supported Plan Colombia is displacing coca production and processing labs back to other Andean countries. Despite the heroic efforts of these Andean countries and the massive financial and technical support of the United States, the total acreage of coca plantations in Peru, Colombia, and

Bolivia has increased in the last decade from 206,200 hectares in 1991 to 210,939 in 2001. Between 1990 and 2000, according to economist Jeff DeSimone, the median price of a gram of cocaine in the United States fell from $152 to $112.

Even when top leaders of drug cartels are captured or killed, former rivals take their place. Authorities have acknowledged, for example, that the recent arrest of Benjamin Arellano Felix, accused of running Mexico's most ruthless drug cartel, has done little to stop the flow of drugs to the United States. As Arellano said in a recent interview from jail, "They talk about a war against the Arellano brothers. They haven't won. I'm here, and nothing has changed."

Arms Trafficking

Drugs and arms often go together. In 1999, the Peruvian military parachuted 10,000 AK-47s to the Revolutionary Armed Forces of Colombia, a guerrilla group closely allied to drug growers and traffickers. The group purchased the weapons in Jordan. Most of the roughly 80 million AK-47s in circulation today are in the wrong hands. According to the United Nations, only 18 million (or about 3 percent) of the 550 million small arms and light weapons in circulation today are used by government, military, or police forces. Illicit trade accounts for almost 20 percent of the total small arms trade and generates more than $1 billion a year. Small arms helped fuel 46 of the 49 largest conflicts of the last decade and in 2001 were estimated to be responsible for 1,000 deaths a day; more than 80 percent of those victims were women and children.

Small arms are just a small part of the problem. The illegal market for munitions encompasses top-of-the-line tanks, radar systems that detect Stealth aircraft, and the makings of the deadliest weapons of mass destruction. The International Atomic Energy Agency has confirmed more than a dozen cases of smuggled nuclear-weapons-usable material, and hundreds more cases have been reported and investigated over the last decade. The actual supply of stolen nuclear-, biological-, or chemical-weapons materials and technology may still be small. But the potential demand is strong and growing from both would-be nuclear powers and terrorists. Constrained supply and increasing demand cause prices to rise and create enormous incentives for illegal activities. More than one fifth of the 120,000 workers in Russia's former "nuclear cities"—where more than half of all employees earn less than $50 a month—say they would be willing to work in the military complex of another country.

Governments have been largely ineffective in curbing either supply or demand. In recent years, two countries, Pakistan and India, joined the declared nuclear power club. A U.N. arms embargo failed to prevent the reported sale to Iraq of jet fighter engine parts from Yugoslavia and the Kolchuga anti-Stealth radar system from Ukraine. Multilateral efforts to curb the manufacture and distribution of weapons are faltering, not least because some powers are unwilling to accept curbs on their own activities. In 2001, for example, the United States blocked a legally binding global treaty to control small arms in part because it worried about restrictions on its own citizens' rights to own guns. In the absence of effective international legislation and enforcement, the laws of economics dictate the sale of more weapons at cheaper prices: In 1986, an AK-47 in Kolowa, Kenya, cost 15 cows. Today, it costs just four.

Intellectual Property

In 2001, two days after recording the voice track of a movie in Hollywood, actor Dennis Hopper was in Shanghai where a street vendor sold him an excellent pirated copy of the movie with his voice already on it. "I don't know how they got my voice into the country before I got here," he wondered. Hopper's experience is one tiny slice of an illicit trade that cost the United States an estimated $9.4 billion in 2001. The piracy rate of business software in Japan and France is 40 percent, in Greece and South Korea it is about 60 percent, and in Germany and Britain it hovers around 30 percent. Forty percent of Procter & Gamble shampoos and 60 percent of Honda motorbikes sold in China in 2001 were pirated. Up to 50 percent of medical drugs in Nigeria and Thailand are bootleg copies. This problem is not limited to consumer products: Italian makers of industrial valves worry that their $2 billion a year export market is eroded by counterfeit Chinese valves sold in world markets at prices that are 40 percent cheaper.

The drivers of this bootlegging boom are complex. Technology is obviously boosting both the demand and the supply of illegally copied products. Users of Napster, the now defunct Internet company that allowed anyone, anywhere to download and reproduce copyrighted music for free, grew from zero to 20 million in just one year. Some 500,000 film files are traded daily through file-sharing services such as Kazaa and Morpheus; and in late 2002, some 900 million music files could be downloaded for free on the Internet—that is, almost two and a half times more files than those available when Napster reached its peak in February 2001.

Global marketing and branding are also playing a part, as more people are attracted to products bearing a well-known brand like Prada or Cartier. And thanks to the rapid growth and integration into the global economy of countries, such as China, with weak central governments and ineffective laws, producing and exporting near perfect knockoffs are both less expensive and less risky. In the words of the CEO of one of the best known Swiss watchmakers: "We now compete with a product manufactured by Chinese prisoners. The business is run by the Chinese military, their families and friends, using roughly the same machines we have, which they purchased at the same industrial fairs we go to. The way we have rationalized this problem is by assuming that their customers and ours are different. The person that buys a pirated copy of one of our $5,000 watches for less than $100 is not a client we are losing. Perhaps it is a future client that some day will want to own the real thing instead of a fake. We may be wrong and we do spend money to fight the piracy of our products. But given that our efforts do not seem to protect us much, we close our eyes and hope for the better." This posture stands in contrast to that of companies that sell cheaper products such as garments, music, or videos, whose revenues are directly affected by piracy.

Governments have attempted to protect intellectual property rights through various means, most notably the World Trade Organization's Agreement on Trade-Related Aspects of Intellectual Property Rights (TRIPS). Several other organizations such as the World Intellectual Property Organization, the World Customs Union, and Interpol are also involved. Yet the large and growing volume of this trade, or a simple stroll in the streets of Manhattan or Madrid, show that governments are far from winning this fight.

Alien Smuggling

The man or woman who sells a bogus Hermes scarf or a Rolex watch in the streets of Milan is likely to be an illegal alien. Just as likely, he or she was transported across several continents by a trafficking network allied with another network that specializes in the illegal copying, manufacturing, and distributing of high-end, brand-name products.

Alien smuggling is a $7 billion a year enterprise and according to the United Nations is the fastest growing business of organized crime. Roughly 500,000 people enter the United States illegally each year—about the same number as illegally enter the European Union, and part of the approximately 150 million who live outside their countries of origin. Many of these backdoor travelers are voluntary migrants who pay smugglers up to $35,000, the top-dollar fee for passage from China to New York. Others, instead, are trafficked—that is, bought and sold internationally—as commodities. The U.S. Congressional Research Service reckons that each year between 1 million and 2 million people are trafficked across borders, the majority of whom are women and children. A woman can be "bought" in Timisoara, Romania, for between $50 and $200 and "resold" in Western Europe for 10 times that price. The United Nations Children's Fund estimates that cross-border smugglers in Central and Western Africa enslave 200,000 children a year. Traffickers initially tempt victims with job offers or, in the case of children, with offers of adoption in wealthier countries, and then keep the victims in subservience through physical violence, debt bondage, passport confiscation, and threats of arrest, deportation, or violence against their families back home.

Governments everywhere are enacting tougher immigration laws and devoting more time, money, and technology to fight the flow of illegal aliens. But the plight of the United Kingdom's government illustrates how tough that fight is. The British government throws money at the problem, plans to use the Royal Navy and Royal Air Force to intercept illegal immigrants, and imposes large fines on truck drivers who (generally unwittingly) transport stowaways. Still, 42,000 of the 50,000 refugees who have passed through the Sangatte camp (a main entry point for illegal immigration to the United Kingdom) over the last three years have made it to Britain. At current rates, it will take 43 years for Britain to clear its asylum backlog. And that country is an island. Continental nations such as Spain, Italy, or the United States face an even greater challenge as immigration pressures overwhelm their ability to control the inflow of illegal aliens.

Money Laundering

The Cayman Islands has a population of 36,000. It also has more than 2,200 mutual funds, 500 insurance companies, 60,000 businesses, and 600 banks and trust companies with almost $800 billion in assets. Not surprisingly, it figures prominently in any discussion of money laundering. So does the United States, several of whose major banks have been caught up in investigations of money laundering, tax evasion, and fraud. Few, if any, countries can claim to be free of the practice of helping individuals and companies hide funds from governments, creditors, business partners, or even family members, including the proceeds of tax evasion, gambling, and other crimes. Estimates of the volume of global money laundering range between 2 and 5 percent of the world's annual gross national product, or between $800 billion and $2 trillion.

Smuggling money, gold coins, and other valuables is an ancient trade. Yet in the last two decades, new political and economic trends coincided with technological changes to make this ancient trade easier, cheaper, and less risky. Political changes led to the deregulation of financial markets that now facilitate cross-border money transfers, and technological changes made distance less of a factor and money less "physical." Suitcases full of banknotes are still a key tool for money launderers, but computers, the Internet, and complex financial schemes that combine legal and illegal practices and institutions are more common. The sophistication of technology, the complex web of financial institutions that crisscross the globe, and the ease with which "dirty" funds can be electronically morphed into legitimate assets make the regulation of international flows of money a daunting task. In Russia, for example, it is estimated that by the mid-1990s organized crime groups had set up 700 legal and financial institutions to launder their money.

Faced with this growing tide, governments have stepped up their efforts to clamp down on rogue international banking, tax havens, and money laundering. The imminent, large-scale introduction of e-money—cards with microchips that can store large amounts of money and thus can be easily transported outside regular channels or simply exchanged among individuals—will only magnify this challenge.

WHY GOVERNMENTS CAN'T WIN

The fundamental changes that have given the five wars new intensity over the last decade are likely to persist. Technology will continue to spread widely; criminal networks will be able to exploit these technologies more quickly than governments that must cope with tight budgets, bureaucracies, media scrutiny, and electorates. International trade will continue to grow, providing more cover for the expansion of illicit trade. International migration will likewise grow, with much the same effect, offering ethnically based gangs an ever growing supply of recruits and victims. The spread of democracy may also help criminal cartels, which can manipulate weak public institutions by corrupting police officers or tempting politicians with offers of cash for their increasingly expensive election campaigns. And ironically, even the spread of international law—with its growing web of embargoes, sanctions, and conventions—will offer criminals new opportunities for providing forbidden goods to those on the wrong side of the international community.

These changes may affect each of the five wars in different ways, but these conflicts will continue to share four common characteristics:

They are not bound by geography. Some forms of crime have always had an international component: The Mafia was born in Sicily and exported to the United States, and smuggling has always been by definition international. But the five wars are truly global. Where is the theater or front line of the war on drugs? Is it Colombia or Miami? Myanmar (Burma) or Milan? Where are the battles against money launderers being fought? In Nauru or in London? Is China the main theater in the war against the infringement of intellectual property, or are the trenches of that war on the Internet?

They defy traditional notions of sovereignty. Al Qaeda's members have passports and nationalities—and often more than one—but they are truly stateless. Their allegiance is to their cause, not to any nation. The same is also true of the criminal networks engaged in the five wars. The same, however, is patently *not* true of government employees—police officers, customs agents, and judges—who fight them. This asymmetry is a crippling disadvantage for governments waging these wars. Highly paid, hypermotivated, and resource-rich combatants on one side of the wars (the criminal gangs) can seek refuge in and take advantage of national borders, but combatants of the other side (the governments) have fewer resources and are hampered by traditional notions of sovereignty. A former senior CIA official reported that international criminal gangs are able to move people, money, and weapons globally faster than he can move resources inside his own agency, let alone worldwide. Coordination and information sharing among government agencies in different countries has certainly improved, especially after September 11. Yet these tactics fall short of what is needed to combat agile organizations that can exploit every nook and cranny of an evolving but imperfect body of international law and multilateral treaties.

They pit governments against market forces. In each of the five wars, one or more government bureaucracies fight to contain the disparate, uncoordinated actions of thousands of independent, stateless organizations. These groups are motivated by large profits obtained by exploiting international price differentials, an unsatisfied demand, or the cost advantages produced by theft. Hourly wages for a Chinese cook are far higher in Manhattan than in Fujian. A gram of cocaine in Kansas City is 17,000 percent more expensive than in Bogotá. Fake Italian valves are 40 percent cheaper because counterfeiters don't have to cover the costs of developing the product. A well-funded guerrilla group will pay anything to get the weapons it needs. In each of these five wars, the incentives to successfully overcome government-imposed limits to trade are simply enormous.

They pit bureaucracies against networks.   The same network that smuggles East European women to Berlin may be involved in distributing opium there. The proceeds of the latter fund the purchase of counterfeit Bulgari watches made in China and often sold on the streets of Manhattan by illegal African immigrants. Colombian drug cartels make deals with Ukrainian arms traffickers, while Wall Street brokers controlled by the U.S.-based Mafia have been known to front for Russian money launderers. These highly decentralized groups and individuals are bound by strong ties of loyalty and common purpose and organized around semiautonomous clusters or "nodes" capable of operating swiftly and flexibly. John Arquilla and David Ronfeldt, two of the best known experts on these types of organizations, observe that networks often lack central leadership, command, or headquarters, thus "no precise heart or head that can be targeted. The network as a whole (but not necessarily each node) has little to no hierarchy; there may be multiple leaders. . . . Thus the [organization's] design may sometimes appear acephalous (headless), and at other times polycephalous (Hydra-headed)." Typically, governments respond to these challenges by forming interagency task forces or creating new bureaucracies. Consider the creation of the new Department of Homeland Security in the United States, which encompasses 22 former federal agencies and their 170,000 employees and is responsible for, among other things, fighting the war on drugs.

RETHINKING THE PROBLEM

Governments may never be able to completely eradicate the kind of international trade involved in the five wars. But they can and should do better. There are at least four areas where efforts can yield better ideas on how to tackle the problems posed by these wars:

Develop more flexible notions of sovereignty.   Governments need to recognize that restricting the scope of multilateral action for the sake of protecting their sovereignty is often a moot point. Their sovereignty is compromised daily, not by nation-states but by stateless networks that break laws and cross borders in pursuit of trade. In May 1999, for example, the Venezuelan government denied U.S. planes authorization to fly over Venezuelan territory to monitor air routes commonly used by narcotraffickers. Venezuelan authorities placed more importance on the symbolic value of asserting sovereignty over air space than on the fact that drug traffickers' planes regularly violate Venezuelan territory. Without new forms of codifying and "managing" sovereignty, governments will continue to face a large disadvantage while fighting the five wars.

Strengthen existing multilateral institutions.   The global nature of these wars means no government, regardless of its economic, political, or military power, will make much progress acting alone. If this seems obvious, then why does Interpol, the multilateral agency in charge of fighting international crime, have a staff of 384, only 112 of whom are police officers, and an annual budget of $28 million, less than the price of some boats or planes used by drug traffickers? Similarly, Europol, Europe's Interpol equivalent, has a staff of 240 and a budget of $51 million.

One reason Interpol is poorly funded and staffed is because its 181 member governments don't trust each other. Many assume, and perhaps rightly so, that the criminal networks they are fighting have penetrated the police departments of other countries and that sharing information with such compromised officials would not be prudent. Others fear today's allies will become tomorrow's enemies. Still others face legal impediments to sharing intelligence with fellow nation-states or have intelligence services and law enforcement agencies with organizational cultures that make effective collaboration almost impossible. Progress will only be made if the world's governments unite behind stronger, more effective multilateral organizations.

Devise new mechanisms and institutions.   These five wars stretch and even render obsolete many of the existing institutions, legal frameworks, military doctrines, weapons systems, and law enforcement techniques on which governments have relied for years. Analysts need to rethink the concept of war "fronts" defined by geography and the definition of "combatants" according to the Geneva Convention. The functions of intelligence agents, soldiers, police officers, customs agents, or immigration officers need rethinking and adaptation to the new realities. Policymakers also need to reconsider the notion that ownership is essentially a physical reality and not a "virtual" one or that only sovereign nations can issue money when thinking about ways to fight the five wars.

Move from repression to regulation.   Beating market forces is next to impossible. In some cases, this reality may force governments to move from repressing the market to regulating it. In others, creating market incentives may be better than using bureaucracies to curb the excesses of these markets. Technology can often accomplish more than government policies can. For example, powerful encryption techniques can better protect software or CDs from being copied in Ukraine than would making the country enforce patents and copyrights and trademarks.

In all of the five wars, government agencies fight against networks motivated by the enormous profit opportunities created by other government agencies. In all cases, these profits can be traced to some form of government intervention that creates a major imbalance between demand and supply and makes prices and profit margins skyrocket. In some cases, these government interventions are often justified and it would be imprudent to eliminate them—governments can't simply walk away from the fight against trafficking in heroin, human beings, or weapons of mass destruction. But society can better deal with other segments of these kinds of illegal trade through regulation, not prohibition. Policymakers must focus on opportunities where market regulation can ameliorate problems that have defied approaches based on prohibition and armed interdiction of international trade.

Ultimately, governments, politicians, and voters need to realize that the way in which the world is conducting these five wars is doomed to fail—not for lack of effort, resources, or political will but because the collective thinking that guides government strategies in the five wars is rooted in wrong ideas, false assumptions, and obsolete institutions. Recognizing that governments have no chance of winning unless they change the ways they wage these wars is an indispensable first step in the search for solutions.

CHAPTER 41

Blowback

CHALMERS JOHNSON

Northern Italian communities had, for years, complained about low-flying American military aircraft. In February 1998, the inevitable happened. A Marine Corps EA-6B Prowler with a crew of four, one of scores of advanced American jet fighters and bombers stationed at places like Aviano, Cervia, Brindisi, and Sigonella, sliced through a ski-lift cable near the resort town of Cavalese and plunged twenty people riding in a single gondola to their deaths on the snowy slopes several hundred feet below. Although marine pilots are required to maintain an altitude of at least one thousand feet (two thousand, according to the Italian government), the plane had cut the cable at a height of 360 feet. It was traveling at 621 miles per hour when 517 miles per hour was considered the upper limit. The pilot had been performing low-level acrobatics while his copilot took pictures on videotape (which he later destroyed).

In response to outrage in Italy and calls for vigorous prosecution of those responsible, the marine pilots argued that their charts were inaccurate, that their altimeter had not worked, and that they had not consulted U.S. Air Force units permanently based in the area about local hazards. A court-martial held not in Italy but in Camp Lejeune, North Carolina, exonerated everyone involved, calling it a "training accident." Soon after, President Bill Clinton apologized and promised financial compensation to the victims, but on May 14, 1999, Congress dropped the provision for aid to the families because of opposition in the House of Representatives and from the Pentagon.[1]

This was hardly the only such incident in which American service personnel victimized foreign civilians in the post–Cold War world. From Germany and Turkey to Okinawa and South Korea, similar incidents have been common—as has been their usual denouement. The United States government never holds politicians or higher-ranking military officers responsible and seldom finds that more should be done beyond offering pro forma apologies and perhaps financial compensation of some, often minimal sort.

On rare occasions, as with the Italian cable cutting, when such a local tragedy rises to the level of global news, what often seems strangest to Americans is the level of national outrage elsewhere over what the U.S. media portray as, at worst, an apparently isolated incident, however tragic to those involved. Certainly, the one subject beyond discussion at such moments is the fact that, a decade after the end of the Cold War, hundreds of thousands of American troops, supplied with the world's most advanced weaponry, sometimes including nuclear arms, are stationed on over sixty-one base complexes in nineteen countries worldwide, using the Department of Defense's narrowest definition of a "major installation"; if one included every kind of installation that houses representatives of the American military, the number would rise to over eight hundred.[2] There are, of course, no Italian air bases on American soil. Such a thought would be ridiculous. Nor, for that matter, are there German, Indonesian, Russian, Greek, or Japanese troops stationed on Italian soil. Italy is, moreover, a close ally of the United States, and no conceivable enemy nation endangers its shores.

All this is almost too obvious to state—and so is almost never said. It is simply not a matter for discussion, much less of debate in the land of the last imperial power. Perhaps similar thinking is second nature to any imperium. Perhaps the Romans did not find it strange to have their troops in Gaul, nor the British in South Africa. But what is unspoken is no less real, nor does it lack consequences just because it is not part of any ongoing domestic discussion.

I believe it is past time for such a discussion to begin, for Americans to consider why we have created an empire—a word from which we shy away—and what the consequences of our imperial stance may be for the rest of the world and for ourselves. Not so long ago, the way we garrisoned the world could be discussed far more openly and comfortably because the explanation seemed to lie at hand—in the very existence of the Soviet Union and of communism. Had the Italian disaster occurred two decades earlier, it would have seemed no less a tragedy, but many Americans would have argued that, given the Cold War, such incidents were an unavoidable cost of protecting democracies like Italy against the menace of Soviet totalitarianism. With the disappearance of any military threat faintly comparable to that posed by the former Soviet Union, such "costs" have become easily avoidable. American military forces could have been withdrawn from Italy, as well as from other foreign bases, long ago. That they were not and that Washington instead is doing everything in its considerable powers to perpetuate Cold War structures, even without the Cold War's justification, places such overseas deployments in a new light. They have become striking evidence, for those who care to look, of an imperial project that the Cold War obscured. The by-products of this project are likely to build up reservoirs of resentment against all Americans—tourists, students, and businessmen, as well as members of the armed forces—that can have lethal results.

For any empire, including an unacknowledged one, there is a kind of balance sheet that builds up over time. Military crimes, accidents, and atrocities make up only one category on the debit side of the balance sheet that the United States has been accumulating, especially since the Cold War ended. To take an example of quite a different kind of debit, consider South Korea, a longtime ally. On Christmas Eve 1997, it declared itself financially bankrupt and put its economy under the guidance of the International, Monetary Fund, which is basically an institutional surrogate of the United States government. Most Americans were surprised by the economic disasters that overtook Thailand, South Korea, Malaysia, and Indonesia in 1997 and that then spread around the world, crippling the Russian and Brazilian economies. They could hardly imagine that the U.S. government might have had a hand in causing them, even though various American pundits and economists expressed open delight in these disasters, which threw millions of people, who had previously had hopes of achieving economic prosperity and security, into the most abysmal poverty. At worst, Americans took the economic meltdown of places like Indonesia and Brazil to mean that beneficial American-supported policies of "globalization" were working—that we were effectively helping restructure various economies around the world so that they would look and work more like ours.

Above all, the economic crisis of 1997 was taken as evidence that our main doctrinal competitors—the high-growth capitalist economies of East Asia—were hardly either as competitive or as successful as they imagined. In a New Year's commentary, the columnist Charles Krauthammer mused, "Our success is the success of the American capitalist model, which lies closer to the free market vision of Adam Smith than any other. Much closer, certainly, than Asia's paternalistic crony capitalism that so seduced critics of the American system during Asia's now-burst bubble."[3]

As the global crisis deepened, the thing our government most seemed to fear was that contracts to buy our weapons might now not be honored. That winter, Secretary of Defense William Cohen made special trips to Jakarta, Bangkok, and Seoul to cajole the governments of those countries to use increasingly scarce foreign exchange funds to pay for the American fighter jets, missiles, warships, and other hardware the Pentagon had sold them before the economic collapse. He also stopped in Tokyo to urge on a worried Japanese government a big sale not yet agreed to. He wanted Japan to invest in the theater missile defense system, or TMD, antimissile missiles that the Pentagon has been trying to get the Japanese to buy for a decade. No one knew then or knows now whether the TMD will even work—in fifteen years of intercept attempts only a few missiles in essentially doctored tests have hit their targets—but it is unquestionably expensive, and arms sales, both domestic and foreign, have become one of the Pentagon's most important missions.

I believe the profligate waste of our resources on irrelevant weapons systems and the Asian economic meltdown, as well as the continuous trail of military "accidents" and of terrorist attacks on American installations and embassies, are all portents of a twenty-first-century crisis in America's informal empire, an empire based on the projection of military power to every corner of the world and on the use of American capital and markets to force global economic integration on our terms, at whatever costs to others. To predict the future is an undertaking no thoughtful person would rush to embrace. What form our imperial crisis is likely to take years or even decades from now is, of course, impossible to know. But history indicates that, sooner or later, empires do reach such moments, and it seems reasonable to assume that we will not miraculously escape that fate.

What we have freed ourselves of, however, is any genuine consciousness of how we might look to others on this globe. Most Americans are probably unaware of how Washington exercises its global hegemony, since so much of this activity takes place either in relative secrecy or under comforting rubrics. Many may, as a start, find it hard to believe that our place in the world even adds up to an empire. But only when we come to see our country as both profiting from and trapped within the structures of an empire of its own making will it be possible for us to explain many elements of the world that otherwise perplex us. Without good explanations, we cannot possibly produce policies that will bring us sustained peace and prosperity in a post–Cold War world. What has gone wrong in Japan after half a century of government-guided growth under U.S. protection? Why should the emergence of a strong China be to anyone's disadvantage? Why do American policies toward human rights, weapons proliferation, terrorism, drug cartels, and the environment strike so many foreigners as the essence of hypocrisy? Should American-owned and -managed multinational firms be instruments, beneficiaries, or adversaries of United States foreign policy? Is the free flow of capital really as valuable as free trade in commodities and manufactured goods? These kinds of questions can only be answered once we begin to grasp what the United States really is.

If Washington is the headquarters of a global military-economic dominion, the answers will be very different than if we think of the United States as simply one among many sovereign nations. There is a logic to empire that differs from the logic of a nation, and acts committed in service to an empire but never acknowledged as such have a tendency to haunt the future.

The term "blowback," which officials of the Central Intelligence Agency first invented for their own internal use, is starting to circulate among students of international relations. It refers to the unintended consequences of policies that were kept secret from the American people. What the daily press reports as the malign acts of "terrorists" or "drug lords" or "rogue states" or "illegal arms merchants" often turn out to be blowback from earlier American operations.

It is now widely recognized, for example, that the 1988 bombing of Pan Am flight 103 over Lockerbie, Scotland, which resulted in the deaths of 259 passengers and 11 people on the ground, was retaliation for a 1986 Reagan administration aerial raid on Libya that killed President Muammar Khadaffi's stepdaughter. Some in the United States have suspected that other events can also be explained as blowback from imperial acts. For example, the epidemic of cocaine and heroin use that has afflicted American cities during the past two decades was probably fueled in part by Central and South American military officers or corrupt politicians whom the CIA or the Pentagon once trained or supported and then installed in key government positions. For example, in Nicaragua in the 1980s, the U.S. government organized a massive campaign against the socialist-oriented Sandinista government. American agents then looked the other way when the Contras, the military insurgents they had trained, made deals to sell cocaine in American cities in order to buy arms and supplies.[4]. . .

Needless to say, blowback is not exclusively a problem faced by Americans. One has only to look at Russia and its former satellites today to see exactly how devastating imperial blowback can be. The hostage crisis of 1996–97 at the Japanese embassy in Lima, in which a handful of Peruvian revolutionaries took virtually the entire diplomatic corps hostage, was probably blowback from Japan's support for the antiguerrilla policies of President Alberto Fujimori and for the operations of Japanese multinational corporations in Peru. Israel's greatest single political problem is the daily threat of blowback from the Palestinian people and their Islamic allies because of Israeli policies of displacing Palestinians from their lands and repressing those that remain under their jurisdiction. The United States, however, is the world's most prominent target for blowback, being the world's lone imperial power, the primary source of the sort of secret and semisecret operations that shore up repressive regimes, and by far the largest seller of weapons generally.

It is typical of an imperial people to have a short memory for its less pleasant imperial acts, but for those on the receiving end, memory can be long indeed. Among the enduring sources of blowback, for instance, are the genocidal cruelties some nations have perpetrated during wartime. Japan to this day is trying to come to grips with the consequences of its actions in China during World War II. Japanese reactionaries are still reluctant to face atrocities committed in China and Korea: the rape of Nanking, conscription of conquered women to serve as prostitutes for frontline troops, and gruesome medical experimentation on prisoners of war are but the better known of these. But given the passage of time and some payment of compensation, many Chinese would probably accept a sincere apology for these events. However, Japanese armies also terrorized and radicalized an essentially conservative peasant population and thereby helped bring the Chinese Communist Party to power, leading to thirty million deaths during the Great Leap Forward and savaging Chinese civilization during the Cultural Revolution. There are many educated Chinese who can never forgive Japan for contributing to this outcome.

Today, we know of several similar cases. In pursuing the war in Vietnam in the early 1970s, President Richard Nixon and his national security adviser Henry Kissinger ordered more bombs dropped on rural Cambodia than had been dropped on Japan during all of World War II, killing at least three-quarters of a million Cambodian peasants and helping legitimize the murderous Khmer Rouge movement under Pol Pot. In his subsequent pursuit of revenge and ideological purity Pol Pot ensured that another million and a half Cambodians, this time mainly urban dwellers, were murdered.

Americans generally think of Pol Pot as some kind of unique, self-generated monster and his "killing fields" as an inexplicable atavism totally divorced from civilization. But without the United States government's Vietnam-era savagery, he could never have come to power in a culture like Cambodia's, just as Mao's uneducated peasant radicals would never have gained legitimacy in a normal Chinese context without the disruption and depravity of the Japanese war. Significantly, in its calls for an international tribunal to try the remaining leaders of the Khmer Rouge for war crimes, the United States has demanded that such a court restrict its efforts to the period from 1975 to 1979—that is, after the years of carpet bombing were over and before the U.S. government began to collaborate with the Khmer Rouge against the Vietnamese Communists, who invaded Cambodia in 1978, drove the Khmer Rouge from power, and were trying to bring some stability to the country.

Even an empire cannot control the long-term effects of its policies. That is the essence of blowback. Take the civil war in Afghanistan in the 1980s, in which Soviet forces directly intervened on the government side and the CIA armed and supported any and all groups willing to face the Soviet armies. Over the years the fighting turned Kabul, once a major center of Islamic culture, into a facsimile of Hiroshima after the bomb. American policies helped ensure that the Soviet Union would suffer the same kind of debilitating defeat in Afghanistan as the United States had in Vietnam. In fact, the defeat so destabilized the Soviet regime that at the end of the 1980s it collapsed. But in Afghanistan the United States also helped bring to power the Taliban, a fundamentalist Islamic movement whose policies toward women, education, justice, and economic well-being resemble not so much those of Ayatollah Khomeini's Iran as those of Pol Pot's Cambodia. A group of these mujahideen, who only a few years earlier the United States had armed with ground-to-air Stinger missiles, grew bitter over American acts and policies in the Gulf War and vis-à-vis Israel. In 1993, they bombed the World Trade Center in New York and assassinated several CIA employees as they waited at a traffic light in Langley, Virginia. Four years later, on November 12, 1997, after the Virginia killer had been convicted by an American court, unknown assailants shot and killed four American accountants, unrelated in any way to the CIA, in their car in Karachi, Pakistan, in retaliation.

It is likely that U.S. covert policies have helped create similar conditions in the Congo, Guatemala, and Turkey, and that we are simply waiting for the blowback to occur. Guatemala is a particularly striking example of American imperial policies in its own "backyard." In 1954, the Eisenhower administration planned and the CIA organized and funded a military coup that overthrew a Guatemalan president whose modest land reform policies were considered a threat to American corporations. Blowback from this led to a Marxist guerrilla insurgency in the 1980s and so to CIA- and Pentagon-supported genocide against Mayan peasants. In the spring of 1999, a report on the Guatemalan civil war from the U.N.-sponsored Commission for Historical Clarification made clear that "the American training of the officer corps in counterinsurgency techniques" was a "key factor" in the "genocide. . . . Entire Mayan villages were attacked and burned and their inhabitants were slaughtered in an effort to deny the guerrillas protection."[5] According to the commission, between 1981 and 1983 the military government of Guatemala—financed and supported by the U.S. government—destroyed some four hundred Mayan villages in a campaign of genocide in which approximately two hundred thousand peasants were killed. José Pertierra, an attorney representing Jennifer Harbury, an American lawyer who spent years trying to find out what happened to her "disappeared" Guatemalan husband and supporter of the guerrillas, Efraín Bámaca Velásquez, writes that the Guatemalan military officer who arrested, tortured, and murdered Bámaca was a CIA "asset" and was paid $44,000 for the information he obtained from him.[6]

Visiting Guatemala in March 1999, soon after the report's release, President Clinton said, "It is important that I state clearly that support for military forces and intelligence units which engaged in violence and widespread repression was wrong, and the United States must not repeat that mistake. . . . The United States will no longer take part in campaigns of repression."[7] But on virtually the day that the president was swearing off "dirty tricks" in other people's countries, his government was reasserting its support for Turkey in its war of repression against its Kurdish minority.

The Kurds constitute fifteen million people in a Turkish population estimated at fifty-eight million. Another five million Kurds live largely within reach of Turkey's borders in Iraq, Iran, and Syria. The Turks have discriminated against the Kurds for the past seventy years and have conducted an intense genocidal campaign against them since 1992, in the process destroying some three thousand Kurdish villages and hamlets in the backward southeastern part of the country. Former American ambassador to Croatia Peter W. Galbraith comments that "Turkey routinely jails Kurdish politicians for activities that would be protected speech in democratic countries."[8] The Europeans have so far barred Turkey from the European Union because of its treatment of the Kurds. Because of its strategic location on the border of the former Soviet Union, however, Turkey was a valued American ally and NATO member during the Cold War, and the United States maintains the relationship unchanged even though the USSR has disappeared.

After Israel and Egypt, Turkey is the third-highest recipient of American military assistance. Between 1991 and 1995, the United States supplied four-fifths of Turkey's military imports, which were among the largest in the world. The U.S. government, in turn, depends on the NATO base at Incirlik, Turkey, to carry out Operation Provide Comfort, set up after the Gulf War to supply and protect Iraqi Kurds from repression by Saddam Hussein—at the same time that the United States acquiesces in Turkish mistreatment of its far larger Kurdish population. One obvious reason is that communities like Stratford and Bridgeport, Connecticut, where Black Hawk and Comanche helicopters are made, depend for their economic health on continued large-scale arms sales to countries like Turkey. At the time of the Gulf War, a senior adviser to the Turkish prime minister said to John Shattuck, assistant secretary of state for human rights, "If you want to stop human rights abuses do two things—stop IMF credits and cut off aid from the Pentagon. But don't sell the weapons and give aid and then complain about the Kurdish issue. Don't tell us about human rights while you're selling these weapons."[9]

The capture in February 1999 of the Kurdish guerrilla leader Abdullah Ocalan exposed the nature of American involvement with Turkey, in this case via a CIA gambit that holds promise as a rich source of future blowback. The CIA term for this policy is "disruption," by which it means the harassment of terrorists around the world. The point is to flush them out of hiding so that cooperative police forces or secret services can then arrest and imprison them. According to John Diamond of the Associated Press, "The CIA keeps its role secret, and the foreign countries that actually crack down on the suspects carefully hide the U.S. role, lest they stir up trouble for themselves." There are no safeguards at all against misidentifying "suspects," and "the CIA sends no formal notice to Congress." Disruption is said to be a preemptive, offensive form of counterterrorism. Richard Clarke, President Clinton's antiterrorism czar, likes it because he can avoid "the cumbersome Congressional reporting requirements that go with CIA-directed covert operations" and because "human rights organizations would have no way of identifying a CIA role." The CIA has carried out disruption operations in at least ten countries since September 1998. In the case of Ocalan's capture, the United States "provided Turkey with critical information about Ocalan's whereabouts." This was the first time some of the details of a "disruption" campaign were made public.[10]

In a sense, blowback is simply another way of saying that a nation reaps what it sows. Although people usually know what they have sown, our national experience of blowback is seldom imagined in such terms because so much of what the managers of the American empire have sown has been kept secret. As a concept, blowback is obviously most easy to grasp in its most straightforward manifestation. The unintended consequences of American policies and acts in country X are a bomb at an American embassy in country Y or a dead American in country Z. Certainly any number of Americans have been killed in that fashion, from Catholic nuns in El Salvador to tourists in Uganda who just happened to wander into hidden imperial scenarios about which they knew nothing. But blowback, as demonstrated in this book, is hardly restricted to such reasonably straightforward examples.

From the hollowing out of key American industries due to Japan's export-led economic policies to refugee flows across our southern borders from countries where U.S.-supported repression has created genocidal conditions or where U.S.-supported economic policies have led to unbearable misery, blowback can hit in less obvious and more subtle ways and over long periods of time. It can also manifest itself domestically in ways that are often not evident, even to those who created or carried out the initial imperial policies.

Because we live in an increasingly interconnected international system, we are all, in a sense, living in a blowback world. Although the term originally applied only to the unintended consequences for Americans of American policies, there is every reason to widen its meaning. Whether, for example, any unintended consequences of the American policies that fostered and then heightened the economic collapse of Indonesia in 1997 ever blow back to the United States, the unintended consequences for Indonesians have been staggering levels of suffering, poverty, and loss of hope. Similarly, the unintended consequences of American-supported coups and bombing in Cambodia in the early 1970s were unimaginable chaos, disruption, and death for Cambodians later in the decade.

Our role in the military coup in Chile in 1973, for example, produced little blowback onto the United States itself but had lethal consequences for liberals, socialists, and innocent bystanders in Chile and elsewhere. On the nature of American policies in Chile, journalist Jon Lee Anderson reports, "The plan, according to declassified United States government documents, was to make Chile ungovernable under [elected socialist president Salvador] Allende, provoke social chaos, and bring about a military coup. . . . A CIA cable outlined the objectives clearly to the station chief in Santiago: 'It is firm and continuing policy that Allende be overthrown by a coup. . . . We are to continue to generate maximum pressure toward this end utilizing every appropriate resource. It is imperative that these actions be implemented clandestinely and securely so that United States Government and American hand be well hidden.' "[11]

No ordinary citizen of the United States knew anything about these machinations. The coup d'état took place on September 11, 1973, resulting in the suicide of Allende and the seizure of power by General Augusto Pinochet, whose military and civilian supporters in their seventeen years in power tortured, killed, or "disappeared" some four thousand people. Pinochet was an active collaborator in Operation Condor, a joint mission with the Argentine militarists to murder exiled dissidents in the United States, Spain, Italy, and elsewhere. This is why, when Pinochet traveled to England in the autumn of 1998 for medical treatment, Spain tried to extradite him to stand trial for genocide, torture, and state terrorism against Spanish citizens. On October 16, 1998, the British police arrested Pinochet in London and held him pending his possible extradition.

Although few Americans were affected by this covert operation, people around the world now know of the American involvement and were deeply cynical when Secretary of State Madeleine Albright opposed Pinochet's extradition, claiming that countries like Chile undertaking a "transition to democracy" must be allowed to guarantee immunity from prosecution to past human rights offenders in order to "move forward."[12] America's "dirty hands" make even the most well-intentioned statement about human rights or terrorism seem hypocritical in such circumstances. Even when blowback mostly strikes other peoples, it has its corrosive effects on the United States by debasing political discourse and making citizens feel duped if they should happen to take seriously what their political leaders say. This is an inevitable consequence not just of blowback but of empire itself.

NOTES

1. "Some Aid Canceled for Gondola Deaths," *Los Angeles Times,* May 15, 1999.

2. Department of Defense, "U.S. Military Installations" (updated to July 17, 1998), *DefenseLINK,* on-line at http://www.defenselink.mil/pubs/installations/foreignsummary.htm; and John Lindsay-Poland and Nick Morgan, "Overseas Military Bases and Environment," *Foreign Policy in Focus* 3.15 (June 1998), on-line at http://www.foreignpolicy-infocus.org/briefs/vol13/v3n15mil.html. According to one report, when the Soviet Union collapsed in 1991, the United States had 375 military bases scattered around the globe staffed by more than a half million personnel. Joel Brinkley, "U.S. Looking for a New Path as Superpower Conflict Ends," *New York Times,* February 2, 1992.

3. Charles Krauthammer, "What Caused Our Economic Boom?" *San Diego Union-Tribune,* January 5, 1998.

4. For documentary evidence, including Oliver North's notebooks, see "The Contras, Cocaine, and Covert Operations," *National Security Archive Electronic Briefing Book,* no. 2, on-line at http://www.seas.gwu.edu/nsarchive. Also see James Risen, "C.I.A. Said to Ignore Charges of Contra Drug Dealing in '80's," *New York Times,* October 10, 1998.

5. Mireya Navarro, "Guatemala Study Accuses the Army and Cites U.S. Role," *New York Times,* February 26, 1999; Larry Rohter, "Searing Indictment," *New York Times,* February 27, 1999; Michael Shifter, "Can Genocide End in Forgiveness?" *Los Angeles Times,* March 7, 1999; "Coming Clean on Guatemala," editorial, *Los Angeles Times,* March 10, 1999; and Michael Stetz, "Clinton's Words on Guatemala Called 'Too Little, Too Late,' " *San Diego Union-Tribune,* March 16, 1999.

6. José Pertierra, "For Guatemala, Words Are Not Enough," *San Diego Union-Tribune,* March 5, 1999.

7. John M. Broder, "Clinton Offers His Apologies to Guatemala," *New York Times,* March 11, 1999. Also see Broder, "Clinton Visit in Honduras Dramatizes New Attitude," *New York*

Times, March 10, 1999; and Francisco Goldman, "Murder Comes for the Bishop," *New Yorker,* March 15, 1999.

8. Peter W. Galbraith, "How the Turks Helped Their Enemies," *New York Times,* February 20, 1999.

9. John Tirman, *Spoils of War: The Human Cost of America's Arms Trade* (New York: Free Press, 1997), p. 236.

10. John Diamond, "CIA Thwarts Terrorists with 'Disruption'; It's Prevention by Proxy," *San Diego Union-Tribune,* March 5, 1999; and Tim Weiner, "U.S. Helped Turkey Find and Capture Kurd Rebel," *New York Times,* February 20, 1999.

11. Jon Lee Anderson, "The Dictator," *New Yorker,* October 19, 1998; Peter Kronbluth, "Chile and the United States: Declassified Documents Relating to the Military Coup," *National Security Archive Electronic Briefing Book,* no. 8, on-line at http://www.seas.gwu.edu/nsarchive; and Philip Shenon, "U.S. Releases Files on Abuses in Pinochet Era," *New York Times,* July 1, 1999.

12. Michael Ratner, "The Pinochet Precedent," *Progressive Response* 3.3 (January 28, 1999).

CHAPTER 42

Oil, Geography, and War

MICHAEL T. KLARE

Of all the resources discussed in this book, none is more likely to provoke conflict between states in the twenty-first century than oil. Petroleum stands out from other materials—water, minerals, timber, and so on—because of its pivotal role in the global economy and its capacity to ignite large-scale combat. No highly industrialized society can survive at present without substantial supplies of oil, and so any significant threat to the continued availability of this resource will prove a cause of crisis and, in extreme cases, provoke the use of military force. Action of this sort could occur in any of the major oil-producing areas, including the Middle East and the Caspian basin. Lesser conflicts over petroleum are also likely, as states fight to gain or retain control over resource-rich border areas and offshore economic zones. Big or small, conflicts over oil will constitute a significant feature of the global security environment in the decades to come.

Petroleum has, of course, been a recurring source of conflict in the past. Many of the key battles of World War II, for example, were triggered by the Axis Powers' attempts to gain control over petroleum supplies located in areas controlled by their adversaries. The pursuit of greater oil revenues also prompted Iraq's 1990 invasion of Kuwait, and this, in turn, provoked a massive American military response. But combat over petroleum is not simply a phenomenon of the past; given the world's ever-increasing demand for energy and the continuing possibility of supply interruptions, the outbreak of a conflict over oil is just as likely to occur in the future.

The likelihood of future combat over oil is suggested, first of all, by the growing buildup of military forces in the Middle East and other oil-producing areas. Until recently, the greatest concentration of military power was found along the East-West divide in Europe and at other sites of superpower competition. Since 1990, however, these concentrations have largely disappeared, while troop levels in the major oil zones have been increased. The United States, for example, has established a permanent military infrastructure in the Persian Gulf area and has "prepositioned" sufficient war matériel there to sustain a major campaign. Russia, meanwhile, has shifted more of its forces to the North Caucasus and the Caspian Sea basin, while China has expanded its naval presence in the South China Sea. Other countries have also bolstered their presence in these areas and other sites of possible conflict over oil.

Geology and geography also add to the risk of conflict. While relatively abundant at present, natural petroleum does not exist in unlimited quantities; it is a finite, nonrenewable substance. At some point in the future, available supplies will prove inadequate to satisfy soaring demand, and the world will encounter significant shortages. Unless some plentiful new source of energy has been discovered by that point, competition over the remaining supplies of petroleum will prove increasingly fierce. In such circumstances, any prolonged interruption in the global flow of oil will be viewed by import-dependent states as a mortal threat to their security—and thus as a matter that may legitimately be resolved through the use of military force. Growing scarcity will also result in higher prices for oil, producing enormous hardship for those without the means to absorb added costs; in consequence, widespread internal disorder may occur.

Geography enters the picture because many of the world's leading sources of oil are located in contested border zones or in areas of recurring crisis and violence. The distribution of petroleum is more concentrated than other raw materials, with the bulk of global supplies found in a few key producing areas. Some of these areas—the North Slope of Alaska and the American Southwest, for example—are located within the borders of a single country and are relatively free of disorder; others, however, are spread across several countries—which may or may not agree on their common borders—and/or are located in areas of perennial unrest. To reach global markets, moreover, petroleum must often travel (by ship or by pipeline) through other areas of instability. Because turmoil in these areas can easily disrupt the global flow of oil, any outbreak of conflict, however minor, will automatically generate a risk of outside intervention.

That conflict over oil will erupt in the years ahead is almost a foregone conclusion. Just how much violence, at what levels of intensity, and at which locations, cannot be determined. Ultimately, the frequency and character of warfare will depend on the relative weight and the interplay of three key factors: (1) the political and strategic environment in which decisions over resource issues are made; (2) the future relationship between demand and supply; and (3) the geography of oil production and distribution.

THE POLITICS OF OIL SECURITY

Many resources are needed to sustain a modern industrial society, but only those that are viewed as being vital to national security are likely to provoke the use of military force when access to key supplies is placed in jeopardy.* There is no question

---

*In 1998, the U.S. National Security Council defined "vital interests" as those interests "of broad, overriding importance to the survival, safety, and vitality of our nation. Among these are the physical security of our territory and that of our allies, the safety of our citizens, our economic well-being, and the protection of our critical infrastructures. We will do what we must to defend these interests, including—when necessary—using our military might unilaterally and decisively" (*A National Security Strategy for a New Century*, October 1998).

that oil has enjoyed this distinctive status in the past. Ever since the introduction of oil-powered warships at the beginning of the twentieth century, petroleum has been viewed as essential for success in war. Before that time, petroleum had largely been used to provide illumination, most commonly in the form of kerosene. (Indeed, many of the major oil companies of today, including Exxon, Mobil, and Royal Dutch/Shell, were initially established in the nineteenth century to produce and market kerosene to the growing urban populations of Europe and North America.) The critical turning point came in 1912, when the British Admiralty—then led by First Lord of the Admiralty Winston Churchill—decided to convert its combat vessels from coal to oil propulsion.[1]

The transition from coal to oil provided British ships with a significant advantage in speed and endurance over the coal-powered vessels of its adversaries, especially Germany. But it also presented London with a significant dilemma: while rich in coal, Britain possessed few domestic sources of petroleum and so was vitally dependent on imported supplies. With a war about to begin, and the reliability of overseas suppliers in question, the cabinet decided—on a strict national security basis—to endow the government with direct responsibility for the delivery of oil. On June 17, 1914, Parliament voted to approve the government's acquisition of a majority stake in the Anglo-Persian Oil Company (APOC), a London-based firm that had recently discovered petroleum in southwestern Persia. With this vote, it became British policy to protect APOC's oil concession area in Persia—thus, for the first time, making the security of overseas petroleum supplies a major state responsibility.[2]

The link between oil and military policy was made even more substantial during World War I itself, when all of the major belligerents employed oil-driven vehicles for combat, reconnaissance, and logistics. The airplane and the tank—oil-powered machines that were to revolutionize the conduct of warfare—were introduced during the conflict. Scarcely less important was the widespread use of motor vehicles to carry troops and supplies to the battlefield: over the course of the war, the British army's fleet of trucks grew from 10,000 to 60,000; the American Expeditionary Force brought with it another 50,000 motor vehicles.[3] It is with this in mind that Lord Curzon, former viceroy of India and soon-to-be foreign secretary, told a group of government and industry officials in London that the Allies had "floated to victory upon a wave of oil."[4]

This perception continued to influence strategic thinking after World War I and in the years leading up to World War II. Believing that the next major conflict would see an even greater reliance on oil-powered weapons than the last, many governments followed the British example by creating state-owned oil companies and by seeking control over foreign sources of petroleum. Britain, for its part, expanded its oil interests in the Persian Gulf area and strengthened its dominant position in Iran (the new name for Persia). France established a state-owned firm, the Compagnie Française des Pétroles, and obtained concessions in the Mosul area of northwest Iraq. Germany and Japan—both of which lacked domestic sources of petroleum—laid plans to acquire their supplies from Romania and the Dutch East Indies, respectively.[5]

Once war broke out, the competitive pursuit of oil by all sides had a significant impact on the tempo and trajectory of battle. In the Pacific, Japanese efforts to gain control over the petroleum supplies of the Dutch East Indies produced mounting alarm in Washington and led, in 1941, to the imposition of a U.S. embargo on oil exports to Japan. This, in turn, persuaded Japanese officials that a war with the United States was inevitable, propelling them to seek an initial advantage through a surprise attack on the U.S. naval base at Pearl Harbor. In the European theater, Germany's desperate need for oil helped trigger its 1941 invasion of Russia. Along with Moscow and Leningrad, a major target of the invasion was the Soviet oil center at Baku (in what is now Azerbaijan). Both efforts ended in failure: the Japanese plan to import East Indian oil was foiled by American air and submarine attacks on tanker ships, while the German drive on Baku was thwarted by stubborn Soviet resistance. With their supplies of oil becoming increasingly scarce, Japan and Germany were unable to mount effective resistance to Allied offensives and so were eventually forced to concede defeat.[6]

After the war, petroleum continued to be seen by military planners as a vital combat necessity. With military organizations placing even greater emphasis on the role of airpower and armored forces, the need for reliable oil supplies became more critical than ever. This influenced the strategic thinking not only of the European powers, which had long been dependent on imported supplies, but also of the United States, which for the first time began to acquire significant supplies of petroleum from outside the country. Fearing that the Soviet Union would seek control over the Persian Gulf area—rapidly becoming the leading source of Western oil imports—Washington established a modest military presence in the region and sought to integrate Iran, Iraq, Saudi Arabia, and other key oil-producing states into the Western alliance. Both the Truman Doctrine (1947) and the Eisenhower Doctrine (1957) included promises of U.S. military aid to any state in the region that came under attack from Soviet or Soviet-backed forces.[7]

Initially, American moves in the Middle East were governed by classical military considerations: to prevent a hostile power from gaining control over a vital resource needed for the effective prosecution of war. With the outbreak of the October 1973 Arab-Israeli conflict, however, the perception of oil as a strategic commodity took on an entirely new meaning. To punish Washington for its support of Israel and to build worldwide pressure for an acceptable outcome to the conflict, the Arab states cut off all petroleum deliveries to the United States and imposed rolling cutbacks on deliveries to other countries. At the same time, the Organization of Petroleum-Exporting Countries (OPEC) announced a fourfold increase in the price of oil. Occurring at a time when petroleum supplies were already under pressure from rapidly growing demand, the oil embargo and OPEC price increase sent a powerful shock wave through the global economy: oil shortages developed in many areas, industrial output declined, and the world plunged into a prolonged economic recession. From this time on, oil was seen not only as an essential military commodity but also as a prerequisite for global economic stability.[8]

The Arab oil embargo was rescinded in March 1974, and the economic crisis gradually receded. Nevertheless, the events of 1973–74 left a profound and lasting impact on the perceived link between oil and the national security of the major industrialized powers. Worried that significant supply disruptions could occur again, the oil-importing countries sought to minimize their vulnerability by searching for new petroleum deposits in more secure locations (the North Sea and the North Slope of Alaska, for example) and by storing large quantities of oil in special reservoirs. The United States, for its part, stored hundreds of millions of barrels of oil in its newly established Strategic Petroleum Reserve.

The American response to the "oil shocks" of 1973–74 was not limited to defensive measures. For the first time, senior officials began talking of using force to protect vital petroleum supplies in peacetime, to guarantee the health of the economy. Specifically, policy makers began to consider American military intervention in the Middle East to prevent any interruption in the flow of Persian Gulf oil. Initially private, these deliberations became public in 1975 when Henry Kissinger, then secretary of state, told the editors of *Business Week* that the United States was prepared to go to war over oil. Although reluctant to employ force in a dispute over prices alone, he stated, Washington would have no such hesitation "where there's some actual strangulation of the industrialized world."[9]

This formulation of Western security interests has governed American military planning ever since. When, in 1979, the shah of Iran was overthrown by militant Islamic forces and the world experienced a second major "oil shock," President Carter was quick to threaten the use of force against any adversary that might seek to impede the flow of oil from the Persian Gulf area. On January 23, 1980, Carter declared that any attempt by a hostile power to constrict the flow of oil in the Gulf "will be repelled by any means necessary, including military force."[10] In line with this principle, known since as the Carter Doctrine, the United States commenced a military buildup in the Persian Gulf area that has continued to this day. This principle has, moreover, periodically been put to the test. During the Iran-Iraq war of 1980–88, when the Iranians stepped up their attacks on oil shipping in the Gulf (presumably to punish Kuwait and Saudi Arabia for their financial support of Iraq), the United States agreed to "reflag" Kuwaiti tankers with American flags and provide them with a U.S. naval escort.[11]

The Carter Doctrine was next invoked in August 1990, when Iraqi forces occupied Kuwait and positioned themselves for an assault on Saudi Arabia. Concluding that Iraqi control of both Kuwaiti and Saudi oil fields would pose an intolerable threat to Western economic security, President Bush quickly decided on a tough military response—dispatching large numbers of American forces to defend Saudi Arabia and, if need be, to drive the Iraqis out of Kuwait. "Our country now imports nearly half the oil it consumes and could face a major threat to its economic independence," he told the nation on August 7. Hence, "the sovereign independence of Saudi Arabia is of vital interest to the United States."[12] A number of other concerns, including Iraq's burgeoning weapons capabilities, also figured in the U.S. decision to employ force in the Gulf, but senior administration officials always placed particular emphasis on the threat to Western oil supplies and the continued health of the American economy.[13]

Since Desert Storm, American leaders have continued to stress the importance of unhindered oil deliveries to the health and stability of the global economy. "America's vital interests in the [Persian Gulf] region are compelling," General J. H. Binford

Peay III, commander in chief of the U.S. Central Command (CENTCOM), declared in 1997. "The unrestricted flow of petroleum resources from friendly Gulf states to refineries and processing facilities around the world drives the global economic engine."[14] In accordance with this outlook, the United States has beefed up its forces in the Gulf and taken other steps to protect friendly powers in the area. At the same time, Washington has enhanced its capacity to intervene in the Caspian Sea region and in other areas holding large supplies of oil.

A similar perspective regarding the role of oil in maintaining economic stability also governs the security policies of other states, including China and Japan. Both of these countries have bolstered their capacity to protect vital petroleum supplies: China has tightened its hold on Xinjiang (a potential source of oil and the site of a rebellion by members of the Muslim Uighur ethnic group) and the islands of the South China Sea (another potential source of oil); Japan has extended the reach of its air and naval forces to better protect its sealanes.

For oil-importing countries, the safe delivery of oil is the basis of their economic security. For oil exporters, however, the *possession* of oil dominates economic thinking. Even at the depressed prices of the late 1990s, the sale of oil was enormously lucrative for those countries; as demand grows and prices rise, the monetary value of oil reserves will climb even higher. In 1997, for instance, the U.S. Department of State placed the value of untapped Caspian Sea oil supplies at a staggering $4 trillion—and oil prices were then considerably lower than they are today.[15] It is therefore not surprising that any state possessing some piece of this latent wealth will view its protection as a vital aspect of national and economic security. . . .

THE INESCAPABLE CONSTRAINTS OF GEOGRAPHY

As older fields are depleted, the global competition for oil will focus increasingly on those few areas of the world that still contain significant supplies of petroleum. These areas will automatically acquire increased strategic importance, as will the transit routes used for carrying oil to distant markets. Clearly, any instability or disorder in these critical areas could impede the continued flow of oil, thus provoking outside intervention. The relative likelihood of conflict is therefore closely related to the geography of oil distribution and to the political environment in key producing and transit regions.

The most significant fact about petroleum, from a world security point of view, is that so much of it is concentrated in a few major producing areas. As shown by Table 42.1, fourteen countries—Saudi Arabia, Iraq, the United Arab Emirates (UAE), Kuwait, Iran, Venezuela, Russia, Mexico, the United States, Libya, China, Nigeria, Norway, and the United Kingdom—jointly possess all but 10 percent of the known world supply. Among these fourteen, the possession of oil is even more highly concentrated, with the five leading producers—Saudi Arabia, Iraq, the UAE, Kuwait, and Iran—together holding nearly two-thirds of global reserves.

The high concentration of petroleum in a handful of major producing areas means that the global availability of oil is closely tied to political and socioeconomic

TABLE 42.1   Global Reserves and Production of Petroleum (as calculated in 1999)

Producer (in order by reserves)	Estimated Reserves (bbl)	Percent of World Reserves	Production, 1998 (mbd)
Saudi Arabia	261.5	24.8	9.2
Iraq	112.5	10.7	2.2
United Arab Emirates	97.8	9.3	2.7
Kuwait	96.5	9.2	2.2
Iran	89.7	8.5	3.8
Venezuela	72.6	6.9	3.3
Russia	48.6	4.6	6.2
Mexico	47.8	4.5	3.5
United States	30.5	2.9	8.0
Libya	29.5	2.8	1.4
China	24.0	2.3	3.2
Nigeria	22.5	2.1	2.2
Norway/United Kingdom (North Sea)	16.1	1.5	6.0
Total	949.6	90.1	53.9

Source: BP Amoco, *Statistical Review of World Energy 1999.*

bbl = billion barrels
mbd = million barrels per day

conditions within a relatively small group of countries. When war or political turmoil erupts in these countries, and the global flow of oil is subsequently disrupted, the rest of the world is likely to experience significant economic hardship.[16] This was made painfully evident in 1973–74, when the Arab oil embargo produced widespread fuel shortages and triggered a prolonged economic recession; the same message was delivered again in 1979–80, following the revolution in Iran. A close look at Table 42.1 suggests, moreover, that such traumas can occur again in the future: a majority of the countries listed in this group have experienced war or revolution during the past ten to twenty years, and many continue to face internal or external challenges.

The epicenter of all this disorder is, of course, the Middle East. That so many of the world's leading oil producers are located in this fractious region has long been a matter of grave concern for leaders of the major importing nations. Even before the discovery of oil, the states in this region were torn by internal divisions along ethnic and political lines, and by the historic rift between Sunni and Shiite Muslims. Once the flow of petroleum began, these divisions were further strained by disputes over the ownership of oil fields and the distribution of oil revenues. This fiery cauldron has been further heated in recent years by the rise of Islamic fundamentalism, the endurance of authoritarian regimes, and deep frustration (among many Arabs) over Israel's treatment of the Palestinians.[17]

Because the Middle East has so often been convulsed by social and political unrest, the major consuming nations have sought to reduce their dependence on Persian Gulf oil by developing alternative sources elsewhere. This is the impulse that led to the rapid development of North Sea and North Slope reserves in the 1970s and, more recently, to the establishment of new production areas in Africa, Latin America, and the Caspian region. "We are undergoing a fundamental shift away from reliance on Middle East oil," the National Security Council optimistically reported in 1998. "Venezuela [has become] our number one foreign supplier and Africa supplies 15 percent of our imported oil."[18]

But while shifting production to these other areas may diminish the importers' reliance on the Middle East, this does not guarantee that the new sources of petroleum will be any less free of disorder and conflict. Colombia and Nigeria, for example, have experienced considerable internal violence over the past few years, while Venezuela is going through a painful and potentially disruptive political transition. Nor is the Caspian Sea area likely to prove any less unstable than the Persian Gulf.

It is true that the development of multiple producing areas allows consuming nations to switch from one source of oil to another when a crisis erupts in any individual area, but the number of such sources are few, and those among them that are entirely free of conflict (or the risk of conflict) are fewer still.

It is clear, then, that a strategy of diversification can succeed for only so long. Ultimately, the oil-importing countries will be forced to rely on the same group of unreliable suppliers in the Persian Gulf, the Caspian, Latin America, and Africa. Like it or not, major importing countries will have to pay close attention to political developments in key producing areas and will have to intervene—in one way or another—whenever local and regional turmoil threatens to disrupt the flow of petroleum.

NOTES

1. For background on the decision to switch from coal to oil, see Geoffrey Jones, *The State and the Emergence of the British Oil Industry* (London: MacMillan, 1981), pp. 9–31.

2. For background and discussion, see ibid., pp. 129–76.

3. Ibid., p. 177. See also Daniel Yergin, *The Prize* (New York: Touchstone, Simon and Schuster, 1993), pp. 167–83.

4. This was said to a celebratory meeting of the Inter-Allied Petroleum Council in London on November 21, 1918. Cited in Yergin, *The Prize*, p. 183.

5. For background on this period, see Jones, *The State and the Emergence of the British Oil Industry*, pp. 208–44; Yergin, *The Prize*, pp. 184–206, 260–308.

6. See Yergin, *The Prize*, pp. 308–88.

7. For background on these endeavors, see David S. Painter, *Oil and the American Century* (Baltimore: Johns Hopkins University Press, 1986), and Michael B. Stoff, *Oil, War, and American Security* (New Haven: Yale University Press, 1980). On the Nixon Doctrine, see James H. Noyes, *The Clouded Lens* (Stanford, Calif.: Hoover Institution Press, 1979), and U.S. Congress, House, Committee on Foreign Affairs, Subcommittee on the Near East and South Asia, *New Perspectives on the Persian Gulf,* Hearings, 93rd Congress, 1st session (Washington, D.C.: Government Printing Office, 1973).

8. For background on these events, see Yergin, *The Prize,* pp. 588–632.

9. Interview in *Business Week,* January 13, 1975, p. 69.

10. From the transcript of Carter's address in *The New York Times,* January 24, 1980.

11. For background on this episode, see Anthony H. Cordesman and Abraham R. Wagner, *The Lessons of Modern War,* volume II, *The Iran-Iraq War* (Boulder: Westview Press, 1990), pp. 277–80, 295–302, 317, 329.

12. From the transcript of Bush's speech in *The New York Times,* August 8, 1997.

13. Alluding to Kissinger's earlier comments, Defense Secretary Richard Cheney told the Senate Armed Services Committee in September 1990 that Washington could not allow Saddam Hussein to acquire "a stranglehold on our economy." U.S. Congress, Senate, Committee on Armed Services, *Crisis in the Persian Gulf Region: U.S. Policy Options and Implications,* Hearings, 101st Congress, 2d Session (1990), pp. 10–11. These hearings represent one of the best sources for information on U.S. security thinking at the time.

14. U.S. Central Command (CENTCOM), *1997 Posture Statement* (MacDill Air Force Base, Fla.: CENTCOM, n.d.), p. 1.

15. U.S. Department of State, *Caspian Region Energy Development Report,* p. 3.

16. For further discussion of this point, see Edward R. Fried and Philip H. Trezise, *Oil Security: Retrospect and Prospect* (Washington, D.C.: Brookings Institution, 1993).

17. For discussion, see the essays in Gary G. Sick and Lawrence G. Potter, eds., *The Persian Gulf at the Millennium* (New York: St. Martin's Press, 1997).

18. U.S. National Security Council, *A National Security Strategy for a New Century* (Washington, D.C.: White House, October 1998), p. 32.

CHAPTER 43

It's Seven Minutes to Midnight

BULLETIN OF THE ATOMIC SCIENTISTS

Chicago, February 27, 2002: Today, the Board of Directors of the *Bulletin of the Atomic Scientists* moves the minute hand of the "Doomsday Clock," the symbol of nuclear danger, from nine to seven minutes to midnight, the same setting at which the clock debuted 55 years ago. Since the end of the Cold War in 1991, this is the third time the hand has moved forward.

TROUBLING TRENDS AND MISSED OPPORTUNITIES

More than 31,000 nuclear weapons are still maintained by the eight known nuclear powers, a decrease of only 3,000 since 1998. Ninety-five percent of these weapons are in the United States and Russia, and more than 16,000 are operationally deployed.

Furthermore, many if not most of the U.S. warheads removed from the active stockpile will be placed in storage (along with some 5,000 warheads already held in reserve) rather than dismantled, for the express purpose of re-deploying them in some future contingency. As a result, the total U.S. stockpile will remain at more than 10,000 warheads for the foreseeable future.

Despite a campaign promise to rethink nuclear policy, the Bush administration has taken no steps to significantly alter nuclear targeting doctrine or reduce the day-to-day alert status of U.S. nuclear forces. If Russia is no longer an adversary, what is the rationale for retaining the ability to incinerate more than 2,000 Russian targets in as little as 30 minutes (or at all)?

Meanwhile, the U.S. national weapons laboratories, with the support of some in Congress, are hard at work refining existing warheads and designing entirely new weapons, with a special emphasis on those able to attack and destroy hardened and deeply buried targets. Although the United States has not conducted a full-scale test since 1992—and the administration says it has no plans to resume testing at this time—it refuses to recognize the overwhelming international support for the Comprehensive Test Ban Treaty (CTBT) and refuses to participate in international meetings to discuss implementing the treaty. Should the required signatories, including India and Pakistan, fail to ratify the CTBT, thus jeopardizing its entry into force, the world will lose an essential tool in halting the further development and spread of nuclear weapons.

Russia and the United States continue to maintain enormous stockpiles of fissile material. Russia has more than 1,000 metric tons of weapon-grade uranium and about 140 metric tons of weapon-grade plutonium, and the United States has nearly 750 metric tons of weapon-grade uranium and 85 metric tons of weapon-grade plutonium. (Just 55 pounds—25 kilograms—of weapon-grade uranium, or 17.6 pounds of plutonium —8 kilograms—are needed to construct a rudimentary nuclear weapon.)

Fortunately, of the hundreds of attempted smuggling transactions involving radioactive materials that have been thwarted since 1991, the vast majority involved materials that were not weapons usable or were of insufficient quantity to construct a nuclear weapon. Only 18 of these cases involved the theft of weapon-grade uranium or plutonium from facilities in the former Soviet Union. At the same time, Al Qaeda operatives were actively seeking to acquire radioactive materials to fashion either a crude nuclear weapon or a radiological dispersion device, commonly known as a "dirty bomb."

The increase in the number of smuggling attempts in recent years serves as a clear warning that surplus nuclear weapons and weapons materials may not be entirely secure. Yet since 1991, successive U.S. and Russian administrations have failed to push for either a full inventory of weapons and materials, or for measures to confirm their destruction. As a result, it is now essentially impossible to verify whether all materials in the United States and Russia are accounted for or whether all weapons are secure. This squandered opportunity has enormous security ramifications.

The U.S. administration's decision to withdraw from the ABM Treaty is a matter of great concern. The administration's rationale—that the treaty is a relic that endangers U.S. security interests—is disingenuous. Regrettably, the United States was unwilling to consider any compromise that would have preserved the basic framework of the treaty, and therefore blocked pursuit of a compromise that would have allowed additional testing but maintained some limits on defenses. Abandoning the treaty will have serious repercussions for years to come.

The crisis between India and Pakistan, touched off by a December 13 terrorist attack on the Indian parliament, marks the closest two states have come to nuclear war since the Cuban Missile Crisis. When the hands of the clock were moved forward in 1998, to nine minutes to midnight, it was in part in anticipation of just this sort of scenario.

Nuclear proliferation continues to pose dangers, both regionally and internationally. Of the countries most often described as seeking nuclear weapons and/or ballistic missiles—Iraq, Iran, and North Korea—North Korea has repeatedly signaled its willingness to turn back, including a decision last year to extend its unilateral moratorium on missile flight tests through 2003. Yet the U.S. administration has abandoned negotiations with that country, and in his State of the Union message, President George W. Bush lumped all three countries together as an "axis of evil," warning that, "The United States of America will not permit the world's most dangerous regimes to threaten us with the world's most destructive weapons." The preference implicit in this statement for preemptive force over diplomacy, and for unilateral action rather than international cooperation, is likely to complicate efforts to defeat terrorism and strengthen global security.

The confluence of the rise of extremists who sacrifice their lives for their cause combined with weapons of mass destruction is an especially worrisome development. So too is the increased awareness since September 11 that terrorists need not manufacture or purchase fissile materials to fashion a crude nuclear weapon or release dangerous amounts of radiation. They need only attack poorly guarded nuclear power plants and nuclear weapons facilities, which contain sizable quantities of these materials. Significantly, President Bush acknowledged on January 29, 2002, that diagrams of U.S. nuclear power plants were found among Al Qaeda materials in Afghanistan.

When resetting the clock we have often noted that the growing disparities between rich and poor increase the potential for violence and war. Poverty and repression breed anger and desperation. Charismatic leaders with easy answers prey on the dispossessed and disaffected, channeling their anger into dangerous and destructive activities. The global community must recognize these facts and do much more to address them. The success of the war on terrorism depends not only on disrupting and destroying terrorist organizations, but also on eradicating the conditions that give rise to terror.

SOME WELCOME DEVELOPMENTS

At the same time, we want to recognize some welcome trends. Since we last set the clock in 1998, the 187 governments party to the Nuclear Non-Proliferation Treaty, including the major nuclear powers, agreed to a comprehensive set of commitments and measures to enhance nonproliferation and fulfill long-standing nuclear disarmament pledges. These agreements were rightly heralded as a political breakthrough, but the real test will be in how seriously the nuclear powers take their obligations to implement the practical steps to which they have agreed. In this regard, we welcome France's dismantling of its Pacific nuclear test site and military reprocessing facilities and commend Britain's research program on verifying multilateral reductions in nuclear weapons as early steps in the right direction.

U.S. funding and technical assistance continues to make significant and cost-effective contributions to international security by working to ensure that Russian nuclear weapons are dismantled, and that nuclear materials and nuclear expertise do not leave Russia. Much remains to be done, however. After initially questioning the value of these cooperative programs, the Bush administration now seeks to increase their funding.

Since 2000, Russia has urged the United States to agree to reductions in the two countries' arsenals to 1,500 warheads each. President Bush's announcement in November 2001 that U.S. "operationally deployed strategic warheads" would be reduced to between 1,700 to 2,200 by 2012—an intention reaffirmed in the administration's Nuclear Posture Review in January—is positive news. It is also the first major commitment to reducing nuclear weapons made by either the United States or Russia since 1997. Although there are serious questions about how permanent these reductions will be, and how long they will take to enact, they are nevertheless an important step away from the grotesque levels of the Cold War.

WHAT IT WOULD TAKE TO TURN BACK THE CLOCK

• As a first step in moving toward a safer world, we urge the United States and Russia to commit to reduce their nuclear arsenals to no more than 1,000 warheads each by the end of the decade. Each side should be free to choose its own means for achieving this goal, but both should commit, in writing, to transparency and verification provisions to ensure that the cuts are carried out and the delivery systems and warheads dismantled. Both countries should commit to storing and disposing of the resulting fissile material in a manner that makes the reductions irreversible. In addition, each side should commit to destroying at least half of the inactive weapons it currently stores within five years, and commit to destroying them all within 10 years.

• These reductions must include tactical nuclear weapons as well. Significantly, the Bush administration's Nuclear Posture Review calls for studying whether the navy should be permitted to retire its nuclear-armed cruise missiles. If these weapons were retired, only about 150 air force bombs stored in seven European countries would remain in the U.S. operational tactical stockpile. We urge the swift retirement and destruction of all tactical nuclear weapons in Europe, and strongly encourage all states with nuclear weapons to begin negotiations to eliminate these weapons worldwide.

• We also urge the United States and Russia to finally recognize the end of the Cold War by abandoning the practice of maintaining thousands of nuclear weapons on high alert, ready to be fired within minutes. This practice, born of fear and uncertainty during the Cold War, is a dangerous anachronism.

• Significantly greater funding must be provided to secure and safeguard nuclear weapons and weapons materials in Russia, the United States, and elsewhere. For example, the current level of U.S. funding to assist Russia with such efforts is less than a third of the $3 billion annual expenditure recommended by an Energy Department task force last year. If weapons materials and expertise are not more tightly controlled, no city in the world will be safe from nuclear attack.

• A Fissile Material Cut-off Treaty must be placed back on the international arms control agenda. Every year that passes without a verifiable means of stopping the production worldwide of nuclear weapons materials makes the task of constraining nuclear proliferation more difficult. In addition, as part of such an agreement, all states with fissile material inventories should declare their current holdings and submit to an international verification and transparency regime that would continuously monitor surplus inventories and develop safe, effective, and permanent disposal options.

Other measures that would increase global stability include a ban on the deployment of space-based weapons, whether designed to damage or disrupt satellites or to attack targets on the ground or in the air; full adherence by all parties to the Chemical Weapons Convention; and the resumption of negotiations on a verification protocol for the Biological Weapons Convention. Stronger international support for the global movement to limit the spread of small arms and to ban land mines, which each year maim or kill tens of thousands of people, most of them innocent civilians, would also be a welcome and necessary development.

The clock is ticking.

Credits

Anderson, Elijah. "Decent and Street Families," from *Code of the Street: Decency, Violence, and the Moral Life of the Inner City* by Elijah Anderson. Copyright © 1999 by Elijah Anderson. Used by permission of W. W. Norton & Company, Inc.

Armstrong, Pat, and Hugh Armstrong, with Claudia Fegan, M. D. *Universal Health Care: What the United States Can Learn from the Canadian Experience,* Copyright © 1998. Reprinted by permission of The New Press. (800) 233-4830.

Bates, Eric. From "The Shame of Our Nursing Homes." Reprinted with permission from the March 29, 1999 issue of *The Nation.*

Bourgois, Philippe. "Workaday World, Crack Economy," from *In Search of Respect: Selling Crack in El Barrio,* second edition. © Cambridge University Press 2002. Reprinted with the permission of Cambridge University Press.

Bray, Rosemary. "So How Did I Get Here?" *New York Times Magazine,* 1993. Copyright 1993. All rights reserved. Reprinted with permission of the author.

Bullard, Robert D. "Environmental Racism," from "Overcoming Racism in Environmental Decision Making," *Environment, Volume 36,* Issue 4, May 1994. Reprinted with permission of the Helen Dwight Reid Educational Foundation. Published by Heldref Publications, 1319 Eighteenth St., NW, Washington, DC 20036-1802. Copyright © 1994.

Commoner, Barry. "Why We Have Failed" is reprinted by permission of the author. Dr. Commoner is director of the Center for the Biology of Natural Systems. His latest book is *Making Peace with the Planet.*

Currie, Elliott. "The Myth of Leniency," excerpted from Elliott Currie, *Crime and Punishment in America.* New York: Henry Holt, 1998.

Ehrenreich, Barbara. "Nickel-and-Dimed: On (Not) Getting by in America." Reprinted by permission of International Creative Management, Inc. Copyright © 1999 by Barbara Ehrenreich. First appeared in *Harper's Magazine.*

Freeman, Richard B. "How Labor Fares in Advanced Economies." In *Working Under Different Rules.* © 1994 Russell Sage Foundation, 112 East 64th Street, New York, NY 10021. Reprinted with permission.

Gans, Herbert J. "The Underclass Label," from *The War Against the Poor.* Copyright © 1995 by Herbert J. Gans. Reprinted by permission of Basic Books, a member of Perseus Books, L.L.C.

Garrett, Laurie. "The Return of Infectious Disease." Reprinted by permission of *Foreign Affairs,* 75(1), January/February 1996. Copyright 1996 by the Council on Foreign Relations, Inc.

Gelbspan, Ross. "The Heat Is On," copyright © 1995 by *Harper's Magazine.* All rights reserved. Reproduced from the December issue by special permission.

Goldberg, Jeffrey. "The Color of Suspicion," reprinted by permission of International Creative Management, Inc. Copyright © 1999 by Jeffrey Goldberg. First appeared in *New York Times Magazine.*

Orenstein, Peggy. "Learning Silence," from *School Girls: Young Women, Self-Esteem and the Confidence Gap* by Peggy Orenstein/American Association of University Women. Copyright © 1994 by Peggy Orenstein and American Association of University Women. Used by permission of Doubleday, a division of Random House, Inc. Permission arranged by Sandra Dijkstra Literary Agency.

Ptacek, James. "The Tactics and Strategies of Men Who Batter," from Albert P. Cardarelli (Ed.), *Violence Between Intimate Partners*. Published by Allyn and Bacon, Boston, MA. Copyright © 1997 by Pearson Education. Reprinted by permission of the publisher.

Rainwater, Lee, and Timothy M. Smeeding. "Doing Poorly: The Real Income of American Children in a Comparative Perspective" is reprinted by permission of the Luxembourg Income Study.

"Reading, Writing, and...Buying?" Copyright 1998 by Consumers Union of U.S., Inc., Yonkers, NY 10703-1057, a nonprofit organization. Reprinted with permission from the September 1998 issue of *Consumer Reports* for educational purposes only. No commercial use or photocopying permitted. To learn more about Consumers Union, log onto www.Consumer Reports.org

Rubin, Lillian B. "Families on the Fault Line," copyright © 1994 by Lillian B. Rubin. Originally published by HarperCollins. Reprinted by permission of Dunham Literary as agent for the author.

Shahmehri, Brittany, "More Than Welcome: Families Come First in Sweden," from *Mothering*, 109, November/December 2001. Reprinted by permission.

Shields, Janice. "Getting Corporations off the Public Dole" is from *Business and Society Review*, 94, Summer 1995. Janice Shields, Ph.D., is director of the Institute for Business Research in Washington, DC. Reprinted by permission of the author.

Silverstein, Ken. "Unjust Rewards," from *Mother Jones*, May/June 2002. © 2002, Foundation for National Progress.

Skolnick, Jerome H., and John J. DiIulio, Jr. "Wild Pitch: 'Three Strikes, You're Out' and Other Bad Calls on Crime" is reprinted by permission of the authors.

Takaki, Ronald. "Asian Americans: The Myth of the Model Minority," from *Strangers from a Different Shore* by Ronald Takaki. Copyright © 1989, 1999 by Ronald Takaki. By permission of Little, Brown and Company, (Inc.).

Useem, Jerry. "Have They No Shame?" from *Fortune*, April 14, 2003. © 2003 Time Inc. All rights reserved.

Wilson, William Julius. "The Political Economy and Urban Racial Tensions" is from *The American Economist*, Vol. 34, No. 1, Spring 1995. Reprinted by permission of the publisher and William Julius Wilson, Lewis P. and Linda L. Geyser University Professor, Harvard University.

Wolff, Edward N. "Recent Trends in the Size Distribution of Household Wealth" is from the *Journal of Economic Perspectives 12*(3), Summer 1998. Reprinted by permission of the American Economic Association.